SETH L. GOLDSTEIN

# THE SEXUAL EXPLOITATION OF CHILDREN

## A Practical Guide to Assessment, Investigation, and Intervention

### SECOND EDITION

# CRC SERIES IN
# PRACTICAL ASPECTS OF CRIMINAL
# AND FORENSIC INVESTIGATIONS

VERNON J. GEBERTH, BBA, MPS, FBINA *Series Editor*

# SETH L. GOLDSTEIN

# THE SEXUAL EXPLOITATION OF CHILDREN

## A Practical Guide to Assessment, Investigation, and Intervention

## SECOND EDITION

**CRC Press**

Boca Raton   London   New York   Washington, D.C.

Ann W. Burgess, *Child Pornography and Sex Rings*, Lexington Books, D.C. Heath and Co., 1984.

*The Donahue Show*, September 22, 1980. Copyright 1980 by Multi-Media Program Productions.

Kenneth V. Lanning, "Child Molesters: A Behavioral Analysis for Law Enforcement", in *Practical Rape Investigation*, Robert Hazelwood, CRC Press, 1987, Boca Raton, FL.

Lori, Steinhorst, *When the Monster Comes Out of the Closet*, Rose Publications, 1994.

Loretta Schwartz-Nobel, "Child Pornography and the Secret World of the Pedophile," *Philadelphia Inquirer*, November 6, 1983.

Suzanne M. Sgroi, *Handbook of Clinical Intervention in Child Sexual Abuse*, Lexington Books, D. C. Heath and Co., 1982.

Roland Summit, "The Child Sexual Abuse Accommodation Syndrome", *Child Abuse and Neglect, An International Journal*, Vol. 7, 1983.

Linda Tschirhart Sanford, *The Silent Children*, Doubleday & Company, Inc., 1980.

Kenneth Wooden, *Weeping in the Playtime of Others*, McGraw-Hill Co., 1976.

## Library of Congress Cataloging-in-Publication Data

Catalog record is available from the Library of Congress

**Visit the CRC Press Web site at www.crcpress.com**

© 1999 by CRC Press LLC

No claim to original U.S. Government works
International Standard Book Number 0-8493-8154-1
Printed in the United States of America    5  6  7  8  9  0
Printed on acid-free paper

# Editor's Note

This textbook is part of a series entitled "Practical Aspects of Criminal and Forensic Investigation." This series was created by Vernon J. Geberth, New York City Police Department Lieutenant Commander (Retired), who is an author, educator, and consultant on homicide and forensic investigations.

This series has been designed to provide contemporary, comprehensive, and pragmatic information to the practitioner involved in criminal and forensic investigations by authors who are nationally recognized experts in their respective fields.

*This book is dedicated to America's missing and exploited sons and daughters and to those individuals whose job it is to help and protect them...*

*To my wife Eileen, without whose love, support, patience and encouragement this project would never have been completed...*

*To my daughter, Andrea Nicole, may she enjoy the innocence of childhood and never face the evil of this crime...*

# Contents

## 4    Child Pornography Investigation                          173

## 7    Search Warrants                                325

# Foreword
# to the First Edition

This book could be a lifesaver. It can help stem the tide not only of "ordinary" child molestation and exploitation but also of the weird, cultish, homicidal nightmares that have so far eluded effective prosecution. Without prosecution and conviction those cases remain reports, suspicions, crazy ideas in the minds of investigators and therapists whose brains have gone soft listening to too many kids. There will be no convictions without solid facts, hard evidence, and proactive infiltration and intelligence. Until "we" are smarter than "they," we will all share the hazards and the backlash of hidden, no-fault crimes. And as long as the crimes remain out of control, the time-proven techniques for working the less exotic child cases will be attacked as the tools of a misguided witchhunt.

There is a crisis in what developed 10 years ago as a new coalition between clinical and law enforcement professionals specializing in child sexual abuse and exploitation. Both groups learned from each other and developed effective teamwork. Carolyn Bailey from Minneapolis taught us techniques of interviewing children with anatomic dolls. Lloyd Martin drew sexual abuse people into a working concern for the exploitation scene I'm indebted to Lloyd for taking me out of the committee meetings and into the street, sharing coffee with his informants, and finding the common ground that helped us all to grow). Ken Lanning teamed with Ann Burgess at the FBI Academy. Toby Tyler and Seth Goldstein worked tirelessly at both ends of California and around the country to teach and to learn.

The present crisis results from learning too much too soon. There is no standard and no consistency from one jurisdiction to another, no uniform funding, administrative support, or priorities for child sexual assault. And lately there is no basis for confidence and control in defining the unexpected chambers of horrors we have unwittingly stumbled into. No one really knows what to look for or how to find it, and in the frustration of failure we have begun to blame one another for our mutual pain.

sounding board for the propositions offered herein. He was one of the few who turned the attention of the FBI to the problem of sexual exploitation

xviii The Sexual Exploitation of Children

one agency to grasp. The media took charge of child sexual abuse in the spring and summer of 1984, with the Jordan and the McMartin cases as the flagships. In the harsh sea of an aggressive defense taunting for a criminal standard of proof the Jordan cases sank like a rock.

Since Jordan, the authorities, the media, and the public have been searching for a scapegoat, a tidy answer to the very complicated, terribly frightening question what really happened in Jordan. The argument advanced by defense has been elaborated and institutionalized in the Attorney General's investigation and the inconclusive impeachment proceedings. What really happened can never be known — because, they say, the investigators, the prosecutor, and the designated therapists were out of line and out of class in their roles and methods. The same teamwork, the same interviews might have been held up as ideal models in the light of conviction, but in these landmark cases there is no room for failure. Either there is a crime or there isn't. If there is no crime, as determined by a trier of fact, then the investigators, both clinical and law enforcement, will be held to answer for inventing a fraud.

These are high stakes and unfair tests, and no one with any sense would buy into such a gamble. But it's our job to be there, and our burden to do it right. The arresting officer in Jordan should have had a search warrant comprehensive for pornography and sexual fetish paraphernalia. The next day was too late. Jurisdiction for taking the children into custody, protocols for interviewing both complaining and uncomplaining children, methods for recording the interviews, orderly preparation for inevitable discovery, countermeasures to predictable defense strategies, interdisciplinary role definitions and communication, rules for information sharing, coordinated media relations — all these controversial areas should have been anticipated, defined, recorded, and authorized. Scott County, Minnesota, like Los Angeles County, California, was not really ready for such a case. With the backlash and frustrations of the Jordan and Manhattan Beach cases, we are now even less prepared, less confident, and drastically more disorganized than we were then.

The Minnesota Attorney General's report had a chilling, alienating effect on investigative teamwork throughout the United States. The team concept was suddenly considered dangerous. Police interviews of children became more hard-nosed, more traditional. Kids clammed up with cops and spilled to their parents and therapists. Therapists and parents were blamed by prosecutors for creating hysteria. Leading questions and cross-germination became the evils that could destroy the case. The legal case took precedent over the family problems, even though there could be no case without primary attention to those problems.

It's time to get back to basics and to relearn from the priceless experience gained during 10 years of unprecedented teamwork and discovery. The skills are available and the record of successes far outnumbers the setbacks. Now, more than ever, the public depends on the police and the courts to set the record straight. Good investigation, independent interviews, clear reports, covert intelligence, specialization of skills, comprehensive search and seizure, due process, compassion for victims, respect for suspects, courage and composure under fire, rest and recreation — all these traditional values are more important now in juvenile work than ever before.

Seth Goldstein is a veteran of these wars. He has been through the best and the worst and he's not about to quit. The lessons in this book are invaluable not only to investigators but to everyone concerned with safety, health, and justice for our most vulnerable and promising citizens. Despite the status traditionally given to homicide, narcotics, and grand theft, nothing in law enforcement and nothing in mental health is more important than the safe, healthy development of our children.

Roland C. Summit, M.D.

are available and the record of successes far outnumbers the setbacks. Now, more than ever, the public depends on the police and the courts to set the record straight. Good investigation, independent interviews, clear reports, expert intelligence, specialization of skills, comprehensive search and seizure, due process, compassion for victims, respect for suspects, courage and composure under fire, rest and recreation — all these traditional values are more important now in juvenile work than ever before.

Seth Goldstein is a veteran of these wars. He has been through the best and the worst and he's not about to quit. The lessons of this book are invaluable, not only to investigators but to everyone concerned with society... and mystified, our most valued assets: our very own citizens. Despite the status that it all gives us about the ravening... beyond that awaiting a law enforcement and cultural... mental health is more important than the safe, healthy development of our children.

Roland C. Summit, M.D.

# Foreword
# to the Second Edition

Since the First Edition of *The Sexual Exploitation of Children* was published nearly ten years ago, managing, treating, and preventing sex-related crimes against children has attracted the attention of a broad spectrum of professionals. In fact, strong argument can be made that since the mid-1980s, no other crime or social problem in American history has been studied, researched, written about or debated, or has presented more training opportunities and scholarly publications, than child sexual abuse. During that time, hundreds of books were published, seemingly on any topic even remotely related to child sexual abuse. There are at least twelve peer-reviewed, scholarly journals which devote at least one-third (and often more) of each issue to child sexual abuse, and two journals which are devoted exclusively to sexual abuse. In addition, nearly every week of the year there is a conference, national or local, being held some place in America, on the sexual abuse of children.

Yet, amid this unprecedented explosion of continuing education opportunities, scientific research and scholarship, there has remained only a single comprehensive text which addresses the investigation of virtually all sex crimes against children: the First Edition of Seth Goldstein's *The Sexual Exploitation of Children*.

In this, the Second Edition of *The Sexual Exploitation of Children*, Goldstein expands and updates his 1987 publication with an application of the best available behavioral science research related to child sexual abuse to the most effective law enforcement investigative techniques. Goldstein's incorporation of the controlling legal ramifications of nearly every step of a criminal investigation enriches this already unique book. In the Second Edition, moreover, Goldstein brings his legal education and training to augment his years of experience as a criminal investigator of child sexual abuse. The end result is a highly specialized, thorough, investigative reference guide.

The publication of the Second Edition is indeed timely. It comes at a time when the child sexual abuse backlash voices are being heard and supported by state and federal legislators. Inspired by the vanguard McMartin

Preschool Case (Manhattan Beach, CA), large segments of our society —
including our law makers, judges, jurors and even investigators — receive
their education about child sexual abuse, children's memory and suggestibility, sex offenders and interviewing children who allege abuse, from the
media's obsession with daycare or multi-victim cases. This, despite the consistently documented finding of the rarity of such cases.

Words like "ritual abuse" or "satanic practices" still result in the media
influencing the direction of a sexual abuse case, particularly if more than one
alleged child victim reports being abused. Any mistakes made by investigators
or prosecutors in these rare cases seem to leave the impression in our society
that such mistakes are very common in all child sexual abuse cases. Good,
thorough investigations and successful prosecutions of child sexual abuse
throughout the country far outnumber the setbacks or reversed convictions.
Unfortunately, the lay public, many professionals who regularly work with
sexually abused children, and now even legislators, quickly point to recent
developments in cases like McMartin, as somehow representative of child
sexual abuse investigations in general. While these conclusions are egre-
giously inaccurate and unfounded, those who investigate and try child sexual
abuse cases in court cannot allow their years of practical experience, no
matter how numerous, to take the place of continuing and updated training
and education.

Seth Goldstein has once again given professionals who work on child
sexual abuse an encyclopedic-like text on how to successfully meet that challenge. Whether the report alleges bizarre cult-related activity or a single child
alleges being fondled, this book should remind all who read it — and hopefully use it daily — of the unique significance of good, sound investigation
of child sexual abuse. Children's safety, emotional well-being, and their very
lives depend on such investigations. Anyone who assesses, investigates, or
evaluates the sexual abuse of children, whether as a law enforcement officer,
a child protective service worker, a clinician, an attorney representing children or a Court, should be required to read this book.

Dr. Roland Summit quite appropriately began his Foreword to the First
Edition by writing, "This book could save lives." Dr. Summit's words remain
the best characterization of the Second Edition.

Thomas F. Curran, MSW, JD
Philadelphia, Pennsylvania

# Preface

This book is written for anyone who is involved in the assessment, investigation, and intervention of child sexual abuse and exploitation. The most successful response to these formidable tasks has been one which involves an integration of disciplines to determine whether abuse has or has not occurred.

This has become known as the multidisciplinary approach. Medical practitioners, clinicians, lawyers, investigators and other forensic specialists, have come together for the purpose of making the best evaluation possible in allegations of abuse. Others who might become involved in recognizing and working with children who have been sexually abused such as teachers, prevention specialists, or care providers, may also find this book invaluable in their work and of assistance in making the multidisciplinary concept work. For this concept to work, each discipline involved in these investigations needs to know what the other needs and what is possible to obtain. Perhaps more importantly, everyone needs to know what the rules are for obtaining that information.

Just as the police officer needs to know that in permitting a sexual assault victim to bathe before a forensic medical examination irretrievable evidence will be lost, so must the medical practitioner be aware that certain questioning practices could invalidate or seriously impair a child's account of events. When a clinician, ordered by the courts, evaluates a child sexual abuse allegation, the total depth of the case must be explored. A shallow inquiry will miss the subtleties and the distinguishing markers that verify or refute the claim.

If a lawyer doesn't know the significance of evidence nor does he recognize the signs and clues that there is more evidence to be found, he is less likely to be able to present a sound case. This will prevent the trier of fact from adequately analyzing the case. This hurts both the child and the accused; for it is to both that we have an obligation to completely, competently, and comprehensively investigate.

There are some preliminary thoughts that must be shared to understand the perspective of the author. Traditionally, it has been believed that only girls are victims of sexual abuse and exploitation. My own experience has been that there are probably as many male victims as female. I have also found that the male victim population has been neglected because of the mistaken belief that they are few in number and that they can handle the problem themselves.

The traditional police approach to investigating juvenile crime or victimization and sexual assault is to assign a female investigator to the case. This is done in the mistaken belief that women are better suited to these tasks. My experience is that although there are many women who are excellent in this situation, simply being female is not a qualification for investigating this type of crime. Both men and women can be very successful in these investigations and equally sensitive to the victim's needs.

In the hope that these misconceptions will soon be eradicated, I use the masculine pronoun throughout the text to help establish the concept that males can be and are victims and that they can investigate these crimes.

I also refer to the child's articulation of his experience(s) as an "account" rather than a "story." The word story connotes a falsehood, something that may or may not be true. An account is a relating of an experience. If we are to begin to believe children, then we should use terms that demonstrate that belief.

This text is written with one priority in mind — the child's well-being. Every technique and procedure suggested here, when applied in the field, should be considered in light of that priority. Whenever the needs of the investigation and the child come into conflict, concern for the child should prevail. In law enforcement, our duty is to protect the innocent. In child abuse investigation, protection of children is the paramount objective. While investigating the sexual exploitation of children — one of the most hideous forms of child abuse — we must never forget this objective.

Seth L. Goldstein

# The Author

Seth Goldstein is a consultant and attorney in private practice. He is the Executive Director of the Child Abuse Forensic Institute, which he founded in 1992. Mr. Goldstein was the Investigator and Project Director for the Child Abuse Vertical Prosecution Unit of the Napa County District Attorney, Napa, California for four years. He also worked as an investigator with the Santa Clara County District Attorney, San Jose, California, for three years. Before that he worked for the Berkeley, California, Police Department for thirteen years — three as a cadet and ten as a police officer. He served in the Patrol, Service, and Detective Divisions of the police department, including two years as a Juvenile Officer.

Mr. Goldstein grew up in Berkeley and holds a B.A. degree from the University of California, at Berkeley. He was conferred a J.D. degree from the Oakland College of Law and was admitted to the California Bar in 1995.

He has formerly been the Chairman of the Northern California Juvenile Officers Association Committee on Sexual Abuse and Sexual Exploitation of Children and has served as the Association's President and editor of its newsletter. He has presented at seminars and workshops throughout the U.S. and Europe, including the FBI Academy at Quantico, Virginia.

He has written several articles on the subject of sexual abuse and exploitation of children which have been published nationally and has received several awards for his work, including the American Bar Association's (ABA) Gavel Award in 1980, the California State Juvenile Officer's Dan Pursuit Award (Officer of the Year), in 1990, and the ABA, Child Advocacy, National Certificate of Recognition for Significant Legal Contributions Advancing the Welfare of Our Nation's Children, in 1997.

Mr. Goldstein has been called to testify as an expert witness in court, including a branch of the Florida Supreme Court, as well as numerous California and Federal legislative commissions and committees. He sat on the California and United States Department of Justice Committees that created investigative and academy curriculum for investigations of sexual abuse and exploitation of children. In April of 1985, was invited to the White House to meet with President Ronald Reagan about the issue of missing and exploited children.

Mr. Goldstein has been a consultant to the International Association of Chiefs of Police (IACP). He sat on the California Attorney General's Violent Crime Information Systems Advisory Group and was a founding Member of the Board of Directors of the National Center For Missing and Exploited Children.

# Acknowledgments

In a one's life there often comes a mentor, a person who stands by, gently directing and suggesting. This person, who has already been down the road you are traveling, looks over your shoulder and guides his protegé by supplying invaluable advice, guidance, counseling, and confidence. I was fortunate to have such a person in Vernon Geberth, the father of the Forensic Series which this text has become part of.

From the very beginning, Vern guided me forward, providing insight, suggestions, and enthusiasm. It is apparent that his vision of a unique body of knowledge collectively drawn together into the Forensic Series has become a reality. It is a wonderful resource for those individuals who protect our communities. I consider myself genuinely lucky to have had the good fortune to know him and to have had the honor to have been invited to be part of this series.

I also want to acknowledge my grandmother Rose, who had enthusiastically volunteered to type and edit the first version of this book. As always, but especially during this project, she continued to encourage and support me through to completion. As she has in all things with me, her love, inspiration, and interest often led to new energy, for which I thank her. At 97-years-young, she is still an inspiration to us all.

I would also like to thank Detective Lloyd Martin (Retired), of the Los Angeles Police Department, for his inspiration and encouragement. Lloyd has made great sacrifices as a result of his dedication to the issue of sexually exploited children and was the one who first opened my eyes to the problem. His was one of the first lonely voices crying out for attention to this issue and is responsible for many changes in the way this nation recognizes it.

I would also like to thank another individual who has done a great deal to change attitudes about the problem of sexual abuse and exploitation of children in America, Supervising Special Agent Kenneth V. Lanning of the Federal Bureau of Investigation. Besides contributing the work on offenders in Chapters 1 and 2 and other material in this text,* Ken has acted as a

---

* The material contributed to this book by Kenneth Lanning also appears as a chapter in another volume in the Forensic Series: *Practical Aspects of Rape Investigation*, edited by Robert R. Hazelwood and Ann Wolbert Burgess.

sounding board for the propositions offered herein. He was one of the few who turned the attention of the FBI to the problem of sexual exploitation of children and prompted change in its investigative emphasis, making sexual exploitation of children on of its "top four" index priorities. Ken has made great sacrifices to train the law enforcement community of this country and make the general public more aware of the problem. He is one of the most prolific and insightful law enforcement writers on this subject. His analysis of the factors involved in sexual exploitation of children reveals the true genius he is.

I would also like to thank Lt. Toby Tyler of the San Bernardino County Sheriff's Department, San Bernardino, California, for his counsel, contributions, and time spent reviewing the working drafts of this text. Without his insight and keen understanding of the problem of sexual exploitation of children, many of the passages that follow might not have made their points.

I would also like to acknowledge Gary Duthler, formerly of the Alameda County District Attorney's Office, Oakland, California, and Captain Jeffrey Miller of the Los Gatos Police Department, Los Gatos, California, for their contributions and time in reviewing the working drafts of this text. Their creative techniques in interviewing the children and offender have helped me greatly in investigations and in teaching investigative techniques.

I would like to thank my father for his provoking thought and his review of the working drafts of this work.

Finally, although I would like to thank all of those who helped produce this text in the many ways they have, I would like to especially thank the following individuals for their advice, encouragement, and contributions:

Howard Davidson, J.D., American Bar Association., Washington, D.C.; Inspector Larry Lindenau, Berkeley Police Department, Berkeley; California; Michael Jett, California Attorney General's Office; Paul Crissey, California Consortium of Child Abuse Councils, Sacramento, California, John Brodie, California Department of Justice, Kee MacFarlane, Children's Institute, Los Angeles; Sue Oliviera, Ph.D. Gavilan College, Gilroy, California; Sgt. Laura Warren, Retired, Fairfax P.D, Fairfax, California; Officers Craig Hoyer and Larry Perera and Sgt. Rick Parker, Hayward Police Department, Hayward, California; Detective. Terry Hall, Indianapolis Police Department, Indianapolis, Indiana; Honorable Ed Jagels, Kern County District Attorney, and his staff, Kern County, California; Sgt. Beth Dickenson, Los Angeles County Sheriff's Department; Lt. William Spaulding, Louisville Division of Police, Louisville, Kentucky; Professor John E.B. Myers, McGeorge School of Law, Sacramento, California; Marcia Morgan, Ph.D., Migima Designs, Eugene, Oregon; Lynn Young, Esq., Napa, Ca.; John Rabun, National Center For Missing and Exploited Children, Arlington, Virginia; H. Joan Pennington, Esq., National Center for Protective Parents, Trenton, New Jersey; Richard

Ruffino, New Jersey Department of Law and Safety; Detective., Sid Ladow, Palm Beach Police Department, Palm Beach, Florida; Thomas F. Curran, Esq., Philadelphia, Pennsylvania; Detective. Carl Stincelli, Sacramento County Sheriff's Department, Sacramento, California; Det. Michael DiMatteo, San Bernardino Sheriff's Department; Inspector Tom Eisenmann, San Francisco Police Department, San Francisco, California; Terry Briggs, Sylvia Felix, Leslie Garland, Neal Kimball, Paula Kuty, Michelle McCoy, Ron McCurdy, and Alan Nudelman, Santa Clara County District Attorney's Office, San Jose, California; Professor Peter C. Unsinger, San Jose State University, San Jose, California; Investigator Ed Hudson, Sonoma County District Attorney's Office, Santa Rosa, California; Inspector William Halonan, Retired, U.S. Postal Inspection Service; Roland Summit, M.D., University of California, Los Angeles; De Kirkpatrick, Ph.D, and my good friend and associate Armand Lareau.

A special acknowledgment to the family of Officer William Grijalva, some of whose work appears in the search warrants section of this text and who died protecting the citizens of Oakland, California. Bill's memory and his efforts to protect children from abuse and exploitation will live long with those who knew him. I am privileged to been able to have him call me a friend.

Finally, a very special thanks to my assistant, friend, and organizer, Lynda Duthler, without whose countless hours of attention to the children and families we serve, on top of putting this text together, I never would have survived.

# Introduction

The role of the police investigator in investigating sexual exploitation of children is that of an objective fact-finder. The investigator's responsibility is to determine whether a crime has occurred, offer protection for the victim(s), gather and preserve evidence that will prove the particular crime discovered, and apprehend and bring to court the individual responsible. The crime of sexual exploitation of children poses some special investigative difficulties that make these responsibilities somewhat more troublesome than in other crimes.

The crime has been misunderstood for many years, and as a result has not been adequately addressed. As law enforcement did with the issue of rape in the early 1970s, we must now recognize the fact that sexual exploitation of children must be addressed in a different manner. This type of crime involves highly specialized techniques for investigation, and because the criminal element may be organized in formal or informal groups, specialized units and investigative training are necessary to address the problem adequately. The underground subculture of persons who sexually exploit children through child pornography, prostitution, and molestation also requires a special response on the part of law enforcement.

## The Difficulties Law Enforcement Faces in Investigating the Sexual Exploitation of Children

Investigations of cases of sexual exploitation of children have revealed that the crime causes great difficulty for investigators because it is multijurisdictional in nature, crosses lines of investigative responsibility within local, state, and federal jurisdictions; requires the use of unique, nontraditional training and investigative techniques, and takes an inordinate amount of time to investigate. In addition, law enforcement may now face new liabilities if it fails to act properly on the problem.

## The Unique Position of Law Enforcement and their Agents in an Investigation

Law enforcement, or any person who is assisting law enforcement in developing information (therefore an agent) on a particular allegation, are in a unique position. The courts need a dispassionate and independent assessment and review of the facts. Law enforcement, generally, is the first to be called to the scene of a reported crime, in this case child abuse. It is their responsibility to look into the facts and determine if a crime was committed in such a way as to remove any taint from the inquiry. They are supposed to be nonpartisan and able to provide a rational recitation of what facts were discovered. This is what they are trained to do. In a crime such as the sexual exploitation of children, law enforcement and their agents must present a conclusion that is not susceptible to impeachment for bias or lack of credibility. They personify honesty, integrity, and the concept that justice is blind and should be fairly applied. If law enforcement leaves this duty to investigate to others outside the realm of child protection, they expose the Achilles' Heel of these cases and, ultimately, harm the child when the case fails to proceed.

In other words, law enforcement should, with child protective services, if necessary, conduct all investigations and inquiries. It should not be left to parents, private investigators, or other entities not officially connected or sanctioned by the investigating officer. To do so leaves the investigation and the information it uncovers open to criticism and attack by a defense attorney claiming that it was improper. In many cases where information is unearthed by someone other than the "objective fact finder" embodied in the person of a peace officer, successful arguments are made to juries that it is tainted.

## The Need for Professional Alliances with Clinical and Medical Communities

This is not to say that law enforcement shouldn't use clinical, therapeutic and medical professionals to assist them in the inquiry process. On the contrary. As will be discussed in Chapter 8, "Case Management," forming an alliance and working relationship with these specialists, who have unique skills to contribute, is essential to a successful case. The subtle points, fine nuances, ambiguous characteristics, perplexing aspects of, special problems peculiar and inherent to sexual abuse and exploitation of children are too technical for a single investigator to comprehend or anticipate. This is a different and unusual problem for law enforcement because no other criminal investigation involves the participation and interaction of so many disciplines. It will require a change in orientation, as most police officers are trained to handle their own investigations and not to seek assistance from anyone, much less, someone outside the "official" police realm. It is my hope that this book will help to demonstrate and persuade those in law enforcement that the way to success in these cases is to form professional coalitions with many people in their community. Not coincidentally, this book is also intended to prepare any person who will be or is working with law enforcement in the investigation of these matters and/or the development of evidence to present to a court of law. I hope it will provide the background and basics that form the mortar to build a foundation for unity between the disciplines.

## A Needed Change in Law-Enforcement Response

The problems inherent in the investigation of the sexual exploitation of children relate to the "conspiracy" that bonds its participants together [1]. Burgess et al. [2] detail the dynamics of a "sex ring," outlining the reasons why discovery, disclosure, or infiltration are so difficult to accomplish. Moreover, the problem has gone underground and involves thousands of people. In 1980, the Northern California Juvenile Officers' Association (NCJOA) conducted an unpublished survey of northern California police agencies. Among other things, it found that incidents of sexual exploitation of children were on the rise and that law enforcement on the whole had maintained a reactive stance to it, simply responding to complaints of violations of the law, rather than ferreting them out on its own. This was largely because so many cases were reported. The problem is that seldom do any of the participants come forward and complain, and therefore only a fraction of the cases come to light.

Not much has changed in the interim. In the 1990s, there are only a few law enforcement agencies that have "proactive" investigative units or investigators dealing exclusively with the crimes. Only the Federal Government has a few investigators dedicated to this full-time, and the rest of the world is not in much better shape. Another difficulty in dealing with this crime is that there is little hope of a cure for many offenders, and they will continue to repeat their offences.

The conspiracy also makes the investigation of child porn very difficult. Often, the porn producers insulate themselves by hiding behind a myriad of dummy corporations, In addition, the sources of child porn are often fly-by-night operators — here today, gone tomorrow. The clandestine method of operation and the statutes the law-enforcement officer must work with often make investigation difficult. It is also often very difficult to locate and bring forward the children involved to testify.

Another reason investigations fail is the manner in which the problem of sexual exploitation of children is handled by law enforcement — it has yet to recognize the conspiracy. Although most police agencies across the country operate on the "specialist system," in which the initial crime report is investigated by a patrol (line) officer and followed-up by a person who "specializes" in investigation of that particular crime, sexual exploitation cannot be properly handled in this fashion. Although most agencies recognize the need for specialists to handle these matters, a study by the National Institute of Justice found that of the agencies it surveyed, 78% sent a "patrol unit" to conduct the initial investigation [3]. In other types of cases, the entire investigation, from initial report through final disposition (arrest or otherwise), is conducted by a specialist. It is this type of investigation that is most successful in cases of sexual exploitation of children.

An analogy can be drawn between the building of a house and the building of a case for the prosecution. In building a house, it is necessary to have specialists in various fields perform various tasks in order to complete the final product. A strong foundation must be built for the house to rest on. A specialist, generally a concrete contractor, builds the foundation. In a criminal prosecution, the police investigation forms the foundation. In investigating crime, the foundation of a case may well be the determining factor in bringing the case successfully through the justice system. That foundation may consist of proper search and seizure procedures, effective interviewing techniques, a complete and thorough covering of the elements of the crime, the successful recovery of evidence, and a thorough knowledge of the manner in which the crime is committed. It also may include an understanding of what the victim is experiencing psychologically and the use of special techniques to assist the victim through the investigative techniques and procedures unique to the crime under investigation. All these factors are part of the foundation of a sexual exploitation case.

Specialized training and preparation of the officers who work this crime problem are also a necessary element. To investigate sexual exploitation cases successfully, specialists who are well versed in all these facets of the crime must be assigned to the case from start to finish.

In most police agencies, the practice of using the skills of specialists to investigate certain types of crimes is common and accepted. Vice, for instance, requires investigators who not only are specially trained to recognize and investigate complicated schemes of narcotic sales, prostitution rings, gambling, and similar offenses, but who can also work in a covert capacity and fit into the type of group under investigation without detection.

Sexual assault and child abuse are also generally accepted as crimes that require the skills and understanding of specialists who recognize the symptoms, are sensitive to the psychological needs of the victims, are specially trained to understand the motive of those who commit the offenses, and know the unique characteristics of the offenses. Like sexual assault and child abuse, homicide is also a crime that requires great amounts of time dedicated to interviewing, gathering evidence, surveillance, or making contacts pertinent to the investigation. Because of the seriousness of homicide and its unique nature — it doesn't occur often and requires specialized evidence-gathering techniques, among other things—it is generally investigated by someone who is specially trained and who is attached to a unit that only investigates crimes of that nature.

The sexual exploitation of children has characteristics of each of the previously mentioned investigative areas. More importantly, the crime problems related to the sexual exploitation of children are varied in nature and often span the boundaries of investigative responsibility, within both local jurisdictions (one or more police departments) and state and federal enforcement agencies. For example, if a child is molested and photographed in sexually explicit acts while being molested, the responsibility for investigation might fall to a department's juvenile unit that investigates child abuse. It may also fall within the investigative responsibility of the same agency's vice detail because of the pornography involved. In addition, the pictures may have been taken in other cities or molests may have been committed out of the city in which the investigation was initiated, all of which may mean that other law-enforcement jurisdictions (local, state, federal) may have investigative responsibility. In each of these situations, officers in the units responsible for investigating one aspect of the offense may not have the training, experience, ability, interest, or desire to investigate the other aspects. As a result, the case suffers, and may be lost.

Another aspect of the offense is a different multijurisdictional problem. The offenses often involve multijurisdictional crime, committed by a person whose travels are limited only by the means of transportation available. Even when the offender has no personal means of transportation, public transit not only carries the person to a "safe community" to commit further crimes without being recognized, but also provides a good source of new victims. Rarely is a case found to involve only one city or county, and it is not uncommon to find interstate as well as international implications.

One of the greatest problems for law enforcement in these investigations has been the lack of coordination and a great deal of ignorance on the part of some investigative agencies. In addition, many law enforcement agencies do not communicate what they find in their investigations to other law-enforcement agencies that might have an interest.

These cases must be carefully planned, carried out, and analyzed for additional leads. Because of the conspiratorial nature of sexual exploitation of children, one case often mushrooms into many others. When the crime under investigation reaches beyond the borders of a local agency, police investigations often stall for lack of resources.

Most law-enforcement agencies consider child abuse a serious problem, but few resources have been dedicated exclusively to it.

## Cases Pose Unique Defenses

These cases also pose unique defenses that must be anticipated at the very beginnings of an investigation (see Chapter 8). If the proper procedures and actions are not taken at the inception of an investigation, there is no turning back and the road to successful inquiry will be laced with potholes and pitfalls. These cases are tough enough without having self-imposed road-blocks to get around.

It takes special training and a sensitivity to the needs of the prosecutor or attorney handling the dependency action to protect the child. Investigators who are not aware of the ramifications of the actions they take in early stages of a case may make it impossible to proceed with legal intervention because of the failure to follow the necessary steps. Again, if this happens, the child suffers. As an example, consider the case in which a four-year-old, living with his father, away from the mother, complained to his daycare provider of incidents of sodomy recently committed by his father. The investigator, who discounted the allegation because it came in the context of a custody dispute, failed to prepare a search warrant to confirm the verifiable aspects of the child's account. The evidence was lost forever and the child remained in the custody of the abusive father. The dependency action was dismissed on the grounds that the mother put the child up to making the allegation because there was no evidence to refute this contention or corroborate the child.

## Children are "Perfect" Victims

Children are a natural for victimization from the offender's perspective.

### Curiosity that Can Kill

Children are naturally curious about everything. As they grow, they become exposed to media depiction of sex that spurs on the natural curiosity about their own sexuality and that of the world around them. The problem is that children are told little about sex by their teachers and even less by their parents. The only way many children ever learn about sex is from their friends. This makes them a perfect target for an offender who befriends them with the intention of exploiting that natural curiosity. Once the offender has the child's confidence, the activity will degenerate into sexual activity [4].

## Children Naturally Follow the Authority of Adults

From the very beginning, children are taught to obey the authority of their elders. The socialization process teaches children that adults are to be respected and followed. An adults' size alone can be intimidating enough to compel a child to comply. Add to this position of authority a person who is a parent, a school teacher, a religious leader, etc., and the child will be even more inclined to follow their bidding. As will be seen, some offenders naturally gravitate to a profession or calling that puts them in supervisory or power positions over children specifically to provide them access and power to control their victims. Those who can't get these positions legitimately often will impersonate such individuals to gain control of their victim; as in the countless cases of people who "flash" badges or use clothing or vehicles that imitate law enforcement officers [5].

## A Natural Need to Be Noticed and Loved

Children have a natural need for attention. They need to be loved. This is what makes them so vulnerable to a child molester who uses seduction as his method of operation. They naturally fall for the attention and care the offender showers upon them. One has only to look at the clown at a child's birthday party. Children will often fight to be the next one to sit on the clown's lap.

The unfortunate thing is that even children who live in "normal" families, where they get the love, attention, and affection that the family affords them, are susceptible to an offender who takes advantage of this need. As in numerous cases, all it took was a trip to McDonald's, the candy store, or to provide the child with something they wanted but couldn't get for themselves.

The socio-economic status of the child makes little difference. If the child has a need for more attention or affection than (s)he is getting, the offender has only to fill the void. Often, children will be willingly trade sex for the offerings of the offender. Clearly, those children who find themselves in families with few resources, who are "on the run," or homeless, are going to be even more susceptible.

With the divorce rate in this country at 50% and the number of broken homes increasing by the minute, it makes children in those homes extremely vulnerable. It is not uncommon to find a parent who is more than willing to allow an apparently innocent relationship to develop between their child and an adult who gives that child attention. The shame is that that relationship is often a ruse that leaves the child victimized and left behind when the offender is through with them [6].

## Natural Response to Resist Parental Authority

As children develop and mature, they enter the phase where they tend to do the opposite of what their parents and authority figures tell them to do. Rebellion is a natural developmental phase that almost all children go through. This is another characteristic of adolescence that makes children vulnerable. When a child is manipulated into doing something that they know their parents will not approve of, they find themselves in emotional limbo, afraid to tell what they did for fear of disapproval or worse, punishment. When the crime involves adolescent boys, this is more of a problem because they often feel they will lose some of their freedom if they reveal their victimization [7].

# The Child as a Witness

At the present time, the issue of children's testimony is under the close scrutiny of the courts. Several major cases have been overturned as a result of the apparent unreliability of a child's testimony presented in court. One could say that this is one area that is now getting the most attention in the courts. The perception of children's ability to testify has changed over the years. At one point children were considered not competent to testify simply because they were children. Now, the courts are more open to providing access to children's testimony and the environment in the courtroom is being adjusted to accommodate children's needs.

There has been a big swing in the perceptions of children's ability to accurately report events in the past twenty years. At one time children were thought by some to be little oracles, upon whose words every investigator would hang awaiting some revelation. The pendulum has swung to the other side where children, especially the very young, were viewed with grave suspicion. The reality is that children are just like any other person who testifies in court. Some are going to be more credible and some less. Each child must be judged on his/her own abilities and characteristics. Experience has found that most children do not lie about sexual abuse, except to deny it ever happened. There are, as with any experience, going to be exceptions to this and children have been found to make allegations that are groundless. The reasons they do are as varied as the children themselves and will be explored in greater detail in later chapters.

Certainly children have more problems in providing accounts of events because they do not understand everything they experience. They don't have enough life experiences from which to draw upon in making sense of what they see, hear, taste, smell, and feel. They have a limited vocabulary. They are easily led to believe things when they are tricked, befuddled, or provided drugs by the offender. However, they must be evaluated like any other witness — on their own merits, not as a class. As will be seen, research has established that children do make credible witnesses. The problem is that it is the general perception by adults that children should not be listened to or their accounts given much credence.

These characteristics and perceptions of them by adults make them easier targets for offenders because the offender will take advantage of this and a poor witness assures less chance of being caught or, at trial, more questions about an offender's guilt.

## Studies Support the Credibility of Children's Accounts

Since the original printing of this text, there have been numerous studies conducted for the purposes of determining how much we may rely upon the accounts of children in sexual abuse and exploitation cases. Surprisingly for many people, even young children have been found to be reliable in recounting "central actions of events that are personally meaningful to them" [8, 9, 10]. As will be discussed in greater detail in Chapter 5, "Interviewing Children," the results obtained from talking with children about their victimization will depend, largely, upon the ability of the interviewer to secure reliable information. This is underscored by Professor John E. B. Myers, J. D., the leading legal scholar in this country on child abuse cases in the courtroom, who concludes that skilled interviewing, conducted by trained interviewers will ensure that children are able to correctly recount their experiences [11].

## A Natural Disdain for the Subject Matter

Child sexual abuse is one of the most repulsive crimes in the codes. It offends the very morals of society. Sexuality alone is difficult enough for people to consciously deal with, much less the idea of children engaging in such activities with adults or one another. This natural disdain for the subject matter makes it very difficult for any professional to deal with. One self-defense mechanism that is part of the human make-up which helps to deal with this is called *Isolation of Affect*. It is this ability to separate the emotional reaction from the factual experience that prevents most professionals from becoming overstressed, emotional bowls of jelly.

In general, professionals in all fields are able to use this self-defense mechanism to get them through the types of cases they encounter, *except,* child sexual abuse. One author has suggested that males have greater problems with this than females [12]. This could be attributed to the fact that there is a repulsion a man feels about the despicable acts of another man (since most offenders are males). Perhaps this is true in some settings, but, it would appear from experience that the problem is not limited to gender. Women in social work, medicine, law, and other professions who hear about and must work with this issue have expressed the same difficulties. The difficulty is that until there is full equity in the professions, males are generally the ones who deal with these issues in law enforcement and in the courts. If the perception is true that men have this difficulty, it could explain the manner in which cases are handled by them. Some cases are given a great deal of attention because the person working on it has a great sensitivity to what's happened. On the other hand, often, just the opposite occurs and the person refuses to adequately respond or investigate or to explore alternatives to the perceived stereotypes involved.

This is toxic work. It is not for everyone and those who are involved should be specially selected, trained, and supervised to ensure a balance in approach to the cases assigned. People have different tolerances for such difficult cases and the emotions they engender. This must be closely watched and monitored.

Those who work these cases must have other avenues to work off the frustrations and emotions the cases create. Hobbies, social activities, and other interests should be a regular part of the professional's life. A change in assignment or duties over time will help to ensure this balance.

One of the main defenses in court for these matters is that the professional is on a "witch hunt." Such a break up of assignment and activity helps to deflect such accusations. The crux of this defense is that the professional is on a "crusade" and cannot see anything but the believed crime at hand, thereby missing other explanations or alternatives. Balance in life, interests, and assignment help to keep the professional "sane" and to avoid this criticism.

The professional working on these issues must also contend with the stigma associated with sexual deviance. There is an abundance of ignorance about sexuality in general, and as a result, those who work on these crimes are often the butt of teasing and ridicule, even suspicion. In subtle and not-so-subtle ways, they are often labeled as "weirdos" or "perverts." Law enforcement, a profession where there are strong stereotypes ingrained in the minds of its members about what a law enforcement officer is supposed to be like, is often affected by this response [13]. However, it is not limited to law enforcement. When people who deal with these crimes meet with others in their field, no one wants to talk about the crimes they must work on. The conversations quickly change once the person mentions that these are the cases they work. They often find that they become alone in the crowd because of the discomfort people feel about acknowledging these crimes exist.

Networking with other professionals who have experienced these problems is of great value. There is a need to debrief, to ventilate, and share the problems with another person who has experienced the same difficulties. For the investigator in a small agency, a therapist in private practice, or someone similarly situated in another profession, this is a problem. Few people are able to talk about their problems with their spouses, family, or friends. It can be very difficult when there is no sympathetic ear to listen. It is hard to talk to supervisors about what the person is experiencing, because of the difficulties in acknowledging the effects upon the individual and the misconceptions about the motivations of people who work on them. One author described an investigator who told him that trying to convey to his supervisor the nature of the problem of sexual abuse and exploitation was like trying to convince the "Air Force of the existence of UFOs" [14].

The symptoms of Isolation of Affect must be carefully monitored. In assessing, investigating, and intervening in sexual abuse and exploitation cases, the emotional effects upon the person working these cases can cause errors in judgement. Mistakes in practice and procedure may cause great difficulties in determining the truth of the allegations down the line when the case comes to court. For example, the violation of an offender's search and seizure rights is no less serious than the misinterpretation of a child's account of events if that mistake infringes upon the accused's liberty interests unjustly or ruins his/her reputation. Conversely, there can be no greater injustice to society, much less the individual child, than to misinterpret a child's claim of abuse as false when its really true, thus leaving the offender in a position where that child or other children are imperiled [15].

## Counter-Transference and its Dangers

According to a U.S. Department of Health and Human Services manual, this issue is only now being discussed in the literature [16]. It entails the professional working on the matter reacting to the facts and circumstances in a manner that adversely affects the case because of previous experiences either in the professional's own personal or professional life. In short, instead of dispassionately and objectively dealing with the facts, the professional jumps to conclusions and makes decisions, not based on the facts presented, but, rather, from the experience and conclusions of the past experience.

This is the exact opposite of the concept of Isolation of Affect. Here, instead of building up an emotional wall to isolate the inner feelings the

It is unfortunate that a parent cannot always be close to their child or children. This inability causes the child to be in constant peril. This generates frustration, fear, and anger on the part of the parents. When the subject of molestation surfaces, that anger can be misdirected at the messenger — be it a professional or a program about molestation. This response is unexpected by most professionals, who would anticipate that a parent would want to know if their child was in jeopardy and want to protect that child.

The sad truth is that people cannot live with the constant fear of catastrophe. It would be totally debilitating if all we worried about was a pending disaster. People who live in earthquake-prone areas can't survive day-to-day thinking only of the fact that the world around them could soon come tumbling down, just as people who live in hurricane or tornado country can't live in constant fear that the wind is going to blow their homes away. Its overwhelming. The same is true about child molestation. People must to believe that their children are safe or, at least, somewhat protected. To shatter that image by forcing them to confront the fact their children are never safe is too psychologically threatening. This response by the public is difficult for a professional to accept.

Lastly, when all is done and the case is sent to the judge, does the offender get the maximum? Does he get sent to a prison for a very long time where no children will be periled by this person? Unfortunately, the answer in many jurisdictions is no. The "three strikes" laws aside, most offenders do not get stiff sentences. This can be as great a deterrent to a professional in all quarters where the purpose is to send the case to court if the case is determined to be genuine. After all of the work, pain, and suffering, the professional goes through to get the case into court, frequently the offender is granted probation, little or no jail time. The message to the professional is: why waste my time and energy? This is the psychological deterrent that prevents many cases from ever going forward — the investigator or other professional dismisses the matter before it ever gets into the "system."

Finally, the main difficulty for professionals working on crimes of child molestation is that society has a "two-faced" approach to the crime. On one they deplore the crime and condemn its perpetrators. On the other, the more common response is to find some other reason to disbelieve or discredit the child victim because its too difficult a subject to consciously deal with.

## Backlash

This text would be incomplete without a discussion of the backlash movement. There are those who call child protection workers self-serving zealots, who in their "witch hunts," step all over the rights of innocent people, both adults and nonabused children [25]. The phrase "backlash" is the term now associated with those who disbelieve there is a serious problem in dealing with child sexual abuse. The term identifies the attack upon persons working to protect children for and with official agencies in prosecution of these crimes.

Myers, in *The Backlash: Child Protection Under Fire*, identifies the "opposition forces" which face child protection workers [26]. The first is "inertial," wherein the bureaucratic resistance interferes with the job the professional must do. This is partially the problem of explaining the "UFO's" mentioned earlier. More importantly, this may be direct undercutting of the professional's ability to function. It may be because of petty jealousies, boundary or turf issues, apathy, and fear of something that is new, or which could bring attention to the agency or individual administrator or supervisor.

The second force is what he terms a "counter-movement" [27]. Here, a group of people have come together to voice their concerns that law enforcement, CPS workers, and professionals connected to investigation and intervention in child sexual abuse cases have gone too far. It is primarily comprised of "wrongly accused" parents and concerned persons, some of whom have been largely discredited for their biases and or direct involvement in advocacy for sex with children. Unfortunately, there are also many legitimate professionals and attorneys, who, seeing a great opportunity to capitalize on this wave of discontent, have made it a practice to work with these groups and those who have been accused of the crimes described herein. Wherever these people go, the media isn't far behind.

However, to write-off these people as fanatics who have little or no power would be a great mistake. The pressure and attention they can bring to a case can cause the "inertial" forces described above to create even greater impediments for an investigator. These roadblocks may surface in the form of preventing any further investigation, of having people removed from their cases, having charges dismissed, and, in the worst scenarios, people reassigned to totally different work.

Another tactic of the counter-movement, and defense attorneys who are associated with it, is to file misconduct charges against the professional(s) involved and shift the attention away from their client. This smoke screen tactic will be discussed in greater detail in the section on defenses. It is mentioned here because it is a symptom of the backlash and the personal attacks made upon the professionals have been devastating to the psyche and careers of many people involved in child protection. This symptom must be anticipated and accounted for by both the individual and the involved agency in the development of any allegation of sexual abuse, especially those that become "high profile" because of the nature of the case or the person(s) accused.

to work a case, and to provide some guidance around the stumbling blocks so often encountered in these cases. Approaches, phases, documentation, and investigative techniques will be discussed.

In preparing this text, I have tried to find as many examples as possible of the successes and failures of my own cases as well as those of the investigators I have had the good fortune to work with. It is my sincere hope that our failures and successes will become your triumphs.

## References and Notes

1. Gerald M. Chaplan, 'Sexual Exploitation of Children: the Conspiracy of Silence,' *Police Magazine*, (Jan. 1982): 46–51.

2. Ann W. Burgess et al., "Child Sex Initiation Rings," *Am. J. Orthopsychiatry*, 51 (1), 1981.

3. U.S. Department of Justice, Office of Justice Programs, National Institute of Justice, *Police and Child Abuse: New Policies for Expanded Responsibilities*, June 1991.

4. Kenneth V. Lanning, *Child Molesters: A Behavioral Analysis*, National Center for Missing and Exploited Children, Washington, D.C., 1992.

5. Lanning, 1992.

6. Ibid.

7. Ibid.

8. Karen J. Saywitz, "Credibility of Child Witnesses: the Role of Communicative Competence," *Topics in Language Disorders*, 1993.

9. Keren J. Saywitz, 1993; G. S. Goodman and A. Clarke-Steward, "Suggestibility in Children's Testimony: Implications for Sexual Abuse Investigations," in *Suggestibility of Children's Recollections: Implications for Eyewitness Testimony*, Dores, J. ed. American Psychological Association., Washington D.C., 1991.

10. A. Tucker, P. Mertin, and M. Luszcz, The Effect of a Repeated Interview on Young Children's Eyewitness Memory, *Australian and New Zealand Journal of Criminology* 23(1990): 117–124.

11. John E. B. Meyers, "Can We Believe What Children Say About Sexual Abuse?" *The APSAC Advisor* (1994).

12. Lanning, 1992.

13. Ibid.

14. Ibid.

15. Ibid.

16. Marilyn S. Peterson and Anthony J. Urquiza, "*The Role of Mental Health Professionals in the Prevention and Treatment of Child Abuse and Neglect*," U.S. Department of Health and Human Services, Administration for Children and Families, 1993.

17. Ibid, p. 39.

18. Ibid.

19. Lanning, 1992.

20. Ibid.

21. Ibid.

22. American Prosecutors Research Institute (herein, APRI), *UPDATE*, 9-7/8, 1996, quoting Michele McKay McCoy, Santa Clara County Deputy District Attorney.

23. Lanning, 1992.

24. Ibid.

25. D. Heckler, *The Battle and the Backlash: The Child Sexual Abuse War*, D. C. Heath, Lexington, MA, 1988.

26. Myers, 1994.

27. Ibid.

28. Ibid.

29. Ann Hagedorn, "Prosecution of Child-Molestation Cases Grows More Wary in Wake of Acquittals," *Wall Street Journal*, 4-15-91.

30. Carol McGraw, "McMartin Fallout: Will it Chill Child Abuse Inquiries?" *Los Angeles Times*, Editorial, 2-3-86.

31. John E. B. Meyers, *The Backlash: Child Protection Under Fire*, Sage, Thousand Oaks, CA, 1994.

32. National Center for Prosecution of Child Abuse, National District Attorney's Association, *NDAA Bulletin*, 7, 1, January/February, 1988.

# State of the Problem

This chapter is presented for several reasons. First, it is intended to provide the reader and investigators with some background information on what is presently going on as it relates to the sexual exploitation of children. Second, and more important, this chapter, like the entire text, is intended to give investigators a foundation for understanding and assessing a case. Last, it is intended to establish common ground, to ensure that the reader and author are speaking the same language and have the same interpretations of terms and understandings of the nature of the problem of sexual exploitation of children

## The Problem Defined

The basis of the sexual exploitation of children is pedophilia — sexual attraction to children. Pedophilia is the attraction to or love of (*-philia*) children (*ped-*) (defined in greater detail in Chapter 2). *Pedophilia erotica* can best be translated as "love of children;" however, its true meaning and general usage now implies the abnormal sexual desire for children [1]. Perhaps the *Pedophile Liberation Front* (PLF), defines it best on their web site:

> "... what exactly is a pedophile? A 'pedophile' is an adult that is sexually attracted to children. 'Sexually' means that this person may like to touch you, rub your body against his, be very affectionate and cuddly. He (or sometimes, she) may also wish to touch your private parts, or have you touch his. In short, a pedophile likes to do with children what everybody else likes to do with other adults" [2].

There are many people with this desire, and several groups have been formed that espouse sex with children. They have written and produced manuals and writings to support their perspective. They have also lobbied legislative bodies and pressed for elimination of age-of-consent laws. One such group, although supposedly defunct, yet still listed on the Internet in September, 1997, produced a pamphlet entitled *Paedophilia* (British spelling) in which it offers the following to explain the sexual attraction to children:

> "... (paedophilia is) sexual love directed towards children.... (paedophiles) can be of either sex or any (sexual) orientation (i.e., homosexual, hetero-sexual, or bisexual).... (some paedophiles) believing that their sexuality is natural, harmless, and an integral part of their personality, would not wish to be changed (of their sexual orientation) even if this were possible — which it is not.... (paedophiles haven't chosen their sexual preference) any more than other people have chosen their sexual feelings. They just find themselves attracted to children [3]."

The preceding quote calls attention to a basic misconception that law enforcement needs to recognize to appropriately and successfully address sexual exploitation of children. What the quote implies is that pedophilia may be a way of life, a lifestyle instead of an illness; or if an illness, one for which there is no cure. The sexual attraction and feelings may be as strongly and deeply rooted as those of heterosexuality, homosexuality, or bisexuality. To try to change or alter a pedophile's sexual persuasion might be impossible. An appropriate analogy is the issue of homosexuality. At one time it was considered a sexual deviation, an illness that could be treated. Regardless of personal opinion, in many societies today it is considered a legitimate life-style. One pedophile group uses this comparison to justify its existence.

> "Much of the medical profession in this country (England) was content, until quite recently, to consider homosexuality an illness. But as homosex-uals have organized themselves to challenge this view, the medical opinion itself has changed. Homosexuals are now widely regarded as ordinary, healthy people — a minority, but no more "ill" than the minority who are left-handed. There is no reason why paedophilia should not win similar acceptance [4]."

Although pedophilia should not be accepted as a legitimate lifestyle, our approach to dealing with pedophilia should acknowledge that it may be a way of life and is a major subculture to be reckoned with. That subculture and its underground of sex offenders and devotees to child sexuality are a major source of the crime problems attendant upon the sexual exploitation of children.

## The Difference Between Child Molesters and Pedophiles

The words *child molester* connote many different things to different people. In the field of criminal investigation these words are generally used to identify a person who would sexually abuse a child.

In conjuring up a visual image of this person, one might find they run the gambit from the dirty old man in the rain coat, loitering around school playgrounds luring children into the bushes to the well-dressed, corporate executive, who nightly rapes his own daughter. The myths and misconceptions about who this person is abound and are described in greater detail later in this chapter. However, for the purposes of this text, we must consider that the offender could be any one of the various stereotypes and then some. He is a person who may use nonviolent, seduction techniques to engage in all manner of sex acts with children. He may be a very pleasant individual who coaxes or tricks children into sexual activity. He may be a power rapist, who forces his child victims into sex. He may be a sadist who gets his thrills hurting children. He may be a masochist, who contrary to the sadist, gets his thrills from having the child inflict pain upon himself. Lastly, "he" may be a woman. Over the last ten years, as this crime has been investigated and researched, we are learning more about female offenders.

This person may be known to the child or a complete stranger. As will be seen later, most offenders are known to their victims and their victims' families. This person may commit only one offense or may be a "serial" offender, committing groupings of crimes. He may be an occasional offender who finds a situation and opportunity appealing and offends when presented with certain circumstances. He may chose children as his sexual object who are prepubescent (pedophilia) or those who are pubescent (hebephilia).

For the purposes of this discussion, a child molester will be defined as a person who is older than his victim and who engages children (as defined by local law) in activity (proscribed by law) that would be considered for sexual gratification of his own desires. For the most part, we will be talking about adults engaging in sexual acts with children of various ages. However, as the crime has been found to be committed by children upon children, one must still consider the fact that older persons, still defined as children by law, could be considered child molesters. Juvenile offenders will not be discussed much in this text, except as they are found to have been victims themselves and are re-enacting their abuse or attempting "master" their own trauma.

The term *pedophile* has been used synonymously with *child molester* in the public lexicon. However, research and investigative practice has found that there are *pedophiles* who are not *child molesters*. That is they don't engage children in *activity* for sexual gratification. As will be seen in Chapter 3, there are persons who focus on children as their sexual object, but never touch them or engage them in contact for sexual purposes. These may be *voyeurs* or *collectors*. The term *pedophilia* is one that, in the colloquial sense, encompasses all persons who get sexual gratification from touching, being, watching, or simply doing things with or about children. This term is a psychological label and may be further defined by the literature of the genre.

The *Diagnostic and Statistical Manual of Mental Disorders*, Fourth Edition (*DSM-IV*) defines pedophilia as sexual activity consisting of "fantasies, sexual urges or behaviors ... involving ... prepubescent children...[5]." The definition also takes in people who "...prefer... exclusively" children in this age group.

The key terms here are *activity* with or *fantasy* involving sexual activity with *prepubital* children that is the *preferred* or *exclusive* sexual stimulant. The *DSM-IV* defines psychological and sexual disorders which it classifies as *paraphilia*. The terms and definitions in this manual are for the purposes of identifying and diagnosing psychological and psychosexual problems in people. The definition was not created as a legal term, but, as become the label most commonly associated an offender who molests children.

The difficulty for the courts in using this term is that once the label is made, it creates an inherent "straw-man" defense. Once it is claimed that the offender is a pedophile, the obvious defense is that he is not. This is done by comparing his behavior and symptomatic characteristics to the model we just constructed, demonstrating that he doesn't have the traits described in the definition. Therefore, it is better for professionals in the justice system to avoid making the label at all, while at the same time knowing and understanding the technical definitions of the words. As used in this text, from here on, the term pedophile will take the colloquial meaning.

For the law enforcement officer and other professional working on solving or proving a case for court, the terms are not as important as knowing the characteristics of the types of offenders and what evidence they will leave behind. For example, there are offenders who prefer children, yet still have sex with people within their own peer group. Does this make them any less of a criminal when they offend against children? Of course not, and, more specifically, one wouldn't dismiss the possibility that the person could have molested a child simply because that person has had sex with another adult.

The reader shouldn't be sidetracked by the fact that there are people who merely have fantasies involving sex with children. This, in and of itself, may not be illegal. As those who investigate crime know, there must be two elements present when a crime is committed. The act and the accompanying state of mind. The typology that is recounted in Chapter 2 will set forth a model for law enforcement to follow in assessing whether the two elements come together. It will also help to predict the type of evidence that will be found to establish those elements. The ability to predict what kind of behavior and evidence is likely to be found is what makes this typology so valuable. The confirmation and finding of the characteristics listed in the typology are what will define the offender's acts and help lead to subsequent conviction.

Although the categories were formulated using psychological terminology and theory, they are not intended for diagnosing the acts and symptoms of an offender. Its author, Kenneth V. Lanning, M.S., a behavioral scientist at the FBI Academy, is the world's foremost authority on the crimes of sexual abuse and exploitation of children, and has graciously permitted the use of the typology of the offender that appears in another volume in the Forensic Series, *Practical Rape Investigation*, by Robert Hazelwood [6]. It also appears in *Child Molesters: A Behavioral Analysis*, published by the National Center for Missing and Exploited Children [7], whom we thank for allowing its use here.

## Characteristics of the Offender

### Pederast

Disagreement exists between experts about what terms are correct in describing the offender. Many offenders who engage in homosexual acts with boys believe they are homosexuals. On the other hand, the homosexual community, for the most part, rejects them and is repulsed by them. For example, one gay man told me, that the subject of "boy-lovers" makes most homosexual's "toes curl."

On the Internet, a boy-lover's homepage, *Paiderastia*, defines pederast as deriving from the Greek, literally translating to "boy love." It goes on to say:

> "Etymologically, the term 'pedophilia' could accurately describe boy-love (*paides*, 'boys' and *philia* 'love'), the word itself has no basis in the historical antecedent of modern boy-love, namely, the ancient Greek practice of paiderastia [8]."

It goes on to quote dictionary definitions as ranging from "homosexual' to 'a man who practices sodomy with boys."

As used here, *sodomy* is the act of anal intercourse, and in a dictionary, a *pederast* is generally defined as an individual who engages in anal intercourse. Another underground publication finds the definition in the roots of the Greek language: *ped*-(boy); *erastes* (lover).

> "…pederast is used to denote the male over the age of eighteen who is erotically attached to boys between the ages of puberty or involvement between a male over the age of eighteen and one between the ages of twelve and sixteen [9]."

## Chickenhawk

*Chickenhawk* or *chicken queen* is a street term for the man who cruises for young males. It is a pejorative term, with a strong negative connotation on the street. The person given this label is not one of the most respected of the underground. Some have referred to this individual as the pedophile who is interested exclusively in boys.

## Other Terms for Offenders

Among the underground, other terms for offenders are used to distinguish the object of their attentions. Terms such as *boy-lover, girl-lover,* or *child-lover* connote the type of children they seek.

## Underground Terms for Children

The underground has also given the children names. Terms such as *kittens, princesses, angels, teens, preteens, moppets, puppies,* and *chicken* refer to the objects of their attentions.

# Pedophilia — A Way of Life

There is a distinct underground subculture of offenders, some of whom have banded together to advocate sex with children and abolish laws prohibiting such conduct. Most base it on the child's right to learn new and different things. The Pedophile Information Exchange, a group supposedly defunct, yet is still listed on the Internet, describe their perspective in early publications:

> "… It is desirable for young people of both sexes that they are able to meet and cope with such situations (sexual contact). A normal development requires broad possibilities of introductions, experiment, contact and initiation…[10]."

Later, it said:

> "…The result (of the prohibitive laws) has been needless harm and suffering of many kinds. Children have been humiliated, ostracized, separated from those they love, forbidden sexual relationships, ridden with sexual guilt, even driven to committing suicide. Some parents, too, have been separated from their children… [11]."

A pedophile said in a television interview after being exposed during a "public" meeting in a San Francisco library,

"We're not going to change. All the therapy in the world isn't going to change a boy-lover into something else [12]."

Another claimed:

"...because of our efforts, the day will come, and come soon, when children will have sex freedom (provided contraceptives are used) of a bisexual nature with other children and with adults. They will be allowed happily to participate in kid porn activity... [13]."

Today, on the Internet, the Pedophile Liberation Front (PLF), spells it out this way:

"...the aim of the PLF (web) site is to promote a sense of pride in those pedophiles whose lives are daily made miserable by the media and by their constant bashing of our community [14]."

Some of these organizations actively have run campaigns for legalization of sexual activity with children. One group's motto is "sex before eight or else it's too late." Their stated goal was: "Child-child and child-adult sexuality if contraceptives are used.. . ." They lobbied legislators to their cause:

"...We hardly touched the surface of child mental health and the harm involve in suppressing child porn. Our group has been active ten years and has been backed by the leaders in the world of psychiatry from the first.
In 1887, Dr. Sigmund Freud discovered that children must have bisexual activity at ages four, five, or eight or else they become antisocial even to the point of being suicidal.... The well-meaning person trying to stamp out child porn do not understand the harm they are doing to children. . . .
We suggest that you... [15]."

Although the group that promoted the former proposals is not as active as it once was, others have sprung up to take its place. In signing off of a posting, this quote was found on the Internet in September, 1997, identifying preexisting groups called "UNCLE" (United Nuptial Child-Lover's Emancipation) and "CAMEL" (Child/Adult Marriage Effort for Legalization), stating that "We don't advocate breaking the law, but *changing it!*" (Emphasis original).

As part of a package of sweeping sexual-assault law reforms, the District of Columbia once examined a law that would maintain criminal penalties for sex between adults and children and teenagers and also for forced sex involving children and teenagers, but would allow persons 12 years and older to engage in sexual intercourse as long as one partner was not more than 4 years older than the other. It would have also removed any legal penalties for sex between "consenting" children under 12 as long as the children were no more than two years apart in age. The law did not pass, yet this is the type of legislation these groups try to enact, slowly eroding the law to their wishes.

Other suggested legal reforms are the abolition of laws prohibiting sexual intercourse, sodomy, and oral copulation with children, as well as the child molestation statutes. One group suggests that this should be done because:

> "... (involvement in sex) makes child aware of VD and its prevention. Parents and non-parents help a child toward good mental health by masturbating it and be encouraging it to masturbate...lack of premarital sex leads to divorce, drug abuse, crime and suicide.... The Houston kid murders and others around the nation result from porn laws that punish adults who gratify sex-begging kids [16]."

The same group claims that:

> "One-half hour after a bowel movement, no fecal matter remains in the anal cavity. The cavity is large enough at the age of 4 for both boys and girls to painlessly hold an adult penis — an act they constantly desire from the adult males they love [17]."

What this should reveal about this group and others like it is that these offenders genuinely believe that what they are doing is right for the child. This is important for an investigator when it becomes necessary to prove intent and to demonstrate that the offender had knowledge at the time he committed the offense that what he was doing was wrong. For example, in a case involving a man and a woman who had molested and photographed their 12-year-old babysitter, investigators found the man with a two-inch-thick master's thesis, with his own handwriting in the margins, on the subject of the benefits of child sex. When he was arrested, the following letter was found in his possession:

> "We are always going to be honest with you _____. We still want you to be a girlfriend to us as well as a babysitter. We need to be able to give you a "pat," "squeeze," or kiss at the door whenever you come and go from our apartment. We want to be able to touch, hug, and kiss you. We want to be able to comb or wash your hair, bathe with you, or "make-out" with you whenever you're around. We know you're somewhat confused about this and all we can do is ask you to trust us. *You* (his emphasis) might feel that we're asking a lot of you but *we* (his emphasis) feel that we're offering you a lot, too. We feel like we're giving you the opportunity to experiment and be a little "free and fancy" by doing the kind of things we wish we could have done when we were your age. We provide a neat little world for you to come

and go as you want. You're free to do as you wish here… everything remains a secret. We want you to need us to help you grow up. We enjoy your young world and we want you to enjoy our older, more sexual world… this *is* (his emphasis) a love letter… because (this letter) could cause problems, we need to ask you to leave it with us, for now. We'll save the letter for you… you may have it when it is safe to do so. P.S. We wish we had known you when you were eight or nine or ten or eleven… We love you! [18]."

Another group dedicated to legitimizing sex with children originally said:

"NAMBLA (North American Man/Boy Love Association) supports consensual sex regardless of age. We oppose age-of-consent laws, and all other laws used to oppress children. We support and encourage young people in their rebellions against antisex regulations imposed on them by adults [19]."

NAMBLA has proposed that age of consent laws should be revised to age 12, but, that a "young person of either sex, between the ages of 8 and 12, should be allowed to consent to the erotic acts of fondling, fellatio, and genital orgasm… [20]."

In a 1994 memo posted on the Internet, NAMBLA, supported the position on "Age of Consent/Pedophilia/Children's Rights" that "governments … abolish the age of consent laws so long as there is adequate protection for your from being sexually abused…[21]."

It supports those who have been arrested and jailed for "nonviolent" sex offenses and believes that if the child consents to the act, it should be sufficient. NAMBLA's San Francisco chapter sent letters to child care providers in the Bay Area encouraging them to accept NAMBLA volunteers to counsel boys in their programs who had been molested.

A paperback "treatise" (so described by its author) on sexual relationships with boys typifies the type of thinking many offenders have. Entitled *Toward A Perspective For Boy-Lovers*, its foreword and introduction speak for themselves:

"This book primarily is addressed to those more serious-minded adult males who feel an existential attraction to young boys. Its purpose is twofold: hopefully to help clarify the life-style of the man who finds himself irresistibly drawn to these special beings, and to offer some conclusions which may aid him to achieve a more ideal goal-oriented life and a better relationship with his youthful friends as well as an improved and enriched world for all concerned [22].

Boy-love is the love for (a): a lad *in toto* (his character, personality, soul, body), (b): the beauty and/or sexual appeal of youngsters, and (c): the sexual pleasure afforded by boys [23]."

The PAIDERASTIA homepage and others list this publication as a reference and "must-read" topic. In fact, PAIDERASTIA, even goes further, creating a "code of ethics" for those afflicted with the "innate love of boys." This publication is one of the many that plot the path for the offender to follow. As its table of contents shows, it is a guide to the uninformed and a means of rationalizing or finding support for the offender's illicit behavior:

I. A Factual Concept
   Dynamics
   1. The place of the boy in the life of the man

***

   4. Sexual union: why it is desired by the man
   5. The psychology of sex in man/boy relationships; how it differs
      between man and boy
   General Nature of the Man/Boy relationship
   6. Legally related problems
II. The Ethics of Boy-Love
   Boy Love in the Context of Ethics

***

   2. The ethics of anal-intercourse
   3. Sex without love
III. A Positive Viewpoint
   On Anal-Intercourse with Boys: A Proposed Ideal Purpose Therein
IV. What Needs To Be Done & How It Can Be Accomplished
   Goals
   1. The boy-lover as an educator
   2. To help the boy mature
   3. To help the boy achieve self-realization
   4. To help the boy with his problems
   5. To serve as an ego-ideal
   6. To serve as the boy's adult friend who promotes knowledge and
      understanding of the role of sex [24].

Investigation to date indicates these "groups" are made up of small numbers of people. Yet, they are vocal about their views.

A member of another group that promotes sex with children through its newsletter and by making connections for people with similar interests posted petitions throughout the city of Berkeley (California) headlined, "You may disapprove of child sex, but please… take your sexual hang-ups off our laws." The intent of the petition was to legalize "nonabusive sensual/sexual activity involving children." Among the laws he listed for repeal was the felony murder rule as applied to those who kill children during a molest. He had also written and attempted to peddle *A Brief Manifesto On Behalf of Childhood Sexual Relating*. Although not arrested, this man was found to have been seeking out the friendship of children in a neighborhood park [25].

One of the most frightening aspects of organized sex with children discovered by law-enforcement officials across the nation is the people who worship the devil. Satanic cults, part of what is alleged to be a strong underground separate from that of the pedophile subculture, use children in their rituals and sacrifices. Children as young as babies are believed to have been molested and murdered in the act of worshiping the devil. As is noted infra, no well-developed, organization has yet to be documented.

## Sexual Exploitation

The definition of sexual exploitation of children is best understood when the crime problems related to pedophilia are discussed. These are child molestation, child pornography, and child prostitution. One of the first documented government examinations of this crime problem that was in 1978, when the Texas state legislature examined the problem of sexual exploitation of children, defining it as a problem that placed children in positions where they were taken advantage of sexually because of their inability to cognitively assess or resist the contact, or were placed into positions where they became dependent on the offender [26]. Since that time, governments throughout the world have finally come to recognize that their children are jeopardized by people who actively seek them out for sexual purposes. A World Congress Against Commercial Sexual Exploitation of Children was held in Stockholm, Sweden, in 1996. In their report on contributing factors, they cite economic injustices, disparities of wealth within and among nations, problems of migration, a move towards urbanization among peoples, and family disintegration as causes. They also cite conflicting family values, as well as contrasting societal and cultural values as contributing to the problem [27]. What it comes down to is it is the illicit desires of adults who take advantage of these problems throughout the world that generate the contacts with children for sexual purposes.

Those contacts, and the basis for sexual exploitation of children, can be broken down into three distinct yet directly related crime categories: pedophilia (the sexual/physical molestation of children), child prostitution, and child pornography. Pedophilia is the basis of the latter two. It is the pedophile who creates the demand for both child pornography and child prostitution.

In most of the literature, incest is discussed separately from sexual exploitation of children and is incorrectly claimed to be a far greater threat to children than extra familial offenses. This is generally because incest has been thought to be something unique to a given family situation. We will discuss our perception of the incest offender in Chapter 2. Psychological theory differs when this aspect of the problem is discussed, on the basis of motivation and the ability to treat the offender. In the past, neither has been considered terribly important for the investigator. For example, one of the major theories regarding the incest offender is that he commits his crime because of factors unique to his family situation. It suggests he limits his activities to the children within the family, and is not as prone to violence as are offenders in extra familial incidents. His motivation may be stress related or due to other breakdowns within family dynamics.

As will be seen in Chapter 3, this isn't always true, and some offenders may even marry into situations with children who are in their target group. Others may create a family for the express purpose of raising their own victims. By using the typologies set forth in Chapter 2, by asking questions such as those suggested in Chapters 5 and 7, and by finding the type of evidence described in Chapter 3, an investigator may have a better chance of seeing his case end with a jail sentence.

The distinction between molestation and prostitution is often not easily made, especially when one considers how formal some of the "sex rings" may become. Ordinarily, prostitution is considered the act of sex for money. However, when the dynamics of child molestation by pedophiles are examined, this definition may have to include the act of sex for the satisfaction of other needs.

Most children involved in prostitution are trapped by the need to survive, having been cast into their situations by abuse, neglect, abandonment, or poverty. The typical street victim of pornography or prostitution has a third-grade reading level and few usable skills. Few, if any, enjoy what they do, and most gravitate to the trade as a means of support and/or survival, often becoming dependent on the offender for everything including emotional needs.

Strangely enough, children find means of both financial and emotional support in prostitution and pornography. They find a distorted feeling of being wanted and a sense of importance that offers, in the absence of true and sincere emotion, a temporary degree of satisfaction. Regardless of the many explanations for a child's involvement, the true and ever-present underlying factor is the addressing of the child's needs for love, friendship, interest, and survival. Study after study has found that prostitutes and porn models do what they do as a means of dealing with an impossible situation. In 1996, the international group examining world commercial sexual exploitation attributed "human greed" as the common denominator between sex with children and adults seeking them out for that purpose [28]. However, Kenneth Wooden said it best:

They share a common bond: all are young, troubled, confused and incarcerated — either in institutions or by drugs, pimps or loneliness [29].

Like the child prostitute, the child molestation victim in the extra familial situation is similarly likely to be looking for a way to address his or her unsatisfied needs. Children still in the home who are seeking satisfaction of these needs may become entangled in sexual activities with adults, seduced by video games, candy, or a trip to McDonald's. One molester had actually visited the home of the children he was molesting and had convinced the parents that he was genuinely interested in the children and was doing good things for them.

Just as molestation and prostitution are distinctly related, so are pornography and molestation. The three form a triad of closely tied law-enforcement problems — problems that traditionally were considered unrelated.

The kingpin of this triad is the pedophile (see Figure 1.1). Pornography and prostitution are only "sidelines" to the sexual desires of the pedophile, and all else becomes subordinate to the act of molestation. In one study, producers of child pornography were found, without exception, to be child molesters, and child pornography was an adjunct to the crime of molesting children. It is clear from experience and the discussions in the literature that child pornography is a by-product of child molestation, and the relationship of child pornography to child molestation is a greater threat to children than has been previously considered. A case that illustrates this is that of a clergyman who ran a farm for wayward boys. He had the boys engage in sexual orgies with sponsors and clients of the farm, which were filmed, and then sold as a memento of the acts that transpired.

This farm is a good example of how the illicit desires of the offender have created networks of pedophiles who seek out children for sexual purposes. These networks often have national and international connections, making this a conspiracy of crime that has not yet been adequately addressed.

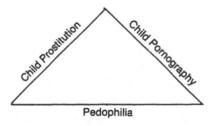

**Figure 1.1**    The triad of law-enforcement problems posed by the sexual exploitation of children.

## Fallacies

To better understand this conspiracy, one must get a different perspective on the problem. As with rape and sexual assault, new directions must be taken to comprehend and successfully address the crime problem of sexual exploitation of children. In seeking these new directions, it is important to recognize that many misconceptions have distorted what we believed to be the truth about the problem. The result has been that many fallacies, believed to be accurate, have misguided law enforcement's posture in responding to the problem. These fallacies can be grouped into three categories: the offense, the offender, and the victim.

## The Offense

FALLACY:   Child molestation is committed by sex-starved maniacs.

TRUTH:   Like rape, child molestation is sexual behavior in the service of nonsexual needs and is generally committed as a result of other psychological factors.

FALLACY:   The crime happens only in "open" cities.

TRUTH:   The crime is widespread and occurs in every community in the country and perhaps in the world.

FALLACY:   The crime problem perils children only when they are playing on playgrounds and alleys.

TRUTH:   Child molestation is not committed solely on the street, in the playgrounds, or near schools. It is committed in areas once considered safe and impervious to the threat of such things — our homes, schools, juvenile programs, and day care centers.

FALLACY:   Child molesters and child pornographers work alone and molest only one child at a time.

TRUTH:   Single incidents are not isolated and often involve or are connected to a number of other offenders and victims.

FALLACY:   If the case surfaces during the litigation of family law matters concerning divorce, custody or visitation, the allegation is manufactured to secure advantage in the civil case.

TRUTH:   Child sexual abuse allegations surface during the pendency of a family law matter because of many factors. The frequency of valid allegations in family law is no different than any other circumstance and the case shouldn't be judged to be false merely because it arises in this context.

## The Offender

FALLACY:   The offender is easily recognized because he looks like a monster, is the troll who lives under the bridge, or is disfigured.

TRUTH:   No such distinction can be made.

FALLACY:   It is easy to recognize a child molester because he is the "typical dirty old man who always wears a raincoat."

TRUTH:   The offender is not dirty, old, or senile.

FALLACY:   Only "criminal types" and people of lower social status commit these crimes.

TRUTH:   The offender may be a well-respected, prominent member of the community. He comes from all walks of life and may be from any aspect of the social spectrum. Child molestation knows no cultural or economic boundaries.

FALLACY:   Children should be warned only to stay away from strangers.

TRUTH:   In the majority of cases, the offender is not a stranger but, rather, someone known not only to the victim but to the family as well.

FALLACY:   Homosexuals molest children

TRUTH:   The offender is not homosexual. Pedophilia must be viewed as a completely separate issue from gender and sexual preference.

FALLACY:   Only men molest children.

TRUTH:   The offender can be a woman.

FALLACY:   It doesn't matter which child a molester goes after, he or she is attracted to any and all children.

TRUTH:   Child molesters have identifiable sex and age preferences.

## The Victim

FALLACY:   We should warn only girls about being molested.

TRUTH:   Girls are not the only target of the child molester. An equal number of boys may be victimized.

FALLACY:   Only lower-class children are victimized.

TRUTH:   Victims are representative of every social and economic status.

FALLACY:   The only way a child could be molested or involved in pornography is by force.

TRUTH:   Children are not forced, compelled, or enticed into acts with threats of harm. They are, in many cases, willing, noncomplaining victims. Some children have actually described the people who molest them as their "best friends."

FALLACY:   Children falsely accuse adults.

TRUTH:   Children rarely make up accusations.

## Magnitude and Scope

### Statistics — The Unknown Factors

The true magnitude of the sexual exploitation of children has yet to be determined. It has been suggested that child molestation is the "perfect crime" because children are singularly vulnerable, easily persuaded to cooperate with molesters, and too ashamed to talk about it with others. Finding definitive statistics is a difficult, if not impossible, task because of the nonuniform reporting of crimes throughout the nation and the integration of child-molestation cases into the broader category of sex crimes/assault by the agencies reporting to the FBI and state governments.

Studies of the numbers of victims and people involved in the sexual exploitation of children provide confusing and misleading information. Most estimates include all manner of sexual assault, including incest, but exclude pornography and prostitution.

Recent studies have revealed that only a fraction of the incidents are reported. It has been conjectured that the problem of sexual abuse of children is of enormous dimensions; however, its national dimensions cannot be adequately measured because of the lack of accurate statistics. Several investigative reports have concluded that the reported incidence is "only the tip of the iceberg" and that the actual incidence is far greater than the reports received.

Like rape, child molestation is one of the most under-reported crimes in the nation, and virtually every study of the crime problem acknowledges the fact that only 1 to 10% of the incidents are ever disclosed.

In a 50-State Survey conducted in 1995 by the National Committee for Prevention of Child Abuse, revealed that there were more than three million children *reported* as victims of child maltreatment, with an estimated 11%, sexual abuse [30] Those figures were about the same in 1996 [31]. The problem with these figures is that they only involve those reported to Child Protective Services (CPS) and the definition of sexual abuse does not include all forms of sexual exploitation.

One of the most telling and respected studies, was a telephone poll conducted by the *Los Angeles Times* in 1985 of 2,627 randomly selected adults. It found that 27% of the women and 16% of the men told of their abuse as children [32]. Another study found that 38% of the women interviewed were sexually abused as children, more than half reported unwanted sexual advances that didn't end in physical contact [33]. A Gallup Poll of adults in Canada found that 22% of adults had unwanted sexual contacts as children and 39% had unwanted sexual advances that never culminated in a physical act [34].

Another Gallup Poll, taken in the USA, found that one million children may have been sexually abused in 1995, by either an adult or an older child. The poll reported that this was *10 times the reported cases* for that same period [35].

Pedophiles themselves claim that 2 to 20 million men are attracted to boys in this country [36]. A study conducted by Dr. Gene G. Abel, Director of the Sexual Behavior Clinic in the New York State Psychiatric Institute, suggests that "child molestation is a more serious and frequent crime than rape." Abel found that the child molesters he studied were "responsible for molesting an average of 68.3 victims, more than three times the number of adult women assaulted by each rapist[37]." In another study conducted in the United States by Abel, it was found that 403 men had victimized over 67,000 children. In Australia, one man was found to have victimized 2,500 boys in his lifetime [38].

Police investigations have also revealed some frightening findings about the numbers of those involved in sexual exploitation of children. As the years have passed, the numbers have only risen to match the sophistication of the individual offender involved. In 1982, police in Los Angeles arrested Catherine Wilson for commercial distribution of child pornography. They found a mailing list of 30,000 customers. In 1997, police in Fort Worth, Texas, arrested a man operating a pornography operation involving children and adults. He had a 150,000 picture library and was receiving over 6,000 photographs a day over the Internet, many of them children [39]. Another undercover operation conducted by a California police officer had over 12,200 child pornography images sent to his computer site in a 7-day period [40]. Barry Crimmins, in testimony before the Senate Judiciary Committee on Child Pornography and the Internet, said he once had so much child pornography sent to him on his computer it took eight-and-one-half hours to "download" it [41]. Police in North Syracuse, New York, broke another child porn ring, finding another mailing list of over 20,000 customers. According to Louis J. Freeh, Director of the Federal Bureau of Investigation, in 1997, in one operation on the Internet, the FBI had generated 200 search warrants, 40 consent searches, 81 indictments, 33 informants, 91 arrests, and 83 felony convictions, and it wasn't over yet [42].

In 1972, Los Angeles police arrested a child pornographer who lived in a two-bedroom apartment. When arrested, one of his bedrooms was stacked floor to ceiling and wall to wall with child pornography and a publication entitled *Where The Young Ones Are*. This publication had no photographs in it, yet records seized revealed that in a 13-month period it sold 70,000 copies at $5.00 each. As the title suggests, it is "a travel guide," listing 378 places, in 59 cities in 34 states and Canada where "the young" can be found. It lists playgrounds, bowling alleys, pool halls, schools, soda fountains, and so on — all places where children either congregate or regularly frequent. It has this notation on the inside back cover:

> "Help us prepare the (next) edition of *Where The Young Ones Are*. Send us listings of places in your home town and our representative in the area will check your listing. It may then become part of next year's publication [43]."

Interviews conducted by police investigators with pedophiles themselves also reveal some startling information. A 52-year-old man told an investigator of 5,000 children he had molested in his lifetime; a 42-year-old Connecticut man told of more than 1,000 children he had molested; and a 62-year-old man, an oil executive with an $11,000-a-month trust fund, admitted to molesting a "boy a day" for 30 years. In Berkeley, California identified incidents more than tripled in a three-year period.

Probably the greatest hurdle the victim must face is the reporting of the incident. Disclosure is the most difficult and threatening step a victim must take and, because of real and imagined difficulties, victims often won't come forward. At the heart of the difficulties lie several factors.

## Embarrassment

A child may be embarrassed about the incident. Sex is an embarrassing subject and not one that people discuss easily when it comes to personal experiences. For adults, who at least have some education and knowledge from which to deal with their feelings and experiences, this is true in situations of *consensual* sexual relationships, let alone coerced or forced. Yet children, who most often have no formal, much less informal, education about sexual matters, often find they have mixed feelings about their experiences, and find it extremely awkward to discuss such matters. Boys who are molested often find that telling others that someone took control of them is an extremely difficult thing to admit because it isn't "manly" to allow such things to happen.

Conversely, *in some situations* if a girl is molested, it is not as threatening for them to disclose. For example, in a case in southern California, a man was involved sexually with and photographed approximately 150 boys between the ages of 6 and 14 years. He was discovered to have over 14,000 photographs of preteen boys in sexually explicit and conventional poses. He was discovered when he took pictures of some girls, who told their parents afterward.

## Fears of Being Responsible or Blamed

Children often feel good during the act because it is pleasurable, but uncomfortable because of the nature of the act and the knowledge or sense that something is wrong. Their inability to resolve this conflict can manifest itself in a reluctance to tell anyone, and gives them a feeling of being responsible for the incidents. The confusion may then induce a fear that they will be blamed for what happened because they "enjoyed" it or in some way allowed it to happen. A 10-year-old girl who was molested starting at the age of 8 years described how she felt:

> ...I was scared and I was uncomfortable and I was very confused. I was afraid to tell my mom. In some strange way, I felt it was my fault. I was afraid my mom would punish me... [44].

## Fear of Being Punished

Children like this girl, especially the very young, may not disclose for fear they might be punished. Most children have been warned not to do "those things" and they fear punishment for doing something they have been told not to. Children — girls in particular — face another dilemma. Those who have gained certain freedoms, such as the ability to stay out late or go to certain places like the movies without supervision, and who are compromised, fear the loss of those freedoms. By disclosing, they admit they can't take care of themselves. On the other hand, boys generally have greater freedoms than girls. The threat of losing these freedoms may be too great to allow them to disclose.

Children who have been involved in the use of drugs or sex for money may feel that they also might be arrested or get into trouble. Those who have committed crimes that are known to the offender, such as burglaries or thefts, or who are runaways, fear they might be caught. In several cases, the offender has been known to entice children to be involved in minor crimes such as these and threaten to expose them if they didn't "cooperate." In one case, a 4-year-old girl was frightened into silence because the offender told her the police would kill her if she told.

## Fears of Exposure or Labeling

Often a child will be afraid of disclosure for fear that exposure might draw censure from peers or parents. Peer-group pressure, called the most influential motivating force in a person's lifetime, easily suppresses a report from a boy who fears the ridicule of his peers by being called a "fag," "queer," or worse. The same is true for the girl afraid of being labeled a "slut" or "easy."

## Fear of the Court Process

Once the incident is brought to the attention of the parents, be it an intrafamilial or extrafamilial situation, the parents often refuse to allow it outside the family, fearing the investigative and court process. This is one of the most important concerns for the law-enforcement investigator and the professionals who deal with the child after the police conclude their investigation. Parents fear what may happen during the investigative and court process, and this fear can permeate down to the child if care is not taken to avoid this pitfall.

## Fear That No One Will Believe the Child

Regardless of age, children fear that no one will believe what they have to say. Children are often brought up to perceive themselves as insignificant, and the size disparity between children and adults doesn't help to make them feel any more consequential. It is not uncommon for the offender to tell the child that no one would believe any accusations the child might make. This is true for all situations, but especially if the child has a discipline problem or has any history of difficulties with the authorities. In any case where the offender is a prominent member of the community or is in a position where his integrity could not be questioned, this problem will create great difficulties for the child.

## Problems for Boys in Disclosure

The socialization or "masculinization" process that boys go through is also an important and strong influence in suppressing disclosure. Boys are brought up to believe that they are supposed to deal with things on their own; that they shouldn't seek help; and, above all, that they shouldn't show emotion. Doing any of these things would be a sign of weakness. As a result, many boys internalize such experiences and tell no one. When they do, they tend to minimize the activity, downplaying the totality of the act and leaving out details because of fears about what people will believe about their "manhood" and ability to take care of themselves.

Greater than the fear of being labeled a homosexual is another concern and reason for nondisclosure by boys: fear of becoming homosexual. The myth that to be molested by a man will cause a boy to become gay is widespread, and the fear of this coming to pass will prevent many boys from telling of their abuse. On the other hand, if the boy is molested by a woman, it is often considered a sign of status and the boy is considered "lucky" or "sowing his oats" early. To complain might negate such a status.

## Family Member Involved

A child is less likely to report an incident when there is a family member involved. When a family member is responsible, the child will experience many confusing feelings, the same as those of the child molested by someone not related to him, yet intensified because of the close relationship. The most common feeling is the love for the offender and the confusion felt about the propriety of the acts. This generally becomes a feeling of betrayal once the child finds out about the wrongfulness of what transpired. A deep sense of guilt may evolve about the subject of disclosure, because the victim is torn between love for the offender and the knowledge that what happened was wrong and that the offender may get into trouble or go to jail.

The victim may have a deep need to protect the offender because of the family ties. The child may fear disruption of the family, and that if disclosure is made, the family may be cast into the street or fall apart. The child then takes upon his shoulders the responsibility for keeping the silence about the abuse. This may be very destructive to the child and the family, often resulting in the child's running away from home or committing suicide rather than face the consequences of reporting the abuse. This fear may be self induced or may have been created by the offender in an attempt to keep the incidents secret.

## Threats Implied or Expressed

Often the child keeps the secret about the abuse because of the threats the offender has made, expressed or implied, about all the things discussed so far. These threats are a great stumbling block for investigators because some of the predictions made by the offender may have already come true before any official ever talks to the child. Once this has occurred, it makes it difficult for the child to continue to talk about the incidents and may, as will be seen later in the discussion on victims, cause the child to recant the accusations. For example, the offender may tell the child that if he tells about the incidents, both the child and the offender may be arrested. In an incestuous relationship, it is not uncommon for the adult to be arrested and the child to be taken into protective custody and kept from the rest of the family, which the child interprets as being arrested. For the child to continue, now missing his family and feeling guilty about the offender's being in jail, is often too much for him to bear. As a result, the child recants, telling the authorities, "I made it up." This will be discussed in greater detail in the section of Chapter 2 on victims.

> ... The first time it happened I was in my room combing my doll's hair. I was 6 and he was 51. He locked the door and said he loved me, but if I told anybody, he'd kill me.... Sometimes I'd start to scream, but he would cover my mouth and no one would hear me.... The only thing I knew was that he had threatened me. I was afraid that if my mother knew, she would kill him and go to jail and I wouldn't be able to see her anymore. Also, I wanted to believe that he did it because he loved me, not like my own dad, who hardly ever saw me... [45].

## Guilt

Children often won't talk about the abuse because of the guilt the offender lays on them through emotional blackmail. The maintenance of silence is often accomplished by the development of guilt experienced by the victim repressing and internalizing the incident(s) because he feels he did something wrong that allowed the offense(s) to happen. Like the rape victim, the child believes that the acts themselves or bad feelings he experiences are the punishment for the wrong he did. It is not uncommon for the victim to suffer in silence for an entire lifetime.

Often those who have a religious background or who have a strong moral upbringing have deep feelings of guilt when they come to believe they have done something wrong. Children also fear hurting the parents, and the guilt that develops as a result of the fear of the parents finding out inhibits children from speaking out. In cases where the offender has established a relationship with the child, the victim also develops guilt because the child fears hurting the offender by disclosing what happened.

Some of the children, regardless of the severity of the abuse, have described the offender as their best friend. Many offenders are expert at this. For example, in a case in California, a boy was kidnapped and kept with the offender for 7 years. During the time the boy was in the custody of the offender, the boy referred to him as "Dad." Even when the boy came forward, it was not to turn the offender in, but rather to prevent the same thing from happening to another boy the offender had kidnapped. In another case, a child molester told of how he would get close to children. He described buying things for the child, taking him places he wanted to go, and doing anything the child wished, making the child feel indebted to him. All these things made it difficult for the child to complain about the offender because the child felt guilty about the good things he experienced and the friendship he developed.

Often in the cases where pictures are taken, whether or not the photos of the child are in the nude, the offender uses them as a means of preventing disclosure by threatening to show them "around" and tell people about what has transpired. In some cases, the offender allows the child to operate the camera through the use of a remote control cord, having the child photograph the action. In the child's mind this further makes the child an accomplice to the acts. The knowledge of what has happened, the guilt the child bears about being involved with the offender, and the fear that others may learn of the details of the intimacies are strong factors in preventing disclosure.

## Secrecy

How deeply ingrained the secret is and the manner in which it was instilled will govern the ease of disclosure. The child's reluctance to come forward in the first place is largely caused by his inability to handle the emotional problems discussed above. Perhaps more important, as it relates to an investigation, it is the ability of the investigator to successfully address these difficulties, which will determine how easily the child tells about what happened.

## Seriousness of the Problem

Florence Rush points out that the problem of adult-child sex has been with us for centuries and that it is not something we have just recently encountered [46]. She traces its history and traditions, outlining its foundations as pedophiles see it. There is little agreement among the authorities about whether organized crime is involved in the child-sex business. Some say that child pornography and prostitution never were part of a "commercial" network; others have said that there is always some element of organized crime where there is a need or desire for such illicit activities.

Child pornography was found to be sold in the "adult bookstores" as early as the 1960s, and by 1976 it became a featured item, made popular by the pedophile's demand. Kids aged 3 to 16 were featured in every conceivable sex act and lewd pose. In 1973, child porn was found to be a commonly advertised commodity in sex magazines. In the early and mid-1970s, the primary source of child porn was the adult bookstore, which sold commercially produced, slick, professionally printed magazines, books, movies, and paraphernalia. In the publications purchased at the bookstores, pedophiles could find mail-order forms that allowed them to select and buy this sensitive material from the privacy of their own homes. These magazines also contained addresses and ordering information for publications created by the pedophile underground, which enabled the pedophile to establish contacts with others who had similar interests. Once contacts were established, pedophiles would exchange magazines, homemade photographs experiences, and the children themselves.

Prior to 1977, child pornography was not illegal to make, produce, or distribute. In 1977, public outcry brought child porn out into the open for all to see [47]. The result was that new laws were passed by the federal government and virtually all states, which specifically addressed the crime problems of sexual exploitation of children. Among other things, these laws made child porn illegal in every way, except mere possession. Some subsequent revisions have made possession illegal. In the 1980s child pornography, largely, went underground, only to surface on the Internet. One can now find virtually every form of child pornography featuring every conceivable kind of sex involving animals, adults and other children ages infant to teen [48]. Child pornography rings have been discovered in Central and South America, Western Europe, Central and Eastern Europe, Asia and the Pacific, the Middle East, Africa, and Australia [49].

Child prostitution is rampant in this country and those elsewhere around the world. One has only to look on the "strips" in local communities to see the young lined up waiting for their "dates." Children with the proper connections can make anywhere from $200 to $1,000 a night. Children as young as 6-years old have been found on the street selling themselves. In fact, the younger the children are, the more money they can ask for, both in selling sex and in making films.

Investigations have revealed that child sex is readily available to Americans in all parts of the world. If the American doesn't have connections to the various "child sex tours" available, all he has to do is go to the areas in other countries, such as "sex bars" or brothels, that cater to his tastes. The World Congress Against Commercial Sexual Exploitation of Children documented sex tourism in the Philippines, Cambodia, Thailand, other Asian countries, North America connecting to Brazil, the Dominican Republic, Sri Lanka, and Eastern Europe. The tours are advertised in slick promotions that include brochures and organized clubs [50].

Child prostitution in Asia has authorities worried. It is estimated that there are 500,000 child prostitutes, 16-years old and younger, in South-East Asia. It has become so well known that pedophiles come from throughout the world to use their services [51]. Another report, done for the United Nations, estimated over 400,000 child prostitutes world wide [52].

Investigations have revealed fake adoption services that will provide a child ready for the asking. In the American underground, all these things already exist; one has only to make the connections.

Prior to 1977, and to a large degree today, child porn was and is propagated by "pirating" or copying films and magazines. Pictures of the material contained within printed magazines and films were copied and sold or traded as original material. This is now being done to the extent that it is conceivable that a child porn model could be seen by his or her own children. Although still illegal, in 1980 the importation of child porn was found to be on the decline compared with previous years. In 1982, commercially produced child pornography was also found to have declined. What this has accomplished is to make the only sources of child pornography the individual pedophile who takes pictures of the children he is involved with and those who "pirate" already existing material. A New York City Police Department investigator said that it would be easier for an undercover officer to buy $50,000 worth of cocaine than to purchase $50 worth of child porn in New York City. Now, one only need have a computer and access to the Internet to get hard-core child pornography in the security and privacy of one's own home.

The pedophile pornographers cater to the perverse desires of the underground, satisfying the sexual fantasies of its members through the medium of pictures. They play on the "innocence of the children and lechery of adults"

[53]. Such titles as *Child Discipline,* a primer on how to derive sexual satisfactions from beating children, and *Lust For Children,* which comes complete with instructions on how to avoid prosecution and claims that a child's screams while being attacked are actually cries of passion, are representative of the type of publication available.

Pictures, magazines, films, and videotapes depicting children in acts of sexual intercourse, sodomy, bondage, bestiality, sadomasochistic acts — boy/boy, boy/girl, girl/girl — sold for as little as $7.50 or as much as $50. The sale of child pornography has been estimated to be in excess of two-and-a-quarter million dollars to one-half a billion dollars annually. The majority of this commercial child pornography is available by mail-order purchase from Europe, yet the material, the photography, contained in these publications comes from the individual pedophile and is not commercially produced. The United States is the "largest single source" of this material [54]. The producers of this type of pornography are often affluent, mobile, educated, and powerful "pillars of the community;" however, most of the material produced, even that depicting children being mutilated and beaten, is produced by the individual pedophile who works out of his home. Now, this material is available through clandestine purchase on the Internet.

## The Turn Toward Violence

In a case in California, a man was found murdered, hog-tied, gagged, and shot numerous times in the head and about the upper body. He was a respected member of the community and no one could provide any possible clue or motive as to why such a terrible thing had happened. It was not until the investigating police agency searched his home and found a cache of child pornography with individual, homemade photos of children in the nude, engaged in sexual acts with adults and children, that the answer was found. The probably motive for the murder evolved not from these photos, but from the ones that depicted young girls bound, gagged, blindfolded, and compelled into sex acts with adults.

The sad truth is that child pornography is being produced in every corner of the world. For example, a comedian, turned children's advocate, Barry Crimmins, spent six months on the Internet posing as a 12-year-old boy. In doing so, he found access to such "chat rooms" that advocated rape, incest, and trade or exchange of child pornography. Some of the rooms were entitled "DadsNDaughters," "Lilboypix," "Have hot stepdaughter," "family fun," "Nudist families," "incest is best," and the like [55].

What concerns many professionals working on this problem is the fact that there is a marked increase and trend toward violence on the part of many of the offenders. More importantly, it must be understood that what is depicted in the pornography of the pedophile underground is what is going on in the streets of this country. Given the fact that material that depicting children in acts of sexual violence commend high prices, it is easy to see what some of the desires of the offenders are. In addition to the pornography depicting children in violent sex acts, there are places where offenders may go to find children who are sold to the individual who prefers violence for sexual fulfillment.

Fortunately, the majority of cases involving molestation, pornography, and prostitution don't involve violence; those that do are a frightening indication of what's going on in this seedy underworld. For example, in Berkeley, a 15-year-old runaway boy was lured to an apartment under the pretext of selling a stolen car. The boy had stolen an old Chevy, torn and battered, and hardly worth a look, much less any money; however, the boy needed money to live. The man led the boy to believe that he could find a buyer for the car, but the boy would have to "clean up" because the "buyer" wouldn't deal with such a "ragtag" individual. He invited the boy to take a shower and took his clothing to the laundry room to wash. The boy heard the washing machine going and assumed that everything was all right. When he emerged from the shower, the man had him lie on the bed while his clothing was drying and offered to give him a back rub. The boy knew what was transpiring, and as the man began to make sexual advances, the boy resisted somewhat, but not strenuously, until the man began to beat him with a whip. It was not until the man attacked him with a knife that the boy fled, naked, from the apartment. Had it not been for a citizen who called to report a naked boy running down the street, we never would have heard about this incident.

The responding officers calmed the boy, but he refused to say what had happened until an officer pointed to a stab wound in his chest (which the boy had been unaware of because of his excitement) and asked how he had acquired the injury. It was only because he became enraged at the offender for stabbing him that he told what happened.

There is much controversy about the exact number of missing children in this country; however, it is an undisputed fact runaways are at great risk for, and very susceptible to exploitation. Unfortunately, this often ends in death as a result of violence related to sex.

Many runaway children lie in unmarked graves throughout this country. A 5-year-old girl in California was kidnaped, molested, and left dead in a ditch. The offender attempted another kidnaping in a neighboring city, but the intended victim was rescued by concerned citizens and the offender was subsequently caught. His arrest disclosed that he had a host of child pornography. Cases such as this are unfortunately too often repeated across the country.

Although investigators have found people who say they have seen children involved in "snuff films" (films showing actual murder or mutilation), no law-enforcement officer has yet seen an actual murder so depicted. In serial murders alone, over 100 children have been killed by people in sex-related murders in the past decade. In 1973, the murders of 27 young men and boys buried in a Texas levee were the start of a frightening trend. In 1979, the murder of 32 young men and boys in a Chicago suburb, the 28 sex-related murders in Atlanta, and the 41 murdered young men and boys who were found over a 3-year-period, nude, along a southern California's freeway — all demonstrate the worst that could happen to the victim of the child molester. Boys are not the only objects of the sex-related killers. The Los Angeles County Sheriff's Office investigated the deaths of at least 10 girls and found photographs of over 500 girls whom they believed to have been "targets" of the murderer. Belgium had one of its most notorious crimes discovered involving the deaths of two young girls, found dead in a "cell" created by the pedophile who murdered them. This crime tore apart the nation, causing extensive changes to be initiated in the government from the top down.

Murder and death are not common characteristics of the pedophile, and represent a small extreme fragment of the sexual activity with children. However, homicide can become an outcome of the sexual act for several reasons. Torture and death may be the only way the offender gets his kicks. In a case in Texas, the only way the offender could become sexually aroused was to tie his victim, spread-eagled to a plywood board, and mutilate and strangle the victim until he climaxed and the victim died. Some homicides occur as accidents during the commission of a sex act, where the offender had not intended to let the victim suffer to that degree. Other homicides occur when the offender is compelled to silence his victims for fear of discovery or extortion, as was the case in the John Wayne Gacy murders in Chicago [56]. Lastly, homicides occur when the parents take "the law into their own hands" when they discover what an offender has done to their children.

## References and Notes

1. Isaiah McKinnon, "Child Pornography," *FBI Law Enforcement Bulletin*, Feb., 1979 and National Center for Prosecution of Child Abuse, *Update*, Vol. 9, No. 1-2, 1996.

2. Pedophile Liberation Front (PLF) 1997.

3. Paedophilic Informational Exchange (PIE), *Paedophilia: Some Questions and Answers*, London, England, 1978, 1.

4. Ibid.

5. *Diagnostic and Statistical Manual of Mental Disorders,* Fourth Edition, (*DSM-IV*), American Psychiatric Associaton, Washington, D. C., 1994.

6. Kenneth Lanning in *Practical Rape Investigation* by Robert Hazelwood, CRC Press, Boca Raton, FL, 1995.

7. Kenneth V. Lanning, *Child Molesters: A Behaviorial Analysis,* National Center for Missing and Exploited Children, Washington, D.C., 1992.

8. Paiderastia, 1997.

9. Parker Rossman, *Sexual Experience Between Men and Boys,* New York Association, 1977.

10. PIE, 1978.

11. Ibid.

12. NAMBLA Homepage, 1997.

13. Rene Guyon Society (RGS) information flyer, 1982.

14. PLF, 1997.

15. Letter sent to a legislator; from the author's case files.

16. RGS, 1982.

17. Ibid.

18. Letter from the author's case files.

19. Statement made at the Lesbian and Gay Pride March, New York City, June 29, 1980. From the author's files.

20. NAMBLA newsletter, Oct. 1991.

21. NAMBLA internet memo, 1994.

22. Dennison W. Nichols, *Toward A Perspective for Boylovers,* Creative Products, Lansing, Mich., 1976, 1.

23. Nichols, 1976, p. 2.

24. Paiderastia, 1997.

25. From the author's case files.

26. Texas State Legislature 1978, Select Committee on Child Pornography, *Interim Report,* 10/16/79.

27. World Congress Against Commercial Exploitation of Children Report, (*WCACSE Report*), U.S.I.S., American Embassy, Strandvagen 101, 11589 Stockholm, Sweden, Homepage 1996.

28. *WCACSE Report.*

29. Wooden, 1980.

30. *The Results of the 1995 Annual Fifty-State Survey,* National Committee to Prevent Child Abuse, Chicago, IL., April 1996.

31. National Committee for Prevention of Child Abuse (NCPCA), *Child Abuse Rates Remain High,* Chicago, IL, April/May, 1997.

32. *The Los Angeles Times* 1985 telephone poll, cited in *Christian Times*, 3/2/86, Oklahoma City.

33. Alfie Kohn, "Shattered Innocence," *Psychology Today*, Feb. 1987 citing Deanna Russell's study.

34. Pedophilia: "The Dark Side of Human Nature," *New York Tribune*, 7/13/90.

35. The Gallup Organization, Press Release, 12/7/95, "Disciplining Children in America: Survey of Attitudes and Behaviors of Parents," Princeton, NJ.

36. Rossman, "Sexual Experiences Between Men and Boys," New York Association, 1997.

37. Eloise Sahols, "Beware of Child Molesters," *Newsweek*, 8/9/82.

38. United Nations, Commission on Human Rights, *Rights of the Child: Report of the Special Rapporteur on the Sale of Children, Child Prostitution, and Child Pornography*, Jan. 17, 1996.

39. *Dallas Morning News*, "Police Raid Shuts Down Internet Porn Site in Fort Worth," 2/19/97.

40. Conversation with Det. Sgt. Toby Tyler, Sept. 1997.

41. Barry J. Crimmins, testimony before the Senate Judiciary Committee, 104th U.S. Congress, July 24, 1995.

42. Louis B. Freh, statement before the Senate Judiciary Committee, U.S. Senate, Apr. 8, 1997.

43. *Where the Young One's Are*, out-of-date publication from the author's case files.

44. Loretta Schwartz-Nobel, "Pornography and the Secret World of the Pedophile," *Philadelphia Inquirer Magazine*, 11/6/83.

45. Schwartz-Nobel, 1983.

46. Florence Rush, *The Best Kept Secret: Sexual Abuse of Children*, McGraw-Hill, New York, 1980, 15.

47. Because of the efforts of people like Lloyd Martin, former LAPD Detective; Dr. Judianne Densen-Gerber, New York psychiatrist and attorney, and others, attention was focused on pedophilia using child porn as the target. Dozens of articles and news stories were written on the subject, bringing this subculture to the surface.

48. Crimmins, 1996.

49. Center on Speech, Equality, and Harm Homepage, 1997, Laura Lederer Executive Director.

50. *WCACSE Report*, 1996.

51. Paul Ehrlich, "Asias's Shocking Secret," *Readers Digest*, 10/93.

52. "A Crime Without Equal," *Miami Herald*, 10/23/94.

53. Rush, 1980, p. 164.

54. R. P. "Toby" Tyler, "Child Pornography: The International Exploitation of Children," presented at The Fourth International Congress on Child Abuse and Neglect, Paris, France, 9/9/82.

55. Crimmins, 1996.

56. Clifford L. Lindecker, *The Man Who Killed Boys*, St. Martin's Press, New York, 1980.

# Parties to the Crime

This chapter is intended to give the investigator some insight into the dynamics of those individuals involved in this crime — the victim and the offender. Knowing their characteristics will help validate observations and conclusions made during the assessment and investigative phases of the case, as well as helping to ensure that the judge or jury reaches the same conclusions at trial. The dynamics of victimization and the reactions of children to their abuse will be discussed. In addition, behavioral, and psychological profiles will be listed to assist in the identification of new or potential victims.

The last section of the chapter will discuss a typology of the offender created for the law-enforcement officer, not to explain the behavior in order to understand it, but rather to help identify and convict people who sexually exploit children. This section will discuss the application of this typology in relation to characteristics that may be observed and in reference to the type of evidence that may be found.

The most important reason to know these characteristics is to be able to dispel the myths and misconceptions held by professionals, lay persons, and court personnel, who encounter these cases. By understanding the alternative causes and manifestations of the behaviors seen in children and offenders, more reasoned and accurate decisions may be made. In particular, the ability to correctly assess the validity and authenticity of claims made by the child and the accused will be heightened.

The author would like to thank Dr. Roland Summit for his review and contributions to the section on victims. In addition, special thanks and appreciation to Special Agent Kenneth Lanning of the FBI for writing and contributing the material which permulates the basis of the excellent section on the offender. Although this section has been edited for inclusion in this text, it is wholly that of Mr. Lanning. The material originally authored by Mr. Lanning also appears in its original form in *Practical Aspects of Rape Investigation: A Multidisciplinary Approach*, by Robert R. Hazelwood and Ann W. Burgess, and *Child Molesters: A Behavioral Approach*, printed by the National Center for Missing and Exploited Children.

## The Victim

In Chapter 1, we discussed the magnitude and scope of the sexual exploitation of children. Children who become victims are the major component of this crime. To learn how to deal with this aspect of the police problem, one must know how to identify the victim and understand why the victim is what he is.

Once it is determined that a crime has been committed, the objective of a police investigation is to prove the offense. To borrow a clinical term, we must do everything we can to "validate" the allegation(s). Dr. Suzanne Sgroi correctly suggests that our "ability to interpret behavior, physical signs, and information" is only limited by our ability to properly recognize the clues of abuse and to thoroughly investigate and document our observations [1]. No one has yet to put this in better perspective. The victims, the accused, and the courts demand nothing less.

This chapter is intended to provide the necessary background and training relating to characteristics of victims for investigators who must be able to properly recognize and investigate allegations of sexual exploitation of children. I will discuss the dynamics of becoming a victim and the after-effects of victimization. Signs of victimization will be outlined to enable investigators to chronicle their observations, which will help to validate the child's allegations. These same documented observations will also help support the conclusions investigators will make during their investigations. An example of how the information outlined in this chapter can be used in an investigation is given in Appendix V. Here, a search warrant was prepared, based largely on the observations of the behavior patterns and symptoms exhibited by the children involved in the investigation made by the family members and the investigators.

## The Dynamics of Victimization

### How and Why Children Become Victims

To say that one specific cause is responsible for children being victimized is to oversimplify the problem. Children become involved in sexual relationships with adults for many reasons. Child molestation has been called the "perfect crime" because children are singularly vulnerable, are easily persuaded to cooperate, and are too ashamed to talk about it with others. In addition, children, regardless of their home situation, are always going to have unsatisfied needs. Quite often, the manner in which these children are seduced is through satisfaction of those unfulfilled needs. With more than 40 million children living in poverty in the world, it's not hard to see that there is a ready source of children for the offender [2].

But the child doesn't have to be from a poverty-stricken home. The sexual exploitation of children is the abuse of children who are powerless, obedient, or cooperative, and who become or are dependent on the offender for many things. This reliance may be for the very basics of life or for a variety of things such as protection, money, approval, love, or care. With the divorce rate as high as it is, this becomes a serious problem for children because they often develop many of these needs.

> You know what these kids on the street are looking for? Love and affection.... You know why 42nd St. [New York] is full of kids? You know why the runaways are coming off the buses? ... It's because something went wrong at home and they're just looking for someone to take care of them [3].

Although the practice is not as common in this country as in others, children have been sold by economically deprived parents who must make the choice of selling what they have or not eating. In one case in California, a welfare family from another state with several children "rented" their boy to a man from Los Angeles for several thousand dollars.

Children are often ignorant about sexuality and sexual matters. What they learn about sex, they often learn from the offender rather than in a legitimate manner. Therefore they are not prepared to deal with the situations they encounter.

## The Problem of the Compliant, Non-Complaining Victim

**The Authority Figure and Satisfaction of Needs.**   For the most part, young children don't often know they can say no to adults. Most comply because they have been taught to obey adults. For both younger and older children, knowledge about sexual issues or their own sexual responses and desires is minimal; as a result they can be taken advantage of through misrepresentation of the acts performed with them. To further confuse the situation, children don't know how to deal with promises made to them of attention, care, and rewards. Sex play is often a source of curious attraction and they are drawn into it with the promise of satisfaction of some need as described earlier. Often their need to understand their own desires is the reason they become vulnerable.

> I was tired of being trash and nobody and feeling like nothing.... I wanted to be me and find out who I was... [4].

Dean Corell, the murderer of 27 young men and boys in the Houston area, was loved like a father by the boy who helped him find, sexually assault, and murder some of the victims. For another boy, he bought a Corvette. Corell was finally killed by the boy who loved him because the boy felt he would become Corell's next victim [5].

The misguided, misinterpreted affection children perceive as genuine from the offender and which they have a natural need for becomes their demise.

An adult woman tells how the man who photographed her from age 9 until 14, molesting her during the same time became a father substitute:

> I had no father. He was there. Physically, I could touch him. I felt protected. I felt wanted. He paid attention to me. He gave me things, took me places. I felt loved and important. For a short while he replaced the father I didn't have until I began to feel taken advantage of. Then everything he did had an ulterior motive — sex [6].

And yet, in another case, a 13-year-old girl had such a confused relationship with her father that she was both his daughter and lover. Her perception was that he was in love with her and that she was in love with him. Her infatuation with him is apparent in her drawings and love notes, found 10 years later after two search warrants were served. The first was served when the allegations first surfaced accompanied by child porn slides. The second was served ten years later, after the original charges were dropped when the girl ran away rather than face her father in court. The drawings and notes were not found until the second warrant was served (see Figures 2.1 to 2.4).

**Figure 2.1**

**Figure 2.2**

**Guilt.** The guilt the child feels after being seduced is often used against him as a blackmail device. Children often feel good about the offender, yet knowing the act was wrong (either knowing at first or finding out afterward), they carry the burden of knowing that if they tell, the offender will be arrested and/or go to jail. In these cases, it is the allegiance they have with the offender that helps to keep them silent. The offender will also often use the guilt against the child for participating in the acts. The child's fear of having everyone know about what he did is often enough to prevent disclosure.

In one case in Southern California, a 15-year-old girl was molested and photographed by her uncle who threatened to expose her by showing the photographs to others. He gave her a note, with photos attached, telling her what he would do if she didn't comply with his requests.

**Figure 2.3**

"Tabby (not her real name), I have every picture I ever took!! I have pictures of the pictures. I have 10 copies of every picture, the copies are everywhere. I haven't shown them to strangers... or given them out on corners. I thought about putting them on windshields in seedy places like X-rated theaters and adult bookstores, but I haven't yet. All I want is 30 min. on film of you and me doing everything possible F_____G, S_____G. Licking....Everything. I have a camcorder and film. If you do this you get all the copies and to watch the film before I watch it.... P.S. There will be no actual intercourse, fake it!!" [7].

The uncle was arrested after the girl complied and made the videos. This note was found during the subsequent search finding the pornography. In addition, the fear that he might hurt his parents may keep the child quiet. Told by the offender that if he tells, his parents will be upset or that the non-offending parent will cry, the child is afraid to disrupt the family.

"I felt [an] appalling realization that I had done something terribly wrong. I felt shame, guilt, and sadness, that I had committed a dirty thing against my Mom and Dad who loved me so much and would be so disgusted with what I had done with this man. I assumed all the guilt. I knew I had to have been responsible..." [8].

Threats of harm to the child are uncommon, but sometimes the offender has told the child he will be hurt if he discloses. In several cases, the offender told the child that if he told about what happened, the child's father would go to jail because he would kill the offender. In others, the child was told that telling would upset the parents, who would be made at him.

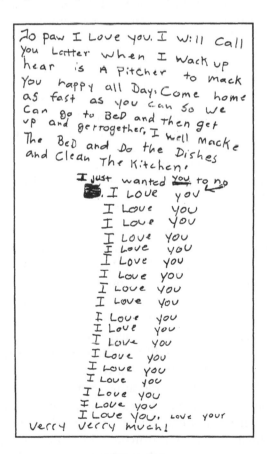

**Figure 2.4**

"My mother is divorced and works nights. Recently her boyfriend started coming over and forcing me to go all the way. It hurts me so I cry, but he slaps me and tells me I'll get over it, and not to tell my mother or she would consider me a whore and kick me out. Each time he does it, the pain gets worse. I'm afraid to mention it to my mother.... I'm so ashamed, but he forces me..." [9].

Even in cases where the child hates the offender with a passion, he keeps the secret because he feels he is to blame and fears the response of others. In a case where a girl was abused by her father and mother from age two through eleven, she described what she was forced to do and how she felt about it during and afterward.

Physically forced to engage in sexual acts with her brother, pictures were taken of them tied together in the "69" position. She was told to say "I love you...I want you so much...Kiss me...Fuck me," and similar things. At age four, she was forced into degrading sadomasochistic bondage. Over time, she was sold to her uncle for the same purpose and, at age 5, was put out to prostitution. She reported hating her father by age 4. She knew that her family didn't care and that she had to get away from them. Although told otherwise, she knew that outsiders also didn't care about her and only were interested in abusing her. She said that she knew saying swear words was wrong, being naked in front of others was wrong, and soon learned that sex organs were "naughty." Regardless of the nature of her abuse, she kept quiet, feeling that others would think she was "bad." She said at age four or five she "realized" she was "different" from other children. When she finally told about her abuse, she had great difficulty relating the incidents [10].

Because the child may have accepted money from the offender (offending fathers also often leave or give money to the child to lessen their own guilt and to help "buy off" the child), the child often feels like an accomplice to the act and responsible for what has happened. It is not uncommon to find that some children on the street are making at least $1,000 a night. Set up through an underground newspaper ad, a man flew from England to Los Angeles and paid $500 to spend one night with a 10-year-old girl. An ad in a child pornography magazine said that the man placing the ad would pay $8,000 in cash to spend the night with a young girl.

But it doesn't require such large sums of money to keep children silent about their involvement. The Los Angeles Police Department arrested a man who invited children to his home, advertising himself as "a human restroom," making the children defecate and urinate in his mouth and paying them for the service. Two of the boys described what they did at this man's home.

"I am nine-years old. I first met Roger between Thanksgiving and Christmas. I met him through Tim and have been going over to his house almost every day.

After meeting him, the first thing that happened was that Roger had me put my hand up his butt. Tim put a dildo up Roger's butt first to make it loosen up. Then he put vaseline on my hand and I put my hand up there, almost all the way to the elbow. I think Tim and Danny were there and did the same thing. He played with his dick when we had our hands up his butt. He sucked on my dick and Tim and Danny's after that.

He has a picture book with pictures of me with my hand up his butt and also pictures of him sucking on my pee-pee. There are also pictures of Danny and Tim.

Last Friday I went to Roger's house and he asked me if I would put my hand up his butt. Tim and Danny were there and I went first. He said if we can get our hands in his butt up to the elbow he would give us $5.00. Nobody was able to do it all the way. He had all three of us do it and take pictures" [11].

Tim also recounted what he did at Roger's house.

"My name is Tim. I am ten years old. I live with my mother. We play games at Roger's and whoever loses had to suck the winner' dick. We play pool and TV pong.

He took a picture of me a few days ago while I was sucking Danny's dick because I lost. Roger says he will give me $5.00 if I can get my arm up his butt to my elbow, and $10.00 if I can get my arm up his butt to my shoulder" [12].

In this case, as in many, the children become hooked on the goodies, and the pleasant things made the other experiences more bearable. Not one child reported what happened to them at this man's home to anyone. The case broke as a result of an informant telling of what happened to other children.

**Peer-Group Pressure.**    Dr. Ann Burgess describes how children react to being involved with multiple offenders and with multiple children, all or some of whom know that sexual acts are taking place with the rest of the group. In what she calls a child sex initiating ring, where one adult is involved with several children simultaneously, the adult uses is legitimate position to recruit and be sexually involved with children. For example, in one case at a junior high school, the boys' dean would penalize boys for misbehavior by getting them involved in a weight-lifting program with him after school. During and after the lifting sessions, he would molest the boys, sometimes in the presence of other boys. All were afraid to tell because of the labeling that would have followed. As in this group, the offender occupies a seemingly valid position of authority and familiarity with the children. In most sex ring cases, the children are rewarded with some kind of psychological, social, or monetary compensation [13, 14].

What is of interest in the sex ring cases is that peer pressure is often the key factor in keeping the child involved and the activities a secret. This bond ensures that children will continue to return to the offender and submit to sex. Within the group, the child finds others with whom he begins to compete for attention and rewards. A loyalty develops that prevents the child from exposing the others for fear of becoming an outcast or for fear of missing what's going on in the group. The child becomes aware that if he tells what is going on he may be harmed by the group and his involvement revealed.

These group dynamics are extremely important for an investigator because when the secret comes out, the degree of cooperation the members of the group exhibit will greatly depend on how the case surfaced. If one of the children in the group lets the secret out, the others often band together and maintain an alliance with the offender, refusing to admit anything. This also may happen if the children are afraid of the consequences of admitting the acts [15].

**Post-Traumatic Stress Disorder.**   Dr. Burgess likens the reaction of sexually abused children when disclosure is made to the post-traumatic stress disorder (PSD) as defined in the *Diagnostic Statistical Manual* of the American Psychiatric Association. In her studies Burgess found that children often relive the event in memory and dreams. Children often exhibited symptoms such as withdrawal from friends and their normal activities, as well as self-imposed isolation from their peer group. Symptoms or behavior patterns would develop after disclosure that were not present prior to disclosure, such as acting out or display or development of fears. Over time, the reactions to the stress situation — molestation — changed, yet were pronounced enough to be recognized as being caused by the abuse [16].

**Brainwashing.**   Children are also "brainwashed" into continuing to maintain the secret and participate in the abusive acts. Their behavior is molded or shaped by the offender to conform to his desires. Consciously or unconsciously, the offender subjects the child to behavior modification in which desirable behavior is rewarded and undesirable behavior is punished. This may be done in subtle or very blatant ways. In a rather celebrated case in southern California, children submitted to abuse after having been threatened by seeing live animals killed in front of them. The offenders told the children that they or their parents would suffer the same fate if they told of the abuse or didn't comply.

Dr. Roland Summit likens this submission to the manner in which American soldiers submitted to the demands of their North Vietnamese captors to denounce the war and their own country during the Vietnam War [17]. They did it to survive, because they were threatened, deprived of their basic needs, and made to feel utterly dependent on their captors. They felt there was no choice but to go along with the demands made on them, even though they were against their deepest beliefs. They could no longer trust or believe in the existence of any prior loyalties or comforts because of the deprivation and constantly repeated, distorted ideas their captors fed them. In response, they developed a mindless devotion and single goal of learning to please and be accepted (loved) by their captors. In short, they were brainwashed into submission.

In the southern California case mentioned earlier, although an extreme example of brainwashing, by making the children terrified of the consequences of not complying with the wishes of the offender, three objectives of brainwashing were achieved. First, fear was instilled in the children of the harm that could come to them or their parents. Second, the children were made to feel helpless to resist or tell of the abuse. Third, the concurrent use of sexual assault was used to ensure humiliation and guilt. All that remained was for the children to accommodate the activity, which they did.

**Threats.** The use of threats of physical force to get children to comply is the exception rather than the rule. Perhaps the child molesters themselves are the best persons to tell how easy it is to seduce children and get them to return willingly without complaint and without force. Here we see just how frequently the molesters' beliefs are used to justify their self-serving image as desired lovers of children and superior alternatives to parents.

In discussing the fact that children are hardly ever "forced" into the acts they perform with the child molesters, one group's publication says:

> As parents know, it's hard enough, even with the full sanction of parenthood, to make children do things they don't want to (do).... Sex between children and adults can arise with surprising naturalness and innocence in the context of, say, a swimming-bath or a summer camp [sic] [18].

Discussing the fact that few children are forced into what they do, another says:

> One can see children's faces reflecting intimidation, uneasiness, and embarrassment more often in family albums than in collections of pedophiles [19].

Still another says:

> "Someone like me has the ability to make a child do or talk about anything
> that they want, whether the child wants to or not" [20].

In cases where satanic worship is involved, the fear factor plays a major role in the seduction of children. The evil figure of the devil himself is used to frighten the children into submission and silence. Here, the ramifications of telling are the threats the children fear the most. They are told that they or their parents will become human sacrifices or be mutilated. Graphic displays of what would happen to the children are played out for them.

## Learning to Live with the Abuse in Order to Survive

In 1983, Dr. Roland Summit described the reaction to being abused in the *Child Sexual Abuse Accommodation Syndrome* (CSAAS) and outlines specific behavior patterns commonly seen in sexual abuse victims [21]. This theory has been accepted in courts throughout the country to explain the reaction of children to sexual abuse [22]. Although it is not intended to be a comprehensive list intended to prove sexual abuse, it is a checklist of some behavioral patterns observed in sexually abused children to help caretakers recognize and understand what the child has been or is experiencing [23].

There has been much discussion in the courts about Dr. Summit's theory on CSAAS since its original publication in 1983, and its subsequent use in court in the form of expert testimony to explain how children react to sexual abuse. For this reason the issues merit some discussion here. The "syndrome" as Dr. Summit both intended it and as it appears here in this text, is presented to provide insight into what the child has experienced or is experiencing, so that common misperceptions about child sexual abuse are avoided. Dr. Summit has formulated a concise and profound description of the common experience of thousands of victims which mirrors and is consistent with the observations of, perhaps, as many, professionals throughout the world in all of the disciplines that work with child sexual abuse victims [24].

It is neither a "litmus test" nor a "diagnostic" tool. It is a set of three-dimensional glasses for the investigator to put on to see the depth of the case and to prevent falling into the trap of a misunderstanding that, in the past, has shrouded what is really happening to children. These patterns of behavior seen after or observed before disclosure, uncovered and documented by the investigation, may be later presented to the trier-of-fact for the same purpose [25]. Its value is offering an alternative rationale to the contention the child is lying when the case involves a child's delay in reporting; a child who gives inconsistent and/or a conflicting account of what happened; and, who, often, recants after disclosure [26]. It makes a better argument at trial for the prosecutor if the investigation documents its characteristics as soon as possible, rather, than having an expert, at trial, months, perhaps, years later, review the circumstances which were experienced before, during, and after disclosure.

The very title of the syndrome Summit describes is indicative of what happens to the child. The child "accommodates" to the abuse to reduce both internal conflict and conflict with the offender, as well as to preserve a relationship with the non-offending caretaker. The child will therefore often return to the offender for more abuse, regardless of its severity or duration, often without ever telling anyone. In other words, the child accepts or submits to the abuse, learning to live with it, because the child is made to feel that there is no other choice and no hope of escape.

Child molestation is similar to sexual assault of adults in that the "normal" response of its victims is to submit. The victim submits because he is in no position to resist and feels helpless in his situation.

**Secrecy and Helplessness.**    Two preconditions must exist for the child to be sexually abused: secrecy and helplessness [27]. The child must feel that what occurs must not be discovered by anyone. In addition, the child must be in such a position that he feels helpless and has few resources to extricate himself from the situation. Because children are small and totally dependent on adult care and approval, they are easily intimidated by any adult who can introduce a sexual secret and alienate the child from responsible caretakers. Even a child with good and loving parents will protect the abuser rather than risk losing a parent's love through disclosure.

**Accommodation.**    Because the child often feels he has no other option but to submit to the acts of abuse, he must find some way to make the acts bearable. the most common way is to go along with it, which is why the child returns to the abuser. The child must find a way to endure his being trapped in the situation and having to conform to the demands being made upon him. The ways children normally adapt to survive in the abusive situation often create psychological and behavioral problems that may persist for life and make it harder and harder for the child to escape or be believed. For instance, children may take over the responsibility of caring for the offender, become sexually aggressive or promiscuous, develop self-mutilating or suicidal tendencies, run away, or become involved in drug or alcohol abuse, stealing, or other delinquent behavior. They may split off separate identities, learn to shut out pain, or even learn to believe and act as if they had never been abused.

**Delayed, Unconvincing Disclosure.**    As a result of the preceding factors, the abuse is often not revealed for a long time, if ever. When it is, it may be viewed with great suspicion or totally disbelieved, not only because disclosure has been delayed, but because of the manner or time of the disclosure. For example, the "disclosure window" must be open in order for the events to be revealed. The child must feel that it is safe to disclose, and often the circumstances that allow for the "window" to open may cast a shadow upon the veracity of the child. This is often the case when a child who has been having behavioral problems accuses someone outside of his family of abusing him. Even more suspect is the report of a molestation made by a child whose parents are engaged in a custody or divorce proceeding. When abuse comes to light under these circumstances, the most common response the child receives is that the adult world discounts the child's allegations.

**Retraction.**    Lastly, often after the child tells the secret, everything that the offender has predicted or that the child feared would happen, happens. The offender is arrested and is sent to jail; the child's parents get upset; the child is arrested (in fact, taken into protective custody, but presumed by the child to have been arrested because he is taken away from his home); the child loses his friends, either because they side with the offender and the child is now considered an outcast of the group or because he is considered a "freak," and no one believes him.

In addition, the child begins to feel guilty about what happened and, as a result, retracts the allegations, saying that the acts never happened or that they didn't happen in the way originally described, minimizing them in some way. The reactions of the parents to the disclosure, the support systems available to the child and the family, and the reaction of the authorities and others when the report is made have an inverse relationship to the retraction — the greater the degree of support, the less likely a retraction, and vice versa. What is important to understand about the retraction, as it relates to why the child becomes a noncomplaining victim, is that the child is more willing to return to the abusive environment than to face the consequences of disclosure. The pain of the abuse is easier to endure than the pain of rejection by family, the general public, and/or peers.

The importance of retraction as it relates to society and to the criminal justice system is that most people would rather believe the retraction than the disclosure. This perpetuates the myth that children typically lie in claiming sexual abuse and that investigators should be suspicious and alert for false claims. A child who has denied abuse during the secret accommodation phase, who makes a late, often impulsive and self-serving disclosure and takes it back as soon as people get skeptical, is not an appealing witness in a criminal prosecution. And a child who tells one parent but is afraid to tell investigators makes it look like that parent is trying to coach false complaints in a custody dispute.

The following is a good example of how the dynamics of the child sexual abuse accommodation syndrome might surface in an investigation. A 12-year-old girl was raped by her "stepfather" while being forcibly held down by her mother, and photographed by the mother while engaged in sex acts with the man. The police report explains what happened in that case.

Audrey told me she had originally disclosed the incidents involving sexual acts with her mother and Paul (her stepfather) because she wanted them to stop and because she hated Paul for hurting her that way. In addition, she was mad at her mother because her mother not only went along with what Paul wanted and forced Audrey to do the sexual acts, but she didn't stop him from doing them. She said she wanted to live with her dad because of what her mother and Paul were doing to her. She felt she would be safe there.

Audrey said that she was surprised when her mother was arrested. She thought that only Paul would be arrested because it was Paul's fault. She thought this because her mother had never done anything like it before she met Paul.

When her mother was arrested she felt very bad, especially when her mother's picture, showing her handcuffed in court, appeared on the front page of the local paper. She said she felt embarrassed both for herself and her mom about the incidents being aired in as much detail as they were in the paper. She felt bad about the publicity also because she thought that everyone would now hate her mother.

Audry said she loved her mother and knows her mother loves her. She always thought that because of that love, her mother had to have been forced by Paul to do what she did. Therefore, when her mother was arrested and put in jail, and Paul wasn't, she got mad because it wasn't fair. She felt it was all Paul's fault, but he wasn't going to jail. (He had fled and disappeared.)

When Audry saw her mother in court, manacled, she felt bad and became worried that that was the way she was all the time. She was also worried about her mother's safety because of what she read and heard about her mother's being attacked in jail, having had hot water thrown at her and so on. She said her sister told her that her mother said the jail flooded where she was and she felt guilty about causing her mother to suffer.

She said that on several occasions she wanted to see and be with her mother, in particular on Christmas. Audry said that she felt bad because now she had to move to another town and go to different schools. She missed her friends in [the small town she originally lived in]. She said that often she wished she had never told what had happened. She said she felt helpless — she couldn't help herself or her mother, she couldn't stop the proceedings, and they had gone much further than she ever thought they would with respect to her mother.

Audry said that ever since she heard at the preliminary examination [first court hearing where testimony was heard] that her mother could be sentenced to a long prison term she felt bad. After she read an article in a paper which said the sentence could be as long as life, she thought she might never see her mother again.

Audry said that at one time her mother had told her that if she ever lost Audry, she would kill herself. Audry thought that going to jail would be the same and her mother would commit suicide. She felt helpless to protect her and unable to prevent such a thing.

Audry said she knew her mother was calling her house and talking to her sister. She said that she answered the phone once and spoke to her mother. Audry said she felt bad about her mother, especially after she talked with her. Audry felt guilty because she thought her mother was in jail because of what Audry had said.

Audry said on several occasions she talked with her sister, Dorothy, about her mother and the case. They discussed what might happen to her mother. Dorothy agreed that her mother might commit suicide and was also afraid that she would be sentenced to life. Dorothy also thought that her mother must have been forced to do what she did.

Audry also said she loved and was very close to her sister. She knew her sister loved and was close to her mother. Audry thought that if anything ever happened to her mother, either she was sentenced to life or she committed suicide, Dorothy would kill herself. Audry was afraid that she would lose both her mother and her sister.

Audry said that after she testified in the preliminary hearing for her stepfather, after his capture, she thought to herself that maybe if she told everyone that she lied and that nothing really happened, she could get her mother out. She thought that everything would be dropped. Audry said she discussed this with her sister and that her sister left it up to Audry what to do.

Audry said that Dorothy once told her about her mother's attorney, who she only knew as Martha. Audry thought maybe she could write Martha a letter telling her the whole thing was a lie and that everything would be dropped. About a month before we talked about this on Nov. 30th, Audry wrote a letter telling Martha that nothing Audry said about her mother and Paul was true and that Audry's mother didn't deserve to be in jail because it wasn't true. She said that Dorothy went out to lunch with Martha after she received the letter. Martha told Dorothy that she couldn't do anything about the charges or the letter. Audry said because Martha couldn't do anything she decided to call me and tell me what she had tried to tell Martha.

On November 30, I met Audry, who was with her sister. Audry told me that everything she had said to me earlier and testified to in court was a lie and that she wanted the charges against her mother dropped [28].

Audrey later reaffirmed her original account and both her mother and stepfather were convicted, based largely on her testimony.

### *Factors Governing How the Child Reacts to the Abuse*

Children react to sexual abuse in a somewhat consistent pattern of behaviors. These are shaped, and the degree of pronouncement of their symptoms are determined, by:

1. The developmental stage of the child at the time of the abuse.
2. The duration of the abuse.
3. The support systems available to the child.
    a. The reaction to the abuse of the child's parents and others around him.
    b. The resources available to the child.
    c. The sensitivity of the intervention or treatment agencies, including the medical examination.
4. The sophistication of the child.
5. The environment within which the abuse occurs.
6. The relationship of the offender to the child.
7. The severity of the abuse.
    a. The degree of physical force used to accomplish the acts.
    b. The nature and- type of the acts engaged in.
8. The degree of participation by the child.
9. The sex of the child and that of the offender.

Virtually all children experience some symptoms of abuse, although they are not always seen or observable. A word of caution should be given before discussing these symptoms. *Neither the presence* nor *absence* of any or all of these symptoms, which may be observed in a child, *should* be considered proof *positive* that abuse did or did not occur. The symptoms should be examined within the context of the situation where they are observed and used to evaluate the likelihood of whether or not the abuse occurred.

**Child's age and developmental level.** The child's age and developmental level will govern how much he comprehends about the abuse and therefore how much it affects him. If the child is too young to understand what has happened to him, the effects will be minimized because he has no comprehension of the consequences. The child's knowledge about sexuality and what he has been told or introduced to will determine how he responds to the abuse. For example, if a 3-year-old girl is molested by a man who orally copulates with the child in a nonviolent manner in the context of a game, it may have a lesser effect on the child than if the same act were performed on a 13-year-old girl who was tricked into performing the act under the guise of receiving a cancer examination.

Yet, because of the developmental challenge the fear of abandonment presents for a 3-year-old, the same act performed on that child, accomplished by threats that she will lose her mother if she tells, may be severely and permanently damaging.

**Duration of the sexual abuse.**   How long the abuse continues will affect the child. For example, if the child was touched only once by the offender, the psychological consequences will be less severe than if the child was involved in multiple touchings over a period of time. This will be discussed in greater detail in Chapter 5 in the section on disclosure issues.

**Reaction of the parents and those close to the victim.**   The manner in which the child's disclosure is received by his parents and those around him will also greatly affect how he responds to the abuse. For example, in numerous cases where young children have been involved, they thought nothing was wrong with what they did until they told their parents or someone else. When the parent or the other person reacted adversely — crying, becoming angry, or not believing — the child's reaction changed greatly. This is why it is so important for the investigator to be sure not to display negative reactions about what the child has experienced. It is also why it is necessary to determine the reaction of the person who first learned about the abuse. If the child anticipates a negative reaction, he is less likely to talk to the investigator with much candor, if he talks at all. It is also another reason why it's important to limit the number of people who have access to the child.

**Resources available to the child.**   If the child has a close relationship with his parents or has friends with whom he can confide and share experiences and problems, the impact will be less than if no such resources were available to him. The support these type of resources provide will greatly reduce the degree of ill effect the child suffers. This is a significant factor for law enforcement because crisis counseling and ongoing professional support services should be sought for all but a very few cases.

**Relationship with the offender.**   The relationship the child maintains with the offender will have a profound effect on the manner in which the child is affected by the abuse. In addition, the power situation between the offender and the child will help to dictate how the child responds [29].

**Degree of physical force or violence.**   Children react to forced sexual acts in much the same way adults do. Consistent with the *Rape Trauma Syndrome,* one study revealed that:

1. 11% of the child victims didn't feel safe where they lived after the incident.
2. 32% showed negative feelings about men they knew.
3. 34% experienced more negative feelings toward strange men.
4. Almost 50% showed fear of being out on the street.
5. 10% of school-aged children developed a "school phobia" (fear of school situations) [30].

**Nature and type of sexual acts.**   The nature of the acts performed with or on the child will also have a great effect on the way the child reacts to the abuse. If the acts involve only touching the child's body over the clothing, the effects will be less severe than if the child was involved in full intercourse.

**Degree of participation of the child victim.**   The extent to which the act was voluntary will also affect the way the crime affects the child. Explaining the differences in voluntary degree, the Queen's Bench Foundation classified child victims into three categories.

1. Coerced victims—who were physically forced to be involved.
2. Passive victims—where there was only one experience, where the child didn't initiate the contact, and where the case was reported immediately.
3. Participant victims— where there was more than one incident and where the offender may have been rewarding the children in some way [31].

The more the child feels responsible, the more pronounced the effects that will be seen.

**The sex of the child and the sex of the offender.**   Once the child has reached an age where he has some concept of sexuality, he will develop feelings about what he should and shouldn't do of a sexual nature. Same-sex sexual contact is one form of sexual contact that is very sensitive, especially for children who are developing their sexual identities and are having the normal confusing feelings about sexual choice. Male victims of sexual assault suffer the same feelings about crimes committed against them as do female victims, but are more reluctant to admit that they've been assaulted and to seek help.

Perhaps because of the socialization process that tells men it is not "manly" to have someone take control of them or that they must learn to deal with their problems on their own, men/boys do not often report sexual assault or abuse. Their fear that they may be branded as weak or unmasculine, even by the professionals they have contact with, serves to suppress the report of abuse and has a significant effect on how the victim deals with the crime after it occurs. This is an important factor in investigations involving boys. Here, women may be better suited for some of these interviews because they may not be as much of a threat to the child as a man.

Victimization of either boys or girls by a woman seems to be especially harmful. Children expect "mommy-type" people to be more caring and trustworthy. A child molested by a woman tends to feel especially unloved and unlovable and will often try to pretend the woman was not involved.

## Profile Characteristics: Effects of Victimization and Symptomatology of Abuse

### Types of Reports/Disclosures

One characteristic pattern that may help to validate the complaint is the manner in which the disclosure is made. Rarely does a child come to the police station, walk up to a police officer, or call the police to say, "I've been molested." The report is generally made to a second party, who makes the report to the police or other authorities.

**Direct reports.**    A direct report is made when the child comes right out and tells exactly what happened. A direct report may be made to a parent, teacher, counselor, nurse, or other person in authority.

**Indirect report.**    A more common type of disclosure is the indirect report, wherein the child tells someone else hoping that they will report it for him. Children often think this takes the responsibility of "breaking the secret" away from them.

A way this often surfaces, is an accounting of what has been happening to the child written in the child's diary or in a letter kept, but, not sent, or in a school journal where a teacher might discover it. The account may be explicit, describing in the child's terms what is going on or veiled, only giving a hint of what is happening. This may be left out where it could be "accidently" discovered by someone or purposely written hoping that someone will recognize and intervene. Examples of these writings are shown in Figures 2.5 and 2.6.

**Disguised report.**    The disguised report may be made in either of the previous two ways, but is generally made by the child telling the story as though it were happening to someone else. Usually this is the child's way of testing what the reaction will be. It is also to see if the abuse will be discovered without *his* telling about it directly, thus lifting the responsibility of disclosing

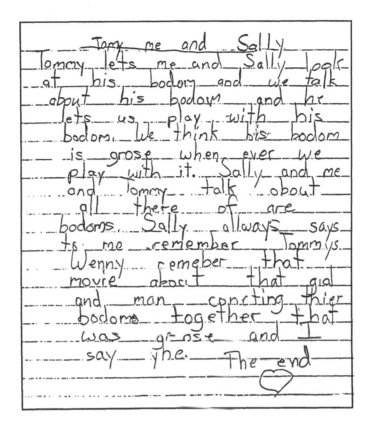

**Figure 2.5** This journal entry was left where the child's mother could find it. This case, detailed in Appendix XI, led to discovering what a neighbor was doing with neighborhood children.

the secret from his shoulders. Here the child tells a teacher, friend, nurse, counselor, or other person, "I have a friend who…," and often makes that person promise not to tell.

### Behavioral Indicators

The behavioral characteristics of sexually abused children can range from living like a normal child to committing suicide. However, some characteristics can be seen regularly enough to identify them as being attributable to sexual abuse. It must be pointed out that the mere presence or absence of any one or all of these symptoms is not proof positive that the child in question has or has not been sexually abused. As the questions in Chapter 8 suggest, an examination for other possible causes must be made. It is possible that some of the symptoms listed next could be the result of poor parenting or other causes.

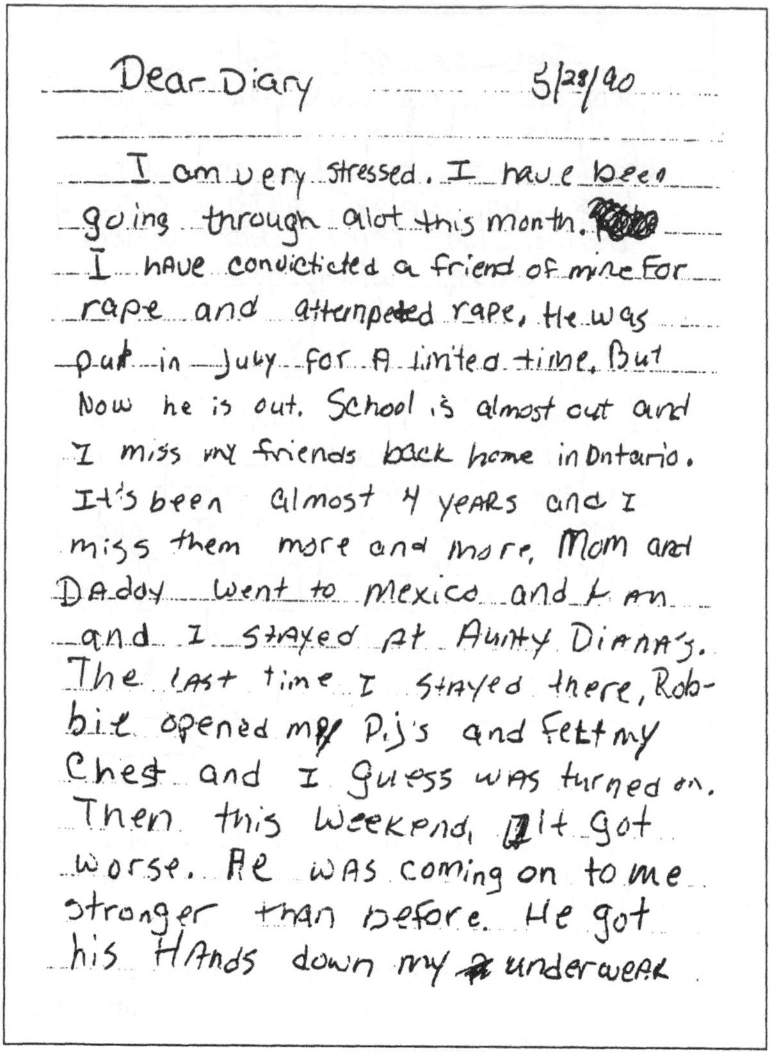

> Dear Diary       5/28/90
>
> I am very stressed. I have been going through alot this month. ~~××××~~ I have convicticted a friend of mine for rape and attempeted rape, He was out in July for A limited time, But Now he is out. School is almost out and I miss my friends back home in Ontario. It's been almost 4 years and I miss them more and more, Mom and Daddy went to Mexico and I an and I stayed at Aunty Dianna's. The last time I stayed there, Robbie opened my P.j's and felt my Chest and I guess was turned on. Then this weekend, I It got worse. He was coming on to me stronger than before. He got his Hands down my ~~×~~ underwear

**Figure 2.6** A note was found in the address book of a 16-year-old girl who was having sex with a well-respected adult. This was found to corroborate her account of the event. (Courtesy of San Bernardino Police Department. .

**Overly compliant behavior.** Often the abused child is taught that to avoid conflict he must submit to anything asked of him. As a result, he carries this behavior outside the home.

**Acting-out/aggressive behavior. Incorrigible or delinquent activity. Prostitution.** These are constant problems with sexually abused children, but they are only some of the ways the child copes with what is happening

Late at night when everyone was sleeping, (after work) Then ~~and to~~ This mornig was almost caught in my bed on top of me in his underwear in my bed. Then Thank god Hank came in when he did. Robbie was so close to having sex with me. Hank came out of the bathroom and Robbie jumped out like a shot. Alexander wants me to go over next weekend because he went to Randys when I was there. I want to go but I'm afraid of Robbie. He is a part of my family and a cop. Theres no one left for me to trust Anymore.

P.S. I Almost lost my bestfriend this month too.

**Figure 2.6 (continued)**

to him. *They do not happen in every case.* Running away from home is the most common characteristic of this nature. Escape is often the only way the child can cope with the abuse. When delinquent behavior is seen, it may surface in several ways. The child may be acting out pent-up anger about what has happened to him and it may show itself in violent attacks. Another common form of delinquent behavior is seeking kicks. For the child who is actively involved in selling himself to others, sex becomes banal and commonplace. An example of this banality can be seen in the portion of a letter written by a 14-year-old girl to a 15-year-old boy who was sexually involved with older men and committing residential burglaries. Here she is writing about her home and what is going on in the summer months. The letter was found in the boy's wastebasket during the service of a search warrant for a series of burglaries.

> "There are about 14,000 people staying at that house. First of all, my dad's girlfriend, her niece is staying there with her baby and boyfriend. Ethan — A's [sic] other son—has his stuff in my room (he's in L.A. doing porno pictures) [32]."

The child needs some activity to stimulate himself and often looks for thrills in committing crimes. Most of the time these crimes are nonviolent and involve malicious damage, theft, burglary, joyriding, or car theft. In the case mentioned earlier, the boy had an apartment full of the property he had stolen, because he had no way to get rid of it except give it away—which is what got him caught.

Aggression may also surface with the child committing a crime against his abuser. In a case where a boy was being molested by a teacher at school, the case came to light when the child punctured the tires of the teacher's car.

Many children turn to prostitution because they have a very poor self image and feel they are not worthy of good sexual relationships. They feel "cheap," and prostitution becomes an outlet for their self-pity, a way of punishing themselves, and a way to express contempt for adults who would pay for worthless favors.

**Pseudo-mature behavior.**    Children often act older than they are. However, this is indicative of sexual abuse when it is coupled with other behaviors described here. It often is seen when the child has had little guidance from his parents and must take care of himself. For example, a 9-year-old boy, son of a mentally disturbed mother with whom he lived, was allowed to roam the streets at all hours and became sexually involved with several adult men. He displayed an enormous capacity to take care of himself in behavior and speech, but didn't really understand the meaning or consequences of what he was doing. In incestuous relationships, a similar behavior pattern may be observed in the child when he acts much older than he really is, taking on the role of an adult in many familial functions and situations.

**Child describes abuse in drawings and play.**    A sexually abused child will frequently re-enact or describe circumstances of their abuse in play, drawings, or in conversation with others where no questioning or inquiry is made of the child. This is both a psychological means of working through the experience and a veiled attempt to have someone intervene (see Figure 2.7).

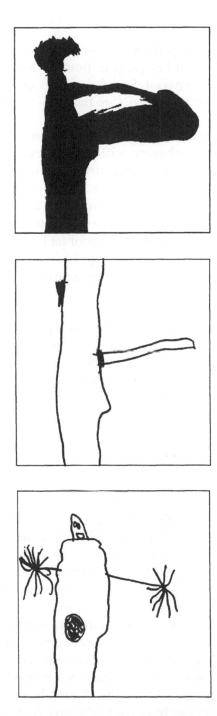

**Figure 2.7** These drawings represent the efforts of a 6-year-old child to work through abuse by her father. They were created when she was merely drawing on a sketch pad which was provided to her in an unrelated matter.

### Hints about Sexuality

In one case, help was sought for a 7-year-old girl who repeatedly pulled up her dress and pulled down her pants in front of her grandparents, despite being punished for the behavior. Such behavior is often considered normal experimentation — and may be so. (See following paragraph.)

**Persistent and inappropriate sexual play with peers, toys, or themselves, or sexually aggressive behavior with others, excessive masturbation, autoerotic behavior, excessive sexual curiosity, and play.**     Sexual experimentation and play in children is a normal behavior; however, it is generally observed to be consistent with the age level of the child. For example, the 3-year-old boy found simulating sexual intercourse with a doll should be considered to be expressing inconsistent behavior for his age. The 9-year-old boy who forces younger children to orally copulate with him in order that they be allowed into his "gang" is displaying an unusual behavior that should be examined more closely.

**Detailed and age-inappropriate understanding of sexual behavior or concepts.**     This is a difficult area because no one knows just what "normal" knowledge should be for children at various levels of development and ages. However, if the child exhibits an understanding at age two or three that the penis should be inserted between the legs and into the vagina and the hips should be rocked back and forth in a thrusting motion, one should wonder from where this knowledge came. Similarly, with an adolescent who can describe oral copulation in experiential terms, questions of the source of this knowledge should arise (see Figure 2.8).

**Arriving early at school and leaving late with few, if any, absences. Frequent absences from school, justified by the parents with little or no regard for the child's school performance (especially when the child is home alone during the day with a father, step-father, or other male figure who writes the excuses).**     In one case, a 13-year-old girl was seduced with the pretext of shooting a spread of modeling photos at a resort town near her home, away from her parents. She was given wine to the point she was so drunk she couldn't "see." She awoke the next morning to find herself in bed with the man. She subsequently became so involved with the man that she left her family home and began living with the molester. He was sexually involved with her and taking pornographic pictures of her, which were published in a European porn magazine. During the 10 months she was living with the man, she went to school only 14 days. She gave far-fetched excuses to the school authorities that were provided by the man, who represented himself as a relative.

**Figure 2.8** In this case, a five-year-old boy accused his father of molesting him. The facts described below and the drawing are the kind of idiosyncratic detailed knowledge of age-inappropriate understanding of sexual interaction that help to determine the child's credibility.

Tommy (not his real name) reported to his preschool owner, in response to a child safety class offered at the school, that he had been hurt by his father. The child also reported the visitation supervisor that his father hurt him "last night." The disclosure came when the supervisor was talking about lying about eating cookies the child shouldn't have. The child, out of the blue, said "my dad lies." When asked what he meant, he said "he says he didn't hurt me, but he did." When asked when, the child said the night before, telling him "he put it there (pointing to his rectum). He put his penit (sic) out here (grabbing his crotch) it came out of his pants." When asked if he was OK, the child "it was hard and stuck straight out" (pointing his arm straight out). He then estimated how long it was by showing the supervisor with his hands spread apart.

The child told his teachers at school, "he caught me in the kitchen and hurt me with his penis in my bottom." The staff noted visible scratches on the inside of his legs.

This was reported to CPS on this date, but they didn't respond for an interview until almost a month later, when the child told his pre-school teacher about his inability to hold fecal matter. The teacher said the boy told her "my daddy was playing the penis game and he hurt me... I can't sit and he put it on there" (pointing to his rectum). The school reported the incident because the child wa s not able to sit down due to the pain.

*(continues)*

**Figure 2.8 (continued)**   The mother's cousin was with the mother when they picked the child up from a visit with the father. She gave him a present to cheer him up and was talking about it when he suddenly said "My daddy hurt me last night.".In response to what happened, he responded "He put his penis back there... it really happened."

Again the mother reported that the child told her "before my bath I was naked without clothes. My dad had his on. He put his penis in here (pointing to anus). It hurt and it did not have a cover on it."

On the way home from school one day, the mother asked the child how his day was. He responded by saying "my dad hurted me." When she told him she didn't think so, he said "yes he did, it did happen." He then said "he went into the kitchen and put on his cover. Its real stretchy, it looks like a balloon and its red."

Sometime in December, the mother reports that the child said "sometime feel Pee go in my bottom when my daddy hurts me."

She also reports an incident in the car where the child again told of his being hurt the "night before," where he described, by squatting on the seat, exactly the position he was required to assume to be sodomized, saying "he was like this, his penis stuck straight out... he grabbed me and pulled me... he stuck it in my bottom."

The mother reports that the child said "my daddy wears a cover on his penis so he doesn't get germs when he sticks it in my bottom". She also reported he said "daddy plays with his penis sometimes, its kind of fat and round."

When asked about his recent visit at his father's, the child responded "it wasn't so good." When asked why, he said "he grabbed my arm real hard and then threw me down like this, wham, and then he hit my back. . . and I hit my head, wham." He demonstrated how it happened for his mother, reenacting it. He showed her a bruise on his head. This was subsequently reported by a doctor who examined him. Photos were taken by the mother.

On one occasion, the child was being taken home by the mother when she noticed another bruise on the child's face. When asked how it happened, the child responded, "I can't tell because my daddy will hurt me."

The school again reported to CPS that the child disclosed he was being sodomized by his father. This time the child had physically reenacted how. He told the teacher "don't tell my daddy put his penis in my bottom,"apparently afraid what would happen if she did.

On another occasion, the mother was getting ready to watch a movie on their VCR, when the child suddenly said "my daddy has movies with big people hurting kids... and big people hurting big people." When asked what he meant, he replied "you know, like how daddy hurts me with his penis... that's how come I know so much about that stuff."He said, "there's a man and then another man sneaks up behind him and hurts him in his bottom."

During the month of February, the mother notes that the child has experienced an increase in his inability to hold fecal matter. He has had frequent "accidents" in his pants.

At school, the child further described the movies as having children younger than him in them. When asked if he could bring one to school, he replied to his mother "oh, so ...(the teacher) could see how my dad hurts me... well he keeps them hidden — somewhere secret."

**Figure 2.8 (continued)**   The boy told the teacher that "my daddy goes to other houses and takes movies of other daddies hurting their little boys." When asked if his father told him this, he said "no, I figured it out because you can't see this on regular TV, it just on my daddy's movies."

The next month, the child reported that his father had taken pictures of him while hurting him. When asked what happened, he drew a picture of himself being sodomized by his father on one side of the page. On the other, he drew a picture of the camera, describing it on "legs." He then drew an image inside the camera, saying that was the picture the camera took.

In the cases of children who are always at school and remain there as long as possible, many of them consider the school a "safe house" where they can feel secure and may find success, attention, and diversion from their troubles. In the case of the child who is often away from school, it is not uncommon to find that the offender is the one keeping the child away from school, fearing that the child may tell someone or that the offender will lose control of the child.

**Poor peer relationships, inability to make friends, sudden changes of relationships with friends at school.**   Sexually abused children often have difficulty in establishing relationships with others in their peer group. They are often isolated from others and have little experience in making friends. Those who are able to establish friendships may have sudden changes in how they relate to their friends during the ongoing abuse because of what is happening to them at the time.

Molested from the age of three to eight, a women tells of her abuse by two uncles and a grandfather. Prefacing the description of her ordeal by saying that she still has bad dreams and wishes her relatives were dead, she says:

> When it happened to me I felt my childhood was robbed. I no longer wanted to be around kids because I felt out of place. Now I'm living my childhood through my four and five-year-old daughters. Every time a man comes around, I watch every move he makes when he comes near my kids, even their stepfather. I want to believe they won't hurt my kids, but they are men and I still remember the pain and hurt I went through [33].

**Lack of trust, particularly of significant others.**   Often the victim of deceit, the sexually abused child learns that it is unwise to trust others. In many cases, the child will expect betrayal and rejection from anyone who displays kindness and caring feelings to him.

**Nonparticipation in school events.**   This is especially true when the child refuses to participate in school gym classes or activities that require the child to dress or undress in front of others. Offending parents will often severely restrict the child's ability to participate in after-school activities (see below).

**Inability to concentrate in school.**    Because of the emotions or bad feelings that come from the abuse, afraid of the consequences of his actions at home, wracked by guilt, afraid of what will happen to him next, the sexually abused child has great difficulty in paying attention to what is going on in school.

**Sudden drop in school performance.**    As a result of the child's inability to concentrate, his performance may change drastically. It is important to determine whether this has occurred, because it may help to pinpoint the onset of abuse.

**Extraordinary fears.**    Of males or females. Of places he has been to before or liked to go to. Refusal to go to school. Fears of showers, restrooms, or bedrooms. Sudden fear of a specific person. Fear of playing alone.

**Overly seductive behavior to other children and adults.**    Often the child learns that to obtain attention or affection or the satisfaction of other needs, he must act seductively or present himself to the offender. This often carries over to relationships with others. It may be seen as the child's actively seeking attention, affection, praise, rewards, and approval. It may also manifest itself in overt sexual advances by touching sexual areas or by making sexual comments.

**Self-destructive behavior.**    Sexually abused children often turn to alcohol or drug abuse as an escape mechanism. It is not uncommon to find that these children become criminally delinquent, hoping to get caught, as a means of punishing themselves for allowing their abuse to happen or, as with prostitution, as a way of self-debasement. Head banging, cutting, burning, disfiguring, scratching, and hairpulling may be signs of self-punishment, tension relief, or an attempt to take control of pain. Starvation or overeating may also be used in order to become unsightly and hopefully immune from sexual relationships.

**Sleep disturbances.**    Nightmares, fear of going to bed, wanting the light on, waking up during the night, and fear of sleeping alone are common. Inability to sleep and changes in sleep patterns also occur.

**Regressive behavior.**    Acting in a way appropriate to a younger developmental level, through which they have already passed, or switching abruptly from one developmental level to another.

**Social or emotional withdrawal.**   Afraid of being rebuked or ridiculed, the sexually abused child often keeps to himself. As a means of escaping his torment, the child may withdraw into his own world and avoid contact with others.

**Clinical depression.**   Unprovoked crying spells and an unusual amount of sleeping are common among sexually abused children. It is not uncommon to find that the child wishes to sleep as much as possible because his dream world is more pleasant than his reality.

**Suicidal feelings.**   Often the child feels he has no escape but death.

**Loss of appetite.**   The child may suddenly, without reason, refuse to eat. This is generally an obvious change in the child's behavior pattern.

**Sudden change in moods.**   Irritability or short temper in a child who was not this way normally are common symptoms.

**Bed-wetting.**   Another sudden change or regression in behavior. The child with this problem will have already passed through the "nominal" age for such a problem and suddenly begin to bed-wet during the night.

**Clinginess.**   Needing more reassurance than usual, the child may physically cling to parents or significant others.
   In a case where a nursery school operator was involved with the children in his care, a girl came home and told one parent that the proprietor had taken pictures of her "butt." The child physically held on to the parents each time the subject of the nursery school was brought up. The parents confronted the owner with the allegation and he admitted taking photographs of the child, later sending them only the conventional photos he had taken to demonstrate the propriety of his acts. The mother saw the other photos 2 years later when the man was finally arrested.
   Other parents described the symptoms they observed while their children attended the school. One mother noticed bruises on her son's back and that he had erections "90%" of the time at home. He had started wetting the bed and having nightmares, all of which cleared up after he was taken out of the school. Another parent found her daughter playing "doctor" with a neighbor child, but asked no questions. Still another mother of a 2-year-old couldn't understand her daughter's continual vaginal rash or her excessive masturbation. She also couldn't understand why her daughter would "French kiss" her.

**Taking excessive baths.**   Sexually abused children have often expressed a feeling of being dirty. In particular, they feel unclean and smelly where the offender has touched them. Behaviorally, this manifests itself in several ways. It is not uncommon to find that the abused child will repeatedly try to wash certain parts of his body. Children have been observed constantly rubbing themselves, as though trying to rub off the spot where they have been touched or where they feel uncomfortable. In some extreme cases, children have tried to cleanse themselves to the point of drawing blood or disfigurement.

**Suffering problems finding his sexual identity or determining his gender role.**   This is most pronounced when boys are involved with men in sexual relationships. Boys who are already having difficulty in sorting out their sexual identity will have many problems if they are sexually involved with adults prematurely.

The following is a good example of how this might show itself. It is also a good example of how several other factors described here may surface in a case.

A 15-year-old boy was arrested for committing a series of auto burglaries. He was connected to a group of boys who were involved sexually with older men. The boy was having regular sex with men in their 50s and 60s.

His parents were in their 60s themselves and were quite conservative for the standards of the day (late 1970s). The generation gap was so strong that the father and the son were unable to communicate, and any attempt to do so usually ended up in a shouting match. The boy's mother would constantly make excuses for the boy and would be there to "catch him when he fell" every time he had a fight with his father or got into trouble.

The boy was sleeping 10 to 12 hours a day. He would stay out until the wee hours of the morning, smoking dope and taking hallucinogens. His excitement was "boosting" cars and running with the street kids who did the same things.

He hardly ever went to class, but when he did, he did poorly because he hadn't studied. When he did study, he was generally ineffective because of the drugs he had been taking, and the result was a very poor showing in class. He could never please his teachers.

At home he could never please his father, who would make ordinary demands upon him to do "chores." His appearance was not pleasing to his father, who was a postal worker. The boy's long hair, dirty clothes, and choice of apparel were somewhat of an embarrassment to his father.

He spent a great deal of time with the men and became strongly emotionally attached to them, as well as physically attracted to them. The problem he expressed was that even while he was with these men, he would encounter girls to whom he would also be sexually attracted. He said he felt great pain in separating or identifying his sexual loyalty [34].

The same problems occur with boys who "hustle" as street prostitutes. They not only are incorrectly identified as gay-oriented by outside observers, they often have difficulty discerning for themselves who they are.

The case described also demonstrates that children, boys in particular, who are experiencing gender identification difficulties, will often be rejected by their fathers (the major male figure in their lives) and be thrust out of the family {emotionally and/or physically). What often happens is that these children turn to male prostitution as a means of finding a ready source of acceptance.

**Serious problems with self-image.**   Sexually abused children often exhibit problems with self-esteem, self-respect, and self-confidence. As a result, they constantly berate and degrade themselves.

A 14-year-old girl tells of being molested and her involvement in pornography:

> "I really feel bad. I feel very low. I respect my body and just ask god every night why did I do this, why? [35]."

**Becoming manipulators.**   Children who have been sexually abused soon find that they have a commodity that is in demand and gives them a power they never knew they had. It is not uncommon to find, upon discovering some need — be it as simple as a desire for some physical closeness — that the child may seek out the offender and initiate the sexual activity in return for the satisfaction of the expressed need. This is important because it often clouds the issue of just who is exploited. What must not be lost in the discussion when this happens is that it is the adult who has initiated the child into the activity, and it is the adult, not the child, who is responsible for preventing it from happening.

> A fatherless 14-year-old boy, who lived with his 14 brothers and sisters on welfare, met a man who owned several video games in neighborhood super-markets. The man befriended the boy, who would visit the man at his home to play video games (free) three or four times a month. This relationship lasted for over a year.
>
> The man engaged the boy in sexual acts by starting to participate in mutual masturbation, which later progressed to other acts.
>
> Over time, the boy began to ask the man for money, which the man willingly gave, feeling a responsibility for the boy as well as being indebted to him. He also wanted the boy to continue visiting him. Whenever the boy wanted money, he would go to the man and ask for it. On some occasions, he was refused.

It didn't take long before the boy realized he could get more money if he threatened to expose the man, and it wasn't long before the man began to pay blackmail money [36].

**Blaming the uncomfortable feelings on the offender.**     Afraid of taking responsibility for the sexual acts and the stigma of being called homosexuals, boys will rarely admit they played an active role in any sex acts. Psychologically speaking, these boys protect themselves by saying it is the offender who is the "weirdo," not them. *"He* sucked *me* off" is a common statement made by such children.

An excellent example of our discussion thus far may be found in the account of a young man who appeared before a U.S. Senate hearing and discussed his becoming a victim at the hands of his uncle:

(He was a victim of)... molestation and pornography abuse that occurred from the ages of 12 to 16.... Alex (the uncle) was a former scout leader, a former Big Brother with Catholic Charities, an elementary school teacher, and a school counselor trained in child psychology. He used to take scores of boys on overnight camping trips, each one carrying a signed permission slip from his unwary parents... the parents actually paid Alex to sponsor the activities.

... He was convicted for molesting five children and sentenced to 6 years in prison.

... At the age of 12... he began taking an interest in me... taking me to ball games with other kids and with other younger family members, and then began taking me to movies by myself.

When I was at my grandmother's house, he would offer to let me spend hours over at his house playing with an assortment of toys, hobbies, and sports equipment which would have fascinated any 12-year-old kid. He let me be alone in his house also so I would become comfortable there.

The next step he took grooming me for sexual exploitation was with photography... first, he took pictures of me clothed, and since everyone knew about Alex's interest and skill in photography, this seemed perfectly normal and, in fact, my family was delighted with the first photographs they received of me.

... (He) then coaxed me to take off more of my clothes. First it was my shirt. He explained how simple and easy it would be. He told me that it would be fun. Then he wanted me to try it without my jeans. Later it progressed to my changing into and out of swim suits and then without my underwear. Finally, fully naked. Then he had me pose naked in front of a camera.

Methodically, always careful to make sure that he could go safely to the next step without [my] running out of the house, Alex led right up to the first incident of molestation, which began with fondling and then led to all the logical sexual acts that could follow.

... He was able to make me feel as if it were myself suggesting what position or what activity to do next. He never physically threatened or coerced me, at least not at first.

Alex realized that this first incident was the pivotal point of my victimization. This was the one time when he knew that he had to act to maintain his control over the situation or I might have left the house and told someone. So my uncle, the school counselor, the man who counseled hundreds of children before me, made me stand before him naked, while he sat on a bar stool in front of me, also naked, and for 45 minutes he subjected me to a lecture about how what had happened between us was completely legal, that I had nothing to be ashamed of. But he went further than that. He told me not to tell anyone and that if I ever did, not only would he go to jail, but that I would get in trouble, and that my parents would hate me.

... I remained silent for 6 years.

... I kept visiting my uncle, even after I knew that there was nothing in store for me but sexual abuse because I thought that's what I was meant to be used for. I felt guilty and horrible. I felt out of place in my clean, loving, trusting home. I didn't belong there with good people. I belonged somehow somewhere else.

... They found thousands of sexually explicit photos of young boys in his home and also many foreign child pornography magazines and films.... On two occasions, he showed me films of young boys my age involved in sexual orgies. Several times, he allowed me to see imported sexually explicit material featuring young boys my age. Eventually he confessed to having molested 5 children....

We refused to cover it up and let it pass unnoticed. Because of this, an entire extended family has strained and become splintered. We were ostracized and rejected by some of the family members who had been such a strong foundation of support throughout the years. The aunt in whom I confided [and who supported him throughout the ordeal also succumbed to family pressure and eventually withdrew her support from me [37].

## Somatic Complaints

Sexually abused children have been found to complain of physical ailments for which there are no apparent causes. These ailments may or may not relate to the specific acts the children are or were involved in and may or may not relate to the parts of the body involved in those acts. Common complaints are stomach aches, headaches, and nonspecific pains.

Often these complaints are caused by the child's desire to receive attention. This attention may be because of the abuse or for other reasons. The child may also see it as a way to disclose the molestation, thinking that the people he tells will "read between the lines" of his complaint and will reveal what has happened.

As with the need to clean themselves, children will also develop "pains" over the areas that have been touched by an offender. There will be no apparent cause of the pain on examination, but to the child the hurt will be very real.

### Family Dynamics

Some other characteristics have been noted in families where the child is sexually active with one of the parents or is known to be involved in illicit sexual activity that is encouraged or participated in by a member of the child's family. As is true for the previously listed characteristics, these characteristics do not occur in every case of intrafamilial sexual abuse, and their presence or absence should not be considered as proof positive that abuse has or has not occurred. Some characteristics of the family of the sexually abused child who is involved with others outside the family unit are also listed.

**Extreme overprotectiveness toward the child.**    The family refuses the child's desires to participate in activities with his peer group. In incest families, the offending parent, usually the father, prevents the child's contact with the opposite sex because he becomes jealous and fears discovery.

**The family is characterized by extreme paternal dominance.**   The father takes control of everything and rarely allows the mother or children to do anything alone.

**The family is characterized by marked role reversal between mother and daughter.**   The child takes on the nurturing and care-taking role when the mother is physically or psychologically absent.

**The family severely overreacts to the child's receiving any sex education in the school setting (formalized class or films, from the school nurse or other children).**   In incest situations, the family does not want the child to learn that what is occurring in the home is improper, and will therefore make every effort to shield the child from the knowledge that might bring the abuse to a halt.

**The family is socially isolated from the rest of the community and attempts to isolate the children.**   Homes in which abuse is occurring must remain intact. To allow a child to participate in activities or circulate among the community might bring the walls of the home crashing down when the child finds out that what is going on at home is beyond the realm of normal relationships.

**The child may be exposed to several men in relationships with the mother. The family offers little or no supervision, controls, or limits for the child. The family unit can be characterized as unstable.**   This may be because either the family is breaking up, is having problems living together, or has poor ties to its members, or only one parent is present.

**The family is from a strict, fundamental religious background that punishes sexual expression or experimentation. The home is characterized as an "abusive" environment, wherein the child is physically abused. The family is characterized as being "sex negative."**   In these families, any questions about sexuality are suppressed and sexual activity such as masturbation is responded to with punishment.

### Physical or Medical Indicators of Sexual Abuse

Physical or medical indicators in sexual abuse cases are often nonexistent for many persons. In most cases, the abuse is reported long after the actual acts occurred; therefore, the body has been able to repair any physical injury that may have resulted from the abuse. Also, the physical body of the child is such that the skin stretches, the orifice opens, or the act itself is one that leaves no physical mark on the body. Therefore, the absence of physical findings should not deter the investigator, *because it is the norm rather than the exception.*

Since the original publication of this text there has been much research and discussion about what constitutes significant medical findings in child sexual abuse and exploitation. Consensus has been reached in many areas and documentation of both normal and abnormal findings has been accomplished. This text is not intended to provide a detailed explanation of the potential medical evidence one might encounter in these cases. This area of medicine has developed into its own specialty. The specialty is supported by prolific articles, texts, atlas', and all amply supported by data to justify its conclusions. The best summaries and digests for non-medical professionals are contained in *Evidence in Child Abuse and Neglect Cases*, by Professor John E.B. Myers [38] and *Investigation and Prosecution of Child Abuse*, Second Edition, National Center for Prosecution of Child Abuse [39]. What both of these authoritative texts agree upon is that the ability to obtain medical evidence in these cases depends ultimately upon the person doing the examination — (his/her) skills, experience, training, and, willingness to accept abuse as a possibility. The more specialized in child sexual abuse the pediatrician who does the examination, the better. Therefore, great care should be taken in the selection of who performs the examination. At minimum, any diagnosis should include: (1) a history, as detailed as possible; (2) an assessment of the child's behavior as discussed earlier in this chapter; (3) a physical examination, preferably with a colposcope; and, (4) lab studies.

The following findings should be considered as strong indicators that sexual activity has occurred:

1. Hymenal disruption, presenting as scars, tears, or abrasions.
2. Injuries of the posterior forchette in girls (area between the vagina and the anus).
3. Significant anal relaxation or the presence of large anal scars.
4. Presence of sexually transmitted diseases and such things as genital warts.
5. Chronic irritation about the genitals.
6. Pregnancy.
7. Presence of semen in the vagina, rectum, or mouth or on other parts of the body.

Other physical/medical symptoms that may, to a lesser degree, point to sexual abuse are painful urination and encopresis (inability to hold fecal matter, generally because of injury or relaxation of the sphincter muscle due to acts of sodomy).

## Other Characteristics

**Often the child is found or observed with unusual amounts of money, new toys, clothes, or other possessions.**   These are either direct rewards from the child molester or are purchased with the money obtained from him. As an example, in more than one case the offender has bought an automobile for the children he is involved with without a parent asking a question. In one case, where the offender bought a 15-year-old boy a brand new, $4,000 motorcycle, the mother of the boy did ask where he obtained it. However, when he told her he traded his 10-speed bike for it, she asked no further questions.

**Often the child will spend more than the normal amount of time at recreation areas, theaters, and other juvenile hangouts.**   Children in this situation are more easily recognizable as they tend to frequent the places where sexual activity is commonplace. They will, in fact, frequent these places because they know of the activity that occurs there. This is important for the investigator because he will be able to identify locations that are active when he finds children he knows are active frequenting the places. In addition, he can identify other children who are involved by their associations at such locations.

**Often, children who are being sexually active with adults will be seen spending an inordinate amount of time in the adults' company.**   This is time they would normally spend with children in their peer group.

As an example of the child who is involved sexually with someone outside his home, what follows is an excerpt from a probation file containing three different reports filed by three different probation officers about a child who was taken to Europe by the man he was involved with. The man also took the child to Disneyland, gave him a car, and let him live with him when the boy left his mother. The man is probably one of the major child pornographers in his area. The boy was arrested on each occasion for "boosting" car stereos. Prior to his being referred to the probation department he had committed three similar offenses, but was sent to "diversion" counseling in hopes of keeping him out of the criminal justice system. When arrested, each time he was found to have stacks of car radios and no place to dispose of them. He was simply "collecting" them.

When the boy was first referred to the probation department, the probation officer wrote under the "discussion" section:

> "The parents are divorced but (the mother) states she has a male neighbor for whom the boys deliver directories and he is a kind of father-figure for the boys and a positive influence on their conduct and attitudes."

The boy was arrested again in December of the same year, and a second probation officer wrote in the section on "family:"

> "He is basically a follower and can easily be led."

When the boy was arrested again six months later, yet another probation officer wrote under "Major Identified Problems:"

> "(The boy)... is the second oldest of four children in a family that is on welfare. (The boy)... seems to be a neglected young man who desperately craves attention from significant adults."

# The Offender

The following sections are largely based upon the typology developed by Supervisory Special Agent Kenneth V. Lanning, of the Federal Bureau of Investigation. It is based upon Mr. Lanning's personal research, investigative experience, and the classifications of offenders which were proposed by sociologists, psychologists, and criminologists. His typology was the first ever created for law enforcement for the purposes of understanding criminal behavior related to sexual molestation of children and abduction of children for sexual purposes. The value of the typology is in creating a set of criteria and symptomology that will help a police officer to track and apprehend an offender. It also lends itself to the identification of potential offenders in the hopes of preventing future offenses by developing strategies for early intervention by arrest. The secondary value in creating this typology is to help investigators anticipate the kind of evidence that may be present in a particular case. It will also form basis for questions of victims and offenders in search of evidence to establish the crime under investigation [40].

A caveat is appropriate at this juncture. The reader should be aware that the presence of any one or more of these characteristics may indicate that the subject under investigation is an offender. Only investigation and the identification of acts and the requisite mental state on the part of the offender will establish whether a crime was committed and the person under investigation is a criminal. It would be a mistake to assume that merely because some of the symptoms and characteristics listed herein are present that the person under investigation is, conclusively, a criminal. On the other hand, merely because none of these characteristics are present does not prove or establish the negative. Because offenders come from so many character types and motivational backgrounds, the absence of these characteristics should not be used to rule out the potential that an alleged offense has occurred.

## Past Perspectives

There have been many psychological theories about what motivates sex offenders [41]. For the purposes of our discussion, we look at people who commit sex offenses against children as being on a continuum. At the ends of that continuum are preferences that range from exclusively attracted to and involved with adults to the opposite end, where the preference is exclusive for children. Within that spectrum, there is also a measure for intensity of sex drive or interest that ranges from high to low [42].

Along that continuum, for investigative purposes Mr. Lanning has created his own dichotomy of offenders. Moreover, Lanning has struggled with the same difficulties that the field has had trouble with since the very beginning of the identification of sexual molestation of children as a crime problem. Defining the difference among offenders is incredibly difficult given the many characteristics and behavior patterns involved in the commission of crimes against children.

However, for the purposes of this discussion, the term pedophile, as used in this typology, will encompass those individuals as we have described them early on in Chapter 1.

## Types of Offenders

Lanning divides the offender types into two categories: "situational" and "preferential." Lanning's typology is the most comprehensive and relevant descriptor of behavioral traits for sex offenders against children that presently exists in the criminology literature. As discussed above, its main purpose is to "identify, arrest, and convict" offenders. The following is presented with the gracious permission of Mr. Lanning and the National Center of Missing and Exploited Children in who's publication Lanning's original work appears.

## The Situational Offender

The situational offender is an individual who does not prefer children, exclusive to any other sexual partner but, who will often engage children in sexual activities for a wide variety of reasons. Although most situational offenders that the author has come to learn about have been involved in more than one incident, their offenses may only involve a singular act or numerous acts with a single victim over a period of time. As Lanning points out, the longer the activity goes on with a single or multiple victims the more difficult it is to determine or distinguish the situational offender from that of the individual who prefers children as their primary sexual object [43]. Experience has shown that the situational offender may molest a smaller number of victims who may be from different families. However, it is possible that this offender may commit crimes against other vulnerable persons within his immediate peer group or who are older. It would not be out of the ordinary for such an offender to be involved sexually with children in his care at one time during the day and then to sexually exploit or abuse an adult in another setting where in he has power over the victim. Situational offenders come from all walks of life and levels of the social spectrum. Lanning divides the behavior patterns of the situational offender into the following four categories: "See Table 2.1."

**Table 2.1   Situational Child Molester**

|  | Regressed | Morally Indiscriminate | Sexually Indiscriminate | Inadequate |
|---|---|---|---|---|
| Basic Characteristics | Poor coping skills | User of people | Sexual experimentation | Social misfit |
| Motivation | Substitution | Why not? | Boredom | Insecurity and curiosity |
| Victim Criteria | Availability | Vulnerability and opportunity | New and different | Non-threatening |
| Method of Operation | Coercion | Lure, force, or manipulation | Involved in existing activity | Exploits size advantage |
| Pornography Collection | Possible | Sadomasochistic, detective magazines | Highly likely, varied nature | Likely |

From Lanning, K., *Child Molesters: A Behavioral Analysis*, 1992. With permission.

**"Regressed."**    This offender has a problem with self-esteem and little or no coping skills. As he has poor peer relationships and, often, he turns to children for sexual gratification as a substitute for a sexual relationship with a peer. Some kind of stress or other family dysfunction is often attributed as the cause of his sexual deviation. Frequently, the child within the family is available which becomes his selection criteria and, because he has access to his own children, then becomes his most frequent victim. This offender's primary method of attaining his desires is to coerce the acts he desires, forcing or cajoling the child into engaging in sexual activity with him by some method. The situational offender may or may or may not collect pornography. Sometimes the content of the pornography collected would be sexually explicit pictures of his victims. This may be with homemade pictures shot by video or still photography.

**"Morally indiscriminate."**    Research by Ken Lanning at the FBI Academy, Behavioral Science Unit, has discovered that this type of offender is being seen on more frequent basis. In this instance, the sexual abuse involving children is a continuation of the pattern of abuse this individual metes out to the people in his life. He is the type of individual who takes advantage of and abuses the people he is married to, those he works with and those whom he considers his "friends." He will do whatever he can that he thinks he won't get caught for including theft, dishonesty and out right abusive conduct. When the opportunity to molest a child presents itself, he does so because he sees no reason why he shouldn't. Lanning points out that the criteria for victim selection is simply a child's "vulnerability and opportunity." This individual would typically simply respond to his urges and has poor impulse control. The FBI has found that he typically uses "force, lures, or manipulation" and may "violently or nonviolently abduct his victims." This type of individual will victimize children that he has no connection to and who are total strangers or anybody else he might have access to including those in his own family.

In incestuous situations, people with this character type may be mothers, fathers, or other blood relatives of the victim. The FBI has found that this type of offender frequently will collect detective magazines or adult pornography involving bondage and sadomasochism.

Perhaps because his normal sexual partners are within his age group, he is most likely to offend with children who have achieved puberty. It is the author's experience, backed up by the FBI's profiling unit, that this individual has little or no conscience or guilt for his offending behavior. When child pornography is found in the possession of persons with this characteristic, it generally is of pubescent children again, perhaps, because they are closest to his natural sexual partners. The FBI has found that he tends to experiment with sex and sexual partners.

**"Sexually indiscriminate."**   This individual is what Lanning describes as a "try-sexual, willing to try anything sexual." This person, in contrast to the morally indiscriminate offender, does have a conscience and specifically seeks out children for sex as a means of satisfying his need to experiment or get excitement. Although he has no specific need or desire to have sex with children, he generally involves them in sex to satisfy his need for excitement and variety. The FBI has discovered through its research that this offender may have other deviant patterns such as being involved in bondage or other sexual deviations that would fall under the categories of paraphilias.

He is likely to be mistaken for a preferential offender because he is involved with so many children. This is often the type of offender that is found to be involved in incestuous relationships with his own children or those within his family unit. The FBI has also found that of the cases its studied, offenders from this category come from the upper echelon of the social economic strata. These individuals are likely to collect and produce erotica and child pornography. If he is a collector, the central themes of that material will not necessarily focus directly on children.

**"Inadequate."**   The FBI has found that an inadequate offender may also exhibit other mental problems such as "psychosis, eccentric personality disorders, mental retardation and senility." This person has poor social skills, is generally isolated from the general population either by choice or by circumstance. If an adolescent offender, this individual might be considered to be shy with few friends within his own age group. If an adult, this individual might be found to be an isolated individual still living at home perhaps relatives or his parents.

## The Preferential Offender

This type of offender has a "generally exclusive, preference" for involvement in sexual activity with children. These are individuals whose fantasies and "erotic imagery" involve children. They are motivated by a sexual attraction and an abnormal desire for sex with children. What makes this characteristic significant for the investigator is that the behavior patterns and conduct exhibited by this offender are extremely predictable. They often appear to be ritualistic in nature following a distinctive pattern of conduct. Because of the compulsion the offender experiences to commit these offenses, they often will commit crimes even when the risk of identification, apprehension, and conviction are high.

The FBI has estimated that the preferential offender may be less frequently seen than those who find themselves situationally motivated. However, research has established that they are more likely to have victimized a large number of children.

Whereas situational offenders may develop what is termed, obsessive/compulsive behavior, that is, they are uncontrollably, forever, thinking about sex with children and feel compelled to act in such a way so as to relieve the pressure they experience. This compulsion may become addictive when the offender finds that the acts he performs gives him pleasure. He may have an intermittent urge that he feels helpless to stop himself act on or he may have constant compulsive, uncontrollable urges that he is, almost, powerless to stop. What differentiates these offenders from the preferential offender is that the preferential offender is exclusively involved with children whereas the situational offender is non-exclusive (they most often have either concurrent or already established sexual relationships with people in their peer group). Another difference is that the situational offender has the transient urge to be sexual with children whereas the preferential offender has more compulsive and ritualized (recurrent, specific acts) behavior with the child. What seems to be a reoccurring theme with the preferential offender is the large quantity and need for new sexual experiences with children. To get an idea of how this manifests itself, one might consider the manner in which offenders are treated for their illicit sexual needs.

In some, the same therapeutic approach that is taken as with drug and alcohol addiction, known as the "relapse prevention" [44]. The intent of the therapeutic model is to reduce the dependency upon, and urge to act on, the impulses the offender experiences. Techniques are given to the offender to apply when the urge strikes in hopes to control their desires. The idea is for them to recognize and identify their urges. They identify what their individual risk factors are related to environment, perception, behaviors, emotions, and thinking. Then they learn methods and strategies to control themselves.

In addition, with the preferential offender, the FBI has found that within the subset of preferential offenders are those who have "age and gender preferences" selecting only certain victims. In other words, a particular offender may prefer one sex, exclusive to all others and within that gender, only children within a particular age group, sometimes spanning between three and five years. What is significant as far as an investigation or inquiry is concerned is that these age groups tend to be around developmental levels and once the child passes out of the stage of development, the offender loses interest in them. They then search for new victims within that age group. This predictability, not only allows the investigator to identify potential victims that need to be interviewed, but provides corroborative and support- ive information once new victims or old victims, as the case may be, are identified by the investigation.

Within the category of preferential offenders, the FBI identifies three behavioral characteristics that consistently appear with the preferential offender. (See Table 2.2.)

**Table 2.2   Preferential Child Molester**

|  | Seduction | Introverted | Sadistic |
|---|---|---|---|
| Basic Characteristics | 1. Sexual preference for children<br>2. Collects child pornography and/or erotica | | |
| Motivation | Identification | Fear of communication | Need to inflict pain |
| Victim Criteria | Age and gender preferences | Strangers or very young | Age and gender preferences |
| Method of Operation | Seduction process | Non-verbal sexual contact | Lure or force |

From Lanning, K., *Child Molesters: A Behavioral Analysis*, 1992. With permission.

**"Seduction."**   As the title implies, this offender accomplishes his victimiza- tion by seducing the child into sex acts. Once again, this pattern of behavior has important connotations for investigation or prosecution of these offenses because of the modus operandi and the ability to admit evidence of like crimes and actions. The seduction process is much as one adult would seduce another adult, using attention, affection, and kindness, often expressed through giving the child gifts and taking them places. Gradually, the child's resistance, sexual inhibitions, and affections are won over, resulting in sexual contact.

As is noted by the description of the victim in the preceding chapter, this offender utilizes the relationship he establishes with his victims as a means of keeping them together, sometimes involving multiple children at the same time.

This individual, often in a position of authority or oversight of children, is often seen as the "perfect" boy scout leader, teacher, or other professional working with children.

A curious characteristic of this offender is the fact that he is often dis- covered when he rejects or begins to ignore one of his victims. It was once observed that this offender's main problem is not finding child victims but getting rid of them when they grow out of his preference range (Lanning, 1992).

The FBI has found that this type of offender has been known to use violence and threats as a means of intimidating his victims into silence. The

FBI has also found that this type of offender is frequently the type of individual who might be involved in a "child sex ring."

**"Introverted."**   This individual is characterized by his preference for children and his inability to develop the interpersonal relationships and techniques needed to accomplish the seduction. The FBI has found that this type of offender will usually turn to strangers and young children.

This individual is very likely to fit the stereotype of the dirty old man in the raincoat, hanging around places where children congregate. He is likely to be found in places where he observes them and will not be involved in prolonged relationships, quickly molesting a child for a very short period of time and then leaving. He may be involved in other criminal acts such as indecent exposure involving children or making lewd or obscene phone calls to children. This individual may also seek out child prostitutes.

The FBI has also found that this individual, being unsophisticated and afraid to engage children in any type of a relationship, might marry a woman with the express purpose of raising his own children to be his own victims, often molesting them as infants.

**"Sadistic."**   This individual, although having a distinct and exclusive preference for children, must subject his victim to psychological or physical pain in order to satisfy his sexual urges. His arousal is heightened by the victim's reaction to his subjecting the child to pain or suffering. This offender is likely to force or lure his victim into compliance. Of all offenders, this type is the one which is most likely to abduct or murder their child victims.

The FBI has also seen a cross-over where seduction molesters may have this characteristic trait.

## Preferential Offender Characteristics

One of the main characteristics of the preferential offender is that he has little social interaction with people within his peer group. The FBI has found that fairly consistently, the offenders of this subgroup are generally 25 years of age or older, never been married, or if they have been, are single when committing the act(s). Often, it is discovered that an offender of this type may have married. After the relationship goes nowhere and/or where the sexual dysfunction of the offender, along with other difficulties in relating to his peer group, interferes, the couple separates and/or divorces. This is extremely important for follow-up purposes if the characteristic exists in a case under investigation. Following a trail of unsuccessful relationships with women in an offender's peer group may yield some significant information.

Once again, for the same reasons, we often find that this offender will be living alone or with parents. For the same reasons, there are limited sexual relations with people in the offender's own peer group and dating is minimal, if at all.

For the preferential offender, the FBI has discovered (and it has also been the consistent experience of the author) that if a preferential offender is married, there often are certain characteristics that appear. As is seen in the case of the situational offender, the individual may marry a dominant woman or, on the other hand, a woman who is passive or weak, not unlike a child. Frequently, the female partner has little need or desire for sexual interaction with the offender. The couple experiences problems which may or may not cause concern on the part of the woman, however, seldom does it rise to the level of identification by the wife of the offender's true interest.

On the other hand, there are offenders who engage in practices with their wives which are indicative of their preferences. It is not uncommon for an offender to ask his spouse to dress and act like a child. It's not uncommon for them to seek out women who have child-like sexual characteristics or ask the woman to shave her genitals to look like a child. It's not uncommon for the offender to ask his spouse to talk and/or engage her in sex play while talking to her as though she were a child or have the woman talk to him as though she were a child.

Lastly, it's not uncommon to find a preferential offender who seeks out a relationship with a woman for the sole purpose of providing a "cover." Here the real purpose for the relationship is simply to maintain the appearances of being "normal." The individual may engage his spouse in sexual relations without any indication of a problem and, even have children. It's not uncommon that this becomes a defense in the courtroom wherein the offender tries to paint himself as a perfectly normal individual who would never consider such deviant behavior.

The next set of characteristics truly set the preferential offender apart from the situational offender and, in fact from society as a whole. When these characteristics are present, an investigator should be alert for the potential that this individual is a preferential offender.

When an adult who is not the parent of a particular child spends an inordinate amount of time with that child, it in itself, is not evidence that this person is a child molester. However, where this individual spends more time with this child to the exclusion of his peer group or others, something may be awry. The FBI has found that one of the major characteristics of the preferential offender is an "excessive interest in children."

That characteristic, along with the fact that the offender spends an inordinate amount of time with children in settings which are really intended for children, should also raise a red flag. For example, preferential offenders tend to frequent and engage children at places where the children ordinarily associate and socialize. The myth that the child molester hangs around school yards, video arcades, shopping malls, and movie theaters has some truth to it, for this is where the offender hunts his prey. An adult spending as much time in these settings as the children do or at more than one child-oriented business for inordinate amounts of time, should raise some suspicions.

### Children as Preferred Sexual Objects

Conversely, where the offender is involved in a sex ring or has multiple victims, it's not unusual to find that there is a constant parade of children in and out of their dwelling. This may be limited to their age and gender preference, to be discussed further below, or may be children of all ages and genders. Simply because an individual is friendly to children does not make him an offender, however, coupled with more characteristics as have been described herein, makes this type of activity suspicious.

Once again, the FBI has found that these offenders tend to have limited relationships within their peer group. This is hypothesized to be because it is difficult for the offender to find adults who are sympathetic to his needs and interests. For that reason, any adults associated with a suspected offender make them come under suspicion for similar interests and involvement. The ability of offenders to communicate so easily over the Internet and through computer bulletin boards should always be a consideration. In situations where other adults are suspected of being involved, efforts to surveil and identify them should be considered.

Another characteristic of the preferential offender is the manner in which he references children. This is often seen in their writings between one another and through their communications over the Internet and computer bulletin boards. They idolize children and frequently consider them to be objects to possess or a project to work on. They use such terms clean, pure, innocent, and impish to describe children.

Lastly, in this characteristic, the trait which labels this offender is that they have a specific preference for children of specific ages and/or genders. The FBI has found that the older the child of preference, the more likely the gender of preference will be exclusive to all others. For example, offenders who were involved with infants and toddlers, may be involved in sexual activity with either/or boys and girls without discrimination. However, an offender who is involved with teenagers is more likely to prefer boys or girls to the exclusion of the opposite sex. A general rule is difficult to articulate in defining the age bracket for this preference. Some offenders may prefer children within a specific age-defined range. Each individual has a unique desire and preference, particular to that individual. Lastly, the preference may not be limited to children, extending beyond the age of majority, however, beginning at a developmental stage prior to that legal change in status.

Lanning also points out that the way the victim looks is sometimes more critical in selection than the actual age of that child as perceived by the offender.

As stated in the discussion regarding situational offenders, the developmental stage of the child appears to be one of the most significant factors in determining which child a particular offender may be attracted to. Puberty is often the most frequent determinate.

As an example of this characteristic, when the author was interviewing a individual who had been arrested for multiple offenses involving nine- and ten-year-old boys whom was later discovered to have been wanted for escape from an institution in another state for a life sentence conviction on similar acts, a question was asked of the offender what kind of children he liked to work with in volunteering for school programs. The offender's response was that he "liked eight-year-olds." It is this type of expression of preference, coupled with the findings that the individual has been involved in activities of a questionable or sexual nature with children, which should identify the individual as a preferential offender. Lastly, it should be noted that this preference is not exclusive. It does not absolutely exclude the potential that the offender would be involved in sexual relations or attractions to other individuals. However, the predominate attraction and preference is for children as described.

### "Well-Developed Techniques for Obtaining Victims"

One of the most frequently reoccurring characteristics which amazes outside observers is the ability of the offender to identify a vulnerable and susceptible target. Within a very short period of time, an offender can observe and/or interact with children and identify his potential victim. Probably more through trial and error than anything else, an offender will do things like saddling up to a child, invading the child's body space, to gage the child's resistance or reluctance to be in close physical contact with another person, particularly an adult. They may engage them in conversation and evaluate the child's need for attention and affection. They may simply watch to see how the child interacts with others in the child's peer group and approach the child accordingly. With amazing precision, it is astonishing to see how quickly an offender works to identify his victim. In undercover situations or simply in observing places where offenders frequent and associate with children, an investigator will see this before his/her very eyes with little attempt by the offender to conceal it.

Another characteristic which falls in this category is the offender's ability to identify with children, more so than with adults. The preferential offender, who is not afraid to get down on the floor and play with kids and pay attention to them finds it very easy to allure a child into their grasp.

As previously discussed in the section on situational offenders, this is especially true when it pertains to the preferential offender. An individual who actively seeks employment or frequents places where children associate and socialize should be considered a preferential offender if other characteristics in his profile are present. In other words, manipulated access to children is a key characteristic. The offender will manipulate the situation or circumstance where he can be in close proximity to and involved with children of his age or gender preference. Lanning describes an offender who married an had a daughter whom he molested. He invited neighborhood girls within his age preference for parties, whom he also molested. He coached a girls softball team, whom he molested. Lastly, he was a pediatric dentist, whose patients he molested.

A related characteristic to that described above is where the offender will engage in activities with children, excluding other adults. Here, the offender manipulates the situation so that he is alone with his child victim. This ploy plays right into modern society's constant conflicts with parents who must balance time with their kids versus their professional and social lives. An individual who shows such attention to their children is often taken as a savior.

One of the early characteristics identified by the Los Angeles Police Department's Sexually Exploited Child Unit is that the offender will seduce children, showering them with attention and affection. The offender will provide gifts, overwhelming the child with things that the child would have not ordinarily have. In fact, as is noted in the discussion with victimization, its not hard to understand why children are torn when they must make a choice to report an offender and thus lose the goodies that come with the relationship.

Yet another characteristic that is not necessarily unique to the preferential offender, it appears in the situational offender as well, is the ability to manipulate children. This is especially true for the offender who is involved in a sex ring with many children at the same time. Here, the offender cajoles, kneads, manipulates, and strokes his child victim into complying with his desires. Lanning says it best in describing the acts as "seduction techniques, competition, peer pressure, child and group psychology, motivation techniques, threats, and blackmail to achieve his ends." What is amazing, is the ability of the offender, whose children grow out of his preference range fairly quickly, to continually find new children and pass others out without being discovered.

Another characteristic, not exclusive to the preferential offender, is that they will develop a hobby and/or interest that children find attractive. For example, the offender may have an elaborate model railroad or frequently go to activities and attractions that are oriented towards children. The unique characteristic to the preferential offender, is that it is not uncommon for this offender to find an activity or attraction that is exclusive for the child in his preferred age and gender target group and developmental stage. It's not uncommon that both the situational and preferential offender may find the supplying of illicit substances such as alcohol and drugs or, even pornography, is a means of achieving his end.

As a segway to the next characteristic, one of the most frequent activities discovered to be engaged in by offenders who molest children is their use of sexually explicit material to lower the inhibitions of children. It is also used as a means of raising the child's curiosity level and orienting their thoughts to sexuality. This is further discussed in Chapter 3, however, it is extremely important because of the evidentiary significance for an investigation. Not only does it provide concrete, crime specific information, it tends to show a conscious course of conduct and provides corroborative facts and detail for supporting a child's contention that they have been abused. It may even provide an additional crime to investigate (production, possession, distribution, providing to minor, etc.). With the wide variety of sexually explicit material available by telephone, computer, over-the-counter and news rack purchase, the manner and method that the child has come into contact with this type of material must be explored to determine whether or not it was the offender who had provided this to the child or whether the child had innocently encountered it.

When this activity is involved, an investigator must consider, as it relates to a possible defense, whether the child will be claimed to have discovered the material by themselves, thereby negating any *act* on the part of the offender. The child is then claimed to have confused and/or made up facts which are being misinterpreted and misapplied to criminal behavior on the part of the accused individual. Here, finding anything that supports the manner in which the material is used is essential. Things like where it was stored, what specifically is contained in the material, who else may attest to similar conduct, fingerprints of the offender on the materials, etc., are very important evidentiary concerns.

## Sexual Fantasies Focusing On Children

Since intent is one of the key elements of determining and distinguishing a crime from an innocent act, the characteristics in this grouping are of critical importance to an investigation. Subtle nuances and facts which identify the offender's true intent in committing a particular act must be examined in the broader context of the facts surrounding the offense.

For example, an individual who touches a child in the context of teaching the child how to dance or handle a baseball bat could be considered totally innocent. But, repeated gropes into the boy's groin or other touching should be highly suspicious. If that individual's home is searched and the walls are found to be covered in posters and pictures of children of the same age and gender as that of the child victim it might raise some suspicions. Likewise, if the home and/or portion of the home is decorated in the same fashion as the child themselves would do and the alleged offender has no children of that age, a red flag is waving. An individual who collects items such as toys and games, posters of rock stars, and stereo equipment that are of interest to children of the offender's target might be of interest in and there are no children in the home should raise some suspicions.

For example, in the case involving a man who later committed suicide after his identification and charging, police found virtually anything and everything related to baseball that a little leaguer would be interested in on the premises of his sprawling estate. It was considered a "mini-baseball park" or playland. Mementos of past games, collections of sports memorabilia, batting cages, and other things which would uniquely be of interest to a boy who loves baseball were found in this man's possession, a "well-seated" individual in his community, who had been sexually involved with young boys for many years.

Another characteristic which is extremely unique to the person who is sexually attracted to children is the need to photograph them. Photographs are taken to record and to preserve the child in their developmental state in which the offender finds himself attracted. Offenders may have literally thousands of photographs of children, not necessarily sexually explicit. However, as happened in one case, a baseball coach took photographs of his swimming team both in still and video recordings. Of the video recordings, he would create tapes of a boy who would commence a diving sequence to walk up to the edge of the board and jump, elongating his body in such a way that the offender found sexually stimulating. The offender would then copy and repeat the sequence over and over again so that when one viewed the tape you could see the same sequence backwards and forwards and in slow motion. This characteristic is described in further detail in Chapter 3.

The link to photographs and molestation through a method of seduction is also apparent in this case where the coach would "groom" his victims. The coach would always have a boy living with him. This worked as a "bait" to legitimize his asking other boys to come over to his home. As the boy living there grew older over the years, he would move that boy out and another one in. Parents would see this man as a "concerned individual" who was "helping troubled youth." The man would use the boy living with him to bring other boys over to see his baseball "wonderland," justifying their staying overnight as being with the boy who was living there. He would then create a skinny dipping situation in the pool with all of the boys present to desensitize the boys to the activity and get the newer boys used to being naked at his home. He rationalized it to the boys as like being in a "locker room" and "no big deal." The peer group pressure worked for him in that the new boys felt compelled to go along because they would not be part of the group or be considered "chicken" (no pun intended) if they didn't. All of this progressed to the point it was just the offender and the victim alone, where he would secretly videotape the boy nude as described in the preceding paragraph above.

The offender will collect pornography or child erotica (a characteristic described in greater detail in Chapter 3). This is one of the most significant characteristics of the preferential offender and must be considered in every case where the offender is suspected to be of this variety. The value of this kind of evidence in determining the true intent of the subject under investigation cannot be over emphasized. With nothing more than a child's bare accusation, the finding of this kind of collection could be critical in deciding what to do.

To summarize this discussion, a perfect example of how the preferential offender thinks and acts is found in Exhibit 2.1, wherein a preferential offender writes about how he would find and seduce boys. In it you see, in his own words (complete with misspellings of the original) the thought process and techniques he would employ to engage and seduce his victims. This was found in possession of a fireman who was never found to be involved in any camp such as that described in this writing. It can be assumed that this was his "fantasy." Yet, the details are consistent with the method that he selected and seduced his victims.

---

## EXHIBIT 2.1

---

"There come a time when children are hungry for adventure. Their innocent enthusiasm and childish fears are all at a high. It is exciting to have the opportunity to influence a beautiful youngster to create an environment of control so that his development is out of his young hands his childs shyness and fears are fun to conquer — no greater satisfaction exists. Like a puppy the litter boy is made to be your willing companion and you must demand his obedience.

The ideal setting for your transform of these children is summer camp where you— have a small group of youths for one solid month. — Within two weeks they will become yours — and your wishes will happen — by the last week every child will be totally yours.

You must carefully decide your intended goals, and set a plan. For me I work to select my new pets with care. I have help in picking my new charges - and research photos and family facts— I place 4 boys in my cabin — less than others — but others enjoy my results so I get every thing I need.

My boys must be very nice looking short hair, cupid bow mouth, wide eyes nice smile — they must be of smooth skin and have a good looking body — with a tight bottom and nice hands. It is important that they not be very masculine and seem like shy and innocents. Being both shy and babylike — they are prone to blushing and giggling and cry at times. They come from small familys of very conservative strict parents and are away from home for the first time. Age of 11 to 13 is ideal so that the child will be on the edge of puburty about to or just starting it. The boy will have just experienced his first curls of pubic hair — usualy blond or light brown and it is like corn silk — short and downey — the childs sexual organs have become larger and fuller, the boy must be circumsized - his feeling is that he is embarrased at its appearance and new size as it is very perky and is hard to hide.

I piked 4 boys — Danny 12, a blond shy boy with an angel face; insecure Timmy also 12 short sandy hair with frecles and a perfect boys body; shy Jimmy a darling 11 1/2 year old — he could have been a girl — giggles and crys easily; Peter the oldest at 13 but just starting puberty and perfect. These were lovely boys and cute to look at. I decided to keep them away from other boys so that they would be totaly mine now I was ready to set my plans

The first week they will be taught to speak in boy talk, to describe their bodys in new ways.

The second week will be spent getting the children out of their clothing and to experience being totaly nude with another boy.

The third week will instill in each youngster sexuality — touching kissing and finally oral sex with an other boy — fello to and sperm

The fourth week the boys will be taught that they are to enjoy their homosexuality with each other freely— each boy will enjoy his first experience with intercourse and anal pleasures.

The final week will allow the boys to entertain adult councilors and to engage in man boy sex play

I began by asking sex education questions, it was wonderful — none had any ideas on sex and their parents were avoiding the subject — since we are all the same age boys you should all be starting puburty — puburty is the time when you stop being a little boy — the first to change is your sex organs — they grow quickly — and your body has to catch up. I explained this is the most fun time in a boys life — if he takes advantage. I explained each had a new way of having fun — they giggled. Did you know that — thats why you are told not to play with yourself because at puburty the pleasure to a boy gos up 10 times — here at camp its ok for you to experiment and try new things — each year boys your age discover pleasure they never dreamed of have you heard of boys describing their penis as a toy — or play thing well they discovered that boys can do all kinds of things with their new pleasure toy and find that other boys enjoy it too — new words appear which boys start to use like come, cream and fuck, suck you see boys at 11 and 12 have all the fun they can have — but have to wait till 15 for girls and dating — so do you know what these young boys do the experiment with ways to have pleasure — most boys experunent with homosexual things — for several years its very normal for a boy to try out his sexuality with other boys his age Because you are healthy beautiful boys you will think about trying a homosexual adventure. If you dont like it you can stop Last year we decided to have our cabin try boy-boy pleasures. And yes all the boys agreed to try — and after 2 weeks everyone was having a good time."

## Application of the Typology

Character traits should not be viewed as mutually exclusive or all encompassing. The patterns of the traits of offenders involved in crimes throughout the world, which have been identified by careful examination, are merely the salient characteristics which help to assess the potential risk, likelihood of evidence, and factors which may help to determine the veracity of allegations made. As was stated earlier in this text, no characteristic, in-and-of-itself, should be taken to identify an offender as belonging to a particular group without careful analysis of the entire circumstances surrounding the crimes. The following observations are made to help investigators and those who assess allegations of sexual abuse in the quest to answer and address the previously described issues.

### "Combination Offenders"

Investigators and those evaluating these crimes should never lose sight of the fact that the preferential offender may also exhibit other problems such as "psychosexual disorders, personality disorders, or psychoses" and be involved in other crimes. This type of offender's sexual involvement with children may also be combined with other sexual deviance such as zoophilia or infantilism. The FBI has found that the morally or sexually indiscriminate situational offender may also have similar traits and interests in sexually deviate activities.

Offenders may be psychopaths, survivalists, and have been known to be serial killers. They all have the ability to con and to kill. Characterized as morally indiscriminate, the likelihood of the preferential offender committing such acts of violence is frightening. Abduction and murder in these situations is not an uncommon experience. A person with no conscience and who has a sexual desire for children could be a very frightening prospect.

## "Sex Rings"

The term "sex rings" was first coined by Dr. Anne Burgess, R.N. [45, 46]. These are cases that involve one or more offenders with multiple children, all of whom are aware of the presence and/or involvement of the others. These kind of cases might involve a day care center, a preschool, a house on the street where children frequent and are drawn because of the activities of the other children and the offenders. At its extremes, it may involve something like a satanic cult or religious sect who might have different individuals all possessing different character types and characteristics of the offenders described herein. When encountering a sex ring, a careful analysis of the facts developed through interviews and investigation must be undertaken to help determine the likelihood of certain types of evidence and the degree of risk to the children and community.

## Female Offenders

The FBI has not found sufficient data from which they might place women into this typology. One thing is clear, from a general consensus of investigators and therapists who work with victims in this area, that there are a larger number of female offenders than are generally thought to exist. They offend against both genders and the ratio of male to female victims in all studies seems to have a larger percentage of male victims over females [47].

The most common response when the offender is identified as a woman and the child as a young boy is not unlike that of a police lieutenant who, upon hearing that a 21-year-old woman was having every conceivable sex act with a nine-year-old boy said, "Where was she when I was a boy." However, the frequency of women involved with girls and women involved with boys is emerging as a crime problem to be dealt with. More and more, women are found to be offending as co-participants with men and on their own. The FBI has found that there are very few who fit the profile of a preferential offender.

One study found that when the offender was a female and in a situation such as babysitting, they often were experimenting or taking advantage of a very young boy where they might have been afraid of engaging in sex with boys who were their own age. It was felt that the motivation was curiosity or experimentation rather than outright sexual interplay [48]. Another study found that female offenders offending against males might be exploiting the male for the offender's own sexual benefit, have a personality disorder, have been severely abused themselves, or have some developmental or regressive behavior problems [49].

It is the experience of the author that when women are involved in these crimes with men, the acts(s) is/are generally motivated by a desire to maintain the relationship or dependency on the offending male. They either are emotionally or financially dependent on the male and, as a result, engage in acts, often luring or supplying their own children to the male, to satisfy this need. Sometimes they act in fear of their own safety, having been threatened by the male into participation. When involved on their own, the same characteristics of the situational offender, generally, apply. Of course, for investigators, the same evidentiary concerns should be examined whether the woman is acting alone or in concert.

## Adolescent Offenders

When the child molestation first became recognized as a real problem, the question of classifying offenses committed by children was not adequately answered. Since the evolution of the theories on why people commit sex offenses, there have been many theories posited as to why children molest other children. For the criminal investigator, the approach should not be that much different than that of an adult offender. What has been found to be true in examining the motivations and patterns involving juvenile and adolescent offenders, is that many of the same characteristics attributable to adult offenders may be found in the young offender. Theories abound as to why they commit their offenses, but, the fact is, they are much the same as adults [50]. Therefore, the same evidentiary and investigative concerns should be employed.

However, there are still those people who excuse the behavior as "normal exploration" or "discovery." In determining whether such is the case, there must be some criteria that an investigator may use to differentiate a knowing sexual act versus a child's inappropriate, yet, not criminal acts. In making this distinction, the following factors should be considered.

1. Age and size disparity between offender and victim.
2. Victim selection criteria (who was the victim and how did the offender get access).
3. Sophistication, number, and degree of the act(s).
4. Any prior victimization on the part of the offender on other children.
5. Any prior victimization on the part of a third party on the offender.
6. The involvement of other parties as offenders or on-lookers.
7. The age and developmental level of the offender.
8. The offender's ability to discern "right" from "wrong".
9. Any psychological disturbance on the part of the offending child.

In any case, the investigation should not be any less intense or complete, simply because the offender in a particular case is a juvenile. One must always consider the child offender a victim himself and one who was influenced by an adult or who has re-enacted the crime he was a victim of.

## References and Notes

1. Suzanne M.Sgroi, *Handbook of Clinical Intervention in Child Sexual Abuse*. Lexington Books, Lexington, MA , 1982, p. 40.

2. UNICEF compiled statistics, "Children as Victims," 1997. Bonwist@IX.net-com.com

3. Illinois Legislative Investigative Commission. *Sexual Exploitation of Children*. Report to the Illinois General Assembly, Chicago, IL., Aug. 1980.

4. United States Congress. *Exploitation of Children*. Hearing. Senate Subcommittee on Juvenile Justice, Committee on the Judiciary, 97th Congress, 11/1/81.

5. Jack Olsen, *The Man with the Candy*. New York: Simon & Schuster, 1974.

6. Conversation with author, 1997.

7. Note provided courtesy of Investigator Michael DeMatteo of the San Bernardino Sheriff's Office.

8. United States Congress, *Child Pornography and Pedophilia*, Hearing of the Permanent Subcommittee on Investigations of the Committee on Governmental Affairs.U.S. Senate, 99th Congress, 2/21/85.

9. Letter to "Ask Beth," in *The Boston Globe*, 7/7/85.

10. Letter in response to article "Women Against Violence and Pornography in the Media,"*Newspage*, Vol. IV, No. 8, Aug. 1980.

11. California Legislature. Senate and Assembly Committee on Revision of the Penal Code. Child Molestation Hearing. Los Angeles, 12/16/80 (testimony of Lloyd Martin).

12. Ibid.

13. Ann W. Burgess and H. Jean Birnbaum, "Youth Prostitution," *American Journal of Nursing*, pp. 832-834, May 1992.

14. Ann W. Burgess, *Child Sex Rings: A Behavioral Analysis*, National Center for Missing and Exploited Children, Washington, D.C., 1988; *see also* Note 29.

15. Burgess, 1988; *see also* Note 29.

16. Burgess, 1988.

17. Roland C. Summit, discussions with author, 1990-1997.

18. Paedophilic Informational Exchange (PIE). *Paedophilia, Some Questions and Answers*. London, England, 1978, p. 4.

19. David Sonnenschein, *What is Pedophilia Anyway?* Austin, TX.: Austin Pedophile Study Group, 1982.

20. Letter to the author.

21. Roland Summit," The Child Sexual Abuse Accommodation Syndrome," *Child Abuse and Neglect: An International Journal*, 7, 1983, pp. 177-193.

22. John E. B. Meyers, *Evidence in Child Abuse and Neglect Cases*, 3rd Edition., Wiley, New York, 1997.

23. Lectures and personal communication with the author 1985-1997.

24. Roland C. Summit, "Abuse of the Child Sexual Abuse Accommodation Syndrome," *Journal of Child Sexual Abuse*, 1:4, 1992.

25. Ibid.

26. Myers, 1997.

27. Summit, 1983.

28. Investigative report from the author's case files.

29. Kenneth V. Lanning, *Child Molesters: A Behavioral Analysis*, National Center for Missing and Exploited Children, Washington, D.C., 1992.

30. Robert L. Geiser, *Hidden Victims*. Beacon Press, Boston, MA, 1979, p. 30.

31. Queen's Bench Foundation. *Sexual Abuse of Children*. San Francisco, 1976, p. 53; *see also* Lanning, 1992.

32. Letter from the author's case files.

33. Letter from the author's case files.

34. From the author's case files.

35. National Broadcasting Company. *NBC News Magazine with David Brinkley*. New York: NBC Television Network, 9/3/81.

36. From the author's case files.

37. U.S. Senate, 99th Congress, 2/21/85; *see* Note 8.

38. Myers, 1997.

39. *Investigation and Prosecution of Child Abuse*, Second Edition, National Center for Prosecution of Child Abuse, (NCPCA), American Prosecutors Research Institute, National District Attorneys' Association, Alexandria, VA, 1993.

40. Lanning, 1992.

41. David Finkelhor, *Child Sexual Abuse: New Theory and Research*, N.Y. Free Press, 1984.

42. Ibid.

43. Lanning, 1992; *see also* NCPCA, 1993 and Note 39.

44. D. R. Laws, ed., *Relapse Prevention with Sex Offenders*, Guilford Press, N.Y. 1989.

45. Ann W. Burgess, *Child Pornography and Sex Rings*, D.C. Heath & Co., Lexington, MA, 1984.

46. Ann W. Burgess, *Children Traumatized in Sex Rings*, 1988.

44. D. R. Laws, ed., *Relapse Prevention with Sex Offenders*, Guilford Press, N.Y. 1989.

47. F. G. Bolton, Jr., L. A. Morris, and A.E. MacEachon, *Males at Risk: The Other Side of Child Sexual Abuse*, Sage Publications, Newbury Park, CA, 1989.

48. Larry Leitch, "Profiles of the Perpetrators," *Networker*, May/June 1992.

49. Ibid; *see also* "Characteristics of Child Sexual Abuse Victims According to Gender," *Child Abuse and Neglect*, 19(8), 963-973, 1995.

50. A. Nicholas Groth, "Patterns of Sexual Assault Against Children and Adolescents," in *Sexual Assault of Children and Adolescents*, Burgess, Ann. W. et al. Lexington Books, Lexington, MA, 1980.

## Additional Reading

American Psychiatric Association, *Diagnostic and Statistical Manual of Mental Disorders*, 4th Edition, APA, Washington, D.C., 1994.

Henry E. Adams and C. David Rollison, *Sexual Disorders*, Gardner Press, New York, 1979.

A. Nicholas Groth et al. "The Child Molester: Clinical Observations," in *Social Work and Child Sexual Abuse*, Conte, Jon R. and Shore, David A. (eds.), Hawthorn Press, New York, 1982.

Erwin J. Haeberle, "Children, Sex and Society" in *Hustler* (date unknown). Reprinted from *The Sex Atlas: A New Illustrated Guide*, Haeberle, Erwin J. Hawthorn Press, New York, 1978.

International Association of Chiefs of Police. *The Child Molester*, IACP Training Key. Gaithersburg, MD., 1967.

Will McBride and Helga Fleischhauer-Hardt, *Show Me*, St. Martin's Press, New York, 1975.

Eloise Sahols, "Beware of Child Molesters," *Newsweek*, 8/9/82.

Linda Tschirhart Sanford, *The Silent Children*. Anchor Press, New York, 1980.

*San Francisco Chronicle*, 5/23/85.

Loretta Schwartz-Nobel, "Child Pornography and the Secret World of the Pedophile." *Philadelphia Inquirer Magazine*, 11/6/83.

# Commission of the Crime

3

## MO Characteristics

Common characteristics of sexual exploitation can be drawn from the vast number of cases that have occurred in this country. In fact, distinctive MO traits have been isolated and appear in varying combinations in most cases. The identification of any one of a combination of these traits in a given case may help an investigator or prosecutor in determining the offender's true desires and intentions.

A prosecutor or attorney who must prove or convince a court that a person acted in conformance with a particular signature trait, committed an intentional act, acted in a conscious course of conduct, had a common plan or scheme, made no mistake, showed consciousness of guilt, is a risk to children, is best suited for a long stay in a protective environment, or, simply, is the person who did the act he was accused of, should pay close attention to the factors and characteristics listed in the following text. Criminal and civil court judges and juries have reported that after hearing an explanation of how, why, and what, offenders do, they are better able to render the decisions they must so often make. It is important for the investigator to identify as many of the characteristics and factors listed herein as possible.

By determining the type of offender being investigated (using the typology given in Chapter 2), an investigator will be able to predict the kind of evidence he will find. As was mentioned in Chapter 2, offenders often collect child pornography and child erotica. Seeking this evidence is an essential element in any investigation.

In order to be able to predict anything, certain basics must be determined. How and where the targeted child is selected must be learned. It will help to predict when and where the next offense will occur and what will be found in the offender's possession when he is arrested. How the child is contacted or located is an important facet of how the crime is committed. The manner in which the child is seduced into performing what the offender desires must be determined. The role and use of alcohol and/or drugs by the offender himself or with children is very important in determining both the offender's mental state at the time of the offense and his level of sophistication. The offender's involvement in and connection to child prostitution is also an important factor in determining his desires and intentions. Last, the manner in which the offender records the events will also be extremely useful in making a determination of his intentions.

## Premeditation

With few exceptions, child molestation is premeditated. This preplanning may be as simple as thinking about a course of action, often referred to as fantasizing, as sophisticated as creating an environment in which a child would be comfortable, or as diabolical as digging a hole in a yard, lining the hole with cement blocks, and creating a cell within which he will keep his captive prey. Finding evidence of such premeditation is not uncommon, including the writings the offender has collected or written himself.

In the example shown in Figure 3.1, a young girl was kidnapped, taken to the offender's home, and molested. She told the investigating officer what had happened. Acting on this information, the officer prepared a search warrant for the implements she described as being used during the assault. When the officer served the warrant he found, among the things she described, the "memorandum" you see in the example. It outlines the assault on the child in exact detail. What is of major interest is that it was written before the assault and displays some of the unique characteristics of child molesters. At the top of the note the offender lists the name by which he knows the child and what he believes to be the child's birthdate. He even refers to the child as a "victim." In his listing of the things he will need for the "case," he includes the Spanish word for gag. Not only does he describe what he eventually did to the girl [in the exact order], but he makes a note to himself to preexamine a place to set his camera's tripod in order to photograph the assault.

Another offender dug a hole in his backyard, lined the hole with concrete blocks, provided an electric light, covered the "cell" with wood, and planted a lawn over the wood and a trap door that provided access to the cell. So well was the cell concealed that after the child escaped and described its location, it took the police three visits to find it. The girl had been kidnapped and held for 5 months and was repeatedly molested over the period of captivity. The offender was a popular individual, whom many in the

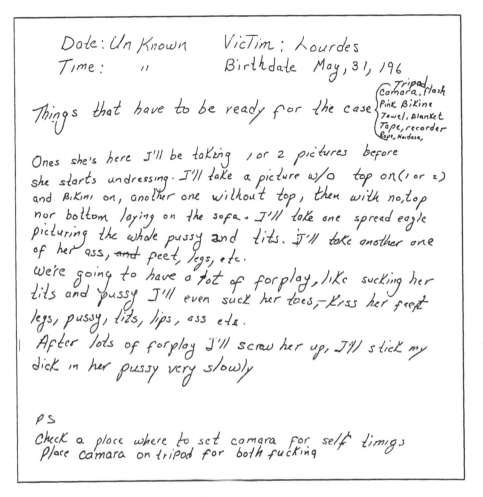

**Figure 3.1** Evidence of premeditation.

neighborhood called "Uncle George." He loved to have children come to his home and allowed them to do anything they wished.

Although some acts are impulsive — that is, the offender commits a particular action without thinking much about it at the time — generally the thought has passed through his mind at one time or another and he develops a strategy in the event an opportunity presents itself. In many cases, the offender will claim that the child misinterpreted the act so that the act appears to be either impulsive or noncriminal in nature.

Premeditation can easily be determined if one examines the circumstances of the incident. In one case, a man was reported to have boarded a transit bus loaded with school children as well as other passengers and sat among the children, near girls aged 10 to 14 years of age. During the bus ride the man's arm would come to rest inside the child's inner thigh or upon her upper leg. By questioning other children in the area, I was able to determine that the man was always among a group of children at the time school let out and had no legitimate business there, that he always sat among the children on the bus, and that he had used his "hand trick" before. In this case, going beyond the incident that was reported, talking to witnesses, and seeking out information about prior acts, it was possible to determine both the aspect of intent and premeditation.

## Relationships among Peer Group

A common experience with child molesters is that they have difficulty in dealing with people in their own peer group on a close personal level. They may be great leaders, social "climbers," or other public figures, yet on a one-to-one basis they often experience problems, which may not be apparent on the surface. Thus, during an investigation it is important to cover the types of relationships the offender maintains. Does he spend more than the normal amount of time with children? Does he have and can he sustain intimate (personal as well as sexual) relationships with others in his own peer group? The answers to these questions may establish the necessary pattern to prove the offender's intent and true desires. Often, as a result of the offender's insecurity among his peer group, he becomes very adept at working with children and quickly becomes a favorite among them and their parents. A foster parent who was taking in and molesting children from at least three different counties turned "F" students into "A" students in a matter of weeks. Perhaps the child molester who wrote the following passage experienced this ability to be good with children.

> I have searched for help for years with no success. I am a "pederast" [I like little boys]. I cannot tell you how difficult it is for me to even write those words. For people who read about child molestation, every individual who has sex with a child ranks among the most evil deviates of our society. Perhaps the act is, but often it is performed by an otherwise responsible, well-adjusted man. Nothing could be further from my mind than wanting to hurt a child. In fact, my greatest joy is working with children, and my success in dealing with them has been remarkable....
>
> I have the problem under control, but the desire still rages within me, and I would like to eliminate it if possible. I know there must be thousands of men like me who are active and would like to overcome this urge, but there is simply nowhere to go for help... [1].

## Nature of Relationships with Children

An interesting observation is the manner in which some offenders relate to their child victims. Look at the kind of activities the offender participates in with the child. In what way does he participate? What role does he take in the activities? Is he a "father-type" overseeing the activity, or does he join in like one of the kids? For example, many offenders try to equate their behavior to the child's. This may be as simple as playing baseball with the child or as involved as dressing up with all of the required protective gear and going skateboarding.

One offender, when entering a subway with the child he was involved with, watched as the boy slipped by the turnstile, avoiding paying the fare. Instead of paying for the boy, as most adults would, the offender slid past the turnstile. In one case, alert parents noticed an offender acting in the same manner as the children and a subsequent investigation revealed sexual misconduct. The man was seen playing with the children in the same manner another child would. He was acting like a child rather than an adult. Concerned, parents called the police.

Conversely, other offenders try to elevate the child's behavior to their own or rationalize that the child is "old enough." They treat the child as though he were in the offender's peer group. These offenders take the children out to activities that are far beyond the comprehension of the child, such as a night at the opera with a 10-year-old. They refer to the child in a similar vein. For example, incestuous fathers often talk as though the girls were replacements for their wives. While one offender was being led from a school where he had been arrested for molesting young girls, he turned to the arresting officer, pointed to an 8-year-old girl, and said, "That's some broad!"

## Associates of the Offender

Another often overlooked MO characteristic is the offender's associates. In one case, police found an offender's address book that contained the listing of names of adult associates, the places where the offender obtained child pornography, and the names of the children he was involved with (in their own handwriting, no less). The offender prefers to associate with those with whom he feels comfortable and those with whom he can share his experiences without fear of rejection or, worse, discovery. These molesters will communicate about their exploits only with those they trust, and thus seek out other adults with similar interests.

Many offenders take pride in their sexual interest and seek out those people who will give them recognition for their accomplishments. Often they are desperate to find someone who understands their relationships with children and to establish acceptance, validation, and friendship. The groups they form or join serve to reinforce their illicit desires. This also works as a communication system. The warning written at the bottom of Figure 3.2 was written in red ink and was the result of a phone call made by someone I arrested on the day before the dated entry.

Boyish-Collegiate Shawn 19 cute boyish face
bl eyes br hair 5'8" 130 very smooth
proportioned swimmer build 7" Versatile
441-         -$35.00 hr. SanFran
David- 771-          $50.00 hr.(Outcalls only)
Italian weightlifter 5'7" 41 chest 27 waist
SanFran(Call 2 days in advance)
Sex Information and Referrals-530-        (Jim)
Super good head for goodlooking guys under
23 (over 18) High school, college, chickenok
San Francisco  552-
Bill 6pm-11pm. 254-
Santa Cruz Beach & Boardwalk
Vic-849-1958 Italian 26yr.old
"Team Mates" "Skate Board Heroes"
Catalog $2.00 State 21 SASE To
Times Square.              West 42nd
Street #        New York, N.Y. 10036
Lg. Negatives- Number 5 67 2 3 9 4
Small Negatives- 17 19 20 13 16 4 20 4 17 18 8 19
Plus Slide of Matthew - Processing of Photos

( May 3rd- Seth Goldstein, Juvenile Dept
Hot for Child Molestation Cases in
Berkeley

**Figure 3.2**   Example of communications and associations of offender.

Practically speaking, if an investigator encounters someone he knows to be an offender in the company of others or is found to be closely associated with others, the officer should try to identify them as well. In addition, the discovery of names and publications of those in the underground subculture of offenders will greatly assist in determining the offender's true interests.

More importantly, the discovery of these names may give investigators new leads to find other offenders, thereby better protecting their community's children.

Particularly during the service of search warrants or other investigatory functions, officers should be alert to evidence of underground communications (Figure 3.3). When children are unavailable, offenders often survive through explicit letters and child pornography. For this reason, they keep correspondence and exchange information "forever," unless a request is made to do otherwise by the correspondent. Recent materials are often kept in order, somewhere nearby, ready for response, much as stamps are collected and traded.

## Contact Points and Methods

Offenders often frequent places where there are children in their target group. This is an extremely important factor for an investigator, because it will help to prove the offender's intent by establishing the profile of the child the investigator should look for in order to identify other victims. This observation can help to establish probable cause to stop, detain, identify, and (hopefully) arrest offenders or potential offenders. For example, in one case an officer observed two known "tricks" (prostitutes) in the company of an adult. The officer was able to stop and detain the adult because of the nature of the location (based on his knowledge and experience of the area), his knowledge of the children's activities, and his knowledge and training regarding the behavior of those who seek out child prostitutes.

Because so many incidents go unreported, one wonders how the offender can pick a child who is a complete stranger and, with few exceptions, know that the child will not tell and/or will go along with him. Does the offender have some kind of radar or sixth sense? The answer, in a manner of speaking, is yes. The offender generally picks a type of child he believes will be receptive to him. This may be a child who is in need, in crisis, or simply involved already. Determining these factors will also help the investigator determine who might be this offender's victim. Offenders themselves give us the best insight into how they gauge which child to approach.

> "I meet up with a group of kids. I single one out first by appearance. I like blond, blue-eyed boys. Then by conversation..." [2].

Another offender, when asked how he seduced his children, said that he would gain their confidence by getting to know them. He started picking up hitchhikers, then went to specific children he described as the type of kid he was when he was young.

**Figure 3.3** (A) Correspondence found in the home of a child molester who was also writing and exchanging letters, stories, pictures, and slides with others. Contained on the pads shown in the upper right-hand corner were fantasy writings by the offender about his desired exploits. In the slide boxes at the bottom right corner were sexually explicit slides he had copied from others people had sent him. In the envelopes were letters from other child molesters who wished to share their experiences with him, as well as his and their photos. Some were several years old. At the top left corner of the figure are envelopes containing photocopies of many sexually explicit pictures used in his exchange. (B) The desk of a child molester who was very organized and orderly. His correspondence was laid out on his desk ready for reply, with the exchange materials (videotapes, magazines, and pictures) carefully sorted.

## Locations Where Children Congregate

Most sexually exploited children are molested by people they know: neighbors, teachers, relatives, or friends of the family. Yet, for the offender who is only interested in "chance" encounters, any place children are to be found is where you will find him. Juvenile hangouts such as pinball or video arcades are prime areas; in fact, these places are listed as good pickup points in the underground publications. For example, the following listing was discovered in a 1980 publication regarding a San Francisco pinball arcade:

> PRIME AREA. Be careful! Big Brother watches. Also, be patient. School days those who ditch abound from 9 AM to 3 PM. Weekends are great—anytime but late at night. Daytimes are best. All ages, and most who frequent are very much in the know, and in fact frequent the place for the extracurricular fun and games to be had. Lots of one hme deals [3].

Pinball/video arcades are such common pickup points for children that the underground has developed its own code that tells the offender which child is there for what purpose. For example, at a local pinball arcade, I watched boys being picked up by "tricks" who would walk to the pinball machine the boy was playing and begin to plunk down quarters, each quarter representing $25, until the boy turned to the man. By the time the man walked out of the place with the boy, he knew what he was going to get and how much it was going to cost.

Although the publication mentioned was intended for those who specifically cruise for boys, its message is clear — children in general can be found in such places. Street gathering points are also good places to find children. A corner in downtown Berkeley is a central transfer point for all transit buses going through the downtown area. It is also the location of the main entrance of the rapid transit subway, which runs through town. When school lets out, the plaza is full of children awaiting their buses. Because it is near the high school, during the day highschool students also frequent the area when they cut class or have free time.

A sergeant who worked the downtown area repeatedly saw a man in his forties talking to boys, all of whom were in the 15-to-17-year-old age group, at different times throughout the day and on numerous occasions on different days. Aware that several child molest cases had emanated from contacts that began in this particular area and knowing that California law prohibits anyone from loitering where children congregate, the sergeant stopped, detained, and identified the individual. The man, outraged, made a complaint to the city's civilian police review board that he was unjustly detained. The board heard his complaint. He claimed that he was a homosexual and that his sexual preference was the reason he was singled out. He even brought his 15-year-old boyfriend to back up his claim. The review board upheld the detention.

Schools, playgrounds, shopping centers, and businesses that cater to children are popular places with offenders. Depending on the age preference of the individual, the offender will be found at places that attract children in his target group. For example, a 28-year-old man was arrested at a Berkeley comic book store for shoplifting. Investigation revealed he was often seen in the store in Berkeley and in Sacramento (the state capital approximately 70 miles away) trying to pick up 14-to-15-year-old boys. Found in his wallet were first names and phone numbers, as well as scraps of paper containing similar information. A photo of two 15-year-old boys was also found. The man told the investigator that his "collection" of comic books was stolen by some children. He was found to have been previously arrested for child molestation in other states. The man told investigators about the pictures in his wallet, describing the "relationship" and "friendship" he had with the boys depicted. He also identified the names and corresponding phone numbers the investigators found in his possession, telling the investigators that the named persons were involved in child molestation activities. The information he provided, along with his identity and the circumstances of his arrest, was forwarded to the appropriate authorities in Sacramento. Approximately one month following his arrest in Berkeley, he was arrested for multiple counts of child molestation by the Sacramento Sheriff's Department. An example of how records are kept and maintained is seen in Figure 3.3.

Another man who preferred 6- to 10-year-old children cruised Berkeley, approaching children at bus stops, schools, and playgrounds. He performed sleight-of-hand tricks for them and tricked them into performing sex acts on him and allowing him to perform sex acts on them. He was easy to recognize because he fit the "dirty-old man" profile, but what made him most identifiable was the "child-molester's kit" he carried (Figures 3.4 and 3.5). It contained everything he needed to entrance children into believing he was a magician. It contained a doll the child could play with while the man played with the child; it had a "magic" handkerchief the child would rub to make things get "bigger" and "smaller;" it contained firecrackers and playing cards. He was arrested on the street after trying to pick up several children while under surveillance. In his pockets was over $67 in Susan B. Anthony silver dollars. His favorite trick was to pull a dollar from the ear or other parts of a child's body to begin his "routine," usually giving each child a dollar. Apparently his fantasy or plan involved more than $67 worth of children, because he had over a hundred Shell gasoline presidential commemorative coins in his "kit."

No respectable child molester's kit should be without candy; his was no exception. He had dice to perform tricks with. He also had a thimble, which

**Figure 3.4** Child molester's kit.

the children would kiss while they closed their eyes, and he would place it on his "thumb" to make the "thumb" disappear and reappear. Finally, he had his "special officer's" badge, which he would use to substantiate that he was a truant officer and that they were in trouble and had to come with him if they didn't cooperate.

Bus benches or places where children are found to be alone are also common points of contact. It is not an infrequent sight to see a man drive up to a bus stop, roll down the passenger-side window, flash a roll of bills, and say "You wanna make some money?" or simply ask a child if he "wants a ride." A child is often followed by the offender from place to place, in a car or on foot, until a safe or appropriate opportunity for an approach is determined.

Locations where children congregate are so well known as pickup points that when asked about the availability of children, where to find a child in a strange city and how easy it would be, one offender said, "Simple, just show me to the nearest convenience store." Everything you ever heard about shopping mall bathrooms is true. The same situation applies to park, department store, and other bathrooms the public has access to. At these locations the

**Figure 3.5**  Child molester's kit.

offender may befriend the child and sustain a prolonged relationship or may only be involved with him for the time he is there.

## Programs that Cater to Children in Offender's Target Group

Other offenders ingratiate themselves into, volunteer for, or otherwise get involved with programs catering to the children of their target group. For example, the following quote is from a man who volunteered as a counselor at various halfway houses and other juvenile programs and was arrested for molesting the boys in his charge.

> "I met a lot of them (the children) when I was working at the center where I was running an "under-21" counseling group...at the center they would introduce me to somebody else. I started off with 3 kids in the group and when I was done, I had 136. That was in a 2-month period. Some of the kids would introduce me to other kids, whether they were in the program or not" [4].

Strangely enough, children themselves often provide the offender with other kids. This may happen in several ways. A runaway in need of a place to stay may be willing to put up with the demands of the offender to have a roof over his head and something to eat. In one case, a home for emotionally disturbed children was constantly having problems with children running away. After several of the children were found and returned, interviews with the kids revealed that a particular individual's address and phone number was well known to the children of the home and that any child was welcome. Like the children mentioned by the counselor quoted above, children, either to be recognized by the offender or to receive rewards or special attention, will go out and recruit or scout out other children to bring to the offender, knowing the new kids will be molested. It is not uncommon for children who are involved with an individual to go out and find others so that they themselves will be left alone. Some are actually paid a "bounty."

In one case, two teenage boys who were runaways were molested by a man who gave them shelter. He also provided them with a refuge they were allowed to return to whenever they wished. When they found that he wanted to continue molesting them, but was also interested in young girls, they began to supply him with a constant flow of young runaway girls. Another case that comes to mind illustrates the sad side of this type of activity. A 14-year-old boy went out, found a 12-year-old, and brought him back to the offender, who then bound, gagged, and kidnapped the child, making him his "sex slave" for two weeks. In this case, the older boy went out to find the younger because, had he not found a replacement, he would have experienced the same fate.

Although the following segment of an article that appeared in an underground publication pertains to boys, it shows the ease with which many child molesters can gain access to the child of their need.

There are ways of being COMPLETELY LEGAL, and still being a quite active and fulfilled boylover.... From your [the man's] point of view, there are many satisfying ways of making contact with boys, ways that are not only socially approved, but encouraged! Big Brothers, Boy Scouts, church groups — the list of organizations goes on.... Whether or not you have a criminal record or other "problems" in your past, there is very little chance that anyone will ever know of your interests or check into your background.... Many men think they are easily recognizable as a boy lover, and that their "cover" will be blown the minute they walk in the door of the YMCA to volunteer. Boylovers come in so many different types and shapes that no common characteristic can be seen on the surface [5].

## Businesses that Involve Children

Businesses that cater to children are also common places to meet them. The YMCA, bowling alleys, and hobby shops are excellent places to find children. For example, a model railroad store had an employee who was attracted to boys 12 to 15 years old. In one case, a man was arrested for molesting children on the street. His business? He drove an ice-cream vending truck around the residential neighborhoods where the children he molested lived. The truck he drove became a ready and "legitimate" means of attracting his victims.

If the offender can't get into such a program or business, it is not uncommon for him to start one of his own. For example, boy scout troops have been formed with the express purpose of providing access, not only for the offender but for others, to the young members of the troop. In a celebrated case in Australia, a pedophile group obtained children under the pretext of a foreign foster parent support group. In Berkeley, a man who represented himself to be a clergyman was adopting orphan "boat people" (refugees from Cambodia and Vietnam), then molesting them. One molester actually started an orphanage to gain access to young girls. When found out, he left and purchased a small private school in another country, where he was found to be giving "medical exams" to the girls. This particular individual was known to move into a poor neighborhood and befriend single mothers with young children, often giving them used household appliances or other "extras" the family might not be able to afford otherwise. He was described as having an excellent ability to determine what people didn't have and needed, then using that need to his advantage.

## Advertising as a Way to Find Children

### Underground Publications

The child molester can often find children through ads in the underground publications. Ads are placed seeking people who have similar interests. The offender will advertise for children to respond or for the adults who have a desire to meet them and/or their children. Although some ads appear to be written by children asking for adults, most are placed by adults looking for other adults with similar interests. "Swingers" publications, those catering to individuals of varying sexual interests, provide information for adults involved in sex with children and for the children themselves. One woman advertised for a man who was looking for a woman with children. Shortly after the woman met the offender, she participated in the molestation of her 11-year-old daughter by forcing the girl to participate in sexual intercourse and oral copulation with the man. In addition, the mother took nude pictures of her 8-year-old son for the man, who represented himself as a "free-lance photographer." The woman photographed the sexual acts with the daughter and, in one instance, actually held the girl down while the man raped her. This case is described in Exhibit 8.1 (Chapter 8).

## Legitimate Publications

**"Help-wanted" ads.** Legitimate periodicals also provide contacts for the subculture of child molesters. It is not uncommon for the offender to advertise for children in this target group by offering jobs. In order to get the child to the location the offender wanted, one employment ad specified that the child must apply in person for a personal interview, at which time the child was molested. A prominent, conservative, major paper in the San Francisco area ran the following ad in its Sunday classified section: "Wanted, teens to pose in costume for Hookers' Ball." The Hookers' Ball is an annual gathering held in San Francisco at Halloween for homosexuals and prostitutes. Two children responded to the ad. They were questioned about their sexual practices with their boyfriends and girlfriends. Arrangements were made for a meeting in Berkeley to engage in sexual acts to be filmed. The advertisers/ pornographers were arrested when the meeting took place. The "personals," "miscellaneous," "miscellaneous employment," and "performing arts" sections of these papers are often used in this fashion.

**Ads for materials or services of a similar nature.** Classified papers that have appeared across the country in liquor stores and thrown on the doorsteps of homes listing secondhand merchandise, garage sales, and personal services are also a source for the offender. A local investigation uncovered a large ring of people who exchanged and made child porn. The investigation was initiated by answering an ad in one of these papers that read: "Wanted — trade or exchange pornography." The ad was placed by a member of the ring who was seeking others to exchange with or sell to. In another case, police found pictures of over 200 children engaged in sexually explicit activity in the home of a man who advertised in a classified listing newspaper, printed and distributed only on Wednesdays: "Models wanted under 5' 4"." After his conviction he was still found to be advertising, but his ad had changed to: "Wanted: models under 5' 4" — must be over 18."

## Community Bill/Notice/Bulletin Boards

Contacts are also made with children and adults who are interested in sexual liaisons by means of notes left on bulletin boards. These bulletin boards are commonly found at places where children and others who see them might be interested in such activities. In Figure 3.6, the note was found in an area heavily trafficked by those who pick up boys.

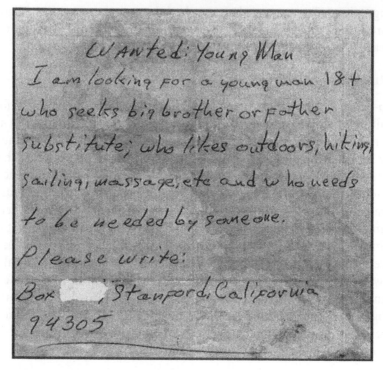

**Figure 3.6**    Bulletin-board notice.

## *On the Street*

Graffiti on bathroom walls where activity involving children can be found provides a ready means of contact. The phone number of a man who was molesting 8- and 9-year-old boys was found on the walls of a downtown McDonald's restaurant on a note offering children a place to stay

One of the underground publications suggests hitchhikers as a ready source of sexual fulfillment. It describes a particular main street as follows: "Same is true of this area — usually something hitchhiking. That which is hitch-hiking is *usually* in the know. Be careful however — be sure of that pick before you do it." The introduction to this publication is a good summary of how to find children.

> Remember, fun is where you find it. You may go to the places listed herein, to find an essentially empty place, or that there is nothing that you like.... you may be there during a slack period or bad time (baseball game that day, parade elsewhere in town, etc.) Go there again before deciding that it is of no yield. Patience *is* rewarding... Keep in mind that Big Brother is always watching you [6].

## Role of Child Erotica and How the Offender Operates

There is a distinction that must be drawn between *child pornography* and *child erotica* two very important manifestations of an offender's object of attention. Pornography has been generally used to reference reproductions of writings, depictions, or oral expression (voice), which has a sexual theme or purpose. This form of expression will be more greatly defined in the following chapter on pornography investigation.

The difference between *pornography* and *erotica*, is that the objects that form erotica may or may not be sexually oriented or even related to the particular children involved in a given case. *Erotica*, means something that provides a sexual stimulation to the particular observer that may, or may not, be unique to that individual. As one author points out, almost anything could be considered *erotica*. Things which have been found in cases throughout the country that might constitute erotica include, electronic tape (video, audio), newspaper clippings, books depicting or describing children, magazines containing references or depictions of children (e.g., *National Geographic*), photos of children or other people, toys collected by the offender, photography equipment, sexual aides, etc. The list could go on and on. The important thing to remember about erotica is that the objects themselves may or may not be illegal and may or may not necessarily relate to children and/or sexual subjects. For example, erotica may include cartoons about child molestation. Found in one offender's home was a clipping from *Hustler* magazine's "Chester the Molester" cartoon. In another, a man found to be involved in infantilism (sex with toddlers) was found to have a matchbook cover bearing the logo of the women's rights organization that depicts two toddlers looking down the front of each other's diapers.

### Collection of Child Pornography and Child Erotica

The collection and maintenance of collections of child pornography and erotica in molestation cases is documented and, almost, universal. This is because of the fantasy aspect of the crime. It can be invaluable to determine the true intent of the offender and to identify the state of mind critical in embellishing the act as a crime.

Erotica also has a second importance when it involves collections of names or depictions of other persons. It will provide additional leads to new offenders and victims. Quite frequently, this type of erotica consists of recitations of acts the offender has committed with the children he has been involved with or names other adults who could be considered principals in the crimes under investigation.

The physical evidence and its value in establishing the elements of the crimes under investigation cannot be underestimated. These writings provide admissions and confessions when they are in the hand of the offender himself. They provide the glue that ties in co-conspirators in matters where there are multiple offenders. They provide the hammer that nails shut the case on an offender who claims he has no illegal intent or purpose when arrested.

The problem is that the items found in possession of the offender that constitute erotica may also be kept in the home of "normal" people who have no such illicit proclivities. How does one make the distinction of purpose? In one case involving a popular school teacher, when the case came to trial, the defense attorney presented to the jury, by way of the prosecution's expert witness, all of the types of things that were found in the offender's home. He brought out a deck of cards, a book on magic, a *Hustler* magazine, pictures of children, a baseball bat, all of which he placed upon the counsel table and asked if these were the type of things that might be found in an offender's home. He then asked if the witness felt this could be indicative of an offender. The answer, of course, is yes, but, the context in which these items were found would be what determines their significance. The items, which the attorney described as his own, from his own home, are not in-and-of-themselves indicative of illicit conduct. It is how they are used and to what significance the offender holds in them that could make them become erotica.

If the cards were used by the offender to get the child to come to his house to play; if the magic book was left where the child could have access to it to become curious about doing "fun" things; if the *Hustler* magazine was left out where the child could find it to become excited or curious about sexual depictions of women and men; if the bat was used as a means of gaining "innocent" touching when the teacher would reach around his target child's body to demonstrate how to swing, each time groping the boy's genitals; then maybe the objects could be considered erotica. But, by themselves, they may mean nothing.

Another example of one of the most commonly found items of erotica are clippings from children's underwear ads from department store catalogs or sales papers. It is one of the most frequently discovered fantasy materials discovered in jail cells of convicted child molesters.

When the ages of the depicted children are examined, it is often possible to determine the age group the offender is most likely to target. These clippings often are pasted into scrapbooks and other documents that are secreted away for fantasy use. This material often is juxtaposed in these books with children who are really in the offender's life. When this is found it is a very good way to demonstrate the potential danger this particular offender poses to those children. The question is, if his fantasy is expressed in this manner, what might he do if he has the opportunity to act out that fantasy?

What is more compelling in establishing an offender's sexual preferences is the fact that even if the offender has explicit child pornography, they often will collect this erotica. What ever the offender has, it is never enough and he is always constantly seeking new stimulation devices. The same is true for child pornography. Offenders will maintain collections to sell or trade to others. They will reproduce the same materials for the purposes of exchange. In one case, a bathtub full of photocopies of child pornography was found for the purpose of trade and exchange. In another, the offender kept duplicates of the pornography magazines he had collected in his car so that he might exchange or trade among the accomplices he met or would encounter.

For searching purposes, it is important to know that these collections are maintained as though the items contained are of great value. They are prize possessions and kept — *forever*. In one case in Los Angeles, an investigator found items the child had seen 14 years earlier. This especially is true when the items are used in the process of seducing the child victims (see Figure 3.7).

Offenders will not destroy anything, including correspondence with others, unless there is an express request on the part of the other party to do so. Even if offenders know the police are coming, rather than destroy their "invaluable" collection of materials, they will store it, give it to a friend, hide it, or *temporarily* secrete it some other way.

Timeliness is always a consideration in investigations of this nature. The fact that evidence of collection was seen at a time remote from the time a search is to be initiated should be of no consequence and this point elaborated upon in a warrant affidavit. Here is an example to illustrate the length of time this material is kept. In 1977, a man was accused of molesting his natural daughter. A search turned up hundreds of slides of sexually explicit depictions of the man with his daughter, with others, and other children. When the girl ran away, rather than cooperate with prosecutors, all of the slides were returned to the man. Apparently sometime after his arrest and subsequent release, there was a fire which badly damaged the man's home.

In 1986, another investigation was initiated and a search turned up not only the original slides, in the same trays, still with the original evidence tags attached, but, also 8-mm movies of the girl with him and other men, engaged in sex acts, missed in the original search, now scarred and scorched by the fire. They also found drawings and love letters not previously known to the authorities written to him by his daughter. (Refer to Figures 2.1 to 2.4 in Chapter 2.)

## What Is Collected

One of the many ways an offender draws children to his home or gets them to return is to provide them with things they don't have or would be unable to obtain easily — books, magazines, or toys. Pedophiles might collect toys or dolls, build model planes or boats, or perform as clowns or magicians to attract children. A pedophile interested in older children might have a

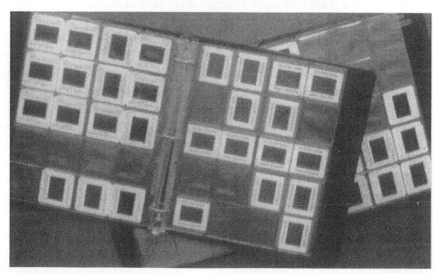

**Figure 3.7**    Here we see how one child molester stored and protected his collection of over 90,000 slides of children he had molested. It was carefully indexed and stored in a fireproof cabinet.

"hobby" involving alcohol, drugs, or pornography. Police have found picture books for toddlers, comic books for teenagers and adolescents, and books that spell out how to perform magical tricks for children. Here, a 10-year-old boy who was molested from the age of 8 tells how he was seduced.

> "At first he was like a dad to me. We climbed mountains, we played Atari. He had three poisonous snakes, he had crickets and mice and a frog. See, he was my friend and he loved me very much. Then he began to do things to me. I kept saying he shouldn't, but he wouldn't stop. He said that if I told anyone, I would not be able to play with the Atari and wouldn't see him anymore... [8].

One case involved a foster parent who was molesting the boys in his charge. Searching his home during the service of a search warrant, investigators found everything for young boys — toys, games, even a freezer full of frozen hot dogs and a cupboard full of Froot Loops.

## Concealing Activities and Identity

A common defense at trial is that the offender didn't know what he was doing at the time he committed the offense. This defense, diminished capacity or insanity, is easily foiled if the proper questions are addressed early in the investigation to demonstrate consciousness of guilt. The same is true when identity is a defense (this is discussed in greater detail in the section on defenses in Chapter 8). By demonstrating an intentional act to conceal their activities, an investigation may establish they knew and understood the wrongfulness of their acts.

Members of the underground use postal boxes, mail drops, and remailing services to assure anonymity and remove themselves as far as possible from the actual transactions. Generally, they use pseudonyms, often making identification very difficult.

It is not uncommon to find that the offender is using his home address for legitimate mailings and his mail drop or work address for material or transactions he is afraid of having discovered.

The clandestine purchase and trafficking of child pornography readily adapts itself to the use of the mails by virtue of the anonymity afforded to both the sender and the addressee. The postal authorities arrested a major distributor of child pornography and seized over 10,000 sexually explicit photos, slides, films, and magazines involving children under 16. The entire business was run through the mail. Another offender not only operated through the mail, but used an elaborate phone scheme to prevent a meeting in person. His calls were forwarded to a "secretary" and set up as conference calls. At the time, the offender was in a state prison. Another case involved international connections. Porn orders sent to Europe were rerouted to this country and packaged in Los Angeles. The distributor then drove throughout the western United States, dropping the packages in mailboxes as she drove through different towns to prevent the source from being traced. The money then went to the Cayman Islands and on to Switzerland. Because of the clandestine nature of the operation, this particular investigation took 10 years to complete.

## The Use of Computers

Home computers and those operated by large industry have been found to be invaluable to the clandestine crimes committed by the pedophile. The fact that so much information can be created and stored in a computer that no one will know about except those who the offender tells or shows makes this invention very useful. Add to this the ability to encrypt (hide) the data and provide an automatic destruct mechanism to the program and there is the perfect device to hold illicit information and data.

Offenders have been found to use home style computers that range in sophistication from those children use in school to highly complex set-ups that have scanning and communication capabilities, in addition to the regular functions a computer does. Investigations and research have found that pedophiles use computers to organize their material. They can build lists, charts, data banks on the things they collect or do. They can scan in photographs, file them by whatever criteria they chose to be reviewed by themselves or others. The compulsive nature of the offender to collect and store this information makes the computer the ideal tool. The significance of this evidence is the record keeping that may be found which will establish identities of victims, offenders, connections to either or both and, in some cases, the offenses themselves. For example, with the storing of scanned photographs, an offender will often write a description of the acts, surrounding circumstances, identities of the person(s) depicted, etc. These can be invaluable in proving or establishing a crime was committed.

By using the computer to research on-line data banks and communicate with others they can "validate" their feelings and desires by communicating with other offenders. The means they do this with is only limited by the resources of the offender. With a modem, as will be discussed in later chapters, the offender can communicate with the world. The fact that they can find someone else with their desires and interests is comforting to them and the computer provides a way to do so in (almost) complete anonymity. In one example, through the forum of the "internet," a group of men, from as many as three different countries, engaged in "on line" fantasies with each other, in a "chat room" they created. This led to the actual, live molestation of a young girl whom one of the group had befriended. The whole transaction was broadcast by computer video connection to all of the group who participated while the one individual carried out sex acts on the child as directed by the others. This was all recorded in the computer system and, subsequently, used as evidence against the men.

The electronic bulletin boards (BBS) and "chat rooms," as will be discussed later in this text, also provide access to one another in much the same way as one would put up notes on bulletin boards in grocery stores or schools. This type of communication is also perfect for the pedophile because of the anonymity it provides. The "postings" on the boards are in the same vein as those in "swinger magazines," only with the potential of instant contact if the e-mail address of the target is being monitored by the person who posted it. For example, one of the major pedophile organizations that publishes its own magazine, created its own electronic bulletin board and website. This would have permitted its members to communicate with themselves and others who might find them through the board postings. Like the CB craze that swept this country in the early 1970s, the electronic bulletin board and "chat rooms" also provide another means of contacting children who have the same computer equipment. Numerous cases have been seen where an offender has met and molested a child contacted through the internet.

Lastly, the computer provides the necessary record-keeping for any business the offender might engage. It is a way to store and retrieve the transactions that have been completed or are anticipated. The evidentiary value of such records should be plain to see. The important aspect for an investigator to consider is whether such equipment exists in the suspected offender's home or business and to what ends it was used. There must be some connection drawn to a criminal act and/or to the equipment before it may be searched for or seized.

As the technological age has advanced, so has the pedophile network using the medium of computers for illicit activities. Through the method of "digitizing" and graphic reproduction by Graphic Interchange Format or GIF, actual images of people may be scanned or entered by direct video camera imaging into computers, and stored on disc or magnetic tape. This data may then be transmitted from one computer to another by modem and phone lines. The images may be still photos or actual motion picture/video action. The information or data may be retrieved by any individual who has a computer either through the Internet, the "information superhighway" or "cyberspace," or directly from the creator in the form of computer discs or tapes. An example of the pervasiveness of the practice is a case in England, where a child pornography library containing thousands of still photos of children some as young as two, was seized. It had been stored in a university computer, apparently maintained by an employee. It was linked by the Internet communications network to the general public and 160 countries.

As noted above, BBS cases have involved the linking of the offender with target children who have been contacted directly through the computer. One case involving such a practice involved a 23-year-old man who met a pair of 12- and 14-year-old boys whom he forced into sex with him. Found on his computer were the records of his contacts with the boys, pictures of nude boys, and a 29-page photo album filled with ads cut from legitimate public domain publications depicting semi-nude children. As is typical of pedophiles, this album also had pictures the offender had taken of children whom he had direct contact with, one as young as three. Clipped to the album was a fantasy or actual account of how he molested or would have liked to have molested an eight-year-old boy and girl [9]. This case is significant, because it reflects a direct connection of the common traits of the pedophile to the modern technology of computer communication, data creation, storage and retrieval.

Phone numbers for BBS may be located in computer magazines, "swinger" magazines, local porn shops, and once discovered, the specialty BBS user groups that cater to pornography, personal connections, and the pedophile underground itself. Websites and addresses are published as "links" on the internet by those who have similar interests.

Covert investigative practices and search warrants are the most successful way to investigate these type of cases. There is a discussion of the covert operations involving BBS and search warrants in subsequent chapters on "Search Warrants" and "Case Management." The discussion in the search warrant section is particularly valuable because it contains an investigation of an offender who was originally investigated for his involvement in transmitting pornography and setting up liaisons with children over the Internet, but, who at the time of the original investigation, had not been connected to any particular crime involving an identified child. It was not until after his publicized arrest, did a parent come forward to report, the heretofore unreported fact that her child had been forced into sex acts with the offender long before the investigation had been initiated. The offender was subsequently convicted of the sexual assault.

## Clandestine Photography

Offenders who photograph their children do everything in their power to ensure they are not discovered. The type of photographic equipment they use often demonstrates their knowledge of the wrongfulness of their acts. Offenders will use cameras that don't require negatives, such as Polaroid or Kodak instant cameras. This also includes motion picture film. If the offender is more sophisticated and has the resources, he may develop and print pictures, operating out of his own photo lab.

A pornographer who ran a business from his attic took prints to an adult bookstore, which used an exclusive service that would develop virtually anything. He also used the services of "fast photo" developing firms that develop and print pictures by machine, hoping to assure secrecy. This is a common practice because of the manner in which the prints are made. In addition, slides, which offer little chance of discovery because they are not printed and are often mounted by machine, are also used by the pornographer for the same reasons.

## Offender is Aware he has a Problem and is Seeking Information

Most offenders, even the dyed-in-the-wool, hard-core pedophiles, have guilt feelings. Two articles about personality problems and difficulties were found in the possession of the "magician" mentioned earlier. One article was about being "what you want to be," which in his case was a child molester who feels good about what he does. The problem was that he didn't. Throughout the articles he highlighted and underlined passages. The most strongly highlighted lines were the ones he seemed most interested in. What he seemed to like was one paragraph that said something like: "Do what you've wanted to do because it's good and you'd like it." It continued: "Don't worry if it makes any sense, do it anyway." The second article was about sexuality and problems people have. Again, the problem he was having was highlighted by his own underlining: "people should be allowed to do what they like because it is generally good. "What he believed the articles were talking about was child molesting. The discovery of this type of material in the possession of the offender is another way of demonstrating that the offender knew that what he was doing was wrong.

## Collecting Books and Writings about Sex with Children

Another characteristic of the offender is the collection of books on the subject of sex with children. In addition to the reasons specified, the offenders will collect these books to sanctify and validate their thoughts and/or actions: if others do it, it must be OK. Finally, the stories and accounts given in the publications provide fantasy material so that the offenders can project themselves into the places of those portrayed. The discovery of this type of material demonstrates an offender's true intent.

## A Compulsive Need to Record Events

The offender will often record the events that have transpired between him and the child, probably because he has such a short time to be with the child. It could also be because he has limited access or because the child will soon grow out of his age range. The recording is generally in the form of pictures, diaries, drawings, or anything that will assist him in recalling the events with the child, to masturbate or to fantasize.

Depending on the sophistication of the offender, he will use whatever is available to him. If he is able to use a computer, entries are often coded so that only he will be able to find what he is looking for. These codes may consist of passwords that will prevent unauthorized access to the records, or encryption, by which the computer will only give gobbledygook without the proper password. Child molesters have also been known to create their own code words and meanings such as those mentioned in the following paragraph. If the offender is not able to use such advanced equipment, he may resort to the simpler forms of recording events using pictures, movies, or videotapes.

### Diaries or Writings

The notes in Figure 3.8 were found in the possession of the "magician" previously mentioned. Note that the names and addresses of the children on the notes were written by the children themselves. Over 200 such notes, torn from various pieces of paper, including some schoolwork, were found in the man's possession. His notations were also found on the notes, in some cases giving the date, time, location, and what was done with the child. His terms for sexual conduct were "magic" and "talent test." The purpose of these notes and records was also to maintain contact with the victims.

As was discussed in the section on associates, child molesters try to keep track of those they were or are involved with. Like anyone who has a relationship he would like to keep, child molesters keep the names, addresses, and phone numbers of their victims and friends. This is very important, as will be discussed in the chapter on search warrants, because this characteristic both gives investigators a way to identify otherwise unknown victims and offenders and supplies a reason to search the offender's home, business, or car. An arrest of a child molester revealed that he had over 200 3 × 5" cards with the names of girls on them, many of them his victims.

Some offenders use a plain calendar or diary to record events. In a case where a child molester was arrested by the U.S. postal authorities, correspondence was found along with child pornography photographs, books, and videotapes. One of the videotapes was a "master" for those the man was distributing. Authorities also found diaries containing detailed accounts of the man's sexual exploits and performance evaluations and ratings of the girls he was involved with.

Perhaps a good example of the maintenance of a diary that contained fantasy and a good example of premeditation, is that of Westley Allan Dodd, who was executed in Washington state for the murder of several boys, but,

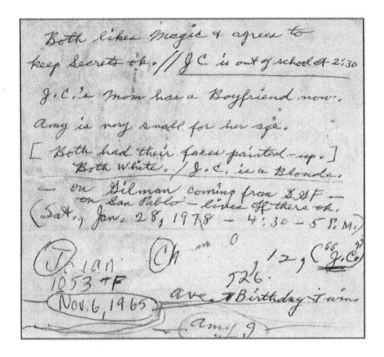

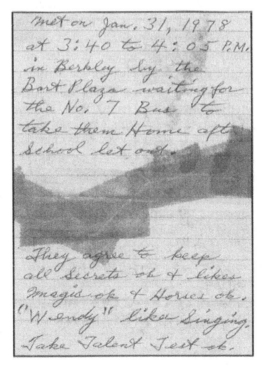

**Figure 3.8** Recording of events.

who had actually killed numerous others. In a letter to the author of *When the Monster Comes Out of the Closet*, Dodd wrote:

> "I arrived in Vancouver already planning to kill boys. I would find a way to bring them to my home, rape them, and kill them... I got a map and drove around town trying to find areas where children might be playing without adult supervision... I walked through the park, paying attention to the terrain, nearby buildings, etc. I went home and started writing down my plans for finding and isolating one or more boys. I re-read the plans and when I didn't like something I changed it... Finally, I felt I had planned for every possible 'emergency' that may arise. I wrote that I had had an erection 24 hours a day for the last few days (while making my plans) and the only way 'to make it soft again' was to find a boy" [10].

## Scrapbooks

One of the more frequent discoveries in searches of an offender's belongings, is a scrapbook containing his fantasies and records, either photographic or written, of his exploits. An excellent example of this was a grandfather who had molested his four-year-old granddaughter in February, 1986. The original report was of a fondling of the grandfather's penis by the child, digital penetration of the child, and, nude photographs taken of the child, some eight months before the investigation was undertaken, in October, 1986.

Investigation revealed that the grandfather had molested and taken photos of the child's mother, her two sisters, in their late-thirties at the date of report, and some of their friends, when they were similar ages. The original photos of the mother and her sisters were found by them and destroyed some 18 years before. The mother described seeing books at home on "nude studies of women" and the book entitled, *Lolita,* when she was a child. What concerned investigators the most was that the grandfather was a professional photographer who specialized in nursery school children.

Several months after the offender had been arrested, a search warrant was prepared and served. It recovered the original book the mother had seen, pseudo-child pornography, the nude study books the mother described, nude pictures of children and the offender, and 8-mm child and adult porn films, all hidden in a specially crafted compartment in his photo lab in the basement of his home. Apparently he had disposed of the photos of the granddaughter when he knew the acts with her were discovered after he was confronted by his daughter, before she reported it to the authorities. However, what is most significant about this case, is the scrap book found among the materials previously described. It contained clipped images from adult pornography, child pornography, and photos of the offender and children whom he was involved with over his life. Perhaps the most insightful clue as to what a threat this man was to children and why he should be committed to a maximum term, were his fantasy writings, written in his own handwriting in the margins, adjacent to the sex acts he had engaged in with his victims. One such passage read:

> "This pretty little body
> By the age of ten
> Had pleasured many men.
> Young fresh flesh
> In love with lust.
> She had done everything —
> At fifteen..." [11].

### Mementos or Trophies

Another way the offender tries to recall events with the children he was involved with is to keep a memento that is unique to the child. Most of the time this consists of photographs. It also includes toys played with, drawings the child made, or an article of clothing. Often the clothing will consist of underwear, sometimes soiled, which the offender uses to fantasize with or show off as a trophy of his "conquests" (Figure 3.9).

Examples of these type of mementos are the drawings and writings kept by an offender can be seen in Figures 2.1 to 2.4. They were drawn and written by the offender's 13-year-old daughter and they were found nine years after

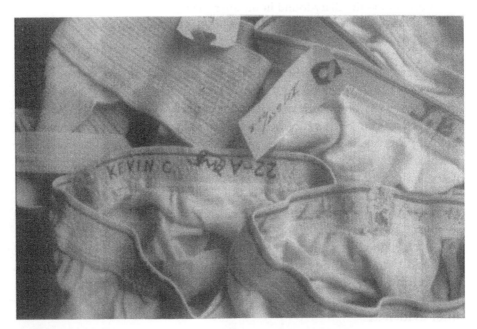

**Figure 3.9** Mementos or trophies. (Courtesy of Mountain View, California, P.D.)

the offender was arrested on the charges described previously in the section on retention of materials collected.

Another form this characteristic takes is clippings from newspapers and periodicals that report the crimes the offender has committed. The maintenance of this record of events serves several purposes. The first is purely ego — he wants to know that he has done something. The second is fantasy. He may relive the experience every time he reads the article. The third is pure curiosity. He wants to know about his victims. Their names, ages, and, often about their family. This relates to both pity and sorrow, but, it is mostly morbid curiosity — he wants to know who he killed and what the family is feeling. This relates to an important element proving his mental state. Here, he wants to know what was reported and what the authorities know about his crime and identity.

Once again, we turn to Westley Allan Dodd, writing after he killed two boys in Washington state:

> "I watched the news *very* (his emphasis) closely. After 4 or 5 days the police were saying 'no clues, no motive, no weapon found, no eyewitnesses, no suspects... I had read that killers return to the scene of the crime, and could be expected to do certain things. I went to work and agreed with the talk in the break room the day after the murders — 'it was terrible — who could do such a thing?, etc.' — After 8 or 9 days, I knew I gotten away (sic) with a double murder. And, in fact, the only evidence to connect me with the murders was the diary found in my apartment.
>
> That scared feeling went away. Within two weeks I was trying to decide what to do with the next victims... [12].

To further highlight how this may be seen is an interesting experience of a patrol officer in Medford, Oregon, on graveyard shift closing what was one of the most heinous crimes in the history of Fresno, California. A six-year-old girl had been brutally sexually assaulted, strangled to death, and set afire; there were no clues. The crime went unsolved for a long time. The patrol officer received a a suspicious person call. He responded and subsequently stopped the offender. All the officer knew at the time was that the person was reported as being suspicious and it was a very late hour of the night. Trying to obtain some identification from the individual, who said he didn't have any, the officer asked him about the bulge in his pocket which contained a wallet. When the offender withdrew the wallet and thumbed through it, he noticed some well-worn newspaper clippings. To make a long story short, the articles were about the Fresno homicide, taken from a local paper after the time of the killing. He was tied to the scene by other evidence.

Another characteristic of this trait is the collection of data or information. An example of this may be seen in Figure 3.10. Here, the offender both recounts his conquests for bragging purposes, while at the same time providing a source of fantasy by using it to recall his exploits.

## Photographs

**Symbolically keeping the child close.** Photographs play an increasingly important role in the molestation of children. If the offender can't take the photograph himself, he will often obtain one supplied by the child. The child molester has a need to record the events of his life and to remember the experiences he has with the specific children he is involved with. A photograph is one of the many symbolic ways of doing this.

**Remembrance, importance, and reduction of inhibitions.** The child molester will take photographs of the child involved in innocent activities such as that in Figure 3.11. This serves three purposes for the offender. First, it creates a remembrance for the offender when he no longer has access to

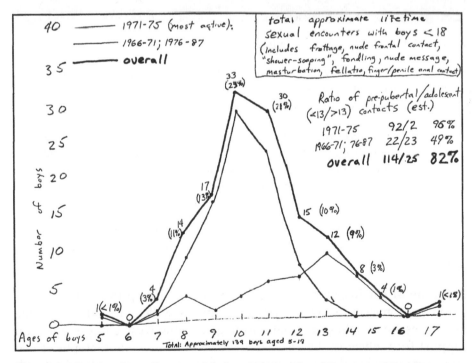

**Figure 3.10** Trophy collection of data or information. (Courtesy of San Francisco Police Department.)

**Figure 3.11**   Photo of a child victim.

the child, and it "freezes" the child at the age of greatest interest. Linda Tschirhart Sanford, in her book, *The Silent Children*, quotes a 34-year-old child molester who describes this characteristic of offenders:

> "I was really into little redhead girls and I'd fantasize about them all the time until finally I had to have one. But they are really hard to find, especially after you hurt them, so whenever I can find one I take her picture first so I can have that later. That's the nice thing about pictures — they never grow old even though the kids do" [13].

Second, it gives the child a sense of importance. Third, it gets the child comfortable with the idea of having his picture taken and lowers his inhibitions in front of a camera.

**Bragging or gaining of status.**   The offender will keep the child's photograph as a memento, often carrying it in his wallet. In addition to the memories, he uses these photographs to gain status, trust, and psychological support from offenders he associates with. In one case, photographs of two boys were found in the possession of a man who was sexually involved with them. When he was arrested, he told of his experiences with the boys as though they were his "lovers" and he was proud of his "conquests."

It is not uncommon for the offender to pull out his wallet and brag to his associates of his sexual prowess to increase his stature, displaying his trophies of the children he has been with. In addition to ogling the photographs, the associates may lend support to the offender by sharing their experiences and feelings about sex with children. It is not uncommon for the offender to display the photograph on his wall for others to see. An inmate running a child pornography operation from his jail cell in Florida had a picture of his favorite "model" taped to the wall of his cell and another in his wallet.

When a picture is taken of the child, the child gets a false sense of importance, which binds him to the offender. One of the major reasons the offender asks to have a photograph of the child is to make the child feel that he cares about him. The child then perceives he has special status in the offender's eyes.

To identify the target group and/or children the offender is involved with, the investigator may have only to look at the walls of the offender's home.

**Demonstrating propriety.**   An insidious facet of the practice of photographing children is the fact that these photographs (both explicit and otherwise) are often used by the offender to convince other children that what the offender wants is OK because he has done it with others.

In one case, a man contacted girls in a shopping mall and asked them if he could photograph them. He showed them an expensive leather folder with pictures of other girls, both dressed and nude, and told them he would make them models. When he was arrested, police found over 100 more photographs of girls and hundreds of names and phone numbers. In addition, they found a host of adult pornography and the type of pornography, called "simulated" child pornography that purports to depict "teens," but actually shows older women dressed and "made-up" to look like teenagers.

**Fantasy.**   Fantasy plays an important role in the molestation of children, and the photograph lends itself perfectly for enhancing the offender's fantasies.

Activities such as the boy skateboarding in Figure 3.12 are common for offenders to photograph because they depict a child in a state of undress. It also is a short step to taking pictures without clothes on. Some offenders are only "turned-on" by a certain type of clothing or a lack of clothing — for example, jock straps, shorts, or sports uniforms.

> I like taking pictures of the kids. Not just pornographic pictures, all kinds of pictures. Even just a kid in gym shorts with maybe a shadow of a suggestion is provocative to me [14].

**Figure 3.12**   Fantasy use of photos.

Photographs of this type showing some skin exposed can best be described as "safe pornography" for the offender. They are often erotic and sexually stimulating for the offender. Even simple "innocent" pictures of children may be provocative if he is unable to obtain more explicit material. However, even though he has the most explicit material in existence, he will still collect this type of picture. For example, a teacher in a junior high school was found to be receiving child pornography from overseas and a search warrant was executed on his home, permitting the seizure of thousands of sexually explicit photographs, magazines, books, movies, and videotapes. The offender had acquired all of this material over 20 years, and also had numerous videotapes of television programs such as "Flipper," "Lassie," and others depicting young boys. What he did with these tapes helps to illustrate how the innocent photograph taken by the offender of a child swimming or in activities wearing only shorts represents child erotica and a sexual stimulant.

One of the "Flipper" programs depicted a scene where the young boy in the program is on a dock near the water at his Florida home. The boy is clad only in a swimsuit and is seen to dive into the water to join the dolphin "Flipper." In the motion to dive into the water, the boy crouches, then springs up and arches into the water, elongating his body as one would when diving into water to prevent a splash. The teacher had used a special-effect feature to stop the action and repeat the entire motion, backward and forward, from the crouch to the entry into the water several times, as though it were an instant replay of a football fumble. In another video segment, from the original version of the movie Tarzan, there is a sequence where a boy, approximately 10-12 years old, runs up to Tarzan and trips over a log. He is wearing only a loin cloth and the cloth is seen to flip up, apparently exposing the side of the boy's buttocks. Even though the film is not very clear about what is seen, the teacher stopped the action as the boy falls forward and repeated the sequence over and over again, backward and forward, from the time the boy runs forward and trips to the point where the loin cloth flips up.

Another aspect of photographs is that offenders create fantasy worlds around the photographs of the children. One man, who was arrested for molesting elementary school children, was found to have the photographs in Figure 3.13 in his home. He met the 10-year-old girl in the photos at a 4-H Club gathering where she was displaying an animal she had raised. He befriended her at the gathering but never saw her again. He asked her to pose for a picture behind a "Farmer John" cutout. She was to poke her head through the hole in the cutout, but she refused. She did, however, agree to pose for a portrait provided she was able to get copies for herself. The montage in Figure 3.13 is the end result of the photograph. Unfortunately, you see it in black and white, but in color it depicts an autumn pastoral scene with the leaves turning colors in the lower portion; on the right, a forest scene with the sun filtering through the trees; on the left, a waterfall with the sun shining through the mist; in the center, a rainbow; at the top, a sunset with a seagull flying across the sky; and in the middle, the girl's picture repeated, now with a flower in her hair, her name across her chest, and hearts on either side. Also found in this man's possession were romantic letters he had written (but never mailed) to this girl about the great relationship and love they were experiencing together in his fantasies.

**Blackmail.**    Photographs, regardless of the innocent nature of their content, are also used as blackmail to keep the child quiet. The threat, expressed or implied, is that if the child tells, the photographs will be found or be put up somewhere where everyone will see and know what happened with the child. This threat is extremely successful in keeping children in line, regardless of age. It works very well with younger children who don't realize that if the pictures are found, the offender will get into trouble. It also works well with the older child, who fears others finding out what embarrassing things he has done with the offender.

**Sexual Stimulation.**    Pictures of naked children or children engaged in sex acts by themselves or with others, including the offender, are primarily intended for the sexual gratification of the photographer and other viewers. When sold, depending on the nature of the action depicted and the age of the child, the photograph may be worth anywhere from $1 to $1,000 per

**Figure 3.13**   Fantasy use of photos.

print. Most of the photographs taken by the offenders are not directly submitted to child pornography publishers. Instead, they are swapped or loaned, usually without fee. Often it is during the circulation among those who share this interest that someone in the group submits the photo to a publisher, who then prints it in a commercial venture. There are, however, some people who take pornographic photographs for the express purpose of making money by selling them. But it has been the experience of virtually all investigators who have worked this type of crime, that if someone takes this type of photograph, he is interested in more than just the money. For this reason, *if photos of naked children are taken, there is a great probability that the child has been molested before, during, or after the taking of the picture.* Therefore, if an investigation reveals photos of naked children, the investigator should strongly suspect that the children depicted have been abused, are in further danger, and *are in need of immediate protection.*

## The Use of Pornography

### *Seducing Children*

Both child and adult pornography is often used by the child molester to seduce the child. In 1991, a study was conducted by the Los Angeles Police Department's Sexually Exploited Child Unit (SECU), regarding the frequency of involvement of pornography in its cases. In a 10-year period of operation, from 1980 to 1989, the cases investigated by SECU detectives of extrafamilial offenders involved pornography over 62% of the time. Of the 320 cases it surveyed, 199 involved pornography, 74 (23.1%) child porn, 69 (21.6%) adult porn, and 56 (17.5%) both [14].

In addition to misrepresenting moral standards, the pornography can be used to demonstrate the acts the offender wishes to engage in. It may also be used to stimulate the child's interest in the depicted activities and lower the child's inhibitions. A girl who was modeling for a child pornographer described how she was able to learn how to pose.

> "...but then you start looking at other pictures and looking at magazines and then you know you can get a certain look..." [15].

Pictures of children engaged in various poses or sexually explicit acts with either adult or child pornography in the foreground or background are commonly found. In Utah, a man kidnapped and murdered several boys. He had used sexually explicit material to arouse the children and took pictures of the boys before killing them. Although it is fairly common to find the child pornographer involved in "buying" or "selling" children, the true and major purpose of child pornography should not be forgotten — *the sexual gratification of the offender.*

## Demonstrating the True Interests of the Offender

The true desires of the child molester can be determined from the type of materials found in his possession. A convicted child molester who murdered several of his victims describes how he sought materials of this nature.

"...Somehow I became sexually attracted to young boys, and I would fantasize them naked. Certain bookstores offered sex education, photographic, or art books of nude boys. I purchased such books and used them to enhance my masturbatory fantasies..." [16].

A small-time pornography distributor who worked out of his attic had thousands of adult pornography pictures; sold audio tape recordings of people allegedly engaged in sexual activities; sold copies of pornographic video tapes; had a small stock of magazines; and had several hundred child pornography photographs. This individual, who received most of his original pictures from his clients, also lived in his attic, with his bed at one end, surrounded by his supplies of pornography and some of his recording equipment, which he could monitor from his bed. Immediately around his bed were various personal effects, but no pornography except for a small envelope of "special" photographs, most depicting children engaged in sex acts and in lewd poses. Although his true desires were never at issue and not established in court, he did plead guilty to distributing child pornography.

Many single-person operations like this exist. The offenders duplicate photos sent to them or take them themselves and sell them in sets of three to five pictures, ranging in price from $5 to $100, depending on the age and activity of the action depicted. Generally there is a delay in mailing because these individuals often work on the run or await a call from the authorities. In most cases of this kind, a teaser for more material is included with the order.

## Genuine Interest in Children

The offender will often have a genuine interest in children — in fact may even worship or idolize them or their image (see Figure 3.14). It is this concern that the child misinterprets as genuine love rather than the selfish use of the child for the offender's own needs. It may manifest itself in various ways. The offender may collect books or articles on child development, child abuse, or child education (see Figure 3.15). It may be seen in the way the offender treats the child he is involved with. Many times the offender will take great pains to ensure that the child is clothed, fed, and well taken care of. The offender may express his concern by equating his love for the child with sexual activity and repress or rationalize away the harm he does the child by emphasizing the positive aspects of his relationship.

These characteristics can be seen in the following quote from a letter sent to a child sex group by a man who likes to be sexually active with 8- and 9-year-old boys:

**Figure 3.14** An offender's bedroom with evidence of child idolization. (Courtesy of the Bergen County Prosecutor's office.)

**Figure 3.15** Evidence of the offender's concern for children.

"I am 23 going on 8, I love children i.e.: [sic] little boys very much and have been experiencing sexual relationships with boys 8 to 10 years old since I was 12... I do a great deal of pediatric and preschool elementary education work in addition to playing with lots of little kids who are my friends... I am especially interested in any available contacts that you may know of out here in California... The one very big complaint I must express is that I am involved with a number of little boys as friends, there has been no sexual contact to speak of yet. After a year and a half of none such relationship it is very frustrating to me [sic]. I do manage to obtain photographs of my friends and even children that I just see around on the street, etc. I love little kids for a lot more than just sexual [sic] but I personally feel that it is just another way of expressing that love just as patting on the head, cuddling or holding hands..." [17].

## The Use of Narcotics and Alcohol

The use of narcotics and alcohol by the child molester is commonplace. What better way to get a child to a place he wouldn't ordinarily go to than to provide him with something he can't ordinarily get? The use of alcohol is mostly limited to the older child; however, it is also a common denominator in some cases involving young children. Drugs, especially those that give a "rush" or stimulate the child, are common among child molesters. Rarely are depressants (other than alcohol) used. On the West Coast, a child molester was arrested for making child pornography, supplying "dope," and providing a place for kids to stay as a means of getting them to his home. Contacts were by word of mouth. He had fled an East-coast state on similar charges of molestation and drug use. When arrested, he was found to have brought his whole collection of materials with him from the East Coast. His arrest was brought about when he tried to start his own child porn magazine.

For the investigator it is important to distinguish between the individual who abuses drugs and alcohol and one who uses either for the seduction of children. The former may claim a diminished capacity defense and/or that the drugs or alcohol caused him to commit the crime. With the latter, it can be shown that the use of the stimulants were part of an established pattern of reducing the child's inhibitions to facilitate sexual arousal. In either case, the investigator must establish the category the offender falls in, through questioning the child and others involved in the case. The elimination of the diminished capacity defense can greatly enhance the prosecution's case, if done early enough in the investigation.

## Methods and Styles of Seduction

### Affection and Attention

For the most part, a child is seduced in the same way as one adult seduces another. The offender takes him places, buys him things, impresses the child with his own personality, makes the child feel loved and indebted to the offender, then becomes physical with the child. It starts subtly, by holding hands, an arm over the shoulder, hand in lap, graduating to more explicit conduct. Generally it takes some time to develop. For example, a teacher was arrested for having sexual intercourse with his daughter; he pleaded guilty and was given a probation sentence with counseling. He was later accused of giving some of his female students inappropriate strokes and touches. Initial investigation suggested that he was never allowed any further by the students. However, given the nature of his background, further investigation should have been pursued to determine if it was likely to lead to more substantial conduct.

The offender will shower the child with attention and affection, often placing him on a pedestal, doing everything the child wants, constantly giving him rewards, praise, approval, and concern, which the offender considers love. An 11-year-old described her abuse at age 9:

> "Not long ago I met a man who was 35 years old. He treated me very fine. He never hit me, we never argued. we always agreed on the same thing. He had a house and a lovely car. He bought me presents, then he took dirty pictures of me and offered me money... I don't really want that... I want a home. I want a mother and a father. I want someone who will accept me and love me for a long time... The man I just told you about, he doesn't want children for long. He keeps finding new ones when the old ones get bigger. I know that he'll leave me soon and I will be alone again. All he really wants are the dirty pictures and the sex. I wish I could stop. I wish I was strong enough to say no..." [18].

Making the child feel special is a great way to gain his confidence. In a major pornography case in California, the offender placed ads in various underground papers seeking people interested in modeling for large sums of money. Most of those who responded were runaways and under the age of consent (18 in California). Even though the offender was aware of this, he would have the respondents fill out an application, have them write in that they were of age, and give them a screen test that required them to have sex with him. He would make them dependent on him by "renting" a room from him. He would constantly tell them that he loved them, making them feel special by giving them "pet" names. He then would get the children involved in sex with his friends, make movies, and take "calls" for sexual services.

Often a child is tricked into performing a sexual act because he doesn't understand the significance of what has transpired. With most young children, the advantage the offender has is that the child doesn't know that what the offender wants is wrong. As Elizabeth J. Roberts, Director of the Project on Human Sexuality, Cambridge, Massachusetts, said:

"The idea of the father-son talk about the birds and the bees is a myth. Ignorance about sexuality still pervades through our society and in homes across the nation. Parents retreat into silence when questions about sex are asked by their children, and as a result children are learning not to ask questions, and to conduct sexual experiments on their own" [19].

## Threats

Most of the time, no threat or coercion is necessary until after the act is completed. Rarely is a threat of harm used to get the child to comply with the act. The only time a threat becomes necessary is to keep the child quiet and to continue participating in what the offender desires. Most threats by the offender are either implied or are subtly broached; seldom do they include violence. For the most part, threats are made that imply negative consequences for both the victim and the offender if there is disclosure. For example, the offender may threaten, "We'll get into trouble if you tell... If you tell, your mother will be upset and we'll never be able to see each other... I'll never see you again."

## Programming

In some cases the child is "programmed" to perform. The child is taught to interpret a certain motion, situation, or act as his cue to perform. For example, in one case a father discovered that his daughter was being molested by a friend of the family when he placed her on his lap and, not knowing the wrongfulness, she began groping his genitals. When he asked her what she was doing, she said that it was what the friend always had her do when she sat in his lap. In another case, a parent discovered that his child had been molested when he complimented her for doing something he liked and her response was a solicitation of oral sex. She was responding the way she had been taught by the person who was molesting her. In yet another case, a 6-year-old boy was repeatedly orally copulated by his father when he visited him. After the police report was made, the boy was taken to a hospital for examination. The doctor noted that immediately on removing the child's pants, he observed that the boy had an erection, as though he were expecting sexual stimulation.

## Misrepresentation of Moral Values

Possessing little experience or knowledge, the child is often easily convinced that what the offender wants is a legitimate activity. It is easy to understand why children acquiesce to the demands of the child molester, considering the vast literature on sex with children and sex manuals that are on the market. These are often left out and available for children to "discover" by accident or are specifically shown to the child by the offender (see Figure 3.16).

**Figure 3.16** Virtually every book on the shelf at or just below the child's eye level are either sex education manuals or books on having sex with children, left there for the child to "discover."

A child who wrote to one of the groups in the pedophile underground probably said it best when he described how he was seduced:

> "A friend of mine in Denver lets me see the *Bulletin* (the publication advocating sex with children that this letter was printed in) and the *Journal* (another publication from the same organization) and other stuff like *Pan* and *Panthology* (a monthly magazine and a book on sex with boys) and... I think they are just about the best stories I have ever read.... his (stories) make me feel good and sometimes I wish I was one of the kids in his story with someone to love me like that. I'm sorry I can't give you my address, but my mom and dad open my mail and they would murder me if they found out about you" [20].)

In many cases, children have been shown films that are either sexually graphic or suggestive. In a gay bathhouse, homosexually oriented child pornography was being shown in the bath's movie theater. Boys were taken there to see the film and were led to believe that it was appropriate behavior. In several other cases, boys were taken to a film called *The Rocky Horror Picture Show*, which is about transvestism. Although the movie has nothing to do with child sex issues, children were seduced by using the film as a starting point for discussion and legitimacy of sexual acts. Children were often picked up for sexual purposes at the theater where the movie was showing.

Another way an offender will misrepresent moral values is by entering into the activity himself, giving the child the idea that it is acceptable behavior. In the case discussed in Chapter 1, of a 12-year-old babysitter who was molested by a man and his wife, they explained the legitimacy of the action to the child in several ways.

First, they took her to a nude beach where everyone took off their clothes, getting her used to the idea of doing the same. Every time the family got together, they talked to the girl about becoming the third partner in a ménage à trois. The man and the woman took showers with the girl. They had her pose for conventional photographs, at the same time showing her pictures of the man's wife with her vagina shaved to "look like a little girl." They took her to see the movie *Pretty Baby* starring Brooke Shields, who was the same age as the girl. The film was about a 12-year-old girl who grew up in a New Orleans brothel at the turn of the century. The girl's mother teaches the child how to sell her "virginity" and become the "Lolita" of the brothel.

The couple also gave the girl a copy of the book *Pretty Baby* and a pictorial biography of Brooke Shields entitled *The Brooke Book*, which contains no nudity. They then convinced the child that what they wanted to do with her was OK by telling her that she could see Brooke in the movie and the book and that they would reenact the scenes that were not depicted in the film. Just in case the child didn't believe it was OK, the woman also undressed and engaged in sexual activity with the child and the man. The child said that at first it was "fun." She felt uncomfortable about going to the beach and taking the showers, but had a good time "dressing up." Her words describing what happened tell it all:

> "...he had pictures of (his wife) in their room and stuff. He showed me one picture of (his wife) that she (sic) was shaved (her vagina). She said that the reason she did that was because she wanted to be like a little girl. They said that (the wife) would pretend she was me..." [21].

The use of child pornography is a common way of misrepresenting moral values. The offender will take pornographic publications depicting children engaged in sexual conduct or poses and tell the child that what he wants is OK because it is printed in a book. Children will comply with the offender's requests, misled by the contention that if such things are printed in books or magazines they must be legitimate.

## Slow/Subtle Exposure to the Concept of Sexual Activity

The effectiveness of constant exposure in order to desensitize the child to the concept of sexual activity is evident in the case of the baby sitter. In a way, it is the offender's way of saying "sex practiced here." By constantly talking to the child about sexual activity, showing him pictures and magazines, or participating in sexual activities in the presence of the child, the offender slowly indoctrinates the child into the world of sex.

An example of this is an "art" poster found in the home of a man who liked 8-to-12-year-old boys. The poster is a series of photographs of a nude boy in various innocuous poses. This poster hung in the hallway so a child would have to see it when entering the apartment. A second example is an "etching" depicting naked young girls in repose, found in the home of a man who went to his neighborhood grocery stores and placed 3 × 5-inch cards on bulletin boards to solicit highschool girls to do household work around his home. Once the girls arrived at his home, he would run around wearing only his underpants, claiming that he had a skin disorder that required constant exposure to the air. While cleaning the man's bedroom, the girls would see the drawing on his wall. During the cleaning sessions, the man would discuss breast cancer and would "show" the girls how to examine themselves. He would also discuss their sexual practices.

Among other things, he supplied them with marijuana and convinced them that they should pose naked for him. He also convinced them to engage in sexual acts with him and others. Later, he would send the photos he and the girls had taken to an individual who was to prepare them for distribution. The offender had these girls conditioned to a point where they would communicate with each other by letter, "comparing notes" on what kind of sex they engaged in or enjoyed.

In other cases, the suggestiveness is quite subtle. As with the books left out for the child to "discover," the offender leaves other hints for the child to pick up. For example, in the trial of a California junior high school teacher who was involved with an 11-year-old boy prostitute, brought to him from Philadelphia through the underground for the express purpose of a sexual liaison, one item of evidence was a composite "magazine article" assembled by the offender. It began with the opening of a *People* magazine article about Brooke Shields and the movie *The Blue Lagoon*; it then continued with more suggestive photos from two *Playboy* magazine pictorials about the same film and other, more obviously adult-oriented movies. The subtle change from innocent to graphic, sexually explicit photographs was clearly intended to be a way of exciting the unsuspecting child, who would pick up the magazine to read about a child idol, Brooke Shields. The "magazine article" would also act as a stimulant for the offender, because the young male star of *The Blue Lagoon* was also shown naked.

## Mislabeling the Activity

Another common method of seducing the child is to misrepresent what the offender is actually doing. This could be by tricking the child into performing a sex act or by using a legitimate activity to achieve physical contact with the child, from which the offender can derive sexual gratification.

In one case, a man who engaged in sexual activities with 8-to-9-year-old boys liked to play a game called "monster," in which he would wrestle with the boys and touch their genitals and other areas, achieving sexual stimulation in doing so. All of this was accomplished without the child's knowing what was actually going on. From this kind of activity, the offender will graduate to more blatant touching. After the child feels more comfortable with the idea of the offender breaking the barrier of "personal space," the offender will advance to sexual play.

An example of this type of molestation was seen in a case in which a man ingratiated himself into a family with several children aged 3 to 8 years, one of whom was a 7-year-old girl. He was introduced to the family by another family member, who had been convicted of child molestation. He would "roughhouse" with the children, constantly playing games that involved physical contact of some sort. On more than one occasion he tried to "teach" the 7-year-old girl how to dance. He would do this by placing the child on his feet facing away from him and holding her hands. In this position, the girl's head came to the level of his groin, and as they danced he would rub his groin against the back of her head and shoulders. The investigating officer, when questioning him about this activity, was able to get the man not only to confess to engaging the child in the dance for sexual stimulation but also to admit to having ejaculated inside his pants during the dance.

A common ploy to trick the child into an act is to tell the child that what is being done is for a purpose other than the real one. For example, a young child was seduced into posing for photographs by being told that the offender was making pictures for a publisher of books for medical practitioners — the pictures were to assist doctors in teaching others about sex.

## Curiosity

Another style of seduction is the generation of curiosity on the part of the child. This is often done by leaving sexually oriented materials out and available to the child, such as the books previously mentioned. The seduction includes the use of sexual aids such as dildos and sex dolls, which are left in areas where children can find them, or the aids are presented to the child to try to stimulate his inquisitiveness. This leads to conversations about sexual matters.

It is common to discover sexual aids in the shape of penises, ranging in size from that of a 4-to-5-year-old boy to oversized exaggerations, in the possession of child molesters. The conversations often degenerate into sexual activity, either in acting out or demonstrating what the aids are used for (see Figure 3.17).

### Rewards and Bribes

A very common style of seduction is the use of rewards. Sometimes the child is told in advance what he will receive if he cooperates with the offender. Other times the offender doesn't tell the child until after the act. Soon the child learns that by doing what the offender wants, he can have his own way, turning the tables and becoming a manipulator. It isn't long before the child gains some control over the activity. From there, it is not uncommon for the child to begin to approach the offender and offer sex in anticipation of the reward. The reward may be as elaborate as a car or as simple as an ice-cream cone, depending on the circumstances. In one case, a man bought a 15-year-old boy a motorcycle, registered and insured it in his own name, and gave it to the boy in hopes of having a sexual relationship with him. We could

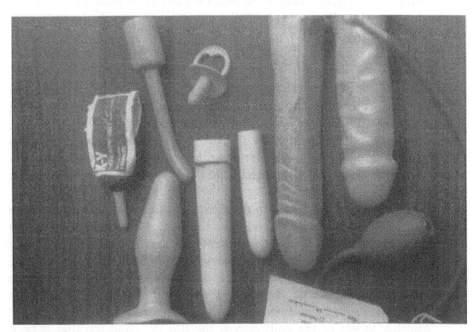

**Figure 3.17**    Items to spark curiosity.

never get the boy to admit having sex with the man, only to disclose why it was bought. In another case, a teacher at a high school bought expensive cars and other gifts for boys she was sexually involved with.

Money is another strong seduction method. The offender who uses it to entice a child usually succeeds, particularly when the child needs the money. In the proper environment, a child can earn as much as $1,000 a night. Ads in pornographic magazines have been seen offering up to $5,000 for one night with a child.

Children are easily lured into big money by promises to make them Hollywood stars. In one case, an offender told the parents of a child that the child could become another Brooke Shields, and told them about the nude photos Brooke had posed for. He took great pains to explain to them that Brooke's mother Terry had her pose for the nude shots at the age of 10 because it was necessary to become successful and have a good portfolio. The hopes of grandeur, and comparisons made by the offender between the child and the child's idols or child movie stars of the time, often make them easy prey. Modem advertising is often shown to the child, especially advertising that accents the sexuality of young children, to convince the child of the propriety of the acts.

The reward scam also makes the child dependent on the offender. Either the offender places the child in a position where the child must "come across" with what the offender wants or he won't eat or have a place to stay, or the offender puts himself in a position where only he can supply the child with what the child wants.

## Blackmail

Blackmail is another way of seducing the child into complying with the requests of the offender. Once the child has been placed in a compromising situation—sexually or otherwise—the offender can obtain some control over the child by threatening exposure. The offender knows that the child feels guilty and is wrought by shame. The offender also knows that most children have very little self-esteem or confidence and they feel helpless in the situation they are in.

If pictures are taken (even nonexplicit), they become a tool not only to make the child comply with the requests but also to keep him quiet about the incidents for fear of discovery and embarrassment. These pictures may not depict sexual activity or even depict the child nude. What the child is afraid of, regardless of what is shown in the photographs, is that someone may discover the nature of the relationship. Here the offender plays on the guilt the child harbors about being involved with him.

Another aspect of the guilt ploy is the fear the child has that if he is discovered, he might be in trouble both for the sex acts and for other things the offender knows the child has done — illegal or not.

A deep concern of many children who have a close relationship with the offender is the fear of being taken away, out of the family situation. This threat may be expressed or implied by the offender or may be developed by the child with no direct threats being made.

## Misuse of Authority

Another method of seduction is the misuse of authority. This may take two different forms. In the first, the offender takes advantage of his power, as in the following example. A Boy Scout leader told the children in his troop, while on several outings, to disrobe. Over a period of time he graduated from fondling them to orally copulating with them. Each time he told them not to tell anyone.

In the second type of misuse of authority, the offender takes advantage of a position of special trust and represents the activity as legitimate, using his authority, stature, and position to convince the children that what he wants is OK. In a case involving a Big Brother who was involved with an 11-year-old boy, the man invited the boy into his bedroom and asked the boy to disrobe from the waist down. The boy complied, not knowing that what was about to happen was wrong. Before anything happened, the activity was interrupted by something. Three weeks later, the offender again invited the boy into his bedroom and showed him an adult pornography film. He then orally copulated with the boy. This scenario was repeated 10 or more times, the boy complying because he didn't know any better. Finally, the man asked the boy to bring in other boys. The boy went to his Scout troop and told a friend about what happened, hoping to get the friend to join him. The friend told his father and the police were called. Examination of the man's application for being a Big Brother showed that he had asked to be involved with boys 10 to 13 years old and boys who were "loners" or needed recognition.

## Methods of Approaching the Child

The child molester pursues his prey with purpose, and a direct comparison between stalking prey and the seduction of children may be made. The offender, once he has targeted a child, will track down and methodically approach the child and begin to work on seducing him. This may be as simple as approaching a child on the street, asking if the child wants a ride, or, as in the following example, catching a child by surprise.

A 10-year-old boy was mowing his front lawn when a man approached him, gave him a $5 bill, then walked away. He returned a few moments later, with the boy still holding the bill in his hand, and said, "I bet you're wondering why I gave you that money." At that moment, the man saw the boy's mother watching them from the window and he left.

The approach may also be as simple as staring at the child until eye contact is established. A smile or conversation follows, much like the way adults meet in bars. Another method of establishing eye contact is the furtive glance, wherein the offender finally catches the eye of the victim after repeated attempts.

Staring at the genital areas of the child, which then generates a conversation, is another method, as is direct solicitation. However, the most common approach is the establishment of a nonsexual relationship with the child.

The offender may also try to establish physical contact with the child in some way, perhaps legitimate at first, then turning to sexual activity. In front of parents, the offender can test his target, simply by putting his arm around the child and evaluating the child as a potential victim. When the offender is a trusted adult, such as a youth leader, the natural reaction of most parents is one of satisfaction and pride because every parent wants others to like their child. This method of approach is common on public transportation, where the offender sits next to his target. It involves invading the child's "personal space," actually touching the child by sitting too close to him. If the child doesn't move away or moves closer to the offender, the next step is for the offender to place his hand or arm in such a way as to "cop a feel" or rest it in an inappropriate place on the child's person.

For example, a man sat beside a young boy on a train, boarding after the child and his mother had sat down. The man sat so close to the child that the child was almost pressed against the wall of the car. After a while the man began to talk to the boy, asking sexually explicit questions and soliciting oral copulation and other acts. This was done in the daytime and a seat away from the boy's mother. At one point, the man reached into the boy's lap and felt the boy's inner thigh.

Another characteristic of some offenders is their tendency to pay more than the normal amount of physical or emotional attention to a child in their company. In situations where the offender has some relationship to the child or his family, this attention is often misinterpreted by the child and others as "affectionate" behavior, when in reality it is both a means of reducing the child's discomfort with touching and a way of testing the child's reaction to the contact. It is very blatant, as can be seen in this example of a relative of a child who wrote to "Dear Abby:"

> "My sister remarried six months ago after being a widow for nine years. The man she married is a handsome, outgoing, successful professional man. A problem has arisen that disturbs me and others of our family... It concerns my sister's son, who is 14 (I'll call him Jeff). At first we were glad that Jeff and his stepfather hit it off so well since Jeff had been fatherless for so long. But we are beginning to think they are too close. My brother-in-law

is very affectionate with Jeff. He hugs him constantly and kisses him too!
When he's near the boy, he reaches out and strokes his shoulder or his back.
And Jeff seems to appreciate and encourage such affectionate gestures [22].

The offender will often conceal his approach by legitimate physical contact or displays of affection such as hand-holding or rubbing the child's
shoulders, back, or head. This is particularly true for the person who establishes a relationship with the child. This type of legitimate touching then
degenerates to feeling the child's sexual areas or buttocks. The child who is
in great need of physical affection misinterprets this as genuine concern.

A variation of the physical contact approach is the use of what may be
perceived as legitimate contact to intersperse inappropriate sexual messages
to the child. This type of activity is often rationalized by the offender as
"teaching" the child what sex is all about or preparing him for later life. In
these cases, the offender begins by touching the child in what appears to be
a legitimate way, but then begins to talk about or do inappropriate sexually
related things. The child will recognize this and be confused, as was this girl
who wrote to "Dear Abby:"

"I am a 13-year-old girl with a problem I can't talk to anybody about. I have
an uncle who everybody thinks is the greatest. He's 39 and married. Lately
he has been pulling me on his lap, feeling me and trying to give me grown-
up kisses on the mouth. He used to be my favorite uncle, but now I feel funny
when he gets near me... I don't have a father... My uncle comes over a lot
and wants to teach me how to drive. I'd like to learn, but I really am afraid
to get into his car and go for a ride because of this funny feeling that comes
over me when he touches me. I don't think it's just my imagination [23].

Once the girl entered the car and sat in his lap to learn the controls, the
way many young children learn to drive, the offender would not only have
the child in the physical position he wanted, but would also have her in a
place where no one but the child could observe or question his actions.

This scenario also contains two other elements of seduction besides
supposed legitimate access to the child's body. In placing the child behind
the wheel, the offender is rewarding her sitting in his lap and enticing her to
return to do something she is excited about and shouldn't be doing. He has
also introduced the element of secrecy. The child is caught in a bind, because
if she does realize she has been molested, she will have to admit she broke
the law by driving, possibly getting both of them into trouble.

Previously in the chapter on the offender, we discussed the preferential
offender's commission of bold, daring, and high-risk acts. Although a persistent pattern in the preferential offender, this characteristic is not exclusive

to him. The characteristics of approach and actual molestation include the commission of the acts in front of others where people would generally not expect such a thing to happen. The general expectation would be that the acts of molestation are committed in complete secrecy with great care taken by the molester to avoid detection. Yet, for two reasons, this been found to be a false assumption.

First, the thrill of getting away with the act done, in many cases, directly in front of others, is in itself a source of excitement for the offender. Second, when discovered, it is often easier to defend against the allegation by claiming (a) it is not possible because of the inherent chances of being caught and that someone would see them in the act, and (b) because it is easier to say that the person misinterpreted what they saw.

Both of these defenses are based upon the erroneous assumption that no one would do such a thing in such a fashion, so therefore, (a) it could not have happened, and thus the complaining witness is discredited, and (b) the observer must have misinterpreted what they saw, and thus the eye witness account is discredited.

For example in Sacramento, California, in a department store, a man wandered through the hardware (life is stranger than fiction) department, drawing the attention of security as he paced back and forth due to his suspicious nature. Thinking he was a shoplifter, the security force followed him by use of a video camera, recording his actions. They watched in amazement as they found he was not interested in the tools, but rather, was stalking an eight-year-old girl, who was shopping with her father and younger brother. She was wearing a two-piece swimsuit which left much skin exposed.

The video tape of the incident showed the man walk up to the child, look around to see if anyone was watching him, then adjust himself (he was wearing a pair of gym shorts and a T-shirt) and fondle the girl three times — twice on the buttocks and once on the front of her body. After the acts, which were committed while the girl was standing directly beside her brother who was beside their father, he is seen walking to, what he thought was a place no one could see him. He turned, profile to the camera, and the bulge from his erect penis was so noticeable that he had to reach into his pants to readjust himself again.

He was detained outside the store by security officers who immediately went to the child and asked her what had happened. Apparently, she either didn't realize what had occurred or refused to acknowledge it. Because of the tape, he pled guilty as charged. Here, this was done with a stranger, in a public place. However, where the offender knows the child, it often happens while on family or group outings. In one case, the offender had the child sit on his lap, watching TV, in a living-room filled with his wife, the parents of the child, and another family. All the while the child was in his lap, he was digitally penetrating her vagina. This happens so frequently, it can be now identified as a distinct MO trait.

This activity may continue over a long period of time and vary in degree. A young girl was molested over a 10-year period by a 70-year-old man; her story exemplifies much of what has been said thus far.

"... When I was eleven-years-old and in the sixth grade in 1969, I joined 4-H and began taking western riding lessons from a farmer/horse trainer who was the horse project leader. His ranch was in (a small town in Northern California). Shortly after I began taking lessons this man began molesting me. His attacks on me continued for months and became more bold as time passed. As a naive twelve-year-old I did not understand what the slang language he used with me meant. As the months turned to years, I realized he was saying he wanted to have sexual intercourse with me and that he had had intercourse with my friend Patty. Patty was my classmate who introduced me to the idea of taking riding lessons. Soon my friend Patty was run off the ranch by this man's wife. Everyone saw (the wife) as the "crazy bitch," because they did not understand how she could be jealous of a twelve-year-old girl. Since this man did not have Patty anymore, he accelerated his pursuit of me. He continued to corner me in stalls and force himself on me by fondling areas of my body. He insisted I be responsive, but I was not responsive. He badgered me for months to let him have intercourse with me. I struggled for over a year to maintain my will not to give in to his incessant harassment. The thought of him overpowering me with intercourse was a nightmare. It would have meant I would lose control of what power I had left to defend myself against him and direct my own life. Finally I was broken and succumbed to his power. I was forced into an act I now know was rape.

After a time he captured not only my body, but my mind and spirit as well. That is to say that I pretended that the sexual attacks never happened. They would happen and I would put them out of my mind as soon as possible so I could get on to riding the horses and the other things I wanted to do. I was not at all in control of my life. He controlled my activities so that all I was involved in was the horses and himself. He was so obsessed with controlling my activities and knowing what I was doing all the time he made me call him every day on my lunch break from school. He made things very unpleasant for me if I did not call him. I tried to break away, but he made threats that scared me and I never got back control of my life.

During four years of this ten-year period I was employed by this man to train horses and give riding lessons. The horses became the only love in my life and he held all the strings where the horses were concerned, since my parents were not in a financial position to back my interest in horses.

When I came to Chico (a small, country-atmosphere, university town she was living in at the time of writing this) I still was not able to break from his clutches. I am from Yuba City (a small California community in the Sierra foothills), which is only one hour from Chico, so I did not make many breaks from home. I was employed by this man through that fall and summer. His sexual abuse of my body and myself continued through this whole period....

I am outraged at my own situation, even more so because I am not this man's only victim. There were other girls before myself and Patty who were victims of the man's perverted behavior. I have also learned that during part of the time period he was assaulting me, he was also assaulting my close friend who took lessons from him and also worked for him. He abused her in the same pattern as he did me. I'm sure I am not this man's last victim. He told me, when I confronted him with the fact that I was no longer going to be forced into anything against my will, that he would find other little girls. It scares me because I know many of the young girls he has taught since then.

I have also found out that his ex-wife knew what was going on, but she knew nothing would ever be done because of the prominent community families involved. As it has turned out so far, she was right. It enrages me to think how long this man has been terrorizing young females and that he thinks it is appropriate masculine behavior. He has always contrived his position to be one of unquestionable authority, supreme protector, and righteous instructor. In cutting such a figure it was easy for him to success-fully prey on impressionable, trusting young girls. Pursuing legal recourse meant telling my family about my sexual abuse by this man. It was very difficult to tell the people I love and who love me that I had been sexually assaulted three times a week for ten years of my life" [24].

## Ritualistic Abuse

Many cases throughout the country have involved children complaining of sexual abuse that appears to be connected to a "ritual" or ceremonial act or series of acts. Some have involved what has been termed "satanic," meaning worship of the anti-Christ or devil. Most notably, the Jordan, Minnesota and McMartin Preschool case in California, involved such allegations. As has been noted elsewhere in this text, these cases were not successful prosecutions. There have been others which were successful. Although, considered "ritual" in nature, they did not necessarily involve satanic worship. There have been cases reported in Florida, California, Colorado, Iowa, Michigan, Nevada, North Carolina, Ohio, Oregon, Texas, Utah, and Washington State [25]. This is important to consider because when faced with such allegations, professionals and the police, who are often more skeptical, will dismiss the disclosures because they are incredulous, involving bizarre and seemingly unbelievable acts.

A study commissioned by the National Center on Child Abuse and Neglect in 1994, found that although there were isolated instances of "lone perpetrators or couples" who used the specter of satan as a part of their method of operation, they found no substantiated reports of "wide spread, well-organized *satanic* rings of people" involved in child sexual abuse [26]. This is significant for several reasons. First, and foremost, we are only interested in the investigation of the commission of a crime — the abuse of a child or children. The investigation of child sexual abuse and exploitation is the focus of the inquiry, not the religious or philosophical outlook of the alleged perpetrator [27]. Robert Barry, Former Director of the Delinquency Control Institute, at the University of Southern California, points out that where there are crimes committed by those who worship satan, law enforcement must use the same techniques to investigate the criminal activity as it would with organized crime, going after the criminal element of the legitimate business they conduct [28].

Second, the fact that there are multiple perpetrators and/or victims (children) involved in an allegation, calls into play the need for additional resources and special practices. The research seems to indicate that although it is important to consider that a case under investigation is part of a larger, more intricate, plan, investigators should not expect to always find such connections and not invalidate a charge simply because no such connections are discovered. This can only be accomplished where care is taken to ensure that evidence is obtained and preserved as quickly as possible so that the perpetrators do not have the opportunity to dispose or alter it.

Third, not all "ritual" acts involve the worship of satan. Many are ritualistic in nature, often involving strange, sometimes repetitive, practices and acts, but, not necessarily religious or an act or worship. The fact that a "ritual" or practice of some sort is involved is important because it will provide tangible evidence to corroborate and support children's accounts. These acts may involve adults and children or any combination of persons. Although the list provided below is a summary of common reported characteristics of reported cases, not everything has been corroborated in subsequent investigations.

Children have described the ingestion of blood, feces, urine and other matter. The remnants of this conduct should leave trace evidence such as stains or physical deposits on floors and other objects, all of which should be looked for. Children have also described mock weddings where they were forced to wear certain garb and which involved intricate decorations and other objects which should be inquired about in interviews and sought in search warrants.

Children have described ceremonies where people chanted, stood in circles, and did other things which involved other children and adults, all of which should be the subject of inquiry with witnesses to corroborate and support the allegation.

In some cases, children have described the killing of animals and humans. The obvious physical or trace evidence, such as hairs, fibers, and fluids, should be sought in such cases as well as checks of files for missing persons, animals, or reports taken by animal control officers and pounds regarding missing or mutilated pets.

Children have described the use of daggers, knives, and other objects in both the actual abuse and the "ritual" involved. Symbols such as pentagrams, inverted crosses, and other designs have been seen by children.

The use of candles and burning lamps are a common experience. The remnants of wax, smoke damage, flame charring, lamp fuels, and matches should be sought and inquired about.

Photographs have also been reported to have been taken and confirmed in some cases.

Practices have been claimed to have occurred in abandoned buildings, churches, and cemeteries. These locations may retain physical evidence and the observation and confirmation of a child's description may serve to corroborate an account.

Children have described masks and special clothing they were compelled to wear and which were adorned by others.

Children have described buildings where the windows have been blackened or covered.

In short, when asked about what to look for, "look for evidence of a crime" [29]. All of the things described above, if they are found as described by children, which may constitute physical acts or conduct, paraphernalia, or other tangible objects, are significant in their ability to corroborate testimony or identify locations, perpetrators, or conscious acts or conduct.

### Purpose of Ritual Elements

Numbers of investigators and clinicians have looked at cases involving ritualistic acts to see how and why the crimes were committed in the manner they were. Of them, the Los Angeles County Commission For Women, Ritual Abuse Task Force, best summarizes the reasons we see such conduct in abuse and exploitation [30]. The ritual elements may be for any one or combination a of three reasons:

1.  Part of a shared belief or worship system in which the victim is being indoctrinated.
2.  Used to intimidate victims into silence.

3. Elements (are introduced to make the allegations) so unbelievable to those unfamiliar with these crimes that these elements detract from the credibility of the victims and make prosecution of crimes very difficult [31].

Although the Commission report describes mind control as a separate element, what it really comes down to is the practices are employed to control and dominate the victims. Under the first theory above, the acts of abuse and ritual are used to make the child want to belong to the group. The dynamics are similar to those discussed in sex rings earlier in the previous chapter. The child will also come to believe that the conduct engaged in is permissible and/or deserved. The Accommodation Syndrome also explains much of the child's involvement in this phase.

Where fear is the inducing factor, the child will come to believe that to go against the belief system and its concomitant acts, will subject the child to unbearable pain, suffering, and, perhaps, death. Children have been subjected to "magical surgery," wherein a bomb was supposedly planted inside them and they were told it would explode and kill them and the person they tell, should they do so. They have been told that they were the recipients of "the devil's heart" in a transplant and it will take control of them if they tell or cause them pain if they don't do what the perpetrators want.

Lastly, either implied or expressed is the threat or implication that what they have been exposed to is so unbelievable that no one will take the child seriously if they tell. Sadly, this is true in many cases. The result is that the child feels utterly helpless and at a loss as to how to get out of the situation [32].

It has been documented that some offenders, who have no connections to any ritualistic group or practice what-so-ever, will purposely introduce an element of ritual for the express purpose of discrediting the child, should the child tell. For example, they mislead young children about what is happening by telling them they are being sodomized by a snake or other animal. They drug the children with hallucinogens and play "tricks" on the mind about what is going on.

In short, there is no easy way to summarize the ritualistic abusive incidents or characterize them into, simple, quantifiable boxes. The key in these investigations is to do basic police work — take the information as it is presented, confer with experts to identify the significance to make criminal connections, if necessary, and try to collect evidence to support or refute the allegations.

# References and Notes

1. "Dear Abby" ©1983, Universal Press Syndicate. Reprinted with permission.

2. Loretta Schwartz-Nobel, "Child Pornography and the Secret World of the Pedophile," *Philadelphia Inquirer Magazine,*. 11/6/83, pp. 12-31.

3. *Boys Together*, Detroit 1980. Out-of-date publication from the author's files

4. Interview from the author's files

5. *Hermes*, Sept./Oct. 1976, as quoted to the Illinois Legislative Investigative Commission, *Sexual Exploitation of Children,* Report to the Illinois General Assembly, Chicago, Aug. 1980.

6. *Boy}s Together,* 1980.

7. Lanning, 1987.

8. Schwartz-Nobel, 1983.

9. "Man Charged with Rape Finds Alleged Victims on Computer Bulletin Board," *American Family Association Journal,* July 1994.

10. Lori Steinhorst, *When the Monster Comes Out of the Closet,* Rose Publishing, Salem, OR, 1994, p. 1.

11. From the author's case files.

12. Steinhorst, 1994, p. 5.

13. Linda Tschirhart Sanford, *The Silent Children,* Anchor Press, New York, 1980; *San Francisco Chronicle,* 12/24/78 and 12/7/83.

14. Schwartz-Nobel, 1983, p. 17.

15. National Broadcasting Company, *NBC Magazine with David Brinkley,* New York: NBC Television Network, 9/3/81.

15. Ralph W. Bennett, "The Relationship Between Pornography and Extrafamilial Child Sexual Abuse," *The Police Chief,* Feb. 1991.

16. Statement by Arthur Gay Bishop to the National Conference on Pornography, Denver, CO, Oct. 1985.

17. Letter from author's case files.

18. Schwartz-Nobel, 1983, p. 19.

19. Sanford, 12/24/78.

20. *NAMBLA Bulletin,* "Feedback," April 1983.

21. Interview with child victim from author's case files.

22. Dear Abby ©1983 Universal Press Syndicate. Reprinted with permission.

23. Ibid.

24. Letter to the author.

25. *Believe the Children Newsletter,* "A Decade of Disclosures: Ritual Child Abuse in the United States," 11:2, Summer, 1994.

26. Child Advocacy Council of San Mateo and Santa Clara Counties, *Newsletter,* Winter, 1995, quoting the *San Jose Mercury News,* October 31, 1994.

27. Kenneth V. Lanning, "Satanic, Occult, Ritualistic Crime: A Law Enforcement Perspective," *The Police Chief,* October 1989, and see *Think Tank Report: Investigation of Ritualistic Abuse Allegations,* The National Resource Center on Child Sexual Abuse, October, 1989.

28. Robert J. Barry, "Satanism: The Law Enforcement Response," *The National Sheriff,* Feb/Mar, 1987.

29. Ibid at Note 3.

30. Los Angeles Commission for Women, *Ritual Abuse: Definitions, Glossary, Use of Mind Control,* March 15, 1991.

31. LACFW 1991.

32. Ibid.

## Additional Reading

Groth, A. Nicholas and Birnbaum, Jean., *Men Who Rape: The Psychology of the Offender,* New York: Plenum, 1981.

Lanning, Kenneth V., "Criminal Investigation of Sexual Victimization of Children," *The APSAC Handbook on Child Maltreatment,* 1996.

Martin, Lloyd, and Haddad, Jill, *We Have a Secret,* Crown Summit Books, Newport Beach, CA, 1982.

Tyler, R. P. "Toby", "Child Pornography: The International Exploitation of Children," Paper presented at the Fourth International Congress on Child Abuse and Neglect, Paris, France, 9/9/82.

# Child Pornography Investigation

4

At the present time, it is illegal to produce child pornography in most countries [1]. According to the U.S. Customs Service, the "traditional source countries are: Sweden, Denmark, and The Netherlands. France, Japan, Thailand, and the Philippines, are considered new sources [2]. In the past, North America, Europe, and Asia were areas where most commercial child pornography was produced. It is now possible to see children from South America, Europe, Australia, Asia, India, and Africa, taken by individual offenders who trek to these places. In 1997, the Center On Speech, Equality, and Harm, researched laws enacted in 165 countries throughout the world, finding very little unified efforts or statutes to comprehensively address this problem. Only 31 countries had laws that prohibited production, distribution, and possession of child pornography. This approach, dealing with all three issues, is proposed to be the most successful in eradicating this problem [3]. The United Nation's Commission on Human Rights, 52nd Session, reported that throughout the world, the problem of child pornography and the use of children in its production is a problem that is not adequately being addressed by governmental agencies [4].

## Legal Approaches to Control

In the U.S., prior to 1977, only two states had laws specifically prohibiting the use of children in obscene materials and performances. Today, virtually all states have such laws.

Federal law had led the way in attacking the various aspects of the criminal problem involving child pornography. It has expanded its prohibitions to include all children to the age of 18; made it unnecessary to prove commercial interests; removed the obscenity requirement; removed the gender requirement for the Mann Act (18 U.S.C. Sec.2423) involving transporting persons interstate for immoral purposes; included advertising as prohibited conduct; subjected the crimes herein to the Racketeer Influenced and Corrupt Organization (RICO) statutes, thereby increasing both the techniques available to investigate and the penalties for violations; made it illegal to possess; provided for civil and criminal forfeitures; and, lastly, expanded the civil remedies for personal injury in these matters [5]. It, of course, remains illegal to import child pornography into this country in all of its forms.

Unfortunately, the states have not kept up with the federal government in its aggressive legislative bent to eradicate child pornography. In only a handful of states is it illegal to merely possess. This one law would make investigations so much easier, as all one would have to establish is that an offender knowingly holds it in his possession. The illicit act becomes the key to the offender's door through a search warrant.

## Conduct versus Obscenity

The concept of obscenity will be discussed in greater detail in the following pages, however, at this time, let us direct our discussion to the most successful way to protect children through investigation of child pornography.

As the United States Supreme Court said in the *Ferber* case, protecting children is a compelling interest [6]. It likened the making of child pornography to an act of abuse in itself and the visual record of that act the perpetuation of further child abuse. In the same case, it permitted the conviction of the defendant without having to prove the subject matter was obscene under the applicable "morals" standard. In short, it was telling us that it is the *conduct* involved which must be prohibited. Conduct it labeled, on its own, as abuse.

Child abuse statutes, including those pertaining to sexual abuse and assault, are classified as crimes against persons. They generally have stiffer penalties and carry higher priorities than morals crimes. Judges and juries, in general, agree that children should be protected with little convincing. There is a greater urgency in dealing with this crime problem as an abuse issue. If a child is being abused, there is both a legal and ethical mandate to stop it and prevent further trauma.

In general, people are not interested in protecting other people's morals. Judges, juries, even most public agency administrations, don't give it the same priority as abuse. So, why fight an uphill battle to convince someone to act in a morals case, when you may present it as an abuse issue, and have little or no resistance? Don't treat the medium in your case as "dirty pictures," treat them as pictorial evidence of the commission of the act of child abuse. If there were photos of a bank robbery in progress, taken by the bank's security cameras, the photos would be evidence of a felony in progress. Your community, and superiors, alike, will give you more support and you will have a greater likelihood of your case being charged with a successful prosecution.

To understand how you might attack the problem in your community, let us examine some of the issues involved in different state statues. Legislative approaches to controlling the problem vary, generally addressing the production and distribution of obscene or pornographic materials involving children. Because of the varying laws in different states and the wide range of possible penalties for the crimes, we will examine other statutes that may apply to the pornography problem besides those that deal with obscenity. These may provide greater penalties, and greater leeway for prosecuting attorneys to make a disposition at trial.

In all states there are sex offense statues that proscribe specific acts. This is helpful in child pornography investigations because the statutes involve prohibited conduct, usually the conduct depicted in the material in question. Most often, the offenses are felonies when the act involves a child, which means that more severe penalties are provided and the investigator can do things he wouldn't be able to in a misdemeanor investigation.

## Child Abuse Statutes

All states have child abuse laws that prohibit certain types of conduct with children. In addition, the state may intervene in certain conduct or situations on behalf of the child's best interests. Although these laws mostly address the issue of "fitness" of the parents to care for a child, they also may apply to anyone who places a child in a position of jeopardy. In most situations where children are used in pornography by a parent, an argument can be made that the child has been placed by the adult in a position where he is in danger because he is being physically (sexually) abused or is suffering emotional distress or abuse. In some states, this line of argument is actually expressed in the statutes as pornography "promoting child abuse." This applies to *any situation* where the child is involved in pornography, regardless of parental knowledge, consent, or indifference. These statutes are generally felonies when there is an injury, and allow for the state's intervention and removal of the child from the situation.

## Child Protection Statutes

There are also statutes intended to protect children from becoming delinquent and to protect them from individuals contributing to their delinquency. The use of children in sexual activities may be considered, in and of itself abusive, as corrupting their morals and therefore causing them to become delinquent. Statutes that protect children from being exposed to such things as pornography and premature sexual knowledge or conduct are often helpful in child pornography cases.

## Child Labor Laws

Child labor laws in most states are intended to protect children from being exploited and/or placed in working conditions that are injurious to their health (now included in some statutes is emotional well being). Generally, these statutes deal with restrictions on the type of work (paid or not) children may engage in, payment, and licensing and inspection of working places. Given the conditions children are often subjected to when they are involved in making child pornography, and the investigative and administrative powers provided to the state in these areas, persons enforcing child labor laws can be very helpful to a police investigator.

## Federal Law on Commerce

Lastly, there is the federal legislation mentioned earlier. Where the conduct involves interstate or international commerce, federal law applies, and the resources of the federal government may be brought to bear on the offender. The FBI, U.S. Customs, and the U.S. Postal authorities may now enter the picture in far more cases than in the past, and a definite connection to interstate criminal activity does not always have to be demonstrated for these agencies to become involved.

## Child Abuse Reporting Laws

In every state there is a child-abuse reporting law requiring that certain conduct involving children be reported to the authorities. These statutes include definitions of what is considered abuse; sexual abuse is included in virtually every statute. These laws define the class of persons mandated to report (generally those involved with children in a professional capacity), the requirements of reporting, and the responsibilities of the person making the report. In most states, failure to report suspected abuse is a misdemeanor. In all states except Wyoming (where the age of consent is 16 years), the definition of a child is someone under 18 years. In several states, photo finishers or photo developers are included in the class of persons required to report.

## Child Pornography and Obscenity Statutes

Today, child pornography laws attack the issue on one of two levels. They either describe certain depictions or actions as "obscene" or define them as a form of child abuse or conduct. In the past, some laws considered the use of children in pornography as safeguarded by First Amendment guarantees of free expression. According to the First Amendment, the state may not interfere with the free expression of ideas. This includes all forms of expression, including photography or their reproduction in magazines or books. This means the prosecutor would not have to prove that the matter or actions depicted in the matter or performance(s) in question fall within the legal definitions of obscenity.

## Miller vs. California

The final product that is sold, exhibited, or displayed is what is subject to examination. In many states, the statutes that address "obscenity" do not differentiate between materials that depict adults and children. Although perhaps easier to prove "obscene," matter depicting children engaged in sexually explicit conduct is not necessarily, per se, obscene. To prove that the matter or performance in question is obscene, the legal test that must be applied is commonly referred to as the "Miller Standard." It is the result of the United States Supreme Court decision *Miller vs . California*, [7]. In order to adjudge something obscene, *Miller* says that *each prong* of a three-pronged test must be satisfied:

1. Whether the average person applying contemporary community standards would find that the work, taken as a whole, appeals to prurient interest.
2. Whether the work depicts or describes in a patently offensive way sexual conduct specifically defined by the applicable state law.
3. Whether the work, taken as a whole, lacks serious literary, artistic, political, or scientific value.

The problem is that not all depictions of children can be easily placed into each of these categories to satisfy the three-pronged test; therefore, some cases fail to pass muster under the constitutional protections of the First Amendment.

## Laws Based on Sexual Conduct with Children

Some states have laws that comply with *Miller,* defining sexual exploitation of children without maintaining the obscenity requirement, but prohibiting the use of children in filming or photographing of specifically defined acts. Other states only outlaw the use of children in the production of materials where specific sexual conduct is involved. Most states prohibit the sale and distribution of matter that depicts what is considered obscene or contains depictions of the specifically defined acts. California has a broader (more liberal) definition of obscenity, but also has specific criminal statutes prohibiting specific conduct involving children that do not have to meet the obscenity standards.

The intent of the legislatures of the individual states that enacted child pornography statutes was that by restricting the production and distribution of child pornography, they would prevent a form of child abuse. They hoped to focus attention on the use of children and not on the final product of the pornographer. The argument has been made over and over again that the use of children to produce child pornography is abuse in itself. Someone who commits an act of child abuse is not protected by the First Amendment, which only protects freedom of expression. The making of child pornography involves conduct — the use of a child — to produce some form of "expression" (generally called "art"). The state has the ability to restrict certain conduct if that conduct involves a combination of expression *and* action (conduct). This is especially true when the state has "a substantial interest in regulating the non-speech or conduct" aspect of the material. Clearly, the state has such an interest in preventing child abuse [8]. This is also true even if the material is adjudged not to be obscene, but is abusive in nature.

### Ferber vs. New York

The landmark case, *Ferber vs. New York* [9] affirmed the right of the state to limit the distribution of material depicting children engaged in certain sexual conduct (regardless of whether the material was legally obscene) because that conduct is abusive in nature. It said that use of children in child pornography "is harmful to the physiological, emotional, and mental health of the child," adding that "prevention of sexual exploitation and the abuse of children constitutes a government objective of surpassing importance" to the right of free expression.

## Elements of Pornography Crimes

Laws forbidding obscenity generally do not mention the word *pornography*. According to the dictionary, pornography is basically writings, pictures, drawings, or other visual media intended to stimulate sexually. *Obscenity*, on the other hand, means something dirty, often described as containing filth or excrement. Using these definitions, it is possible to have one without the other. Not all pornography would be considered legally obscene. Therefore, for those who must work with a law that applies the obscenity standards to child pornography, a thorough understanding of the elements of obscenity is imperative. Investigators in states that don't apply the obscenity standard to child pornography but have laws that follow the *Ferber* case must know what acts fall within its purview.

## Jurisdiction, Venue, Statute of Limitations

In either situation, the first things that must be established are jurisdiction, venue, and that the crime was committed within the statute of limitations. *Jurisdiction* means the location in which the crime was committed, and determines which agency has investigative responsibility. Establishing *venue* means determining the court that has jurisdiction to try the violation(s). *Statute of limitations* refers to the time frame in which legal proceedings must be initiated after the crime is committed or discovered, depending on how the criminal code applies to the specific statute violated.

## *Miller's* Community Standards

Under the *Miller* decision, the first prong of the obscenity test involves establishing "community standards" against which all of the matter may be compared. We won't discuss the everchanging theories of what constitutes community standards, but I will say that primarily the term "community standards" implies an area greater than just the locale in which the case is tried. However, there have been cases throughout the United States where the local (town or city) norms were used as a means of determining standards. I mention this because investigators and prosecutors are often reluctant to pursue cases, thinking that they are limited to the geographic area in which they live in which the "standards" will be drawn. Clearly this problem must be researched by individuals who consider undertaking a pornography investigation, and I cannot anticipate what situation every investigator will face in his community.

I will leave this subject with the comment that proving that something is obscene in a particular area might be much more difficult than if it were evaluated in another area.

## *The Matter as a Whole*

In each part of the *Miller* test of obscenity, the term "taken as a whole" is mentioned. This means examining the matter under scrutiny in its entirety. It is not possible to take only some portion of the matter and determine that it falls within the definition of obscenity, because the rest of the material may have some purpose or benefit to the community at large.

In *Miller*, there is a reference to engaging in prohibited conduct pertaining to local statutes. This may vary from state to state, but the acts described therein are most commonly sexual intercourse, sodomy, oral copulation, bestiality, and something akin to lewd exhibition of the genitals. Each of the sexual acts may be actually depicted or only simulated. Statutes that follow *Ferber* also have similar prohibitions and definitions of conduct.

### Value Test

The *Miller* test also includes an evaluation of whether or not the matter possesses some serious value as art, makes a contribution to science, is of educational benefit, or makes some political statement. Therefore, it may be necessary to get beyond the issues of art, science, education, and politics and prove that the *sole purpose* of child pornography is the sexual stimulation or arousal of the offender or the rest of the child molester population. In discussing this aspect of the standard, it must be shown that the primary purpose of the child pornography in question is to perpetuate the victimization of children — to blackmail children, lower the inhibitions of children, spark curiosity, demonstrate the propriety of the acts, and entice children to become involved in the acts. In doing so, it will be possible to demonstrate that the material has no valid or contributory purpose or value.

## The Medium of Depiction

Careful attention must be paid to the type of material limited by the statute. Most laws follow federal guidelines, which include "films, photographs, negatives, slides, books, magazines, or other visual or print medium." Some laws also prohibit certain sexual conduct taking place in "live performances" (which may or may not fall within the definition of obscenity).

## The Level of Involvement

Another concern in deciding how to attack the problem is determining the role played by the individual the investigation has focused on:

1. Is he the person who actually takes the pictures; if so, what is done with them?
2. Is he the person who develops and prints the films; if so, where does he get them and what does he do with them?
3. Is he the person who makes or prints the matter in which children are depicted in sexually explicit poses?
4. Is he the person who transports and delivers the matter or is he the person who shows or has the matter shown to others?
5. Is he the person who simply buys or obtains the material from others?

Each of these types of offenders will require a different approach and will present the opportunity to get at someone else in the chain. The manner in which this individual is approached will greatly affect the chances of getting to the rest of the chain.

## The Age of Consent of the Child

Individual states have different ages of majority and consent. They also have different definitions in their statutes as to the age of children who may not be used in obscene activity. Be sure you check the ages listed in the individual statutes, as they may differ from the age of majority or consent within your own state. In addition, the age of the child involved may determine the penalties and/or the type of prohibited conduct. This is where the federal authorities may be able to help. If your local or state statute has an age limitation that prohibits action in a case where the child is older than your laws specify as actionable, a federal statute may apply. For example, if your state only restricts conduct involving children under 16 and you have a photograph mailed to you of a child over 16, but under 18 (which falls within the federal prohibition), the postal authorities can act under the federal laws governing use of the mails.

## Sexual Purposes of Viewer

Some states have also included within their definitions of obscenity or illicit conduct the prohibition of the use of children in the production of matter that is intended for the "sexual gratification or stimulation" of any person who might view the product. This is helpful, as it recognizes the true purpose of child pornography.

## Scienter

Another element that must be proved in child pornography cases is that of *"scienter,"* or guilty knowledge. This means that the person being prosecuted knew or reasonably should have known that the child involved was under the stated age or that the matter depicts a child under that age. This means that if the matter is a magazine or book, it will be necessary to demonstrate that the person being prosecuted knew that it contained within its pages a minor (of stated age) depicted engaged in the prohibited conduct. If conduct is under scrutiny, and that conduct involved a child under that stated age, it must be shown that the person involved a child under the stated age and it must be shown that the person knew or reasonably should have known that the child was under that age.

# Legal and Evidentiary Concerns in Child Pornography Investigations

Child pornography can be viewed as an evidentiary product of the crime of sexual exploitation or child molestation and should be treated as such. We have a greater responsibility than simply confiscating contraband in the investigation of child pornography cases. Our ultimate goal must be the prevention and elimination of the sexual abuse of children through the medium of child pornography. Therefore we must go further than simply dealing with the materials seized at the moment. We must seek out its source, identify the children involved, and identify and prosecute those involved in the making of the material.

## Protection and Care for Children Involved

An integral part of the process must also be insuring that the children who are identified are provided appropriate counseling and follow-up care, because child pornography has serious effects on the children portrayed. Discussions and research on pornography often focus on the effects on the viewer rather than on the effects on the child subject. The latter is particularly crucial in evaluating the harm of child pornography.

Children used in pornography are desensitized and conditioned to respond as sexual objects. They are frequently ashamed of and/or embarrassed about their portrayal in such material. They must deal with the permanency and wide circulation of this record of their sexual abuse.

Some types of sexual activity can be repressed and hidden from public knowledge; child victims can fantasize that some day the activity will be over and they can make a fresh start. Many children, especially adolescent boys, vehemently deny their involvement with a pedophile, but there is no denying or hiding from a sexually explicit photograph or videotape. The child in a photograph or videotape is young forever; therefore the material can be used repeatedly for many years. Some children have even committed crimes in attempts to retrieve or destroy the permanent records of their molestation. The difficulty in trying to achieve the goal of child protection is what often makes these investigations fall short of successful prosecution.

In situations where the *Miller* standard must be met, cases often fail to get beyond the charging prosecutor, because the material under scrutiny contains at least one section that might have some "scientific, artistic, educational, literary, or political" value. The most common defense in obscenity cases is the offender's claim that there was no intent to be obscene, only to educate, be artistic, or perform some scientific study.

Given today's lax moral standards, it is very difficult to convict someone on an obscenity charge. The problem is that neither we as individuals nor the general public at large can determine what is obscene. This must be done by a judge or jury, and only after the matter in question has had "its day in court." Even though we believe that children are "psychologically" harmed merely by posing for pictures in the nude for someone's sexual gratification, it is unclear whether or not such posing would fall within the definition of obscenity under the *Miller* standard.

## Technical Defenses

Homer Young (one of America's leading authorities on obscenity investigations [now deceased]) found that obscenity cases are most often lost because of the following technicalities: (1) illegal search and seizure; and (2) chain of evidence broken; investigators unable to sufficiently identify when and where the evidence was seized.

Young points out that the worst enemy in these investigations is your fellow officers who want to "help out," who destroy or misplace evidence, and who tamper with or move evidence [10]. Evidence collection is a paramount concern, and begins with the initiation of the case investigation. Consider what kind of evidence you will encounter, i.e., its size and volume. What will you need to carry it away, package it, and review it?

## Evidence Log

To eliminate some of the arguments often raised at the trial, an evidence log should be created to ensure that all access to evidence is documented from the time of seizure to the time of court presentation. This should include where the item(s) was/were seized, who seized it, who was present, where it was reviewed. Each item should be labeled with the time and date seized. If the evidence is opened for any reason, examined, or removed from the evidence area, an appropriate notation should be made in the log. This means continuing maintenance of the log after the evidence is turned over to the prosecutor. Access to the material should be limited, regardless of where it is.

## Proving the Child is a Minor

One of the greatest difficulties in child pornography and exploitation cases is proving that the child was a minor at the time of the production of the material. It is difficult primarily because the identities of the models are generally not known. Some state laws permit proof of the model's age through the use of expert testimony.

## Proving Intent to Distribute

Proving intent to distribute is also very difficult. It will often require many of the same article to make the charge stick. This is where the knowledge of how the child molester works and the ability to bring his actions into perspective come into play. In some states, intent to distribute is legally defined as three or more of the same items in the possession of the person under investigation [11].

## The Uncooperative Child Witness

Another problem is that children used in child pornography often don't want to get involved in prosecuting the offender. They deny that anything happened to them, even when the photographs are shown to them. They will often say that the pictures depict someone other than themselves, even if the offender has admitted taking the photographs. The children involved in child pornography experience the same psychological problems as incest victims and must therefore be cared for exactly the same way as other sex crime victims.

A California police detective received a call from a photolab in their city reporting they had found 37 slides depicting a young boy in various states of undress, mostly nude. There were no sexually explicit shots, only the boy standing in a shower in various seductive poses with a "semi-erect" penis.

The detective was able to identify the family involved, finding the boy lived with his parents. He prepared and executed a search warrant, discovering hundreds of slides of naked boys, including some more of the original boy, locked in a box by the boy's father.

When the detective interviewed the boy, he immediately denied he was the one in the photos. He finally admitted it was him, but denied any sex acts had occurred with his father, defending his father as not being a "homosexual." Of course, the father also denied any sexual activity.

It took several interviews of both parties before the detective was finally able to obtain the confidence of the boy and the full details of his abuse, which involved oral copulation by the father upon him, fondling, and digital penetration of his anus by his father on numerous occasions.

## Sources and Types of Child Pornography

### Hard- and Soft-Core

Pornography can generally be broken down into two basic types that can be used to define the action depicted. The first is often referred to as "soft-core" pornography. Here, the material does not show actual sexual acts. It includes depictions of naked people and people involved with others in sexual acts. However, soft-core pornography only shows simulations or depictions that veil the act by interposing the body or other object between the camera and the action.

The second type is often referred to as "hard-core" pornography. In this type of matter, the actual act is explicitly depicted. It includes the depiction of penetration and ejaculation.

The type of acts depicted in child pornography are limited only by the imagination. In single activity, children are depicted naked, in various poses accentuating the genitals or simply posed in "normal" activity. It may show them engaged in simple manual masturbation or using foreign objects. In activity with others, children may be depicted in sexual acts with children and/or adults. The activity may be with one or more individuals or with animals. Child pornography, like of the adult world, also involves violence, wherein children are tortured, beaten, and physically abused for those who are interested in sadomasochistic acts or "discipline." It also depicts children tied up, bound, and gagged for the "bondage" crowd. Although no police officer has ever seen a commercially produced or distributed "snuff film" involving an actual mutilation and murder of children, these films are a highly sought-after commodity.

## Commercial and Homemade Child Pornography

Another distinction in child pornography involves the manner of production and distribution. Commercial child pornography includes matter that is professionally produced and printed, generally in large quantities, with paid models and production staffs. The main difference between this and other types of pornography is that this matter is produced with the intention of making money. This matter comes in various forms, including magazines, films, videotapes, and single pictures or sets of pictures.

Homemade child pornography is produced and distributed by either an individual or groups of individuals who produce it at home and distribute it by trading it or selling it among the underground or keep it for themselves. The major reason for producing this type of matter is for sexual gratification of either the individual producer or others who may see it. The type of matter this group produces is generally limited in scope by the sophistication of those within the group.

Both types of pornography may be produced in original form by the individuals involved or reproduced from existing material. The extent of commercial child pornography is only a very small part of the overall problem. Very few of the many individuals who make their own child pornography ever send it to a commercial producer. Clearly, the number of people who use this homemade material for personal use and exchange outnumber the commercial producers.

There is another facet to the provision of material to commercial producers and distributors. Although the original taker of the pictures intends to use the photos only for his own pleasure or for exchange, he has no such assurances from those to whom he sends them. It is not uncommon for the party who receives the material in "exchange" or on "loan" to send it to a commercial pornographer after copying it.

## Technical and Simulated Child Pornography

The Federal Child Protection Act of 1984 defines a child as anyone under the age of 18. Therefore, a sexually explicit photograph of a 17-year-old girl is *technically* child pornography. However, such a photograph might be of sexual interest to more than pedophiles.

The production, distribution, and, in some cases, possession of such child pornography should be investigated under appropriate child pornography statutes. However, the investigator should understand that the consumers of such material are not necessarily pedophiles.

On the other hand, sexually explicit photography of 19-year-old or older males or females are not legally child pornography. But if the person portrayed in such material is young looking, dressed young, or made up to look young (hair in pigtails, shaved vagina, etc.), the material could be of interest to pedophiles. This is *simulated* child pornography, designed to appeal to the pedophile, but is not legally child pornography because the individuals portrayed are over 18.

What is worse, it is now possible to "morph" a picture that is not considered to fall under any act into one that might. For example, a popular child actress was posed in a natural setting wearing age-appropriate clothing. The image was altered by computer to depict her in the nude. Computer technology has allowed such alterations to become commonplace and the laws are having difficulty keeping up with it. At present, such an act would be illegal in the United States, but, not necessarily anywhere else. In its report, on the Child Pornography Prevention Act of 1995, Congress found that computer generated child pornography poses the same threat to the well-being of children as photographic pornography [12].

## Manner of Distribution

The manner of distribution of both types of material varies. However, because of the laws governing such distribution, it is done in a clandestine fashion. There are basically three methods of distribution: hand-to-hand, travel, and mailing. In hand-to-hand distribution, those involved in the transaction generally know each other. The buyer/trader either knows the seller from post experience or has been referred to him by someone the seller knows. For example, in the few commercial pornography shops that still handle child pornography transactions, the store will not sell to anyone unless it "knows" the buyer from past experience. In the underground exchange, people doing the trading, buying, and/or selling are just as leery as the commercial operators because of their awareness of police "sting" operations. For this reason, the majority of transactions are done through the mail. Child pornography is advertised in underground publications or by the commercial producers themselves in "poop sheet" mailings and the pornography itself. The majority of exchanges occur through an informal network within the underground. The mail-order business offers virtual anonymity to both the seller and the buyer.

Because of the illegality of the production of child pornography, it is generally done in secret. Individuals who take pictures of children they are involved with tell the children not to say anything and take great measure to ensure that the pornography is not discovered. Their collections are hidden in various ways to avoid discovery, and they use the type of production equipment that will ensure they are not found out accidentally.

The use of instant developing film and cameras, videotape, and home labs for developing and printing their material is extremely common. In this country, some people use the "fast photo" services (which use mechanical devices to develop, print, and package the film and prints) to avoid discovery if they are not sophisticated enough to do it themselves. For example, a man was found to have given 185 35-mm color slides of boys 16- and 17-years-old involved in sexual activities to a drugstore photo service for developing. The slides were discovered by computer failure. The man was found to have sold the pictures he had previously printed from the slides to child pornography producers, who in turn published them in magazines. Police also found that he had advertised the photographs in underground publications. It is believed that North America, in particular the United States, provides the largest single source of child pornography photos to commercial producers. Western European nations are second, with Asia and the rest of the world not far behind.

## Amateur Sources

With few exceptions, all commercial producers of child pornography are dependent on the individual amateur producer for new materials. The commercial operators therefore advertise within their own publications and those in the underground for the "amateur" to send them material. Depending on the content and age of the child depicted in the material, an individual may make as much as several hundred dollars. Here is a typical ad in a child pornography magazine calling for submission of materials:

> Turn your old pre-teen photos to money. We pay top price for amateur photos, even imperfect ones. Your contribution will be greatly appreciated and will help us continue this series. As an extra bonus, we aim to bring an amateur photo column in our next issue [13].

Rarely, however, will amateurs use their own personal photos for commercial purposes. When they do, they are proud of their ability to secure such photographs and they want to show off. In a case where a 23-year-old man was arrested for molesting two girls, aged 8 and 7, he was found to have a large quantity of child pornography depicting young girls. He was also found to have taken many nude pictures of local girls. The authorities found a letter from the man to a pornography distributor, expressing his hope that his own little daughters, aged 2 and 3, would appear in the magazines when they got older.

## Commercial Production and Distribution

Child pornography producers will often exchange photos for pornography subscriptions. With the increased attention by the authorities to child pornography violations, both the people who make the original material and those who produce commercial pornography have had to reduce their activities as far as open exchange is concerned. For example, *Lolita*, perhaps the most popular child pornography magazine, had to reduce publication from one issue a month to one or two each year because of limited access to new materials.

Commercial child pornography imported into the United States is generally smuggled in. A common method is for the purchaser to buy several other pornographic publications, not necessarily considered contraband, and see if they are intercepted by the authorities. If there is no interference, the buyer will make another purchase, ordering both the child pornography and the other type of material at the same time. The seller will package the child porn inside the material that is less likely to be seized, hoping that the authorities will only look as far as the material that is normally not seized.

Another way of smuggling child porn into the country is to represent it as something that is non-pornographic or unrelated to the pornography trade. It is not uncommon to find child pornography concealed within other printed matter, such as travel guides to Europe. When packaged, the legitimate printed matter is placed on top and on the bottom of the packaging, where it will most likely be examined. The child pornography is then slipped into the center of the package between the "cushions" of legitimate material. It is also not uncommon to find that child pornography is imported by concealing it inside furniture, pottery, and other items.

To avoid detection, pornographers and their subscribers do many things to make identifying them difficult. Both use fictitious names, and almost all of them use post office boxes or mail drops as mailing addresses. Knowing that customs officials in many countries target certain mail for examination originating from countries that produce child pornography, the producers of the material often reroute their mailings through nontargeted countries. For example, with the heat placed on mail coming into the United States from certain European countries, Canada has found that it has been receiving a high volume of child pornography. A recent report noted that 37.4% of the seizures of child pornography in Canada in 1983 came from the United States, the rest from other countries. The same report said that the seizures revealed that a similar amount of pictures and magazines was discovered in the mailings [14].

According to William Von Raab, Commissioner of the U.S. Customs Service, in 1984, 85% of all imported child pornography seized by Customs originated in The Netherlands, Denmark, and Sweden [15]. According to INTERPOL, Germany was the major producer, The Netherlands and the United Kingdom were the major distribution centers, and the United States was the largest market. Statutory changes in these countries have shifted the production and distribution to South East Asia [16]. The problems in enforcement in the Asian and European countries are that definitions of obscenity are different, and the age ceiling for involved children varies from country to country. It is apparent that because of the lax nature of the laws, heavier enforcement efforts in the U.S. and the U.K., and their own lack of enforcement, child pornography production has increased in those countries. Still, another report by the Center on Speech, Equality and Harm, indicates that in the 1990s, there are no child pornography laws in the countries formerly part of the Soviet Union and that due to economic and social problems, child pornography production may increase there [17].

To stretch their profits and because of the difficulty in obtaining new materials, commercial child pornographers use the same photos of the children they obtain over and over again in different publications. When they run out of new material, it is not uncommon for them to plagiarize other's pictures right out of the publications themselves — copyright laws are seldom a problem for the child pornographer. For example, a child pornography publication entitled *Boys Will Be Boys*, depicting boys in color in sexually explicit acts and poses, was produced in Europe. An enterprising employee of a governmental printing house in San Francisco reprinted the magazine page for page in black and white and sold it as his own. Because of the chances of being caught by using commercial photo-developing firms, the photocopying machine has been pressed into service to provide quick reproduction. In one case in San Jose, California, investigators found thousands of photocopied pictures of children engaged in sexually explicit conduct, most copied from magazines. Many had been copied several hundred times and were tied together with rubber bands, ready for distribution.

## Medium of Production

The type of medium used to produce child pornography may vary according to the sophistication of the offender. All manner of visual print media have been found to contain child pornography: photographs, slides, videotapes, motion pictures, magazines, newsprint, drawings, and comic books/cartoons. A child-porn operator was found to have over $20,000 worth of photography equipment. Found in his possession were over 90,000 color slides of child pornography. Investigators found that he had traveled outside the United States to obtain children as photo subjects. Another child pornographer was found to have both photography equipment and videotape duplication equipment. Through his business records and customer files, he was found to have done several hundred thousand dollars worth of business in a year's time and was found to have over 300 master tapes and films containing child porn. Another arrest found a pornographer with films, video tapes and equipment, and a computer to keep his records straight.

Because of the large market for the illicit material and the knowledge that no one will complain, there are a large number of "rip-off" operators who purport to be child porn suppliers. If the requesting party is lucky enough to get something from these people, the material they send is either of adults made up to look like children or nothing like the materials ordered. Virtually all of these people use postal drops as mailing addresses, making identification difficult when complaints are made.

On occasion, the parents of the children involved may enter the children into the activity. In one case, a parent "rented" his child for a 9-month period for $3,000. In another, the parents gave written permission for their three sons ages 12 to 15 to engage in pornography trips. Many states have special criminal penalties for parents who do this.

Some say organized crime is involved in making and distributing child pornography in the United States. Others say the mob won't touch it because either it is too hot or it goes against their moral standards. Those who know say that in other countries organized crime is a major influence and source of support for the market. Many child pornography producers are in the market solely for the money. However, most do it because it gives them some sexual gratification. These individuals either molest the children they photograph or use the materials they get from others for their own ends as well as for making money. Determining the real motive for being involved in child pornography may be as easy as looking at whom the pornographer associates with (children or adults).

Those who collect pictures will keep them in places (car, home) where they are readily available for exchange should the opportunity present itself. In one case, a daycare provider was arrested for importing child pornography and molesting children in his care. In his car were found numerous child pornography magazines, some of them in duplicate and triplicate for exchange. Offenders also keep a good accounting of the material they have, both to document their collection and to prevent duplicate purchases. These records may be as simple as a notebook or as sophisticated as a computer filing system.

## Investigative Techniques

Each case will vary according to the type of individual under investigation. Although the techniques will vary between the investigation of a commercial distributor and the individual producer of child pornography, law-enforcement concerns remain the same — to identify the children involved and seek a child molestation violation first, then to pursue a pornography violation if the molestation charges can't be substantiated, or both. The discussion in the following sections will center primarily on the pornography investigation, as the molestation investigation is addressed elsewhere in this text (see Chapter 8).

For the most part, investigators have found that traditional police investigative approaches have not worked in child pornography violations. Because of the clandestine nature of the underground, innovative ways have been developed to expose those involved in the making and distribution of the material. However, the time-honored methods of researching and documenting those involved in similar acts, such as adult pornography violations and narcotics traffic, still provide the foundation on which the rest of the case will be built.

### Investigating the Underground

The very nature of the underground dictates an approach that is a combination of an intelligence case, an undercover narcotics operation, and a gambling or mail fraud case. Child pornography cases are vastly different from adult pornography investigations because the child pornography operator doesn't usually advertise commercially or openly. They are generally very cautious about performing any transactions and will most often do business only through word of mouth and personal contacts. For this reason, investigations must be conducted with close cooperation between local, state, and federal agencies. Each must offer its resources and information systems to the other, or the case may fail because of lack of adequate intelligence. If the investigation is discovered by the person(s) under investigation, rest assured that the elements of proof will not be established.

Local police and sheriff's agencies are responsible for investigations of cases that occur in their jurisdictions, and some state investigative bureaus exist to handle cases that go beyond normal city and county lines or involve multiple jurisdiction violations. The FBI is responsible for cases involving the transportation of child pornography over state lines, and cooperates with the postal inspectors in mail violations; however, the Postal Service has primary jurisdiction over violations involving the mails. The United States Customs Service (Department of the Treasury) is responsible for the enforcement of violations of this country's duty laws and for preventing the importation of certain contraband, including child pornography.

Child pornography investigations should be treated like all other secret undercover operations, and it is essential that tight control of any information regarding the cases be maintained to prevent leaks. In one case that broke in the morning, the material was moved while the police prepared to raid the location where the pornography was being produced and stored. By the time the police arrived to serve the search warrant, the material was gone. The word had gotten out to members of the police agency and the suspect was warned. In another case, because of the transmission of the location of the suspect's residence over the police radio, when the police set up a raid and awaited in a concealed place for enough manpower to assault the location, the suspect and his material were gone by the time help arrived. The discovery of police scanners in possession of those involved in this illicit activity is becoming more and more common.

Child pornographers don't trust many people, so the direct approach of walking up to them and asking for child pornography will rarely work. In situations where the police suspect an individual is involved in the making, selling, or exchanging of child pornography, the most successful approach has been an indirect one, where the investigating officer doesn't identify himself as a police officer. With this type of approach, it is less likely that the subject will discover that he is the subject of an inquiry. The indirect method includes pretext interviews, where the officer passes himself off as something other than a member of the law-enforcement community; also the use of pretext mailings, wherein the officer represents himself as a member of the underground seeking out whatever materials are available. Another indirect method may be the use of an informant or other reference source of information. When use of the mail is involved, both Customs and the postal authorities have found that "controlled deliveries," wherein the questioned package is delivered to the suspect in such a way that it remains under constant observation, are the most successful investigative tools.

## Information Gathering

In any clandestine operation, the key to success is knowing as much as possible about the individual(s) under investigation. One method of gaining information about those under investigation is surveillance. With the use of this method it is possible to identify the main operators or frequenters of the location being watched. This may include the owner of a business or the person(s) living at the location, if it is a residence, and those who come to make transactions or to be involved in the making or distribution of the materials in question. The problem with surveillance is that it takes much time and manpower; sufficient resources must be allocated or the operation will be of little value. This brings up the problem of adequate briefing of those involved and the development of modes of communication, signals, dress, code words, and manner of relief. Another problem with surveillance is the finding of adequate vantage points. Most places will not be as easily surveilled as simply by sitting outside and watching what goes on. In addition, a log must be kept that adequately reflects all actions by those being watched (Figure 4.1).

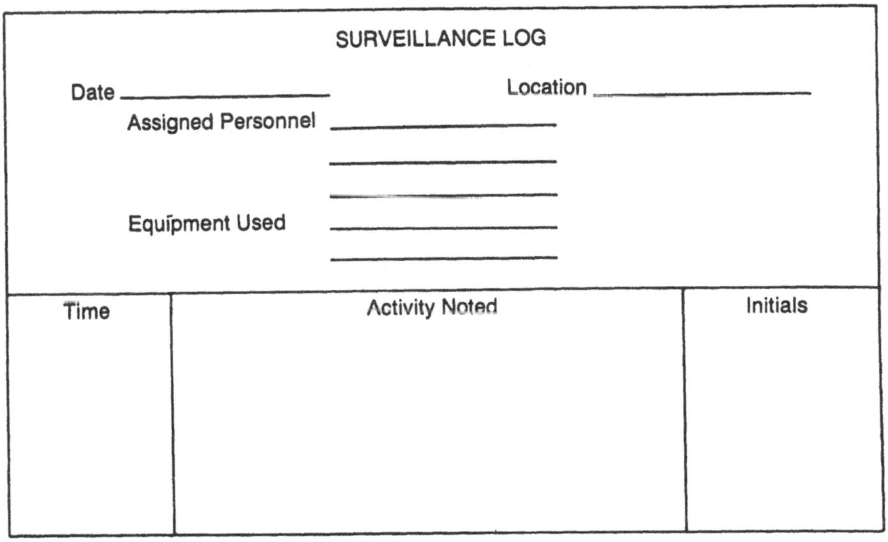
SURVEILLANCE LOG

Date ____________ Location ____________

Assigned Personnel ____________

____________

____________

Equipment Used ____________

____________

| Time | Activity Noted | Initials |
|---|---|---|
| | | |

**Figure 4.1** Sample surveillance log.

To prove scienter and identify those involved, at the same time surveillance is being conducted, a thorough background investigation should be done on all individuals known to be involved and who are subsequently identified through observation or investigation. It should begin with record checks of the major federal agencies working child pornography cases. The FBI has its own information systems containing the names of those it has investigated or who have come to its attention through violations of related laws. The Postal Service maintains a similar list, and the Customs Service also maintains a seizure list of those both sending and receiving child pornography. Finding a subject's name on any one of these lists can be extremely fruitful, both in the substantiation of the element of intent and to establish a pattern of behavior. If possible, IRS records should be sought, as they may establish who is in control of a given location as well as what business the person(s) under investigation are operating. State and local police contact files should not be overlooked, especially field contacts where the names of other persons in the suspect's company are noted.

Most public utilities' files are open to the police investigator. Information contained in these files may reveal the names of the subscribers at a location under investigation. The files may also give employment information about those paying the bills, as well as previous addresses, references, and spouse's maiden name, if any. Telephone company records may include all of this information and, more importantly, records of long distance and toll calls. These may be used to tie in other individuals or locate persons involved with the suspect.

The Post Office can determine to whom mail destined for the address in question belongs and from whom it came, by the use of a mail cover. It can also tell you who is supposed to be receiving mail at any given address. Commercial credit firms can provide a wealth of information regarding those to whom the suspect is indebted and with whom he deals, as well as where he works and lives. In addition, they may provide bank affiliations that can trace the travels of the suspect through the use of his bank cards.

Banks are also another good resource for the investigator. A person's checking account can be of great assistance to prove purchases and sales of materials, as well as the existence of large or frequent withdrawals and deposits. Savings accounts may provide similar information. In addition, bank loans for property may help to establish locations where the suspect has been and where evidence may be found. For major operations, payroll records may reveal former employees who would like to provide information on the suspect.

## Public Records

There are many sources of information that are open to the general public and hold a wealth of information that may be of use in this type of case. At the county level, the Tax Collector or Assessor will provide the name(s) and address(es) of property owners. The Registrar of Voters will give you the names and addresses of voters, and can provide the birthdates of the occupants of given residences, as well as signatures for examination. The County Clerk and Recorder will have records of real estate transactions, births, deaths, and marriages. The Court Clerk will have all records of civil and criminal cases, corporations, fictitious name statements, and divorce actions.

At the state level, the Department of Motor Vehicles can provide physical descriptions, addresses, and signatures, and often pictures, fingerprints, and social security numbers. It also can provide information regarding the ownership of vehicles and descriptions. The Secretary of state and Department of Corporations will provide addresses and names of officers and shareholders of any business formally incorporated in a state. The Controller will hold names of all who would be indebted to a state. The Department of Education will provide information regarding the credentials of employees working in schools regulated by the state and may have inspection authority over certain educational institutions. The Department of Social Services will have information on certain care facilities such as licensed daycare or sitting services and foster care programs. It also has certain inspection privileges. The Department of Labor may have child protection responsibilities under a state's labor laws that empower it to regulate and inspect the work conditions and situations of children under certain ages. State medical boards or departments of consumer affairs may have certain regulatory responsibilities for medical facilities that may come in handy in trying to find out about a medical practitioner. The Department of Real Estate will have records on who holds deeds to certain properties, along with the owners' addresses.

At the federal level, Bankruptcy Court will reveal the assets, debts, and background of parties engaged in bankruptcy actions. The Securities and Exchange Commission maintains records on fraud investigations regarding stocks and security transactions. The Department of the Interior maintains records of homesteads, public land filings, maps, and legal descriptions of property owned by individuals.

Also available to the investigator are public directories listing persons living within certain geographical areas. City and reverse directories serve an investigator well in providing information not always available through other sources. Newspaper morgues and Better Business Bureaus also hold invaluable information.

### Finding Child Pornography

Child pornography, for the most part, is an underground commodity that rarely surfaces unless it is reported by a noninvolved party. The most successful techniques of investigation. entail covert operations because of the nature of the distribution methods. Ads placed in the underground journals for the geographical area an investigator is interested in may help to locate some material. The same type of ads might be entered in legitimate publications such as newspapers, classified ad papers, or shopping newspapers. In some areas, child pornography may be purchased under the counter at pornography shops where the "client" is known and for the right price. When suspected child pornography is encountered under any of the circumstances listed and it appears that the operation is only a sales outlet and not a producer, one should make or attempt to make purchases rather than simply seizing the material. It may be best to make several purchases to ensure that the elements are not only complete, but affirmed in more than one transaction. In addition, the demonstrating of sales will provide charges for which there is often a greater penalty.

**Covert letter writing.**   One of the most successful investigative techniques is covert letter writing. Names to write to may be obtained by looking through an arrested subject's address books or through the various mailing lists seized by law-enforcement agencies throughout the country. Although now highly suspected by the underground, the unsolicited letter is a common way to develop evidence of a violation. Offenders are almost compulsive in what they say to complete strangers, thinking they will have support from them or be introduced to a child or new material. Disarm and reassure the person to whom you write by telling him that you are not a police officer or a member of any law-enforcement agency. This way he feels he cannot be "entrapped," and it will help to make him feel more comfortable with you. Often the offender will ask for "good faith" proof of your intentions, asking you to send him something pornographic. Try not to use material from other investigations unless you know you will be retrieving it immediately in a search warrant or other situation.

It is unethical to continue to exploit children by using in investigations pictures of children seized in other cases and that have not already been commercially reproduced and distributed on a wide scale. If for some reason we lose control of the pictures sent to an individual, we continue the cycle we are trying to break. It may be more acceptable to use photos in which the faces are not identifiable. There is probably nothing wrong with "pirating" photos from already extensively distributed, commercial magazines and using them, as this is a practice already used by the underground. When you are involved in correspondence with a suspect, do whatever he says to establish and maintain his trust. As soon as he trusts you, he will be more apt to give you evidence of the violation you seek. Keeping the defense of entrapment in mind, the practice of covering the truth with those you correspond is acceptable and often the only way to gain their confidence.

There are several ways of getting evidence of a violation with this method. The first is to use the federal statutes when the pornography is sent through the mail, using a controlled delivery and a federal search warrant to enter the suspect's home. This highlights the need to coordinate and involve federal agencies in your case from the start. Another is to get the person to mail you the material at an address in your own community from a mailing site also in your community, and get a local search and/or arrest warrant. The preferred manner is to get the offender to tell you about how he is/was molesting a particular child and/or children, and to send you pictures of the events or children themselves. For example, in one case a child molester boasted in a letter to an investigator about several acts of molestation with a 9-year-old girl and provided the investigator with photos of himself and the girl. In another case, a molester sent police pictures of the children he was involved with in his daycare center, showing him having sexual contact with the children. Both of these molesters were arrested on local charges and found guilty of child molestation.

**Child pornography search warrants.**    This subject will be addressed in greater detail in Chapter 7 on search warrants. However, just as in every child molest case you would prepare a search warrant looking for corroborative evidence, so must you prepare one in a pornography investigation. In the child pornography search warrant, the affidavit must contain a detailed recounting of the facts and observations that will enable the judge to make an independent assessment that there is probable cause to believe a crime has been committed (molestation) or that the material falls within the purview of obscenity or child pornography statutes. During the service of the warrant, be sure to limit the movement of suspects at the scene and watch what is said in their presence, to avoid any allegations of misconduct in court as well as to avoid tipping them off to what you know already. I try not to effect an arrest until the last possible moment, so that I can complete my search and know what evidence I have before I talk to the suspect. I try to encourage the suspect to stay at the scene to assure himself that we don't do anything improper and that we take care of his property. By having him stay at the scene "watched and restricted by a police officer), I am not forced to book him and permit him to make phone calls because technically he is not under arrest. Because most searches take a considerable amount of time, this relieves the pressure of interviewing him immediately.

## *Identifying the Participants*

A major problem in child pornography investigations is identifying the children and others depicted in the pictures. An assessment must be made as to which photographs you will spend time on trying to identify the participants. If he is cooperative, asking the offender to identify those depicted in the pictures will get the best results in the shortest amount of time. Each identification must be corroborated by an independent source, preferably the persons depicted. Caution should be taken to cover the sexually explicit portions of the photographs if at all possible, as this causes great concern among those depicted when they find out how you identified them. If the offender won't cooperate, the children involved must be asked to identify others, if you are lucky enough to have identified any of them.

If you are unable to identify the children through these means, you will have to try another way. One of the best ways is to have the juvenile officers of your agency examine the photos. School resource officers and any beat officer who might have worked in the area where you believe the children are from are also good resources. You may wish to try officers from neighboring agencies or create an informational bulletin with only the faces of those found in the photographs, with physical descriptions including unique tattoos or body marks. Examine the yearbooks of the schools with children of the ages involved. Keep in mind that pornographic photos are often old and that the search should cover several years prior to the time the photos are discovered. As a last resort, try showing the photos or, better yet, blowups of the faces of the children to the staff at schools in your area. Try to select photos with a minimum of sexual activity in order to protect the children. If it is necessary to show pictures with sexually explicit action, be sure that they are masked in some way to prevent the viewer from knowing what is going on.

Should the schools not pan out, you might consider the neighbors in the immediate area the suspect is known to frequent, where he lives, and where the incidents are believed to have happened. A technique used by Sgt. Toby Tyler, San Bernardino County Sheriff's Department, San Bernardino, California, is to confront the offender with the photographs in question and ask him where they came from and who is depicted in them. With Miranda out of the way, Toby tells the suspected offender that if the offender is unable to identify the pictures, he will have to show the pictures to the offender's neighbors and family. The obvious fear of ridicule, embarrassment, and exposure often secures cooperation.

In a rather celebrated case in Los Angeles, a packet of photos containing pictures of a man and woman sexually molesting a girl who was two- or three-years-old, was found in the street. In an unusual step, but, necessary in the case due to the fact that there would have been no other way to identify the child, much less the adults, the police went to the courts and obtained an order allowing them to release portions of the photos showing separately, both, the adults and the child. The news media carried the pictures in papers and news programs across the country. Within minutes of the broadcast, the child was identified as having been cared for in a baby-sitting setting by the adults in the pictures. The adults were also identified by people who saw the photos, more incriminating evidence found when a search was conducted, and the adults were arrested. The parents of the child were totally unaware of what had happened to their child.

Should you not be able to identify the photographs by any of the methods described, you must decide which photographs you will try to identify. One consideration is determining whether the photographs are originals or pirated material. If the photograph is copied from a magazine, close examination should reveal the printing process dots, the telltale signs of a pirated print. The age of the print may also be an obvious sign that identification of the children depicted is a lost cause. Look for the dates the developer often prints on the back or edges of the print. Often the offender himself has written dates on the print, sometimes in code. Sometimes he even includes the child's name. Be aware that the date may be misleading because the photo is a reprint of a negative made a long time before or a copy of something also taken long before.

Lot numbers on instant developing film help to determine the date the photo was taken and give an idea of where the film was purchased. They may also help to determine where the picture was taken. The lot numbers are coded to give the date of manufacture and the site of distribution. With these facts, you have a better chance of determining venue and statute of limitations. The fact that this type of film also has a short shelf-life will assist greatly in deciding these issues. Dated prints help; however, examination of hairstyles, clothing styles, and the types of things in the background, such as automobiles, license plates with dates, and/or locations, may help to date pictures. You may also establish these things by looking for publications purposely or inadvertently left in the picture that may help to date the photo, by the use of photo enhancement. Whenever vehicles are depicted, try to read the license numbers and contact the registered owners to see if they can help to identify the locations and/or participants.

### Identifying the Source of the Pornography

Whenever photographs are found in an investigation, they must be carefully examined for as much information as possible. You must examine the prints themselves to see if you can match them up with a camera or the developing and printing devices you might find in the possession of your suspect. Provided the camera hasn't been used too much since the photographs in question were taken, film can be matched up with the camera that took the photographs much as a bullet can be matched up with the gun that fired it. As the film moves over the film gate of the camera, striations are left on the film, similar to the rifling in a gun's barrel. These can be matched up for positive identification. This will work for instant cameras also, provided they haven't shot a lot of film. In a case in California handled by Sgt. Tyler, the shadow of a hair caught inside the lens system of a 35-mm, single lens-reflex camera was found on every photograph the camera took. Comparisons made of the camera, found with the same hair permanently sealed in the camera, were proof positive that the photographs came from that particular camera. In addition, the printing easels for enlarging of prints from negatives often have unique characteristics that can be matched up to the prints they make.

Defects in the edges of the printing easel, when compared with the prints it makes, will show the same markings.

In cases where magazines or other materials have been printed, careful analysis of the printing plates should be made. In the offset printing process, a plate is made, generally out of a piece of thin metal, which is pliable enough to bend around a printing drum. The printing on the plate is made by photographing the material to be printed. A photographic negative impression of the material is then chemically transferred to the plate. Any evidence of this process such as the negatives, "cut-outs" (portions of the material cut out and attached to the printing transfer materials or negatives), plates, or printing machinery should be secured as evidence and held for comparison with the material it is suspected to have produced.

## Analysis of the Photographs Involved

Another concern you should have when examining photographs found in a child pornography or molestation case is that of multiple pictures taken at the same session. Examine the photo(s) you have:

1. Do they appear to be part of a series? Is the child fully clothed in one shot and totally naked in another?
2. Is the child only partially clad? Does it appear as though there is a distinctive pattern in the posing such as the slow removal of clothing or a progression in the sexual acts?
3. Does it appear that there are certain steps missing in the sequence (you see the girl taking off her blouse step by step, but the last pictures show her naked)?
4. Have you found the negatives that made the prints you have found?

By making this analysis, you may open the way for a search warrant asking for what you believe to be in the suspect's possession, such as the rest of the pictures or negatives. By analyzing the pictures, you will develop questions based on what you see in the photographs that you will want to ask the children who are involved—questions such as who was present and who took the pictures. Having the child confirm the sequences of the pictures is also important. The numbering on the negatives will help corroborate the child's account by confirming the order of events. What was said by the suspect is of great importance in determining intent and knowledge. What the suspect did at the time of the photo session is also important, especially if he was involved sexually with the child or if he masturbated during the photo session.

Each photograph must be examined for things contained in the background and foreground that may assist in identifying the suspect, the location, and the victim. What does the photo show? Where was it taken? Who is in it? All of these questions must be answered. Identify evidence you want to ask for in your search warrant. Try to pick out the most unique objects as well as some of the common ones. Be sure you have made an attempt to identify the number and identity of all those involved in the photo session. Examine all reflecting surfaces to see if the photographer or other models might be depicted in the picture unbeknownst to him or her.

An example of how important this can be is seen in the court marshal of a major in the Air Force who had been discovered bringing sexually suggestive photos of a young girl into a photo developing firm in a neighboring town. The 35-mm pictures were discovered by the firm when they were developed. The major was identified because he drove an Air Force vehicle to the drive-in drop-off and, unfortunately for him, picked an alias that caught the attention of the authorities in the neighboring town. It happened to be the same name as their deputy Chief of Police.

The pictures depicted a young girl apparently sleeping on her back, no underwear on, with her knees unnaturally propped up, leaning outward, and to each side, so that her vagina was exposed directly to the camera. There were numerous photos, several depicting the lips of the vagina spread apart, exposing the inner portions of the genitals.

A search warrant was issued and the results netted more photographs, this time they were Polaroid, of the same girl, in the same poses, in the same locations. A video tape was also discovered. It dimly depicted the girl on several occasions, in the same positions, in the same locations, with a single lamp on in the background. However, when she turned over or moved, the camera suddenly was turned off. On one occasion, just before the camera was shut off, when the girl stirred, there was a sudden panning of the camera down and to the side, as though he was hiding it from being seen.

His explanation was that he was testing his cameras for low-light production and that he had only done it once, when the girl spent the night at his home. She was the daughter of a friend of the family who was also in the Air Force.

When I examined the pictures, looking at the backgrounds, we found that there were what appeared to be, at minimum, three different rooms. The wallpaper, furniture, and wall hangings were different. The girl had some scabs and bruises on her knees in one series of photos, but, they were in various stages of healing or nonexistent in others.

The bedding was also different in several of the series, depicting a print pattern on the sheets in one, not in another, and yet, another print pattern on the pillowcase, different from the rest, in another series. The girl was also wearing different sleeping ware in each series.

The problem the prosecutor had, originally, was demonstrating that he had touched the girl and that it occurred on more than one occasion. In addition, we had to demonstrate his interest in the girl's position was both placed and for sexual purposes, in other words, a conscious course of conduct. It didn't take much to show the girl's clothes and the covers had been pulled up and that he obviously treasured his encounters so much that not only did he take the pictures with a standard 35-mm camera, but, in case the photos didn't come out, he took the Polaroids. If that wasn't enough, he had the video to back it all up. Once we analyzed the points discussed above, he had his case.

Another example of identifying the perpetrator and location is a case in Philadelphia, where a music teacher tricked a nine-year-old girl into performing oral sex upon him at school. He had told her she was demonstrating how various reed woodwind instruments could be identified by touching them with a person's tongue. The entire act was videotaped, but all that could be seen was the girl's face, the offender's hand, and his penis.

Investigators examined the tape and immediately recognized the music room blackboard of the classroom in the background. They heard children's voices in the background, apparently coming from outside the classroom. The principal of the school recognized the teacher's voice on the tape. To cap the investigation, the teacher wore a monogrammed cuff on his shirt, bearing his initials.

When examining the pictures, you should look not only for a progression in the activity depicted, but for a progression in the locations where the activity occurs. For example, in a series of 39 35-mm photos, a babysitter shot several sequences showing a definite progression of sexually explicit pictures of his 5-year-old charge. In the first pictures she appeared playing with a dildo in an obvious sexual fashion, in addition to being posed with her dress being slowly hiked up to reveal her underpants. In later shots, the action moved to a couch, a bed, then to a chair. In each sequence the sexual activity became more graphic, and the suspect was eventually depicted actually molesting the child. The progression of sexual activity was accented in this case by the moves to the locations where sexual activity would normally occur (sofa and bed). In addition, on examination of the photographs, it was noted that the camera was out of focus on several of the prints when the child was engaged in some of the more explicit self-stimulation. It was apparent that the suspect was not paying attention to taking the pictures at that juncture because he was distracted by something else, his own sexual excitement.

That series of photos also clearly demonstrated that the 5-year-old had been told to pose in the sexually explicit activity. It was not natural for her to have assumed the poses without some type of prompting or demonstration by the use of other pictures or magazines. This is common with children, even those in their teens. If the offender wants a certain pose, often he will have to demonstrate the pose himself or show it to the child by using other photographs or magazines. If this appears to be the case, it again gives you something to search for and enables you to confirm the child's account.

## Connecting the Offender to the Pornography

A sure-fire way to connect an offender to the pictures you find in his possession is to find the negatives for them in his possession. In every search where you suspect the offender to have taken photographs, look for them.

In cases of correspondence or distribution, consider evidence found in the offender's possession that will tie him to the materials you suspect came from him. Compare the ink and paper of the materials you found at his home or business and the materials you received through the mail or purchased. Don't overlook handwriting, printing, and typewriter comparisons. Perform fingerprint evidence examinations on any correspondence sent to you or any evidence seized or found during service of the search warrant. Do the same for books, magazines, covers, internal pages, and price tags [top and bottom]. Fingerprint cash boxes, typewriters, computers, packaging materials, and anything that might have been touched while being used by the producer or distributor of child pornography.

It's not uncommon to find bloodstains on materials that are mailed or found at the scene, caused by paper cuts, film, film containers, and packaging. Care should be taken to preserve and analyze properly this valuable evidence of personal identity. Another good type of evidence of identity is hair and fibers. Comparisons can be made of any fiber or hair samples found on the materials or within its packaging with those found at the arrest site. Consider any rope or string used in packaging for possible comparison. Consider examining any tool marks found in the packaging, such as marks made by the metal crimping tools used to wrap wire around packages and the ends of tape dispensers. Collect any rubber stamps used in mailing or for printing any messages within the correspondence or mailings found. Consider paper comparisons of the letters sent or found during the investigation and those found in the offender's possession. Don't forget to consider the possibility of comparing inks used in pens or printings found in materials obtained during the investigation.

Collectors and makers of child pornography know how damaging the discovery of their material can be in court and therefore take great pains to hide the material from others and, in particular, the law. Where and how such evidence can be hidden is limited only by the imagination and resources of the person involved. False walls have been found in closets, hallways, bookcases, and around electrical appliances and switches. Check the pockets of clothing in closets and in drawers. Check between the pages of books and under and in furniture. Check the floors of closets. If there is a rug, pull it up and see if it comes up easily. If it does, consider the possibility of a false floor.

## Establishing Control of the Material

One of the best ways to establish who has control of the material is the "controlled delivery." This method, generally conducted by members of the Postal Service, places the material directly in the hands of the person intended to receive it, thereby reducing the possibility of contamination. When dealing with the mail, liaison should be made with the U.S. Postal Inspection Service and controlled delivery should be considered.

## Documentation

It is extremely helpful to diagram exactly where each item of evidence was seized (see the discussion in Chapter 7 on search warrant preparation). It is also helpful to show where the offender was at the time of arrest in relation to where the evidence was found. In pornography (as in virtually all other investigations), investigative reports should contain only observations, no conclusions. The reports should reflect in a narrative format the true facts of the case, ensuring that the elements of the crimes to be charged are carefully covered.

In any pornography case, photos should be taken of the interiors of all rooms, especially anywhere a sex act might take place, such as beds, couches, and rugs. These photographs should be kept indefinitely in case pornographic photographs that may have been taken at the same location later turn up. In one case, an FBI agent found that it was extremely helpful to photograph the offender reading the search warrant (a contention was made that the bad guy never saw the warrant).

## Follow-up Investigations

Once a search warrant has been served or the offender has been arrested, the work of corroborating what witnesses and victims have said begins. All of the evidence gathered at the scene of arrest or on the offender must be examined to determine if the offender was involved with other persons or in other offenses. All leads arising from the arrest or service of the search warrant must be followed up to ensure connections are made to the necessary elements of the crimes. Interviews should be conducted with those who were not interviewed earlier because of the sensitive nature of the case and the possibility of notice of the ongoing investigation being given to the offender. Neighbors, relatives, and suspected associates should be interviewed to determine what they know about the offender and his activities. Lastly, any law enforcement agency that might have an interest in the offender should be contacted. The authorities in any place the offender has inhabited or is believed to have inhabited in the past should be contacted and told of the investigation to see if they have any leads or information regarding your case, and to inform them of the arrest in case they are working connecting incidents. It might help to surveil the offender after he gets out to see to whom he goes and if his travels after release lead you to other offenders or conspirators.

## Other Ways to Control Child Pornography

If you suspect child pornography is being sold or shown at a particular location and you can't legally get in to verify it or you wish not to reveal your investigative interests, consider others who can do so within their official capacity. The fire department of your community generally has wide inspection authority in public places. Tax assessors, building inspectors, and the like can also do some "scouting" for you in a legal manner. Without falling into the pitfall of selective enforcement, these individuals can also help to "clean up" a problem area by finding violations of codes that only they can enforce.

## Resources

Excellent materials and technical assistance are available from several sources in investigation and prosecution of child pornography cases.

> The Obscenity Law Center, Suite 239, 475 Riverside Drive, N.Y., NY 10115, 212 870-3232;
> The National Obscenity Enforcement Unit, Criminal Division, U.S., D.O.J., 10th & Constitution Avenue, NW, Washington, D.C. 20530;
> The National Center for Missing and Exploited Children, 2101 Wilson Blvd., Suite 550, Alexandria, VA 22201, 800 843-5678;
> Dept. of Treasury, U.S. Customs Service, Child Pornography and Protection Unit, Washington, D.C. 20229

## References and Notes

1. *Reuters World Report* (wire services) Jan. 18, "Sweden Weighs Clampdown on Child Pornography," April 11, 1994; Dutch to Tighten Laws Against Child Pornography."

2. U.S. Customs training materials distrubuted to author, Feb. 1988.

3. *National Legislation on and International Trafficking in Child Pornography*, Second Edition., Center on Speech, Equality, and Harm, Minneapolis, 1997.

4.  *Rights of the Child: Report of the Special Rapporteur on the Sale of Children, Child Prostitution and Child Pornography,* United Nations, Geneva, 1996.

5.  *Obscenity Enforcement Reporter,* 1:4, 5 (Nov. 1988); *see also* "Child Pornography and Prostitution: Background and Legal Analysts," National Obscenity Enforcement Unit, U.S. Department of Justice, National Legal Resource Center for Child Advocacy and Protection, Covenant House, and the National Center for Mission and Exploited Children, Washington, D.C. (Oct. 1987).

6.  *New York vs. Ferber,* 458 U.S. 747 (1982).

7.  *Miller vs. California* 413 U.S. 15 (1973).

8.  American Bar Association, *Child Sexual Exploitation: Background and Legal Analysis,* rev. ed. Washington, D.C.: National Legal Resource Center for Child Advocacy and Protection, 1984.

9.  *Ferber vs. New York* 454 U.S. 1052 (1982).

10. National Legal Data Center, *Techniques in Pornography Investigation,* Thousand Oaks, California, undated.

11. Louisiana Rev. Stat. Ann. Sec. 14118 (Suppl. 1981).

12. U.S. Congress, 104th Congress Senate Report 545, Aug. 27, 1996.

13. U.S. Congress, *Child Pornography and Pedophilia.* Hearing, Permanent Subcommittee on Investigations of the Committee on Govenmental Affairs, Washington, D. C., U.S. Senate, 99th Congress, 1st Session, Part 1, 11/29-30/84.

14. S. P. Petruzzellis, "Child Pornography: An Incurable Problem?" Paper presented at Red Deer Community College, Toronto, Canada, May 1984.

15. Ibid.

16. World Congress Against Commercial Sexual Exploitation of Children, (*WCACSE Report*) USIS, American Embassy, Strandvagen 101, 115 89 Stockholm, Homepage, 1996.

17. Center on Speech, Equality and Harm, *National Legislation on Child Pornography,* Minneapolis, MN, 1996.

## Additional Reading

Citizens for Decency through Law, Inc., *The Preparation and Trial of an Obscenity Case: A Guide for the Prosecuting Attorney,* Phoenix, AZ, 1988.

John E. B. Meyers, *Evidence in Child Abuse and Neglect Cases,* Wiley, N.Y., Third Edition, 1997.

Shirley O'Brian, *Child Pornography,* Dubuque, IA, Kendal/Hunt, 1983.

*Obscenity Law Bulletin,* National Obscenity Law Center, N.Y., 1996.

U.S. Attorney General's Office, Commission on Pornography, *Final Report,* USIS, American Embassy, Strandvagen 101,115 89 Stockholm, Homepage, 1996.

# Interviewing Children

5

## Building a Foundation

Fundamental to interviewing children is the foundational structure of the interview itself. The investigator must know his own shortcomings and how well he functions in this type of setting. If the investigator does not have an understanding and acceptance of the background problems the victim has faced, the interview may reflect it in a very negative way. Either the child will not be able to articulate what happened because the investigator is unable to use proper techniques to help the child, or the investigator will improperly interpret what the child does or says. In addition, if the child is approached in the wrong manner, with little effort made to make him feel comfortable about discussing the incidents, the end product will again be poor. Appropriate measures must be taken to establish a rapport with the child and to use the rapport-building process as a means of setting the stage for the remainder of the interview. This will determine the strategy the interviewer will follow to encourage the child to express the details of the incidents.

I have purposely not taken a specific approach to discussion of the evaluation of the developmental level of the child. Instead, I have incorporated checks about developmental levels concerning cognition (mental ability to comprehend and report), memory, reasoning, concept formation, and ability to articulate (language) what happened to the child into the different areas of questioning listed herein.

The author wishes to acknowledge and thank Toby Tyler, San Bernardino County Sheriff's Department, and the following individuals, whose techniques and suggestions helped provide the material for this chapter: Ether Amacher, Nashville; Eli Breslin, San Jose; Dr. David Corwin, M.D., Beth Dickinson, Los Angeles Sheriff's Department; Gary Duthler, Alameda County District Attorney's Office; Peter Graves, San Jose Police Department; Hon. Pam Isles, Orange County Municipal Court; Paula Kuty, San Jose; Kay Lantow, Berkeley Police Department; David Lloyd, J.D., Jeffrey Miller, Los Gatos Police Department; William Spaulding, Louisville Police Department; and Bill Whiskle, San Jose Police Department.

I have also not specifically listed "a method" to interview children. This text is intended to provide alternatives and choices that may be utilized to facilitate a child's telling what happened to him from which it is possible to make a determination whether abuse occurred or not. It is a compilation of many techniques and methods, all of which may or may not work for an individual case. The key is flexibility and the ability to use as many tools available to the interviewer as necessary to accomplish the task. For more specifics regarding reliability of children in accounting for what has transpired with or to them, I commend the articles and publications listed in the references section of this chapter. Here, I will merely summarize, in general terms, their findings as they relate to the approaches I recommend in interviewing strategies.

I have also not separated techniques to approach specific age groups, except to note where certain concerns should be considered with the specific technique discussed. For the same reasons above, the goal is to have as many tools as possible to approach each child, not to apply rigid or specific parameters to an child because the child is a specific age. Caveats and warnings are discussed with potential problems which might be encountered with a particular age when using a particular technique.

In short, what I have tried to do in this chapter is to heighten the interviewer's "communicative competence" [1]. For it is the ability of the interviewer to access what the child has experienced that is important. If the child has something to tell and if the interviewer is unable to communicate successfully with the child, there is no point in the interview, because it will cause great problems for the child in the future and will endanger the ability to successfully litigate a case. As stated above, there must be a sound foundation from which to build an interview. From that base, the case may be formulated. The National Center for the Prosecution of Child Abuse conducted a study on what were the deciding factors in successful prosecutions of child sexual abuse. In short, they found that the determining factor was the effective collection of *verbal evidence* [2]. It all begins with a verbal account from the victim.

This text is written primarily for the police investigator. However, as the techniques discussed here are universal, they may be used by anyone dealing with a child victim. For this reason, I will review the roles of those who might be interviewing a child victim. The police officer's main interests will be criminal in nature, with protection as an additional concern. The officer will have to determine if abuse is occurring or has occurred, and, if so, by whom. In the process, he will gather evidence, consider whether the child is in further jeopardy, and make a decision about protective custody. A social services worker may be concerned only with the protection issue, a lawyer with the trial details, and a nurse or doctor with the degree of the abuse to determine the treatment.

Each official representative of a child protection agency (police, social services, probation, district attorney) must recognize that he can have no preconceived ideas about the child or what has happened to the child before he interviews him. If the professional who conducts the interview does not consider the needs of those who will ultimately contact the child, and if improper techniques are applied, serious problems could arise. The child may refuse to cooperate later on, and the opportunity to retrieve the information that could have been obtained at the initial interview will have been lost. If repeated interviews are held with the child on the same subjects, there will be a greater chance of confusing the child and obtaining statements that appear to be contradicting or inconsistent. Therefore, careful consideration must be given to the type of information needed from the child and ways of obtaining that information to avoid holding additional interviews.

## Concerns Regarding Reliability

If there is any area which is most susceptible of successful attack by a defense attorney, it is the interview process. Therefore, it is one of the most litigated issues and the one which receives the most scrutiny. The most likely target for casting doubt upon what the child has recounted is, not the child, but, the person(s) who the child has talked to. To directly attack the child might generate sympathy for the child and disdain towards the attorney, which would flow to the defendant. So, the focus becomes the secondary source of the damaging information — the person(s) who obtained it. Here, the alluring theories which could be claimed as having tainted (leading, suggestive, intimidation, encouraging, pleasing, etc.) the child's account, are applied to discredit the source. This makes the interview techniques and results obtained fertile ground for a defense attorney to plant the seed of doubt.

It must be conceded that there have been and are mistakes made by interviewers in investigations. Well-intentioned as they are, people make mistakes. Its a fact of life. Its also a fact of life that an attorney is going to exploit that mistake for all its worth to make it appear better for his client. This is said because there are also good techniques that produce information that certain people would rather not have exposed. Defendant's don't want children to tell what happened to them. The techniques are aggressively attacked by attorneys as misleading and contaminating. They attack the technique on two levels. First, they claim the questions produced something that didn't happen. Second, and the most important point to remember, is they then claim the child *adopts the new fact* as having happened and part of his experience. This is the *False Memory* argument. It is the way the defense tries to discredit a convincing account made by a child in the courtroom. They claim the interview process produced the memory and that is why the child is so convincing.

It doesn't mean that the techniques should be eliminated per se, merely because defense attorneys don't like them and they are capable of producing incorrect results. What it means is that whatever techniques are utilized must be used with the understanding and expectation that they are controversial and subject to question. They should be used only when other techniques are ineffective, and, even then, as minimally as possible. Careful documentation of every interview and/or contact with the child must be made to assure this defense argument is not effective. The effect of the technique is what is important. Measures must be taken to ensure that the proper effect is produced.

For example, what is most commonly attacked by attorneys is the leading question with young children where the interviewer must direct the child's attention to a particular subject because free recall isn't working. To assure that the question and its response is as free from interpellation as possible, measures such as those described herein to obtain as much specific detail should be employed. It is important not to be defensive about using and explaining the use of the techniques that are the focus of courtroom attack. The legitimate reasons why the techniques need to be and were used should be matter-of-factly presented to justify their use if questioned in court.

Even the court's have realized that leading questions are necessary. Many states have codified a exception in their evidence law that permits attorneys to do that very thing. The question is how much, if any, has the method influenced what the child has said. As of the time of this writing, one state supreme court (New Jersey) has required a "taint hearing" in a case involving a nursery school investigation wherein numerous very young children were interviewed, resulting in a 163 count criminal trial and conviction. Reversing the conviction and sending the case back for a new trial, the court found the techniques used by investigators to be beyond the "standards" accepted by professionals and law enforcement communities [3]. It specifically was concerned with whether the techniques used were "so coercive or suggestive that they had the capacity to substantially distort the children's recollections, and thus compromise the reliability of the testimony" [4]. Although the practices of the investigators in the case may have been well meaning, the court used the following factors to consider to determine that the techniques used were not appropriate:

"lack of investigatory independence; the interviewer's preconceived notion of guilt; leading questions; lack of control for outside influences; whether the interviewer is a trusted authority figure; the use of repeated questions; vilification or criticism of the defendant; tone of voice; threats; praise; cajoling; bribes; rewards; and, peer pressure [5]."

Regardless of whether the court's characterization of the case is correct, it is now the law of New Jersey and through legal doctrine, will undoubtedly be argued in other states. Therefore, it is imperative that to assure that the outcome in this case is not repeated. To help understand what the court decided, here are the findings the court made regarding the record it was provided on appeal. It found that "few children volunteered information that directly implicated the defendant" spontaneously, nor did they "provide details" even after encouragement. The interviewers had no special training relating to children. Interviews conducted early in the disclosure process were not recorded. Notes of the interviews were disposed of and not available for court. Investigators were not impartial. There was "repeated and incessant interrogation" of children. In the record was evidence of "threats, cajoling, and bribing. Positive reinforcement was given for inculpatory statements and negative for exculpatory." Apparently "vilification of the defendant" was observed in the record by the court [6].

This case typifies the technical arguments made against interviewers' techniques. It also underscores that fact that the process is an easy target, because the arguments made by the defense sometimes have merit. As infrequently as it does occur, children may sometimes be lead to make statements the interviewer is looking for. The defense attorney's job is to convince a trier-of-fact that it has occurred in the case at hand. Our job is to interview children to determine what, if anything, has happened to them, without influencing their account, and, therefore, to provide as little as possible for the attorney to argue about. All of the concerns of the New Jersey court are addressed in the following text as they relate to the techniques described.

As Professor John Myers concludes in this discussion of "Can we Believe What Children Say Abuse Sexual Abuse," it is not necessarily the lying child we are concerned about, but, rather the child who is not abused who, believing it, says he is because of some external influence [7]. There is some research indicating that, "in rare cases" children may have had their memories influenced to the extent that they describe abuse that never happened, but, which they truly believe [8].

All in all, the research indicates that children, even young children as young as three have good memories and the ability to accurately recount things they have experienced [9]. The danger is the failure of an interviewer to properly identify when he is being overly suggestive. The literature reflects wide, disparate, and varying opinion on the ages and extent of the ability to provide suggestion which would adversely affect a child's account of what happened to him. This leaves the interviewer with the dilemma of whether to not to use the techniques which have been proven to properly and correctly assist children in relaying their accounts, yet, which are potentially suggestive or leading. It is a delicate balancing act extracting accurate information from the child that is an aid in accessing the child's recall without adversely influencing him.

As will be discussed in each instance where leading questions are to be considered, in many cases, it is the only way to determine what happened. What the research has determined is that as many as 80% of children who have been abused initially deny or are reluctant to talk about what has happened to them [10]. In order to overcome the natural and, in some cases, imposed reticence to disclose their abuse, it is necessary to use some techniques that could be considered suggestive. As will be discussed later, other developmental impediments also require the use of these questions.

Karen Saywitz, reports that, in an "interview orientation," when children were given the admonitions and requests for clarification listed below, in the laboratory experiments, their ability to correctly recall and relate their experiences was improved [11].

First the child was told that questions will be asked which the child may not know the answers to. The child was told that this is expected and that if it happens the child should feel free to tell the interviewer he doesn't know the answer. The child is told that the interviewer only wants to know the truth and what really happened.

Next, the child was told that it was permissible not to answer if the child felt uncomfortable with a particular question. The child was encouraged to tell the interviewer when that happened.

Then the child was told that the interviewer might ask a question that the child didn't understand. The child was given permission to ask for clarification or state he didn't understand.

Lastly, the child was told that some questions might be asked more than once because the interviewer might forget he had asked it already. The child was told that it wasn't expected that the child should change the answer, just to answer the best he could remember.

These preliminary parameters discussed with the interviewee are an adaptation of the Cognitive Interview Technique, first popularized by R. Edward Geiselman [12]. Saywitz offers another set of suggestions for improving the quality of the answers.

Since children are not familiar what the purpose of and how an interview works, and more particularly, with what an interviewer is seeking, she suggests an exercise, not related to the abusive incidents. In this exercise, the child is asked to think of another set of circumstances that he could tell the interviewer about. For example, the child is asked to recount his experience at a recent birthday party he attended.

The child is asked to remember and visualize a particular event at the party, such as the gift giving or exchange. Then the child is asked a series of questions about what the child saw and heard from or about what the other children gave the child whose birthday it was (it could also be his own birthday). He is also asked to describe the room, cake, etc. The questions get more particular when the interviewer asks what the child gave the birthday celebrant, how the child and the celebrant reacted, what was said, etc. The important point here is to avoid the words "pretend" and "imagine", as they might infer you want the child to make up events. It must be emphasized to the child he is to describe things which he personally experienced and which happened in his presence. I would suggest that the child be told that the reason he is being asked to recount what happened in this manner is to help him remember what happened. He should also be told not to guess at anything.

Then the child is told that he will be asked about what happened to him (the abuse, if any) by telling it in total, without out stopping, from the very first incident to the last. He is instructed to tell as much as possible, in narrative form, describing or providing as much as he remembers, leaving nothing out, even the things he might feel are unimportant.

Next, after the narrative, the interviewer asks specific questions regarding details of anything he sees needs elaboration or clarification.

Then the child is asked to recall the events in a different order, starting first at the end, then from the middle. Prompts are provided such as "what happened right before that?," in order to prevent the child from jumping too far backward in time. Then he is told to start at the beginning again.

Lastly, after all of the child's memory is exhausted, the child is asked to view the incidents from another person's perspective. They were told to "put yourself in the body of... and tell me what the person saw."

This last area is of great concern because it may be developmentally difficult for very young children to assume the perspective of another. It is also troublesome because, it requires the child to use his imagination, something which could distort or provide opportunity for influencing his account of the events, thus tainting anything further he might say at that time or in the future.

This whole technique may have the same problem with very young children, for the same reasons and should be used with great care and only after discussion with the child's therapist, if there is one, or professionals on your multidisciplinary team who can make such evaluations and judgments.

Lastly, in what follows, within the context of both interview questions and later discussions of evaluating or validating an allegation, I have extracted criteria from what has been termed "Statement Reality Analysis" [13] as adapted by Brian Tully, Ph.D. [14].

## Child Interview Problems

### Not "Cut-Out" to Interview Children

Perhaps the most important point to be made about interviewing child victims of sexual abuse is that not every individual is cut out to perform well in this work. An investigator may be superb at finding out the facts in cases where there is little contact with traumatized victims, or he may be excellent at dealing with the anxious adult sexual assault victim. However, children present certain unique difficulties when it comes to sitting down and discussing the intimate sexual details of their abuse, and not every investigator can do it.

### Emotional Crime

The investigator should not be ashamed, nor should he feel inadequate. This type of crime is an emotional one, and the deepest feelings within the investigator, regardless of how controlled he thinks he is, can interfere to the point of placing the investigation in jeopardy. Some investigators avoid the task by getting someone else to do their interviews. The dedicated investigator and the one who seeks to master his skills and emotions is the one who finds ways to confront and cope with his limitations. He is also the one who learns to adapt to whatever situation he is faced with. He is the one who is able to use whatever technique is best for the situation he finds himself in. It is absolutely essential that the investigator not only keep his emotions under control, but also leave those emotions in the report folder on his desk when he is not on the case.

### Victims Are Children

Besides the emotional issue that creates difficulties for an investigator, there is another problem an investigator might face in an interview setting. Children create difficulties for some people, and not every person can successfully handle cases involving children. Some can relate to children under a certain age; some are better with children over that age. The point is that because of their age and lack of sophistication, children are often difficult to deal with for people who have no understanding of a child's limitations. The conscientious interviewer will seek to understand these limitations and overcome his own inability to cope with them. He must be aware of this own phobias, dislikes, and limitations.

This is what Saywitz calls the adult's "communicative competence." She lists the following as the criteria for a competent interviewer:

1. Ability to interact with the child without bias in a manner and level the child will understand, taking into account the child's "conversational rules and concepts;"
2. An ability to account for the age of the child and the child's language skills;

She then describes the child's "communicative competence" as:

1. The ability to convert what the child remembers into verbalization that is able to be understood by others.
2. The ability to recognize when he doesn't understand a question.
3. The ability to "reason."
4. The ability to separate "fact from fantasy."

Lastly, she points out that it is imperative that the child have some understanding of the legal system and be able to withstand the stress of the investigative and court process [15]. This is what the adaptation of the cognitive interview process described above is intended to address.

## Interviewer Not Flexible

The successful interview will be one in which the interviewer finds the most comfortable techniques for himself and the child. Experience has shown that in interviewing child sexual abuse victims, it is necessary to throw most traditional police techniques out the window. There is no one successful technique or approach. The successful interviewer will have a handle on as many techniques as possible. The investigator who uses only one style of interviewing won't get very far.

## Adaptation of Non-Traditional Techniques

Some of the most successful techniques of interviewing child molest victims have been established within the therapeutic community. Used by clinicians, these techniques assist the child in expressing what has happened to him with minimal additional trauma. Today, law enforcement is adapting these communication techniques to fit its needs. The primary difference between therapeutic and law-enforcement interviewing techniques is that the law-enforcement approach is directive and objective. It is a method that requires the interviewer to control the content of the interview by directing the victim/witness's attention and concentration to specific concerns, as opposed to allowing for rambling accounts. It is also a quantifiable interview process in which certain objectives must be satisfied: the elements of the crime must be established; the answers to the questions "Who? What? When? Where?" and, often, "Why?" must be found.

Therapists and investigators use the same techniques to obtain the truth, but the therapist's approach is one of inference and conclusion based on clues provided by the child. It must be understood that the suggested use of these methods is not intended to make the law-enforcement investigator an evaluator. The law-enforcement investigator must use these techniques to obtain *facts* to support conclusions that will be made by protective services and the courts.

Before I discuss the specifics of interviewing children, one final point must be made. The medical profession has its Hippocratic oath, which says, in effect, that the help shouldn't hurt the patient nor should the medical profession bring to the patient something he didn't already have. Clearly this applies to the interviewing of child molest victims. Not only must we take great pains not to inflict further pain on the child victim as a result of our contact with him, we must also be sure not to influence the child in any way. In particular, in the interview it is incumbent on us to be absolutely certain we do not lead the child unnecessarily or suggest the answers we seek. In other words, the purpose of whatever is said or done with children is to make them feel comfortable *talking about what happened*. It must in no way influence what the children say, except to help bring out the truth.

## Background:  Influencing Factors

### Sensitivity

The interviewer must have some understanding of the background problems the child has faced and be sensitive to the plight of the victim (see Chapter 2). This must include an understanding of why the child is in a given situation and the reasons for nonreporting. It must also include the recognition of "acting-out" behavior as a symptom and as indicative of the abuse, rather than an indicator of ulterior motive or some other psychological problem (see Chapter 2). Most importantly, the investigator must understand that his own reaction to the child's inability to come forward, and his observations of the symptoms exhibited by the child as a result of the abuse, may make him reluctant to pursue an interview or investigation thoroughly.

## Interview Stress Syndrome

The result of this reluctance is "P.I.S.S. Poor Performance"—a syndrome that afflicts police officers, prosecutors, probation officers, protective service workers, physicians, and many other professionals. "P.I.S.S." is an acronym for *Police Interview Stress Syndrome* (also known as the Prosecutor, Probation-office, Protective-service-worker Interview Stress Syndrome). What causes this syndrome is the difficulty in talking to children about such sensitive things as intimate details of how they were molested. First, the social taboos that prohibit talking about sexual matters inhibit the investigator's ability to discuss the matter openly. Second, the investigator's ignorance of how a child perceives sexuality at different developmental stages may improperly restrict the manner in which he approaches the child. Third, the investigator's inability to establish a common vocabulary with a child who has a limited understanding of technical and common terms may hinder an interview. Fourth, the investigator's own moral "baggage," which may include a perception of the case as being filthy and the child as being unclean or dirty, greatly restricts the investigator's ability to grasp the child's predicament. Last, the investigator's ignorance about his own sexuality and body parts creates a block to communication.

It has been said that child molesters talk to children about sex. "If they don't do it (talk to kids about sex), they won't get it (sexual activity with kids)" [16]. It's clear that we, as information seekers, are in the same boat. If we don't talk to the children about what happened to them, we are not going to get what we need. We must overcome the reluctance, resistance, and distasteful reactions we encounter in ourselves when it becomes necessary to interview a child molest victim if we are to be successful.

## Easing the Pain of Disclosure

The interviewer should keep in mind that the child must not be upset or hurt more than the abuse itself has done — a difficult task. The child is going to have problems in disclosure. "Reliving" the incident(s) will be traumatic. Breaking the silence imposed on him by the offender will be extremely painful. However, done effectively, getting the child to tell as early as possible will prevent later pain.

Many therapists insist that it is good for the child to tell about the events. In doing so, the child gains control of the situation, which he did not have before. The investigator can assist in the healing process by providing the child with the ability to disclose. The manner in which the interview is conducted will determine, in large part, how it affects the child. The investigator who interviews rather than interrogates the child will reduce the chances of interview trauma. By remembering that the child is not a "little adult" and has different capabilities than an adult, the interviewer will minimize the degree of discomfort the child will experience.

## Recognizing Child's Difficulty

The investigator must be aware that the child will become anxious as the interview focuses on the abusive incident(s). This may manifest itself in several ways. The child may verbally try to avoid the subject. He may engage in all manner of avoidance behavior, such as playing or fidgeting with whatever is within reach. He may also complain of pains or discomfort — for example, "My ears hurt." The child's body language may reflect tension or discomfort. This is important to know and recognize because these reactions may be mistaken for those of a lying or uncooperative child. Investigators should be cognizant of the dynamics of victimization (previously discussed in Chapter 2 and 3) — that certain reactions should be expected and understood as normal for a child molest victim — so that mistaken conclusions will not be drawn.

With few exceptions, the initial and some subsequent interviews will only scratch the surface of what actually occurred. The more often the abuse occurred, the greater the number of interviews that will be needed. The first account will never include all the details. The best way to determine what has happened to a child is to allow as much time as necessary for the child to feel comfortable with the interviewer and the idea of talking about the events. Ideally, this will take several interview sessions. Most of the time, however, the ability to conduct interviews over several days will be curtailed by the need to protect the child and secure evidence, and the growing caseload of the investigator. Therefore, the investigator should consider ways of conducting a prolonged interview, allowing for appropriate breaks for play or rest before resuming questioning. What must be carefully avoided is creating a situation where the child is held until he reveals something about the molest. This will be discussed in more detail later in this chapter in the section on timing and pace.

As the interview progresses, the investigator may uncover more offenses than were originally reported. In the beginning interviews, the child probably will only tell part of what happened, until he trusts the investigator. This will occur when he sees that he is not punished or ridiculed, or that his parents or the investigator don't react adversely. This may be a conscious or subconscious testing of the interviewer by the child to see how he will react. The child will also begin to remember more as the pressure about the secret's being disclosed is relieved. That release of pressure — the Child Sexual Abuse Accommodation Syndrome notwithstanding — will also be facilitated by the child's seeing that the world doesn't come down around his ears after he discloses. All of this will assist the child to feel better about talking about what happened.

## Factor's Affecting Disclosure

The manner in which disclosure is generally made is like the peeling of an onion. Each layer removed reveals new details. The child will first tell of the least threatening details. He will tell of meeting the offender and going places or doing things with him, and may reveal some aspect of the manner in which he was seduced by the offender, omitting any activity or inference about his willing participation in any sexual acts. This may happen during the first interview or subsequent interviews, or when other contacts are made for other purposes such as serving papers. This is one of the main reasons a child molestation victim should be re-interviewed and allowed the opportunity to give more details after the initial interview.

Whenever child molestation victims are interviewed, the investigator must consider several factors. He must examine the circumstances of the abuse to determine just how much the incident has affected the child. This will also help to determine where the child stands in relation to those involved in the incident and his own family. For example, as discussed in Chapter 2, the child's age will determine greatly how much the incident affects him. If the child is too young to understand either the wrongfulness of the act or the significance of what occurred, this will greatly influence the way the interview is conducted. If the child is aware of either or both of these factors, that too will determine the way the child is approached and how the interview is conducted.

Another factor is that of the age of the child at the time of the incident vs. his age at the time of the report. A child who reports the incident several years after its commission will have more difficulty remembering what happened. The child may also appear to be in much greater control if he reports the incident a long time after its occurrence, and not display the symptoms generally associated with abuse. If the child is much older when the incident surfaces than when it actually occurred, it may create other credibility problems for him. His use of sophisticated or age-inappropriate language may cause people to be less likely to believe him, because it may appear as though he made up the incident. This is especially true if he shows no visible signs of emotional disturbance from the abuse or no emotion when talking about it. The longer the delay in telling of the abuse, the greater the chance of his having a credibility problem. This air of disbelief is often apparent to the child and may cause some anxiety within him, creating a strong block to communication.

The interviewer must also consider the physical and emotional developments of the child:

1. Did the child feel that the activity was physically comforting or stimulating?
2. Does he have any feelings about the offender or activity that will influence the way he relates it to the investigator?
3. Will the child become emotional when discussing the incident?
4. How will he handle the stress of talking about it?

The child's understanding of sex will have a great influence on the way the child is approached by the interviewer:

1. Does the child understand the sexual significance of the act?
2. Does the child know the difference between the sexes?
3. Does the child understand the concept of stimulation and its relationship to what occurred?

Other factors that will greatly affect how the child reacts to the incidents and the interviewer are:

1. The stability of the child's family.
2. The relationship between the offender and the child.
3. The fears the child holds about disclosure.
4. The threats of violence or death.
5. The degree of brutality or nonviolence of the incident(s).
6. The child's attention span.

If the child's family is not supportive of the child and is split over what to do about the allegations, the child may have difficulty in telling about what happened. If the offender is a relative, this may be a greater problem for the child because the family may be split both on what to do with the offender and on the issue of believing the child. If the offender is close to the child, it may be very difficult for the child to disclose to anyone, much less a police officer he doesn't know. An attack by a stranger is often easier for the child to speak about, because there is less threat of retaliation and little or no relationship has been developed.

The child's fears about what might happen if he tells about the abuse will greatly affect the ease with which the interviewer is able to get the child to discuss it. If the child fears that something will happen to him or someone else because of what happened or because he was threatened, he will be less likely to discuss the incident(s) freely.

Finally, the developmental level and attention span of the child will determine how the interview is conducted and how long it will last.

## Symptoms Seen in Disclosure

Some symptoms of abuse will surface during the interview. The extent to which the symptoms will be seen will vary depending on all of the factors discussed in this chapter and in Chapter 2. For example, the child may experience fear — fear of you, of the court process, of the offender, of the fact that his parents may be hurt, or just plain fear of the unknown.

### *Withdrawal*

A common response to abuse is withdrawal. This may be caused by the desire to forget and/or suppress the incident(s). This is common in cases where the offender is a family member or a close friend. The child may withdraw because of the discomfort of the incident(s). He mentally extricates himself from the uncomfortable situation of the abuse to make it bearable. In this way he creates a mental block that prevents him from remembering what happened. Removing himself mentally while talking to you will be an easy way to prevent his reliving the pain he experienced too many times.

He may also withdraw because of his unfamiliarity with the interview surroundings and procedures. For this reason, don't expect the child to talk easily to you in a cold, drab, police setting. Lastly, he may withdraw because he is embarrassed. He may feel uncomfortable talking to you because you are a stranger, and it is difficult discussing embarrassing things with a stranger. Avoiding talking about an embarrassing situation helps him alleviate the discomfort.

### *Embarrassment*

Embarrassment is also another symptom of abuse. The child may be embarrassed about what occurred, embarrassed for his parents, or embarrassed for falling victim to the offender. The child may also feel guilty. He may feel that through the abuse he was being punished for doing something wrong. Children experience emotional pain, if not physical pain, as a result of the abuse. The problem is that children often associate pain with guilt. They feel that if they do wrong they get punished (experience pain), which then translates into, "If you hurt after the incidents, then you must have done wrong." For example, a child may feel he will be punished for accepting the enticement of the offender. He may feel especially guilty if he is wondering whether his own sexuality had anything to do with the incidents. This is a common problem when the child has experienced some confusing sexual sensations and/or emotionally comforting or satisfying feelings during the abusive incidents.

### *Confusion*

Some children are genuinely confused about the whole thing. They know something unusual occurred, but they are confused about the fuss because they don't understand or feel the violation or the wrongfulness of the act(s). Guilt may also be caused by another conflict the child is trying to resolve. Children are often told by others that if they are touched sexually it will hurt. The confusion is cause because, although they expected pain, they often experienced pleasurable feelings. This confusion is extremely important for the investigator to understand and recognize, because he must not assume that the experience was bad or painful for the child.

## Non-Judgmental Questions

It is equally important that the investigator not impose or project his own feelings about the incident. To do so may negatively affect the child. The investigator must be aware that if the offender was involved in any kind of relationship with the child, there is a great chance that the child will be defensive about the offender. For this reason, make absolutely no judgmental comments about the offender in the presence of the child.

The parents may help prevent some of these problems from becoming great hurdles by accompanying the child into the interview setting. They can reassure the child as the interview progresses and provide support for the child as well as for the interviewer in trying to get the child to express difficult concepts. The problem is that parents can be equally destructive if they are not sensitive to the issues or supportive of the investigator's efforts, so the investigator must make tactical decisions in each case. This will be discussed in greater detail in the strategy section of this chapter.

## Level of Understanding

We discussed above the fact that many children don't understand the sexual nature of the incidents. Children often don't understand sexual excitement or its relationship to stimulation. Therefore, the child does not understand the sexual significance of an event and generally views the assault on a strictly physical level. This means that all questioning will have to relate to experiential terms the child can understand. For example, when talking to a child about an erection and trying to get the child to express what he saw, the questions will have to go something like this:

Q:   You said you saw your daddy's pee-pee. What did it look like when you saw it?

The answer you will most likely get with this question, which is intentionally vague to avoid being leading (see discussion of leading questions later), is "What do you mean?" The follow-up sequence to this question might go something like this:

Q: Was it always the same?

A: What?

Q: Was your daddy's pee pee different any of the times you saw it?

A: Yes

Q: How was it different?

A: I don't know.

Q: Was it stiff, was it floppy, or was it something else?

Note that at this point, rather than asking if the father's penis was a different size as well, only the question about texture was asked. It is important not to cloud the issue with children and not to test more than one concept at a time. Follow-up questions should cover the question of size and matters:

A: It was both.

Q: When was it stiff?

A: Some of the time it was stiff.

Q: At what time was it stiff? When you first saw him or after?

A: Sometimes it was stiff when I first saw him and sometimes it was after.

Q: How was it before you saw it stiff?

A: It was soft.

Q: How do you know it was soft?

A: I felt it.

Q: Do you know what made it stiff?

A: No.

Q: When it was soft at first did you or your dad ever do anything to his pee pee?

A: Yes.

Q: What was done and who did it?

A: Sometimes he would rub it and sometimes he would have me rub it.

Q: Show me on the doll how he made you rub it?

From here the questioning should continue by returning to the description of the penis with questions such as: was it "big or small," "hanging down or sticking out," and any other questions that might be pertinent to the incident(s). Each series of questions should relate directly to something the child could feel, see, hear, taste, or smell.

## Rapport Building

All the considerations mentioned will be of no value if no effort is made to make the child feel comfortable—with the interviewer and with the idea of talking about what happened. Earlier, I spoke of building a foundation from which an interview can grow. Understanding where the child has been and is now (emotionally) is only a small part of that foundation. The rest is the rapport that the interviewer will be able to build with the child. When the interview hits spots that appear to threaten its success, the child will balk and the interview will fall to produce the needed results if no such rapport exists. There are some very simple techniques for building rapport and establishing a strong bond with the child. Most require little time and/or effort.

## Breaking Barriers

When you first meet the child, offer your hand to shake his. As has been described, a child has various feelings about what has happened to him. One of these is that he feels unclean. Shaking his hand will help, in a nonverbal way, to assure him that you don't think he is dirty.

An investigator must do everything in his power to interview the child in the manner he would like someone else to interview his own children. Regardless of how the investigator feels about the child he must interview, he will find that someone loves and cares for that child. He must consider how he would want his own children or relatives interviewed if such a thing were to happen to them. The investigator must try to deal with the children he interviews accordingly. In trying to conform to this suggestion, it has been my experience that it is important to consider the reasons the child is in the situation he is in, and to accept him for what he is rather than making judgments. Making judgments will narrow an investigator's decision-making capabilities and will act as a roadblock to building the necessary rapport.

As police officers, we must often play the role that best suits the situation in order to resolve some of the conflicts we are called on to settle. Interviewing children is no different. I suggest that if an investigator cannot genuinely accept some of the suggested techniques that follow, and he doesn't have the luxury of getting someone else to do his interviews, he should act as though he does accept them. I say this with one caveat—if he cannot act in a way that is convincing, he shouldn't act at all. Nothing is more apparent to a child than someone who is "acting" about caring for him. So, be careful!

## Showing Concern

One of the easiest ways to establish rapport and trust is to demonstrate concern. The investigator should let the child see that the investigator genuinely cares for him, that the investigator is concerned for his welfare. Because children communicate in limited ways, a technique that helped produce this effect was having some snacks or cookies with you when you met the child. Like offering a person who is visiting you a cup of coffee, it was a courtesy and a form of nurturance that demonstrates, in a tangible way, "I'm thinking of you" or "I care." This is an area of high controversy. The "snack" shouldn't go beyond the initial contact, before and apart from the interview, because it may appear as thought he child was answering your questions simply to get more snack or food.

This practice is most controversial in situations where the defense position is that the child was trying to please the interviewer by answering questions the way the interviewer wanted. The defense is also raised when a toy or gift is provided the child, such as a teddy bear as has been provided many children by agencies as a means of trying to comfort them in a time of need or sadness.

There have been several cases where children have been alleged to have made up allegations just to get the teddy bear or other reward. Where food or candy is the means of making the child feel comfortable, the defense position becomes the child made up what was said so that the child could get more candy. In one case, an offender who was charged with multiple counts on several children was acquitted of all counts, largely, because the police agency had given teddy bears out to the children who reported abuse. Those reports were suddenly made in the early days following the original case, which probably was valid. The jury found him not guilty because it believed the children merely wanted new teddybears.

## Physical Touch

Another way to establish rapport with the child is to use physical affection. This can also be used to support the child. Letting the child set the limits, allow for "controlled touching" during the interview. Start by placing your hand where the child can reach out and touch it. During the interview you may want to demonstrate your support for the child in a difficult area. You may reach out and gently touch the child on the back of the upper arm as you talk to him. These "tentative touches" will help you to gauge whether or not the child will accept physical consolation. For example, after accepting these tentative touches the child may be crying. To demonstrate your support and comfort the child, you may want to put your arm around the child's shoulder and pat him on the back. You may want to hold is hand at a troubling time or hold him as you talk to him. If necessary, you may want to cuddle him or have him sit on your lap. All of these touches and any other supportive touches you may think of will assist in creating a bond between you and the child. The only caution here is that you must be sure that both the kind of touching you want to use and the timing are appropriate. *Remember:* the reason he is talking to you is because *someone took advantage of some kind of touching.* Whatever you do, be sure that the touch you initiate is one that is not threatening and will be accepted by the child willingly and without reservation.

The investigator must be prepared for the possibility that some touching may be initiated by the child. Especially with younger children, physical contact will be desired for support and assurance. A child may climb onto the investigator's lap and may even display seductive behavior. This may be rubbing the interviewer's leg while talking to him, or straddling the investigator's leg and thrusting his hips as in intercourse. The investigator must be prepared to have this happen without reacting in a way that will upset the child.

During the interview, children may begin to masturbate or begin to touch themselves while talking, especially when describing pleasurable parts of what happened. Although this type of behavior should be documented in the interview report, it may be best not to call it to the child's attention, as it could be construed as a reprimand and cause the child to freeze up.

### Discussing the Child's Fears

Earlier, we discussed fears the child may have as well as confusion about what happened and the investigative process that may follow. The degree to which this affects a child will depend on the child's age, and whatever is done to address this concern must be appropriate for that age. A simple way to eliminate both the fear and confusion, while at the same time establishing some trust with the child, is for the investigator to explain his role. Tell the child what you do and why you're there. You might spend some time talking about yourself, establishing some common ground or shared experiences. Ask the child if he ever met a police officer before. Let him know you are human, that you eat, drink, sleep, and can feel pain. One of the things I do is let the child pinch me to see that I am just like he is—real! I try to let him know that he need not fear me.

### How to Dress

If you are in uniform, remember that the child may be distracted by it, if not afraid of it. The best and preferred way to interview a child is in plain clothes, such as comfortable jeans or similar attire. If you must do it in a uniform, do something to make the child comfortable with you and to lessen the uniform's impact.

### Use of Position as Police Officer

A technique I have used is to show the child my equipment. In particular, school-age children are intensely interested in how things work. Use the child's curiosity as a means of gaining rapport. Kids love to see your handcuffs and radio and know what kind of gun you carry (don't take it out of its holster). Start by asking them if they have any questions about your uniform. If they are comfortable with you as you are, go on to another subject. A preferable way to interview a child if you are in uniform is to take off your gunbelt, badge, or anything else on the uniform that would create a distraction before you meet the child, and put it out of sight. This will also allow you better freedom of movement. Taking off your gun will also help to prevent the defense attorney from claiming that you intimidated the child. Remember, some children will fear you anyway because they have been threatened that the police will harm or arrest them.

Another technique I have used to get the child to be comfortable with me is to ask the child if he ever saw a real badge before. It is an excellent way to express to the child in a way he can understand that you would like to make him feel comfortable with you. Most of the time I have found that all the child can see on a uniform is the badge, and a friendly opportunity to see it up close—hold it in his hand—is rarely refused. This works just as well when the investigator is wearing plain clothes. Because children love to play "dress up," once the child is holding my badge, I ask him if he would like to wear it. The only responses I have ever received are smiles. In one case where I had to interview several children in the same family at their home, they ended up arguing over who was going to wear it next while waiting for me to talk with them.

Another badge technique is the use of the "deputy" or "assistant" badge, which is made of paper or cardboard and is used by community relations divisions of police departments for children to wear. As a way of making friends, the child may be "deputized" and made the investigator's "partner." The child may then be told that he and the officer are "partners" and that partners, as a matter of respect and concern for each other, share secrets or don't keep things from one another. The officer may then tell the child a "secret" and ask for one in return. A variation of this technique worked well with an officer who was interviewing a young girl who wouldn't tell him about her abuse. He did have the trust and cooperation of the child's sister, who was 2 years older. He "deputized" her, giving her a paper badge. In the officer's presence and with his assistance, she interviewed her younger sister for him, obtaining a detailed account of the events.

One technique, developed by Captain Jeffrey Miller of the Los Gatos Police Department, Los Gatos, California, is that of introducing oneself as a "secret policeman." The technique works well with children who understand and can be charmed by the concept of secrets. It is a successful way to establish rapport and trust and facilitate the telling of the child's experiences. His technique requires that the officer be introduced to the child as a "friend" of the family, with no reference to his being a police officer. Before the interview, he takes time to explain how he wants to be introduced by the parents and what role he wants them to play in the interview, if any. After drawing, playing, or reading to the child and discussing and explaining the concept of good and bad secrets, the officer determines whom the child likes and respects. This accomplishes two things. It gives the officer a brief view of how the child perceives those around him, in particular the offender. It also determines for the officer how the child perceives the police, because one of the people he asks about is a police officer. If the child tells him he doesn't like the police because they arrest people and put them in jail, it's natural to ask who the child fears might go to jail. This may give the officer a glimpse of the child's self-image and what the child fears might happen to him, or it may offer some insight into the fears the child has about what might happen to the offender.

When the officer is confident that the child does not have an insurmountable dislike for the police, the officer tells the child that he has a secret he would like to share with the child. He tells the child that he is a "secret policeman," explaining that he is the one that children tell secrets to. He tells the child that is the reason he wears plain clothes and drives an ordinary car, unlike the other policemen. He takes the child out to his car (which in Det. Miller's case has all the accoutrements of an undercover police car) and lets the child see the hidden radio, siren, and special emergency lights rigged into the headlights. After allowing some time for the child to become enamored with the idea of knowing a "secret policeman," the officer asks the child if he would feel comfortable in sharing a secret now that the officer has shared one with the child.

What this technique does quickly and in a nonthreatening manner is explain the officer's role. In explaining your role, it is important to tell the child that you talk to children who are in situations similar to the one at hand. In doing so, you accomplish two things—you let the child know you have done this before and he should feel comfortable with you, and you show him he is not alone, that this is something that also happens to others. At the same time you can side with the child, telling him you are there for him. He needs to know that someone will be his advocate, that someone will believe him, especially someone who is not within his family unit. By revealing your interest in the child, you show him you can be that person.

## Other Techniques

Regardless of your technique, the ultimate goal is to get the child to like you. Through the demonstration that you are concerned for the child, it should happen naturally. Consider beginning the interview by asking the child about school, hobbies, friends, and activities. Play with the child. Do something fun first. Don't zero in on the incident until rapport is well established. Be sure that you reaffirm your rapport and relationship in all subsequent interviews before you begin re-questioning.

## Non-Verbal Communication

Nonverbal communication will play a significant role in establishing rapport with a child. It's not just what you say, but how you say it. Your actions will oftentimes speak louder than your words. As police officers, we often fall victim to the fault of being in a power position, so that we carry ourselves in such a way that we set ourselves apart from others. Our demeanor, body language, and speech convey an air of superiority. If we are to be successful in interviewing child sexual molestation victims, this must not be one of our personality traits.

Normally, when we speak with others, we try to approach them on the same physical level. What we ultimately try to seek is the same eye level. In doing so, we establish some common ground. Neither person is given the advantage of being physically higher than the other. A very successful way to establish rapport with a child quickly is to come down to his physical level. An adult can intimidate a child merely by size; therefore, something must be done to equalize the child and the interviewer and reduce the size disparity. This may mean that you must kneel or crouch to come down to the child's eye level. However, I don't suggest this method if you intend to speak with the child for any length of time. A better and easier way to accomplish this is to sit on the floor, where the child feels more at home anyway. You may even wish to lie on the floor to get your head closer to the child. This will quickly give the child a sense of control—you're in his domain—and will help him to relax.

By simply sitting or lying on the floor you have, without saying a word, conveyed to the child that you are "one of us." You will also have demonstrated to the child that you are open to hearing what he has to say. You can help maintain this feeling by adopting the child's body language. If the child sits "Indian style" with his legs crossed in front of him you might consider doing the same. You might also consider taking on some of the mannerisms of the child, not necessarily mimicking the child, which may be interpreted as false, but using some of the gestures children use in talking or playing.

Whatever you do, be sure your body language is read as being open and willing to hear whatever the child has to say. Avoid bored mannerisms such as leaning against walls or furniture, drumming your fingers on a surface, or leaning back in a chair. Be careful not to assume an authoritative stance or position when facing the child, such as standing or sitting with crossed arms, giving stern looks, or continuously staring or glaring. By crossing your arms you are telling a child you are not open to receiving information. Such positions should be avoided.

Wherever you sit while conducting an interview, you must maintain a position of "openness." That is, you must appear to be willing to accept anything and have the appearance of being flexible. To accomplish this, here are some things not to do:

1.  When seated on a chair, try not to cross your legs.
2.  Whatever you sit on, try to avoid facing the side of the child.
3.  Don't straddle a chair with the back facing forward.
4.  Don't sit on or behind a table or desk.

All of these positions place a psychological or physical barrier between you and the child that will create a block to the flow of information. Good sitting positions are slightly to the side, at a diagonal but facing the child, or directly in front of him. When sitting on a chair, it is best to be bent slightly forward, with your legs spread apart at about 10 o'clock and 2 o'clock. This position connotes openness, interest, and concern.

## Avoid Distractions and Interruptions

Listen closely to the child's language and use the same words he uses in discussing the events with him. It is extremely important that you pay close attention to the child when interviewing him. If you have a radio or pager on, turn it off. If you are in an office, disconnect the phone. All interruptions should be eliminated, if possible. The reasons for this should be obvious. This should be done as a simple matter of courtesy, just as you would do with any other person. Children don't know that when the alert tone is broadcast on your radio, your attention is immediately given to the broadcast that follows the tone. The same is true for the pager. The phone is a bit more obvious, but many investigators rudely allow these interruptions.

Consider the child's reaction to the interruption of the interview. If the child continues talking through the radio broadcast or page, unaware that your attention has slipped, and then you ask a question he has already answered or covered during your brief distraction, he concludes that you don't really care because you weren't listening. This can seriously set you back in the interview process. It doesn't have to happen if you take precautions to avoid it.

## Eye Contact

Another sign of respect for someone is eye contact. If you can establish and maintain eye contact, you will demonstrate support, interest, and encouragement without saying a word. Just be careful not to stare or glare.

## Avoid Reactions that Disclose Your Feelings

Be sure to avoid accusing or critical comments about the offender. Remember, many children still have some strong feelings about the offender and will defend him to the hilt. Avoid judgmental statements about what has happened. You must also not show emotion or react if the child tells you something that is personally upsetting. He may interpret your reaction as a judgment of either the offender or himself and it could influence what else he says or doesn't say. If you react by only smiling, the child might feel that what he said is what you want to hear, and will therefore continue to tell you only similar things, hoping to please you. Conversely, if you react by frowning, he may cease telling you things he feels will upset you.

## Dealing With Anxiety and Guilt

The concept of providing positive reinforcement for the child to tell the truth about what happened will be discussed in greater detail later in this chapter. If you sense some defensiveness or protectiveness about the offender or what happened, try offering some statements that will help to reduce the child's anxiety. Here are some statements that have worked for me in the past:

> It's not bad to tell what happened.
> You can help X by telling what happened.
> You will feel better if you tell, even though it's hard to do.
> At the same time you can relieve guilt by asking:
> Do you feel you might get into trouble?
> Do you feel it was your fault?
> Do you feel you are to blame?

A more subtle way to establish who is to blame for what happened is to ask, *after disclosure is made*:

> By the way, if X had not done this to you, do you think we'd be here talking?
> If X had done nothing to you, we wouldn't be here talking, would we?

This technique works well because it directly assigns responsibility in a way the child can understand. Even if the child tells you he doesn't fear getting in trouble or feel that he is to blame, reassure him he is not. Continue to do so throughout your contact with him if it seems appropriate.

Another technique to relieve guilt is to tell a story about fault. Give an analogy with a child who is on a bike and who gets pushed down by the neighborhood bully. Ask the child whose fault it was that the child on the bike fell and hurt himself. Try to get the child to see that he is not responsible for his pain. Try to get the child to assign responsibility and have him say in his own words who is to blame. Throughout your contact with the child, have him associate responsibility for the offense with the offender, including what happens to the offender if he is convicted. In addition, reassure the child that the consequences of what happened belong not only to the offender but also the judge. It is very important to convince the child that his testimony did nothing to jeopardize the offender.

Another way to approach the subject of responsibility is to tell the child that it appears there is a "problem" and that you would like him to help you figure out what it is. Being very careful not to attach any significance to the size of the problem or the number of times the incidents occurred, try to get the child to figure out what he thinks the problem is. Many times children, especially those aged 8 through the teens, will realize that the number of times an incident occurred or the size of the problem is equal to the serious-ness of the problem—i.e., the length or type of sentence. A child who realizes this is more likely to revert to protective devices. Try temporizing language such as, "Right now I don't know what will happen to [the offender] because someone else decides that later. Right now I need to know everything that happened so we can figure out what the problem is. Then we can figure out how to solve the problem."

It is equally important that you not make predictions about the outcome of the investigation and/or trial if the subject comes up. Always put the onus onto the offender. It at all possible, try to avoid discussions about court (this subject will be discussed in greater detail later).

Even after you have placed the responsibility on the offender, you may have some problems with the child on this subject. Oftentimes, the child is concerned about the offender because he doesn't want anything bad to happen to him. This may occur even if the abuse was severe. You may use this to your advantage by playing on that concern and the child's desire to help. One common trait among children is their desire to help adults. Tell the child that what he tells you will help the offender. I often tell the child that the offender needs help. I explain that often the result of the child's telling what happened is that the offender gets help. If the child asks whether the offender will go to jail, I answer that sometimes that is the outcome, but that he will get help in jail. I also explain, if necessary, that sometimes jail will be help in itself. I always try to put the best light on a bad thing when explaining it to the child.

One way to address this with children is to ask them what happened when they do something wrong. They generally will respond by giving some negative consequences. Explain that when adults do something wrong, it may be necessary to punish them too. Tell them that because we can't spank adults, take away their allowance, or make them go to bed without dinner, we have to punish them in another way. Often this punishment is a way of helping them not to repeat what they have done. This will better prepare the child for what may happen at the conclusion of a trial.

## Positive Reinforcement

As the interview progresses and the concerns mentioned here surface, I use a technique to encourage the child to continue talking. It is a behavior-shaping technique and is commonly attacked by defense attorneys as molding the witness. If done carefully, it is by no means solely a technique that molds behavior. It is a successful way to comfort and support the child and at the same time *reinforce the talking, not what is said.* It is called *positive reinforcement.* Use positive reinforcement as much as possible during the interview. Periodically compliment the child and reassure him that he is doing OK.

It often helps to use positive reinforcement after the child has passed through a difficult time in the interview. For example, if the child has struggled to describe a particular event, after you ask another question not related to the event, it would help to reassure the child that he is doing well. During the rapport-building process and during the interview as a whole, it is a good idea to praise the child for talking with you. Tell him that he is courageous to talk about such things and that you are honored to be talking with one of the children who have the courage to tell and to be so open about what happened to them.

Take great care to avoid accusatory questions. Remember that your inflection and tone of your voice can be interpreted as being accusatory and/or guilt producing. Avoid any question that begins with "why." For instance, "I'm not sure I understand this. Can you explain it?"

## Interview Concerns

The interview should always include discussions of several issues. Ask the child if he has any questions. Give the child an opportunity to voice any concerns prior to starting the interview. This will assist in instilling trust in you. Try to identify the expectations of the child once the crime has been revealed. In a very tactful way, try to determine why the crime was reported. This is an important statement to get from the child at the beginning of the investigation. The child's articulation of one of the following reasons for reporting will assist greatly in validating his allegations.

## Disclosure Issues

Generally, you will find that the crime is reported for one of three reasons. First, although difficult for the child to articulate, is that he wanted the abuse to stop. Second, the child may want the offender to be punished. Last, and most frequent, he wants some help for the offender. The circumstances that permit disclosure may cast a shadow on the real reasons the child came forward. As I said about the window of disclosure in Chapter 2, the time must be right for it to occur. Often the child tells when a driving force pushes the disclosure to the surface. This may be simply because the child feels safe, or it could involve stronger emotions such as anger, jealousy, vengeance, or vindictiveness.

Another facet of disclosure that must be discussed is how the incident came to light. Most cases are reported through secondary parties. Often the child doesn't consciously tell what happened. He may confide in a friend and that friend tells, resulting in the case being reported. The child may then become hostile, for two reasons. The first is that, consciously, he did not wish to disclose and he is concerned about telling what happened. The second is the sense of betrayal he now feels about the person who let the cat out of the bag, and that sense of betrayal may be transferred to you. In discussing how the case came to be discovered, you may be able to bring this hostility to the surface and try to divert it.

Encourage the child to discuss his feelings about what happened. Regardless of age, it is necessary that each child be given the opportunity to acknowledge how he feels. You will demonstrate your concern for the child and your sincerity simply by asking. In doing so, you must give him permission to tell what happened, to feel angry or have other emotions, and to talk about them. Assure the child that he is not alone. When telling the child that you have talked to others, reassure him that you know how difficult it is for him. When to do this in the interview process must be left to your judgment. Usually it is best addressed when it appears as though the child has hit a communication block. Like the questions listed earlier relating to trouble, blame, and fault, pose the question as a possibility and reassure him that it is normal to feel these emotions or have these concerns.

Having the child express why he reported the incident will both determine what the relationship is between the child and the offender and demonstrate your concern for the child *and* the offender. It is a good way to lead into other areas of discussion in the process of gaining rapport. While talking to the child about the investigation and the case, don't lie to him. On questions that are related to negative feelings or negative aspects of the investigation, build on the positive points, as was mentioned earlier regarding the possibility of jail.

## Promises

Be especially careful not to make promises you can't keep. Promises made about the offender's being or not being arrested or convicted can create problems for you and the child by betraying the child's trust if the opposite of what you said happens. A common statement made by investigating officers that often backfires is the promise that "you won't have to testify." Just as frequently unreliable is the promise that "court will be OK." Remember, once the case leaves your hands, it is out of your control. This means three things. First, you may not be there when the child has to go to court and you will not have the opportunity to prepare him for the disappointment you set him up for by making the promise you made. Second, and perhaps more important, you have no control as to whom the case goes to. The people who receive the case may not be as sensitive to the child's needs as you. Last, don't make the mistake of telling the child that no one will know what he tells you.

All too often this promise is made without explaining that everyone down the investigative/prosecutorial line will know, and that if the case goes to court, anyone who is interested can find out by attending the court hearings. When this question comes up, as it inevitably will, simply tell the child that few people will know and that you and other people will do everything in your power to keep it that way. In any case, this should not be discussed with a child until the child brings it up. There is no sense in bringing up a concern the child doesn't have. Perhaps the biggest mistake some investigators make is either not telling the parents about what happened or telling the child that the parents won't know. This will be discussed in greater detail later on.

## Explaining Why Certain Questions Are Asked

A child must be told during the interview that the reason for asking certain questions—in particular the specific personal questions and questions about the sex acts—is not that you don't believe him or that you are curious. He needs to have an understanding of what you're doing when you talk to him— that you are trying to determine what the problem is. To eliminate fears and confusion, he needs to understand the procedures you follow and what to expect from those who will follow you. The details need not be delved into, but the child should at least know that the reason you are asking the questions and taking notes is that you will have to report to someone else. He should be told that the information will be kept as confidential as possible. He also needs to know what to expect next, such as when he will next hear from you or who the next person in the chain will be. Consider that the more the child realizes the implications for the offender, the more likely he will begin to hedge.

The preceding concerns are important for most cases, but they are paramount when talking to adolescents. For example, a case involved a man who hired highschool girls to do phone soliciting for him. He pressured them into sex acts with him and to pose for pornographic pictures after giving them cocaine. Although well-intentioned, the investigators made some major blunders. This caused no end of trouble for the prosecutor because of the disappointment of the "breaking of the promises" the children thought had been made and the misinformation they and their parents had been given. The problems encountered in this case as a result of these errors should demonstrate why it is so important for the investigator to ensure that the child knows what will follow and what to expect.

Everything that transpired between the police and the girls was discovered after a preliminary hearing at which the children testified and the defendant was held to answer. Before going to trial, interviews with the children and the defense attorney were set up in order to try to get a plea from the defendant. At the meeting before the interviews, it was discovered that one of the children who came in with her father would not talk to the prosecutor. In discussing this with her and her father, it was found that she had been advised by her father not to talk because he thought she was going to be prosecuted for the narcotics violations. Her father had never been told about the sexual aspect of the case or his daughter's involvement in the sex acts.

It was also found that several other of the girls were hostile toward the police. Once the interviews with the other girls began, the reasons became abundantly clear. One girl complained that one of her friends told her she had been shown pictures by the police of the girl naked and involved in sex acts with the defendant. Apparently, the friend saw these pictures when the police were trying to identify girls involved with the defendant. Another complained that the officer told her that no one would ever know about what she told him. Still another told the defense lawyer that she was told by the police that she wouldn't have to testify and that she was angry because she had to testify in open court at the preliminary hearing. All of the girls were extremely hostile toward the prosecution because of what happened, and openly told the defense attorney that they didn't want to cooperate with the prosecution. The hostility may have come from other sources, but the police certainly gave the girls ample justification for it.

Adolescents usually question values and beliefs they have been taught. They will often distrust police officers on the surface, yet want very much to talk to them. They may show a facade of bravado or hostility that is often a bluff to cover feelings of shyness, inferiority, or insecurity. Children often relate better to their peer group and outwardly may have a minimum rapport with adults. For these reasons, it is important not to threaten them or put them on the defensive. It would also be a mistake to rule them out as a source of information. It simply means that you will have to work harder at gaining rapport with teenagers than with any other age group. They are people approaching adulthood who want to be adults, but cannot quite handle it. The best way is to approach them as though they were adults—appeal to their sense of responsibility and of defending their rights.

## Protective Custody

Finally, in building and holding rapport, nothing will be as difficult as explaining why you have to take a child into protective custody. The child must understand why he is being taken out of the home. Many parents and children think the child is being "arrested." This can have a devastating affect on the child and the relationship you might build with him. In attempting to mitigate this with very you children, one officer explains to the child that he is going to a baby sitter for a while, and reassures the child that he hopes the child will be home soon. The difficulty with this technique is that it could set the child up for a great disappointment if he is away from home for a long time. Care must be taken with this technique.

In the following example, both the reasons for explaining protective custody and the need for establishing rapport are clearly illustrated. Although well-meaning, an officer unnecessarily frightened a child and her parents in the process of taking the child into protective custody and trying to interview her. The result was a hostile family who refused at first to allow any further cooperation by the child.

After a school presentation by a child assault prevention program in a local community, an 8-year-old girl told the rape crisis counselor that her natural father had been molesting her over a period of time. She said that her father had engaged her in sexual intercourse, oral copulation, and digital penetration of her vagina. She also said that her father, who no longer lived with her, was molesting the 6-year-old daughter of his current girlfriend, with whom he was now living.

The officer immediately went to the 6-year-old's school and pulled her out of class unannounced. With too little introduction about what the interview was to be about, he questioned her about her father's sexual involvement with her. Naturally, she denied that anything had happened—the father had threatened her and told her not to tell anyone. Unable to reach her mother, the officer took the child to the police department and subsequently to the children's shelter in protective custody, not explaining to the child enough about what was happening or why. He left his card at the school for the school authorities to give to the mother when she came to pick up the child. When the mother came to the school later that day, she was told that the police had picked up the child and she was given the officer's card. She called the police station, but by that time the officer had gone for the day. No one knew anything about the case, so the mother called the children's shelter. Because the officer had not left any information about the child, the shelter was afraid the mother might be involved and refused to release any information about the child's whereabouts. Unfortunately, the week before all this happened, the child's school had sent a warning notice to parents about a man who was posing as a police officer and trying to pick up children. Needless to say, the mother was upset, not knowing if her child was actually in the shelter.

The child was at the shelter overnight. It wasn't until late in the afternoon of the following day that her mother was able to pick her up. The following day, the probation officer—cases of this type were handled by probation rather than social services—tried to contact the family. He was referred to the family's attorney (a distant relative who worked for the federal government), who wanted to know why the child wasn't read her rights and why she was taken into custody without a warrant. He told the probation officer that he had advised his relative not to cooperate. The probation officer tried to explain, but when he went to the home again he found that the family would not cooperate, even after being threatened with the loss of the child again. They didn't want anything to do with the police.

Because the probation officer didn't want to alienate the family any further than necessary, he correctly held off, knowing that the defendant was out of the home. We both returned later, after I talked to the attorney and explained California's law relating to protective custody. We almost had to force our way in the door. After about an hour, they allowed us in and we sat down to talk to the child. At first she was hesitant to talk with us. She clung to her mother as though we were the "boogie men" who might whisk her away again. We spent another hour explaining to the child what happened and why she had been taken into protective custody. It was all we could do to keep the child from threatening to do something to the police officer who had taken her into protective custody. Because we had spent so long with the child, I made an appointment to return another day.

When I returned, I spent about 45 minutes talking with the child and explaining what I did and why I was there. We also discussed her interests, activities, and anything else I could think of. In the last 15 minutes, I gave the child a coloring book. She immediately began to color it with the crayons I had brought. I colored with her for a while, then left, leaving the coloring book behind and making another appointment to return in a few days.

At the next meeting, I colored with the child again for a while and talked about the things she had done since we last saw each other. I then gave her a blank piece of paper and asked her if she would like to draw something. She said "yes," and I asked her if she like to draw people, intending to see how she related to her family. Again she said "yes," and immediately began to search for a color she wanted to use. She leaned over the table and began to draw a stick figure, first drawing the head, then the body, then the extremities. Finally, she drew the face, making a pair of eyes, a nose, and a smiling mouth. When she had finished, she sat up and smiled. I asked her who it was. She replied by smiling again and pointed at me. In the following two sessions she confided in me that her "father" had digitally penetrated her over a two-year period.

What might have helped in this case was personal contact with the mother and a different approach to interviewing the girl at first. The subsequent interviews reveal what might have been a more successful approach.

## Strategy

In child molest investigations, it is best to keep the number of times a child is interviewed to a minimum. This will assist the child in recuperating from the abuse and prevent the child from being further traumatized by having to relive the incident(s) through interviews. It will also minimize the chance of getting conflicting statements. One tested way to ensure that the child will have to face a minimum of interviews is to plan what needs to be asked of the child before interviewing him. Let us call this "strategy." But strategy is more than just planning. It is a form of tactics, something we as police officers are not unfamiliar with. Tactics are the means used to accomplish a stated goal. In interviewing children, the goal is to obtain a coherent statement of what happened to them. The means are the methods we employ to get the statement. Let us see how using strategy can assist in gaining the information we seek.

## Planning

In planning for the interview, it is necessary to know the age of the child and have some idea of the child's developmental stage. It is important to obtain some other background data on the child that will assist you in determining how to approach him:

### Background of Disclosure

1. What is the relationship between the offender and the child?
2. How does the child relate to others? Children? Adults?
3. What activities does the child like to participate in?
4. What type of fears does the child have?

I then consider the setting in which I will talk to the child and the methods I will use to get him to express what happened. I consider how to approach the child and exactly what questions I want answered. I will know as many of the facts of the case as possible. One of the things it is important to know is the mental state of the child at the time of disclosure and at the time I wish to speak with him. I also want to know the circumstances of disclosure:

### Disclosure Circumstances

1. To whom and how was it reported?
2. What was the relation of disclosure to the activity, action, or incident the child was involved in at the time of disclosure? In other words, what prompted the child to disclose when he did?

3.  What was the reaction of the person to whom the disclosure was made?
4.  What was the child's reaction to making the disclosure?

It is important to know if the child was upset at or subsequent to the time of disclosure. It is equally important to find out if the person who received the report became upset in the presence of the child, because the child may expect the same of you.

In order to determine this, find the person to whom the child first disclosed. From him, find out exactly what the child said. The precise words are invaluable because children often do not associate the abuse with the experience—they block the bad parts out of their memory. Your use of the precise words the child used in a previous disclosure will allow you to directly "tap into" the incident. With most young children, questions will have to be right on target, because children cannot relate to abstract thought. Your knowledge and use of the exact words used in previous disclosures will assist in re-creating the account. By contacting the person to whom the first report was made, you will also be able to assess the mind set of the child. As is noted in Chapter 8, be sure to memorialize what is said. With this knowledge, you should be able to judge how, when, and where to approach the child.

## Alternative Approach

There is another school of though on the practice of obtaining information prior to interviewing the child, which is intended to counter the defense argument of leading the child and contamination of the child's account. Several law-enforcement agencies and many child abuse screening programs use this technique. Instead of the original investigator conducting the interview, another person who is given minimal or no background information conducts the interview. This is to ensure that the responses of the child are validated by the generation of information in a "controlled, sterile" environment with minimal outside influences. The problem with this type of interviewing is that it takes time and manpower, commodities that investigators often lack.

It also means that the child may be interviewed more than is necessary. The technique uses a follow-up interview when it is necessary to confirm or explore information already developed. Although it is possible for the interviewer to be monitored by listening in or watching through a two-way mirror, and then to confer during a break, this prolongs the interview process. The technique may not be practical in situations where time is of the essence, where the child being interviewed is young and has a short attention span, or where  the information needs to be obtained as quickly as possible. It should only be used in a few select cases. This is because it is often necessary to use the precise words the child used in prior disclosures to re-create the account or to get past the child's denial stage. It is also invaluable to have background information in order to know what questions to ask and what avenues of investigation need to be explored.

There will be times when a particular investigation will come under much scrutiny from the press, public, or one's superiors. This technique was developed to protect the integrity of the investigation and the interviewer in such cases. The major problem it creates is unintended inconsistent statements—when the child gives different accounts of events because the interviewer either words the question improperly or the child misunderstands what is being asked. In politically sensitive cases, where time isn't of the essence and the manpower resources are available, this technique might be considered.

## Recording the Interview

One of the most controversial issues in investigations of sexual exploitation of children is the tape-recording of the child's interviews. Clearly the most accurate record of the child's account is a tape recording. Not only does it eliminate the need for taking notes and allow for greater concentration upon what the child is doing and saying, but it captures word for word what is being said. Recording prevents the investigation from being attacked on the grounds that no one knows what went on in the interview. It will be there for all to hear. If videotape is used, it preserves the nonverbal clues of abuse that are so important in establishing the child's credibility. It also eliminates the need for repeated interviews by others in the "system chain" who need the same information.

Recording the child's interview has some other advantages as well. The child may refresh his memory by listening to the tape at a subsequent time. The tape may be used to confront the offender with the child's own words without the child's being present, which often results in a confession or plea. The tape may also be used to help convince unbelieving relatives of what has happened and the need to proceed. A tape recording may reduce the likelihood of retraction because the child knows that what was said is permanently preserved and that he will not be able to say the investigator "misinterpreted" what was said. On the other hand, the tape may be used to impeach the child should a retraction occur, and the judge or jury will be able to see and/or hear the interview in its entirety to evaluate it for themselves. For the investigator, mistakes made during the interview both in the wording of questions and in strategy may be reviewed along with the things that worked, to prevent repetition of mistakes in future interviews.

Recording a child's interview may be detrimental to a case. The child may be intimidated by the recording, which may inhibit his disclosure and allow him to alter his account because he is afraid of what others will think when they hear or see it. In one case, whenever the girl who was being interviewed answered a question, she glanced or actually looked at the recorder before answering, even though she said that she didn't mind being recorded. In another case, I mistakenly used a video camera for an initial set of interviews, and the young boy who was being interviewed repeatedly hid from the camera or glanced at it before answering each question. This was not observed during the interview itself, only when the tape was reviewed. Later I found out that he had been photographed by the offender.

Although such occurrences should still be memorialized in the form of police reports, a tape that depicts a child in a stage or denial or confusion about the events could cause some difficulty in court. A tape of this nature could easily become "defense-oriented evidence," to be used to impeach the child's later testimony.

Conflicting statements are prime ammunition for the defense attorney to use to impeach and discredit an opponent's witness. Using a child's own words and likeness to impeach him can be devastating for the child.

## Credibility Concerns

Perhaps one of the best ways to minimize the attack on the child's credibility is to try to eliminate the cause of conflicting statements. Rather than recording the initial interviews with children from the very beginning, a "pre-interview" should be conducted to be sure the investigator understands what the child is saying. The content of this "pre-interview" should be either covered again in the taped interview or memorialized in the form of a report. What must be avoided in the interview that follows the "pre-interview" is the recounting of what was said by having the officer ask the child questions that must be answered by only "yes" or "no." "*A little while ago you gold me that Mr. X touched you in an area you didn't like, is that true?*" Too often this type of re-interview sounds as though it was rehearsed or manufactured. Efforts should be made to recapture the same spontaneity that was present in the previous interview. Open-ended questions should be asked, just as though you didn't know what the answers would be: "*Do you know X?*" "*Were you ever with X?*" "*Can you tell me what happened at X's house?,*" etc. The interviewing of others who have already talked with the child will also help to eliminate the conflicting statements, because the interviewer will have a better idea of what statements have been made and know what kind of questions to ask to confirm them. In addition, you will have a better idea of what has occurred and how to approach the child properly so that you don't negatively influence him, as I did in the interview with the boy who was photographed.

## Multiple Victims and Offenders

There are some problems with the making of tape recordings in cases where there are multiple victims. In this type of case, the need to validate the child's statements by memorialization in the form of a tape recording is less than in a case where there are no other victims. The need to record is not as great because other children will, generally, corroborate the original child's account independently. Although the recording may help to assure that the proper account is attributed to and associated with the proper child, it will increase the chances of documenting conflicting accounts provided by different children. This may be good in that it will allow for the trier of fact to examine the interviews in their entire context and make an evaluation based upon what is heard or seen. On the other hand, it may contribute to the defense arguments by providing too much to shoot at.

Another problem with taping arises in cases where there are multiple offenders named. In the preliminary interviews and investigations where a child names several offenders and one of them is arrested and brought to trial before the rest are fully investigated, this information may become available to the additional parties, thereby "letting the cat out of the bag" too soon. Where no tape exists, the reports reflecting the account provided by the child should contain only the information related to the offender(s) who will be charged in the instant action. Any reference by the child to others who are not immediately arrested or who will be investigated in other cases should be considered for documentation in a new case or report that does not pertain to the instant case under investigation.

## Documenting Emotion

The use of videotape will greatly help to eliminate the "Mr. Snuffelupagus Syndrome." Mr. Snuffelupagus, the imaginary friend of the *Sesame Street* TV program character Big Bird, was very real to Big Bird and the TV audience, but who would disappear whenever any of the other cast members would appear [17]. Very often in sexual abuse cases, the molestation is conveyed very convincingly to the interviewer when the original and subsequent disclosures are made. However, in the process of reducing the account to reports and through repeated interviews and hearings, often that realism and sincerity, like Mr. Snuffelupagus, is lost. If the interviews can be videotaped, not only will the child's words be heard, but the nonverbal responses may be seen as well.

This can be very helpful to the court (judge and/or jury) in evaluating the veracity of the child's account, as well as to clinicians who might have to evaluate the child at a later time. In some states, exceptions to the hearsay rules have been made to allow for the use of such recordings, clearly a reason to utilize the technique if the practice is held to be constitutionally valid. However, even though the law will allow for a tape's admission in court, most of the time the child will still have to testify.

If the interviewer's practices are called into question, the existence of the tape recording will show any errors in relation to the entire interview, and their results may be evaluated in their proper context. If there were no errors, the existence of the tape will reaffirm the propriety of the interview.

## Location for Videotaped Interviews

The best place to conduct taped interviews is a location where it can be done unobtrusively or clandestinely, where the child is unaware, at first, of the recording equipment. The difficulty is that most places where interviews of children must be conducted are not conducive to such recordings. If the camera or tape recorder must be in a place where the child is aware of its presence, some acclimatization time must be allowed for in the rapport-building process. Sometimes allowing the child to see the tape recording through his own TV is a way of enchanting the child into cooperating with the notion of video recording. Great care must be taken to assure the child that the interview is not being "broadcast" and that only a select few people will ever see it. Allowing the child to hear his voice on a tape recorder often works to get him to feel comfortable with the idea. Some children are overly sensitive to the idea and others are not. Most, if the recording is made as a matter of fact, will ignore the camera or recorder after the interview gets underway.

Ideally, the best way to conduct a videotaped interview is to have an interviewer and a camera operator who will follow the child's actions as he moves. However, if a room with a two-way mirror is not available, the presence of the second person may create difficulties for the child. A way around this is to get a camera that has the capability of viewing a wide perspective while keeping everything in focus. This means that the child must be kept in a certain area during the interview, or that if he moves, the interviewer will have to move the camera. A monitor that depicts the recorded action may be helpful in these cases, or, on the other hand, it could also create an insurmountable distraction. The placement of the child and the camera is also important. Any and all actions, expressions, and comments the child makes or engages in must be recorded in such a fashion that they are visible to the camera. This means that care must be taken regarding where the child sits and where others place themselves. The placement and type of microphone used must be such that even the softest voice is picked up.

## Decision to Record

The ultimate decision to record or not to record interviews should be made by the investigator, with all members of the criminal justice and child-protection systems having input into the final outcome. The positive and negative aspects of such a recording should be weighed carefully in making this decision. In addition, the child's developmental stage, chronological age, verbal skills, and possible fears should all be weighed and evaluated against the possible benefits or disadvantages. With very young children, the use of recording may be more easily accepted than with teenagers. The older the child is, the greater the chance of his understanding the ramifications of what he says and of the recording. The greater the fear of what the results will be (people thinking ill of them, or what will happen to the offender), the greater the chance of the recording's influencing what they say and how they say it. Some children have been known to "play" to the camera, become very formal or rigid, or simply be inhibited by its presence. In these cases, perhaps clandestine recording should be attempted. If a decision is made to allow for the recording of children's interviews, one last caution should be made. Tight controls should be instituted upon the use and release of the contents and the tapes themselves to prevent their falling into the wrong hands. As highly publicized cases have revealed, money is no object to the obtaining of court evidence for the media or for other nonlegal purposes. The taping of interviews of the kind conducted in sexual abuse cases warrants the utmost in security for the privacy of both the victim and the accused. Any tape recording should be retained until the case has been adjudicated and the appeal period has passed.

To be certain that such a technique is valid in your state, check the criminal or penal code statutes addressing wiretapping and eavesdropping. For example, the federal statute authorizing this practice is U.S. Code Title 18, Section 2511.

An excellent discussion and listing of the pros and cons of videotaping interviews is contained in the American Prosecutors Research Assn's manual, *Investigation and Prosecution of Child Abuse* [18]. The conclusion that one can make, based upon all this well thought out contrast in viewpoints, is that the decision should be one that is not taken lightly.

## Interview Setting

It is important to plan the interview setting and the arrangement of the child. The ideal setting will not be the same for every case. The best location is a special room, separate from the "official" domain, and could be at a school, church, park, therapist's office, the child's home, or the police building (the location of last resort). It must offer privacy and afford proper distance between the child and the interviewer. It should be free of obstacles such as desks, filing cabinets, and big tables. It should be free of symbols of power. It should be comfortable—a place where the child feels safe, where his physical and emotional comfort is assured. It should be free of distractions and absolutely not an area associated with trauma or abuse. The decor should be soft, bright, and cheerful. The windows might be frosted to ensure privacy and minimize distractions. It should have a soft floor covering and little or no furniture. It should have no official trappings, and perhaps children's drawings on the walls.

If the interview is conducted at the child's home, great care should be taken to ensure that it is not conducted in the room where the abuse occurred. Distractions that might be caused by parents or relatives should be eliminated, preferably by closing the door. The problem in conducting interviews in the home is that there will be connections to the abuse wherever the child is. This may intimidate the child and compromise the quality of information he is willing to impart.

The same is true for interviews conducted at a children's shelter, and especially at the investigator's office. In both of these settings, the child will feel alienated. Something must be done to make the child feel comfortable with the setting if the interview has to be conducted in either of these places. Perhaps rearranging the furniture will help. With teenagers, having both the child and the interviewer sitting on chairs adjacent to each other might make the child more comfortable. If this is not possible, placing the child at the same corner of a table as the interviewer might help to close the distance between them. For some teenagers, and most younger children, sitting on the floor may be even more comfortable. For very young children, throwing a sheet over a table and sitting beneath it in a "fort" may be a good way to discover and share "secrets." Dolls and other play things may be left around the room to soften the atmosphere.

One excellent interview room I am familiar with is in a therapist's office. It could easily be a "soft-interview" room in a police department; it contains toys, pillows, a sandbox, puppets, dolls of every description, clay, drawing materials, and a two-way mirror. It is carpeted and is brightly colored with appropriate wall decorations. It is quiet and devoid of outside distractions.

**Figure 5.1**  Interview room.

In selecting an interview site, tailor the location to the needs of your case, but give the child a sense of having some control over the situation. In other words, ostensibly give the child a choice but steer him to where you would like to have the interview. Each situation will be different. For example, the adolescent presents some unique problems. He needs to establish his own identity outside the family. It may be why he got involved with the offender in the first place. Often, the adolescent will talk easier outside the home. The warm-up rapport building might be conducted at a cafeteria or McDonald's over a shake and fries. Be sure not to select a place where the child will think his friends will see him. He will be sensitive to being seen with "the man" (the police), fearing that his friends may think he is "snitching" or know the real reason he is talking to you. Once the child is comfortable with you, get to the details. McDonald's is not the appropriate place for details with adolescents; for this, you may wish to go to your "special room" or to a secluded park or restaurant.

## Parents

Parents present another set of problems for you. It is essential to evaluate the parents' feelings about the incident in order to anticipate and prevent any adverse reactions. It helps to prepare and discuss all aspects of the interview with the parents prior to the actual interview. This discussion should be held away from the child to prevent him from seeing or hearing the parents' reaction. It's not uncommon for you to have to "win over" the parents and gain their confidence. To do so, consider giving them the reasons for and the topics of your interviews. Tell them the manner in which you will conduct your interview. Never forget that the parents may bring a great deal of pressure to bear upon the child either to cooperate or not. Either way, you don't want the child to be influenced by them in a way that may be detrimental to your investigation. What you want most is their support for the child without their telling him what to say.

One decision that must be made is whether or not the parents should be present during the interview. You must consider whether the parents will influence the child in any way. Will they inhibit the child from talking because the child is too embarrassed or fears punishment, or will they cue or prompt the child? Will they react in a noticeable way or will they support the child?

It has been my experience that it is often best to interview the child without the parents present. However, with the very young, that may not be possible. Most parents will want to be present. In discussing the interview with the parents evaluate these concerns and have the decision arranged with them before you offer it to the child. This will prevent conflicts in front of the child. Even if the parents wish to be present and you have agreed, when you begin to talk to the child outside the presence of the parents, offer the option again. If the child doesn't want the parents present, the investigator should assert that desire without foisting it on the child. Tell the parents that the child doesn't want to hurt them and that it's good for the child to be able to protect them by talking to you privately.

What I try to do is first give the choice to the parents, which makes them feel somewhat in control of the situation and a little more comfortable with me. Then I tell them that children often feel better without them there, and try to get them to agree to let the child decide for himself. Talk common sense to the parents. Ask them how they would feel talking about their own sexual experiences in front of their parents. Explain that the child may be experiencing guilt because more happened than has been told, and that the child may fear that they will be mad because he lied by not telling all or that he denied some of what happened. Most of the time this works. When you offer the choice to the child, allow for his concerns by acknowledging them verbally. Try to convince him to talk to you alone by telling him that his parents will be outside the room and that he can call them at any time he wishes.

When you first speak with the parents, evaluate their reaction to the incident(s). You will have to deal with their emotions just as you will have to with the child. Parents experience grief, which is often a combination of fear, sorrow, and anger, and you must be prepared to recognize it for what it is. When you first encounter the parents, allow them to ventilate. Get them to talk about the child and family. See if they bring up the topic of the molest themselves. If they don't, you must decide whether you wish to get into a discussion on it. It has been my experience that it is better to discuss some aspects of the molest with the parents. In particular, I try to get the parents to talk about what symptoms the child is showing, if any. This accomplishes three things. First, in an indirect way, it tells the parents I care about the child. Second, it shows them that I know what I am talking about. Third, it diverts the parents from their immediate feelings and gets them thinking about helping their child by looking for signs of problems and/or improvement. Assure the parents that everything being done by the authorities during the investigation will be done with the child's best interests in mind. Calm them by assuring the child is safe.

Perhaps the most common emotion experienced by parents is guilt. They feel responsible because they weren't there or because they didn't adequately prepare the child for what happened. This is true in both intra- and extrafamilial molestation. It may also be present in mothers who are sympathetic to the offending father. Instead of protecting the child, however, the guilt manifests itself in denial, wherein the mother refuses to believe that it could have happened or that she could have allowed it to happen.

Guilt is a natural reaction to this type of crime. It comes from the deep-rooted human need to make sense of things, to assign responsibility. Unfortunately, it is also accompanied by blame. Guilt is a form of self-blame. It is a painful emotion, and to avoid pain the blame is often turned toward someone or something else. A common target is the police: "Why weren't you there to prevent this?" or "There's never a cop around when you want one." You will have to try to relieve this feeling as best you can. Most importantly, you will have to ensure that the child doesn't become the target. Just as with the child you placed responsibility on the offender, tell the parents where the fault lies.

When you encounter a hostile parent, especially a mother, consider whether that parent may have been a victim at one time. She may be experiencing some difficulty with the fact that the child is getting all this attention but when it happened to her, no one cared. Without revealing this possibility, let the parent know that the child will need support and that the parent can help to share the child's special feelings. Be sure to get the parents' assurance that whatever the child tells them will not be told to anyone except you or other professionals involved in the case.

Whichever option you take regarding the parents' presence during the interview, have the parents tell the child it's good to tell you about the incident(s). This will help to relieve the guilt or blame the child may be experiencing and will instill trust in you. In some cases it will be helpful to include a trusted or supportive adult in the interview. This could be a parent, teacher, counselor, or friend. Have them introduce you to the child as their "friend," someone nice who helps them and who they want to help the child. The very young child depends totally on the family for all physical and emotional needs. You will have a difficult time in separating the child from the parent, and you may be forced to include a parent. To ensure that no influence is exerted by the parent, consider placing the parent behind or beside the child or putting the child on the parent's lap. In this position, the parent will be able to give support to the child without coaxing or coaching him, which would present the defense with an argument in court.

## Joint Interview

There are other considerations in deciding whether or not to interview the child alone. A joint interview with other members of the criminal justice system may prevent the need for re-interviewing. The disadvantage of this style of interviewing is that the child may be intimidated because he feels outnumbered. This is where the interview room with the two-way mirror comes in. Others may sit behind it and view the interview without being noticed. Their input may be considered during breaks with the child. What-ever the choice is, the needs of the child must always be balanced with the needs of the interview.

## Demeanor and Ethnic Representation

Part of the strategy of the interview should be your demeanor—how you are going to present yourself to the child. It will be to your advantage to make friends with the child, so the softer you appear, the more likely you are to get the child's cooperation and trust. The more comfortable you appear to the child, the quicker he will become comfortable with you. In other cases, a firm, directing approach may work. Regardless of how you feel about the child, the offenses, or the offender, be in control of your own emotions and reactions to prevent delaying the account or inhibiting the child from talking. If you react adversely, it will be as if the parents had done so. The child may become uncomfortable or stop him talking all together.

One aspect of interviewing child victims is often overlooked because we feel we can relate to anyone, regardless of race, creed, or color. With sexual molest victims, some interviews may be more successful with a cultural match of interviewer and child. For the same reasons, if you use dolls in the interview, consider using dolls with similar ethnic representation and hair color because some children have difficulty identifying with dolls of other ethnic groups.

## Evaluating the Child

Another aspect of your strategy should be in evaluating the child's developmental level. How well does the child read, write, count, tell time, and identify colors and shapes? How does the child relate to others in his world? Determining these factors is an easy task and can be accomplished without the child's even knowing that it is being done. It may be done during the rapport-building process in a very subtle manner. You must determine how well the child relates to his own experiences and expresses those experiences in order to be able to correctly assess your approach to the child. Do this by asking questions about time:

> What time is it?
> What is today's date?
> What time does school start/end?
> What time do you (eat, nap, sing, etc.) at school?
> What date is your birthday?
> What do you do before you go to bed?
> What do you do before you go to school?
> What do you do after you get to school?
> What do you do after you get home in the afternoon?
> How many months are you in (or out of) school and can you name them?

Ask questions about family activities and holidays, like when they occurred and what was done. How long the child has lived in his present home is another good way of determining the child's understanding of time. Confirm the answers with the parents to be sure they are correct.

Asking questions about numbers helps to establish the child's ability to relate to other entities:

> How many children are there in your class?
> How many brothers/sisters/relatives do you have?
> How high can you count? (Allow the child to demonstrate for you.)
> How many fingers or toes do you have?
> Ask questions about spatial relationships:
> How many rooms does your home have?
> How big is your bedroom?
> Where is your school and how far away is it?

One of the things that should be done when talking to children for the purposes of evaluating their ability to convey, in oral form, experiences they have had, is to have the child describe both the location in which they are when questioned and a previous, non-abusive incident. As noted, check the description of the event with the parents or an adult (reliable witness) who may confirm the account. This may be accomplished at the same time or using the techniques described earlier involving the Cognitive Interview technique. This will help to forestall an a defense argument that the child is incapable of accurately describing past or present events.

## Timing

Another important consideration involving strategy is timing. The interview should take place as soon as possible after the event or disclosure. The longer the delay, the greater the loss of details. You must also be sure to allow enough time for the interview. In some cases, especially where the child is young and has a short attention span, you must plan for several sessions. It's possible to conduct the sessions on the same day or on successive days.

Time of day is also important. Young children pose special problems in conducting interviews because, unlike adults, they are unavailable at certain times of the day. This doesn't mean physically available, because they are in school or otherwise occupied, but rather because children cannot be counted upon to "have it together" at certain times of the day. For example, 7 P.M. is not the time to interview a 5-year-old. In general, younger children are best interviewed in the early morning or early afternoon. Be sure the interview doesn't begin before nap time; if in the afternoon, be sure the child has had a nap. Also be sure that you are not interrupting the child's nap schedule and that the child has eaten recently.

Young children develop a schedule or routine that provides them with security and stability. This is especially true for preschool through second graders. Something that disrupts that schedule may also disturb the child. Allowances must be made for these schedules, and the interview should be done when there is the least chance of interference. If this is not done, the child may react to the interview in a way that taints the information he provides. For example, if the child is anticipating going somewhere, he may try to expedite the interviewing process by answering the questions the way he thinks the interviewer would like. Conversely, if the child is upset about having his routine disrupted, he might clam up and not say anything.

School-age children are sometimes better interviewed after school. If they are taken out of class they may be too distracted by thinking about what they are missing. The opposite may be true for the adolescent. School is often a good place to interview if you can assure privacy. This means that the location not only affords privacy, but also prevents other children from knowing that the child is talking to the police. I have found that some children like to miss class, and this can be a way of joking with them to get them to feel a little more comfortable with you: "I hope I'm getting you out of a class you didn't really want to be in."

Another aspect of timing in interviewing is pace. The best way is to conduct the interview as though you have all the time in the world. Allow time to pass and allow silence. It shows that there is no pressure. Silence is a very helpful tool for the interviewer. In conversation, the tendency is to fill space or silence with words. The use of silence, in the form of pauses, can help to encourage the child to talk. The intention is to try to convey a relaxed, unhurried attitude. If you appear rushed, you will seem to be anxious or uncomfortable and the child will pick this up immediately and react accordingly.

Finally, how long the interview will last may vary with each case. A determining factor will be attention span. Assume that children from 5 to 7 years old will not be able to go more than 30 to 40 minutes. This is where several interviews will be necessary or where play breaks should occur where you distract the child for at least the same amount of time you talked, before resuming to the interview. This is where experience comes in. During the interview you must be sure to control the activities of the child and not allow his attention to wander. Another factor is the number of events or incidents the child must describe. If there are many, it may be best to break up the interview into blocks where you only talk about certain aspects of the incidents in each segment. The child's vocabulary will also determine how long the interview will last. If the child is unable to articulate very much, it may not be very fruitful to continue talking to him. Last, you must pay attention to the degree of emotional exhaustion the child is experiencing in recounting the events. If the child is getting too tired, it may be best to take a break and start anew in the next session. A fatigued child may give unreliable information.

## Getting the Child to Express Himself

How you will get the child to express himself can also be considered part of the strategy. For each child the mode of communication may be different, and you will have to adjust your method to the child's developmental level. Children learn to communicate in predictable patterns. At first they communicate through expression and gesture. Soon they begin to play out what they wish to convey. They play with dolls, draw pictures, or role play. As they develop language capabilities, they pick up meanings of words in broad concepts. Slowly they develop sophisticated language and a finer understanding of the meaning of words. This can pose a problem for the investigator because he must realize that a child's use of language may be misleading. Children may use words that imply they understand more than they actually do. In other words, their verbal skills and vocabulary may be greater than their intellectual ability. For this reason, "assumption checks" are extremely important.

An assumption check is a test to be sure that the person you are speaking with understands what you are saying, and vice versa. For example, when a child uses a word to describe what happened to him (even if the word is as simple as "private" or as commonplace as "penis"), you must confirm that the two of you are speaking about the same thing. Especially in describing the genitals, to be sure you understand correctly, have him point out on a doll or drawing the things he is describing. This way there will be no misunderstanding about what the child meant (see later discussion on aids).

When you begin to talk to the child, have pen, crayons, and paper handy. The drawing materials will give the child something to do while you are talking with the parents and will provide a controlled distraction. Once you have him drawing, it will be easy to use the medium to express the experience.

## Breaking the Silence

Breaking the silence of the child's secret may be the most difficult task you will face in the interview process. Your tactics must concentrate on this goal. Technique will vary, depending on the degree of the abuse, the age of the child, and the relationship of the child to the offender. One way to accomplish this is allowing for the child's feelings. The technique, called "reflecting," acknowledges the child's concerns and emotions in order to demonstrate to him that it is all right to share the experience. What is being said is that the interviewer has some insight into the child's emotions. The intention is to encourage the child to open up:

> I could understand that you might feel _____.
> You might be concerned about _____.

## Denial

A common experience an investigator will encounter in interviewing the child molest victim is denial by the child. Denial is a psychological defense mechanism every person uses to protect himself from discomfort — the individual refuses to either acknowledge a thought or experience or entertain its possibility. In child molestation this can be because the child has been told to keep the "secret" or because he is afraid, embarrassed, or simply reluctant to discuss the intimate details. It may surface in different degrees. If the child has not yet told anyone about the experience, and the investigator is the first to discuss it with him, he may refuse to admit it happened until he overcomes the need to deny. Children will also continue to deny even if they have already told of the experience. Both responses should be expected and should not cause concern; it simply means that the interviewer must switch tactics and try something else.

The fact that the child is in the denial stage should not deter an investigator from proceeding. All avenues of questioning should be explored. Independent evidence such as medical findings, pornography, or another victim may surface and sustain a criminal complaint. The offender may confess. Regardless of the inability to sustain a criminal complaint because of denial, the investigator has the responsibility to protect the child or others who may be exposed to the offender. By stopping simply because the child won't admit to the abuse, the officer may be unduly imperiling the child.

Recognize that this reaction to the abuse is normal; it simply means you will be forced to work around it. When it happens, don't confront the child; rather, try again in a different way, back off and go on to another subject, or digress and work on rapport some more. Reapproach it later in a different manner or, as we discussed earlier in this chapter, employ the words the child originally used to make the disclosure. Another way to reapproach the child on the issues he is reluctant to talk about is to confirm your understanding of previous statements the child has made. For example, "Didn't you tell so and so?"

With children it is often necessary to be firm about what you wish them to do. Interviewing them is no different. When you first encounter denial during the interview, "test the water" to see how deep it is. The child may be willing, if pressed, to continue, and is simply testing you to see how far you are willing to go. As mentioned, either change direction or ask the question in another way. It's OK to be firm, and don't hesitate to direct the child if necessary to keep him on track. Try acknowledging the child's discomfort and continue with the questioning. See what the reaction is. You have only to be careful not to push the child too hard. You will develop a sense for this as you gain experience.

Certain developmental characteristics should be taken into account when you decide how to approach children. Denial may be mistaken for some of these characteristics, or vice versa. Preschool children tend to be emotional, spontaneous, and have little internalized limits. This means that they will need more direction than other children. They can be stubborn and quarrelsome. Pitting yourself against them is a losing proposition. Sometimes a firm direction will work, but you may need a parent or other friendly adult who can help you if you are unable to extricate yourself from a situation with an argumentative child. It may also mean that you have to give up and try again at another time.

The adolescent presents different problems. Denial will be a common response, especially from a teenager, because of his fear of exposure. Peer-group pressure and the fear of others finding out will be a strong suppressant of the experience. The adolescent will also be undergoing significant emotional and physiological changes that will be affected by the abuse. Mood swings will be very apparent and may compound the problem of reluctance to report what transpired.

## Confirming the Authenticity of the Account Through Questioning

You will find that children are often interested in obscene things. For this reason it is extremely important that you confirm anything that relates to the child's description of sexual organs or sexual acts. This is no simple task. Keep in mind that a common defense move is to allege the child said what he said because he was curious about or intrigued by the genitalia on your dolls, rather than because he had seen the real things somewhere else. Another common defense is that the child saw something depicting what the child said on TV or on videotape .

If you are unable to corroborate the child's account by finding a witness to the crime(s), you may have to approach it from another angle. Try the process of elimination. Ask the child where he first saw genitals; if he uses a word to describe them, ask where he learned the word. It would be ideal if he tells you he saw them on the offender and/or that the words he used were told him by the offender. Even if the child tells you that he first saw genitals on the offender, ask the child if he ever saw them anywhere else. Remember, be general first, then ask specific questions. If the child doesn't offer the response that he saw them on TV, a video, or anywhere else (books, magazines, etc.), specifically ask about those possibilities to rule them out. Also, ask the parents if the child had access to anything that might have given rise to the report. By conducting the interview this way, you short-circuit any avenue of defense on this issue at trial that might give a juror sufficient doubt to acquit.

## Watching Your Own Reactions and the Child's Affect

Regardless of age, once the child begins to discuss the incident(s) with you, you must refrain from showing any reaction other than encouragement to talk. Your reactions should only be supportive, no matter how repulsive or upsetting the facts are. A social worker who lectures on how to interview child molest victims cautions investigators against "flinching and flushing." Be prepared to hear anything and to say anything without hesitation. For example, if a child begins to tell you about how he orally copulated with the offender and the offender made him eat feces, your response should be something like: "Thanks for sharing that with me. I know it must have been hard for you to tell me." Virtually any other response might be considered as judgmental and could trigger the child into silence.

As the interview progresses, pay close attention to the child's reactions to your questions. Watch his body language. The psychological term for the physical reaction to emotional feelings is "affect." As he gets down to the "nitty-gritty," you are likely to see him stiffen up and become distracted easily. Watch for disassociation at this point. With the young, it may come in a way you'll easily recognize because the child will suddenly talk about something far from the subject matter. It also may set in more subtly, and be recognized by the child's blank stares or by one-syllable responses. If this occurs, you must draw him back because you don't want to be trapped by single-word answers to your questions.

If you notice that the child appears to be drifting or not making sense, do not cross-examine, accuse, or threaten him. If you do, you will assume the mantle of the abuser. If you have questions about the veracity of what he is telling you, reassure him that you believe him by telling him: "I know it's difficult for you to talk about this, but I really need to hear what you have to say. Telling me the truth will help both of us." It may be important to note in your investigative report your observations of the child's affect and how it changed at certain points. It will help to explain why the interview unfolded as it did.

Never reveal your true feelings. If you still feel you're not getting the truth, have the child explain without confronting him with your suspicions. Ask him to "clarify" a few points by telling him: "It doesn't make sense to me. Can you explain . . . Last time you said X. This time you said Y. How do explain this?" Try to determine if the child has been threatened. Ask him if he told everything on the previous occasions he was interviewed. Ask him if he was afraid to tell you what was just said or what he wants to say.

In breaking the secret, it is important to recognize that the child will have ambivalent feelings about the offender and the incident(s). The child may have had some good experiences with the offender. If the offender is a parent, the attachment may be unbreakable. Sometimes the good things that came from the relationship appear to the child to outweigh the bad. The good feelings about the relationship may make it harder for him to tell you. With school-aged and adolescent children, peer-group pressure and same-sex-loyalty may create problems for the investigator, who must break into a sex ring where silence is part of the ritual, tradition, or rules of belonging.

Here, the denial takes a different twist. It becomes a means of protecting the offender or the group.

Once you have determined how the child views the offender and the incident(s), you will be able to determine what tack to take. If the child is fond of the offender, work with the non-offending parent (in the case of a parent-offender). Have the parent support the child and echo what you tell him. Act as though what the offender did is "no big deal" so that the child will not feel hesitant to cooperate. If the child dislikes the offender, it will be easier to get information and his cooperation. Support the child by confirming that he is not in trouble but the offender is. Reaffirm the need to solve the "problem" you have been talking about. The school-aged child is generally very sensitive about justice, especially about himself. He is still naive enough to believe that if he is wronged, someone should get punished.

## Discussing the Court Process

Try to avoid discussing court with any child or parent. Both child and parent will be extremely sensitive on this issue. Parents probably fear the court process more than the child does, but the child will soon catch on. This is especially true for the child who likes the offender. If you must discuss testifying or court, try using analogies. For example

1. Ask the child what happens at school when an argument breaks out on the playground. Explain to him that what happens in court is the same as when the playground director or teacher comes over and settles the fight.
2. Ask the child to consider himself the judge or jury, and decide who he thinks will look bad. (Use some caution with this ploy; with an insecure child it could backfire.)
3. Tell the child that the judge is just like a preacher: he wears a black robe and likes children.
4. Talk in terms of TV programs the child has seen.
5. Tell the child that "people go to court to take care of problems" ... it's a place where you must explain what the problems are ...
6. Tell him the judge helps to solve problems, but he needs to hear the facts first-hand from the person who knows them best.
7. In referring to the judge, tell the child that the judge keeps the rules and doesn't let anyone else talk while the child explains the problem. Only one person is allowed to talk at a time and the person who started the problem must to be still and listen.

You must let the child know that the offender will be there, but reassure the child he will be safe. Tell the child that no one will think he is bad and that the judge will know all about the case. Most important, tell the child that he won't be alone, that he will have some supportive people in the courtroom.

## The Crying, Restless, Shaking Child

Most children, regardless of age, are going to experience some agitation or discomfort while being interviewed. How that discomfort manifests itself will depend, among other things, on the age of the child and how uncomfortable he feels. When this discomfort occurs, measures must be taken to get the child through it. If the child continues to exhibit behavior of this sort, it indicates that he is experiencing some anxiety or stress that may influence what he says. In all cases, the interviewer should acknowledge the discomfort, yet be firm and try to get the child to pass through the emotion of the moment. Be sure to tell the parent or support person who is present with you during the interview that this could happen and how you want him or her to handle it.

If the child begins to cry, comfort him, first with words, then with physical support. After acknowledging the reasons for the child's crying, try to have the child regain control of himself. It is not helpful to allow the child to continue crying. If the child is unable to stop crying, a break is appropriate. After the break, if the child still continues to cry, another attempt later on is in order.

For children who become restless and appear to be unable to concentrate, clear direction is in order. The interviewer must take control. If the child doesn't respond to the directions to pay attention, a break should be considered. If, like the crying child, the child continues to be distracted, time should be taken to talk about something else, or the session should be stopped. It will do no good to get the child upset with the interviewer, and may harm future endeavors. For the hyperactive child, a playroom may be too much. In this case, a neutral setting with limited distractions should be used. The interview should also be much shorter than with a normal child.

If the child begins to shake or manifest other physical reactions, an attempt should be made to bring the child out of the agitation. If it is not possible to get the child back on track, the interview should either pause or cease.

In the case of a mentally retarded child, the interviewer must assess the developmental age of the child and deal with him at that level.

# Techniques to Facilitate the Child's Expressing the Incident(s)

We have thus far discussed the background problems children might have, the need to build rapport with the child, and the need to develop a strategy to draw out the child's experience(s). How do these three considerations assist in getting the child to express what has happened to him? No two children are exactly alike, and the manner in which they feel most comfortable in expressing the incident(s) will reflect those differences. Once the investigator has researched the child's background and established a relationship with him, during which an assessment of the child's capacity to communicate has been made, the investigator should be able to judge what techniques would best elicit the child's account of the events. One of the most difficult judgments will be when to enter into the subject.

## Broaching the Subject

The investigator must gain access to each child individually. If he brings up the topic of the abuse and meets resistance, sometimes it is wise to back off and return to it later; other times he can try to approach it in a different manner. To get the details, it is best to begin with an open-ended question to get the child going. A simple statement such as "tell me what happened" will often be sufficient to launch the child into a rambling account. During this time, make no interruptions, take no notes, just listen. While listening, watch the child's nonverbal behavior and affect for signs of discomfort and reenactments of the abuse.

In one case during an interview, a young child was observed to be holding a large marking pen and rubbing it up and down as though stroking a penis in masturbation. Later, she was seen to be inserting the pen in and out of her mouth as though engaged in an act of oral copulation. This was going on while she was talking about being abused, but the action appeared to be totally unconscious and the child did not relate at all to what she was saying.

While talking to children you may observe motions of the body that might be reenactments of their abuse, such as thrusting of the hips consistent with intercourse. If this type of activity is seen, it should be noted in the police report as observed behavior.

## Proper Phrasing and Questioning Technique

The way questions are asked is extremely important. We want to ensure that we do not in any way provide the answer we seek (leading questions) and we must ensure that our questions and the responses we elicit are beyond impeachment. A leading question is one that directs or suggests an answer:

"He touched you there, didn't he?" A question that contains information not provided by the child might also be considered leading. To avoid leading, begin as outlined earlier, using an open-ended question, and avoid interrupting the child. Use the technique of "hiding the leaf in the forest" by starting with general questions. The aim is to get the child to spontaneously say the words that describe his abuse, before you have to use them:

> "Do you know why I'm here?"
> "Do you know so and so?"
> "Were you ever at _____ ?"

Become increasingly more specific as you progress:

> "I often talk to children who have had things they want to talk to someone
>    about."
> "What do you know about so and so?"
> "What did you do at _____ ?"
> "Did he touch you there?"

When dealing with specifics, the best way is to begin with open-ended questions:

> "Where did it happen?"
> "When did it happen?"
> "What did it feel like?"

Once you have received answers to the key questions, rephrase the question several different ways to be sure you have an accurate understanding of what was said. You can get the same result by the use of an assumption check to be sure of your interpretation of what the child said or meant. The spontaneous responses you obtain will both assure you of the child's sincerity and that you didn't lead him to the answers.

Another aspect of leading questions is the inclusion of a factor that has yet to be established (assuming facts not in evidence). This is a common mistake in questioning children. The questions must have as little information content as possible to ensure that the child is responding from his own experience. In asking questions, tell the child as little as possible because the information contained in the questions may give the child some insight into what you are looking for. This could create a problem if the child anticipates what you want to hear and answers accordingly.

> WRONG: "Some children tell us that Mr. X did Y. Did that happen to you?"
> RIGHT: "Did Mr. X do anything to you? ... (if yes) What did he do?"

A way to minimize the ill effects of leading questions is to give the child several possible answers. I like to use humor in my interviews because I find it helps to break the ice and make the difficult seem easier. For example, whenever I have to get a child to describe ejaculate (which is already a sensitive subject), I use a little humor. I use a multiple choice question like this: "Was it like water, hair conditioner, Jello, Cheerios cereal, or something else?" This accomplishes several things. First, if the child picks the cereal, I know I have problems. Second, if the child selects one of the other options, it tells me the child can relate to the concept of different textures. After the child picks one or more of the options, follow-up questions are then asked about details the child would only know if he had experienced the sensations he is asked to describe. These include questions relating to touch, color, smell, taste, and observation. If the child picks none of them, I ask the child if he can compare it with something he is familiar with.

The multiple-choice question also avoids a dichotomous question format in which the child feels obligated to select the "best" answer of only two choices, even though it isn't at all like what happened. A big mistake is made by interviewers who approach the child believing they already know what has happened and try to confirm it with the child. Because misconception and misunderstanding are so common in communicating with children, it is absolutely necessary to approach each child as though it were a new experience. Using the information obtained from witnesses and evidence found in a case is of great importance in determining the questions to ask children. But assumptions should not be made about what has occurred, or serious problems could arise. For example, if a child was molested in a garage, but the investigator learned (incorrectly) from other children that the incident occurred in a bathroom, the questioning might not include the garage as the option.

"Did it happen in the bathroom, the bedroom, or the livingroom?" The child, faced with a set of answers that does not include the correct option, feeling that he must please the interviewer, and wishing to get the interview over with, will give the "best" answer, thinking:

> "Well, I was in the bedroom with the man, but nothing happened there. But he asked me if it happened there and I wasn't in the bathroom or livingroom. Maybe the bedroom is what he meant?"

and he will answer:

> "It happened in the bedroom."

A better way to frame the question is to include another option, such as "or something/where else?" This leaves an opening for the child to give the answer that is most correct from his perspective. It doesn't limit the alternatives.

Some interviewers prefer not to use multiple choice questions at all, because it is possible that the child isn't developmentally able to discern or distinguish alternatives or options. It also may prove confusing, because of the manner in which the offenses were committed and the child is unable to accurately identify which part of your question is the best answer according to what happened to him. This is mostly a problem with very young children, but, could prove to be an obstacle with children who are reluctant to talk and with developmentally challenged children.

The decision to use multiple choice questions should be determined by talking to people who have talked with the child and by conducting the developmental level evaluation discussed above.

I then follow-up this question with detail-seeking inquiry such as: "Was it like any of the other things mentioned and, if so, which one?" If I am asking questions about location, the child would be asked to describe the room or location he mentioned.

I then ask about color, taste (if applicable), and temperature. It is very important that you only test one concept at a time and not mix them. The problem with multiple-choice questions is that some children, at varying developmental stages, may not be able to relate to the concept of "or" questioning. This will have to be tested for in some way during the process of evaluating the child's ability to relate to the interviewer. In addition, the choices offered the child may all be correct or there might be more than one correct answer. The phrasing of the questions must be very carefully done to ensure the child's understanding.

## Playing "Dumb"

One technique that I find works in a variety of situations and in several different ways is what has been dubbed the "Columbo" approach. It's a simple ploy in which the investigator plays dumb. Even if you have handled the investigation from the very beginning and you know every facet of the case, tell the child that you "haven't read the report, don't know anything about the case, and would like the child to fill you in." When the child has to repeat the account over and over to people he thinks should already know about it, he may get the idea that no one believes him or they wouldn't continue to question him. The Columbo approach will prevent the child from getting the idea you don't believe him. It will also call upon the child's natural desire to help, and may make him more cooperative.

## Pauses

Another technique that often encourages talk is the use of pauses. If you ever have the opportunity to be interviewed by a good journalist, you'll see how he gets people to talk. After he asks a question he pauses, after you finish giving him an answer he pauses, after he makes a statement he pauses; in fact, whenever he wants to trap you, he pauses. The reason is simple. The human brain tells the mouth to fill open space in conversation. Whenever there is silence there is a natural urge to fill that space with something. Often what is said to fill that void is spontaneous, less thought out than the rest of the conversation.

Spontaneity is good in child interviews because it bespeaks sincerity, especially when it concerns details the child couldn't have known about unless he experienced them. In addition, as mentioned earlier, the technique relieves pressure and conveys ease.

## Leading Questions

Eventually you may need to use leading questions because most young children can't think abstractly and you will have to "hit the nail on the head" to elicit the answer. It is impossible to question a child and not have to rely to some degree on the leading question to elicit the needed information [19].

With a child who is in the denial stage, questions that assume more than has been established may be the only way to bring him to acknowledge what has happened. The child may think you already know what has happened and feel more comfortable in discussing it with you. For example, in several cases where I suspected that the child had engaged in oral copulation with the offender but didn't say anything about it on his own, I asked, during the discussion about ejaculate, what it tasted like. On more than one occasion I caught the child off guard and he responded by telling me.

The use of these confirming techniques will minimize the ill effects of these questions. When you find it necessary to ask leading questions, you must also validate the answers by the use of follow-up questioning that will bring out detail the child can express only because of his experience(s).

Here is an example of just how specific the questions must be in order to obtain the whole account. The first question is general, so general the child doesn't connect it to the abuse. It is then followed by a specific, somewhat leading question, which "hits the nail" squarely on the head:

Q: Did he put anything inside you?*
A: No.
Q: Did he put his (*penis/pee pee/finger*) inside you?
A: Yes.

---

* This question shows how an inartfully posed question might provide a confusing or contradictory answer. If the question was first worded "Did he put any part of his body inside of you?," the answer might have been different. The detail-oriented follow-up question, "What part?" might have produced a more significant answer.

Other questions of an experiential nature are:

1. How did the ejaculate come out (*in a stream or all at once*)?
2. What did the ejaculate feel *like (wet, creamy, warm, sticky, not like urine or water)*?
3. What color was the ejaculate (*white, creamy, clear*)?
4. What did the offender look like afterward (tired, breathing heavily, etc.)?
5. What did the offender do afterward (*cleaned up, rolled over, went to sleep*)?
6. What did the penis look like (*circumcised — like a bullet or helmet; noncircumcised — like a fire hose*)?

A problem may arise when the child is asked if the penis was hard or soft. Penises when erect are, to adults, hard because they know that when flaccid they are soft. But to a child, the penis, when erect, is still soft, stiff, but not necessarily hard compared with a rock, which is the likely comparison he will draw. The best way to word a question like this is to couch the words in terms of whether the penis was "sticking out, hanging down, stiff or floppy."

## Pronouns

One consistent problem with the younger child is the confusion of pronouns. You must be certain you understand and clarify exactly who the child is referring to in all references. Also be sure to confirm that the child knows the difference between sexes if it is relevant to your case. The last thing you need is a female or male child to get confused over the existence or nonexistence of the genitalia in describing what happened if the offender was a member of the opposite sex. Remember, some children don't know the difference.

Here is an example of an assumption check in a typical interview situation:

Q: Did he put "it" in your pee-pee hole?
A: Yes.
Q: What do you mean by "it"?
A: His pee pee.

Here is how confirming detail questions would be used to follow-up this sequence:

Q: What do you mean by his pee-pee? (anal Can you show me where his pee pee is on this doll?
Q: What did it feel like?
A: It hurt.

## Avoidance Behavior

A common type of response is avoidance behavior. As soon as the conversation becomes uncomfortable, the child begins to look for a distraction or a way out. How you deal with it will depend solely on the situation and the people. Don't hesitate to try to push on. You'll be surprised at the results.

It is very important to be very matter-of-fact about whatever you say or do and that any comment be encouraging. Active listening techniques, such as nodding the head in an affirmative fashion, repeating the last words of the child's sentence, and other positive verbal responses, help to keep the child talking.

## Use of Media Aids

It is often necessary to use visual and sensory aids to assist the child in describing the incident(s). Most children don't have the sophistication or verbal skills to relate the details of the abuse. Therefore, any technique that allows them to more easily describe what happened should be used. Young children communicate best by showing.

The use of symbolic methods of portrayal will assist in the child's expression of the event(s) with a minimum of trauma. The pitfall in using techniques of this type is the leading nature of the questions that may be necessary. The degree of leading can be carefully minimized if done correctly. When it becomes necessary to confirm what the child is saying, some form of demonstration technique is used. The phrase "show me" is used as a way of getting the child to recount what happened in a nonleading fashion and to confirm your understanding of what the child is saying. This will be covered in greater detail when we discuss the use of interview aids. The question should be formulated like this: "Would you please show me where you said he touched you? Show me what he did."

## Role Playing

Since children communicate best by showing or demonstrating, reenacting the event(s) can often help the child convey what happened. The use of puppets, dolls, and toys, and a technique called "role playing," are very effective in drawing out the child. However, when role playing, the interviewer must avoid the use of the word "pretend" in describing what he wants the child to do. It's alright to describe the technique to the child as a game, but emphasis must be placed on the fact that it is a game in which the child reenacts what actually happened. When using role playing, every aspect of the interaction must be recorded in as much detail as possible, explaining precisely what the child says and does.

The advantage of role playing is that it helps to relieve the guilt the child bears about the event(s) by describing it as though it happened to someone (something) else (the doll or a toy) or by telling about the incident(s) through the mouth of another (the doll or toy). This technique is called "guilt transfer." As the name implies, responsibility for the incident(s), which the child has wrongly placed upon himself, is shifted to the object (toy, doll, etc.) used in the technique.

Several role-playing techniques may be used to the interviewer's advantage, depending on the situation and the child. In the simplest case, the child is asked to demonstrate on an appropriate doll what he did or what the offender did to him. The child indicates on the doll where the touching occurred or demonstrates by manipulating the doll.

Another technique is called "reverse role playing." Here the child assumes the role of the offender and directs you to take on the role of the child and reenact the incident(s).

The problem with puppets, dolls, and toys is they are three-dimensional. They are real; perhaps, too real. This in itself may create a block for the child. Therefore not every child will be able to make use of the technique successfully. Another problem with this technique is that it may be difficult for the preschool child to relate to the role others play. Children of this age often have a perception of the world that places them in the center of things, only relating to events they become a part of by how it affects them or how they felt about it at the time. They don't have the capacity to relate to other's feelings or to take on another's role because they don't understand what that person might have been feeling or doing. Each child must be evaluated individually in relation to this problem.

An example of how this type of role playing works can be seen in the case of a 4-year-old who was suspected of having been molested by his babysitter. The child had been told not to tell of the incidents and was extremely hesitant to discuss what had occurred. The officer who did the interview struggled with the child for a long time, trying to find something the child felt comfortable with to allow for disclosure. Eventually, he asked if the child knew anyone else who knew what happened. The child said no one knew about it, but the officer persisted and began asking if any of the child's toy characters knew. When he arrived at a "Mickey Mouse" toy, the child "lit up." Asking the toy what happened, with the child assuming the role of "Mickey Mouse," the officer was able to get the child to describe several incidents he was involved in. This child was still experiencing some guilt about the disclosure later in the day, as evidenced by a comment he made to his mother. He told her that "Mickey" was bad for telling about what happened. This interview is described in Appendix V, demonstrating the techniques in obtaining a search warrant.

Another role-playing exercise that works well with young children is for the child to confront the offender, whose part you play. A set of toy telephones often works well with this technique. It helps the child feel safer when "confronting" the "offender" and provides a "vehicle" to do so. Try denying the offense, and see what kind of reaction you get. Insist that the child is lying, and record the results. With this exercise, a supportive "wind down" session must follow immediately afterward, with a discussion of what should be done with the offender. This exercise probably should not be done with a weak victim or one who already fears that no one will believe him. School-aged children are able to do well with these techniques because they are better able to see themselves in the role of others than are-preschoolers.

## Correct Practices

Before I discuss the types of aids that can be used with these techniques, I will first discuss the way to use them successfully without leading the child unnecessarily. Whenever the child is asked to demonstrate on a doll he is told to "show" what happened, without any further prompting. If the child talks about what happened first, he is asked to confirm what he said by demonstrating. This is one of the first ways you should try to get the child to express the incident(s). As mentioned earlier, the spontaneous nature of the responses should help to ensure the sincerity of the account. Often the child will not manipulate the dolls because he is afraid of them or too embarrassed. He will want you to do it for him. In this case, two techniques work well to avoid impeachment.

The first technique uses the "Colombo" approach when the child tells the interviewer what to do by saying, "you know what I mean." The interviewer simply plays dumb and, by inaction, gets the child to manipulate the dolls, which either the child or the interviewer holds. The second technique is similar, but is used when the child will not or cannot demonstrate physically and must describe to the interviewer what occurred. With this technique, when the child tells the interviewer what to do, the interviewer intentionally does it wrong. If possible, the interviewer does it wrong several different ways, until either the child corrects the interviewer, or in exasperation confirms the incident by doing it himself.

Often, when interviewing a child, we probe by "shooting in the dark," not knowing what the answer will be to the questions we ask. As has been discussed, it is important to avoid questions requiring only a "yes" or "no" answer. However, because it is often necessary to hit directly on the meaning you seek when questioning certain children, the probing question becomes a problem, especially when using media as a means to get the child to express himself. As in our discussion of the leading question, when asking the probing question it is best to give multiple choices, from which the child selects the best one. With media (dolls, puppets, drawings, etc.) it is necessary to do the same.

For example, suppose you believe the child you are interviewing has been touched in the genital or sexual area. When asking the probing question about where the child was touched, begin by pointing to another part of the body, asking if he was touched there. I suggest a variety of places such as the head, the back, the hands, the neck, the bottoms of the feet, the nose, and ears, some of which the offender might have touched. This permits both yes and no answers rather than setting up the child for either yes or no to all the questions. After getting several yes and no answers, move to the genitals or sexual areas of the body. Continue on to other areas, looking for other "no" answers. This helps to assure the defense that you didn't just wait for the answer you were looking for. Whenever the child answers "yes," ask the child to explain when and the circumstances under which he was touched. This both takes the sting out of the sex-related touches and helps to validate the child's account by preventing the defense argument that you only asked one question regarding sexual touches and that the child was led to the answer.

## Puppets

Using puppets is a great way to talk with young children. The theatrical nature of this medium often helps to break the ice and makes the rapport-building process a bit easier. This technique is used by some judges in *voir dire* (qualification) of children on the witness stand. Children are intrigued by adults who use puppets, and this can be used to your advantage. The puppets can be as elaborate as you can find in the toy stores or as simple as faces drawn on paper bags. Making the puppets can also help to building the rapport that is so necessary to make the technique work.

In selecting puppets to complement your collection, be sure to include some that could be interpreted as "threatening" or "scary" as well as those that are "meek" or "friendly." The puppet the child chooses to play with often can tell a therapist much about the child's self concept. This can help the child later both in therapy and in the courtroom if expert testimony is used. When introducing the puppets, tell the child that they can help the child tell what happened, that "they can talk for you." In a role-playing situation, you can use the puppets to say (for you), "Something might have happened to you that made you feel *uncomfortable/funny/strange*." Can you tell me about it?"

## Dolls

Dolls are very useful in getting the young child to demonstrate what happened. Its amazing how quickly a child picks up and relates to a doll. There are some techniques in using dolls that will make them easier to use. First, when you introduce the dolls be sure to establish who they belong to. This helps to reaffirm that the dolls will be going with you when you leave. Nothing is worse for you when you leave than having a crying child who insists on keeping "his" dolls. This is easily done with an introductory statement such as, "I have some dolls who help children like you talk to me." Some people suggest describing the dolls as "friends," but, as Marcia Morgan, in *How to Interview Sexual Abuse Victims Including the Use of Anatomical Dolls* [20], points out, this may be a "loaded" term because the offender may have used those words or the term "special friends" to seduce the child. This could cause consternation in the child or identify you with the offender. To avoid the child's mistaken belief the dolls are his, Morgan also suggests, when you are preparing to leave reminding the child that the dolls are yours. Do this by saying that just like they helped the child, they are very special and that you will need to keep them to help other children.

This approach also accomplishes the secondary purpose of telling the child that others have used these dolls, so "it's OK" to talk with them. Just be sure not to tell the child anything about what was said by the other children, why they used them, or who the other children are.

### Anatomical Dolls

If you use anatomical dolls, you must first consider the fact that they are a controversial technique. Some people characterize them as suggestive and invoking of sexual fantasy, thus creating false reports of abuse. Before anatomical dolls were created, some attorneys claimed that when a child identified the place he was sexually touched by pointing to the groin, buttocks, or breasts of the dolls, that it wasn't possible to be sure they meant the sexual parts. They are probably the same individuals who claim that the interviewer "misunderstood" what the child said when there is no demonstration on an anatomical doll by the child to confirm positions, movements, and acts committed upon them. In other words, regardless of the technique used, there is going to be some objection. The point is to use the dolls in a manner that minimizes the legal issues created, while at the same time, maximizes their effectiveness in facilitating a child's account of events.

The research doesn't support the contention that the dolls suggest sexual activity or that children will automatically begin sexual play with the dolls and thereby begin to make up sexual stories. In fact, it supports the position that, when used properly, it neither invokes false reports nor does it sexualize the child's play with the dolls. Michael D. Bradbury, District Attorney of Ventura County, California, reviewed three studies involving childrens' behavioral interaction and interviews following a staged incident he concluded that the dolls did not lead to false reports of molestation [21]. In the most comprehensive discussion of evidence in child abuse cases, Professor John Myers says that dolls are "a useful adjunct to the complex task" of determining if children have been sexually abused.

The important thing to remember is that the dolls are only a means to assist in making the determination of abuse. They are not a test nor are they conclusive evidence of abuse when a child does things with them that appear to be sexual in nature. As Morgan says, it is the verbalization of what happened to the child, coupled with the demonstration and confirmation of acts described, that makes them so valuable [22].

The value of the doll is in clearing up the ambiguities of what a child is describing. This is accomplished by giving them something with which they can demonstratively articulate/explain things they find difficult to do otherwise. They also provide a springboard from which a professional may begin to ask questions when he sees the child doing something that appears to be indicative of abuse. All that is required when such activity is observed is to ask the child what he is doing and/or how, where, and with whom, did the child learn that behavior. In very young children, the dolls give some insight as to what may have happened by observing their play when the child is too young to articulate the incident.

If a child is able to provide a good description with sufficient detail, the dolls may not be necessary. In anticipation of the controversy discussed above, some professionals choose to wait until the child has already disclosed something of a sexual nature before introducing the dolls. If clarification is required, they are used, if not, they're not.

If they are used in this fashion, the identification of the body parts should be put off until determination is made that they will be needed. On the other hand, in a case where the child does a good job of articulating what happened, regular dolls or drawings may be used to identify body terms. This is because sometimes you think you have all the information verbally, but when the child demonstrates with the dolls, you discover additional information. For example, the child may say the offender had sex with her, but demonstrates vaginal and anal penetration.

If you do elect to use anatomical dolls, it is important that you acclimate the child to the dolls before you get into discussing what happened to him. Have the child undress the dolls and name the body parts. In the process of naming the parts, the child will be exposed to the differences in your dolls and may not be so intrigued with them when it comes time to describing what happened to him.

Finally, in short, no one says you must use anatomical dolls. In fact, the child's own dolls often work as well, if not better, because the child will be more familiar with them and have little or no fear of using them. In a pinch, stuffed animals such as teddy bears or similar toys with the proper appendages will suffice. Dolls may be used with a victim of any age if you fear that the child will be embarrassed about the incident. However, the way you go about introducing and use the dolls will vary with the age and sophistication of the child.

## Sand Tray

Another borrowed therapeutic technique is the use of a sand tray. It is simply a miniature sand box that may be used on a table or on the floor. How the child plays in the tray with various toys may help to show how the child feels about himself. What the child builds in the sand tray should be described, in detail, without interpretation, as well as the toys he selects to play with.

Often seen in the use of the sand tray are symbolic displays of fears, separation, loss, and aggression. A molested child often feels guarded and restricted. These feelings often manifest themselves in the sand tray by the child's encircling a character representing himself in sand. If the young child to be interviewed is nonexpressive, this technique will sometimes generate something to talk to the child about. The tray also offers a different medium in which the child or interviewer may draw the figures of persons for the purpose of identifying body parts or places touched. A distinct advantage the sand tray has over drawing is that it can easily be "erased" and drawn over or corrected. This is a helpful way to prevent "leading" with drawing, as will be noted later. Photographing the end result of the play might help for later court presentation and expert evaluation.

## Clay

The use of clay is an art therapy technique. The child is given clay to play with and, as with the sand tray, what the child does with the clay and the implements he selects to play with must be noted in detail without interpretation. Often the child's aggression is displayed by his interaction with the medium. Like the sand tray, the clay may also be used to make figures, and its pliability allows for greater detail in demonstrating how the genitals looked to the child. For example, one technique is to have the child make a figure of a person. Ask the child to name the parts. When he comes to the genitals, have the child make them, or direct you to make them, exactly how he saw them (flaccid or erect).

The report in Exhibit 5.1 was filed by a therapist who worked with a four-year-old boy who was having difficulty moving his bowels. He had been sodomized repeatedly over a long period of time by his father.

## EXHIBIT 5.1 CLAY TECHNIQUE REPORT

_____ began the session with play in the sandt ray. He again "crashed" his airplanes into the sand, then built a "castle" surrounded by a "dry moat." He poured water into the moat and on the castle, with the result that the castle and configuration of the moat dissolved. He messed up the sand, saying he didn't want to play anymore. I brought out the clay for him and he began to pound it with the mallet and cut and stab at it. He did not like the water I had wet my own piece of clay with. He became very squeamish about the water, discarding the wettened clay. During this process I was saying things like, "You don't like the wet clay. You don't want to touch the wet clay. How does it make you feel when you touch it? Does the wet clay remind you of something you don't like?" I wasn't getting any answers, but a lot of vigorous aggression toward the clay with the cutting and pounding was much in evidence.

I suggested we throw clay at the wall. I threw a piece at the wall and it stuck there. _____ was excited by this and began to throw at the wall. I then said, "Can you think of someone you're really mad at or who bugs you that you'd like to hit?" He replied without hesitation, "my daddy". I said I would draw a picture of him on the wall, asked him what he looked like, if he had a beard or moustache, and whether I should make him with a smiling face or a mad face. _____ said to make him with a mad face, which I did. I then threw a piece of clay at the face and said, "Don't be mad at me, don't hurt me." _____ threw, also saying, "Don't hurt me." I asked. _____ "How does daddy hurt you? What does he do to you that you don't want him to, that you don't like?" _____ answered "He puts his fingers in my bottom." I tell _____ to throw clay at the face and say, "Don't put your fingers in my bottom." _____ does this with some relish, saying, "Don't put your fingers in my bottom." I then say, "what else do you want to tell daddy to stop doing to you?" He has the idea now and he says as he throws, "Don't put your penis in my bottom." He is enthusiastic now and throws more and more clay repeating, "Don't put your penis in my bottom, ever!" I ask, "What else does daddy do to you that you don't like. Tell him." _____ throws and says, "Don't suck my penis, either. Don't do that." He throws and repeats the above about the penis in the bottom several more times until the clay is used up and the face is pretty well obliterated.

## Anatomically Correct Drawings

There are numerous publications on the market specifically written for use with the next technique to be described. When you find that the use of the dolls or other techniques are not suitable for a particular child, consider the use of drawings or pictures that depict people. These illustrations may be less threatening to the child. Some books feature anatomically correct drawings; others are medical or educational materials on related or unrelated subject matter with drawings or pictures of people that will be appropriate for the identification needed in a child molest investigation. You can also use any magazine or newspaper containing drawings or pictures of people (Figure 5.2).

## Coloring Books and Abuse-Prevention Materials

One medium that has worked exceptionally well for me is coloring books. Give the child a coloring book supplied by your local police agency dealing with

**Figure 5.2**    Anatomically correct drawings. (Courtesy of Los Angeles County Sheriff's Department.)

child safety rules and crime prevention. Have the child draw in it while you talk to the parents, then use the coloring book figures to have the child note where any touching took place. The advantage of this type of coloring book is that it introduces the police officer in a subtle manner and in a positive light. Most recent police coloring books have a discussion about "good touching" and "bad touching," which, again subtly, introduces the subject to the child.

I try to use a coloring book with a story line involving some kind of secret. I let the child draw in the book; I may color with him. This gets me close to the child and better able to build some rapport. After the child has had an opportunity to color in the book, I ask him if he would like me to read the story. Seldom is the offer refused. After I read the story I discuss with the child the "good" secret involved in the story and see if he is affected in any way. If the child does not offer any statement about his abuse, I then offer to read another story from a prevention coloring book. Sometimes, especially with the very young, this process takes several sessions. After the prevention story, which includes a discussion about "good" and "bad" touching as well as the concept of disclosure, I reinforce everything I said in my warm-up with the child and reassure him that if anything happened to him, it would be alright to tell me.

With few exceptions, this technique has been very successful with pre-school and school-aged children. When the session is finished, I leave the book with the child. If any of the drawings are needed for court evidence, I simply tell the child I will need to have them to show to others, and we make an agreement that I will keep the pages for him and that he can have them when we are finished.

## Drawing

Another art therapy technique is drawing. The medium used with this technique is only limited by the means and imagination of the investigator using it. Like the sand tray and the clay, a "blackboard" that uses felt pens works well. Some investigators use the full-sized newsprint drawing pads used by artists. Others use plain typing or binder paper. However, binder paper is lined, and though the lines are not suggestive, they do provide a form of measurement and scale. It is often better to let the child create his own scale; some say the relationships of the body parts and figures drawn may be better analyzed in this fashion.

I also use the end rolls of old teletype paper. Children love it because they usually have never seen a roll of paper like it and they can draw on it "forever." For court purposes, whichever technique is used, all products of the interview should be memorialized (photographed or videotaped) and/or made a permanent part of the case. Notes should be made on the drawings of what the child said about them (written by the child if possible), with the date and time witnessed by the interviewer.

If the child is reluctant to draw, start by having him draw a squiggle on the paper. Then ask him what it looks like. Have him finish the picture. A variation of this technique is having the child scribble all over the paper, then asking him to pick out shapes he sees in the drawing. After he completes this task, you can begin to talk about what was drawn. Although deep discussion with the child about the significance of the drawings should be avoided by the lay person, it is important to pay close attention to the shape of things he draws or finds significant. When analyzed by therapists, many of the drawings made by a molested child are found to have sexual overtones. The lay person may, however, have an idea as to the direction to proceed in based on his own observations and evaluations of the drawings.

There are several variations on how to get a child to draw a figure on which he may show where he was touched or where he touched the offender. One way is to draw a figure of the same sex as the offender and ask the child to identify the body parts. The method that must be used in this situation to prevent leading the child, as with all body-part identification techniques, is to have the child play a "game" in which he identifies all the body parts, not just the genitals. The format should follow that of the probing questions discussed earlier. It can begin like this: "This is a head. What is this/what goes here?", working down the body until the genitals are reached and continuing on to the toes, without attaching any particular significance to any specific part if possible.

The follow-up sequence to these questions should be something like this: *"Have you ever seen toes/elbows/knees? How many? Does everyone have them? How about a tummy? Have you ever seen one?"* If the child identifies the genitals, the same questions could be asked in the same fashion: "Have you ever seen them? How many....?" etc. From talking about the genitals, the discussion might go into details if the child chooses to, or the discussion can move on to other things. Using this method, the interviewer should be able to evaluate the cognitive level of the child, as well as determining how much the child knows about the fine details of the body. It also will allow for acceptable conversation about the genitals because it will neutralize the impact of discussion about them.

Another method is to have the child draw a stick figure of the same sex as the offender (do not tell him what he's doing; just ask him to draw a man or woman) (Figure 5.3). When he has completed this task, have him draw a stick figure of himself. After the child has identified the parts of the body (leaving out the genitals and sexual areas of the body), have the child indicate on the drawing where he was touched or where he touched the offender. If the child will not draw the figure himself, draw one yourself and have him copy it. Do the same for both the offender and the child.

When neither you nor the child can draw a human figure very well, another technique that works well in helping the child to identify areas of violation is to draw a figure of a "gingerbread man" (Figure 5.4). If you can't draw one, try tracing the outline of a gingerbread cookie cutter. Then, by having the child identify the body parts in much the same ways as described earlier, the discussion can move to where he was touched and where he touched the offender.

**Figure 5.3**   Stick figures drawn by a 5-year-old girl and the interviewing officer. The report submitted about this interview might have read as follows: "At this point I drew two stick figures on yellow note paper. I explained to Andria that the larger stick figure represented Dave and the smaller stick figure represented her. I then asked Andria if she could draw two similar stick figures. Andria took my pen and drew two stick figures directly under the ones I drew. I then asked Andria if she could mark on her stick figure of Dave where his 'pee pee' was. Andria drew a small line between the legs of the stick figure of Dave. I then asked Andria to draw a circle on the stick figure of herself where Dave touched her. Andria drew a small circle between the legs of the stick figure she drew of herself. The drawing was retained for evidence." (Courtesy San Jose Police Department)

Yet another way to get the child to draw a figure is to ask him to draw a figure of anybody he wants. See who the child draws first, then ask him who else they would like to draw, until he gets to the offender. Spend a little time talking about each person the child draws. If he draws the offender first, ask why. If none of the drawings are of the offender, and the child is reluctant to continue, ask the child why he hasn't drawn the offender. This may launch you into the discussion you wish. If the offender is a family member or close friend, another way to approach this is to have the child draw a picture of the family/ neighbors/family friends along with the family, and see if and how the child portrays the offender. Ask the child about the relationships between the people he draws. Be sure to have the child draw a picture of himself. The child's self-image may often be revealed by this type of drawing.

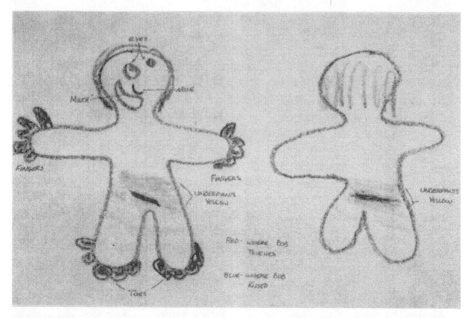

**Figure 5.4** Gingerbread man drawn by the officer and marked by the child. The officer used the figure to have the child name the body parts and labeled them as she identified them. He then had her mark the drawing with different colors where the offender touched and kissed her. He had her use lighter colors to depict her clothing and darker to show where the child was touched (the dark shows through the lighter color). (Courtesy Los Gatos Police Department.)

An example of how the drawing of the offender works can be seen in a case in which an officer asked a child to draw the offender (who was white), then asked her to mark on the drawing where she was forced to touch him. The child spent a great deal of time making the drawing, using a wide variety of colors. After some time, the child stopped and was clearly searching for something, moving the crayons about, lifting the box of crayons, and shifting papers, about when the officer asked what she was looking for. She replied "a black crayon," which she equated with being "dirty." He quickly found one, and the child immediately drew in the man's penis.

Another type of symbolism that commonly surfaces in these cases is the drawing by the child of disproportionate-sized figures of the child and the offender. This also may be seen in the child's drawings of appendages and sex organs. Here he either draws in oversized genitals, omits them, or omits arms and legs. These type of drawings help to demonstrate the child's perception of himself and the events he was involved in (Figure 5.5).

Many young children, especially preschoolers, have trouble remembering things. Their memories are "spotty" and they lack continuity or organization.

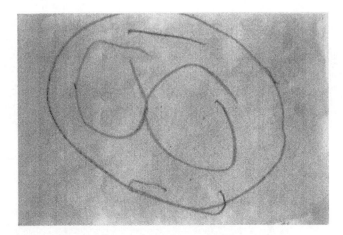

**Figure 5.5** In this case, a 4-year-old boy drew a picture of the offender. In all his depictions of other people such as himself, his parents, and the investigators, he included legs and arms.

Their recollection is often triggered by something they associate with the experience — a familiar sight, sound, or the right question. They are usually able to vividly recall isolated events. One way to refresh their memories is to take them back to the place where the acts took place. This can be a very traumatic experience for a child, so other ways should be tried first. A better way to do this, without actually returning to the scene of the crime, is to have the child draw the location where the events took place. Have him draw his home or other place where the incident(s) occurred. Then, have him tell you — drawing at the same time — what happened. Photos of the home or location in question may help to accomplish this. Figure 5.6 is an example of how a child used drawings to illustrate what happened to her in this fashion.

## Doll House

Another method of returning the child to the scene without actually going there is the use of a doll house. Have the child "re-create" the environment of his home using a doll house. It will be necessary to have dolls of the appropriate size, along with appropriate furniture for rooms in a typical home. Building blocks that are similar in size may be used for furniture if necessary (Figure 5.7). First, have the child arrange the doll house to resemble his home or the place where the incident(s); occurred. Have the child describe the home, naming the various rooms. Questions may then be asked about where the incident(s) took place, and specific details can be followed-up as the account is given.

a

b

**Figure 5.6** (a-e) An 11-year-old girl's drawings of events as she remembered them: **(a)** she and her father sitting in his car on the front seat, where he molested her while the family was inside the house; **(b)**, some sexual play between herself, her sister, and a friend where they all were rubbing each other.

c

d

**Figure 5.6 (continued) (c)** her father would require her to sit next to him so he could fondle her while watching TV; **(d)** shows a time when her father had her come into his bedroom and rub his genitals under the towel he was wearing;

e

f

**Figure 5.6** (*continued*) (e) a trip she and her father and sister took during which her father molested her sister in the front seat of the car while driving; the victim was in the back seat listening to a stereo on headphones. (f) A 3-year-old's drawing of a room in which she was molested. The large figure in the middle is a couch/bed where the incident occurred. The other figures outlined at the top and left are pieces of furniture, a window, and a TV. The dark squiggly lines on the right represent the red rug on the floor (drawn in red by the child). When arresting officers arrived, they found the room exactly as drawn. (Courtesy Los Gatos Police Dept.)

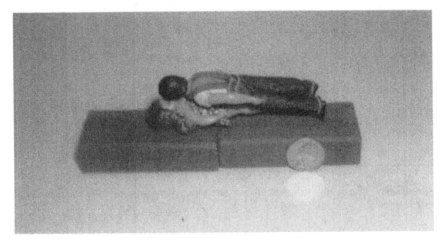

**Figure 5.7** Typical placement of dolls in a doll-house reenactment.

## Blocks

During interviews on the subject of molestation, children often experience mental blocks that prevent them from being able to remember or articulate what happened to them. Several techniques work well in overcoming the blocks. Here the "Columbo" approach may serve you well. When the child says, "You know what I mean," feign ignorance. Insist on the child showing or describing the incident to you. If the child continues to be reluctant, make ridiculous statements or ludicrous suggestions and see how he reacts. For example, if the child refuses to talk about how the offender touched him, ask if the offender touched him with his elbow, toes, and so on. Humor, again, may bring about the transition you need.

Another technique is role reversal. Tell the child that "adults get confused," and emphasize the point that the child can assist you. If the child balks at continuing to discuss a particular topic, try asking questions with key words missing or with the final word left off:

"Would he _____ to you?"
"What did he do to your _____ ?"

Ask the child if he is embarrassed. Reassure him that you have heard it before. Reassure him that it's OK to say the words. Children are often afraid to use certain words because they have been told that the words are forbidden. If you encounter this, have the child's parents tell him that it is alright to say the words. If he is still embarrassed to say the words, have him write them down (see Figures 5.8 and 5.9).

If the child can't write, ask him to whisper the words in your ear. Later this can be developed into a stage whisper. If you're using a taperecorder,

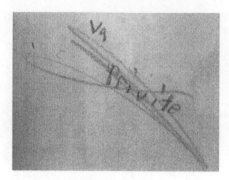

**Figure 5.8**    The word written by a young girl who was too embarrassed to say aloud where she was touched.

**Figure 5.9**    These drawings depict what an 11-year-old was too embarrassed to say out loud. When asked what she was forced to touch first, she wrote the word she couldn't say out loud (**a**). Then she indicated where on her body she was touched. When asked to describe what she had written looked like, she had difficulty, and drew what it looked like "before"(**b**) and "after" (**c**) her touching it.

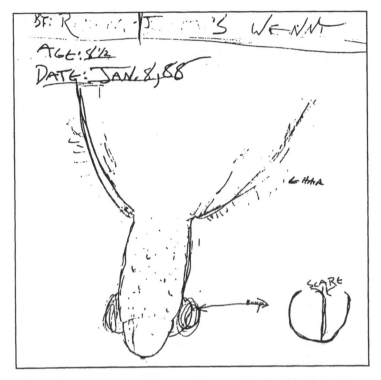

**Figure 5.10** This 9-year-old, was told by the offender that he had a vasectomy and he asked if she wanted to see it. She drew a picture of what she he showed her.

have him whisper the words he's embarrassed or afraid to say into the microphone. Stop the tape (after announcing the time and purpose) and play it back to the child. Turn the recorder back on before there is any further conversation, and (after giving the time), ask him if what he heard was what he said, if it is what he meant, and if it was the truth.

If the child repeatedly says he can't remember, try asking him to close his eyes and think about the event. Ask him to tell you what he sees. This is a good technique to relieve guilt, because he sees the incident "from the outside."

As has been mentioned, in accessing the child's account of what happened, it is often necessary to relate the questions to concrete concepts he understands. What often happens is that the child develops a block because the questions asked don't pertain to his experience. This commonly happens when the interviewer asks questions like:

"Did X do anything to you which hurt?"
"How did he molest you?"

To avoid this problem, questions about molestation should be worded using terms that relate to touching. The use of words that connote pain assume that the incident was painful but as we have found out, virtually all such experiences do not physically hurt the child. Avoid the word "molest" around children. First, most children have no idea what the word means. Second, it pins a label on the child, and if the child does understand what it means (generally associated with "damaged goods"), he might be unwilling to admit it happened because he is afraid of being labeled "damaged goods." In addition, "molest" means various things to various people—ranging from being the victim of a flasher to actual sexual contact. If the child thinks that it is something other than what happened to him, you will find it difficult for him to relate to your questions.

## Time Relationships

One of the most difficult tasks in the interview will be to establish time relationships, a crucial element for prosecution. Unfortunately, too many people think it is absolutely necessary to obtain an exact date and time. In some states, this may be true. For the most part, all that is necessary is to have the child describe specific events within a specific period of time. In cases of chronic abuse with many incidents occurring, if the child can say that the incidents happened during the summer months of a particular year, this should be sufficient given that he can articulate some particulars of the separate events.

Children relate to time differently from adults; they associate their actions with events. Therefore, when questioning children about what happened to them, ask about each event in relation to something that happened about the same time. This might relate to school activity; play (inside/outside); TV shows; family activities prior to, during, or after the events; holidays or vacations; and also the offender's activities, prior to, during, or after the events.

If the child refers to a specific activity, confirm it with a teacher, parent, or any other person who might be able to corroborate the child's account. If the child associates the activity with a TV show, put a copy of the television log from a newspaper into evidence. Also call the television station to confirm that the show was aired on schedule.

## Specifying Criminal Acts

There are other ways to specify the acts. Ask the child what he was wearing at the time of each event, what the offender was wearing, what the weather was at the time, and the rooms or location where each event took place. Then separate the charges into specific acts that took place at different times or during the same incident, for example: "Bathing-suit Incident," "Rainy Day Incident," "Bathroom Incident," "Rubbing Incident," "Tongue Incident," etc.

## Determining Degree of Coercion

It will be extremely difficult for the child to express the degree of coercion used by the offender to keep the child from telling about the incident(s). It is possible to approach this question from several angles. Ask the child if "someone"— don't lead — told him not to tell about what happened. Ask if anyone threatened him in anyway or if he was warned that something might happen to him, his parents, or anyone else if he disclosed. Ask him if he was told that what happened was a secret or say to him, "How did you figure out that you shouldn't tell?" If he is hesitant, tell him you weren't told not to tell *me*, were you?

## Closing the Interview

Closing the interview correctly is almost as important as beginning it correctly. To prevent any attack by the defense about disclosures made after you leave the child, ask him if there is anything else he would like to tell you "now, today, tonight, etc." This will leave the door open for later revelations. It is important to leave the child with a good feeling about disclosure. He should feel good about you when you leave so that when he sees you again, the good feeling between you continues.

Instead of simply leaving after talking about what happened, spend some time "debriefing" the child. Talk about some of the fun things you discussed earlier during the warm-up session. Praise him for making the disclosure, and remember that a great deal of pressure will be brought to bear on him now that the incidents have surfaced. Reassure him that you will support him, and decide how his parents will be told what you have uncovered. Tell him you have a responsibility to inform his parents, but that you will support him and be his advocate. Let him choose how you will tell his parents. Tell him you will sit with him when he tells them, you will tell them yourself, or you will let him tell them alone. Even though you know the child won't call you, give him your card. It's a great way to maintain communication and reassure the child symbolically that you'll be there for him if necessary. Besides, kids love to have a police officer's business card.

When you inform the parents about what you have learned, tell them what you told the child, in front of him, so that it reaffirms your support for him. Out of the presence of the child, tell the parents what to expect in the way of behavioral changes and symptoms. Tell them that their observations will be very helpful in determining how the child comes through the experience. I suggest that you not tell them that what you are really looking for is corroborative evidence that an expert may testify to in court. Let them think that you are giving them this information because you are concerned about their child.

I also suggest that you discourage the parents from questioning the child about what happened. However, I do recommend that you encourage the parents to sit down with the child and tell him that they support him, believe him, and are willing to listen to him should he want to make any further revelations or discuss the matter further with them. It is also important to suggest that the parents try to shield the child from family members or other persons who might want to discuss what happened with him. I always recommend professional counseling, and that the only people the parents and child should talk to about the incidents are me, the prosecution team, and a therapist.

In summary, to be successful in interviewing child molest victims, it is necessary for the investigator to be cognizant of his own capabilities and shortcomings, of the background problems the child may have faced, and of the symptoms of abuse. From this understanding, the investigator may structure his interview, developing a relationship of trust with the child, at the same time assessing the child to determine how he will approach the subject of the molestation. Once he has decided on a plan of approach, he will try the techniques he feels are best to assist the child to express his experiences. Finally, in order to leave the door open for him to return and for the passing of the case to the prosecution or therapist, the investigator should be sure to leave the child on a high note. By accomplishing all of these aspects of the interview, the investigator will have ensured that the child's needs have been met and protected, at the same time meeting the goals of the investigation.

## References and Notes

1. Karen Saywitz, "Credibility of Child Witnesses: The Role of Communicative Competence," *Topics in Language Disorders,* Aug. 1993.

2. NCPCA update as reported in *For the Children,* California Consortium for the Prevention of Child Abuse, 1:2, Aug. 1990.

3. *State of New Jersey vs. Michaels,* 625 A.2d 489, N.J. Super. 1993.

4. John E. B. Meyers, "Child Witness Law," *The Guardian* 16:3 National Association of Counsel For Children, Summer, 1994.

5. *State of New Jersey vs. Michaels,* 1993.

6. Ibid.

7. John E. B. Myers, "Can We Believe What Children Say About Sexual Abuse," *APSAC Advisor*, 7:1 at 5, Spring, 1994.

8. Ibid, citing E. F. Loftus, "The Reality of Repressed Memory," *American Psychologist* 48, 1993.

9. Stephan J. Ceci, and Maggie Bruck, "Suggestibility of the Child Witness: an Historical Review and Synthesis," *Psychological Bulletin* 113:3 (1993); Karen J. Saywitz, "Credibility of Child Witnesses: The Role of Communicative Competence," *Topics in Language Disorders* 13:4 (1993); Dennison Reed, "Enhancing Children's Resistance to Misleading Questions During Forensic Interviews," *APSAC Advisor*, 6:2, 1993.

10. Myers (1994) citing T. U. Sorensen, and B. Snow, "How Children Tell: The Process of Disclosure in Child Sexual Abuse," *Child Welfare* 70, 1991.

11. Karen J. Saywitz, "Enhancing Children's Memory with the Cognitive Interview," *ASPAC Advisor*, Summer, 1992.

12. R. Edward Geiselman and R. Fisher, "Interviewing Victims and Witnesses of Crime," National Institute of Justice, *Research in Brief*, Dec., 1985.

13. Udo Undeutch, "Statement Reality Analysis", in *Reconstructing the Past: The Role of Psychologists in Criminal Trials*," Trankell, A. ed. Stockholm, Sweden: P.A Norstedt and Soners, 1992.

14. Senior Force Clinical Psychologist, Psychology Unit, Royal Hong Kong Police Force, in "Special Care Questioning," *FBI Law Enforcement Bulletin*, Nov. 1985.

15. Saywitz, 1993.

16. The Honorable Pam Iles, lecture before the California District Attorney's Association, Los Angeles, 1993.

17. In 1985, because children were interpreting the fact that no one on the TV program believed Mr. Snuffelupagus existed as meaning that no one would believe them when they described unusual events (such as molestation), the producers of the TV show changed the character premise to allow for others to recognize and acknowledge the character.

18. Investigation and Prosecution of Child Abuse, 2nd Edition, National Center for the Prosecution of Child Abuse, National District Attorney's Association, Washington, D.C., 1994.

19. Recognizing this need, California courts have an exception in the Evidence Code that permits such questions of a witness in court. Several other states also have such exceptions.

20. Marcia Morgan, *How to Interview Sexually Abuse Victims Including the Use of Anatomical Dolls*, Sage, 1994.

21. *Prosecutors Perspective*, American Prosecutors Research Institute 2:1 at 2, Jan., 1988.

22. Morgan, 1994.

## Additional Reading

Bradbury, Michael, editorial: "Prosecutors Perspective," American Prosecutors Research Institute 2:1, Jan., 1988.

Berliner, Lucy and Stevens, Doris. *Special Techniques for Child Witnesses.* Seattle, WA, Harborview Medical Center, date unknown.

Clausen, Janie M., "Using Anatomically Correct Dolls", *Law and Order,* March, 1985.

Freeman, Kenneth R. and Estrada-Mullaney, T, *NIJ Reports,* at 2, Jan./Feb. 1988.

Friedemann, Virginia, M. and Morgan, Marcia K. *Interviewing Sexual Abuse Victoms Using Anatomical Dolls: The Professional's Guidebook.* Migima Designs, Inc., Eugene, OR, 1985.

Goodman, Gail S, "Children's Use of Anatomically Correct Dolls to Report an Event," "Children's Testimony: Research and Policy Implications," papers presented a Society for Research in Child Development Convention, Baltimore, MD, April, 1987.

Gorline, Lynne L. and Ray, Mary M. "Examining and Caring for the Child Who Has Been Sexually Assaulted." *MCN,* Mar./Apr. 1979, pp. 110–114.

Everson, Mark, et al., "Functional Uses of Anatomical Dolls in Sexual Abuse Evaluations," paper presented at Program on Childhood Trauma and Maltreatment, University of North Carolina, Chapel Hill, June, 1993.

Everson, Mark and Boat, Barbara W., "Putting the Anatomical Doll Controversy in Perspective: An Examination of the Major Uses and Criticisms of the Dolls in Child Sexual Abuse Evaluations," *Child Abuse and Neglect,* 18:2 at 113, 1994.

Faller, Kathleen and C., Corwin, D., "Children's Interview Statements and Behaviors: Role in Identifying Sexually Abused Children," *Child Abuse and Neglect,* Vol. 19, No. 1, pp 71-82, 1995.

Faller, Kathleen, *Child Sexual Abuse: Intervention and Treatment Issues,* U.S. Dept. of Health and Human Services, Administration for Children and Families, 1993.

Faller, Kathleen, "Types of Questions for Children Alleged to Have Been Sexually Abused, *APSAC Advisor,* Summer, 1992.

Faller, Kathleen, "Child Interviewing, Child Maltreatment," *APSAC Advisor,* May 1996, August 1996.

International Association of Chiefs of Police, *Interviewing the Child Sex Crime Victim,* Training Key. Gaithersburg, MD, 1975.

Morgan, Marcia, *How to Interview Sexually Abuse Victims Including the Use of Anatomical Dolls,* Sage (1994).

*Prosecutors Perspective,* American Prosecutors Research Institute 2:1 at 2, Jan., 1988.

Schreiber, F. Barry and Middel, Judthye Kay. *Child Abuse: Police Intervention.* MTI (date unknown).

Whitcomb, Debra, *Accuracy of Children's Memories,* Child Victim as Witness Project, Newton, MA. (1992).

Tully, Brian, "Special Care Questioning," *FBI Law Enforcement Bulletin*, Nov., 1985.

Update, NCPCA, as reported in *For The Children*, California Consortium for Prevention of Child Abuse, 1:2, Aug., 1990.

Whitcomb, Debra, *Credibility as Witnesses*, Child as Witness Project, Newton, MA, 1992.

Whitcomb, Debra, *Techniques for Improving Children's Testimony*, Child as Witness Project, Newton, MA, 1992.

# Interviewing the Offender

This chapter is intended to give an investigator some insight into interviewing the child molester. It is not intended to be a comprehensive chapter on interrogation but, rather, a compendium of experiences that have proved successful for me and those I have had the honor to work with. Like the strategies and techniques described for the interview with the child victim, these techniques may not be right for every investigator.

Like the interview with the child, no specific method or style of interview will be recommended. I will only describe successful practices, approaches, and specific techniques which may be adapted to an interviewer's already existing method or style. Just like children, offenders come in all sizes, shapes, and from as varied a background as any other offender. No one method or style will work and the astute interviewer will be able to adapt his approach to the particular circumstances he is presented with.

As discussed earlier, sexual assault has been termed a "psychological crime" — a crime caused by the mind or its workings. This can be used to the advantage of the investigator because the criminal, unless he is a psycho/sociopath, generally will carry with him guilt, fear of discovery, and some "emotional baggage" from his past, all of which may be used against him in an interview setting.

Interviews with these individuals are genuinely a challenge because the offender generally has not committed his crime for the same reasons as a

The author would like to acknowledge that many of the techniques listed in this chapter are those of Gary Duthler formerly of Alameda County District Attorney's Office, Oakland, CA.The author would also like to thank Ken Lanning for writing and contributing the material which forms the basis for the section on the offender's reaction to identification.The material originally authored by Mr. Lanning appears in its original form in *Practical Aspects of Rape Investigation: a Multidisciplinary Approach,* by Robert Hazelwood and Ann W. Burgess, and *Child Molesters: A Behavioral Approach,* published by the National Center for Missing and Exploited Children.

burglar, car thief, or purse snatcher, and has different reasons for refusing to acknowledge his crime(s). For example, the common thief generally commits his crimes to satisfy his need to get money, dope, food, or a place to live. The sex offender on the other hand, expresses himself by acting on urges and desires caused by his inability to deal with life's problems, or out of some deep-rooted psychological problems he has not been able to resolve. Both the thief and the child molester will deny because they are afraid of prison, because their employer will not trust them, or because they may lose their job.

The thief, unless he is a kleptomaniac, knows his problem is caused by a need he can recognize and deal with in a conventional way—find a job, get on welfare, marry a rich woman. Not so the sex offender. He is perplexed by the reasons he commits his crimes. His urges and desires stem from a base need that cannot be satisfied in a conventional way: he isn't going to find children who are old enough to marry. Because his fantasies and actions are shunned and condemned by society, he is left confused and perplexed at his predicament. Even the hard-core pedophile who finds himself "irresistibly drawn" to children and who actively promotes sex with children, often has deep-seated feelings of guilt, confusion, fear of discovery, and dissatisfaction with his sex and social life. Unlike the thief, he cannot simply stop his acts by finding another source for them. His acts will never be legitimate.

Unlike the interviewing of a thief, there are other elements within the offender's personality that can work for the investigator: the offender's desire to get help; his love or caring for the child, his desire to talk to someone and get some understanding and/or acceptance. In the interview setting, if the investigator is able to draw out the psychological feelings and emotions the sex offender experiences before, during, and after the acts he commits, the investigator is going to be successful because these facets of the offender's personality are generally those he talks little about, those he is most interested in having understood, and are the things he most wishes to resolve. The problem is that the offender wants to talk about his feelings but will be afraid to discuss them with an investigator for fear of the consequences of going to jail, or worse. This is where the techniques described next will be of help.

## When to Give the *Miranda* Warning

Do not give the *Miranda* until you are ready to interview the offender about the crime. A lot of investigators — mistakenly — automatically give the warning as soon as they arrest someone. This often cuts off valuable information before the investigator has had an opportunity to obtain it. Delaying the warning will afford the offender time to make spontaneous statements/admissions/denials and to ask questions, all of which are admissible because you didn't elicit them and you didn't intend to talk with him.

If the offender begins to talk about the offense(s), stop him, giving him positive reinforcement by complimenting his desire to talk and supporting his decision to cooperate, but tell him to wait until you're ready. This is like "plugging the dam." It will create pressure in the offender by holding back his desire to talk. When you begin to discuss the case with him (therefore releasing the plug), the release of pressure may cause him to say things he might not have said right at the beginning.

The way I accomplished this every time I arrest someone was by completing the booking sheet before I spoke with the offender about his crime. I did this because I wanted to have every bit of information I could before I approached him. I never varied from this practice, so that if there ever was a question about the propriety of my *Miranda* warning, I could honestly say I always did it that way and for that purpose. Another advantage of filling out the booking sheet is that it allowed the offender to get an idea of who I was before I talked to him, the offender got to see a bit of my personality and it allowed me to build some rapport with him.

## Giving the *Miranda* Warning

You must establish that it is in the offender's best interest to talk with you. Before reading him his rights, emphasize them and your desire to protect him. Imply that it is possible the child made up the allegations, and you want to hear his side. Emphasize that you are conducting an impartial investigation and that it's just as much your responsibility to determine that a crime didn't happen as to prove it did. If he invokes his rights, give him your business card and tell him you are willing to listen to him should he change his mind. Be sure to leave him on a good note so he will be encouraged to talk with you later.

Some investigators have found that it is best to hold off on making an arrest of the offender, as noted later in this text. This negates the need to give a *Miranda* warning. A suspect will be more willing to discuss his situation when he thinks he can explain away the accusations. An arrest, of course, will put him on the immediate defensive. This makes giving a *Miranda* warning somewhat problematic. Although, amazingly, most sex offenders will waive (consistent with the experience in most other criminal investigations) their *Miranda* rights, the potential of an invocation must be considered. Therefore, thought ought to be given to not interviewing the offender in such circumstances that require a warning. As should the decision of when to arrest, this should be discussed with your local prosecutor for local interpretation of the current case law and accepted practice.

## Offender's Reaction to Identification

There are common responses to identification and confrontation an investigator should anticipate. These characteristic responses have been repeatedly observed by investigators throughout the world when an offender is identified and confronted. The preferential offender, as described in Chapter 2, by Ken Lanning, is more likely to react in one or more of the ways herein described. Lanning also found that there may be certain responses that could be anticipated. Having these responses in mind an investigator may be better able to plan his approach and tailor his interview style to the individual to be interviewed, thus increasing his chances of success in helping the offender to acknowledge what he has done. What must be considered in making this assessment, is how intense will the response be. In most circumstances, the greater the degree of risk to the offender, the greater in intensity of the response. In other words, the person who has the most to lose often has the most intense reaction.

### Denial

This is the most common response to an accusation of child sexual abuse. It may be anticipated in all settings. Directly confronting the denial is generally not successful. However, by evaluating the response by the accompanying emotion, one might be able to formulate a way to ease the pain of admitting what was done. For example, if the response is surprise or shock, the investigator will have a greater chance to permit a discussion than if it is indignation and anger.

The former set of emotions are not necessarily a shutting down of conversation. They may be openings to explain how the act(s) could have been "misinterpreted" by the child or other person who reported it/them. On the other hand, with the latter, it may be the offender's way to intimidate or feigned to throw the investigator off.

Denial may be complete or partial. He may claim to know nothing about what happened or try to offer alternative explanations. He may immediately offer the defense of misunderstanding or mistake, providing another way to see the act(s). As was noted in our discussion of public attitudes it is not uncommon for other people, such as relatives, co-workers, and so on, to come to the defense of the offender with the same responses. In order for an admission or confession to be obtained, an investigator must work to overcome the denial response. Techniques to do so are described in this chapter.

### Need to Minimize Acts

This is a self-defense mechanism employed by someone who thinks that it is possible to reduce the seriousness of what was done. It may be a genuine feeling or feigned to reduce culpability and the wrongfulness of what was done. He will underplay his act(s), either misquoting the actual number or seriousness of what he has done. The tactic is sure to include a denial of any criminal intent, admitting some form of conduct. It may also depreciate the nature of the acts, admitting those which he feels are less serious, such as misdemeanors versus felonies. This is a tactic that can work in the investigator's favor because it will give a starting place to accepting the concept of responsibility and, therefore, an opening to admitting or confessing to the entire conduct.

## The Need to Justify or Excuse One's Behavior

Another self-defense mechanism, an offender will often try to justify in his own mind that what he did wasn't wrong or, at least, so bad. He will say that he "loves" the child or the child's family. He might explain that he was doing what every father should do for their children, teach them about sex. He might claim he was answering the child's need or was "seduced" by the child. It will involve some form of "reason" why he did what he did. This form of shifting responsibility to the child is common among the preferential offender and may also be a good starting point for an interview once it surfaces. Once again, like minimizing, it offers an admission of the conduct, but, shifts the blame to the child.

## The Fabricated Response

The stories offenders make up are as fantastic as they are false. They span from the plausible explanation where an offender gives a different version of what happened to outright outrageous claims such as a man who was supposedly experimenting with camera angles when he took pictures of his infant daughter sucking on his penis while he held the camera on his chest.

The variation on the theme of these lies often takes quite a while to spin and to unravel, but, that is just what needs to happen. The offender needs to be given the opportunity to spin the story for as long as possible, then to have the door shut by asking questions that pick away at its plausibility. The follow-up is to let the fabricator continue with another spin until there are several versions that will help to demonstrate the conflicts in the account and the facts. The need for follow-up to disprove these accounts is also very important.

The interview tactics and strategies should concentrate on getting the offender to elaborate, in as much detail as possible, exactly how he came to be in the situations he is trying to fabricate an explanation for, so that he will be held firmly to this story in court. If he later varies from his explanation, regardless of how ridiculous it is, the interview information will help to demonstrate the falsehood. The more lies and different explanations are given the better.

## Mental Illness as a Defense

This response involves the offender's taking the position that he is sick or mentally unbalanced. The response generally won't be the first offered to the investigator. It will be offered when the investigation continues to the point of arrest or prosecution. This will take the form some description of urges that they can't resist or voices they hear; compelling them to do certain acts. The key with this response is to assure that the offender is given an opportunity to explain exactly how the "interference" with his mind caused him to commit the acts alleged. Time should be allowed to permit the explanation of as many instances as possible of this trait and its effects.

The impairment must have occurred at the time the crime was committed and so impaired his ability to control himself that he couldn't stop himself. If he is able to provide examples with adequate witnesses to these instances, they must be confirmed or refuted by further investigation.

## The Need for Sympathy

Here, the offender will try to get people to feel sorry for him. A form of excuse, it is the jury's pity he seeks and the hope that those who view him will use it to mitigate his punishment. Surprisingly, this is a very effective approach for the "normal" looking offender. As happened in one case, he evoked the sympathy of the jury when they acquitted him merely because they were too afraid to send such a "nice" man to prison.

If the offender makes the claim that he is a respected member of the community and brags of all of the organizations he belongs to, the investigator should question him in detail about people he would use a references. They should be sought out and interviewed as soon as possible, to nail down what they know and think about the offender and to prevent them from being influenced by him.

## The Attack Response

This is the theory of "a good defense is a good offense." This has a very destructive result to its victims. Here, the offender takes the offensive and attacks every person connected with his case. Harassment, threats and personal attacks on the individuals involved, all are part of this response. The idea is to apply pressure to those witnesses and agencies who are taking the case to court. This has been the strategy of several organizations created to support those they feel are "falsely accused." Once ties are discovered to these organizations, great care need be taken to assure all investigative steps are completed as soon as possible to prevent the negative impact such pressure can create for a case. The pressures applied by this practice can dissuade witnesses from cooperating and change testimony of others.

When this tactic is anticipated or recognized, investigators must be careful of divulging any information that may provide the offender with the identities of the accusing children or witnesses, or any information that may be used by the offender to attack the investigation before it is complete or the offender is eligible to receive "discovery" of evidence.

## Suicide

One other reaction should be anticipated in all cases. An offender, especially from a middle class background, who has no prior arrest, should be considered a high suicide risk any time after arrest. In an interview situation, an investigator must realize that this possibility exists and be aware of the offender's demeanor and ability to carry it out. In a case in California, while the police were serving a search warrant and the offender was waiting to be interviewed while sitting on a couch behind the investigating officers, he reached for, cocked, and fired a gun into his head, killing himself before anyone realized what was happening.

In another case involving a police officer as a suspect, the arresting officers arrested him at his workplace. They took his weapon, only to be surprised he had another, with which he killed himself within in inches of the officers.

In yet a third case, apparently unable or unwilling to shoot at the police, the offender confronted investigating officers with a shotgun, only to be killed by the police detectives.

## Rapport Building

For the same reasons that rapport is developed with children who are interviewed, time must be spent on developing rapport with the offender. If the offender thinks you're a nice person, he will be more likely to cooperate with you. The rapport-building process must begin as soon as he is contacted. If he is to be arrested and transported somewhere, calm him when placing him in a car by explaining that nothing will happen to him. Confirm, openly, the absence of threats and abuse. Bring him into the station through a rear door and tell him that the reason you're doing so is to avoid his becoming embarrassed. Remember, on the way to and in the police station, he believes that everyone who looks at him thinks he is a child molester and despises him. Acknowledge this concern and reassure him that no one does.

If you are emotionally involved or excited at the time of the arrest, leave him alone and allow yourself to calm down and relax before you talk to him.

He will pick up any tension that exists between you and interpret it as a threat. As you would do with children, be sure to place him in a room where he cannot look out and others can't look in. Leave him in the company of another officer or person. This will ensure that he doesn't try to commit suicide and will provide a means of keeping his anxiety level where you want it by providing a reminder of your presence in the room. It may also provide an opportunity for spontaneous statements to be heard.

Give him some time to relax and think about what is coming next. His anxiety level will be highest immediately after his arrest. Given time to sit and not be bothered by anyone, will calm him down and his curiosity will begin to work on him. This may open up the conversation when you return.

Like children, the sex of the investigator may have some bearing upon the ability to develop a good rapport with the offender. Being male may be threatening because the offender may fear the ire of another man. Self-concept is a very important factor in interviewing sex offenders, child molesters in particular [1]. How a man might perceive him will deeply effect his self-concept, because he wants people to like him. Someone he thinks is a threat to his concept of self, of which he may be deeply ashamed, will be an unlikely successful interviewer.

On the other hand, a woman may be as great a threat. The maternal image may be either comforting or a threat. In drawing men and women, child molesters were found to often make the woman larger than their male figures and void of sexual characteristics such as breasts and broadened hips [2]. The fact that many molesters are narcissistic or egocentric and emotionally immature people, likens them very much to a child's developmental level. As such they may fear an adult authority figure in either the form of a punitive male police officer, but, perhaps, harbor even greater fear from a woman.

This fear may be cultivated if your style is to heighten the offender's anxiety level. However, as is noted herein, the most successful interviews with child molesters, come from a calm, relaxed, and unsuspecting subject. Therefore, it is suggested that such anxieties be considered and dissipated if at all possible.

## Fears of the Offender

In child molest cases, the offender has different fears than a thief. His need to deny is amplified by what he stands to lose; therefore, denial can be anticipated in virtually every case. In addition to the fears of what may befall him from his family and job, he knows he is the "scum of the earth"; when talking to you, he fears that you feel he is not worthy to be the "dirt on the bottom of your shoes." He fears abuse by the police and the system and, subconsciously, may even desire it He fears that he will be sent away for life or will get the death sentence. He has seen or heard of the movie "Short Eyes," and knows that to be a child molester violates the "honor code" of convicts and that he will be abused in jail.

Just how much fear the molester has of going to prison can be seen by the following experience I had with one molester. The term "Short Eyes" is the name given child molesters in prison. An award-winning documentary, "Short Eyes," on "a day in the life of a child molester" was made in the New York City prison, The Tombs. It begins by introducing the viewer to a man arrested for child molestation who admits he is a child molester, but that he didn't commit the crime for which he was arrested. The man is abused throughout the day; finally, he has his throat slashed by the other inmates. I went to see the film with my wife and an associate and his wife. Seated four rows in front of us and about two seats to our right was a child molester I had been investigating for several months. He was involved with 8- to 12-year-old boys. He was unaware of our presence, and we watched him as the movie progressed. When the molester in the film was abused, we watched as the man wriggled in his seat. At the close of the film, when the film showed the molester being murdered, we watched as the man actually convulsed in his seat. At the end of the movie, when everyone else had left, we remained at the back of the theater and watched as the man, still quivering, sat in his chair for several minutes. I arrested him several weeks later and told him that we had seen him there and saw how disturbed he was. I asked him how it affected him and he told me that it scared him so much he didn't molest a child for two weeks.

The fact that most child molesters are nonviolent should not lull you into complacency about officer safety. The "fight or flight" syndrome never applied to anyone more than the child molester. All he sees in you is the key to his cell. He should be afforded all the safeguards you would give any other potentially violent offender, and should be considered a high escape risk, without overdoing the harshness of the security aspect. In one case, a molester jumped out of a second-story window.

The investigator must also consider the possibility of physical violence. It would be a terrible mistake for any investigator to think that all child molesters are passive, inadequate people who are easily intimidated. There have been cases where the arrested child molester was a survivalist with a massive arsenal of weapons and explosives.

To allay the offender's concerns, minimize his fear of going to jail by telling him that few who are sentenced actually go to prison. Talk about the good aspects of being discovered, such as the treatment he can now get. Use a tactful approach, keeping in mind that if he is approached in a harsh manner he will probably withdraw. This has the advantage of being unexpected, and the offender will be caught off guard, expecting to be ridiculed and despised.

## Putting the Offender at Ease

After the offender has waived his rights and before you go on to the interview, put him at ease by playing on the angle that he has a problem and demonstrate your desire to help by telling him that you desire to hear both sides of the story. Don't immediately begin talking about the offense. Acknowledge his loneliness and uncomfortable feelings by telling him that you understand many people have such feelings and it makes his life very difficult for them. For example, one molester said that he often felt, "Why me, I'm the only one" (with this problem). He acknowledged that he had deep feelings of loneliness and low self-worth. After the act, he said that he felt like the lowest life on earth and could have crawled into a hole in the ground because he felt so low.

Past experiences mean a lot to the offender; often they are what got him started. Ask about them. Since many offenders have been molested as children, you might consider discussing this with him at some point. Talk about his relationships with his mother, parents, girlfriends, and his background. Spend as much time as necessary to demonstrate your "concern" for him and why he is in this position. Once you have him talking, there is a greater chance he will continue when it comes time to talk about the offense. Empathize with him and acknowledge what a hard life he has led. Some officers cry if necessary and others pray with the offenders. Do whatever fits your style and beliefs. Put down your pen and paper until you feel you have sufficient rapport and have had him run through his story once. If you immediately begin to write things down while he talks, it may inhibit and/or distract him because he will wonder what you think is so important about what he has told you.

## Strategy

If there are coparticipants, interview the weakest first. If you believe that one has more culpability than the other, consider interviewing the less involved party first. This will give you an advantage over the second individual because he too will know that the first is the weaker or has less to lose. If two investigators are involved in the interview, prearrange a signal to let the other know who the subject bonds to. That investigator should do the actual interview.

One technique I have found to be very successful when acknowledging that the offender has a problem is to tell him I know very little about the subject, I have "just read one article" on it, and I'm concerned about the people who do "such things" and the children involved. I tell him I want to learn more about the problem and that perhaps he can help me. This technique may do one of two things, both of which can help you. It will establish a bond between you and him because he genuinely thinks you are interested in helping him, or he will think you're a "chump" and he can manipulate you. This is beneficial to you because he will think he is in control, which will give him a false sense of confidence.

Another important aspect of your strategy should be to deemphasize the criminal or negative character of topics the offender will be uncomfortable with. Don't call it "rape," call it sexual intercourse or whatever term he uses. Don't use the term "child molest," refer to the allegations as "touching." Minimize his responsibility and the seriousness of the crime by saying things like "its not your fault," "its not that bad," or "you didn't hurt anyone." Be sure to avoid accusatory language.

Be attuned to his body language. Watch for signs of tension. Listen to his voice and speech pattern as he goes over things that are of great concern to him. Watch for signs of breaking down, such as his head dropping and other visual signs of submission.

The Behavioral Analysis method has this theory down to a science. Once the bodily movements and traits are observed, techniques to permit him an "out" or plausible explanation should be employed. Studies on proxemics and kinesics (territorial limits and body language) have shown that there are certain signs a person gives in non-verbal behaviors during interviews and interrogations that can help to recognize what is going on in the person's mind. It has been found that there are visible clues in people's expressions which may help to detect a person who is lying [3]. Yet, people, in particular police officers and judges, have very little success in accurately recognizing when a person is lying. This also underscores the fact that as an investigator, the responsibility is to gather facts, not make determinations of truth or falsity. The value of recognizing when someone is lying is the cue to ask questions, the answers to which will either discredit or support the interviewee.

One theory of inquiry is to disprove the statements made by an offender rather than to try to prove he is a molester. This is a very important concept as has been mentioned several times in this text. The investigator's job is to be a neutral fact finder. It requires that the investigation continue after the interview of the offender to assure that all statements made by the offender, just as those made by the child, where possible, are corroborated or disproved.

Again, like the interview with the child, the setting is extremely important. The same rules apply. It must be quite, private, and offer few distractions. It should be void of institutional and authoritative signs. If you use your office, take down the jokes on the wall about "hanging," "shooting," or otherwise doing harm to the child molester. Consider interviewing the offender at his home. I have had some success in interviewing offenders in their homes because they feel comfortable and less threatened than in my office or an interview room. A good place to begin is talking with him about general and background matters that may not require a *Miranda* warning. Often, interviews over the phone are successful in getting some information and admissions because of the offender's comfort at home. After you get him talking, you can invite him to the station, where you can get to the more important matters. Phone interviews should be avoided unless there is no other way to do the interview. Too many of the non-verbal clues are missed.

A friend of mine often says that the best interviewer for a child molester would be a child. A child is less threatening, and the offender can relate better to him because he may think he can manipulate him. Your attire and demeanor are extremely important in interviewing the offender. Do everything in your power to avoid being threatening. Plain clothes, preferably comfortable attire, is desirable for this task. There should be little of the "police aura." If you are in uniform, take off your badge and gunbelt; if in plain clothes, take off your gun, badge, handcuffs, keys, and anything else that might be associated with authority. Be sure they are well out of sight. Whatever you wear, it should appear professional, neat, and clean; this is good way to project an air of competence and confidence. It is also important to demonstrate your honesty and demand the same from him.

I can't count the times I have listened to taped interviews where the officer starts by sitting down with the offender and says, "Now let me tell you what your daughter/the neighbor girl/your student told us," then goes over the allegations one by one, asking, "Did you do anything like that" or "Is there anyway she could have misinterpreted something you did?" Understandably, with few exceptions, most offenders deny any wrongdoing.

In one case, an officer from a local agency asked for my assistance in a case where a man had been sexually involved with an 8-year-old boy he had met while the boy was in a Big Brother-type of program. The boy, now 15, told of how the man engaged in sex acts with him, and described numerous things that we sought in a search warrant. After searching the man's home, we decided to interview the man in his home because we felt he might be more comfortable there. The officer was one of the nicest guys you want to meet; however, he was African-American and built like a tackle for the L.A. Rams. We were both dressed in casual clothes, which was appropriate for service of a search warrant. The offender was in his 50s and a frail, white, conservative individual. He waived his rights with little problem, but the officer immediately began to review the allegations the boy had made and asked how the boy could make such claims if they weren't true. Needless to say, the man denied any wrongdoing. He even denied being with the boy during times we had documented by independent means.

During the entire interview, the man was chain smoking. His arms were crossed in front of him and his voice quivered each time he gave a narrative response. After we took a break, I began to talk to the man, first qualifying myself by saying that I "didn't know much about this case or this type of problem" and was asked to assist because they "just needed another person to help." I told him that I couldn't "understand why these things happen" to such nice people, pointing out that I had seen all of the boys' club materials in his name, his boy scout leader's uniform, and all the pictures of him with boys who clearly respected him. I asked him about the military medals we found in his closet, which he told me came from his participation in the Korean War.

We discussed his family, with whom he was still living, and I complimented him on his home and parents. We discussed the boy and the relationship they had. I had him describe the boy and tell me how much the boy had grown, matured, and learned since they first met. We discussed the relationship with the boy and how much both the boy and he loved each other. Suddenly he turned to me and said, "Can I talk to you alone?," at which point the officer left. Within 45 minutes, he confessed to all of the allegations except one, which he said he "couldn't remember." He also pleaded guilty to all counts in court. This interview is reported in Exhibit 6.1.

---

## Exhibit 6.1 Investigator's Report

---

DEFENDANT: EARL E. BOSTON

I assisted the Palo Alto Police Department in the service of a search warrant I obtained on the 20th of this month signed by The Honorable Judge Forman.

After the service of the warrant, Detective Bill Williams of the Palo Alto Police Department began interviewing the defendant after obtaining a Miranda waiver. I joined the interview and listened as Detective Williams explained to the defendant the facts of the case as he had understood them.

Boston denied all of the allegations Williams made regarding the claims made by the victim in this case.

I talked with the defendant regarding his relationship with the victim, and after a short while the defendant asked that I speak with him alone. At this point, Williams left.

As soon as the Detective left the room, the defendant asked me if he could speak with me in confidence. I told him no, and explained to him that I was a police officer assisting the Palo Alto Police Department in their investigation, emphasizing the fact that speaking to me would be the same as speaking to Detective Williams.

The defendant asked me, qualifying his question by first stating that he wasn't admitting anything, what might happen to him. I explained to him the fact that we presently held a warrant for his arrest with a bail of $5,000.00 for one count of felony child molest. I also explained to him the possibility that the charges might be increased, including several other counts. The defendant asked me if he would go to jail and I told him that the case was not mine and that the decision would rest with the investigating officer; however, he would have to be booked into jail on the warrant one way of the other. We also discussed the possibility of him obtaining an OR (own recognizance) release.

The defendant asked if he were to make a statement whether that would determine whether or not he went to jail. I told the defendant that I was not in a position to make that decision as it was not my case and that regardless if he made a statement he would probably be eligible for an OR release. I did tell him that it might look better for him if he cooperated. I repeatedly told him that I could make no promised on the outcome of the case or charges nor could I make any promises about his making the statement, which he then made.

The defendant told me that he had first met the victim when the victim was approximately 7 years old. His first sexual encounter with the child did not occur until approximately 1 to 2 years after that. He said that he had met the child through a counseling program and had become very close to him.

The first time he remembers anything sexual occurring with the victim was when the two were wrestling around on the floor and they "both sensed excitement." He said that they both became confused about the feelings and stopped seeing each other for about a year.

I then discussed with him the specifics of the allegations as outlined in Detective William's report. The defendant admitted that oral copulation occurred often but not as often as the victim claims, each time the two saw each other. He also admitted that he had engaged in what he described as "mutual masturbation" each time they had oral sex, describing the action as he rubbing the victim's penis and the victim rubbing his. Again, the frequency of this was often, but not as often as the victim claims.

The defendant believes that after the victim moved to Santa Rosa in the summer, he had only seen him approximately 1 to 2 times a month. In reviewing the incident described by the victim involving "Ron" and the masturbation and oral copulation activity which occurred near the end of November or December of 1983, the defendant denies that it ever happened. He also says that he doesn't know a "Kevin" as described by the victim nor does he have any of the photographs the victim described.

When discussing the incident the victim describes as occurring in the victim's mother's home in Santa Rosa during the first week of January, 1984, the defendant says that he does not remember it.

After taking the oral statement, I asked that the defendant submit to a tape recorded statement, at which point he discussed the prospects with his mother and elected to see an attorney.

Before I left, the defendant specifically asked me to call the victim and tell him that he was not angry at him and that he still loved him.

During the interview the defendant repeatedly told me that he did not intend to hurt the victim in any way.

## Techniques

I have already discussed some interviewing techniques to use, in the sections on rapport and interviewing the child victim. I will review some of the methods that work well in both interview situations.

Use open questions that require narrative responses and allow more information to come out:

"How did...?"

"What did…?"
"Tell me about…?"

Echo the interviewer's responses, using active listening techniques. Pausing and using silence are very successful techniques. Use open, broken sentences that the offender can finish for you:

"What did X…?"
"What about the…?"

One of the greatest mistakes investigators make in interviewing offenders is not knowing when to shut up. This is a fine art, and determining just when to stop talking is difficult, but you don't want to give the offender any information or a way out until he has refused to do otherwise. Many investigators mistakenly do this too soon in the interview. If information is provided by the officer too soon, the offender may commit himself to a defensive stand and it may be more difficult to get him to come out with the truth.

Perhaps we are led to believe that if we don't get a confession or admission [4] we have failed. One of the best things that can be accomplished in an interview is getting the offender to lie by giving you alternative stories. This is good when you go into court because it locks the offender into stories he must explain if there are differences in the facts and his accounts.

Although the technique of allowing him to lie is very good, it is important not to confront him immediately with his lies. He may clam up in frustration or steadfastly stick to his story because he is backed into a corner and fears the consequences of admitting a lie. He may also fear losing face. If, after a while, he doesn't allow himself an out by providing an alibi or by admitting some minute responsibility, give him an out. Give him an excuse and let him build on it. Let him talk while you write down what he says, getting as many different accounts as possible: the more elaborate and complicated his lie, the better. Then break down each account with its errors and inconsistencies, and have him explain each one, point by point.

Like the case discussed in Exhibit 6.1 or any case where the offender has a relationship with the child, have the offender describe the child, pointing out his good points, especially his integrity. Then ask the offender why the child would like about the allegations. If it is an incest case and the parent loves the child, ask the parent if he wants to accuse the child of lying in front of a jury. A successful technique to get the offender to confess is to play for him the audio or videotape of the child's interview if you have recorded it.

An example of a successful interview (shortened and edited for this purpose) may be seen in Exhibit 6.2. Here, the detective began to immediately confront the offender, who was being interviewed in jail after his arrest by uniformed officers, after the *Miranda* warning was given and waived. I watched the offender's body language, and actually saw him recoil in his chair, at the same time his body began to stiffen and tense up.

At that moment, I interceded and began to redirect the interview to less threatening matters. No sooner than we began to discuss the non-threatening aspects of his history and began to personalize the interview, he relaxed and slowly began to admit what he had done.

He had admitted his touching of the children to one of the parents of the children already, saying he was sorry, but, denied it to the responding uniform officers. The purpose of the interview was to try to ascertain if there were any more incidents or victims he would be willing to admit to as well as to get him to confess to the case at hand on tape.

In the margins are the techniques used with descriptions of the nonverbal cues we saw. He pleaded guilty shortly after formal court charges were filed.

## Pretext Interviews

This technique is one which requires careful preparation. In the situations where an investigator is working "undercover," phone calls, letters, or other communications (such as by computer modem) may be initiated wherein admissions and confessions are sought.* They can be very successful when the offender is unsuspecting and, strangely enough, even when they know an investigation is underway.

Thought should be given as to how to approach the offender in a manner that will not raise his suspicions. In the situations where a child has been communicating with the offender, a tape-recorded phone call wherein the child confronts the offender directly with what he has done often produces great results. This has also worked with parents confronting the offender.

The only thing which must be considered is the Sixth Amendment right to counsel and when it attaches. The Fifth Amendment rights as they relate to Miranda and when an invocation has occurred or when the person would be considered in custody is also important. The defense argument which has been successfully raised that the technique has produced "coerced," "involuntary," statements as a result of threats made to go to the authorities should also be considered.

Approaching him with the idea that he needs help and that the person confronting him is willing to see that he gets that help, may be an opening.

The person making the confrontation should never present the offender with a question such as "… did you do it?" as this will give him the opening

---

* This technique requires checking on local law regarding evesdropping and wiretapping statutes. Some states prohibit this practice. Be sure to have a prosecutor or agency attorney research your state's law before employing this practice.

## Exhibit 6.2

SG: Mr. B before we do that (talk with him) I want to turn this on so that there's no question about what is said. I want to protect you and by making sure that what we hear is the same thing that we write down. OK? Is that all right?

B: OK

DM: Mr. B, you have the right to remain silent... Do you understand each of these rights I...(full *Miranda* given)

B: Yes, I do.

DM: OK, having these rights in mind, do you wish to talk to us now?

B: We'll start at least.

DM: OK. The reason, what we need to talk to you about is, going back on, on 12/13/87, December 13, 1987...

SG: Actually, I was just thinking, maybe we can do something else first before we do that?

DM: Sure.

SG: Would that be all right? Talk about something else for a minute? How long have you been in Napa County?

DM: Since July.

SG: Since July. OK. And you lived someplace else before that? Where did you live before you lived here?

B: San Jose.

S: San Jose?

B: I think. Year, San Jose.

S: OK, how long did you live in San Jose?

B: Well, we did some moving around in that area. At the last address it seems like it was about a year, although I...

Here we begin to demonstrate our concern for him and assure our fairness. By telling him you're recording the interview and assuring you're reporting it accurately, you are establishing a benefit-advantage of talking to you. You are able to get his side of the story and enable him to show the children/witnesses are lying.

He sat upright, against the back of his chair. His muscles visibly tensed.

Gives the appearance of giving him control at the same time demonstrating concern. The major benefit here is that this gets him talking. By talking about non-judgmental, non-threatening subjects, he will feel comfortable talking and when the interview becomes strained due to the threatening subjects, he is more likely to continue talking. It is the beginning of building the foundations of a line of communication.

The objective at this moment is to relax the subject at the same time obtaining information about where he has been in the past for our background check in search of new victims and other crimes.

The number of moves could mean that he had offended in a community and fled in fear of discovery or was actually discovered.

*(continues)*

## Exhibit 6.2 (continued)

S: In the City of San Jose?

B: Yeah

S: OK, and did you always live in San Jose?

B: No, it was Morgan Hill before that, and Campbell...

S: Campbell. OK, and about how much time were you spending in that area? About what years? Do you remember?

B: No, I don't remember the years.

S: Before that, where were you living when you got married?

B: In Watsonville.

S: Watsonville. Boy, you've really gone around the state.

B: Yeah

S: What do you do?

B: I'm an electronics technician.

S: Technician. That explains why you were living in San Jose.

B: Yes, and going to school off-an-on and that kind of thing. Ended up with a lot of little moves here and there.

Through these non-threatening questions, he is finding it's easy to answer and talk to me. At the same time I am developing information, I am searching for some common ground, something to show him my personality and a bond between us.

This was intended and said as a sign of respect for seeing a lot of the state. He responded by sitting forward, resting his hands on the table, leaning towards me.

By echoing his answers, I was demonstrating to him I was listening. His response to my comments demonstrated he felt I was listening to him — engaging him, a surprise to most sex offenders who expect you to despise them and reject anything about them. If he thinks I'm listening to him, it's easier to talk to me. It's a continuing effort to build the line of communication.

He was proud of his job and his association with the firms he worked for.

S: I just moved, well actually, both of us are from the Santa Clara area. You lived in?

D: San Jose

S: San Jose. I worked in San Jose for a long time. We can understand why you left San Jose.

B: Yeah (laughs)

I found the common ground — traffic, congestion, and the general dissatisfaction with the cost of living in a metropolitan community. More importantly, I was showing him respect building his ego/self image by sharing our mutual experiences.

S: There's no reason to be nervous. I can understand you probably are a little uncomfortable about talking to us.

It worked. His body was now relaxing, you could see his shoulders drop.

## Exhibit 6.2 (continued)

B: Sure, when it involves your future, you always get a little anxious

By identifying the cause of his anxiety, he didn't have to try to hide it any longer. It allowed him to relax. It showed my understanding of his problem — that he wasn't such a bad person.

S: Sure, sure. The reason I was asking where you're coming from is perhaps it will give me an idea of … your family and so on. You are married— once?

Again, showing our concern for him.

B: Just once. The first time.

S: What does your wife do?

B: She is a supervisor at the college laundry.

He's very relaxed and talking freely. He has become animated, moving his hands and arms about when he talks.

S: Where are your working now or are you working?

B: I'm working for a temporary service which has provided me a job a firm in Petaluma.

S: So you're commuting between here and there… Do you know why we're here?

This doesn't confine me to the crimes reported, maybe he's thinking of other offenses?

B: Yes I do.

S: Tell me what you think we're here about.

I am asking open-ended questions hoping he will use incriminating terms to answer the questions. I'm also "hiding-the-ball", keeping him in the dark about what I'm looking for.

B: The case involving the family in Angwin.

S: Can you tell me what happened?

B: I think I'd prefer not to.

I found a sensitive point.

S: OK. Are you concerned about what might happen if you do? Is that what you're concerned about or what is it?

By identifying the concern I hope we can bypass it as we did above. It also permits me to be honest with him in hopes he will be honest in the answer. It works, he tells me exactly why he is afraid.

B: Year, I kind of made it real difficult for myself before by just spilling everything. So, I, you know, I'd rather hold that reservation, just…

S: What do you mean before?

B: I'm sure that you've probably checked and know that I have a previous incident.

Yes, but we didn't want him to be concerned about it.

## Exhibit 6.2 (continued)

S: Well, let me ask you this without asking any particulars about what happened. You talked to the parents, I guess they talked to you after what happened. Did you tell them the truth when you talked to them?

He had confessed to the parents and I wanted to confirm he was telling them the truth (on tape, locking him into his account to them) for impeachment, if necessary. Although I won't use "particulars" I will use fact patterns that are the same.

B: For everything that we talked about, I don't think we discussed the actual incident at that time.

He didn't remember his confession, good. It means that he could corroborate the father to whom he confessed if he made a second confession.

S: Did you like to them at any time in terms of when you talked to them?

B: No. The family were friends of ours for awhile. You know starting after we moved up there and they are good Christian people and come to talk to me the night of the incident and so I didn't have any reason to hold things back from them. I valued my relationship with them.

S: You're living now with, who is living at your house now?

This is a deflection — a way of distracting him from his anxiety re answering the previous question about the Angwin family. It allows him to continue on talking about something less stressful until I can bring him back to the subject I really want to know about.

B: My wife and son.

S: Other than that family in Angwin, and Sue (another victim), was there anybody else that we should know about up there? That you would like to talk to us about or share with us?

B: No.

A test to see how far, if at all, he is willing to go in making an admission.

This is the *Columbo* approach, hoping he'll fill in the blank at the same time minimizing the importance of the information.

S: What about the kids in the apartment house that you had over to your house? Can you tell us anything about what happened with them or would house be willing to talk to us about other kids that were there? I forgot the name of the apartment complex. It was an apartment complex you lived in, right?

B: Yeah. Actually, I'd prefer not to.

Found another sensitive point.

S: Is there a reason you don't want to talk about those?

B: Again, reserving my options.

## Exhibit 6.2 (continued)

S: All right, what are your plans now as soon as you get out of here?

Another deflection. Change in subject to divert his attention from the subject.

B: My, I don't know what my specific plans, our specific plans are. They will be, whatever we do will be for the purpose of getting help for myself, because its been a difficulty I've had for awhile. I don't like this kind of lifestyle and I'm ready to do about anything I need to do to correct it and get back on a...

But he opens it himself — he's admitting he has a problem. It's now my job to establish it's a sexual perversion.

S: By lifestyle you mean that you don't want to expose yourself anymore?

Direct question to assure to ambiguity and a test to see if he's willing to discuss it.

B: That's exactly right.

S: That's understandable. That must be a real difficult thing to live with.

Bingo!, he's admitted his problem. Now it is possible to show that we feel sorry for him and maybe he'll want more sympathy and tell us more.

B: It is and we have several options that we're considering (he goes on to describe them, naming a sex therapy program in the process)... I'd like to check into at least.

S: What kinds of things have you tried to stop yourself?

B: I've been in counseling with a psychotherapist for quite some time. It appeared to and I think it did, help for quite a while. It's been four years since the last incident before this came up. The other ones had been fairly close together like within a year or a-year-and-a-half every time. And so it appears to at least helped. It wasn't useless. I used to do something more serious, more intense. So at this time whatever plans we had are on hold until, because it's not going to do much good to make plans for the rest of my life until I get this under control. When I do, then, then I can go on with the rest of my life and not be worried about this all of the time and my wife won't have to live with this kind of thing.

He's indirectly admitting his touching here. He's telling me that he really isn't so bad. I shouldn't dislike him — he's different. He can control himself most of the time.

S: What kinds of things have they tried to do to get you under control? What kind of things did they suggest that you do?

Here, I'm hoping he'll get specific with the criminal acts he's been involved with.

## Exhibit 6.2  (continued)

B: It's basically recognizing the problem itself. What it entails and the steps that lead to it, and recognizing those steps. Begin able to stop them before they get to the uncontrollable point. Because there's a point when, a point-of-no-return when you don't have the power anymore. It's a little like alcoholism. It's a compulsive behavior and after an alcoholic takes a drink, its all over for him.

S: Go ahead.

This is his counseling showing through, it's part a rationalization/excuse and part a confession he has a serious problem. It tells the interviewer he may be willing to talk more about it.

I encourage him to continue as he looked up at me as if to ask shall I go on.

B: Also, OK, there's a program that he recommended to me in gaining a balance in my life in the spiritual and mental and physical aspects. And when those areas are in balance, its much easier to be in control of myself.

S: So what would happen? You would get an urge to expose yourself or something or other, and they would tell you a specific thing to, how to deal with that? What would happen? What would you do?

Now he's adopted my language ("OK," which I've unconsciously repeated throughout the interview)

I'm hoping he'll tell me specific instances, so it's a test to see how far he'll go at the same time wearing away his resistance to talk about the acts. If he answers about previous occasions that I have no power to do anything about he is doing several things. First, he is testing to see my reaction. Will I change my demeanor and ridicule or dislike him? Second, he is trying to ease out an acknowledgment of pain on his part. If he can do this, it will be easier to admit the present case. Third, it is reducing his anxiety about admitting his problem to a police officer. If he tells, the result will be it will be easier to continue.

B: Well, it doesn't usually manifest itself in a sudden blatant urge to expose myself, but for one reason or another, I might get a sexual input of some kind and then get thinking about it and from there get fantasizing and its a series of steps that take that route. And then when I'm deep into it and I'm looking for some kind of fulfillment then it would come out in the way of exposing myself.

He's now admitting the key motivation for many sex offenders and demonstrating he has a conscious awareness of his criminal acts. He's also admitting a degree of premeditation. I've removed his fear that I will reject him.

## Exhibit 6.2 (continued)

S: Well, it sounds like, I don't know anything about this, like I said its kind of fascinating. If, it obviously goes more than just exposing yourself.

B: Yes

S: You have the desire to have the people touch you or to touch others, I assume.

B: Well, yeah.

S: Or is it limiting to a particular...

B: It kind of varies from situation to situation. Its not something that is ever planned ahead of time, and sit down and think, now I can do this and this. Its more like an alcoholic, he's just going to have one drink and from there, you know it's not planned, it just snowballs.

S: Well, for example, can you give me an idea, again I'm just, I'm really kind of must curious about this. Do you have an attraction to, some little kid will just kind of walk in or something and all of a sudden you get an idea or is that how it works?

B: Not in a normal situation because I've had a difficulty when I see a child obviously it brings back thoughts of the difficulties that I do have and that kind of thing, but, its not an immediate uncontrollable urge. That follows the previous steps and then if an opportunity presents itself that's when it becomes a problem.

S: So what do you do? What do they ask you to do?

B: Part of it is recognizing that I have a lot at stake, a lot at risky by going ahead with what I would like to do and sometimes that has been effective. There are other times when I have allowed myself to get so involved in fantasizing and that kind of thing that I'm not thinking rationally. I've found myself in a situation where I say that this is ludicrous, this is suicide, and yet I was going ahead with it. Somewhere my rational mind was back there screaming but, again...

I'm lowering my status in his eyes, building him up and trying to get him to want to "help" me understand "his" problem. This gives him "control" and a feeling he can fool me.

He knows now that he has talked about his "problem", softening the impact to himself about making a total admission. If I already know about his problem, it will be easier to tell me.

I'm setting up the facts of the instant case where he touched the children, not just exposed himself. And he goes for it. The "hook is set", now it's necessary to bring in the actual facts of the case.

*Columbo* again and a draw back to the facts of the case.

I want to know what he did when he molested the kids in the instant case. Will he tell me?

I've softened the problem he has by showing compassion and a "genuine" interest in his problem. If his self respect is restored it will allow him to admit. He is now not afraid of my reaction to his act.

## Exhibit 6.2 (continued)

S: It's sort of like what happened with these kids, I take it? ... So you... get an urge to go farther and touch or anything like that? Get involved in any other kind of interplay with them?... To touch or to do other things? Again, I'm just curious? You know, you really didn't do anything really bad. You didn't hurt the kids.

B: Yeah, to touch ...In the way I look for acceptance... Its always done in a way of... whatever the child is comfortable with.

S: Interesting. What kinds of things have you done with kids?

B: As I say, those times are pretty typical (pointing to our police reports which we've now placed on the table).

S: Obviously you get some excitement if they touch you, right? I guess. Based on the things I've read?

B: Yeah, that would be part of it, although it's not part of the scenario...

S: ...for example, let me ask you a question. After this thing up on Angwin when the girls ran out of the door and there you were in your altogether,... they saw your penis?

B: Yeah.

S: ... and like when you were roughhousing with the kids. That must be a real turn on for you...?

B: ...it is... like the Calistoga incident, the neighbor girl was over and we played...

S: Do you ever have urges for your own child?

B: No. Number one he's a boy (he likes girls) and as I mentioned that's not nearly as much of a problem... That's totally different. That's a little like having an attraction to girls but your sister and your mother just don't fit into that category... Too close.(we talked about other characteristics of offenders to confirm the research and our own learning)

To reassure him that I don't feel ill of him I verbalize it. He had the second child find a small toy he had hidden in his front pants pocket, near his penis.

An admission. He's looking for reassurance he's not a monster — he can control himself. He wouldn't force or hurt a child.

Now admitting to what is in the report.

Establishing lack of mistake, intent, premeditation, conscious course of conduct.

If there was a question before, it's not now.

The approximate facts of the exposure case.

Confession! By way of an adoptive admission.

Facts of the touching case.

Admission!

Here's an opportunity to both nail the offender down on the types of problems he has so he can't later refute them, at the same time learning about how they feel and commit their crimes for yourself.

## Exhibit 6.2 (continued)

(after concluding the two hour interview with
more discussion re his acts and background and
our saying goodbye)

B: Thank you for your understanding. Would you
please call my wife for me and tell her I love her.

The sign of a successful interview
and an open door if we need more
information later.

to deny. Just as the investigator does in an interrogation, the presumption in
the conversation should be that he committed the act, to provide the offender
with an opportunity to respond. The confrontation wording should be formulated around the elements of the crimes committed.

Given the fact that most confrontations will occur when the offender is
at home or work, on a phone, Miranda shouldn't apply unless the offender
has been formally charged. Nor should the laws of confessions apply when
no reference is made to the authorities' involvement. However, this is where
the defense will get a grip on the case if it appears as though the threat of
arrest or its subsequent consequences are made by the confronting party.

A statement such as "I just had a teacher tell our class that your touching
me on my vagina is wrong," followed by a "pregnant pause" to permit him
to respond will be much better than following it with, "... and I am thinking
of telling her/the police/CPS about what you are doing."

However, if the investigator were to confront the offender with the statement (in the context of seeking his cooperation and help in stopping what he
is doing and helping the child through the difficulties the child is having with
what the offender has done) in a covert fashion as the child's counselor/teacher,
"X has told me about your having oral sex with her and I would like to help
you both," there is less of a likelihood this argument will be successful.

Of concern is the argument which has been successful in many cases that
the child or adult making the confrontation becomes an agent of the police
and therefore the rules of coerced confessions apply.

The defense position in these cases is that the ploy is likely to produce a
coerced confession or admission because the threat of exposure of a false
allegation is as great as a real one due to the negative consequences the
accused will face in his life. They claim he is likely to lose his family, his job,
friends, and social position.

Remember, the basic principle of this technique is to produce circumstances under which it is most likely the accused person will tell the truth.
The counter to this defense argument, when made alleging the accused

admitted only to avoid exposure, is that the confrontation was made to provide an opportunity to get at the truth. Why would the accused person not want the authorities to determine the truth, by investigation if necessary since the child has already made the allegation?

As stated above, the key is to have the caller confront the offender with an unequivocal statement that includes the elements of the crime and see what he does. Adoptive admissions, wherein a discussion follows the confrontation that includes comments about the details of what has been said by the child is as valuable as a direct admission. In one case, a 12-year-old girl confronted her grandfather on the phone, telling him that "your oral sex with me has got to stop," resulted in the response, "I know honey, I was planning to tell you that tomorrow."*

A tacit admission, where the offender doesn't deny the confrontation, but rather, goes on talking to the witness is also valuable. For example, a 14-year-old, said during a later portion of the conversation, after she confronted him, "Do you know what its like to watch a program on TV where they are talking about a child being molested by someone they know and think that everyone in the room is looking at you, knowing it happened to you?," to which he replied, "I know."

The manner of confrontation is only limited by the creativity of the witness and the investigator. Two examples of successful confrontations with offenders are presented in Exhibit 6.3 and Exhibit 6.4. An excellent article on this technique appears in the *APSAC Advisor* [5].

This technique is also discussed in Chapter 8 on case management when to initiate this practice.

## Ending the Interview

Regardless of how much or little the offender has cooperated or has admitted, be sure to avoid "dumping" him when you leave. Before concluding the interview, thank him for his cooperation and debrief him a bit to lower his anxiety level. Ask him if he has any questions or concerns. For example, in the case in Exhibit 6.1, when I asked the Big Brother if he had any questions or comments he wanted to make, he asked me to tell the victim that he was sorry and that he still loved him. Leave the door open to later contact by giving him your card. Then, to help you in the future, ask him before you leave what made him want to talk to you. Find out what worked, so that you can try it again.

---

* Although this practice and technique is one of the most successful in securing admissions, confessions, and convictions, consideration must be given to the child's mental health. This is a controversial technique that should be done with mental-health professionals involved in the decision-making process.

## EXHIBIT 6.3 A MOTHER CONFRONTING A BOYFRIEND ABOUT HIS HAVING SEX WITH HER SON.

Mom: I found that letter last week. And the things you did with Bobbie and we have to do something about this. His father could take him away from me if he finds out and you know Bobbie. Bobbie can't handle this. I mean he doesn't need things like that. I mean he might tell someone at school and the school would have to do something.

BF: Okay

Mom: And I don't know what to do...

BF: What to do? Its over, its finished, Okay?

Mom: How will I know you won't do it over again?

BF: By trusting me.

Mom: Okay.

BF: Can we talk about it this afternoon?

Mom: No, I want to talk about it now, why did you masturbate him?

BF: I didn't, its not true what's in the letter.

Mom: Then why did you write it?

BF: Bobbie is weird and I have to, to, encourage him. I , I have... part of its he needs that sort of thing.

Mom: Why?

BF: Bobbie has a problem I guess that, worst than we think of, any of us know about. And he, he, he likes to hear things like that. Bobbie and I take a shower together, Bobbie and I did lie in front of the fire, and , and get... dry off. Or stood in front of the fire I should say and dry off. That did happen.

Mom: And what else happened? I mean Bobbie has really been quite upset this week...

BF: (later in the conversation) I'm, I'm, I'm, an honest person, I'm not, I'm not a child molester. I'm not a mean, ugly person.

Mom: But you were touching my son.

BF: Yes.

Mom: In places where you shouldn't have touched him according to that letter.

BF: Would it matter if I said he liked it. That he wanted me to...

Mom: No

BF: Okay, then I've made a terrible, terrible error then cause I though it was, ah, I thought it was something that he, I shouldn't say enjoyed, but he allowed, he let, he, he let me do, he, he wanted...

Mom: ...you're 48- years-old and he's 10. How's he supposed to go against an adult? He's been raised to do what adults tell him to do.

BF: Yeah.

Mom: I mean, how long has it been going on?

BF: Not long. It's, it's not a big thing. It's not part of my whole life... It's just something that occurred, ah, ah... I shouldn't say occasionally, occasionally okay, that it's not happened often. Once, twice, three times...

## Exhibit 6.4

A 13-year-old girl confronting her Mother's boyfriend regarding digital penetration.

Witness (W): (Earlier confrontation in conversation)

Clay, I have something to ask you. I have a rash down there. Is it possible to get AIDS from you sticking your finger in my vagina?

Suspect (S): (continuation of conversation)

Beth, I'm telling you, I haven't made love to another girl for over a year, so there's no way in the world, okay. If you're really concerned about it, then next week I'll take you somewhere and I'll pay for an examination...

W:No, Clay, I've — I've already gotten an examination down at the health department.

S:What did they say then?

W:They didn't — they don't know yet, they haven't gotten the results. But, Clay, I don't know what to do, if you, you had cum on your finger and if it went up inside me, then I don't know what to do because you could get AIDS from it.

S:Will you quit saying that.

W:No, I'm serious, Clay, yeah, I read it in the *Enquirer.*

S:So what are you gonna do?

W:I don't know.

S:Are your going to tell your Mom about that?

W:I don't know, that's why I'm calling because I don't know what to do. I'm gonna die if I have AIDS or VD or something like that.

S:Alright, now you listen to me. If you go tell your Mom about it, then, there's gonna be a whole lot of trouble. First of all, you're gonna be in trouble and they're gonna be mad at you forever...

W:They're not going to be mad at me.

S:Well OK, if you don't mind seeing me go to jail and never seeing me again...

## Types of Statements

Statements taken by police officers are generally attacked on three grounds: the investigator misinterpreted what was said, he mistranscribed what was said from a tape, or he wrote it wrong. Anything you can do to avoid attack on these grounds will greatly enhance a statement's success in the courtroom. An oral statement, where you take notes and then write a report, is the easiest to attack. A written narrative — one that you write and make deliberate mistakes that the offender must review, correct, and sign — is the best type of written statement. Having the offender write a statement by giving him a pencil and asking him to write down what happened is generally not worth the paper it's written on because he will seldom include the things you need.

A statement where you ask the questions, he answers, and you record it (audio or video) is good. Some people suggest doing this only when you know what the answers are going to be. They suggest that the statement shouldn't be recorded until you have conducted the entire interview and are reviewing the facts. Others prefer to have it all on tape. The problem with this is that something embarrassing might be said by you that you would rather not have in front of a jury, and that you never know what the offender may say.

Perhaps one of the most convincing aspects of an interview is the subject's body language. Just as we pointed out in the section on interviewing children, the same is true for offenders — their body language and facial expressions tell all. The video recording of the offender not only locks him into his version of what happened by memorializing it in such a clear and definite way, it gives the trier of fact something else to judge the truth with. They see the delivery and diction in each statement and can judge for themselves whether the offender is lying or not.

In a study by the National Institute of Justice [6], with no uncertain terms, defense attorneys opposed video taping because it gave the State a "strategic" edge. They said they could successfully attack or impeach written or reported interviews more easily than when it is video taped. They could create more ambiguity where there was no image to look at to support the interpretations the prosecution was making.

For example, if a suspect was to say, after a long pause, in answer to a direct question, that he had touched a child as was claimed by the child, hanging his head after nodding in an affirmative response, it would be difficult to argue that the investigator misunderstood the answer and that the offender actually denied any touching.

Videotaping also picks up things that might not be noticed by the investigator at the time such as injuries/bruises/marks or torn clothing. In review of the tape at a later time, these may be seen and explain or support contentions made long time later at trial.

Whichever technique you utilize, it should be done in a clandestine manner if possible. The admonishment should be recorded along with the waiver. If for some reason you have to shut off the tape, acknowledge the time going off, back on, and the reason for going off. Be sure not to talk about previous criminal conduct or background at the same time you discuss current, chargeable events, as it will have to be excised from the tape and it will make it sound altered. It is better to talk about these issues at a time when it won't interfere with the overall interview. The advantage of taped interviews is there is no question of what was said, the offender's demeanor comes across as it really is, you don't have to take notes, and therefore are able to concentrate on questioning.

In documenting the interview in your reports, tell exactly what you did by summarizing the conversations which were not recorded and reporting in detail what was said regarding the offenses.

## Polygraph Examinations

The polygraph provides an excellent opportunity to get "another shot" at the offender in an interview situation, and is an excellent tool for the investigator of a child molest case. Given the proper background information about what you know and need to know, a polygraph operator can elicit very important information for your case. Be sure the interview is tape-recorded. Have the operator talk about background information and the fears of the offender, all of which can be used to help you talk to him later, or assist the prosecutor in the courtroom during cross-examination by revealing some of the facets of the offender's defense early on in the investigation.

## Notes and References

1. Myron, R. Chartier, "Five Components to Effective Interpersonal Communications," *The 1974 Annual Handbook for Group Facilitators*, 1974.
2. Shawn A. Johnston, "The Mind of a Molester," *Psychology Today*, Feb. 1987.
3. Debi Howell, "Detecting the Dirty Lie," *The San Francisco Examiner*, 8/8/93.
4. The difference between a confession and an admission is that a confession contains all of the elements of the crime and an admission only part of them.
5. Ray Rawlings and Dana Gassaway, *APSAC Advisor*, 6/3/93, American Professional Society on Abuse of Children.
6. William A. Geller, *Videotaping Interrogations and Confessions*, National Institute of Justice, Washington, D.C., March, 1993.

## Additional Reading

American Professional Society on Abuse of Children, *The APSAC Handbook on Child Maltreatment*, Sage, Thousand Oaks, CA, 1996.

American Professional Society on Abuse of Children, *Child Maltreatment*, "Child Interviewing" Parts I and II, Sage, Thousand Oaks, CA, May, Vol. 1, No. 2, 1996; August, Vol. 1, No. 3, 1996.

Barker, Philip, *Clinical Interviews with Children and Adolescents*, W. W. Norton, New York, 1990.

California Attorney General's Office, *Research and Evaluation, Final Report*, Child Victim Witness Investigative Pilot Projects, Sacramento, CA, 1994.

Cantlay, Lynne, Ph.D., *Detecting Child Abuse: Recognizing Children at Risk Through Drawings*, Holly Press, Santa Barbara, CA, 1996.

Goodman, Gail S. with Bottoms, Bette L. Editors, *Child Victims, Child Witnesses: Understanding and Improving Testimony*, Guilford, NY, 1993.

Faller, Kathleen Coulborn, *Evaluating Children Suspected of Having Been Sexually Abused*, Sage, Thousand Oaks, CA, 1996.

Magnotte, Mike, "Child Sexual Assault," *Police Magazine*, at 56, March, 1994.

Miner, Edgar M., "The Importance of Listening in the Interview and Interrogation Process," *FBI Law Enforcement Bulletin*, June, 1984.

Meyers, John E. B., "Child and Adult Memory," *The Advisor*, American Professional Society on Abuse of Children, Chicago, Summer, 1992; Vol. 5, No. 3.

Nissman, David, et al., *The Law of Confessions*, Bancroft-Whitney, 1985.

Rawlins, Ray, Gassaway, D., "The Telephone: Tool or Tort," *APSAC Advisor*, 6:3, 1993.

Rudy, Leslie, & Goodman, Gail S., "Effects of Participation on Children's Reports: Implications for Children's Testimony," in *Developmental Psychology*, American Psychological Association, Wash., D.C., 1991 Vol. 27, No. 4 527-538.

Strentz, Thomas, "Proxemics and the Interview," *The Police Chief.*

Walsh, Bill, "Interrogation: Important Tool For Law Enforcement," 3:2, July/Aug. 1994.

Whitfield, Charles, L., *Memory and Abuse: Remembering and Healing the Effects of Trauma.*

Zulawski, David E., and Wicklander, D. E., *Practical Aspects of Interview and Interrogation*, CRC Press, Boca Raton, FL, 1993.

*Investigation and Prosecution of Child Abuse*, National Prosecutors Research Institute, Washington, D.C.,1993.

# Search Warrants

7

The search warrant is one of the most under-used tools available to the investigator. Unfortunately, because of the difficulty in obtaining one, unfamiliarity with the process, lack of understanding of what it can accomplish, or the knowledge that it is possible to obtain one, the search warrant is often disregarded or discounted. This chapter is intended to review the function of search warrants in investigations of sexual exploitation of children and to demonstrate the benefits of using them in every case possible. Because the success of many a case rests on the amount of evidence available, the discussion will briefly review the concept of search and seizure law in order to show how the types of search warrants obtained in cases of sexual exploitation of children can best be used. We will discuss how to obtain a search warrant in these cases and what should be contained in the affidavits for search warrants, and offer some suggestions on serving them to maximum advantage.

## Definitions

Under the Fourth Amendment to the United States Constitution, individuals are protected against unreasonable searches and seizures without warrant. These warrants must be based on probable cause, with particular descriptions of places and things to be searched and/or seized. A search warrant is an order in writing, signed by a magistrate, commanding a police officer to search for whatever is described in the warrant and to bring it to court. The test of probable cause is what would a reasonable man, under similar circumstances, conclude or believe. In arrest situations this means that the facts in support of the arrest must demonstrate that a crime was committed and that a particular individual committed the crime. In search warrants, that probable cause must demonstrate that whatever is being pursued will have evidentiary value and that it will be found where it is being sought. In child molest cases, it is also extremely helpful to establish information that would lead one to believe and entertain a strong suspicion of guilt of the accused. This will provide the magistrate who signs the warrant with a greater basis of information upon which to rest his conclusion.

In all states, there are limits on what can be sought with a search warrant. Of these, the following are the most relevant in cases of sexual exploitation:

1. Property or things (instrumentalities) used as a means of committing a felony.
2. Property or things (instrumentalities) that are in the possession of any person with intent to use it as a means of committing a public offense.
3. Property or things (instrumentalities) constituting evidence that tends to show a felony has been committed or tends to show a particular individual committed a felony.

Some states include other things that can be sought in a search warrant, loosely described as anything pertaining to the production of child pornography.

## Search Purposes

In a search warrant, an investigator will be seeking evidence relating to his case. Evidence is defined as anything offered to the senses to prove or disprove the existence or nonexistence of any fact that may be in controversy. Evidence can consist of documents, testimony, or real (tangible) evidence. In the affidavit of the search warrant the investigator must demonstrate the relevance of the evidence he seeks. Relevance is defined as being of consequence to the action. In court, this evidence may be used to impeach a defendant or rehabilitate or support a witness.

In cases of sexual exploitation of children, the search warrant may have one or more purposes in seeking evidence, all of which must be carefully spelled out in the affidavit so that there is no question about its validity. One of the benefits of the use of search warrants, especially in "minor" offenses, is the fact that evidence discovered during service of the warrant often may develop charges of a more serious nature.

### Corroboration

A constant problem in these cases is the credibility of child witnesses, who are constantly attacked by defense attorneys. Using the statutory terms mentioned, one aim of seeking evidence by a search warrant is to corroborate a victim's account and demonstrate that an individual or group of persons committed a crime by finding certain property or things that were used as a means of committing a felony or that tend to show that a felony was committed and that a particular individual committed a felony. This may also be done by finding property in the possession of any person with intent to commit a public offense.

The type of evidence sought, such as a picture depicting the offender and victim engaged in a sex act, will not always prove a particular criminal act but, rather, will corroborate the child's account. This is accomplished by finding things the child describes, demonstrating that the child's testimony is reliable and that the particular individual either possessed the items found with the intention to commit a public offense or felony and/or committed a felony. This type of evidence could consist of the camera used to take the pictures, the bedspread on which the acts took place, sexual aids used in the act, or other paraphernalia commonly used to seduce children.

## Intent and Scienter

One of the most common defenses in child molestation and pornography is lack of intent in or knowledge of the acts and/or content of the materials. Therefore, another aim of the search warrant is to demonstrate scienter (guilty knowledge), intent, and the true purpose and desires of the offender—in other words, using the statutory definitions, finding evidence that will demonstrate that the person possessed things that will tend to show that they were held with the intention of committing a public offense or a felony and/or that would tend to show that a particular individual committed a felony. Evidence of this nature could consist of membership in a child sex group; evidence to show who is getting satisfaction from the acts, such as diaries or letters; evidence that shows a connection to goods or materials sent by the offender; and evidence that demonstrates prior conduct, production, and/or distribution such as pictures, letters, writings, or other documents.

## Protect the Child

The search warrant also becomes a way to protect children by identifying victims who otherwise might not come forward because of the situations they find themselves in. This element should be emphasized as much as possible in every search warrant affidavit and, in particular, when seeking the identities of children and offenders you don't absolutely know exist. This concern may help to justify an intrusion and overcome the right to privacy when the interests of the children and offender are weighed by the judge.

Appendix III is an example of how this can work in a search warrant situation. In the case under investigation, the identities of several children were sought because during questioning of the victim and several witnesses it was learned that the offender may have been involved with other children, none of whom was identified. The need to identify and protect those children, as well as establishing that the offender's behavior and actions were consistent with several characteristics of child molesters, provided the probable cause to search the man's home. This case is a good example as it involves a *single* offense with a *single* victim, with *no physical evidence* seen or known of. But by establishing the offender's behavior to be consistent with the characteristics of child molesters, I was able to obtain a search warrant for his home, asking for many things that I didn't know in advance were there.

## Offender's Identity

Lastly, the search warrant becomes an investigative tool with which to prove that the individual in question is committing crimes. This can be done by finding evidence that will identify the individual under investigation and others who are committing the same crimes, as well as those who are victimized — in other words, finding evidence that tends to show that a felony was committed and that particular individuals committed a felony.

In cases where the identity of the offender is not known, such as serial stranger molestations or abductions, the search warrant is an invaluable tool to identifying and proving a particular individual is the offender. A special format for these warrants will be presented that builds a case, brick-by-brick, formulating a basis to believe the individual under investigation is responsible for the crimes under investigation.

## Discovery of Other Crimes

Service of search warrants helps to link cases and open up others; it often provides an opening into the subculture or underground. Rarely does one case limit itself to those under investigation; more commonly, cases will mushroom or snowball into greater numbers.

## Types of Warrant Affidavits

The aim of a search warrant is to provide independent review and approval by a neutral party (the judge) of an intrusion by search. The judge will base his opinion on the facts the investigator provides in the affidavit supporting the warrant. As with any other case, in sexual exploitation of children, the investigator must lead the judge to the conclusion that the circumstances contained in the case under investigation support the need to look for evidence pertaining to the case at a given location. This can be accomplished in several ways. The best way to develop probable cause is to demonstrate the investigator's expertise and plainly recount the facts, then draw conclusions based on that expertise and the facts. In most states, the tests of sufficient probable cause in an affidavit will either be the "two-pronged" test of *Aguilar v. Texas* [1], *Illinois v. Gates* [2].

The "two-pronged" test of *Aguilar* consists of very simple criteria. First, the information contained in the affidavit must be factual, based on verifiable information, not conclusion, and contain some or all of the underlying circumstances from which the affiant made the conclusion that the probable cause to search exists. This prong also ensures that the conclusion that probable cause exists was based on personal knowledge and that the source knew what he was talking about. Second, the affidavit must demonstrate why the information is reliable or credible.

The *Gates* test is much broader, basing the conclusion of sufficiency of probable cause on a judge's "common sense". Unfortunately, some judges don't have the same "senses" as police officers, and there is nothing to ensure that one judge will have the same "senses" as another. Therefore, many prosecutors recommend that when a search warrant affidavit is written, the author should make it conform to the guidelines of *Aguilar*. Should the affidavit fail on these grounds, the prosecutor may still defend its sufficiency under the *Gates* case.

The affidavit examples that follow conform to the *Aguilar* standards. Even though a child victim is considered to be "reliable" without corroboration under *Aguilar*, examples of how to corroborate a child's account within the body of the affidavit will be demonstrated because of the consistent attacks on children's credibility and the reluctance of many judges to accept children's testimony. The inclusion of this information is not only intended to support the child, but to create a "general picture" of what the individual under investigation is really about. Finally, it must be realized that such corroboration often may not be easily obtained and that *it is possible to obtain a search warrant without it.* Because not every investigator feels comfortable with the final affidavit format that will be recommended, we will discuss some alternatives, their disadvantages, and demonstrate how to develop an "expertise" affidavit format.

## Straightforward Listing of Facts — Totality of the Circumstances

In simple cases that do not involve more than one incident or report, the investigator may lay out the facts of the crime and name in the affidavit the evidence he seeks, based on what he has found, what the victim saw, and what a witness or witnesses saw and told him. This type of warrant will list in a straightforward manner what happened and the findings of the investigation. For example, in the following affidavit, after the officer listed her qualifications and gave some background on the case, she described the circumstances of the reported incident:

Elisabeth told your affiant that on the day of the incident, Mr. Williams returned to her grandmother's apartment and began talking to her and MacSems about modeling and band equipment. She said that Mr. Williams offered her $50 an hour to model. She said that she compromised with Mr. Williams, telling him she would model for $35 an hour.

She said that when the latter fee was agreed upon, she and MacSems were given wine and asked their ages by Mr. Williams. She said that she told Mr. Williams that she was 16-years old and MacSems was 14 years old. She said that Mr. Williams began talking about his band and how the male and female members of the band engage in both heterosexual and homosexual relationships. She said that Mr. Williams asked if she and MacSems would like to have lesbian sex. She said that Mr. Williams initially had told her he wanted her to model only in a "sexy" manner and would require no totally nude poses.

She said that when they arrived at Mr. Williams apartment, MacSems went into another room with another man, while she and Mr. Williams went to his bedroom to model for photographs.

She said that as the modeling session progressed, Mr. Williams requested she pose with only her jean skirt and jacket on, with her breasts exposed. She said the modeling session ended at approximately 1545 hrs, and Mrs. Williams soon arrived at the apartment after that.

She said that she went into the bathroom and put on a white corset and stockings for the next modeling session. While she was dressing, Mrs. Williams entered the bathroom and began feeling her breasts and kissing her on the mouth. She said that she left the bathroom and began to model in "sexy" poses for Mr. Williams.

She said that at approximately 2000—2100 hrs, she was served some food by Mrs. Williams. She said she began to feel drugged and sluggish after eating while she was modeling for another photography session. She said that during this session she was only attired in a wet T-shirt and, later on, only a towel.

She said that after the modeling session, she was tired and lay down on a mattress in the living room, with MacSems leaving the apartment at the same time. She said the next thing she remembered was being awakened by Mrs. Williams, who was kissing and touching her body while taking off Elisabeth's clothes. She said that Mrs. Williams began to stick her finger in Elisabeth's vagina while licking her vaginal area. She said that she tried to push Mrs. Williams away but was unable to because her body would not move and her arms "felt like rubber."

She said that she did not know how long Mrs. Williams was with her. She said that when Mrs. Williams left, Mr. Williams, who had been watching from the couch, lay on top of her nude. She said that while Mr. Williams touched and kissed her, he also forced his penis into her vagina. She said that she couldn't resist because she felt too numb to move or push him away. She said that she fell asleep, awakening about 45 minutes prior to the arrival of your affiant (on an earlier call, which launched this investigation). She said that she left her watch, bracelet, high school ring, and shoes at the Williams' apartment.

MacSems also gave a statement that said basically the same thing as that made by Elisabeth. She did add the following. She said that Mr. Williams attempted to kiss her mouth approximately three times while inside the apartment. She said that both Mr. and Mrs. Williams kept touching and rubbing her thighs. She said that she left at around midnight. She said that prior to leaving, Mrs. Williams was asking her to stay so that everyone could take their clothes off and climb into bed together.

The problem with this type of warrant is that the officer, with no further qualifications, assertions, or conclusions, based on training or experience, could only ask for things mentioned in the narrative—for example, the camera, film, pictures of the girls and offenders, the girl's watch, jewelry, clothes, and the clothing worn during the posing. Nothing else that could prove the true intent or interests of the offenders could be requested because no justification was listed in the affidavit.

## Facts Developed from Investigation — Known Offender

A judge can be convinced that evidence will be found at a given location if he is presented with a pattern that points in the direction you wish to search. For example, in the next affidavit, the investigator begins by laying out events that led to the discovery that an individual was inclined to be involved with children, was sexually oriented toward children and, finally, was molesting children. The affidavit lays out in the chronological order the events that led to the offender and what the investigation revealed, and gives the judge a view from the investigator's position, to assist him in making the necessary conclusions. Throughout the affidavit, statements by the witnesses and observations made by the investigator begin to lay the foundation for seeking certain items of evidence.

Your affiant is a police officer of the Berkeley Police Department and has been acting in that capacity for approximately six years. Presently your affiant is assigned to the Juvenile Bureau of the Berkeley Police Department as a Juvenile Officer and has been so assigned for approximately the past 18 months. Presently, your affiant is responsible for the review and subsequent investigation, if necessary, of cases involving sexual exploitation and sexual molestation of children.

In your affiant's capacity as previously mentioned, your affiant had occasion to review several reports and obtain information regarding an individual known as "Theodore B. Underdog, 1234 Virginia St., #1, DOB: 1-2-55, and his involvement in activities which constitute crimes against children defined in the California Penal Code section 288. In order to get a full grasp of the background of this case, the following summary and details of the offenses are offered.

On October 11, Underdog approached your affiant at the Berkeley Police Department, applying for a position as a "Big Brother" in a counseling program run by the Juvenile Bureau of the police department, of which your affiant is the Director. Underdog completed a background application, identifying himself as listed above. He listed his vocational goal and vocation as being an ambulance paramedic and child care worker. Among other things, he described his experience as being involved with pre-school and elementary level children, child abuse, autism, crippled and mentally retarded children, as well as being a voluntary aide in pediatric care. He indicated that in the past two summers prior to his making the application he was employed in doing a lot of work with children in his free time. Your affiant asked Underdog if he had any particular age preference with whom he liked to work, to which he replied, 12 or under.

In November, Officer Ross, a Juvenile Officer in the Juvenile Bureau of the Berkeley Police Department, received a telephone call from Ron Paulson of the People's Clinic, a medical clinic in Berkeley, regarding Underdog. Paulson indicated that Underdog had gone to the clinic and filled out a referral card for a group which Underdog called the "Homosexual Pedophilic Group." The referral card, according to Paulson, stated that the group met at the First Oversized Church at 1st and D Streets, in San Francisco. Paulson also told Officer Ross that the card indicated that anyone interested in the program should contact Underdog at a number which your affiant determined to be Underdog's home phone number. According to Paulson, the card listed the group as being "for those who are sexually involved with little boys."

Ross further indicated that Paulson told her that an unidentified woman from the clinic called Underdog to confirm the validity of the referral service. Paulson told Officer Ross that the unidentified woman determined that the group was not a self help group, but rather, a recruitment group.

In March and April articles appeared in the *Local Gazette, Bay Area Tribune,* and *East Bay Times,* respectively, featuring a story about Underdog and his association with a group known as "Teddy Bears of the Nation." In the *Gazette* article, Underdog's photograph appeared depicting his collection of teddy bears. In the article in the *Tribune,* Underdog's photograph appears with several teddy bears, a child who is identified as Detrick Smith and another adult who is identified in the article as Jay More. *The Times* article features a photograph of Teddy Underdog and a teddy bear as well as a second photograph which depicts several teddy bears, More, and another young child who is identified as Kathleen Stevens of Apple Creek.

In May, Theodore Underdog reported a theft from his residence which was investigated by Officer Lee of the Berkeley Police Department and recorded under report 123456. The report describes the following items as taken:

1. (1) black looseleaf notebook, approximately 5″ × 7″ divided into five separate sections. The contents of this notebook included addresses of preschool and daycare centers, emergency medicine, parks and recreation, "Teddy Bears of the Nation," pediatric care, pediatric, and miscellaneous personal information.

2. (1) 8″ × 10″ color photograph of a young boy mounted on a piece of cardboard.

In May, Leo Ring and Annett Wall of Oakland contacted Officer Moore of the Sex Crimes Detail, of the Berkeley Police Department, regarding Theodore Underdog. They said, as detailed in her report on the matter, that they had come into possession of a notebook which belonged to Underdog. They gave the notebook to Officer Moore and told her how they had come into possession of it. According to Wall, Underdog was working for a referral counseling service known as "Oranges," and Wall had gone there where she met him, approximately one month prior to Officer Moore's interview. Wall said that she met Underdog at her home at a later time. Wall said that Underdog told her his "life story." She said that he talked about having a bad sexual experience with an older male when he was a child, which later developed into his wanting to have the same relationships with small children. Wall also said that Underdog told her that he liked little boys between the ages of 4 and 10 years. Wallace said that because she had a youngster who was four years old she became upset, at which time Underdog left. After Underdog had left she noticed that he had left the notebook which she gave to Officer Moore.

Officer Moore gave that book to your affiant when she discovered that your affiant had already been conducting an investigation regarding Underdog's activities. Your affiant looked at the notebook and found an 8″ × 10″ color photograph of a young male juvenile approximately 7 or 8 years old who was naked. This youngster was standing with his hands behind his back, genitals exposed, facing the camera. Your affiant further noted that contained in the notebook were lists of names and locations as described in the theft report taken by Officer Lee. The list of names contained names of young children who were involved in various programs, school activities and other organizations. Most of the ages of the children, as denoted beside their names in many instances, ranged from age 3 to 17.

Your affiant also found a page with the handwritten heading of "Berkeley Unified School District, Wilson Elementary School, SRV

Program." Your affiant knows, having worked with the school district, that SRV is the abbreviation for Student Resource Volunteer. The same page lists, in handwritten print, "Date began January, ... Project title—School Resource Volunteers..." Below the aforementioned writings were listed 27 names, among them Detrick Smith's, including his address and phone number, Asa Jose's, and a Zeke Schwartz's. The following was written at the bottom of the page: "As of March 5th, voluntary services have been terminated." Your affiant found Smith's name on another page in the book which contained names of public parks.

Your affiant found the following handwritten notations on one of the last pages of the notebook: "Boyish collegiate, Shawn, 19, cute, boyish face, blue eyes, brown hair, 5-8, 130, very smooth, proportioned swimmer build, seven inch versatile, $35 an hour, San Francisco" and "Super good head for good looking guys under 23 (over 18), high school, college, chicken okay, San Francisco." Both had phone numbers written beside them.

Your affiant knows, from training and experience, that these notations are consistent with the "personal ads" used by the child molester underground to communicate with one another and that "chicken" is the term used by the underground for boys under 18 years of age, generally street prostitutes.

Of importance and interest to note, on the same page, written in red ink, was the following: "May 3—Seth Goldstein, Juvenile Department, *hot* for child molestation cases in Berkeley."

Thus far, the investigator has given some background on what is known about the offender, slowly building a case by demonstrating the offender's predilection or inclination to be with and, perhaps, molest children. With the information provided and limited expertise listed by the investigator to this point, he does not have enough to support an arrest or search warrant because sufficient probable cause has not been established to believe a crime was committed. More must be obtained. However, this background information accomplishes two things. It begins to establish probable cause by laying the foundation for the judge to see who the offender really is and it begins to support the children who will give their accounts of how they came to know Underdog and what he did to them.

In May, Detrick Smith, White Male Juvenile, 7 yrs old and Aaron Jones, White Male Juvenile, 8 yrs old, were brought to the Hall of Justice by their parents at the request of Officer Moore. Officer Moore initiated a report which she recorded under case 12346 which your affiant had occasion to review. Your affiant read that she spoke to Smith first, indicating that he said "Teddy makes us take off all our clothes everyday when we go over to see him." Smith described Underdog as being a person who lives approximately four or five blocks from his home, someone who was a friend of the family, and someone who he had met through a friend at Wilson Elementary School. Smith said that Underdog, whom he called "Teddy," had told him to bring another of his friends over so that they could play at his house and that he could do that at anytime he wanted. Smith said that he and Jones went to Underdog's house every Thursday and Saturday. He said that not until the second time that he went to Underdog's house did Underdog suggest that they "play a game." Underdog told them to take off all their clothes and told them that the game was called "monster." He said that Underdog unzipped his pants and had both boys simultaneously fondle his penis. He also said that at the same time, Underdog fondled their genitals as well.

Smith estimated that this activity occurred at least 10 to 15 times within a two week period and that each incident lasted approximately one hour. Smith said that after they had visited Underdog on about 5 or 6 occasions, each time they would come to his house Underdog would demand that they take their clothes off, which they did. Smith said that each time this was done, Underdog would then undress himself and have Jones lay on a couch and Smith on the floor. Smith said that Underdog would climb on top of Jones, who was lying prone on the couch and, on Jones' back, do what Moore described as "simulate intercourse." According to Moore's report, Underdog would rub against the body of Jones with his penis until he ejaculated. Her report indicates that Underdog would then get down on the floor with Smith, having Smith lay in a prone position, whereupon Underdog would rub his penis against Smith's buttocks until he ejaculated again. According to Moore's report, after Underdog ejaculated at least two times, the two boys were allowed to put their clothes back on and play with some of the stuffed animals which Underdog kept in his home.

Separately, Officer Moore asked Jones what had happened and he gave a similar description as to the events described by Smith. He indicated that the incidents of sexual play occurred at least 20 times. According to Officer Moore, Jones described the ejaculate as "yukky white liquid" that came out of his (Underdog's) "dick." Both boys told Moore that each time they were at Underdog's apartment, they were there together.

Officer Lee told your affiant that in May he recontacted Underdog regarding the alleged theft of his book. When questioned further regarding the contents of the book and photograph, Underdog requested that Officer Lee discontinue his investigation.

Up to this point, the investigator has established the elements of child molestation (in this case, a felony, in California) and corroborated his victims through testimony given independently by each child. Although great suspicion of the guilt of Underdog has been developed, very little has been mentioned as evidence that may be searched for to corroborate the children. Still more investigation is necessary.

In May, Smith and Jones came to the Hall of Justice and were interviewed by your affiant regarding the crimes being investigated by Officer Moore. Your affiant asked both Smith and Jones if there were any other adults involved or if they knew anyone who associates with Underdog. Both of them replied that Underdog's roommate, whom they only knew as "Jay," was present at the time of the sexual play and that he "did a nasty" as well. Both Smith and Jones said that "Jay" had told both of them to take off their clothes and said something similar to "show me your penis." They stated that "Jay" also took off his clothes and that, although he did not touch them, he was present during the time that Underdog did. Both Smith and Jones said that this happened numerous times; however, they were able to pinpoint only one instance which occurred around the date that the Tribune photo was taken.

Both Smith and Jones said that a friend of their's, Asa Jose, 7 yrs, also knew Underdog and that they believed he had been in Underdog's house as well. They said that this was so because they had seen a drawing which had Asa's name signed at the bottom of it. Both said that another juvenile, 7 years old, with a first name of Zeke, who attends their school, was at Underdog's home and knew him.

Both Smith and Jones said that the last time that they were at Underdog's home was about one week ago.

Now the investigator has established a greater reason and need to get into Underdog's home. He can search for evidence which will identify Underdog's coparticipant, the stuffed animals mentioned previously, the picture drawn by Asa, and information that will further identify Asa and Zeke. All of these things will help to demonstrate that Underdog committed a felony (child molestation), by supporting the children's accounts of what happened, identifying More, and identifying Underdog's home. However, there are other things to be searched for, creating an even greater need to search Underdog's home.

Smith told your affiant that Underdog had taken three photographs of him, the first two taken approximately the first day after they met. He said that both of them were in front of his own home and that the third one, taken approximately one day or so after the first photographs, was taken in Underdog's living room. He said that he was fully clothed in each photograph, however, Underdog had repeatedly asked him to take off his clothes so that Underdog could take a picture of him in the nude.

Jones said that Underdog had also taken three photographs of him, the first being shortly after they met. He stated that his was taken in front of a sofa bed store at the corner of University and Milvia. Jones said that this was taken in the daytime and he was fully clothed, however, Underdog repeatedly asked him to allow him to take pictures of him in the nude. Jones said that the second photograph was taken approximately one week after the first picture and was taken in Underdog's living room by his couch. He stated that he was clothed at the time, but was requested to take off his clothes. Jones said that the third photograph was taken approximately one day after the second, in the same place, wearing different clothes.

Both Smith and Jones said that while they were at Underdog's apartment, they would play in his room with toys which Underdog allowed them to use. They described them as being a fire station and garage made by Tonka Toys, approximately the size of two typewriters. They also played with a dump truck and three ambulances which they believed were made by Tonka Toys, as well as a fire truck which they thought was a Fisher Price product. In addition to those toys, they played with a toy train which had a track for it which they described as having three cars and an old style engine. They described the entire length of the train as being 24" when totally assembled. They also indicated that they played with numerous stuffed teddy bears, which they estimated to be 40 in number, which were on shelves in Underdog's room.

Both Smith and Jones said that they drew pictures which they last saw around 5-11, hanging in Underdog's room. Jones indicated that he had drawn a picture on the second day that they had gone to Underdog's house, drawing it on an $8^1/_2$" × 11" piece of paper (using a piece of office paper as comparison) in which he drew mountains, trees, clouds, and a house. He described the picture as being drawn with crayon with brown, black, green and white crayon. He stated that he signed his name by printing "Aaron." He said that he last saw it hanging on a sliding door of Underdog's closet in Underdog's bedroom.

Smith said that on the first day he had gone to Underdog's house, he had drawn a picture in crayon as well. He described it as being of two racing cars, orange, red and black in color. He said that he signed it by printing "Detrick" at the bottom. He said that he last saw it somewhere near May 11th hanging on a wall in Underdog's bedroom.

Both Smith and Jones told your affiant that Underdog had shown them a book which depicted nude boys and girls their age, babies, kids older than they were, as well as adults, which they described as being approximately 10" × 14", approximately $^3/_4$" thick. It was described to your affiant as having a white cover and the letters "SHOW ME" in big black letters across the top and the picture of a naked boy and girl below it on the front cover. Both Smith and Jones said that Underdog told them they could look in the book at any time they wanted to.

Both Smith and Jones said that Underdog had shown them two photographs, one of which they identified as being the nude photograph found in the notebook which was given Officer Moore and your affiant. They described the second photograph as depicting a boy, 6 to 7 years old, standing nude in a river or lake who was splashing in the water. They said that there was another boy in the background who was playing with a ball. They said that this second boy was naked also.

The children described to your affiant the camera used by Underdog as that listed in the search warrant attached to this affidavit.

In June, your affiant contacted Dr. Steven Gil, Principal, Wilson Elementary School and Alice Lemert, White Female Adult, 40 yrs old, Instructional Aide. Lemert said that approximately Wednesday or Thursday of last week, at approximately 12:30 or 12:45 hrs, she observed a White Male Adult, mid-twenties, dark brown hair, wearing blue jeans and a tan sweater or shirt, sitting on a 10-speed bike near the fence line of the playground. She said that he stayed at this location for approximately 10–15 minutes and was talking to several of the children there. She said that she was unable to speak to him prior to his leaving, however, she spoke to a student whom she only knows as "Paul" who told her that the individual had told him to remove all of his clothes so he could take his picture. She said that there was also a girl who witnessed this whom she only knew as "Lotus."

Dr. Gil said that he had identified that individual as Underdog by talking to another student who had seen him at the time, but whom he was unable to remember the name of. He said that Underdog had served as a Resource Volunteer during the Fall of '78 and when he discovered that Underdog was trying to get children to come to his house as well as exhibiting some other strange behavior, he discontinued Underdog from the program. He identified "Lotus" as Lotus Davidson and identified Zeke Swartz, but was unable to identify "Paul."

As of the time of this writing, your affiant has not had an opportunity to contact any of the aforementioned students; however, this incident is mentioned to demonstrate further involvement on Underdog's part.

All of the reports which have been written thus far have been attached hereto and incorporated herein for reference.

With this affidavit format, a section listing all of the affiant's qualifications and expertise should follow. Examples of how to list expertise are given in Appendices I, II, and XI. After the listing of the affiant's qualifications, conclusions should be drawn about what the affiant expects to find and why. For example:

It is from this training and experience that your affiant has found that people who commit such crimes against children as have been referred to in this affidavit and in the attached reports often keep in their residence phone books, lists, or registers with the names and phone numbers of the children they are having contact with. In one such case your affiant investigated, these "numbers" consisted merely of pieces of paper torn from various other paper materials. The fact both Smith and Jones told your affiant that they had observed Underdog write their name and phone numbers in a small phone register, in addition to the fact that your affiant has found several of the names connected with this investigation in the notebook given to your affiant by Officer Moore, causes your affiant to believe, based on expertise and training, that further lists, phone books, or notes are in Underdog's possession or in his residence.

The problem with this type of affidavit, for the most part, is that it limits what can be requested for seizure to that which the investigator can establish is known to exist by testimony or investigation. The format greatly limits the ability to predict "associative" type of evidence so frequently found in these cases.

## Totality of the Circumstances — The "Puzzle Concept"

This concept was first developed and "coined" as the Puzzle Concept by Inspector Larry Lindenau of the Berkeley Police Department and applied to serial rapes and other sex crimes committed in the City of Berkeley. Its use has become standard practice where the identity of the serial offender was unknown until sufficient evidence could be mustered to support searching and/or arresting a particular individual. Its basis is what has come to be known as offender profiling, something to be discussed in greater detail in the following chapter on case management.

### Building Blocks Complete the Puzzle

The formula for this approach is treating each bit of evidence found in the cases already experienced as a piece of a puzzle that will eventually coalesce to formulate a clear picture of the identity of the offender. For example, in one case a child reports a molestation by an old man, carrying a distinctive satchel from which he withdrew some candy. A second case is reported where a child saw the man had on a shirt which was monogrammed with the initials "P.O._." Yet, a third and forth case provide adult witnesses who describe the man as in his 50s, 5-6/10, 150/160 lbs, graying hair, below the collar. In each case he was wearing a distinctive golf hat. As the cases pile up, a distinctive MO emerges, wherein the man approaches elementary school children on the street near parks, playgrounds, and bus stops, showing them "magical feats" using variously described props taken from his "bag of tricks," engaging them in sexual acts under the guise of his magic. His favorite trick is pulling a silver dollar from the ears of his victims.

On a surveillance detail created for the purpose of apprehending this offender, an officer stops a man near an elementary school playground who is wearing a golf hat, is 5′ 7″, 155 lbs, has gray hair and his name is Ped O. File. In his pockets are found over $60.00 in silver dollars.

This is an oversimplified description of the case described earlier in this text in Chapter 3, but it presents the facts in a straightforward, logical manner, piling fact-upon-fact to lead to the inevitable conclusion that the person stopped is likely to be the offender. Connections to specific evidence in each crime report in the series are drawn and a warrant affidavit is drafted for the search of the offender's home/vehicle.

An excellent example of the way this type of warrant may be put together in the case of a stranger, hot-prowl (residents present during the commission of the crime), burglar/molester, may be seen the in the work of Sergeant Laura Warren (Retired) of the Fairfax, California, Police Department shown in Appendix XIII (a reconstruction of the actual warrant). Over a period of several years, she developed a profile and facts that connected the offender to the crimes involved. She used every conceivable lead and source of information to characterize this offender and tie him to the crimes she was investigating, culminating in one of the most comprehensive investigations and case presentations in Marin County history. The resulting conviction was the payoff.

## Expertise Affidavits

Another type of affidavit is one that leads the reader to entertain certain beliefs based on the information the investigator has developed and reported within the affidavit. This type of affidavit uses the investigator's experience and training to help the judge reach the same conclusions. This is the preferred format for child molestation search-warrant affidavits.

In determining probable cause, the law doesn't place the man of ordinary care and prudence and the experienced officer in the same class. Circumstances and conduct that might not arouse the suspicion of the man on the street may be highly significant to a trained police officer. Facts in a given case may not mean anything out of the ordinary to a judge; however, by demonstrating a special knowledge or significance in the affidavit, an officer may cast a different light on them. The affiant must set himself up as an expert in the affidavit. In an affidavit, this expertise may come from the affiant or from a recognized "expert" — for instance, a criminalist who compares ballistic evidence in a homicide investigation.

If a victim is found to have been shot with a .22-caliber weapon, and a ballistic comparison is made at a crime lab on a particular weapon seized by investigators from a suspect, the results of the comparison may be described in an affidavit for a search warrant. All that must be done is to list the expertise of the ballistics expert in the affidavit, and ensure that the conclusions are not overboard and have a factual basis (described in the conclusionary statement). An example of how this may be accomplished is found in Appendix I. Here, one police officer uses the expertise of another to make conclusionary statements.

An example of where this might occur is in determining the age of children depicted in photographs who the investigator is unable to identify. Through the use of a pediatrician, approximate ages may be established. What the affidavit should include is a description of the doctor's background, how long he has been in practice, how many children he has examined, and on what observations he bases his opinion. He should be able to describe the children's physical development, muscular appearance, and overall build, in relation to the age he believes them to be. He should describe the presence or lack of public hair and its developmental characteristics as it relates to the age he estimates they are.

The affiant may use his own expertise to make conclusions. For example, any police officer who has been through a police academy knows that if a man is arrested after making repeated sales of cocaine to an undercover operative, and that cocaine was packaged in small, waxed paper bundles, a search of the person's home base will probably turn up more than cocaine, money, and waxed paper. The officer would know, from training and experience, that cocaine is "cut" with various agents, is weighed or divided in some manner, is packaged in various forms, that the salesperson must keep a record of his orders or sales, and that the officer will find evidence of this in a search. Therefore, laying out why he knows this to be true he can, in a search warrant, ask for certain types of evidence even though he hasn't seen it. The same may be done with child molestation warrants.

It is also possible to list only those characteristics that apply to a given case. The disadvantage of this technique, however, is that it will limit the type of things the officer will be able to search for. When all of the characteristics are listed, all of the things shown in the checklist, which will be discussed later, may be sequestered.

The format for the affidavit that will be recommended will include particular characteristics of the offender and crimes that have been discussed throughout this text. They are not to be considered exhaustive nor the only characteristics that may or should be listed. Investigator's individual experiences may not cover all of these characteristics. You may view these characteristics with different interpretations, or other characteristics may be known. If this is the case, all that need be done is to replace those that are not consistent with your experience and replace them with something that is. Similarly, if you know of some characteristics that are not included, they should be added. *Do not list anything you do not feel comfortable explaining.* If something that is listed is not within your experience and you do not understand its meaning, you might consider using the expertise of someone else who can explain it.

This affidavit format has three sections: the expertise section, the characteristics section, and the probable cause section.

The intention of this format is to list what we know about the offenders and their offenses that will justify asking for particular items of evidence. Not every characteristic will be seen in each case investigated. It is *not* necessary to have *every characteristic* within the body of the *probable cause section* of the affidavit to *satisfy the test of probable cause* to ask for certain items of evidence. Through the use of the language suggested the same types of evidence in every case may be requested for seizure, providing all the characteristics are listed in the expertise section and that at least some of the characteristics listed are demonstrated to exist in the recitation of the probable cause in the affidavit. If none of these characteristics exists in a case under investigation, this affidavit format should not be used. However, one of the preceding styles should be.

The most important consideration in drafting this type of warrant is that *clear connections* are drawn between the evidence sought, the crime under investigation, and the belief that the evidence will be found where you are asking to search. This was the downfall of a capital case involving a serial offender in California that subsequently overturned his death sentence [3]. There is now a much larger body of case law on the books regarding the validity of this affidavit format than when it was first utilized. Although this makes it more likely to withstand the scrutiny of the defense attorney, it is a better policy to be conservative in approach. If there is any question at all about what to ask for and what may be asked for, consultation with the prosecutor who oversees such cases and concerns should be sought. It is always wise to consult with a prosecutor in drafting these warrants anyway, because it would be a terrible shame to lose significant evidence that would have protected a child when such problems could have been avoided in the drafting.

A mechanical application of the language described, as "boiler-plate," in this text will surely result in disaster when challenged. The language suggested in this text to justify request for search and seizure is intended as a guideline, not a "fill-in-the-blank" form. Therefore, careful examination of the facts of each individual case and what is to be sought must be undertaken. If there is a doubt regarding what may be asked for, a supplemental warrant affidavit should be considered. Once the original warrant is issued for that evidence the investigator feels sufficiently certain will be found, it may be served and anything subsequently found as a result, that is not contraband, may be requested for seizure in a supplementary warrant affidavit.

This would require either a telephonically secured warrant or the security of the scene while it is obtained. A telephonic warrant supplement may be obtained from the same judge simply incorporating the original affidavit in the new warrant request with the new facts discovered during the search forming its grounds. An excellent resource in the preparation of these warrants is the National Center for the Prosecution of Child Abuse, Alexandria, Virginia and the National Center for Missing and Exploited Children, Washington, D.C. Both have publications which detail both the format and supporting legal precedent for this concept [4].

## Establishing Expertise

In this section, the investigator must list everything he has done or seen that might relate to his ability to draw conclusions as an "expert." It should begin by identifying any academy training that pertains to the subject of sexual assault and child molestation. Any specialized training should be spelled out. Formal and informal discussions or meetings with other professionals pertaining to the issues of sexual assault and child molestation should be mentioned. This should include role-call training and meetings held to discuss crimes of this type and their solution, conducted by neighboring law-enforcement agencies. The number of investigations conducted should be listed, with a breakdown of the number of victims and offenders interviewed. If the investigator has authored other search warrant affidavits, they too should be listed. Any reading or research the investigator has done should be listed. If the investigator has taught, lectured, or written anything on the subject of sexual exploitation of children, this should be listed. If the investigator has testified as an expert in court or other forums, this should be listed. If an investigator uses this format on a regular basis, it is helpful to consider making a copy of the expertise section and use it in each warrant, updating it as necessary.

Following the section on expertise, a listing of known characteristics of the crime and offender should be made, prefaced by the statement that they are based on the investigator's "training and experience." It is also permissible to include a brief explanation of each characteristic as it is listed. The reason for listing these characteristics first is to educate the judge and give him an idea of how to interpret what he reads in the affidavit. It is like giving a person a pair of glasses that makes everything look three-dimensional. Without the glasses, what is seen looks flat, with no definition or significance. With the glasses, everything makes sense and takes on its true form. The judge, given the glasses before he begins to read the affidavit, will have a better chance of seeing what you want him to see than if the characteristics were listed at the end of the affidavit or not at all, and he was left to draw his own conclusions.

## Characteristics of the Crime and Offender

Although throughout this text we have discussed the offender as being a pedophile in terms of his behavior, great care must be taken by the nonclinical professional to try not to diagnose offenders. Because pedophilia is a clinical term used for people who present certain psychologically significant characteristics, it is important to avoid mentioning it in an affidavit. In the past (as can be seen by the sample affidavits), it was common to describe the subject under investigation as a pedophile. However, this often created problems when the case came to court or when evidence asked for in the search warrant affidavit was not found. By naming the individual as a pedophile, it gives the offender an immediate defense: "I am not a pedophile," which clouds the issue in court. To avoid this, it is better to describe the crime in terms of experiences with those who commit similar crimes.

The following list of characteristics should precede the probable cause section of the affidavit, with the introductory paragraph as listed here:

As a result of your affiant's training and experience, I have learned that the following characteristics are, generally, found to exist in varying combinations and be true in cases involving people who buy, produce, trade, or sell child pornography; who molest children and/or who are involved with child prostitutes:

1. There are persons whose sexual objects are children. They receive sexual gratification and satisfaction from actual physical contact with children and from fantasy involving use of pictures, other photographic or art mediums, and writings on or about sexual activity with children;

2. These people collect sexually explicit materials consisting of photographs, magazines, motion pictures, video tapes, books, and slides, which they use for their own sexual gratification and fantasy;

3. These people use sexually explicit materials, including those listed above for lowering the inhibitions of children, sexually stimulating children and themselves, and for demonstrating the desired sexual acts, before, during and after sexual activity with children;

4. These people rarely, if ever, dispose of their sexually explicit materials, especially when it is used in the seduction of their victims, and those materials are treated as prize possessions;

5. These people often correspond or meet with one another to share information and identities of their victims as a means of gaining status, trust, acceptance, and psychological support;

6. These people rarely destroy correspondence received from other people with similar interests unless they are specifically requested to do so;

7.  The majority of these people prefer contact with children of one sex, as well as in a particular age or developmental range peculiar to each individual;

8.  These people engage in activity or gravitate to programs which will be of interest to the type of victims they desire to attract and will provide them with easy access to these children;

9.  These people obtain, collect, and maintain photographs of the children they are or have been involved with. These photos may depict children fully clothed, in various states of undress or totally nude, in various activities, not necessarily sexually explicit. These photos are rarely, if ever, disposed of and are revered with such devotion that they are often kept upon the individual's person in wallets and such. If a picture of a child is taken by such a person depicting the child in the nude, there is a high probability the child was molested before, during, or after the photo taking session because the act of the posing is such a great sexual stimulus for the individual;

10.  These people use such photos as described above as a means of reliving fantasies or actual encounters with the depicted children. They also utilize the photos as keepsakes and as a means of gaining acceptance, status, trust, and psychological support by exchanging, trading, or selling them to other people with similar interests. These photos are carried and kept by these people as a constant threat to the child of blackmail and exposure;

11.  These people cut pictures of children out of magazines, newspapers, books, and other publications which they use as a means of fantasy relationships. These "cut-outs" help to identify the age and sexual preference of the person under investigation;

12.  These people collect books, magazines, newspapers, and other writings on the subject of sexual activities with children. They maintain these as a way of understanding their own feelings towards children;

13.  The people who are afraid of discovery often maintain and run their own photographic production and reproduction equipment. This may be as simple as the use of "instant" photo equipment such as Polaroid makes, video equipment, or as complex as a completely outfitted photo lab;

14.  These people go to great lengths to conceal and protect from discovery, theft, and damage their collections of illicit materials. This often includes the rental or use of safe deposit boxes or other storage facilities outside their immediate residence;

15.  These people often collect, read, copy or maintain names, addresses, phone numbers or lists of persons who have similar sexual interests. These may have been collected by personal contact or through

advertisements in various publications. These contacts are maintained as a means of personal referral, exchange, and commercial profit. These names may be maintained in the original publication, in phone or note books, or merely on scraps of paper;

16.  These people often keep the names of the children they are involved with or with whom they have had sexual contact. They maintain these names in much the same manner as that described in the preceding paragraph and for much the same reasons;

17.  These people use sexual aides such as dildos fashioned after a man's penis of various sizes and shapes in addition to other sexual aides in the seduction of their victims. They often utilize these as a means of exciting their victims and of arousing the curiosity of the children;

18.  These people maintain diaries of their sexual encounters with children. These accounts of their sexual experiences are used as a means of reliving the encounter when the offender has no children to molest. Such diaries might consist of a notebook, scraps of paper, or a formal diary; depending upon the resources available to the offender, they may be contained on audio tape or computer entries in a "home computer";

19.  These people collect and maintain books, magazines, articles, and other writings on the subject of sexual activity. These books and materials may be on the topics of human sexuality, sexual education, or consist of sex manuals discussing or showing various sexual acts, positions, or sexual activities. These books and materials are used as a means of seduction of the victim by arousing curiosity, demonstration of the propriety of the acts desired, explaining or demonstrating what the offender desires to be done, and as a means of sexual arousal on the part of the offender— particularly when naked children are shown or depicted in the materials;

20.  These people often use drugs as a means of inducement to get a child to a particular location such as the offender's home. Alcohol is also used in this fashion. Both drugs and alcohol are also used as a means of seduction, reducing the child's inhibitions and for sexual excitement;

21.  These people often collect and maintain artifacts, statues, paintings, or other art medium which depict children or young persons in nude poses or sexual acts. These are kept or "left" in places where the victims can find or "discover" them;

22.  These people obtain and keep things of interest to their victims. These may consist of magazines, books, and toys for the age level of the victims they desire to attract and may be as complicated as video games, toy train sets, and computers;

23. These people often keep mementos of their relationship with specific children as a means of remembrance. These may consist of underwear or other garments or things which are unique to the relationship they had with the child;

This section should end with a statement asserting that these characteristics will provide evidence that will fit within the criteria which permitting the issuance of a search warrant.

> All of the materials requested for seizure will identify children who are being sexually exploited through child molestation, child pornography, and/or child prostitution. The materials will also identify other adults who are engaging in the sexual exploitation of children by these means. In addition, these materials will demonstrate the sexual proclivity, inclination, preference, and activities of the person(s) under investigation, providing evidence that will tend to show that the person(s) under investigation has committed felonies, to wit, sections

An example of how to present an affiant's expertise and these characteristics is reflected in the first pages of Appendix XI. Note how detailed each element of experience is shown. The purpose of this section is to demonstrate to the judge that the affiant is an *expert in the field* and is qualified to make judgments and opinions that will help the judge to recognize the crimes under investigation, the connection(s) to the evidence involved in those crimes, and that the evidence sought will be likely to be found where and when the search is performed.

Finally, following a recitation of the facts uncovered in the investigation, at the end of the affidavit, a synopsis of the characteristics involved in the case at hand is drawn into a further discussion of the profiles created by Ken Lanning in Chapter 2. This is intended to assure that the direct correlation is made between what the offender has done, what the evidence is that demonstrates the characteristic, and what evidence will be expected to be found as a result of the characteristics observed. As was mentioned earlier, the problem courts often find when reviewing warrants such as these is the affiant fails to make connections between what the offender does and the evidence sought. This format addresses this legal issue.

## Developing Probable Cause: Totality of Circumstances

### Circumstances that Would Lead One to Believe

The probable cause section of the expertise affidavit may take several forms and may be used in several ways. Its primary function is to collect facts and make evaluations and conclusions that ordinarily would not be allowed in the body of an affidavit. One of the ways to accomplish this is to reach the necessary conclusions based on circumstances that would lead one to believe there is reason to search a particular place or person.

## Actions by the Offender

One circumstance that can be examined is the actions of the offender. The facts that must be brought to light in this type of affidavit are anything that casts the shadow of suspicion on the offender. Appendix IV shows how probable cause was developed over a four-year period, recounting the actions of the offender as revealed through investigations conducted during that time:

Another example of actions of the offender is depicted in the affidavit in Appendix XII. Here, an undercover operation was the investigative technique used. Correspondence and covert meetings were the basis of the warrant affidavit. The officer recounts each investigative step and draws the connections to the crimes under investigation and the evidence he sought.

## Demonstration of Pattern of Behavior

In the preceding examples of search warrants and the appendices, examples of how to demonstrate a pattern of behavior on the part of the offender are given. This is an extremely important aspect of the probable cause section of the warrant in both an expertise and conventional affidavit. What is important to note is that it is not enough to simply list in the affidavit that the individual has a prior arrest or conviction for the same thing. What must be done is to examine the previous incidents for any similarities, connections, and patterns. Whatever is found which will show a propensity to commit these crimes and which could be construed as relevant should be included within the affidavit.

## Actions of Suspected Victims

With very young children, often the only clue to their victimization is their behavior, which is observed by parents or others, including the investigator. Coupled with whatever an investigation can develop, the identification and notation of the behavioral characteristics such as those discussed in Chapter 2 can help to justify a search when the expertise format is used in an affidavit. Appendix V shows an example of how this was used in a day care situation.

## Seizure of Pornographic Materials

The United States Customs Service routinely seizes child pornography at ports of entry for violation of federal law. Using the expertise affidavit format, it may ask for items other than the pornography it will deliver in conjunction with the Postal Service. Another way for a local police agency to accomplish this is to write an affidavit based on the seizure and what is found at the time of the controlled delivery. Appendix VI offers an example of how this is accomplished.

## Correspondence with Suspected Offender

Correspondence with suspected offenders is an investigative technique that will be discussed in Chapter VIII. Depending on the content of the correspondence, search warrants may be obtained for evidence of child molestation or pornography. The emphasis in this type of warrant, and in a warrant written after the discovery of pornographic or suggestive photographs of children at photo-processing firms (discussed below), should be the need for protection of children who are possibly being abused. Appendix VII shows an example of how this may be accomplished with the expertise affidavit format.

## Photographs Seized from Photofinisher, Justifying a Search of an Offender's Home

As noted, another set of circumstances that may justify a search is the discovery of pornographic or suggestive pictures of children found during the processing or sales of developed pictures by photoprocessing firms. The expertise format works well in this situation because it helps to demonstrate the need to protect the children suspected of being abused who are depicted in the pictures. The use of this format is not always necessary, but it is recommended. In most cases, it will be necessary to prepare a search warrant to seize the photos themselves from the photofinisher. Appendix VIII gives an example of how to prepare an affidavit of this nature.

There are two approaches an investigator may take in preparing an affidavit in a case such as this. Taking into consideration the factors that will be discussed in Chapter 8 on case management, an investigator may try to identify and interview the people depicted in the photographs, or he may simply prepare the affidavit based on information he develops that provides sufficient probable cause for believing that the location to be searched will contain evidence to identify those depicted or involved and the evidence asked for. In the *latter case,* the *photos themselves,* with supporting information developed by the investigator, *may justify the search.* Regardless of which affidavit format is used, the affidavit must contain a description of the nature and content of the pictures.

Appendix IX demonstrates how a warrant was obtained using the latter method and an expertise format. Note how much time was taken to demonstrate the connections between the two packets of pictures and the location to be searched. No interviews *were* conducted with any of the suspected abusers or abused children before the search. The descriptions of the house to be searched matched that in the pictures.

## Descriptions of the Property

To comply with the constitution, descriptions of property must be as specific as possible. With sexual exploitation of children, this is often difficult. A general rule in preparing any search warrant is to name any and all things that might be reasonably connected to the items you wish to seize. For example, if a gun was used in a crime, it is reasonable to ask for ammunition, cleaning equipment, a holster, and even the original box it came in. The checklist that follows corresponds to the characteristics described previously. When preparing a search warrant affidavit, one has only to use this list and add anything else that applies to the particular case.

## Search Warrant Seizure Checklist

1. Camera equipment and video equipment intended for the taking, producing, and reproducing of photographic images, including but not limited to: cameras, instant developing and otherwise, video production, lenses, enlargers, photographic papers, film, chemicals (*include specific description in addition to above if you have one*).
2. Phone books, phone registers, and correspondence or papers with names, addresses, or phone numbers that would tend to identify (*specific name, description, age or sex*) or any other juvenile (or adult if applicable).
3. Photographs, movies, videotape, negatives, slides, and/or undeveloped film depicting nudity and/or sexual activities involving juveniles with juveniles, juveniles with adults juveniles with animals, if applicable), that would tend to identify (victim(s) or any other juvenile or adult.
4. Photographs, movies, slides, videotape, negatives, drawings, and/ or undeveloped film that would tend to identify I *victim(s)* or any other juvenile or adult.

5. Correspondence, diaries, and any other writings, tape recordings, or letters relating to any juvenile and/or adults that tend to show the identity of juveniles and adults and sexual conduct between juveniles or adults.

6. Magazines, books, movies, videotapes, and photographs depicting nudity and/or sexual activities of juveniles or adults, including (*specific description*) as well as collections of newspaper, magazine, and other clippings of juveniles that tend to demonstrate a particular sex and age preference of (*suspect(s)*).

7. Magazines, newspapers, classified ads, and other publications or writings that contain names, addresses, and phone numbers of individuals who have similar sexual interests and that would tend to identify persons, adult and juvenile, who are involved with (*suspect(s)*).

8. Sexual aids consisting of "sex toys" such as rubber penises, dildos of various sizes, shapes, and construction, vibrators of similar design and construction, and (*specific description of items known about*).

9. Articles of personal property, toys, drawings (*whatever applies to your case*), played with, belonging to or made by (*known victim(s)* described as————.

10. Safe deposit keys, bank statements, billings, and checks tending to show the location and identity of safe deposit boxes and storage facilities of any person involved in the sexual exploitation of children through child molestation, child pornography, and child prostitution, consisting of, but not limited to: file cabinets, mail envelopes, items of mail.

11. Indicia of occupancy consisting of articles of personal property tending to establish the identity of the person or persons in control of the premises located at ————, including, but not limited to, rent receipts, canceled mail, keys, utility bills, and telephone bills.

## Computers

When investigating sexual abuse and exploitation, as was discussed in previous chapters, computers are commonly used by offenders for various purposes. Seizing such equipment is problematic for several reasons:

1. The descriptions of what to be seized cannot always be as particularized as might be necessary to withstand overbroadness and scope of search objections.

2. Because what you are looking for is something the offender doesn't want you to find, chances are it won't be labeled so you will readily identify it. This raises a question of what you will be able to properly seize.

3. Many computer offenders have "fail-safe" systems that can destroy the sensitive data you want to find if proper steps aren't taken to open files or turn on or off the equipment.
4. Operating and knowing what to do with the equipment may require expertise beyond that of the investigating officers. This is important because careful explanation and detail must be taken to explain what will be sought in the warrant and why it needs to be taken.

Fortunately both local law enforcement, as well as state and federal agencies, now have experts on staff, who are working "high-tech" crimes. There is a professional association of High-Tech Crime Investigators and Communications Fraud Control investigators. Contacts with these organizations may be made through any Economic/Computer Crimes unit in major law enforcement agencies or state and federal agencies.

One such expert is Franklin Clark,* a Criminal Investigator for the Pierce County Prosecutor's Office. He teaches investigative techniques at numerous programs throughout the country and is a recognized expert in computer-related crimes. A copy of a search warrant affidavit created for a bulletin board case is included in Appendix XIV. In this affidavit, Clark lays out the necessary details on the connection to computers and computer communications as it relates to the crime he was investigating. His description of the equipment sought and articulation of the probable cause for seizure are a model to follow.

The U.S. Customs Department suggests that some methods to establish probable cause to seize computer equipment include determining that the subject under investigation is employed or associated with a computer business or occupation. He might be receiving computer or high-tech magazines and publications. His telephone toll records may reflect calls to computer bulletin boards. Telephone company records may reflect several numbers to his home or business that could be checked to determine if computer equipment is operating on them. Observations by covert operatives or direct surveillance might confirm computer use. Lastly, a computer may be found during a search where it was not previously known to exist.

They suggest that, if possible, the computer should be described by brand name, model, with a description of all storage devices and records, as listed in the warrant mentioned above prepared by Clark.

It would be wise to take a computer expert with the search team where one is expected to be found. This will ensure that any data will be safely preserved and the equipment disconnected without damage to the system or the data. If necessary, a request should be made in the affidavit to authorize

---

* Co-author of *Investigating Computer Crime* (CRC Press) a companion text in this series.

non-police personnel to accompany the search team for this purpose if law enforcement personnel are not available to handle this task.

## Staleness

There are no clear cut rules about when information relating to a case may be considered stale; it depends on the nature of the unlawful act and the type of property sought. What must be demonstrated is that the things asked for are of the variety and type the offender would ordinarily keep for periods of time and that the information is current. It is possible to use expertise to demonstrate the reason why information would still be valid over time. This may be accomplished by use of the characteristics previously listed that carefully describe why the offender might keep the things he does. if used, they should sufficiently establish timeliness.

One way to update stale information is to present recent corroborative evidence showing that criminal conduct or conduct similar to that under investigation is still continuing. In one case in Southern California, a man approached the police when he found that the boy scout leader who had molested him six years before was still a boy scout leader. He described in detail the type of evidence that he had seen when he was at the offender's home. The investigator did some surveillance and determined that children were still trooping in and out of the offender's home, and he sought a search warrant. Found in the offender's home were all the things the man described, including evidence to tie the offender to many new offenses.

In one case I prepared a search warrant affidavit at the conclusion of a two-year investigation that documented molestations as long as eight years prior to the time the warrant was issued. The degree of background investigation that was necessary to update the information to establish the likelihood that the offender was still actively involved in criminal acts was lengthy, creating a 42 page affidavit.

Connections were made to past associates of the suspect and their relationships with other children were established. This was updated to show on-going contact with children in the same age group and with the suspect. Surveillance identified where the suspect was living and the warrant was obtained. This warrant service is discussed in Figure 7.1.

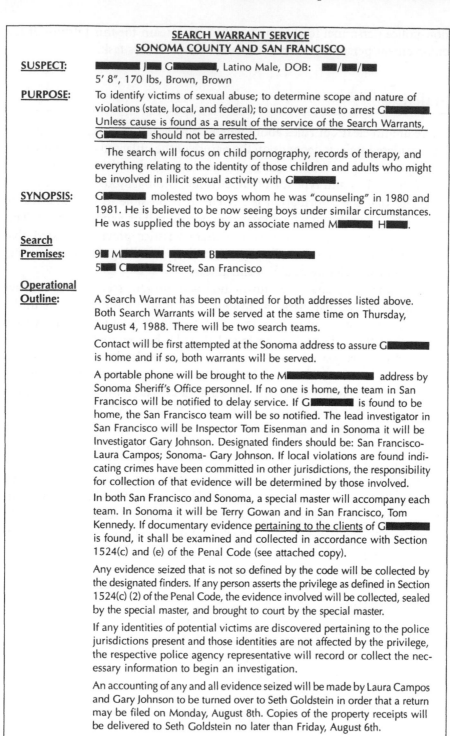

**SEARCH WARRANT SERVICE**
**SONOMA COUNTY AND SAN FRANCISCO**

**SUSPECT:** ▆▆▆▆ J▆ G▆▆▆▆, Latino Male, DOB: ▆▆/▆▆/▆
5' 8", 170 lbs, Brown, Brown

**PURPOSE:** To identify victims of sexual abuse; to determine scope and nature of violations (state, local, and federal); to uncover cause to arrest G▆▆▆▆. Unless cause is found as a result of the service of the Search Warrants, G▆▆▆▆ should not be arrested.

The search will focus on child pornography, records of therapy, and everything relating to the identity of those children and adults who might be involved in illicit sexual activity with G▆▆▆▆.

**SYNOPSIS:** G▆▆▆▆ molested two boys whom he was "counseling" in 1980 and 1981. He is believed to be now seeing boys under similar circumstances. He was supplied the boys by an associate named M▆▆▆ H▆▆.

**Search Premises:** 9▆ M▆▆▆ ▆▆▆ B▆▆▆▆▆▆
5▆ C▆▆▆ Street, San Francisco

**Operational Outline:** A Search Warrant has been obtained for both addresses listed above. Both Search Warrants will be served at the same time on Thursday, August 4, 1988. There will be two search teams.

Contact will be first attempted at the Sonoma address to assure G▆▆▆▆ is home and if so, both warrants will be served.

A portable phone will be brought to the M▆▆▆▆▆▆ address by Sonoma Sheriff's Office personnel. If no one is home, the team in San Francisco will be notified to delay service. If G▆▆▆▆ is found to be home, the San Francisco team will be so notified. The lead investigator in San Francisco will be Inspector Tom Eisenman and in Sonoma it will be Investigator Gary Johnson. Designated finders should be: San Francisco- Laura Campos; Sonoma- Gary Johnson. If local violations are found indicating crimes have been committed in other jurisdictions, the responsibility for collection of that evidence will be determined by those involved.

In both San Francisco and Sonoma, a special master will accompany each team. In Sonoma it will be Terry Gowan and in San Francisco, Tom Kennedy. If documentary evidence pertaining to the clients of G▆▆▆▆ is found, it shall be examined and collected in accordance with Section 1524(c) and (e) of the Penal Code (see attached copy).

Any evidence seized that is not so defined by the code will be collected by the designated finders. If any person asserts the privilege as defined in Section 1524(c) (2) of the Penal Code, the evidence involved will be collected, sealed by the special master, and brought to court by the special master.

If any identities of potential victims are discovered pertaining to the police jurisdictions present and those identities are not affected by the privilege, the respective police agency representative will record or collect the necessary information to begin an investigation.

An accounting of any and all evidence seized will be made by Laura Campos and Gary Johnson to be turned over to Seth Goldstein in order that a return may be filed on Monday, August 8th. Copies of the property receipts will be delivered to Seth Goldstein no later than Friday, August 6th.

**Figure 7.1**    An actual case example of pre-search organization.

Any evidence collected in San Francisco will be retained by Tom Eisenman unless it is more expeditious to handle it otherwise or it is protected by an asserted privilege.

Any evidence collected in Sonoma will be retained by Gary Johnson unless any of the above applies or there are violations found that occurred in other jurisdictions. In that case, reasonibility for collection and retention will be decided between the agencies present.

## PERSONNEL

### Sonoma County Sheriff's Office
Phone:   (707) 527-2118
Detective Spence Martin
Detective Dave Sederholm
Identification Technician

### State of California
Department of Consumer Affairs
Phone:   (415) 573-3864
Investigator Gary Johnson
Investigator Laura Campos
66 Bovet Road, Suite 230
San Mateo, CA 94402

### Special Masters
Tom Kennedy
Phone:   (707) 575-7715
Terry Gowan
Phone:   (707) 578-8988
Napa County District Attorney
Phone:   (707) 253-4211
Investigator Seth L. Goldstein

### U.S. Postal Service
Phone:   (415) 550-5775

### Federal Bureau of Investigation
Phone:   (415) 553-7400
Agent Tom LaFreniere

### Walnut Creek Police Department
Phone:   (415) 943-5872
Detective Jerry Whiting

### Concord Police Department
Phone:   (415) 671-3176
Detective Paul Arno

### Contra Costa Sheriff's Office
Phone:   (415) 646-4583
Sgt. Dave Long (or Designee)

**Figure 7.1 (continued)**

---

<u>**SEARCH TEAMS**</u>

**San Francisco:**
  Tom Eisenman
  Laura Campos
  Tom Kennedy
  Jerry Whiting
  Tom LaFreniere


**Sonoma:**
  Gary Johnson
  Seth Goldstein
  Spence Martin
  Dave Sederholm
  Scott Morrell
  Paul Arno
  Conta Costa Country Sheriff's Designee


<u>**MEETING INFORMATION**</u>

<u>**Date:**</u>        Thursday, August 4, 1988

<u>**Time:**</u>        6:30 a.m.

<u>**Locations:**</u>   **Sonoma:**
                Sonoma County Sheriff's Office Sub-Station
                16715 Sonoma Highway
                Boyes Hot Springs,
                Phone:   (707) 996-9495

                **San Francisco:**
                Contact Investigator Tom Eisenman
                San Francisco Police Department
                Crime Scene Investigations
                Phone:   (415) 553-1819

---

**Figure 7.1 (continued)**


# Additional Concerns

## Attachments to the Affidavit

It is often a good idea to attach various items to the affidavit to give the judge a first-hand opportunity to evaluate the probable cause. If photographs are involved, especially if age is a question, bring them to the judge for his evaluation. It might not be a good idea to attach copies of the photos to the affidavit as they become a matter of public record and anyone can see them. This might cause undue embarrassment to the children involved. If a magazine or other materials are involved, bring it to the judge for him to get a flavor of what you are dealing with. When correspondence is involved, attach copies of letters that are relevant. The child's drawings should be attached.

## Identifying Those in Control of the Premises and the Evidence

When conducting the search, look for the things that will establish and identify those in control of the premises and the items seized. Mail, identification, canceled checks, bankbooks, fingerprints, and photographs all help to establish who's in control of the premises.

## Tips on Service of the Warrant

One of the most important concerns in investigations of this nature is preventing the offender learning of the investigation and destroying evidence. Because children often let the "cat out of the bag" intentionally or nonintentionally by informing the offender that the police know what is going on, it is a good idea to act as soon as possible on the information received. As soon as enough information is available to obtain a search warrant, it should be sought and served. Many a case has suffered because of delays in the time between the information's coming to light and the service of the search warrant.

Consider the use of telephone search warrants whenever this is a problem. They are no more difficult to obtain than conventional warrants, only requiring a conference call and a tape recorder. They come in handy when the warrant doesn't contain all the items you find at the search premises. All that is necessary is to describe the new items in a supplementary warrant affidavit, which may be issued by the same judge who signed the original warrant.

## Marking the Evidence for Identification

In searching homes, offices, or other areas, one of the most difficult tasks is identifying who found what, when, and where. It is often helpful to draw a diagram of the location to be searched and note which investigator searched which areas. Mark each room or area with a letter or a number unique to that room or area. then mark each piece of evidence with that number or letter and its own corresponding number, so that it is easy to determine where the evidence was found. For example, if a house has a livingroom, a bedroom, and a garage where evidence was seized, the livingroom might be marked A, the bedroom B, and the garage C. A series of porn magazines found in the livingroom might be marked A-1, A-2, A-3, and so on. Pictures found in the bedroom might be marked B-1, B-2, B-3, and so on. If any of the rooms have many areas where evidence is found, they might be numbered with roman numerals to indicate where they were found. For example, the bedroom may have three dressers, a closet, and four trunks. The dressers might be numbered I, II, II; the closet IV; and the trunks V, VI, VII, VIII, respectively. Evidence found in the dressers might be numbered A-I-1, A-I-2, and so on.

## Photographing Scene for Later Identification

During the service of the warrant, photograph all areas where sexual acts might occur. Photograph beds, couches, floors with floor coverings, and all four walls of each room. This may later establish where pornographic pictures were taken.

## Concerns Regarding the Offender

Be sure to serve the warrant when the offender is at the location you wish to search. If necessary, wait for him to come home or to his office if that is the location of the search. This will prevent premature discovery, flight, or destruction of evidence. It will also ensure that you find whatever evidence he may have on his person before he has time to dispose of it.

A big problem with the service of search warrants in child sex cases is the extraneous personnel who "arrive" at the scene. It is important to limit the number of persons at the search sight to be sure that the evidence is not contaminated or destroyed. This will also help to prevent intimidation or any other influence on the offender that might prevent him from cooperating or confessing. After the search has been conducted is often the best time to interview because the offender is most vulnerable emotionally.

A good example of how to serve a warrant involved a case in which a boy scout leader, Big Brother, and YMCA swimming instructor was arrested for molesting several boys in his neighborhood. Found in his home were films, picture, books, and diaries of his exploits. The investigation began when one boy began telling of the acts with the man. A search warrant was obtained and served while the man was gone. A call was placed to his work, informing him that his house was being burglarized, and he was confronted when he arrived home. A confession was obtained after he curled up on the floor and began crying.

## Concerns About Commercial Distributors

It is not proper to seize certain materials that may be protected by the First Amendment without a hearing. This doctrine is called "prior restraint." This applies only if the materials in question are sold openly to the general public. If they are sold surreptitiously, no prior restraint protection exists.

To avoid prior restraint problems in search and seizure cases, buy one copy of each publication that is suspected to fall within the purviews of child pornography, and supply it to the judge when the warrant is sought. Describe its content in the affidavit exactly as if the material in question was a film being shown at a theater or other location. When searching the premises, if you find other materials that you believe to be obscene and are available to the public, a new search warrant must be obtained. An example of how to write a search warrant for a theater is shown in Appendix X.

## Organizing the Search

Searches in child sexual abuse and exploitation cases can be very confusing because of the large number of people involved and the large volume of material that must be examined at the scene, not to mention the amount of evidence seized.

Details should be worked out ahead of time about who does what and who will be responsible for various tasks (see Figures 7.1 and Figure 7.2).

---

**SEARCH WARRANT SERVICE**

TASK                                                  ASSIGNED

LOG OF OFFICERS ON PREMISES

EXAMINE SCENE FOR SCOPE OF VIOLATING AND SEARCH ZONES

DIVIDE TO SEARCH/REVIEW SCENE

REJOIN TO DISCUSS WHAT FOUND

DETERMINE IF IMMEDIATE FOLLOW-UP REQUIRED

DIVIDE SEIZURES INTO THOSE THAT ARE NECESSARY TO REVIEW IMMEDIATELY FOR FOLLOW-UP

---

**Figure 7.2** A sample form designating assignments to what tasks and what will be done during the warrant service.

## Serial Offenders

A search warrant affidavit format to use when investigating serial offenders is shown in Appendix XIII. Its design is further described in the following chapter on case management.

## References and Notes

1. *Aguilar vs. Texas*, 378 U.S. 108, 114, 1964.
2. *Illinois vs. Gates*, 462 U.S. 213, 1983, 76, LE 2d, 527.
3. *People vs. Frank*, 38 Cal. 3d 711, 1985.
4. Kenneth V. Lanning, *Child Molesters: A Behavioral Analysis, 1992* and *Investigation and Prosecution of Child Abuse*, National Prosecutors Research Institute, 1993.

## Additional Reading

Chrystie, Richard J. and Schirr, Robert. *Search Warrants: A Manual*, California District Attorney's Association, June 1977.

Clark, Franklin and Diliberto, Ken, *Investigating Computer Crime*, CRC Press,Boca Raton, FL, 1996.

McGuiness, Robert L. "Search and Seizure of Obscene Materials., *FBI Law Enforcement Bulletin*, October 1983, pp. 25-3 1.

# Case Management

Thus far, we have built a foundation of understanding about the dynamics and definitions of the crimes of sexual exploitation of children. This chapter suggests ways to properly investigate these crimes by applying correct investigative practices and procedures through case management.

Like any other complicated crime such as homicide, rape, or child abuse, the sexual exploitation of children is difficult to investigate. Simply documenting the elements of the offense(s) will not suffice for a thorough investigation, nor is investigating it as easy as simply asking who did what to whom, when, where, how, and why. Investigations of sexual exploitation of children take time and — to ensure that every base is covered — planning. This chapter is offered to help the investigator avoid the pitfalls faced by other investigations. It will suggest principles of investigation that have proven successful in other cases, and will try to explain why other methods have failed, in hopes of preventing their reoccurrence. Finally, it will suggest some record keeping and reporting techniques to maximize the amount of information that must be gathered in cases of this type.

## Investigative Goals

For the police, the primary goals of any criminal investigation are in order of priority: to determine if a crime has occurred, and if so, determine who committed it; to gather evidence to prosecute this individual; to arrest him. In sexual exploitation of children investigations, another goal is added and the priorities change. The investigator must determine if the child has been molested or exploited, then determine if the child is at risk and/or needs protection. This determination, and *protecting the best interests of the child* during the investigative and prosecutorial process, have the highest priority.

It is important to emphasize that proper investigation will enhance a child's credibility through documentation and verification of his account. It

361

will also determine, in the long run, whether or not there will be a successful prosecution.

Child sexual abuse cases can be difficult to prove. Most of the time, it becomes the child's word against that of the adult. Furthermore, there are many problems for children in testifying in court and this experience may be traumatic for them. Although research has shown that in many cases testifying in the case can be beneficial for a child, this is not always the case. Recent legislative and procedural changes in the manner in which children are permitted to testify may also lessen the potential trauma in testifying. However, the testimony of the child should be considered only if there is no other way to prove the abuse. The objective should be to try to prove the case without having the child testify.

The reality of most, if not all, cases is that the child will have to present some testimony. However, after the interviews are over, the evidence carefully evaluated and assessed, the investigator will consider if there are any other investigative avenues open which might produce evidence which could prove the case without the testimony of the child. Another way this can be accomplished is by amassing so much evidence, its sheer weight causes the offender to plead guilty. This is a difficult objective, but it should be the investigative goal.

## Team Approach

Some of the most successful investigative approaches in this country have used a "team approach." This method employs a multidisciplinary team of investigators who represent all the disciplines who have an interest in this crime problem. Each understands the needs of the others, from both working together and/or training together. They jointly approach the case, dividing the responsibilities among themselves in a manner that best suits the case. This prevents problems such as a social worker making contact with the suspect before the police have begun to investigate, then having evidence lost or witnesses' stories tampered with.

For example, in a case of intrafamilial abuse, a police/social worker team would approach the case together, making contact at the same time. Follow-up investigations by both the social worker and the police officer would be conducted in the same fashion. In this way, any information obtained by either will immediately be known to the other, and the problems of confidentiality and inability to learn about the information in the social worker's file will be eliminated.

In the case of a single offender, extrafamilial abuse case, the investigation may be conducted by the same team, with the social worker providing for the needs of the child while the police officer conducts the investigation. What this arrangement requires, and many jurisdictions do not have, is a good working relationship between social workers and the police. It also requires specialized training so that both the social worker and police officer are aware of what the other does and how he goes about it. It also requires that both the social services agency and the police agency have an agreement that one or the other will take responsibility for the investigation. In most cases, it should be the police because they are the information gatherers, and whatever is done in an investigation will eventually affect how that information is obtained.

Most teams have a law enforcement/probation/social services (child protective services) worker combination. Others also use members of the prosecuting attorney's staff, the FBI, the U.S. Postal Service, and U.S. Customs in varying combinations. Often medical and clinical professionals who have been specially prepared and trained may become part of the team.

This helps to eliminate the need for repeated interviews, and ensures that the investigative goals for each agency, which normally are different and achieved at different times, will be better served. For example, it is not uncommon to find that the social services investigation may finish before the criminal investigation has been completed, and the child is released from protective custody and returned home. This, needless to say, can cause great problems for the police, who may have not had the opportunity to complete all of the interviews with the child, who is now thrust back into an environment that is not always supportive. With the team approach, either the decision to release the child is reached jointly or the coordination of the investigation eliminates the conflict. In situations where the interests of one of the disciplines are at odds with another's, the close working relationship between the members of the team will facilitate a joint decision.

Another advantage of the team approach is that it provides a pool of investigators who are able to respond to cases involving multiple victims and offenders, without straining other investigative resources. This will better prepare the investigative agencies to engage in investigations of the magnitude of preschool or other organizational abuse situations in which as many as several hundred children might be involved. In cases such as these, because of the chances of cross-germination and contamination (discussed in greater detail later in this chapter) or loss of witnesses and other evidence, investigations must move quickly to protect and secure evidence. The "task-force" approach will work well in this situation because multiple tasks can be performed simultaneously. The pool of investigators and coordination of services immediately available will greatly enhance the capability of responding to other difficult cases such as those with very young victims because of the specialized training and experience of the team members.

When members of the task force come from various disciplines — such as social welfare or clinical fields — there must be a careful examination and clear understanding of the roles they are to play. They must know whether or not they are to play an investigative or therapeutic role. The two are not necessarily mutually exclusive and they can complement an investigation well, but the methods used to obtain information in a therapeutic mode are somewhat different and can cause evidentiary problems if applied to the other mode. Any person, including a clinician, who is going to be used to obtain information that will be used in court, must be well-versed in what constitutes proper questioning and investigative techniques, and be prepared to document and testify about his actions. It is unwise and unfair for law enforcement to ask this person to take on a task he is not prepared for.

Figure 8.1, is an example of a letter spelling out the responsibility of a therapist who was used in an investigation as an adjunct supportive resource

---

Dear Pat:

Enclosed please find a three paragraph summary of the police reports which formulated the statement of probable cause for arrest and source of facts in the Juvenile Petition relating to the three children.

Please note that the information which you have been provided is intended for therapeutic purposes only. Please do not discuss the contents of the report or the tape with the children. It is absolutely essential that you not tell one child what another child has told the police or yourself.

Prior to our leaving, we admonished the children about speaking to each other about what happened to them and what they have told their therapist, myself, or the police. I urge you to reiterate that warning when you speak with them. I have encouraged them to speak with you and your colleague, Wally about what happened to them as individuals. I have also told them that the reason that they may want to speak with you is because it will make them feel better. I emphasize this to you as your contact with the children should be strictly therapeutic and not investigative.

We acknowledge and want to emphasize that your role is to help the children work through their feelings about what happened to them and to make them feel better about their unfortunate experiences.

At this time, I would also like to thank both you and Wally for providing both a psychological and physical environment which allow the children to feel comfortable enough to speak with us. It is my belief that without you and the

rapport you have developed with those children, we would not be in a position to properly prosecute this case.

Please do not hesitate to call if you have any questions about the content of this letter or the information you have been provided.

---

**Figure 8.1**   Sample letter to therapist.

in an investigation wherein an uncle was molesting several of his nieces and nephews. The purpose of this letter was to both articulate and clarify the therapist's role in the investigation and to provide written evidence of the relationship that therapist was to play in the case. Should it have become an issue in court, it would have been used to demonstrate the insulation measures taken in the case.

## Preliminary Investigation Concerns

### Nature of Response

All investigations of sexual exploitation of children should be conducted in person. Telephone interviews are not sufficient to assess cases or properly secure information nor should someone else be asked to do it for you. One of the most widely publicized and condemned child sexual abuse cases in American history had many of its problems begin by the following letter sent out by the investigating law enforcement agency:

> This Department is conducting a criminal investigation involving child molestation (code cited). Mr. X, an employee of the (school), was arrested on (date provided) by this department.
>
> The following procedure is obviously an unpleasant one, but to protect the rights of your children as well as the rights of the accused, this inquiry is necessary for a complete investigation.
>
> Records indicate that your child has been or is currently a student at the (school). We are asking your assistance in this continuing investigation. Please question your child to see if her or she has been a witness to any crime or if he or she has been a victim. Our investigation indicates that possible criminal acts include: oral sex, fondling of genitals, buttock or chest area, and sodomy, possibly committed under the pretense of "taking the child's temperature." Also photos may have been taken of children without their clothing. Any information from your child regarding having ever observed Mr. X to leave a classroom alone with a child during any nap period, or if they have ever observed Mr. X tie up a child, is important... [1].

It doesn't take much to imagine the shock, indignation, fear, and anger which must have filled the parent reading this portion of the letter sent them by the police department. You can bet that emotion was carried into the interviews with the children. This, and many other mistakes by many people involved in the case, led to the ultimate failure of the case. The reasons this case failed speaks to the need to carefully assess, plan, and respond to an allegation.

Similarly, when a report is made by a teacher at a school who suspects that one of her pupils has been sexually abused by a parent, the allegation can't be assessed by the social worker or police detective calling the home on the phone and asking questions. Yet, this is still the manner in which many cases that are not considered an "immediate risk" are handled. There are not many absolutes in criminal investigation, but, there is *absolutely* no case that can be investigated in this fashion.

## Manner in Which Cases are Generated

Approaches to cases of sexual exploitation of children will vary according to the way they are reported. For example, investigations and interviews where the investigator has an idea what happened (child/children already disclosed) will be greatly different from those where he doesn't. Cases of sexual exploitation of children may be generated in several ways. Most reports or complaints will come from the general public. These may be about a particular child who has either disclosed his involvement or is exhibiting characteristics that lead the caller to make a report. Reports may also be about a particular individual who has drawn the attention of the general public because of his interest or involvement with children, but there are no identified victims. Reports may be generated from observations by a diligent beat officer or may come from another case already under investigation. Whatever way the report is made, the first important step is to try to establish and verify as much information as the urgency of the situation and time permits. This will assist the investigator in making critical decisions as quickly as possible.

In most states, there are requirements that if a case of suspected child abuse is taken by a law-enforcement or other "child protection agency" (social services, probation department, etc.), the case must be "cross-reported" to at least one other agency. This is to ensure that the case is properly handled and that all of the necessarily involved agencies act together. Figure 8.2 depicts a typical reporting "track" of a reported case of suspected sexual abuse.

In many cases of sexual exploitation of children, a report will not be made by the public because the investigating officer will have "generated" the case himself based upon information he has developed. Often the identities of the children are not known at the outset of the investigation, and much investigation is necessary to determine who is being victimized. For example, here is an outline of the investigative process from a case file where a retail photo processing firm discovered 24 photographs of girls aged 7 to 11 years old, filmed in the nude in suggestive poses.

1. Seized photographs from photo finisher, thereby obtaining suspect's name (may require a search warrant; see Appendices VIII and IX).
2. Discussed case with D.A. (not a necessary step, however, where the defense is likely to be overzealous prosecution, the team response may defuse it.).
3. Selected schools to contact to based on ages of children in pictures (important to do so without embarrassing children).
4. School employees identified children.
5. School provided addresses and family background (may provide significant lead information, as parents and relatives must be considered as suspects.)
6. Information led to parents and children (in this case parents not involved).
7. Children admitted their involvement during interviews (expect denial from many children, even with pictures.)
8. Prepared and served search warrant.
9. Discovered cache of child pornography depicting the subject children and others (case turned out to be suspect's children and their friends.)

Figure 8.3 depicts the "normal" investigative flow of a case of child sexual abuse or exploitation where the identity or suspected identity of a victim or victims is known. It applies to both intra- and extrafamilial cases.

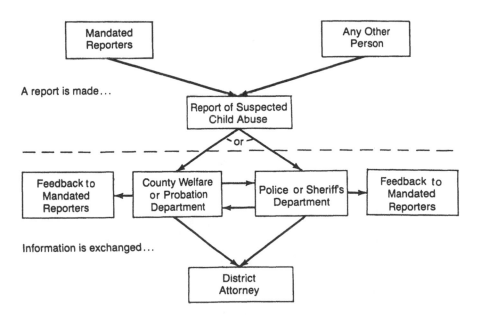

**Figure 8.2** Typical reporting "track" for a case of suspected sexual abuse. (Courtesy California Department of Justice).

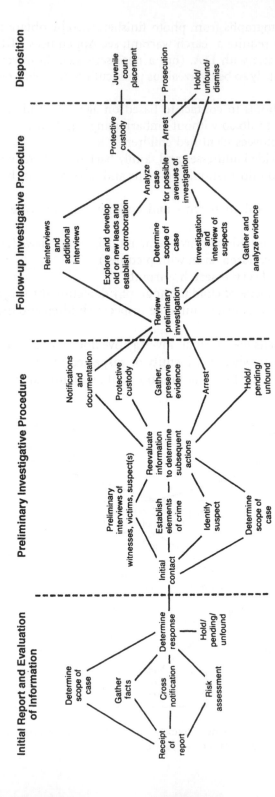

**Figure 8.3**  "Normal" investigative flow in a case of child sexual exploitation where the victim's identity is known of suspected.

In the Initial Report and Evaluation phase, the report is received by either the law enforcement or social services agency. In a simultaneous or immediately sequential act, the agency both cross reports to those agencies it is mandated to inform and conducts a background check on the names already identified in the case. This helps to direct the nature of the response and arms the investigator/responder with some information upon which he may base later decisions. Once this is done, an attempt to determine the scope of the case may be made and the amount of manpower that will be needed can be established.

By gathering preliminary facts such as identifying the parties involved with subsequent records checks conducted including an review of the claims being made, an assessment of risk can be concluded. From this, it is possible to determine how quickly to respond to the allegation.

Having done this would have saved the child in the following example a lot of trauma.

In a case involving a neighbor man who lived in the area, a young child reported the neighbor had molested him. The mother was unsure of the veracity of the allegation because the child had been untruthful in the past and was exhibiting behavioral problems. Unsure of what to do, she called the police for advice.

It wasn't until the graveyard shift arrived that the case was assigned. A uniformed, inexperienced, patrol officer who responded and was told of the mother's suspicions and the child's complaint. The officer interviewed the child and concluded the child was lying. After some lengthy interrogation, the child was then arrested for making a false police report.

Later in that week, hearing of the child's allegations, several other children reported to be victims of the man accused by the child. A *subsequent* records check by detectives investigating the case found that the man accused by the original child was a previously convicted, registered sex offender with sex offenses against children in his history.

It is important to note that in each phase of the investigation, the investigator must consider the scope of the case. It means that the investigator must be assessing and reassessing the information received constantly to be sure that his actions will not create negative consequences.

## Sensitivity of Responding Investigator(s)

The child may be further traumatized by an investigator who inappropriately responds to the child or the child's parents and who questions the child's credibility as in the example above. Developing rapport with the victim and the family is one of the most important aspects of this type of investigation. The investigator must be sensitive to the needs of all concerned in the family. Use of professional support people, such as rape crisis, victim witness workers or court-appointed special advocates, may help to facilitate this if they are brought to the initial meeting with the officer. Psychologists and other therapists may be used at the initial stage or be referred to, and they will help to provide support for the child and family, develop the elements of the crime, maintain continuity throughout the process, and keep the family on the prosecutorial tract.

Failure to establish this trust and rapport with the family causes the family to lose faith in the police investigation. This may compel them to begin their own investigation which will cause no end of problems with contamination and cross-germination, not to mention outright loss of evidence which will be discredited if found.

For example, in the McMartin Preschool case, parents banded together and met on their own. They conducted their own investigations, including an archeological dig under the preschool which may have uncovered significant evidence. However, because it was done so late in the case and the fact it was conducted by the parents, the results were discredited and disregarded.

This is an important facet of the investigation. The maintenance of contact with the family throughout the process will help to eliminate fears they may develop, and will demonstrate that the system cares about them. Properly used, professional support people can also help to limit the number of people who have access to the family and child by insulating them from inquisitive members of the family and friends. Generally, the family should be discouraged from talking to the child about the abuse because any information the child provides could be tainted.

The family or other concerned persons should be referred to professional support people or the police investigator for information about the case. This is important because it can be devastating for a child to face repeated questioning. In cases of multiple victims and offenders, where factions form of those who believe the children (generally parents of the children) and those who don't (generally members and supporters of the program, school, or friends of the accused), the professionals can help to provide the support the victim and his family need.

If there are multiple victims in a single case, consideration of sending the children to different therapists may be in order. The investigator should try to ensure that no group therapy sessions are conducted with children who are involved in the same case. The same is true for the gathering of parents in group sessions. If any children or parents in a case involving multiple victims get together to talk about their experiences, it may impair the credibility of the children's accounts because of the element of cross germination.

If an investigation is to be conducted by therapists in cases of multiple victims, consideration should be given to having different therapists from different offices do the interviews. This will help to ensure that the conclusions reached by the independent clinicians will be supported.

## Initial Contacts

Once the investigator arrives to investigate a complaint, the first task is to access the situation and initiate the appropriate response. If the crime has just occurred, the reporting person should be located, and the location and condition of the victim determined.

Should the offender be on the scene, he must be isolated and the crime scene protected and preserved. If the offender has fled, steps should be taken as soon as possible to identify and locate his whereabouts. The relationship of the offender to the victim should be established in the process of obtaining this information.

If it is an incest case or a case where the a victim is known or related to the offender, the location and condition of any siblings must be determined. Their safety must be considered and steps taken to interview them as soon as possible. In cases of incest or where the offender is known and is not on the scene, trying to locate him immediately may not have the same priority if there is no evidence to be lost. However, this can *never be assumed*, as there is often more to the allegation than is first reported and steps must be taken to assure the offender doesn't have the opportunity to destroy/dispose of evidence such as photos, clothing, sexual aids, etc.

Although it may be helpful initially to seek out the offender's whereabouts to assure he is not able to destroy evidence, contacting him to be interviewed may not be the wisest move, as it may be more advantageous to learn as much as possible before finding and talking with him. In most cases, he should be the last to know of the investigation.

The identification of any witnesses should begin. They should be separated from the presence of others who are involved. Care should be taken in selecting a support person the victim feels comfortable with. This may be a relative, who will have information that ought to be obtained first, out of the presence of the child. This may mean that someone else must be with the child during this quick interview.

## Interviewing Victim(s) and all Potential Witnesses

Each witness should be interviewed separately and away from any others. Try to avoid "cross-germination," contamination of accounts by witnesses comparing notes with each other or telling others what they have told the police. Never tell a child specifically what another child has said about the abuse. If it becomes necessary to confront a child with what has been said by others because it conflicts with what the child is saying (generally the case when children deny the abuse), try to avoid leading the child until you have no other option. Be prepared to explain in court what was done in great detail. Exact word accounting by tape recording or word-for-word transcription into your report may help to support the propriety of your interview techniques.

If the abuse occurred in a school or other organization setting, not only should the other students in the child's class or group be interviewed, but those in past classes should be considered. Children who have already passed through the classes or programs will have a greater ability to describe what happened, not only because they are older but because they are in a safer environment and may not be influenced as much by the offender(s). Present and past staff members should be interviewed.

Their accounts may be considered more reliable because they have no interest in the present case.

In an incest case, the siblings of the victim should be interviewed, both those who currently live in the home and those who don't. Ex-spouses or "significant other's" and child of any previous relationship/marriage should also be sought out and interviewed in person.

All residents of a home where an incest case occurs should also be identified and interviewed, in particular the non-offending parent. In extra-familial cases, examine the characteristics of the victim(s) and try to "profile" who the offender would target. By creating a "victim profile" in your mind, you will be able to select those children you should interview first and those who should be left as a "long shot." Relatives and neighbors should be interviewed. In short, anyone who may be able to shed light on the case should be sought out and talked to. As early as possible in the investigation, establish that the offender could have done what he is accused of, or had access to the child, as the child claims.

In both intra- and extrafamilial exploitation cases, factions and alliances form quickly. Generally they form around the victim and the offender. There will be those who believe the children and those who support the offender. Every effort must be made to interview those who might be able to shed light on the case before they have a chance to side with the victim or the offender. This is best accomplished at the time of the initial disclosure, when everyone is either shocked and surprised at the incident or feels that the offender "needs help." Interviewing them early in the investigation will "nail down" their statements and prevent them from altering their stories as a result of influence from the child or offender.

Recording these interviews helps to assure accurate reporting and anticipates the need for impeachment if they change their account(s).

Parents can become a problem. When interviewed, their confidence must be sought, both in the investigator and in keeping what they are told to themselves. It is not a good idea to tell the parents of children too much. Experience has taught us that even though parents say they will not betray a confidence, they often compare notes with other parents and, sometimes, the children involved. Most of the time they do not do this maliciously, but rather do it to learn as much as they can about what may have happened to their children. Clearly, this creates a problem with contamination of the information they uncover. As discussed in the section on interviews in Chapter 5, care must be taken in how parents are handled.

Attempts should be made to keep the parents under control. Often parents want to confront the offenders, do their own investigations, or have meetings with other parents and children. Parents who are allowed to do these things will contaminate anything they find and may tip off an offender or interfere with an ongoing investigation. Most of the time this problem arises when the law-enforcement agency has lost credibility with the parents or the parents feel that not enough is being done. Maintaining communication with the parents will prevent this from happening. Here are some questions to ask:

1. If the victim reported the molestation to a household member, what specifically did the child say?
2. What was the victim's demeanor when he made the report of the molestation?
3. What is the witness's relationship to the suspect?
4. What is the witness's attitude toward the suspect and toward the allegation that the suspect has committed acts of child molestation?
5. What is the witness's attitude toward the victim — e.g., does the witness believe the victim to be a truthful child? If not, what does the witness perceive as the motive of the child to fabricate?
6. Have there been any behavioral changes in the suspect or the victim?
7. What is the attitude of the child toward the suspect?
8. What is the attitude of the suspect toward the child?
9. Have there been any recent or ongoing problems between the child and the suspect? Has the suspect shown any unusual interest in the child?
10. Has there been any change in the victim's performance or conduct at school?
11. Has the child complained of pain or soreness, particularly in the vaginal or anal areas?
12. What is the child's medical history?
13. What is the name and address of the child's physician? (This information will facilitate the subpoenaing of the child's medical records.)

14. What schools has the child attended, and when? What are the names of the child's teachers during those years? (This will help establish the period of the molestation and will facilitate the subpoenaing of the child's school records.)

15. What opportunity did the suspect have to commit the crimes at the times alleged? Did the suspect have access to the child? Is the child frequently alone with the suspect?

16. When and where did the incidents reported by the child occur — i.e., if the child reports that he was molested while the family was at the beach, when did the family go to the beach, who was present, where was the beach? If the child reports that he was molested while the suspect and the victim were together in the backyard, when were they together in the backyard?

17. What are the drinking and drug habits of the suspect?

18. Is there any conflict in the home? Is the child aware of it?

19. Is the child aware of what effect the report of molestation might have on his living or custody arrangements?

20. Has the suspect ever previously been accused of child molestation? If so, when, where, and to whom?

21. Has the child ever been molested previously or made any allegations of molestation in the past?
    a. if so, when, where, and to whom?
    b. does the child know anyone who has made such allegations?
    c. if so, what are the circumstances of that incident?
    d. is the child related to or friends with the person who reported that incident?

22. Where did the child acquire any awareness of sexual matters, and is it possible the child was exposed to anything like what he describes?
    a. is there a possibility that the child is participating in sexual activity?
    b. if so, with whom?
    c. are there sexually explicit matters in the home?
    d. does the family watch the "Playboy Channel" or other cable type of pornography TV station?
    e. does the family have a video recorder and does the child have access to it?
    f. has the child had opportunity to observe sex acts of other family members?
    g. if the child describes sexual intercourse, oral copulation, sodomy, or other bizarre sexual practices, has the child ever been in a position before to observe such activities?
    h. is the suspect inclined toward such practices?

23. If the child describes the use of foreign objects — e.g., vaseline, condoms, pornography, etc. — are there such items in the home?
24. Has the witness/relative noticed any of the following behavior at any time during, after, or presently, by the child?
    a. overly compliant behavior
    b. acting-out/aggressive behavior
    c. pseudo-mature behavior
    d. hints about sexual activity
    e. persistent and inappropriate sexual play with peers, toys, or himself, or sexually aggressive behavior with others
    f. detailed and age-inappropriate understanding of sexual behavior (especially by young children)
    g. arriving early at school and leaving late, with few, if any, absences
    h. poor peer relationships and the inability to make friends
    i. lack of trust, particularly with persons who are important in his life
    j. nonparticipation in school and social activities
    k. inability to concentrate in school
    l. sudden drop in school performance
    m. absolutely "perfect" child
    n. extraordinary fear of males (in the case of a male perpetrator and female victim)
    o. seductive behavior with males (in the case of a male perpetrator and female victim)
    p. seductive behavior with females (in the case of a female perpetrator and male victim)
    q. running away from home
    r. sleep disturbances
    s. withdrawal
    t. clinical depression
    u. self-destructive behavior (self-inflicted injuries, etc.)
    v. suicidal feelings
25. What are the sleeping arrangements in the household?

## Who Conducts the Child's Interview

This is a question that frequently draws as much controversy as the content of the interview itself. There are those who believe that the police should never interview children because they are not properly prepared or trained to do so. On the other hand, there are those that believe that the social worker/therapist interviewers are not sufficiently trained to conduct interviews that will stand up in court. To address this controversy, numerous programs throughout the country have created centers with "Interview Specialists" to conduct interviews of children where abuse is suspected.

The American Professional Society on Abuse of Children, in a point-counter-point article, in *The APSAC Advisor* [2] discussed this and a conclusion that can be drawn is, its a difficult decision and depends on the resources available and the training *each discipline* is provided. The key is *training*. Regardless of who conducts the interview, that person must be properly trained in developmental stages of children, proper questioning techniques, the legal issues involved, and the needs and expectations of an investigation as described in this text.

On the one hand, interview centers where the child is interviewed by a specialist and the interview is videotaped can be incredibly successful. The ability for all involved disciplines to be on hand to view the interview from behind a screened area or window is a wonderful way to minimize the need to reinterview a child and to maximize the ability to obtain the necessary information.

On the other, there are some detractors with this concept. The reality is that most areas of the country cannot afford the money to create such a center or the personnel to conduct such interviews. Even if they can, subsequent interviews must be conducted in most cases and to return to the interview center is not always feasible. This, in itself causes problems. Rarely is there a case where the all details of abuse are disclosed in the initial interview. There are virtually always questions that arise later that must be answered.

What happens is that the child has developed rapport with an interviewer who is not able to continue to conduct interviews later in the investigation. The interpretation of what the original interviewer discovered is often lost in the change of personnel when a second interviewer (law enforcement or social worker) steps in for follow-up interviews. These points have been the major reasons it has been recommended there be a minimal number of interviews and a limit to the number of people actually conducting them. This process would therefore seem to go against the concept of reducing interviews and numbers of people involved in conducting them.

This problem also feeds into a defense argument that credibility problems are raised because the subsequent interviews are not video/audio taped in the same fashion, if at all, like the initial interview was. A common defense position is to cast doubt upon the subsequently obtained information because there is no "clean" record of what the information is and how it came out. When there are differences/inconsistencies in accounts made by the child, the claim is then made that the initial or subsequent information is suspect. Another defense position commonly taken when this problem arises is that there is something to hide.

There is also a problem when the initial interview is not productive, another common experience. As is known about children's disclosures, they don't always want to discuss the details of their abuse and the initial interview may only end up being an opportunity to establish rapport. For the same reasons mentioned above, follow-up interviews are problematic because of the need to return to the interview center and have the same interviewer conduct the new interview.

These are only some of the problems inherent in the concept. They are not insurmountable nor are they reasons, in-and-of-themselves, why the concept shouldn't be considered. With almost universal agreement, one thing can be said about the interview specialist concept: when it works, it works. From San Diego, California, to Washington State and across the country at interview centers like the Huntsville, Alabama program, at the National Child Advocacy Center, people applaud the results.

In California, in 1988, the Child Victim Witness Judicial Advisory Committee, issued its *Final Report* [3] with strong recommendations to adopt this type of interview approach. A follow-up study in 1994, conducted by the Child Victim Witness Investigative Pilot Projects (programs created as a result of the recommendations of the aforementioned Judicial Advisory group), found that the concept is highly successful [4]. A flow chart describing the suggested role the interview specialist plays in a dependency and criminal investigation is seen in Figure 8.4. In practice, the actual order of the interviews conducted by the specialist has varied from being the initial interview to subsequent follow-up interviews. Each case is taken individually, however, the intent is to conduct the interview with the specialist as soon as possible to avoid any potential for loss or contamination of information.

Another comprehensive discussion of the different approaches involved in developing child abuse cases for court can be found in *The Child Victim as a Witness: Research Report* [5]. In studying the outcomes of intervention in abuse cases, this report reflects that there are several approaches to the problem of who interviews children. There are positive and negatives to every approach. The one thing that is clear is a multidisciplinary approach is generally best and those who interview children need to be prepared for the task in the fashion discussed in this text.

## Identify All Children the Offender May Associate With

Every effort should be made to identify the children whose names are found in possession of a suspected offender and who appear in photographs or videotapes, even those fully dressed. This is especially true if these items appear to have been produced by the offender himself. Each of these children

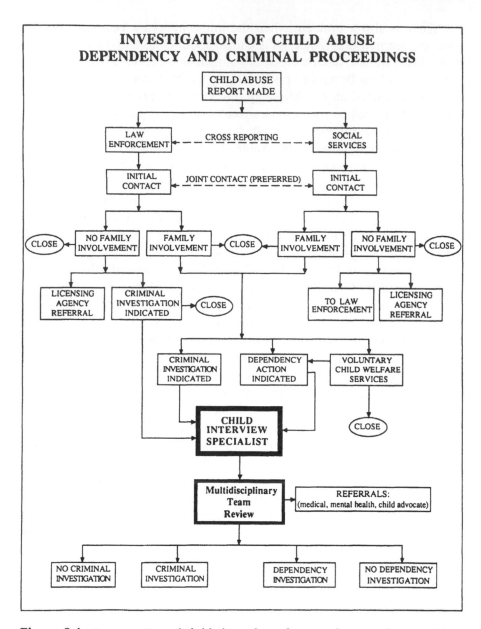

**Figure 8.4** Investigation of child abuse dependency and criminal proceedings. (From the California Victim Witness Judicial Advisory Committee, *Final Report.*)

is a potential victim of sexual abuse. However, this identification must be done discreetly in order to avoid potential public embarrassment of the children, whether or not they were victimized. Sometimes the offender makes the identification unbelievably easy by labeling his photographs with names, descriptions, addresses, dates, and even the sex acts performed.

## Pretext Confrontation

At this point, before contacting the offender, the investigator should consider the potential of a pretext confrontation such as that described in Chapter 6. A monitored confrontation done by a parent by phone or "wire" can save hours of interrogation and often, if a confession is obtained, produce a plea, thus sparing the children from a trial.

The offender is most vulnerable to making an admission or confession at the time he discovers he has been found out. The opportunity to present him with a set of circumstances that are most likely to motivate him to tell the truth is what should be the objective. He will be seeking a way out of his predicament and may want to try to convince his victim or the parent of the victim (maybe even an employer if in an institutional setting) that he can be cured and he will stop.

The concern in using this technique is first, safety, then feasibility. Is the child old enough to carry it off? Is the parent calm enough to do so? Is it possible to "play-act" the role of a therapist/teacher/counselor and accomplish it without non-professional help? Is the equipment available?

The best manner in which to conduct this technique is to use an "in-line" recorder which takes the signal directly from the phone and not an induction coil over the earpiece. The clarity and certainty of catching all that is said makes it worth it to purchase such a device and have it attached to the phone at all times.

If a face-to-face confrontation is contemplated, the same considerations apply. If a "wire" is used, all the precautions taken in any covert operation should be employed to assure the safety of the persons involved and function of the equipment. Children should not, generally, be used in this type of confrontation because of the traumatic impact it may have. In addition, the risk to their safety is paramount in the decision. Too often children have been used in this fashion and they have been abused again or are otherwise traumatized by the offender.

Before using this technique, investigators must research the law in their respective states regarding wiretapping and eavesdropping. Most states permit one-party-consent, which allows the person making the call/confrontation to consent/agree to the confrontation and then there is no violation of privacy under the "unreliable ear" theory of law.

## Covert Correspondence/Communication

Another successful technique that should be considered at this juncture is the covert investigative technique involving communication with the offender by ads in underground publications, mail, or computer. With the Internet in as widespread use as it is and its apparent lure of pseudo-anonymity, computer communication is as lucrative a target for the investigator as the mails. One merely needs to know that the offender is using it.

At this juncture in the investigation, this technique should only be considered where there is no immediate threat to a child and where there is no potential of loss of evidence.

These type of "sting" operations are often utilized by U.S. Customs, the Postal Inspectors, and specialized units in various police agencies throughout the country. The same legal concerns in vice investigations regarding entrapment and identity of the offender apply where the communication is done covertly and not in person. Investigators should research the prevailing law in their own jurisdictions before engaging in this practice [6].

Two other concerns arise in these cases that must be considered to protect children. The first is the "exchange" or "sale" of child pornography. For a law enforcement agent to send child pornography in an investigation of this nature is perpetuating the child's victimization who is depicted in the pornography. Efforts to avoid this practice should be considered and only previously, widely published material should be used for this purpose.

Lastly, a problem arises when the investigator has secured sufficient information to arrest the offender, but, to make an arrest would expose the operation and the subsequent loss of other "potential" or actual offenders "on the line." This issue should be resolved in favor of immediate arrest when the crime is established to assure that no further victimization occurs.

A case like this caused some serious problems. A child was kidnapped at gunpoint and raped by a person who had previously had a pornography crime established against him through correspondence. The person was not arrested because of the fear of exposing the ongoing sting and long after the establishment of the elements of the molest crime he committed the kidnap offense.

Needless to say, the civil ramifications of acts such as these could be devastating to an officer's career and pocketbook.

This technique is discussed in greater detail in Chapter 4, "Child Pornography Investigation."

## Interview of Offender When Named

All too often, investigators jump into an interview with an offender without preparation. This may deny the investigator valuable information that could help him successfully obtain a confession. If the investigator is able to talk to the child's or offender's relatives or review other cases in which the offender was involved, perhaps interviewed, he might learn from the child's family, the prior reports, or from the investigator, who handled them and how best to approach the offender. Researching the offender's name and making a review of the cases in a MO log or pin map, which identifies other crimes (further described in this later in this chapter), if appropriate, before the investigator talks to the offender may indicate that the offender is responsible for more than the one case being investigated. This will give the investigator the upper hand when he talks to the offender. Record checks should be made for:

1. Warrants.
2. With other police agencies where the offender might have had contact or lived.
3. With the state justice agency responsible for sex registration.
4. With the child abuse registry or state intelligence unit on sexual assault cases.
5. With the social services agency that handles child abuse.
6. If appropriate, with any of the federal law-enforcement agencies that might have an interest, i.e., the FBI, Postal Inspection Service, or U.S. Customs.

Always try to interview suspected offenders. If, as they often do, they talk to you and give you some story about why they couldn't have done what they have been accused of, try to prove what they tell you.

If they lie, the objective is to demonstrate how what they saw/did/say couldn't have happened the way they claim. As Terry Hall of the Indianapolis Police Department says, "prove they are a liar, not a child molester" [7].

Talk with their spouses, friends, neighbors, and co-workers. Ask them the questions listed above under "Interviewing Victim(s) and All Potential Witnesses."

The same principles apply to interviews of both offenders and children. Separate offenders and talk to them alone. Try to avoid cross-germination or contamination. If an offender confesses, independent corroborative evidence of the elements of the crime should be sought out to ensure that the confession is admissible. If one accused person points at another, even greater efforts should be made to corroborate the claims of the first. In this situation, an offender's predicament makes his statements highly suspect because he may try to make others look worse in order to make a better case for himself. It must be remembered that child molesters are first-class manipulators and liars.

A technique that Terry Hall has used is to have the offender write the child an apology if he won't confess or admit what he has done. Even though he won't make any admissions about what is claimed by the child, explain to him that the child obviously thought the offender did something wrong. Maybe he could set things straight by writing an apology which you will carry back to the child? You will be surprised what you get. What follows is a reconstructed, excerpted version of what one 37-year-old offender wrote to his nine-year-old victim. He stated that he "didn't do this," but would write a letter of apology so that she wouldn't think that she had done anything wrong. Note the inadvertent admission it contained.

---

Dear Cindy,

You will have to understand that grown-ups have big problems, problems that make them do things that they wouldn't ordinarily do. These problems take a while to work themselves out and make the adults act in a way that's different from what you're used to. Don't let what has happened get you down. Go on with your life as I will mine.

I'm sorry for any bad feelings that you have...

Signed _____

P.S. This does not mean that I did it [8].

---

## Forensic Medical Examination

In every case involving a child who has been assaulted or abused within 72 hours of the disclosure, a forensic medical examination, with emphasis on gathering biological evidence, should be made to avoid irretrievable loss of the evidence, if any exists. A colposcopic examination should be done on any child who says he was molested. It is not uncommon that such a medical examination reveals a greater degree of abuse than the child initially reports. For example, in one case semen was found in the child's mouth, between the teeth, as late as seven days after the event. The child had said nothing about oral sex.

All attempts should be made to acquire such evidence if the capability of collection and analysis is available. Examination should be made of the child for samples of loose hairs, fibers, debris, lubricants, and fingernail scrapings. In other words, the same examination preformed on a victim of rape should be considered for a child molest victim whenever appropriate. The same should be done with the suspect when arrested.

Even if the abuse was alleged to have occurred long before the disclosure, a forensic examination should be conducted. The degree of intrusive examination procedures should be left for the medical examiner to determine, depending upon the severity of the abuse, what external physical findings they are able to see at the time of the examination and the history provided by the child and the child's parents.

If fondling on the external genitalia or oral sex is the only type of activity alleged, the likelihood of internal findings may be minimal (keeping in mind that children don't tell all that happened to them). However, an intrusive procedure may be more traumatic and less productive in this type of setting, depending on the circumstances presented to the examiner. Each case must be analyzed on a case-by-case basis.

The investigator must ensure that before leaving the hospital, the medical report jibes with the information contained in the crime report or that he has at hand. it is not uncommon for a nurse or doctor to have obtained different or more information. It is also not uncommon for a nurse or doctor not to understand the technical terms for certain sexual acts or simply misunderstand the child's descriptions of what happened and therefore to mislead the child when questioning him about the acts. In one case, a nurse wrote on the sexual assault reporting form that the child did *not* engage in cunnilingus after the child had told the investigator that she had been orally copulated. When questioned about the discrepancy, the nurse discovered she didn't know what oral copulation was and had asked the child the wrong question.

For the significance of the medical findings in individual cases, investigators should talk with the examiner following the completion of the examination and after the examiner's report is filed. There is often a different report written than what is told the investigator. This is most often attributed to misunderstandings between what the investigator thinks he heard about technical findings and what the writer intends by what is written, even though they, in reality, mean the same thing.

With pre-verbal children (under the age of two), this kind of forensic medical evidence may be very important because behavioral symptoms may be the only way for the investigator to demonstrate that abuse occurred.

For the significance of what findings are discovered by the examiner, the investigator must first ask the examiner. Then consult with an expert if necessary.

What must be always kept in mind: *"Its normal to be normal."* The majority of cases will have no medical findings. This by no means establishes that no abuse occurred. The body heals quickly and often leaves no trace of trauma.

Excellent resources regarding medical findings and their significance may be found in the following publications:

"Examination Findings in Legally Confirmed Child Sexual Abuse: It's Normal to be Normal," Adams, Joyce, in *Pediatrics*, Vol. 94, No. 3., Sept. 1994.

*Evaluation of the Sexually Abused Child*, Heger, Astrid, Oxford, (1992).

*Evidence in Child Abuse and Neglect Cases*, Second Edition, Myers, John E.B., Wiley, (1992).

*Investigation and Prosecution of Child Abuse*, Second Edition, National Center for the Prosecution of Child Abuse, American Prosecutors Research Institute, Alexandria, VA (1993).

*Child Abuse: Medical Diagnosis and Management*, Reece, Robert M., Lea & Febiger, (1994).

## Evidence Gathering

Evidence gathering begins with the initial response and preliminary investigation, and continues, if necessary, through the prosecution of the offender.

Many types of evidence are presented in cases of sexual exploitation of children. The investigating officer lays the groundwork for introducing them. Evidence is both direct — that which proves the fact directly — and circumstantial — that which proves the facts through inference. The evidence ranges from the various types of testimonial evidence to the different kinds of physical abuse.

Evidence sought in cases of sexual exploitation of children may be used for various purposes, so it must be focused on the needs of the case. The major reasons for seeing evidence in these cases is to prove that a crime occurred, corroborate the child's testimony, prevent as many avenues of defense as possible, and identify the responsible offender(s).

The Attorney General of the State of Minnesota, Hubert Humphrey III, said in a report on the Scott County investigations in Jordan, Minnesota, that "Belief that a child is telling the truth, by itself, cannot support a criminal conviction or establish proof beyond a reasonable doubt" [9]. Because in many states people believe this is true, authorities have the responsibility to gather as much evidence as possible in addition to the victim's statements.

In these cases, investigators must move quickly to protect and preserve evidence once information indicating a violation of law surfaces. In some cases, as stated previously several times in this text, it may require the use of a task-force approach to perform multiple tasks simultaneously.

Another factor that must also be considered is that the police have an affirmative duty to preserve evidence they find. For example, if biological evidence is secured, it must be stored in such a fashion that it can be examined by the defendant when the case comes to trial. If it is not, not only may it not be possible to use it, it may force the dismissal of the case.

Analogous arguments by defense attorneys have been made concerning the need to record all interviews with children. The position is that because no recording was done, there is no way to test the veracity, accuracy, and completeness of the statements made by children. Some lower courts are listening to this and it has affected how the case has gone. This should be of major concern in the decision whether or not to audio or videotape interviews and local interpretation of case law should be sought by any investigator doing these cases.

Several publications have been produced by defense attorneys, training programs, and advocacy groups on how to defend against allegations of abuse. All emphasize the need for quick and thorough investigation. In short, what they are saying is that the time to nail down and secure evidence is as soon as possible. If the investigator doesn't, you can bet the defense will.

## Anticipation of Defenses

One of the most important aspects of these investigations is the necessity of trying to anticipate the defenses the offender may make to cover himself. By systematically addressing these concerns, the investigation almost automatically falls into order. In some cases, knowing which defense to prepare for will be easy because the offender will give a statement and explain why his story should be believed. In others, it may not be so easy. But even if the offender makes a statement that appears to fall into one or more of the defense positions listed next, it is important to prepare for the others, because the offender may either try a "shotgun" defense using two or more defense arguments at a later time in court, or he may change from one to another.

It can be assumed that each piece of evidence will be examined to see what defense may best be used to cast doubt upon its validity. Anyone who followed the O.J. Simpson case can understand why this is so important. This tactic is very common when the defendant or his attorney sees that the investigation was inadequate or that the situation may better lend itself to another line of defense. Remember, the defendant in a case need only establish a reasonable doubt to walk out of the courtroom at the end of the case. The prosecutor must prove the case, each element, beyond all reasonable doubt.

The following defense arguments are not intended to be all-inclusive. They merely suggest different variations of several common defense positions taken by accused molesters in statements made to police investigators and in the courtroom. With them are offered the types of evidence that must be gathered in order to counter or determine the validity of their claims. Most of this evidence must be obtained at the preliminary investigation or initial interview stage, or it may become contaminated or lost forever.

### *Identity*

Identity usually surfaces in this form: "It wasn't me; I don't know the kid." this defense can be easily countered if the investigation produces witnesses who can place the child with the offender, or if photographs depicting the offender and child together are found. However, not many cases in which this defense is used are lucky enough to have such evidence. The child's fingerprints in the offender's car, home, or on personal property, which the child can describe as being touched and belonging to the suspect, can often connect the two. Biological evidence obtained at the time of the initial investigation consisting of biological trace evidence, hair, fingernail scrapings, and other "rape kit" evidence can help to point the finger at the offender.

DNA evidence should always be considered when identity is at issue. The strength of this particular evidence cannot be overestimated and whenever other trace evidence of physical contact is possible, it should be sought. Often overlooked in these cases is bedding, clothing or objects the offender would clean off with and so on. These cases must be considered in the same vein as any other sexual assault.

Unique descriptions of the offender's person consisting of characteristics that the child could know only if he was in a position to observe them, often help to prove identity. They might consist of the notation of scars, body marks, deformities, and specific descriptions of the offender's genitals. If the child can tell if the offender has a circumcised or non-circumcised penis, it may help to verify that he saw it. However, most children don't understand that there are differences.

Lastly, and often overlooked, is the description the victim provides of the interior of the offender's car or house. Also overlooked is the child's revelation of unique things about the offender's history. This might consist of things the offender told the child or facts the child would only know by them being revealed by the offender. If the victim can describe unique characteristics of the contents of the offender's car or home, and the investigation verifies the observations, it lends credence to the child's account.

For example, a victim in one case described the offender's car in which she had been taken for a ride, kidnapped, and raped. Not only did she give a good description of the exterior of the car, including a license number that led to the identification of the offender, but she described its contents, including a blanket the offender had folded up in the rear of the car, out of view from the outside and that only someone who was in the car could have seen. This helped greatly in supporting the victim's account of kidnap when the offender denied knowing the victim at all.

Whenever identity is at issue, prior acts may be admissible. Anything that would indicate a common plan, scheme, or MO are important to look for in other acts committed by the person under investigation. All of the things described in Chapter 3 should be considered.

Opportunity to commit the offense(s) is also important to establish. Even though no one saw the offender with the child, if witnesses can place the offender in the same place as the child and be able to isolate the child with the offender by eliminating anyone else who might have been with the child at the time the crime(s) is committed, it could establish this element.

Consciousness of guilt evidence also is very important when there is no independent witness besides the child. Whatever the offender does to cover up or try to dissuade others from believing he might have committed the crime could be used to establish this element. People he talked to before and after the offenses might provide leads or incriminating evidence. This would be especially true if he tried to establish an alibi when one didn't exist.

If the offender admits anything that the child says surrounding the offenses, it may be sufficient to prove identity.

### A Word About "False" Report Statistics

In the 10 years since the 1st edition of this book, numerous studies have been conducted trying to ascertain how many reports of abuse are false. The problem in making such a determination is that child abuse allegations are classified differently between the states. All states collect data on the number of reports of abuse and their dispositions. To complicate the problem even further, although most states have written criteria on how to properly determine which category a particular case falls into, individual differences and interpretations make this classification system even more complicated to interpret. Another complication is that many of the states use the same words to denote different outcomes and the generic term surveys that are used to collect the national data will not allow for the differences in definitions.

In all states, there are basically three potential dispositional outcomes. The first is that the report is found to be valid or true. The second is that it is not. Its the third category that causes most of the problems and that one is that which connotes a finding that it cannot be proved or disproved. For example, the first classification category may be classified as "substantiated" or "founded." The second may be "unsubstantiated" or "unfounded." The last may be "unsubstantiated" or some other term.

Given these problems, the most reliable studies that have been conducted reviewing individual or multiple state reported statistics indicated that about eight percent of the reports made by children about abuse are fictitious [10]. This means that they had no merit whatsoever. Other studies have found similar results [11]. Although as a class, custody/visitation cases are lumped into the categories listed above, research studies on this individual subject have found some differences that must be considered before conclusions may be drawn. We will discuss custody/visitation cases separately further in this chapter.

### It's A False Report

The incidence of children making reports that have no merit is extremely rare. Yet virtually every defense attorney who defends an accused molester tries to place his client in the position of being falsely accused. The ABA also finds that the problem in declaring a report "false" is a matter of definition of the term "false." One dictionary lists nine different gradations of the term, ranging from totally without merit to mistaken or incorrect, and it is in this light that the discussion of "false reports" should be examined.

The responsibility of the investigator is to determine whether what is alleged to have happened did or did not occur. Every investigation must try to determine if an allegation of molestation is valid, to the best degree possible. One of the best ways to do this is to "test" the facts against the potential defenses. We have just discussed the identity defense, which pre-supposes that a crime was committed, it merely says "I wasn't the one who did it." Its a "false report," on the other hand totally refutes that any crime was committed.

Generally, false allegations of child molestation cases fall into five cate-gories. This is important to recognize because not all "false allegations" have no merit to them. Depending upon what the investigator is able to establish, the degree of incorrect or fictitious information that is intertwined may or may not discredit the rest which is true.

1. The totally false report, which has no merit at all.
2. The partially false report.
3. Misinterpreted actions by the offender.
4. Displaced assignment of responsibility.
5. Second-party reports.

**The Totally False Report.**   The totally false report involves a situation where none of the allegations is true and the report has no merit. Most of the time, these cases involve some ulterior motive on the part of the child, or adult influences on the child. It may be that the child is using the report as an "attention getting device," where the child is saying, in effect: "Give me some attention. I was molested." This type of report may also involve ven-geance, spite, or manipulation, whereby a child accuses a person of commit-ting the act so that the accused will do what the child wishes — for example, a child reporting that a teacher molested him, because the teacher didn't pay him enough attention (romantically or otherwise).

A word of caution. It is not uncommon for a child who has been molested to discover that his sexuality is power. That is, he knows he can use the giving of his body as a means of getting what he wants. For example, when the offender says he will reward the child after the sex act, the child learns it is not hard to get what he wants by offering or withholding himself. The child soon realizes that he has the power to control the offender in other ways through the use of his sexuality, perhaps even to put the offender in jail.

## Custody Disputes

In cases of older children, generally in their teens, the totally false report might involve a child who no longer wants to stay with a caretaker or wants to stop visitation rights. Most younger children won't have the sophistication to understand the consequences of making such allegations. However, just because there is a custody dispute, this should not imply that it is a false report. Often the conflict in the dispute opens the window to disclosure. This happens either because the anger within the child bubbles to the surface or the child fears returning to the offending parent. It may also occur when, in the care of the nonoffending parent, the child feels safe from the abuser and therefore discloses.

Of the many cases handled by Child Protective Services, police, medical, and clinical professionals, no allegation is more difficult to investigate than sexual abuse arising in the context of marital discord. These cases cause more frustrations for investigators than any other because of lack of evidence, possible biases, and the acrimony between the parties.

One of the main problems is investigations of these allegations take an inordinate amount of time. This is compounded when the child involved is young — too young to be able to articulate what has happened in one or two sittings, the minimum amount of time to spend with them in a preliminary phase of the investigation.

Police and social workers assigned to child abuse investigations are already inundated with cases that are difficult enough to prove when a child is accusing an adult. When added credibility questions surface in custody/divorce cases, it makes the cases even more likely to be unsubstantiated or unfounded. The special questions that must be paid particular attention to in these cases are:

1. Who did the child first disclose to?
2. What triggered the disclosure?
3. When did the first disclosure occur?
4. How did the original disclosure surface?
5. Why the child is telling now (at a particular juncture in the family law case)?
6. How many people have talked to the child?
7. What exactly was said by the child?
8. What exactly was said by the inquirers?
9. How, if at all, has the aforementioned affected what the child is saying?
10. What evidence is available to confirm or refute the allegation?
11. What evidence is available to confirm what the child is saying?
12. Are there any alternative explanations for the child's behaviors and what (s)he is saying?

These allegations often surface in circumstances that impugn the veracity of the disclosure and the stakes are high — an improper allegation may ruin the reputation of an unjustly accused person, yet, an unrecognized valid allegation may subject the child to continued abuse.

There is no denying that there have been malicious, false allegations, made in these circumstances, although the statistical probabilities of a false report are much less than most people commonly believe. Statistical reviews of the incidence of child abuse allegations arising in marital relations courts reveal that as few as 2 and as much as 10% of litigated cases involve claims of abuse [12]. That same study found that of the 169 cases reviewed, 14% were found to have been deliberate false allegations [13]. A follow-up study, involving 9000 families, found a similar result in numbers of cases involving abuse allegations. It found a range of 1 to 8% involved sexual abuse allegations [14]. As have other researchers, the California Judicial Council (CJC) investigation into such allegations found that there were legitimate reasons why an allegation would be made, although it was later found no abuse actually occurred [15]. That same CJC report found that false allegations are not common, "although they sometimes occur" [16]. In short, it would be a mistake to automatically discount an allegation that arises in the context of a marital relations/family law litigation situation.

There are basically three types of cases.

1. Those where there is a sincere, legitimate and valid allegation made which is true because the abuse actually occurred.
2. Those where there is a sincere, legitimate, and valid allegation made which is a misinterpretation of some behavior or statements made by the child.
3. Those where there is a deliberately false allegation made.

The problem is that the manner in which the parent makes the allegation is very much alike in all of them. The dilemma, then, has become how does the investigator determine which type of allegation (s)he has and whether abuse has occurred?

Although all of the practices and concerns regarding sexual abuse allegation investigation must be considered while conducting an inquiry under these circumstances, the following practices must be considered above all the rest.

When a complaint is made, the police must be notified immediately. Interviews with the reporting party (not always the estranged parent) must be conducted and seek to identify the source of the disclosure and separate it from the supporting parent, if possible. For example, in one case a three-year-old child of divorced parents who were sharing custody of him was observed at his preschool drawing at a table. He was obviously experiencing discomfort kneeling over the table and so a teacher suggested he sit down. He replied he couldn't because his "bottom" hurt, at which point the teacher asked if he wanted to go to the bathroom. The child again responded he couldn't because it hurt too much. When asked why, after some shifting and clear reluctance to talk, the child told of his father sodomizing him. Here, the disclosure came from the child independent of the supportive parent and was not volunteered until after the teacher made the inquiry. It is these characteristics, coupled with the emotion, fear, and hesitancy, that made it credible. More importantly, it was identifying these characteristics which helped to support the child's claim and refute the claim of fabrication made by the offending parent.

Considering the posturing of the parties and influences exerted upon the child, witnesses, relatives, and others who the courts will use to evaluate the facts, proper investigatory steps must be taken immediately upon the receipt of the disclosure of abuse or any subsequent information gathered is likely to be of questioned value. Keeping all of the questions listed above in mind, four investigative concerns must be addressed simultaneously at this juncture in the investigation:

1. Is it possible to prevent contamination by witnesses and involved parties talking to one another or is there a chance of alliances being drawn once the "secret" is out?
2. Is it possible to secure an admission or confession on the part of the offender before he learns of the investigation and tries to intimidate the child or witnesses or begins to confabulate a story?
3. Is it possible to prevent the destruction of evidence by the offender or his supporters (often the non-offending parent) before he learns of the investigation?
4. Is there any medical evidence available?

The first is a time, space, and logistics problem. Are witnesses in such situations where they will call or talk to one another? Are there sufficient number of investigators who are able to quickly do interviews to nail down statements to prevent changes in accounts, perceptions or influences by involved parties?

The second is a matter of getting as much information about what happened and confronting the suspected offender as soon as possible. Most incestuous parents will admit their acts if approached properly. Denials are the most common responses investigators get when confronting the suspected offender when he has done it but won't admit it. Therefore, the most successful technique an investigator can employ is one which will encourage the offender to tell the truth. This means he must not be threatened by the consequences of talking with the police or CPS worker. The most successful technique to accomplish this is the pretext confrontation, conducted by the child victim or, if too young or incapable, the non-offending parent. This technique is further described earlier in this and Chapter 6.

The main concern is the personal safety and mental state of the person doing the confrontation. In one case, a child called her father and told him she thought she had venereal disease from the sexual intercourse they were having. His response was that it was impossible, because she was the only one he had been having sex with. In another, a mother confronted the father about the sex he was having with his daughter by asking what she should tell the authorities who were now inquiring. The response she received was to "tell them it was a mistake, I shouldn't have done it."

The third concern is the securing and preservation of evidence. Considerations of the initiation of a confrontational recorded pretext-interview with the accused must be examined at the same time a search warrant is considered. Hard evidence consisting of corroborative facts in the form of concrete, tangible, evidence or admissions or confessions of the offender, must be sought in the earliest stages of an investigation. Besides a confession or admission from the mouth of the accused, there is nothing that can be more convincing than corroborating what the child has told. The clearest example of this is when the offender takes pictures of what he does (a frequently overlooked question in incest cases). The phrase "a picture is worth a thousand words" must have anticipated the doubts cast upon children who accuse their parents of sexual abuse. However, even the slightest corroboration consisting of finding the lubricant or condom the child claims was used in the hiding place the offender keeps it is very compelling.

Lastly, medical examinations should be conducted as soon as possible. The body often heals itself too fast for documentation. Therefore, immediate medical examinations with colposcopic, photographic documentation are a must in every case.

Additional concerns arise in these matters. Backgrounds need to be done on all crucial witnesses and the accused. What connections do they have with the parties involved? What opportunities did the witnesses have to observe or interact with the child or the parties? What behaviors did they exhibit before the disclosure? What were the circumstances of the disclosure? What exactly was said? Who was present? These questions (all basic areas of inquiry in any abuse case) and many more need to be answered to assure that any decision made by the courts is made with the most complete, reliable, credible evidence possible.

Of special concern in these matters is the fact that interviews must be conducted in person. Evaluations of risk conducted by phone are not only inappropriate they are worthless. There is nothing that can substitute for a direct, visual, in-person examination of the facts. The inquiry should not stop until all avenues of investigation have been explored. These responsibilities must not be delegated to anyone other than unbiased, independent, trained professionals. In other words, if a complaint is made by a mother that her child is displaying or exhibiting unusual behaviors, she should not be told to go back and further question the child. This is also true for third parties. If a teacher reports that a child has said something or is doing unusual things, (s)he shouldn't be told to go back and get more information. If either the teacher or mother questions the child improperly or misperceives what is said, unnecessary doubts may be cast upon the case and the child improperly discredited.

In all cases, especially in custody/visitation cases, some specific reasons why a report might be false should be considered.

**Spite.** The child may be acquiescing to a parent, who for some other motive, might be pressuring the child to make the allegations. This pressure applied to the child may be for several reasons. In some cases, the parent desires custody of the child to "get back at" the other parent or has another score to settle with the spouse. In others they might be seeking an advantage to justify their taking custody [17].

**Misinterpretation.** When misinterpretation occurs, the parent may project their own fear on the child, thereby misinterpreting the behaviors seen in the child or what the child has said about the "incident." Still, in others, there is fear of abuse because of what the parent has experienced themselves with their spouse. In these cases, often present in abusive situations, the accused parent may have been a batterer or abuser, having assaulted the protective parent physically or sexually. Also just as prevalent, the protective parent may have experienced sexual abuse themselves as a child and is misinterpreting the signs in the situation at hand as abuse.

What must be considered here is that there is a possibility of these cases actually being true allegations. An adult who has been abused as a child often finds themselves in relationships where the pattern of abuse repeats itself.

**Contamination/leading question.** The child may interpret a suggestion made during the adult's questioning of the child, as something that actually happened. For example, in one case where a child reported being molested, and the offender later pleaded guilty, the child was questioned by a rape crisis worker to whom he had disclosed. Once the child had reported the incident, the worker asked the child some questions about the specifics of the events. She asked if the offender had kissed the child by sticking his tongue into the child's mouth. The child told her that he had not. Later, during the questioning by the police investigator, the child told the officer that the offender had kissed him by sticking his tongue in his mouth. The question arises: Did this happen or was it suggested in the questioning of the child by the rape crisis worker? This case had a plea on different grounds and facts.

The problem in these cases is that after specific questions are asked, it is not uncommon for the child to remember more specifics. The difficulty is trying to establish the child is recounting what happened to him rather than something he picked up on in the questioning process (see Chapter 5 for more details on reliability and questioning information).

**Conditioning and programming.**    The defense attorney may seek to attack the investigation on the grounds that it was the "well-intentioned" police or parents who "conditioned" or "programmed" the child to respond in the manner in which the response was made.

For example, recent attacks on police investigations have centered on the officer's and parents' giving the child rewards for disclosing the events. It has been claimed that the child is being told or is learning that if he "tells more" he'll "get more." Neither the officer nor the family should be defensive about this.

In testimony, the responses to questions on these points should be forthright and affirmative, explaining that any rewarding was done to make the child feel comfortable discussing the events and to encourage the child to tell the truth. For this reason, care must be taken to be sure that the child is not given too much "special treatment," such as being treated too differently, given gifts, or allowed to stay home from school where inappropriate. Just as the child may become a manipulator with the offender to get what the child wants by offering sex, care must be taken to avoid the few children who may try to bargain for their testimony.

In other cases where no rewards were involved, the defense may take the position that the repeated questioning and or manner in which the questions were asked has created the child's account of events.

Here, it is imperative that the child's account be corroborated as much as possible by seeking out facts or people who can verify as much of the account as possible. This may involve the search for concrete facts that back up the child's account or finding people to whom the child has spoken before any questioning was conducted by the parent, social worker, or police.

**Child's claim made to cover an indiscretion.**    In other cases of false reporting, the child may be trying to cover up for something he did. For example, a child may have cut school, come home late, gotten pregnant, and report that she was kidnapped and molested to avoid being punished.

**Fantasy.**    Lastly, the child could fantasize the event. Here the child believes that what he is saying actually happened. The problem with fantasy is that, although children do fantasize, their fantasy is based on their experiences — on what they observe, see, or hear. This is why it is important to determine what the child is exposed to in the home or elsewhere. For example, a little girl reported that she was molested, having been involved in sexual intercourse. However, she couldn't provide the details of the acts with any credibility, misdescribing how they occurred. Investigation revealed that she had been sleeping in the room next to her mother's bedroom and that she had heard her mother on several occasions engaged in sexual activity with men.

On the other hand, too often it is concluded that the child fantasized an event, when in actuality, what the child is trying to do is make sense of what he has experienced. Children, especially the very young, have great difficulty in expressing themselves. This is compounded by the fact that they do not understand or comprehend their abuse. When they try to convey the events, they are often incorrectly dismissed as fantasizing.

When fantasy is the suspected defense, the child should be questioned about things which are not related to the abuse. If the child can describe in a cogent manner the surroundings at the time of the abusive acts or other events that could be corroborated independently, it will help to make the child more credible and undercut the claim the child is unreliable. This is especially important when the child is claiming abuse in a ritualistic case where bizarre acts or activities were involved. The investigator must realize that the child has been in a world that no one can relate to or understand. This technique of "normalizing the situation," will help to ground the child's account of events by making them sound more normal.

One technique which utilizes this practice, is to have the child describe a full day's events from start to finish. An advantage of this technique is that things the investigator didn't think to ask about may come out.

An additional problem with what could be termed fantasy, is when very young children report things which are impossible to believe or which are disproved by the facts. This generally falls into the category of exaggeration, discussed in the interview chapter. The exaggeration takes the form of embellishment on what really happened to the child.

This happens because the child feels he has done something wrong or he feels he needs to make himself more believable. For example, he may exaggerate the degree of violence visited upon him by describing bizarre acts that would leave scars or marks where none are found. This has often been observed in custody situations where the child is placed in the same room with the accused parent for the purposes of seeing how they interact with one another. Because of the genuine love that still exists between the child and that parent and the inherent need for children to be loved by their parents, the child might say that the parent didn't do anything wrong and later claim that the accused parent forced him to say that. In one case it took the form of the child telling the mother later that the father (the accused parent) had whispered in his ear to say what he said. The session was videotaped and there was no evidence of the father doing such a thing.

Later, the child explained that he didn't want his dad to be mad at him and that is why he made the exonerating statement. He also said that because he didn't want to make his mother mad at him, he told her that the father made him say it. In this particular case, as with many others with divorcing parents, the child feels he is in the middle of a tug-of-war and wants to please both parents.

In any case where statements are made that appear as though the child has fantasized or "made up" the facts, they must be closely examined to see if it is possible to establish what motivated the child to make that particular statement. In short, if the child has made some statements that are not true and some which are, those facts which are not verifiable shouldn't be disregarded. This will clearly affect the child's overall credibility, but, by itself, should not be sufficient reason to totally disbelieve what a child reports.

**The child is fabricating as a defense.**    Often the offender makes the statement, or the defense attorney takes the position, that the child is lying. This defense takes several forms:

- The well-meaning police, social worker, therapist, put the idea in the mind of the child.
- Mom wants custody and therefore made the child believe it happened by repeated questioning.
- Mom alienated the child against the father to the point the child made up the story.

This is the leading question argument where it is inferred that the questions posed by the investigators or others involved in the case caused the child to say what is claimed. To counter this defense it will be necessary to isolate the statements made on occasions before the questions were asked. The problem is that when the child's account is consistent over time and in subsequent interviews, the defense will also make the claim that it was the initial questioning that "implanted" the idea in the child. They will suggest that is why the child keeps repeating it. They even will go to the extent of claiming that the child actually believes that the claimed acts happened because they have been repeatedly questioned about it and it has become part of their consciousness.

The only real counter to any of these arguments made by the defense is the corroboration of as much as possible of what the child has claimed. As was discussed earlier in this text on the studies done about children's reliability, it will be difficult for children to describe unique experiences unless they have actually been involved in them. It is therefore incumbent upon the investigator to have the child describe as much detail and support as much of that detail as possible.

Having the child describing sex acts in an experiential fashion, places gone and things done, unique descriptions of the offender's body, and so on will help to refute this defense. Establishing the lack of the motive on the part of the mother to have the child make the claims also helps to counter this defense. Background investigation on the type of relationship the mother has with the father and the manner in which she refers to the father while in the presence of the child should be conducted, talking to anyone who might have witnessed this. Friends, relatives, neighbors, co-workers, siblings, or anyone else who the family knows should be contacted and questioned.

This is one of the reasons why recording the interviews with the children is helpful. The recording will place things in context. Emotion and the child's affect will be evident, especially if the sessions are videotaped. It will help to establish the sincerity of the statements.

The problem is that often follow-up interviews are not recorded. The defense then has the opening to argue that what is developed outside the taped/documented interview was the product of the influence of the interviewer. This is a situation where the discussion on recording in this text should be considered.

**"I know the child, but it didn't happen / The child has a motive to lie."** Here, in addition to work on corroborating the account, the potential motives to lie must be examined. This can be very difficult as some allegations are likely to be subject of this defense and it will be very difficult to disprove an ulterior motive. For example, a foster parent was accused of molesting a recently placed teenage foster child. The foster child claimed that she had been raped by the parent. She had been having great difficulty in other homes and had continued to have similar difficulties in her present placement situation. The investigating social worker had grave concerns about the potential manipulation of the situation that could have been going on with the child making the allegation simply to be moved out of the placement home. The social worker considered this and when the foster father later confessed corroborating the child's account, this defense was foreclosed.

To support the child, biological evidence can help immensely. If semen is discovered in the victim's vagina, mouth, rectum, on the child's clothing, surface of the offender's car seat, the child's or offender's bed, floor, or other surface, and is typed within the offender's biological groupings through DNA or other genetic markers, it can be quite damaging.

This, among other things, is the reason a medical examination, using such equipment as the colposcope, may reveal injuries that can help to corroborate the child's account. Observations by a physician of bruises, or injuries consistent with the child's account of the event(s), will help to corroborate the child's account. In one case where a mother was told by her young son that his father was sodomizing him on visits, she observed bruises on the child's inner thighs. This was verified by the child's pediatrician and became crucial in supporting the child's account.

In another case, in an investigation that spanned eight years, an investigator was able to find a former employee of a furniture store who corroborated claims that the owner had been sodomizing boys on the store's premises. She remembered seeing small bloody hand prints on a mattress that was leaning against a wall as though a boy had been leaning against the mattress with his legs spread after having touched his bleeding anus. After finding numerous victims who also corroborated the claims of assault, the owner committed suicide.

Pregnancy, with or without blood typing, helps to confirm the child's testimony. Similar or matching strains of sexually transmitted diseases or herpes found in both the child and the offender can lend credence to the victim's account. As mentioned in Chapter 2, the child's behavior at or about the time of the incident(s) is bound to change, and observations of those behavior patterns made by others are extremely helpful in supporting the child and determining what happened.

This is another reason why it is necessary to do everything possible to establish the accused lied in his statement to the authorities and others. Rather than demonstrate he is a child molester, if it can be shown that he is a liar and is not to be trusted, it will help take the onus off of the child.

**Fresh complaint doctrine evidence.**    It is not uncommon for a child to tell someone about the incident(s) after they occur. Although he won't necessarily be able to use the exact words, he will try to tell what happened to him. For example, a child might tell his mother: "Daddy makes me do things that I don't like." In most cases, the mother assumes this means that the child is making conventional complaints about doing what the father wants him to do. The mother won't understand or suspect that the child is referring to something more serious, and therefore will not give much attention to the complaints. But both the child and the adult may remember that the child made the complaint at or about the time of the incident(s).

This is evidence of "fresh complaint" and is, in most states, a valid exception to the hearsay exception and would be admissible.

The theory of the exception is that when something so traumatic as a child molestation occurs, the child would want to tell someone about it. In this context, it is considered more reliable because it, generally, would be said by someone without reflecting upon it or with the opportunity to fabricate. Evidence of this nature is of great importance to an attorney in presenting a case in court because it tends to corroborate the fact that something happened at or about the time the child made the statement.

Furthermore, it will be important to have some description of the child's affect, general demeanor, and behavioral traits at the time this statement was made. As has been stated in other places in this text, the observations of the child's behavioral traits exhibited at the time these statements are made could be crucial in helping to determine credibility.

It is also not uncommon to find that the child has told a friend what happened because he hopes someone else will reveal the secret for him but, either because the friend was told not to tell or for other reasons, no one is told at the time. In some cases, particularly incest, the child may have written about what happened in his diary. Finding this type of information, either by asking the child or anyone who had contact with him at the time of the events, is very helpful in corroborating the victim's account.

**Spontaneous statement exception.**   In many states, the diary described above may also be admitted into evidence under another doctrine called the Spontaneous Statement or Sudden Utterance. Here, where the statement was made under the stress of excitement or the moment (hurting from the abuse, anger as a result of an denial made by the offender when confronted, fear of the offender's reoffense, a cry for help in oral or written form). What must be determined and described are the circumstances that existed at time the statement was made or, as in the diary, written. Previous statements by the child made about the abuse and circumstances surrounding it should be sought out to provide this type of corroborative evidence.

**State-of-mind exception.**   In this instance, the writing disclosing the abuse in the form of a diary or other statements made at or about the time of the alleged acts will help to refute the contention the allegation is false. This is evidence of the child's state of mind at the time the statements were made. The statements could be used to show why there was no report made or why when one was, it was later taken back, as often seen where the Child Sexual

Abuse Accommodation Syndrome is involved. When emotional outbursts or withdrawal are seen, it can also be used to determine explain why a certain course of action was taken by a child.

Discovery of these statements made before the parents, police, or therapists intervened will also help to support the propriety of the investigation and protect it against attack when allegations of leading or placing ideas in the mind of the child are made. People who may have had these statements made to them might be teachers, parents, friends, or professionals involved in the criminal justice system.

Another variation of the fabrication defense is, "Yeah, I know the kid, but it didn't happen the way he claims." This is helpful for the prosecution because it often involves an admission of some sort. The offender will say that he was with the child and that they were involved in some activity, but not of the kind the child described.

In a rather celebrated case in California, the alleged offender admitted having a teenaged girl over to his apartment and giving her his car to drive home, but denied having sexual relations with her. He insisted that she had tried to seduce him and said that he rebuked her on numerous occasions. He convinced a jury of it and was acquitted. In cases like this, the actions observed by others of the offender and the victim before the incidents are very important in developing the pattern. Witnesses must be sought out and interviews conducted with anyone who can describe the kind of a relationship the offender had with the child. Any signs of affection that were observed must be noted. If there were none, that fact must be documented. The amount of time the two spent together is important, as well as the type of places they went to.

### The Partially False Report

Another category of false report is the partially false report. In these cases, some or most of the allegations are true. However, the child embellishes the account, or minimizes the facts in some way (tries to make them sound less serious). In general, children lie for the same reasons that adults do — to make themselves look better. It may be to get out of trouble or to impress someone — telling about child molestation does neither. All the reasons that prevent the child from telling about the sexual abuse work in favor of preventing him from making false allegations — he doesn't look better and it certainly won't impress anyone. However, it is not uncommon for a child either to not tell about all the events, or to change the facts to make himself look a little better. Children who have some relationship with the offender may minimize the degree of the abuse either because they don't want to get him into too much trouble or they don't want people to think ill of him. Others minimize the degree of the abuse because they think people either won't believe them or because they are embarrassed about what happened.

On the other hand, children who embellish may fear that they won't be believed, are afraid that they will appear responsible for what happened, and want to make the crime seem more serious than it is because to them it appears to be minor. These children may fear that because of the way they were seduced, no one will believe them. They fear that because they repeatedly returned to the offender who molested them people won't like them or will think they are stupid. They also fear that if the crime isn't a serious one, no one will care or do anything. These are the children who often add violence or threats to what actually happened, such as a 9-year-old boy who said he fought and hit the offender to prevent the abuse.

The point that must be emphasized with these cases is that these children have been molested; they only alter the facts.

**Cross-contamination/germination.** This defense is just as the name implies. It is premised on the belief there is something that has tainted the product. The defense implies that the results brought into court are not to be trusted because they have been damaged in some way.

The simple definition of the contamination defense is that something like the influence of a parent or another child who made a similar claim has altered or otherwise affected the statement of a child. It generally applies to statements made by children because they are an easy target to imply they have been influenced in some way. Children are not always consistent in what they say, as has been explained previously. These inconsistencies, which are fodder for an impeaching attorney's gun, are exploited by the attorney claiming the inconsistency is a result of someone's influence.

That influence could be the form of questioning when "leading questions" are asked. Here, the argument is made that the child heard some portion of the question that contained a clue as to what the inquirer was "looking for" and that the child answered to please the questioner.

It could come in the form that the child was repeatedly questioned by someone or a number of people and that the child was answering the questions merely to satisfy what he thought the questioners wanted so they would stop.

It could come in the form that the child was merely following along with what the child thought the questioner wanted period, with no specific source of information that could have given the child an idea as to what the questioner wanted, other than it wasn't what really happened

The cross germination defense is a different twist on the same theme. Here, like the term implies, it hinges on the fact that the child developed an account of events that is different from what really happened. Or it may imply that nothing happened and the child has simply made it up because someone has impregnated the child's mind with the false idea that something did.

For example, in a case with a 16-year-old girl who recanted what had happened to her by her father, the defense claimed that she had made up the story because she wanted to "belong" with her peers. It turns out that several of them had disclosed to the girl that they had been molested. She even denied the nude pictures her father had taken of her which were inadvertently found by the mother.

The counters to these arguments are all of the above mentioned techniques intended to provide corroboration and, most importantly, independent support of the child's account of the facts. Recording the interviews by videotape is a good technique to forestall this defense. It often helps to have some insulation between children in cases where multiple victims are involved — different therapists, different interviewers, and so on.

The identification of specific instances where the child has said the same thing before could help to support the later statement made in court. This could have been statements to others at the time of the event or later, in reporting. Prior consistent statements are exceptions to the hearsay rule for rehabilitation purposes and may come into evidence to refute the charge of recent fabrication.

**False memory.** Although the false memory argument hasn't hit the area of young victims as hard as it has in cases where adults later recall event of when they were children, it is a common claim when there is much time that has elapsed between the events and final disclosure.

Here, as in the germination claim, the argument is one that the child has a genuine belief which was created in the therapist's office, in some other therapeutic environment, or in the process of inquiry. They then explain all of the "realistic" qualities observed in the child's demeanor, behavior, and affect, as the child's being led to believe this is all true and therefore it explains why you would normally believe this "poor, misled" child.

Once again, the counter to this is the independent corroboration and independent sources developed in investigation described in other parts of this text.

**Misinterpreted actions of the offender.** Children do not have the experiences of adults and the ability to always understand what is going on around them. Even adults often misinterpret the actions or meanings of other adults, so to expect a child, regardless of age, to always correctly interpret an action of an adult is unrealistic. In this type of false report, the investigator, by thorough investigation, will find that something has occurred, but the child or someone else incorrectly assessed it to be abusive. Investigation reveals that the incident was legitimate or "innocent" in nature. Bathing or showering, an affectionate hug, squeeze, or pat, or some other activity are the most common examples. The problem is that this is often the precursor to molestation or "grooming" behavior seen in offenders. It is difficult to distinguish a genuinely innocent act from one intended to seduce a child or that which provides a ruse for illicit contact.

Here, repeated acts over time with accompanying behaviors that indicate the person's intent will help to make that distinction. Other victims will help to establish true intent. For example, an elementary school teacher who liked to have girls sit on his lap claimed that he was merely showing affection by rubbing their bodies, inadvertently touching forbidden body parts and areas. He did this to hundreds of girls, often in front of the class during movies shown in a darkened room. He gave them candy, took them on fun excursions, and otherwise appeared as though he was genuinely concerned for them.

His "affectionate" touches included running his fingers down the child's pants and into their body openings, massaging undeveloped breasts, and, in one case, actual rape and oral copulation of an elementary school girl enrolled in his class. Although numerous allegations were made over time about this man's behavior, his steadfast insistence of innocent intent and his selection of specific problem children as victims (which almost automatically discredited their complaints), helped to prevent any official action to be taken.

He wasn't officially discovered until long after the children had graduated from elementary school and numerous other children, spanning several school years in time, came forward to complain. His guilty plea in two separate jurisdictions was still denounced by his supporters, who insist his conviction was improperly motivated both by the children and authorities.

**Displaced assignment of responsibility.**    When a child is afraid of the person who is abusing him, either because of threats or because of the possible consequences of reporting the abuse, he may pick a "safe target" to accuse in order to prevent repercussions. This type of displaced assignment of responsibility, or "transference," may manifest itself in a report of abuse or rape to cover up a pregnancy caused by the child's sexual activity. These cases are generally characterized by the fact that the child can't describe or identify the person who did it. In one case where the child did identify the person who allegedly committed the act, it was impossible for it to have been the right person because of the nature of the acts and the location and times they allegedly occurred. The child accused teachers of molesting him. Investigation revealed that the location — a boys' bathroom — and the times — during classes — made it highly unlikely for the events to have occurred in the way the child alleged. However, the boy's behavior and demeanor were consistent with a molest victim and did indicate that something had happened to him. The question is, what and by whom?

**Second-party reports.**   In second-party reporting, it is not uncommon to find that the suspicion is not valid. This type of case involves the child who was molested and believes that a friend or friends were also molested because they were known to be with the offender. It may also be a case where the suspicion comes from observations made by a teacher or other person who comes in contact with a suspected victim. In this type of case, some or all of the children in question are found, by investigation, not to have been molested.

It is unfortunate, but parents or other caretakers in cases where custody/visitation are at issue, sometimes mistakenly believe their children have been abused because they misread the signs. The allegations surface in an environment of suspicion, distrust, highly charged emotional disagreements, many of which involve sexual infidelity or other sexual dysfunction. These situations are difficult to discern the true from the misdiagnosed allegation because, often the behavioral signs are similar. A genuine belief may develop based on observations of behavior signs described in this text that have little or nothing to do with abuse and all to do with the traumatic environment the child is in.

This is why immediate investigation searching for the corroborative elements described earlier is important. Witnesses who can support the child's account, physical and medical evidence are paramount. Incriminating or exculpatory statements made by the accused are important as well. In short, the concerns discussed previously in this section regarding family law matters must be considered and addressed.

## Evaluating the Possible False Report

When an investigator encounters a report whose validity he questions, or knows that the defense will attack it on the grounds that it's a false allegation, the use of the following evaluations criteria might ensure that the proper action is taken. The truth is encoded in the mind at multiple levels. This means that the sensations, emotions, and observations of a child who has been abused should reflect his abuse. The investigator should consider the following factors in assessing the case.

1.  If there has been a disclosure made prior to the investigator's involvement, is there an exact (audio/video) simultaneous record available to evaluate the criteria listed below? Is there any record of the disclosure made previous to this investigator's involvement?
2.  Can the child describe events/acts to which he wouldn't ordinarily be exposed?
    *   Unusual knowledge of sexual matters or acts.

- Is there any idiosyncratic detail which would help to determine experiences versus observations such as descriptors involving the senses like it was "sticky," "salty," it "hurt."

3. Does the child describe characteristics consistent with abuse, such as the style of seduction or manner in which the crime was committed? For Example:
    - Says the offender told him it was a secret.
    - Says the offender called it "sex education."

4. Is it physically possible for the things the child described to have happened?

5. Do the things the child describes exist?

6. Does the child show the emotions and characteristics that generally accompany abuse and disclosure?
    - exhibits sudden behavioral changes in the past.
    - re-enacts abusive acts in play by self or during interview (e.g., inserts pen in mouth simulating oral copulation by inserting the pen, in-and-out).
    - tears during disclosure.
    - fear (both during disclosure and in general).
    - anger (same as above).
    - avoidance behaviors (same as above).
    - reluctance to discuss intimate details.
    - anxiety (same as above)
    - nervousness
    - discomfort
    - sadness
    - uses developmentally age appropriate/inappropriate terms. (e.g., "Daddy sticks his peanut in my poo-poo hole")

7. Does the child exhibit incredulity at questions regarding the intimate or distasteful aspects of the crime that he would have experienced if it actually happened to him?
    - semen in the mouth.
    - oral copulation of the vagina, anus, or penis

8. Does the child fit into the profile of the false reporter?
    - a bright adolescent.
    - has an axe to grind with the offender and/or a motive to lie (consider this of parents also).
    - is overly angry.
    - alleges vaginal intercourse only, with absolutely no other activity.
    - alleges overly bizarre behavior and acts that have little relationship to stimulation.

9.  What was the context of the statements made by the child?
    - were they spontaneous or in response to direct questioning?
    - what was the context of the question posed?
    - what was the context of the answer provided?
    - was the statement produced in the context of therapy, and if so, was it volunteered?
    - was the statement produced in the context of questioning and if so, was there any affect on the statement?
10. What corroborative facts exist?
    - physical evidence.
    - medical evidence.
    - statements or documents.
11. What has been the response of the alleged offending party?
12. What statements has he made to others?
13. What opportunity did the alleged offender have to commit the offenses?
14. What is known about the alleged offender and his background?

An example of the considerations which should be made may be seen in Figure 2.10. Note the idiosyncratic detail the child offers describing conduct, sensation, and physical evidence consistent with abuse.

Before leaving the subject of false reports, one last point must be made. It hurts the child and the investigator if the investigator covers up or ignores any possible conflict in a case. It hurts the child because the child may be confronted with the conflict on the witness stand at trial and be devastated because it is an unexpected attack. It hurts the investigator because his credibility will be damaged in this and later investigations and prosecutions.

If conflicts are discovered in a case, they should be presented in the police report in a factual manner. If there is a question about what should be presented in a police report, consult your local prosecutor for his opinion about the matter in question. The existence of conflicts doesn't necessarily mean that the case shouldn't be filed; it just means that the case won't be as cut and dried as it might be.

### Diminished Capacity or Insanity

Another common defense is that the offender didn't have the mental capacity to formulate the criminal intent to commit the crimes he is accused of at the time he committed the acts. This may either surface as a diminished capacity or insanity defense. What must be demonstrated here is consciousness of guilt, as described in Chapter 3 in the section on the lengths an offender will go to conceal his acts. What must be demonstrated to the court is anything that can be interpreted as a conscious, intelligent acknowledgment that the offender's actions were improper exhibited at the time the crime was committed. Any doubt an investigator can cast on the offender's claim that he wasn't capable of formulating the necessary intent at the time the act was committed can help to destroy his credibility. This defense usually takes the form of, "I was crazy. I didn't know what I was doing because I was drunk/on drugs/have the Vietnam Delayed Stress Syndrome, etc."

This is a good defense to work against because it involves either an admission or total confession, and hangs the offender's responsibility upon his inability to recognize the wrongfulness of the act at the time he committed it. Most child molesters convict themselves with this defense because they often reveal their recognition of the wrongfulness of the act, either when they are involved in the act itself, or immediately afterward when they tell the child to keep the "secret" or warn him not to tell anyone. The offender's reassurances of the legitimacy of the act(s), given to the child at the time they occur to overcome the child's resistance, may also help to establish knowledge of the wrongfulness of the act. Often the measures the offender takes to keep the crime a secret will also demonstrate this knowledge. What will help to establish this is determining and describing the measures he took to cover up the crime — before, during, and after:

1. Where does he contact the child when he finds him?
2. Is it from behind the bushes or other type of concealment?
3. Does he try to conceal his face or identity in some way?
4. Does he try to change his voice in some manner?
5. When he molests the child, does he do it out in the open where everyone can see him, or does he take the child into the bushes with him, around the corner away from everyone else, in his car to a remote location, or does he turn out the lights so no one will see it?
6. After he commits the crime, what does he do with the child?
7. Does he tie up the child so that he can't get away and report him before he escapes?
8. Does he drop the child off in a place where the child can't possible make a report because it's in the middle of nowhere?
9. Does he try to conceal the body or child after he leaves him?
10. Where does he put the pictures he takes of the child?
11. Are they in the same places as his "family" photos?
12. Are they hidden away somewhere where only he can get them?
13. What measures did the offender take to prevent his being discovered?
14. Did he use an alias, postal box, mail drop, or remailing service?
15. Did he give his own address in the correspondence, or did he use a "coded" address when advertising?
16. If he took pictures of children, where did he keep them?

17.  Were they hidden or in a readily available location?
18.  What measures were taken to create a hiding place?
19.  Did he build a false wall, floor, or hidden storage area?
20.  What kind of camera equipment did he use?
21.  Was it the type of film that develops immediately after taking the picture so no one will discover it in the developing process?
22.  Was it videotape, which requires no developing?
23.  Does he develop and print his own film?
24.  If he develops his film through a photo service, where does he have it done?

## Acts Don't Have the Necessary Intent

Still another defense is offered when the offender claims he did the act he is charged with but says he did it without the necessary intent or he wasn't engaged in a conscious course of conduct. To commit a crime, the act must be coupled with the requisite mental state or mens rea. In other words, this defense involves confessing to the act, but claiming it was done for some other reason. The confession may be in the form, "I did it, but I didn't have the required intent because I was doing something else," "I didn't know what I was doing;" or "I was forced to commit the act," etc. For example, in a case where a man groped the inside of the thigh of a boy who was "helping" him work on a plumbing job in a bathroom, the man claimed that he was "reaching for a tool" on the floor and "brushed" the inner thigh in the process. In another, the offender claimed that he didn't have the required intent because "I thought it was my wife," yet in another, the offender claimed he was asleep.

It is important to demonstrate/establish in these cases that the act was knowingly performed for sexual gratification. The child should be questioned about what the offender did during the act, in particular anything that is sexually oriented. Did the offender rub his (own) genitals, expose himself, or do anything else that indicates his sexual stimulation? It is also important to establish what the offender said during the act(s). Clearly, any reference to his excitement or interest in sexual matters would be relevant. For example, the plumber incident described above was committed while the man was asking the boy about his sexual experiences with age mates.

If the offender uses legitimate activities to conceal his acts, it is extremely important to try to get the child to articulate all of these elements because in cases where the activity may be consistent with a legitimate action, the court must and often does take the interpretation of innocence. To do this, it is often helpful to look for a pattern of action or conduct such as those described below.

This may also be accomplished with the discovery of evidence that will demonstrate a predilection to children, such as that described in Chapter 3. In addition, any evidence that will demonstrate that there is a pattern and, therefore, a predisposition for children, will help to corroborate the child's story and prove the offender's true interest.

Another way to demonstrate a conscious course of conduct is to demonstrate that the offender acted with a purpose, plan, or scheme. For example, in photographing children, child molesters and pornographers generally begin in a manner that will not alarm the child and that will ultimately seduce the child into compliance. As will be discussed further in this chapter in looking at the role of photographs and pornography and in the section on seduction methods, the order in which the photographs were taken may be important to demonstrate a plan. What should be examined are such things as the manner in which the offender progresses from one stage to another. Did he start with snapshots, go to swimming suits or underwear, then nude, and finally lewd or sexually explicit poses? An example of the claim of this defense may be seen in Exhibit 8.1 where he claimed he was asleep.

---

## EXHIBIT 8.1    INITIAL POLICE REPORT FILED BY A LINE OFFICER

---

C. (age 4) stated she was awakened sometime during the night, during which time she was lying on her right side. C._____ demonstrated that position, as well as the following, to Taylor and myself, while she was laying on the livingroom couch. C._____ stated that James pulled her panties down to her ankles (C._____ pointing to her ankles), lied her straight on her back, then on her left side towards him. C._____ stated that James then touched her bottom(pointing to her butt). At that point, C._____ stated she told James, "don't do that", with James replying, "what did I do?". C._____ stated James asked her if she needed to go to the bathroom. C._____ also mentioned that James touched her vagina and stomach, pointing to those areas), then pulled her panties back up.

According to Toni, James told her that on the night of 12/26/87, he went to bed late. James advised Toni that he slept with C._____ James stated he remembers dreaming that he was making love to his girlfriend, T._____, then woke up sometime between 0400–0500 hrs., 12/27/88, discovering that C._____'s panties were down and his hands were between her legs. James stated his pants were also down and he was "hard" (erected penis). Toni stated she asked James if C._____ was awake, and, if so, what was she doing?

---

**EXHIBIT 8.1   (CONTINUED)**

---

James stated C._____ was awake, her eyes were open and she was sucking her thumb. James stated he couldn't remember anything prior to waking up, but remembered saying "fuck", as soon as he woke up. at that point, James stated C._____ said "daddy, you said a bad word". James stated because he now realized what he was doing, he pulled C._____'s panties up, then asked C._____ what he had done. James stated C._____ said he was feeling her. James stated he asked C._____ if he had done anything else, with C._____ saying no. James stated he told C._____ he had a bad dream, that what happened was a mistake and that he felt bad about it. James stated he told C._____ that they would never sleep on the same bed again.

Toni stated at first, James told her he told C._____ she shouldn't tell anyone about it. James stated he then told C._____ that she can tell her mommy everything, and that she should tell her the truth. James told Toni that at approx. 0900 hrs., that same morning, C._____ told him he shouldn't have said a bad word and asked him if he remembered what he did.

There are two advantages of finding other children who, independently, give similar accounts or who say that the offender said or did similar things to them. It can show/demonstrate intent by demonstrating a similar plan or scheme, while at the same time, providing corroboration to the original allegation. What's more, if other offenses are established, it will provide additional charges to file.

## Mistaken Age

In many cases involving the teenaged child, the offender tries to claim he thought the child was over the age of majority. It is not enough to have the child say that he told the offender he was under the age of majority. Other evidence must be brought in to support the fact that the offender should have known the proper age of the child. If the investigation can show that the offender repeatedly picked up the child at school, this may be easier to prove. If the offender can be shown to frequent places with the child where only children in the victim's age group go, this may help to demonstrate knowledge of age. The age of other children with whom the offender associates may also help to prove this. Lastly, admissions made by the offender to friends, other children, and neighbors may help to establish this fact.

## Protective Custody Considerations

Removal of the child from the home often becomes a necessity, especially if the offender is a parent and there is little or no support for the child. The problem with this is that the child feels he is being punished because he is the person removed from the home. This creates difficulties in investigations because the child often will refuse to cooperate after being taken out of the home. It can also present some problems if the child refuses to admit any abuse and is kept in custody because it is felt he is at risk. In a celebrated case in the Midwest, some children were not interviewed until after they had been in protective custody for some time and were told that if they wanted to go home, they must tell about their abuse. Eventually the children said they were abused, according to authorities, because they wanted to return home. This cast a shadow on the veracity and integrity of the children's accounts and the investigation.

Many professionals feel that serious consideration should be given to leaving the child in the home if at all feasible. This should only be done when the child's family supports him, where there is no threat of contact with the offender, and constant contact is maintained with the family to ensure this remains the case. When children are taken into protective custody, every attempt should be made to limit the access others have to them to prevent "interrogations" that could be construed as coercion or that may contaminate the statements made.

Questioning of the child should be conducted only by the investigative staff assigned to the case. It may be suggested to foster parents that they give the child the opportunity to discuss his feelings about the abuse if he wishes; but they should be discouraged from questioning him about what happened. They should support the child's desire to tell, and should call a member of the investigative team to talk to the child. Rewards for disclosure should be minimized and special privileges carefully and sparingly given to prevent the child's making up details to get special consideration. In any case, no promises, except that of assurances of the child's safety, should be made or implied when talking to the child.

One way around some of the protective custody issues is to try to use the least restrictive alternatives possible. If the child can be released to a relative who supports the child and who will keep the child safe from the offending parent or any influences of the parents, this option should be tried. In this situation, the child will feel a greater degree of comfort as the surroundings and support systems available are familiar and respected. Whatever is done with the child, the impact on the case of taking the child into protective custody must be considered.

## When to Arrest the Offender

The same considerations about when to arrest the offender — such as flight, destruction of evidence, and so on — will apply in cases of sexual exploitation of children as in any other type of case. The major considerations are how the arrest will affect the investigation, and is it necessary to protect the community. For example, if the father in an incest case is arrested, often the family will close ranks to protect him and will not cooperate with the investigation whereas, had he not been arrested, they might be more cooperative. In extrafamilial cases, if it is found that the offender is actively seeking sexual liaisons with children and that any delay in arrest or apprehension will peril more children, every effort should be made to arrest the offender. This is why if a correspondence case reveals a possible victim, regardless of whether it will expose a "sting operation," immediate measures must be taken to arrest the offender and/or protect the child.

## Major Case Investigation: Managing the Unmanageable

In a case where there is a single victim, single offender or a small number of victims and a single offender, the techniques described thus far will serve the investigator well. However, where the case begins to blossom into multiple victims, multiple offenders, large distances with multiple locations, it becomes more complicated for a single investigator or team to handle.

For example in the McMartin investigation in Los Angeles, there were over 200 interviews that had to be conducted within a period of several weeks once the case surfaced. This posed a serious problem for a small agency to handle and subsequently it was handled by a team of investigators.

The form that the team takes can vary, depending upon the resources available to the investigator and the philosophy of the handling agencies. The important thing to recognize is that there are going to be times where such a team is necessary.

What the McMartin case and many others throughout the country established is that there must be a contingency plan in place *before* such a case happens. Much like the Mutual Aid plans in place for riots, fires, and other public disasters, a plan needs to be in place to handle the major case when it is reported. Roles of the players in this team should be carefully spelled out in a memorandum of understanding. The use of specialists in interviewing children and offenders, evidence gathering, record keeping, investigative strategies, etc., should be considered and prearranged to be available when the call comes.

The manner in which this team responds and conducts business may vary depending upon the make up of the team. An excellent discussion of a concept of multitasking, while addressing the many concerns of a case of this nature is found in *Team Investigation of Child Sexual Abuse* [18]. In this text, they describe the necessary team concerns and organization. More importantly, they describe *Macro Case Investigation*, a term they coined. This type of investigative team is very unique and its approach, in a perfect world, would be ideal.

Another good discussion about the problems of team investigation is contained in *Joint Investigations of Child Abuse* [19]. This publication discusses the kind of considerations most agencies must face in these cases and the problems in creating team approaches.

## Follow-up Investigations

Any follow-up should concentrate on obtaining all of the information not possible to obtain during the initial investigation phase. If the initial investigation was conducted by someone other than the investigator who is later assigned to handle the follow-up, that investigator should examine the case as though he were starting anew. He should review all of the reports and actions taken, to ensure that all the necessary steps were taken. He should try to avoid reinterviewing the child because each interview escalates the potential for confusion and conflict in accounts given by the child. It also increases the chances of further trauma experienced by the child. Generally, the safest practice is to reinterview the child by reviewing with the child the police report pertaining to the child's statement to ensure its accuracy and to see if the child can recall any new details. This will help to reduce the chances of confusion and conflict in recalling the events. The same techniques used in interviewing the child at the initial interview should be used in any subsequent interviews.

## Reporting and Documentation

Accounts of the children and witnesses should be written in their own words. Quotes should be used as much as possible. The investigator should avoid personal opinions and conclusions in his reports; any observations of this nature should be kept separate from the official reports and conveyed in memo form or verbally to other criminal justice personnel. Any premature conclusions or opinions made in a police report may be very damaging to both the case and the officer's credibility.

A detective sergeant wrote in a report of a case that he (correctly) concluded that a child was lying to him when she denied that her father had sexual contact with her. He also went on to describe how articulate and responsive she was, concluding that she was an "intelligent" child and that she was able to understand the situation and respond in a "programmed" fashion. In court, after the child took the stand, his conclusions were used to attempt to destroy her credibility, with the defense taking the position that the officer had programmed her, not the father. What should have happened in this circumstance is that the investigator should have recorded the answers in the factual, specific, and precise manner they came out. This would have prevented the defense from getting into the "opinion" evidence, and would have reduced the negative impact of this conclusion coming from an "authoritative" individual such as the investigating officer.

The same is true for the "qualifying" of a child to ensure that he understands what truth is. Qualification is an examination the child must pass in court before a judge who will determine if the child's testimony may be heard. What is examined is the child's competency to understand the significance of the oath he will take to testify truthfully, not his credibility. The child must demonstrate two things:

1. His ability to understand that he must tell the truth and that it is wrong not to do so.
2. He understood what happened to him and can communicate it in a coherent fashion to the trier of fact.

There is much debate whether this practice should still be used in court. The trier of fact is often denied the child's testimony, although the child understands the tested concepts, because the child cannot convey that understanding to the judge who qualifies him. Many contend that ultimately this prevents the trier of fact from evaluating the child's credibility. The decision to cease doing this test should be one an investigator should consult with his local prosecutor's office about. However, if an investigator must do the test, it should not be reflected in the police report, as it is an opinion. Like the other opinions, it should be conveyed to the prosecutor in the form of a memo or, better yet, verbally.

Factual observations should be included. These might consist of the notation of injuries the victim displays, or other evidence of trauma such as torn, soiled, or disarranged clothing and hair, or smeared make-up. The child's demeanor during the interview should be recorded in factual terms. If he cries, hesitates to talk, avoids answering questions by changing the subject, and so on, it should be documented. How the child feels about talking about the events should also be reported, using the child's own words. For example see Exhibit 8.2.

---

## Exhibit 8.2

---

"He volunteered 'my dad hurt me, you know'. He was hurt by running upstairs, he slid down, he 'hid', 'he (father) found me and hurted me.' 'He put his penis in my bottom and he hurt me.' 'He (the boy) was hiding, 'behind the door,' 'He unzipped his zipper, took his penis out and he hurt me.' This incident occurred 'in the family room', that 'no one else was present.' 'I ran away from him'. The father caught him and put him in the bathtub 'and he hurted me again.' 'He hurted me again' when out of the bathtub. (the boy) states that his incident occurred when he was '4 years old.' After he was out the bathtub 'he pulled down my pajamas, brushed

## Exhibit 8.2 (CONTINUED)

his teeth, 'dad read some stories'. When asked where father hurt him, (the boy) said 'down there…private parts…it hurt when he put his penis in me.' that it 'felt not good.' The worker pointed (to) some abrasions on his knees and asked how those feel - 'not good.' The worker asked who's family room… 'my dad's family room.' (the boy) states father didn't say anything to him during the incident, (but the boy) said 'stop but he wouldn't listen.' (the boy) indicates that fathers penis 'it's really long and it's round" and its skinny.'

Reports should be written to reflect any relevant information gained at a meeting or interview. To not do so may undermine the credibility of the investigation because it implies that things are being hidden. It is not necessary to write everything word for word, only to cover the discovery of new or relevant information and/or report the topics that were discussed. If nothing comes from an interview, the notation might read, "Discussed X with (the child), nothing new said." A sample form is shown in Figure 8.5.

Original notes should be maintained in accordance with department policy or law. Tape recordings should be maintained in the same fashion as all evidence. Some agencies have found that providing the prosecution with word-for-word transcriptions is helpful, but expensive. A report sample is shown in Exhibit 8.3. It could have more specific descriptions of how the sex acts occurred, but otherwise, it is a good example of how complicated and involved a multiple victim case can get.

### Making the Complicated Case Easier to Comprehend

In complicated cases where there is more than one victim, multiple incidents, or multiple offenders, a case summary might help to ensure that the points the investigator wishes to bring out are highlighted. This should be in addition to the police report. Charts showing the relationship of the "players" in the case or the type and number of offenses may also be helpful. This type of accompanying material helps to ensure that the prosecutor and anyone else who becomes involved in the case, after the investigator is finished with it, makes the proper connections and, more importantly, sees all the points the investigator feels are important. When this type of graphic charting and summary is completed, it helps the defense attorney to see how fruitless his going to court will be. An example of a case summary format can be seen in Figure 8.6.

As the instructions show, all that is required is a review of the facts of the case. An example of how one may be utilized is shown in Exhibit 8.6. This case involved incest, with two victims and multiple offenses over a period of time.

```
                       CHILD INTERVIEW REPORT


                         Date    |  Time Start  |  Time Finished
Rapport Building _____

Interview _____|_____|_____


Location/Room _____
_____


Persons Present/Location _____
_____
_____


Taped Y/N  Audio _____ Video_____


Media Used:
         Dolls_____Drawings_____Puppets_____
         Other _____

Report filed Y/N        Investigator's report_____Other_____

Miscellanous: _____
_____
_____
_____
_____
```

**Figure 8.5**  Child interview report form.

## Exhibit 8.3

IN THE MATTER OF: JAMES L. BUSH 3-23-70 (A MINOR)

*(names and addresses have been changed)*

VICTIM: Jeremy L. Sorat (13)

COUNT NUMBER ONE:

OCCURRED: ON OR ABOUT JUNE 1ST THU 30, 1980, ON A EVENING, APPROX 10 P.M., AT 1234 POPE AVE, NAPA, IN THE BACK YARD.

CHARGE: 288(a) CHILD MOLESTATION

ACT: ORAL COPULATION UPON THE VICTIM

COUNT NUMBER TWO:

OCCURRED: SAME AS COUNT NUMER ONE

CHARGE: 288(a) CHILD MOLESTATION

ACT: ORAL COPULATION PERFORMED BY VICTIM UPON THE MINOR

COUNT NUMBER THREE:

OCCURRED: ON OR ABOUT SEPT 1982 THRU JAN., 1983, 1234 PINE LANE, CALISTOGA, IN VICTIM'S BEDROOM

CHARGE: 288(a) CHILD MOLESTATION

ACT: ORAL COPULATION UPON THE VICTIM

COUNT NUMBER FOUR:

OCCURRED: SAME AS COUNT NUMBER THREE

CHARGE: 288(a) CHILD MOLESTATION

ACT: ORAL COPULATION PERFORMED BY THE VICTIM UPON THE MINOR

COUNT NUMBER FIVE:

OCCURRED: SAME AS COUNT NUMBER THREE

CHARGE: 288(b) CHILD MOLESTATION COMMITTED BY FORCE

ACT: ATTEMPTED FORCED SODOMY UPON THE VICTIM

VICTIM: Jason M. Sprat 2-19-74 (12)

*(continues)*

## Exhibit 8.3   (continued)

COUNT NUMBER SIX:

OCCURRED: ON OR ABOUT SEPT., 1982 THRU JUNE, 1983, 1234 POPE AVE, NAPA, IN MINOR'S BEDROOM.

CHARGE: 288(b) CHILD MOLESTATION COMMITTED BY FORCE

ACT: FORCED SODOMY


COUNT NUMBER SEVEN:

OCCURRED: ON OR ABOUT JULY 31, 1984, 1234 POPE AVE, NAPA, IN MINOR'S BED-ROOM.

CHARGE: 288(b) CHILD MOLESTATION COMMITTED BY FORCE OR THREAT OF BODILY HARM.

ACT: FORCED SODOMY


COUNT NUMBER EIGHT:

OCCURRED: ON OR ABOUT JULY 19, 1983, 1234 PINE LANE, CALISTOGA.

CHARGE: 288(b) CHILD MOLESTATION COMMITTED BY FORCE.

ACT: FORCED SODOMY.


VICTIM: Rebecca A. Sprat 7-18-74 (9)


COUNT NUMBER NINE:

OCCURRED: ON OR ABOUT JUNE 1, 1985 THRU JUNE 30, 1985, 1234 PINE LANE, CALISTOGA.

CHARGE: 288(b) CHILD MOLESTATION COMMITTED BY FORCE OR THREAT OF BODILY INJURY.

ACT: FORCIBLE ORAL COPULATION UPON THE VICTIM.


COUNT NUMBER TEN:

OCCURRED: SAME AS COUNT NINE.

CHARGE: SAME AS COUNT NINE.

ACT: FORCIBLE ORAL COPULATION BY THE VICTIM UPON THE MINOR.


COUNT NUMBER ELEVEN:

OCCURRED: SAME AS COUNT NINE.

CHARGE: SAME AS COUNT NINE.

ACT: FORCIBLE RAPE BY INSTRUMENTALITY

## Exhibit 8.3  (continued)

COUNT NUMBER TWELVE:
OCCURRED: SAME AS COUNT NINE.
CHARGE: SAME AS COUNT NINE.
ACT: FORCIBLE RAPE

VICTIM:  Timothy D. Davis 6-28-73 (12)

COUNT NUMBEER THIRTEEN:
OCCURRED: ON OR ABOUT JUNE 1, 1982, THRU AUGUST 31, 1982, 1234 POPE AVE, NAPA, IN THE MINOR'S BEDROOM.
CHARGE: 288(b) CHILD MOLESTATION COMMITTED BY FORCE
ACT: FORCED SODOMY.

COUNT NUMBER FOURTEEN:
OCCURRED: SAME AS COUNT THIRTEEN, EXCEPT ON THE BARN ROOF.
CHARGE: SAME AS COUNT THIRTEEN.
ACT: SAME AS COUNT THIRTEEN.

COUNT NUMBER FIFTEEN:
OCCURRED: SAME AS COUNT THIRTEEN EXCEPT AT THE VICTIM'S HOME ON OLD SONOMA RD, NAPA, IN THE BATHROOM.
CHARGE: SAME AS COUNT THIRTEEN.
ACT: SAME AS COUNT THIRTEEN.

COUNT NUMBER SIXTEEN:
OCCURRED: ON OR ABOUT SEPT. 1, 1981 THROUGH SEPT. 30, 1981, AT THE VICTIM'S HOME ON OLD SONOMA RD, NAPA.
CHARGE: 288(b) CHILD MOLESTATION BY FORCE OR VIOLENCE
ACT: FORCIBLE RAPE

VICTIM:  William "Billy" E. Davis 12-26-70 (15)

COUNT NUMBER SEVENTEEN:
OCCURRED: ON OR ABOUT OCT. 1, 1985 THRU DEC. 31, 1985, 1234 POPE AVE, NAPA, IN THE MINOR'S BEDROOM.
CHARGE: 288a (d) ORAL COPULATION COMMITTED BY FORCE OR FEAR.
ACT: FORCIBLE ORAL COPULATION UPON THE VICTIM.

## Exhibit 8.3   (continued)

COUNT NUMBER EIGHTEEN:

OCCURRED: SAME AS COUNT SEVENTEEN.

CHARGE: SAME AS COUNT SEVENTEEN.

ACT: FORCIBLE ORAL COPULATION BY THE VICTIM UPON THE MINOR.


COUNT NUMBER NINETEEN:

OCCURRED: SAME AS COUNT SEVENTEEN.

CHARGE: 286 (2) (c) SODOMY COMMITTED BY FORCE OR FEAR.

ACT: FORCIBLE SODOMY.


COUNT NUMBER TWENTY:

OCCURRED: ON OR ABOUT JUNE, 1983 THRU SEPT., 1983, 1234 POPE AVE, NAPA, ON THE BARN ROOF.

CHARGE: 288 (b) CHILD MOLESTATION COMMITTED BY FORCE.

ACT: ORAL COPULATION COMMITTED BY FORCE OR FEAR.


COUNT NUMBER TWENTY-ONE:

OCCURRED: SAME AS COUNT NUMBER TWENTY.

CHARGE: SAME AS COUNT NUMBER TWENBY.

ACT: ORAL COPULATION COMMITTED BY THE VICTIM UPON THE MINOR BY FORCE OR FEAR.


COUNT NUMBER TWENTY-TWO:

OCCURRED: SAME AS COUNT TWENTY.

CHARGE: SAME AS COUNT TWENTY.

ACT: FORCIBLE SODOMY.


STATEMENT OF FACTS


The minor's family was at one time close friends with the families of the victim in this case. They had met through and continued to associate with each other as a result of their church affiliations. For one semester of class, from Sept., 1982 to Jan., 1983, the minor attended the same private school, along with his brothers and sisters, as the Sprats. This school is a "one room schoolhouse" which is operated and taught by the Sprats at the Calistoga address.

The minor spent a great deal of the time with the families of the victims, often staying overnight with the victims at their homes and the victim often spent overnight sojourns at the minor's home.

## Exhibit 8.3 (continued)

Sexual acts began occurring between the minor and the victim as long as seven years ago and continued to the time when the first disclosures of the incidents described herein were made.

During the time that the minor was attending the school numerous incidents occurred which bear upon the potential threat the children felt he posed to themselves. They also attest to the behavioral signs of abuse in both the minor and the victim.

The minor was constantly picking on the children in the school. He was seen to be making lewd gestures towards the other children and upon himself, such as rubbing his groin in such a fashion as to simulate masturbation or self-stimulation. He would also make suggestive comments to the other children in the school.

He dominated the other children, virtually all of whom were younger than he. He had great difficulty in getting along with the other children and was often hitting, kicking or bullying the other children in some way. He would "retaliate" upon the victims for "acts" they were supposed to have done to his brothers or sisters. In short, he was described to have terrorized most of the victim children so much, so that none of this behavior ever came out until after he was arrested and the children felt safe to tell about it.

Virtually all of the victim children voiced a fear of the minor, describing him as being much bigger than they and violent either during the commission of the sexual acts or in other situations (association or play). With few exceptions, the children all said that they feared being physically harmed by the minor, regardless of whether or not he actually threatened them.

The incidents occurred at the minor's home and the homes of the victims. In all but a very few of the incidents, they occurred with singular victims and there were no witnesses to the acts.

The incidents surfaced after Rebecca Sprat disclosed to her brother what was happening to her and he told a friend who told her mother. The mother told the Sprat parents and they began to investigate by questioning their own children and, subsequently, the Davis'.

The Sprat family had lived in three different cities over the period of time that the abuse occurred. They first lived in Vallejo moving to Napa in 1977. They then moved to the Calistoga address in Dec., 1979.

The Davis family lived in several locations in South County, living on Smithe in American Canyon until March of 1980. They then moved to a ranch on Old Sonoma Rd., in Napa, in June of 1980. On Sept. 25, 1983, they moved to their present address in Pope in Napa.

The Davis family has only been attending the school run by the Sprats since Sept. of 1985.

INVESTIGATION:

On 3-5-86, I interviewed Jeremy L. Sprat at his home. He told me that the minor engaged him in acts of mutual oral copulation, which he described as "sucking penis'" over the past six or seven years. He estimated the number of separate incidents as being approx 20 in number. He

---

**Exhibit 8.3**   (CONTINUED)

---

said that these acts occurred in the minor's bed, Jeremy's bed, and once or twice in the minor's "fort" which was made of wood pallets and situated in his backyard. Most of the time the incidents would occur at night when he and the minor would stay over night at each other's houses.

He said most of the time the minor would get him to perform the acts by coercing him into it by saying things like: "Do it or I won't be your friend...Don't be a whimp." On one occasion (described in detail below), the minor forced him into an act of sodomy by physically overpowering him.

Other times when they slept over at each other's houses, the minor would make sexual advances and Jeremy would say "no." He said that when he refused the minor wouldn't pursue it. He also said that sometimes he wouldn't allow the minor to reciprocate in the acts of oral copulation.

He said that he was afraid to tell at first. He also said that he was too embarrassed to tell about it. What prompted him to tell was when his sister, Rebecca, came to tell him what was happening to her. Even then he didn't tell anyone in authority, but rather, told a friend who in turn, told her mother. He also didn't tell about what happened to him, only what happened to Rebecca. He said that he was too embarrassed to tell about himself and it was his parents to whom he first disclosed when they asked him.

This happened at a party in June of last year. He told Kerry Choice, who is a friend of his mother's.

He said that in order to get him to perform the acts, the minor told him, on several occasions, that he had done the similar things to Billy Davis.

He said that on several occasions he saw *Playboy* magazines in the minor's "fort" and under his bed. He was able to properly describe the content of *Playboy.*

He said that the minor bragged to him about having a bigger penis than he, about getting *Playboy* magazines, and being able to ejaculate when Jeremy couldn't. Jeremy doesn't believe anyone else heard these claims.

Jeremy said that just before the molestations came to light, the minor had bragged about having sex with girls, admitting that he had sexual intercourse with several girls at the school he was going to at the time. Jeremy believes this to have been Vallejo Christian.

Jeremy said that the sexual acts stopped about one to one-and-one-half years ago when the minor tried to get him to orally copulate the minor and he refused.

When asked how he felt about what happened to him, Jeremy said that he was afraid about being "caught" because he knew that what they were doing was wrong. He didn't like what the minor was doing to him.

## EXHIBIT 8.3   (CONTINUED)

Jeremy said that the first incident occurred just after he had moved into his new house in Calistoga. He estimated this to have been approx two months after they had settled in. He believed that he was about seven or eight years old. He described the incident to have occurred on an evening when the two were staying over night at one or the other's home.

He said that the minor asked him to "suck his penis" and that he refused. He said that the minor pleaded with him until he did.

Jeremy said that after he performed an act of oral copulation upon the minor, the minor told him that if he ever told about what happened, the minor would "beat me up."

He said that the act was performed while they were laying in bed. Jeremy did it to the minor and then the minor performed a reciprocating act. He said that acts lasted for about 10 minutes, but neither of them "sucked" for the entire time.

He described the minor's penis as "sticking straight out" and that it was "stiff."

The second incident he remembers occurred in the minor's "fort" in his backyard in Napa. It occurred aprox six months after he moved to Calistoga, in the nighttime, after dark, perhaps around 10 P.M. It was in the summertime because he was out of school. He believes he was eight to eight-and-one-half years old. He said that he was visiting the Bush family with his mother.

Jeremy said that it started by the minor's asking him "Do you want to do it?' When he declined, he said that the minor continued pressuring him until he acquiesced.

He said that the minor had him perform an act of oral copulation, using the terms described above. He said that the minor told him to stop. Once the minor took his penis out of the victim's mouth he would begin to rub it himself until he ejaculated. He described the minor masturbating himself until he ejaculated upon the ground.

He said that he learned the term "ejaculation" from his mother when he was describing what had happened.

He said that after the minor ejaculated he offered to "let me do you", meaning that he was asking to perform an act of oral copulation upon the victim. Jeremy said that, being afraid, he allowed him to do so.

He said that by this time, after having been involved in the aforementioned sex acts and the manner in which the minor was acting, that he understood he should not tell about what happened.

The third incident he remembers occurred three to four years ago. He said that it was after school started, around mid-fall. It happened when the minor was staying overnight in Jeremy's at his home in Calistoga in his bedroom. In discussing this with his mother after the interview,

---

## Exhibit 8.3   (continued)

---

we determined this to be the school semester of Sept., 1982 thru Jan., 1983, due to the fact that it was the only semester that the minor attended the school.

In this incident the mutual oral copulation occurred much in the same manner as in the previous incident described above. However, on this occasion, the minor asked Jeremy if he would allow him to "stick my dick in your butt." The victim refused, but the minor tried anyway.

Jeremy described this act as the minor was grabbing the victim forcefully and pushing him over and trying to insert his penis in the victim's anus. He said that it happened so fast and with such force that he couldn't stop him. Jeremy said that he resisted after he was turned over and that the minor stopped as a result.

He said that the last acts of oral copulation occurred approx two months before he got the nerve up to say no. He said that he believed these acts of mutual oral copulation occurred in his home, on an overnight stay.

On the same date I also spoke with Jason M. Sprat. He said that the minor forced him to do work or chores that the minor was supposed to do and that the way he forced him was to either spank or threaten to spank him. Jason said that he was forced to engage in acts of sodomy with the minor on at least three occasions. He said that he also saw *Playboy* magazines in the minor's possession. On one occasion he was with the minor's brother, Mathew, and saw the minor reading the magazine while sitting on his bed in his bedroom.

He said that after each act the minor would warn him not to tell by threatening to "kill" him. He said that he first told about what happened to his parents when they asked him about it.

He remembers the first incident to have occurred when he was in the fourth grade when both his mother and the minor's mother were teachers. He believes he was nine or ten years old and that it occurred at the minor's home. It occurred on an afternoon. He believes that he was wearing a pair of shorts and a short sleeve shirt.

In discussing this incident with his mother after the interview, we determined that it must have occurred between Sept., 1982 and Jan., 1983 because James was in kindergarten and Jason must have been in the third grade.

He said that his mother was out looking at property and had all of the kids with her at the time. They had stopped at the Carter's for lunch.

He said that the minor took him to his bedroom to "show (him) something." Once in the bedroom, the minor physically threw him on the bed. The minor told him to take off his pants and he felt that if he didn't the minor would beat him up. He said that the minor pulled down his own pants and "stuck his penis in my rear end."

Using a Cabbage Patch doll and a teddybear, he demonstrated the positions he and the minor were in. Demonstrated his being forced to lay face down on the bed with the minor laying on top of him.

## EXHIBIT 8.3 (CONTINUED)

He demonstrated the minor's movements by rocking the hips of the toy in the manner the hips would move in intercourse.

He described the minor's penis as long, "stuck straight out", and stiff. He said that when the minor inserted his penis in the victim's rectum, it "hurt."

He said that when the act was completed, the minor told him he would "kill" him if he told.

Both went out to play afterwards and began to play. He said that "Aunt Taffy" (the minor's mother) and his own mother were in the house at the time of the act.

He said that afterward he was afraid and that his "read end hurted." He said that he told his mother that it hurt, but said that he had hit it on something. He said that she told him that it would get better soon.

The next incident he described happened about a year ago when he was going from the fifth grade into the sixth. It happened in his bedroom on a summer evening, about a month after he had gone on a camping trip near a lake with his Aunt Julie.

After the interview, his mother helped to place this camping trip to have been on or about July 31, 1984, around the time of her sister's birthday.

On this occasion, another act of sodomy occurred like that described above.

The next incident he described occurred approx one-and-one-half years ago. It happened on the weekend day of a birthday celebration held at his home for Rebecca. Present at the house were the Davis', the Bush's and the victim's two sets of grandparents. The incident happened after the family had cake and ice cream.

Talking with the mother after the interview, we were able to place this as happening the week of July 19, 1983.

On this occasion, one act of sodomy was performed in the same fashion as on previous occasions.

I also talked with Rebecca Sprat. She said that she was forced to "suck his penis" more than 20 times. She said that most of the time all of the incidents occurred at the minor's house.

She said that until she told, she thought she was the only one that the minor was doing these things to. It wasn't until she saw Mathew "sucking" the minor's penis the day she told her brother about what was happening to her that she realized that there was someone else who was being abused.

She said that on each occasion where she was forced to commit acts with the minor, he told her that not only would he kill her if she told, but, that he would kill her mother and father as well.

---

## Exhibit 8.3   (continued)

---

She said that she was forced to engage in acts of sodomy with the minor on at least ten to twenty occasions. She described the acts and feeling pressure by his penis on her rectum and that it "hurted."

She said that the minor "stuck a pencil" in her rectum on at least five occasions.

She estimated that she was forced to engage in sexual intercourse with the minor on no less than 10 occasions.

She also estimated that the minor had performed acts of oral copulation upon her on more occasions than she was compelled to do it to him. She said that he would "suck" on her "Pee-Pee" and that he would stick his tongue inside her "Pee-Pee."

With the use of the doll and teddybear, she confirmed the locations of the body parts she was describing and simulated the acts he was forced to engage in.

She said that on numerous occasions, for little reason or no provocation, the minor would punch or hit her in the head. On many occasions, the minor would actually pick her up and throw her around. She described one occasion where the minor actually picked her up and threw her on the couch and then molested her.

She said that she has seen the minor bathing his sister, Christina alone and slapping her violently when she doesn't do what he wants.

She also said that on one occasion, several years ago, she saw Mathew "sucking" the minor's penis at their "hide-out", but didn't tell anyone because was afraid of the consequences of telling. She said that he had threatened her not to tell anything about what he had done. She said she forgot about this incident when she told me earlier that she didn't know of anyone else who was abused.

Although she didn't have a word for ejaculation, she described the minor as having done it in the bathroom on one occasion when he assaulted her. She said that "white stuff came out" of the end of the penis, slowly, "spilling" over the head. She said that it was thinner than "pee", but that it didn't come out for as long a time as "pee."

She described the minor's penis as long, stiff, and that it stuck straight out. She said that it had hair on it and I had her draw a picture of where the penis was and where the hair was on it. She drew in the hair as being on the shaft of the penis. She said that it was sparse hair, comparing it to the density of the hair on my arm.

She described the last incident to me as occurring in her mother's bedroom closet, on the floor, occurring on the date that she told her brother about the abuse, in the evening.

She said that the minor told her to cooperate or he would kill her. He engaged her in oral copulation with her laying on her back and then he had her switch positions and she orally copulated him.

## Exhibit 8.3 (continued)

With the doll and teddybear, she simulated the positions. She also confirmed the positions of the body parts she described by use of the toys. During the positioning of the dolls, she rotated the hips of the toy representing the minor to simulate the action he was engaged in during intercourse.

She said that when she was orally copulating the minor, he forced her head down on the penis, even though she was choking and gagging.

She said that he forced his finger into her "Pee-Pee" and that it hurt.

She said that he orally copulated her three times, switching positions between each act. She said that she orally copulated him twice, switching positions after he stopped her to do something else.

She said that while she was laying on her back, he inserted his fingers into her vagina, using his "little" finger, showing me her pinkie. This only occurred once.

She also said that at the same time, after doing the other sex acts, the minor forced her to engage in sexual intercourse. She said that his occurred three times, again, stopping between each act before resuming.

I also spoke with James Sprat. He said that he was forced to engage in oral copulation and sodomy with the minor, but was unable to estimate when any of the acts occurred. He said that the acts occurred at the minor's house and told of several acts of oral copulation and sodomy. He used the dolls to reenact the positions he was forced to be in and described what happened to him.

He said that the minor would yell and threaten to hurt him to get him to do what it was the minor wanted. He also said that the minor told him that if he ever told, the minor would beat him up.

On 3-6-86 I spoke with Timothy D. Davis. He said that he has known the minor since he was born. He described the minor as a friend of the family.

In cases where the location of one room relative to another is important, diagrams of the crime scene should be made. In the case described in Exhibit 8.4, the relationship of the mother's bedroom to the brother's bedroom was clearly an issue because the boy supposedly heard his sister crying and screaming while he was in his bedroom and she was being assaulted in the mother's bedroom. A diagram was drawn of the second level of the house to show the close proximity of the two rooms.

In cases where the relationship between the individuals involved is important and confusing, charts may help to make them easier to understand. Figure 8.7 is an example of a linkage chart that shows the relationships

```
┌─────────────────────────────────────────────────────────────────────────┐
│                      BERKELEY POLICE DEPARTMENT                           │
│                                                                           │
│             CASE SUMMARY FOR PROSECUTING ATTORNEY          No. .............│
│                                                                           │
│   Defendant _____ Age _____ Charge _____  │
│   Defendant _____ Age _____                          │
│   Arrested By _____ Date _____ Hour _____  │
│                                                                           │
│                                       Where Was Crime                     │
│   Where Arrested _____ Committed _____  │
│   Complainant _____ Address _____ Phone _____ │
│   Victim _____ Address _____ Phone _____ │
│                                                                           │
│   INSTRUCTIONS:  USE ONLY ONE SIDE OF PAPER. IF THERE ARE MORE THAN TWO DEFENDANTS, USE PLAIN │
│   PAPER AND INCLUDE THE INFORMATION CALLED FOR ABOVE. THE FOLLOWING DATA SHOULD BE SUMMARIZED IN │
│   THE ORDER AND UNDER THE HEADINGS SHOWN.                                  │
│                                                                           │
│        STATEMENT OF FACTS                                                 │
│        EVIDENCE                                                           │
│        WITNESSES   (NAME, ADDRESS, TELEPHONE AND TESTIMONY THAT CAN BE GIVEN RELATIVE TO │
│                    STATEMENT OF FACTS ABOVE)                               │
│        DEFENDANT'S CRIMINAL RECORD                                        │
│        REMARKS                                                            │
└─────────────────────────────────────────────────────────────────────────┘
```

**Figure 8.6**  Sample format for a case summary. (Courtesy of Berkeley Police Department, Berkeley, California.)

between children and the offender, a foster parent who was molesting them. It is intended to demonstrate the way the children were introduced to the offender. This case involved 18 victims and multiple acts in various locations throughout the state of California.

## EXHIBIT 8.4  CASE SUMMARY (NAMES AND ADDRESSES CHANGED)

Victim:          Susanne _____, WFJ 9 yrs        Albany

                 John _____, WMJ 24 yrs          Albany

Defendants:      Walter Smith, WMA 42 yrs          LKA Oakland

                 Joanne _____, WFA 40 yrs        Albany

Statement of Facts:

Joanne _____ is the victim's natural mother. The victim lives with her mother and her brother Joan (14). Joanne _____ met Smith through an ad in a paper and was later married in November. Smith lives in Oakland and comes to stay with his wife on Tuesdays, Thursdays, and holidays. On weekends Joanne goes to stay with her husband in Oakland.

Shortly after the marriage Susanne was forced to become sexually involved with Smith. Her mother compelled her to cooperate with him and actually engaged in sexual acts with both her daughter and Smith at the same time. On many occasions she physically prevented her daughter from screaming or crying by holding her hand over her daughter's mouth while Smith was attempting or actually having sexual intercourse with her. During the act she also held her daughter's legs down.

## Exhibit 8.4 (continued)

Joanne would require Susanne to sleep in the same bed with her husband and take away her clothes when he was visiting. Susanne was not allowed to return to her room until the morning after the sexual activity.

Joanne also had Susanne pose for pornographic pictures. Over 100 pictures were taken with Susanne posing in positions where she was spreading her legs and her labia with her fingers. She was also photographed by her mother while orally copulating with Smith.

Joanne also photographed her son in the nude, sitting on his motorcycle, genitals exposed.

Around Easter, Susanne told her brother that she was "having sex" with her stepfather against her will and that she was being forced to sleep with Smith nude. On July 14th, while visiting her father, she told her father's girlfriend. Shortly afterward the case was brought to the attention of the Albany Police Dept.

Det. Jones investigated the case and took both Susanne and John into protective custody. He also interviewed Joanne. He prepared and served two search warrants, finding nothing of significance.

Evidence:

Diagram of floor plan of house; medical exam; photos of locations.

Witnesses:

John will testify to his seeing his sister going into the bedroom of his mother and stepfather on numerous occasions. He will testify to the fact that he heard his sister crying while in that bedroom and on one occasion when he heard his sister cry, he heard his mother tell her to be quiet. He will testify that his sister told him that she was being forced to participate in sex acts. He will testify that his mother took pictures of him while he was nude, intending to give them to Smith. He will testify that Smith is a photographer.

Georgia, Susanne's natural father's girlfriend, will testify to the fact that Susanne was upset and distraught about the forced sexual activity, and to what she was told when this all came to light.

Summary of Offenses:

On or about the week of Dec. 5–11, Joanne took nude pictures of her son which depicted his genitals for the purposes of satisfying the lust or passions of her (then) boyfriend, Smith.

On or about Dec. 2nd at 9–9 PM Joanne compelled Susanne to take off her clothes and sleep with her (now) husband, Smith, who tried to rub her back while she lay beside him.

On or about the weeks of Dec. 12–16/Jan. 3rd, Joanne forced (by threatening to take away privileges and personal property) Susanne to take off her clothes and perform oral copulation upon Smith by licking his penis while she (Joanne) also did the same.

On the same night, Joanne made Susanne sleep, naked, in the bed with and beside Smith, who was naked. He lay beside her with his erect penis against her buttocks while he rubbed her vagina with his left hand.

The next morning, when Susanne awoke, her mother forced her to copulate orally with Smith while she (her mother) did the same.

On or about the weekend of June 10th, 11th, and 12th, while on a camping trip along the San Joaquin Delta, Susanne was forced to copulate orally with Smith while a photograph was taken by Joanne.

## EXHIBIT 8.4 (CONTINUED)

On or about July 9th or 10th, at approximately 2–3 PM, Joanne forced Susanne to submit to sexual intercourse with him. Aware of what was going on, but outside the house (Oakland), was her mother.

On or about July 12th about 8 PM Susanne was forced to engage in an act of sexual intercourse with Smith. During the act her legs were held down by her mother and her cries squelched by her mother putting her hand over her mouth.

On or about Christmas Day, Easter Sunday, Mat 5th (or mother's day), May 10th, June 19th, and February 28, 1983, Joanne took nude pictures of Susanne in lewd poses or for the purposes of satisfying the lust or passions of Smith.

Defendant's Criminal Record:

Smith has a prior arrest for drunk driving in San Jose. CII shows no other arrests. FBI inquiry has not returned.

As of this time, no record has been found on Joanne.

Remarks:

Photos were taken of the Oakland home by Det. Jones. A medical exam was performed. As is noted above, although Susanne said that she was forced to perform sexual acts with Smith *on each and every occasion* that he visited the Albany home, we were only able to establish dates or approximate times for the incidents listed above.

Seth L. Goldstein, Investigator

9:55 PM

## Proving Intent

An element of child molestation, and therefore establishing that a crime was committed, is proving the intent of the offender — that is, he intended to do something sexual vs. an "innocent" act or an act for another purpose. It is often difficult to demonstrate intent when only one incident is reported. However, it is more difficult for the offender to explain his repeating the behavior when it is found that there are either numerous incidents with a single victim or multiple victims and/or multiple incidents with those children. *This is important because seldom is the offense under investigation the offender's first or the only one involving the child reporting it.*

Few incidents are isolated, and it is not uncommon to find other children or offenders involved. Sometimes it is possible to find connections to the underground, or other individuals connected to the offender. The discovery of this information, and interviewing of the children involved in multiple incidents, can both help to prove intent and corroborate the original complaining child's testimony.

An example of how this might have helped to convict a teacher of a junior high school can be seen in a case described in the search warrant in Appendix

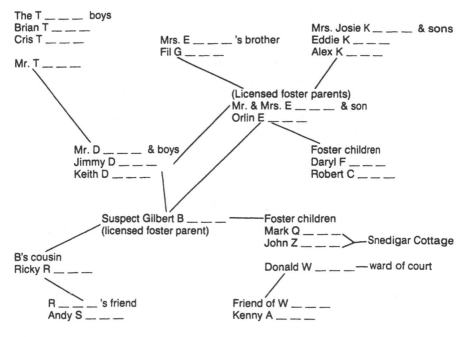

**Figure 8.7** Linkage chart. (Courtesy Hayward Police Department [CA].)

III. In this case, the investigator only interviewed the child involved and the witness who was immediately at hand, the boy's father. The boy claimed he was molested by a man who talked to him about sexual matters and who "groped" him while the two were working in a bathroom. When the original complaint was investigated, neither the field officer nor the follow-up detective interviewed the boy's brothers, who both told the boy's father after the incident surfaced that on other occasions the man had said similar things to them. Both the brothers and the parents of the boy also described other boys seen in the company of the offender at various other times who were in the same age group as the original victim.

Unfortunately, this information came forward three days before the misdemeanor trial, when the deputy district attorney who was to try the case interviewed the victim. Although the search warrant was drawn up and signed by a judge, the attorney decided not to serve the warrant because it might have been construed as harassment if nothing was found, and would have made both the police department and the district attorney's office look as though they were trying to intimidate the defendant into not proceeding with a trial. The brothers' information was important but appeared to be "self-serving;" it was discounted by the jury, which acquitted the teacher. However, had this information been developed at the time of the initial investigation it might have proved very damaging when the other boys the offender was seen with were identified and interviewed, especially had they said they were also solicited or had they told of being molested.

This case is also an excellent example of how certain answers to questions — which will be suggested next — can help secure a search warrant for corroborative evidence. In this case, note that the original incident described by the complaining boy was a single, minor offense. Although by California statute it was a felony, it was charged as a single misdemeanor. As a result of the answers to many of the questions that follow, a search warrant was obtained for a single-incident molest with little or no known evidence to speak of.

## Corroborating the Victim's Account

According to the American Bar Association (ABA), the premises that underlie the need for corroboration in child molestation cases are:

1.  That sex offenses have unique problems of complainant credibility.
2.  That children have unique problems of complainant credibility.

David Lloyd, writing for the ABA, says that the need for corroboration is also:

1.  To overcome societal myths.
2.  To fulfill the requirement of the state (in some states).
3.  To avoid a reversal following a conviction on the basis of insufficient evidence [20].

Just how damaging independent corroborative statements that provide support for a single victim's account can be is demonstrated in the case of an attorney who had been accused of "groping" a young boy he was counseling in a church program. The defense based its case on the fact that the child was a "problem child" and clearly had falsely accused the lawyer, who was an "outstanding citizen" in the community. Using the profile of the identified victim, the investigators researched all of the names of children the lawyer had had contact with. After interviewing about 30 boys, the investigators found seven new victims who were molested in much the same fashion as the one who originally reported the crime. As soon as the lawyer learned of the success of the investigation, he pleaded guilty on the first charge and served time in state prison.

Corroboration also assists in supporting the complaining child's credibility. One point must be made, however, before discussing this topic. One of the greatest difficulties encountered in cases of child molestation is the fact that *seldom is there any corroboration*. Cases most often involve a one-on-one situation, with no witnesses to the act or evidence that will directly prove the acts occurred. Corroboration may consist of physical instruments or evidence of abuse; concurring accounts or observations of other witnesses; or incriminating statements made by the offender. Such evidence may prove the act itself in a direct fashion or it may support the child's allegations through circumstantial evidence. In addition, this evidence can be used to demonstrate a propensity or abnormal sexual desire for children (a necessary element of the offense). The search for this evidence must be begun before or at the same time charges are filed or an arrest is made in order to avoid destruction of or tampering with evidence.

Corroboration can also be established by finding things the child describes in the home, vehicle, or at the location where the incident occurred. In the discussion about the identity defense, we see how this helps the victim. Here the officer seeks to find evidence that can, independently, confirm facts supplied by the child and identify the offender.

An example of this is a case in which a teen-age girl was walking home from school with her books in her arms. She was kidnapped by two men who dragged her down to a creek. They forced her to take off her clothes after knocking the books out of her hands, forced her into several acts of oral copulation, raped her, and left her. After the offenders were gone for a while, the girl finally found the courage to get dressed, walk to a neighboring home, and report the incident to the police. The responding patrol officer did a great job of documenting the incident by reporting what the victim said happened to her. However, although he described the victim's clothing as being soiled and gave a description of the minor bruises she displayed, he did little else to establish the necessary elements of force or fear. The officer made no attempt to locate the crime scene. The detective who got the case the next day saw the problem and did locate the scene. He found the books scattered about where they had fallen. He also found a receipt on the ground from a fast food restaurant that was clearly recently dropped on the ground as it displayed no signs of weathering. Being the thorough investigator he was, he took the receipt and had it examined for latent prints. Prints of the index finger and thumb of one of the offenders were found.

Clearly, the investigator did an excellent job. The problem with this great piece of evidence was the amount of time that had passed between the rape and when the receipt was found. The defense in this case would have little difficulty in coming up with an argument that would discount the receipt's discovery. However, again to the detective's credit, he was able to interview the offender and get him to confess and name his co-participant, which resulted in a guilty plea.

## Question Checklist for Corroboration

1. Did the child ever tell about the incidents and to whom? What did they tell them?

**Comment.**   Be sure to determine how (what words were used) and under what circumstances the child told whomever was told. It might help to have the child describe what the reaction was on the part of those he told. It may explain why the complaint wasn't made sooner.

2. Have the child describe the offender, his home, or his car in as much detail as possible, noting unique or unusual observations of the offender's person (scars, birthmarks, etc.), clothing, house (furniture, decorations, linen, etc.), or vehicle.

**Comment.**   Try to search for, verify, and document as much as possible. The most trivial point may become crucial at trial.

3. Determine the number and specific acts committed by both the victim and the offender.

**Comment.**   This is one of the more difficult questions for the child. As mentioned, the entire story may never be learned as the child may be embarrassed about certain aspects of what happened. The problem is that there are generally only two people who know what really happened — the offender and the child. If the child doesn't tell everything about what happened, the offender may come up with some way of explaining some of the activity the child has hedged on, and make the child appear to be lying when questioned on the stand. Every effort must be made to secure as much information as possible about what happened. the advantage of establishing more than one offense is that the crimes may be charged "stacked" on each other. This may accomplish two things.

    a. It will assure that the offender is off the street longer if convicted.
    b. It may induce a plea bargain.

It may be accomplished in several ways.

    a. Finding multiple victims.
    b. Establishing crimes with the same victim, but on different occasions.
    c. Establishing crimes with the same victim, same incident, but different acts.

4. Determine how the offender induced the child to perform or submit to the acts and exactly what words were used by the offender.

**Comment.** This is extremely important because in the case at hand it may not be possible to secure a complaint or indictment from the prosecutor because there is too little evidence. However, if within the statute of limitations, another offense is uncovered with a different child and it is found that the crime was committed in exactly the same manner, with the same MO, not only might the investigator be able to get the complaint or indictment on the new case, but on the original as well. In addition, enhancements (additional penalties) may apply if the offender used force or threatened the child. Threats may be established in several ways. They may not always be expressed; therefore, an implied threat may satisfy the enhancement requirement. The age, education, and mental facilities of the offender will be considered in determining the degree of threat. The position of trust, dominance, and authority will all be examined when looking at the child's perception of the events. To establish this element, the following questions should be asked:

a. How does the child feel about the offender?
b. What was he afraid of?
c. Was he threatened? If so, with what?
d. Why as the "secret" withheld?

Like threats, the element of force may also enhance the charges. It may be established in several ways. For the most part, force, for enhancement purposes, is substantially different from the force necessary to accomplish the act. In evaluating the degree of force, look at these criteria:
a. The age of the child.
b. The size of the victim vs. the size of the offender.
d. The sophistication of the child.
5. Distinguish and establish dates and times of incidents.

**Comment.** It is not necessary to have exact dates and times. All that is necessary is to establish a "window" of time. What must be done is to get the child to articulate separate, distinct incidents within a period of time. The charges must be specific enough so that the offender can tell one from another. For example, if the child can say that he was molested three times, sometime between the time he had is last birthday and the last Christmas — even if this covers a year — and he can articulate some specific details about the molest, it should be sufficient for charging.

Distinguishing the events may be established in several ways. It may be accomplished by the acts themselves. If the first time the acts involved only touching the child's genitals through the clothing, the second involved mutual masturbation, and the last involved everything previously described *and* oral copulation — this differentiates the events significantly enough to demonstrate that they are independent of one another. The same is true if the order of events can be distinguished. For example, if the same acts occurred each time, but in a different order, this is sufficient to distinguish the incidents.

They may be differentiated by time or location of the event. For example, if the first incident occurred in the boy's living room, the second at the offender's home in his living room, and the last in the offender's bedroom — this separates them sufficiently. If the first event occurred in the morning, the second in the afternoon, and the last in the evening — this, too, is sufficient.

The acts may be distinguished by the clothing the child wore at the time of each event. If the child wore his red pajamas in the first incident, a pair of shorts in the second, and blue jeans and a shirt in the third, and he can articulate this — it is sufficient. The same is true for the clothing of the offender.

What was said at the different incidents may distinguish them. The activity before, during, or after, each event may distinguish them. The people who were present may distinguish them. In short, anything that separates one event from another is sufficient to distinguish them for charging. The greater the number of distinguishing factors, the better. Don't stop just because you've established one; try to develop as many as possible.

Finally, establishing times or dates is not as hard as it might appear. Children relate to time differently from adults. They associate time or days with events. When trying to establish the hour of the day, ask the child questions relating to the child's activity during days in general and/or the day of the incident in particular. For example, if the child is preschool aged and you are trying to establish when a particular event occurred during the day, ask if he remembers the specifics of the day in question, and place the incident within the rest of the day's activities. If the child can't remember the specific things, use general activities that occur at the same time each day by asking the child what he did before or after the event. Was it before or after breakfast, lunch, or dinner? Was it before or after his nap?

This also works well for establishing the dates of the incidents if they occurred over a period of time. Ask the child to estimate the dates or days the incidents occurred on in relation to other things he did. For example, in a case where a child says he was molested each weekend his father visited him over a period of three years, he might be asked to distinguish as many incidents as possible by questions that establish the incident in relation to birthdays, holidays, trips, vacations, etc. The report of the interview should reflect how the dates were established (in relation to the events they are associated with). In doing so, it makes the dates more believable as children seldom come up with dates on their own.

To firm up the dates when the events occurred, the investigator has only to consult with the parents, school, or others with whom the child was at the time of the events in question. Talking with a nonoffending parent is always a good idea when trying to establish the location and time frame of the incidents. In one recent case, the investigating agency took an unnecessary report that should have been another police department's investigation. A field officer took the original report of a child molest in which a four-year-old girl accused her father of molesting her over a period of one year. The only incident she was able to describe in any detail was one where she was on a bed with her father and the mother was in the bathroom. Neither the field officer nor the follow-up detective talked to the mother to confirm what the child had said, by asking if the mother remembered the incident or if she knew where the incident occurred. Not until the mother was interviewed prior to court testimony was it discovered that the incident in question occurred in another county.

6. Determine if sexually explicit material or drugs were used and, if so, for what purpose (how), where they are kept, and have the child describe them in detail for seizure.

**Comment.** Questions should be asked to determine if, in what manner, and what kind of material was used. Then the child should describe it in as much detail as possible for seizure. Included should be the place it is kept. The same is true for drugs. Once the use of this type of contraband has been established the justification for obtaining a search warrant is already accomplished. All one has to do is fill in the details about the molestation. Finding what the child describes in the place he describes it is strong evidence to support their account.

7. Determine if the child was photographed, if the offender asked to take pictures of the child, or if a photo was given to the offender.

**Comment.** As mentioned in the discussion on identity, the discovery of the child's photo among the offender's possessions greatly lessens the chance the offender will say, "It wasn't me." In addition, although the child might have been photographed in explicit sexual activity, the child may only own up to having a conventional picture taken. Having the child tell you that the offender has his picture gives you a reason to search.

8.  Ask if the child saw any pictures of other children. Make attempts to identify the children after the search warrant is served and they are found.

**Comment.**  If the child has seen photographs of other children, this will support the need to identify and protect those children. It will also help to justify the need to obtain a search warrant.

9.  Ask the child if the offender has a diary or a computer.

**Comment.**  It would be nice if the child could describe what he saw in the diary or the computer — if he was lucky enough to have seen one of the other. If not, merely the knowledge that either of these things are kept by child molesters may justify asking for them in a search warrant as they will help to identify and protect the children the offender is abusing.

10.  Ask the child if any other children were present during any of the acts or at any other times.

**Comment.**  Again, discovery that other children are known to the offender establishes the need to identify and protect those children.

11.  Ask the child if he knows of any other adults who participated in the acts or associated with the offender.

**Comment.**  Obtaining this information will identify other offenders and, again, give purpose to getting a search warrant. In addition, by finding a coparticipant, it may provide a situation in which one offender points the finger at the other and makes some damaging statements.

12.  Ask the child if he ever gave his address or phone number to the offender and, if so, how it was recorded.

**Comment.**  This will help to connect the offender and the child. It also provides something to search for to corroborate the child's story.

13.  Ask if the offender ever went to the child's home or called the victim on the phone.

**Comment.**  If either of these occurred, the child's address and/or phone number must be recorded somewhere in the offender's possession. Discovery of this evidence will link the two. During the service of the search warrant, look in the offender's phone book issued by the phone company to see if there is any notation at the victim's family name.

14. Ask the child if he saw any other children give their names or phone numbers and inquire if and how they were recorded.

**Comment.** See comments at No. 10.

15. Ask if the child played with any toys, read any books or magazines, or played with or saw anything else that you might search for to prove the child was where he says he was.

**Comment.** Discovery of these types of items will support the child's account and help to demonstrate the offender's intent. See the second example of affidavit format discussed in Chapter 7 on search warrants, which shows how this can help establish probable cause to search.

16. Ask if the child left any belongings in the offender's place, home, car, etc.

**Comment.** The discovery of any of these type of items will corroborate the child's story and help to eliminate the identity defense.

17. Obtain a detailed account of the crime in the child's own words.
    a. Did the child see semen and can he describe it?
    b. Was the suspect's penis pointing straight down or straight out, etc.?
18. Determine, as specifically as possible, if there was penetration of the vaginal or anal openings.
19. Determine if the victim experienced pain during the sex acts or afterward.
    a. Did the child see blood in his underwear after the molestation?
20. Determine if the child reported to anyone that he was in pain.
21. Determine if foreign substances or objects were used, such as vaseline, condoms, etc. If so, where were they obtained and placed after the act?
22. Determine if the child or offender wiped himself after the act and with what.
23. Determine if the child had ever been molested by anyone else; if so, by whom?
24. Determine the attitude of the victim toward the offender; if the attitude is one of dislike, is it based on anything in addition to the molestations.

25.  If there is any type of dissolution of marriage action or child custody proceeding in progress, determine what the child's understanding and involvement is of the proceedings and his attitude toward it.
26.  If the report was delayed, try to have the child articulate the reasons why.
27.  Ask the child if they keep a diary and check it to see if there are any entries regarding the incident(s) under investigation.

**Comment.**  A diary such as that shown in Figure 2.5 and 2.6 would be invaluable to establish timeframes, state-of-mind of the child in question, and may, establish fresh complaint evidence if shown to or was left out for someone to find.

Events listed in the diary may be confirmed with others who were involved in them to confirm that the diary is reliable and timely kept. If the events involving the molestations are at times where others are able to confirm the circumstances surrounding the molest(s), it will help to corroborate the child's account of events.

The diary found in the case in Figure 2.6 involved a teen and a cop, both credibility issues in-and-of-themselves. A well-planned pretext call and confirmation of other matters reported by the child and confirmed by the diary secured the conviction.

## Investigative Steps in "Whodunit" Cases

Developing leads or a course of action in cases where the offender is unknown is often haphazard, and closure of a case may depend on the arrest of the offender in a subsequent case. The pity about this approach is that it means a child must be molested again before the offender is apprehended. The following is offered in the hope that it will help identify the offender either before he acts or as soon as possible thereafter. It is recognized that the suggestions offered here are optimum and time-consuming, and for agencies with a large volume of cases, may be unreasonably so. However, if even one approach can be used, it may help to prevent a child from being abused. The start is to build a profile of cases and characteristics of the offender. Begin with what you already know.

### Sex Registrant and Parolee Lists

If your state is lucky enough to have a sex-registrant requirement, when a child molester comes to register or your agency receives notice that a child molester is moving into your community, take the time to introduce yourself to him. If he doesn't come in on his own or you're out when he does, pay him a visit. Let him know you care. He might decide to move somewhere else. Many prison systems notify police agencies in whose jurisdictions parolees will be released. When such notification is received about a child molester, take the time to introduce yourself to his parole agent. Whenever you receive either notice of the sex registration or parole release, research your files or those of the agency who arrested the offender for the sex offense he was convicted of and any other contacts he is known for. Get to know the kind of crime he commits and maintain a file with his registration reports or other investigative reports, which will be available should a similar crime be committed. Create a line-up book and add his picture to those of known molesters. In many prison systems, release data is available (upon request) on offenders by offense. Generally, these are provided in computer print-outs.

## Field Interview Contacts and Suspicious Activity File

Maintain a file of the names and descriptions of individuals stopped and identified for activities or circumstances that connect them to this type of crime. Keep track of nuisance offenses and cases involving no crime but that are suspicious in nature, if they relate to child molestation. Research those names and keep records of those found to have sex crimes backgrounds. Add their photos to the line-up book. Communicate with the patrol division of your agency when you develop information about possible offenders.

For example, on several occasions children have been approached by individuals for what clearly is intended to be sexual purposes. In one case, a man pulled to the curb in front of a young boy who was sitting at a bus bench after school. The man was driving a flashy new car. He rolled down the window on the passenger side and asked the boy if he wanted a ride home, at the same time flashing a roll of bills at the boy. The boy refused and wrote down the license number of the car, which he gave his parents when he arrived home. They called the police. The detective who later reviewed the report transmitted the information to the patrol division in hopes the man would be spotted again and identified. He retained the information for future reference because the license number was found to be invalid.

Documenting this type of information will also help to provide the probable cause necessary to detain others who later make similar approaches or are seen loitering in the same area.

## MO Log

Using a ledger sheet with as many different columns as possible and a large enough line for some details, it is possible to create a log that will assist in connecting the MO of one case to others. This log should contain as many cases on one sheet as possible, listed in chronological order, to facilitate the review and comparison of the cases. At the minimum, it must contain the date, time, day, victim's name, race, sex, location, incident summary, suspect description, vehicle description, and case number. If the case is connected to others, such a notation should be made. If an offender is identified later in a case that is listed as unknown, the log should be updated with the new information. It is also useful to have the case disposition (closure through identification, convicted, no arrest, etc.) listed to keep a track record. The use of this technique will facilitate the easy transfer of information to a pin map. A simple MO log is shown in Figure 8.8.

## Pin Map

One of the oldest tracing techniques used by law enforcement today is the pin map. Time consuming as it is, it helps to establish patterns and relationships in a visual manner that is beyond comparison. It may be possible to use a computer to perform this function, at the same time as it collates the rest of the information into files such as those suggested in this chapter. Using a map of your city, and with the use of different colored pins, a pin should be placed at each location where an incident occurs; where a registered sex offender lives; the location of an arrest; or an area of suspected activity in pornography, prostitution, or molestation. Analysis can be made each time a new entry of any type is made to see if there is a relationship to other entries.

## Moniker/Alpha File

When names or monikers (nickname, alias) surface of persons other than those who are known to be involved in a current investigation, these names should be maintained in such a way that they can easily be retrieved later. One way to do this is to maintain a file. The value of keeping this type of information is that it may either connect cases or individuals at a later time, or may provide the probable cause needed for a search warrant. Examples of how this assisted in investigations can be seen in the search warrants in Appendices IV, VI, and XIII. A 3 × 5″ card file system works well for this purpose, a computer might work better. The entries should contain the name of the individual, his aka(s), a photo should be attached to the card, and it should contain any related names. All names should be cross-indexed. The entry should list a brief synopsis of why this name appears in the file, and should reference the card to a case number or file folder. It should contain the initials of the person making the entry so that if a question arises about the entry, the original person who knows about it may be identified. A sample of what it might look like is contained in Figure 8.9.

## MO Log

| Date/ Time/ Day | MO Caracteristics/ Incident Description | Subject Description | Location of Occurrence | Vehicle Description | Case Number | Victim Description | Related Cases? Misc. Facts |
|---|---|---|---|---|---|---|---|
| | | | | | | | |
| | | | | | | | |
| | | | | | | | |
| | | | | | | | |
| | | | | | | | |
| | | | | | | | |
| | | | | | | | |
| | | | | | | | |

**Figure 8.8** Sample MO Log.

```
Last name, first, middle initial, AKA(s)          Date
Address, phone, local and state ID numbers
Physical description
Brief notes re connection
Associates/connections
Case number/folder                      Initials of
                                        person making
                                        entry
```

**Figure 8.9**   Sample entry in a moniker/alpha file.

## Alpha Lists

It is not uncommon that during investigations, names will be found in the offender's phone books or on his mailing lists. Most of the time they are already in alphabetical order. If listing them on cards or in a computer as suggested is not practical, a photocopy of them should be made for later reference.

## Street File

It may be useful to maintain addresses of offenders, suspected offenders, and known locales for activity in a file for reference. If incidents are reported that involve an unidentified offender, correlations may be made that will help to identify him.

## Phone Numbers

If time permits, because so many offenders keep phone numbers of other people who do what they do, a record keeping system that correlates these numbers might prove helpful.

## Vehicle File

The need for this file hardly needs explanation. Descriptions of known vehicles used by offenders should be listed along with those that come from cases where no identification has been made. By keeping the two types of descriptions in the same file system, it will be easier to make the necessary connections.

## Report File or Case Folder

Investigations of sexual exploitations of children often take months, if not years, to complete. They are generally complicated investigations involving contacts made with numerous persons, often with multiple interviews of the same people. For this reason alone, care should be taken in the creation of a case file system. A case file, which may be as simple as a manila folder containing all of the pertinent information, should be opened for every reported child molestation, missing person, suspected prostitute, pornography model, or suspected offender who comes to the investigator's attention. The file should contain an activity log or narrative summary of actions carried out. The log will eliminate duplicated efforts and will act as a checklist when it is time to determine when and if certain steps were taken in the investigation. It should indicate follow-up objectives or leads with notations that show the results of the actions taken on them. This will assure step-by-step accounting for later court testimony, should it be necessary. Often it is helpful to use different color pens, asterisks, and so on to highlight important leads or details.

The results of the record checks made on the offender's prior record or the checks made on other involved individuals should be kept in the file. They should be dated so that if an update is necessary, there will be no duplication of research. It should contain all reports obtained from your agency and others contacted. Related internal organization memos, such as requests for assistance to other units in your agency, should be included. Any other pertinent information such as newspaper clippings regarding those involved in the case should be included also. A composite description/listing of serial/single offenses should be circulated in poster format. See Figure 8.10 as a suggested format for a poster.

## When Offender is Suspected but No Victim Has Surfaced

If information is developed that provides a name of an individual who is suspected of molesting children, but no children are identified as victims, steps must be made to develop a case. The first step should be to complete the record check as indicated earlier. A background check should be done to determine his employment and activities. Surveillance may accomplish this, and also establish traffic patterns of children coming and going from his home or apartment. The surveillance itself may be sufficient to provide probable cause to search his home, depending upon what information is already at hand.

For example, in Los Angeles, police received information from a confidential reliable informant who told them that a particular individual was molesting children in his home. Police set up surveillance on the individual and saw a boy and a man enter the home. They waited for a short time, and when the boy did not emerge from the home, they knocked on the door, identifying themselves and their purpose. After receiving no answer, they forced entry.

```
SAMPLE POSTER FOR DISTRIBUTION TO LAW ENFORCEMENT AGENCIES AND/OR
POSTING IN PUBLIC PLACES

                        ANYTOWN POLICE DEPARTMENT

                        INFORMATION WANTED
                   ON CHILD SEXUAL MOLESTATION

      ┌──────────────────────────┐   ┌──────────────────────────┐
      │                          │   │                          │
      │   PHOTO/COMPOSIT DRAWING │   │  PHOTO/DRAWING OF VEHICLE │
      │        OF SUSPECT        │   │                          │
      │                          │   │                          │
      └──────────────────────────┘   └──────────────────────────┘

   SUSPECT DESCRIPTION/NAME:

   Age:          Race:        Ht.   Wt:        Hair Color:        Hair Lngth:

   Complexion:             Scars/marks, etc:

   MO/INCIDENT DESCRIPTION:

   DATE/DAY/TIME          LOCATION              VICTIM DESCRIPTION
   (May be repeated for a series listing each incident with a highlight of the similarities and cross-
   over charateristics)


                   IF YOU HAVE ANY INFORMATION
                             CONTACT:
                       OFFICER/DETECTIVE:
                       TELEPHONE:
                       CASE NUMBER:
                       WARRANT NUMBER: (If Applicable)
```

**Figure 8.10**  Sample poster for distribution to law enforcement agencies and/or posting in public places.

Although these circumstances are somewhat unique, they highlight one of the main objects of the investigation — the safety and well-being of children. If a police officer has reason to believe that someone is in danger or a felony is being committed, he has the right, under the emergency doctrine, to force entry into a dwelling without a warrant if necessary.

If there is not sufficient cause to act based solely on surveillance, once it is begun, efforts may be made to identify and interview those who frequent the place in question. If this is not successful or more is needed, carefully planned interviews of the offender's neighbors should be attempted. The trick here is to do it without alerting the offender, a difficult task because the loyalty of those interviewed cannot be assured. This should be left as a last resort.

## Protect Investigation and Evidence

Whatever techniques or procedures are used during the investigation, great care must be taken not to tip your hand. If it is necessary to leave the scene of the crime or a place where evidence is suspected to get a search warrant, freeze the scene until the warrant is obtained. Attempt, either through consent or by warrant, to immediately search for evidence at or before the time the offender learns about the investigation. Too often valuable evidence is lost because the offender is interviewed and the officer leaves to obtain a warrant, leaving no one to protect the scene or valuable evidence.

## Proactive Investigation

A successful way to deal with the sexual exploitation of children is to initiate investigations based on information developed rather than waiting for complaints of molestation directly. This proactive technique will put the underground on the alert in the community in which it operates and will best protect those children who don't report their involvement or who are trapped in their situations.

One method of proactive investigation is to engage the offender in correspondence as though the police officer were another offender [21]. The underground is aware that the technique is in use. However, there is little they can do to verify the identity of those they correspond with because they are at the mercy of their desires to communicate with others with their interests and their need to be sexually involved with children. All an investigator who wishes to engage in this method of investigation needs to do is read the correspondence he finds in the possession of the offenders he arrests. The MO is easy to follow, and experimentation will help to mold an investigator's style.

When the investigation must be conducted within the borders of the police jurisdiction, and letter writing is not feasible, covert operations may be fruitful. Figure 8.11 shows a case analysis schematic of a common investigation where a victim has not been identified.

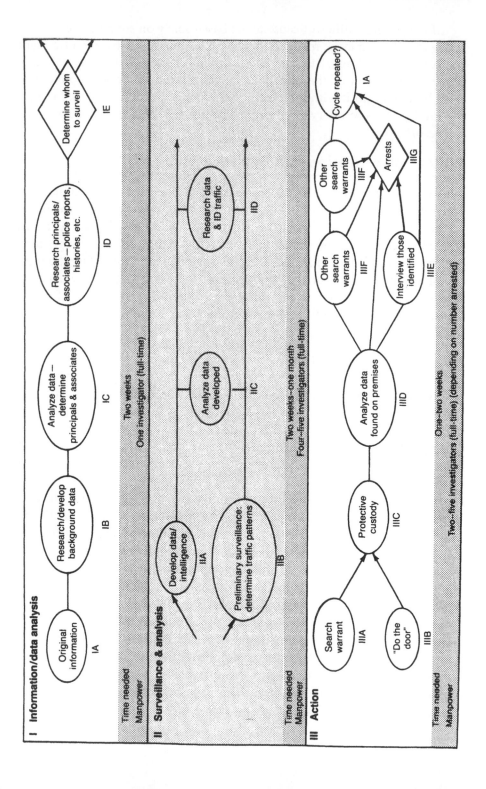

**Figure 8.11** Link analysis chart of a case with no identified victim. **Phase I**, which may take as short a time as a day or as long a time as several months, generally averages 1 to 2 weeks. It is the information-generation phase and begins with a lead, however developed, to an individual who is suspected of being involved with children (marked **IA** on the chart). Phase **IB** involves researching and developing background data on the lead. Phase **IC** may be concurrent with IB but most often follows it, and is the analysis of the data to determine who are the principals in the case and their associates. Following closely or running concurrently with phase IC is phase **ID**, which involves the gathering of information on those identified as being principals and/or associates. The final phase is **I.E.**, which is a critical control point that determines on whom to act. Generally at this phase there will not be sufficient information to move for a criminal complaint or indictment, and surveillance must be initiated to attempt to establish it. However, if, as is true for any point in this process, probable cause develops that is sufficient to establish a crime, appropriate action should be taken. At phase **I.E.**, the decision must be made, based upon all the information developed to this point, as to who will be surveilled.

**Phase II** is surveillance and analysis of information on the individuals involved. As many people as manpower allows may be surveilled at one time. Phases **IIA** and **IIB** may occur at the same time, and involve the developing of data and intelligence based on the work of preliminary surveillance teams. A portion of this data should be the establishing of traffic patterns so that time is not wasted watching a sleeping or inactive subject. As information is developed from the surveillance, such as license numbers, descriptions of persons, and mail covers, it must be analyzed on an ongoing basis. Traffic coming and going from the subject under scrutiny should be identified in whatever way possible. Photographs should be taken of the contacts made at or with the offender's home/office/vehicle that is surveilled (phases **IIC**, **D**).**Phase III** involves actions taken based on the information developed in the preceding phases. It may involve the forcing of entry or the initiation of search warrants; subsequent taking of children into protective custody; the analysis of data found during the search warrant service; interviews of the children or others identified as a result of the warrants; the initiation of new search warrants; or the obtaining of arrest warrants or making arrests without warrants. Information generated as a result of the arrests and/or search warrants may start the cycle all over again.

# When Investigation Involves Multiple Law-Enforcement Agencies

Operations will often involve multiple police agencies from local or federal governments. The involvement may be as short as a couple of hours or as long as several months. Either way, all involved should have a good understanding of their roles and responsibilities.

This may be accomplished with written agreements in contract form such as a Memorandum of Understanding or an oral agreement when brought together for a short duration or operation. When there are significant tasks or responsibilities to be divided up, a written agreement is preferred, such as the operational order created for a case described in Exhibit 8.5.

---

## EXHIBIT 8.5 OPERATION ORDER

---

PURPOSE:

Using a federal search warrant, to enter the primary residence of the suspect. The search will focus on child pornography, both commercial and personal. Attempts will be made to identify any local victims, if found, and to arrest any suspects involved.

SYNOPSIS:

On 15 June, a parcel was intercepted by U.S. Customs in San Francisco, California. The parcel contained pornographic magazines with pictures of young children engaged in sexual activity with other children and adults. U.S. Customs then notified the Palo Alto Police Department. The parcel was to be delivered to a male adult at the Palo Alto Hamilton Post Office Box ____.

A background check on the subject showed another similar mailing. In July another parcel was intercepted. This parcel contained two (2) pornographic magazines depicting bestiality.

The suspect occasionally resides with a woman and a young female at 991 ____ . Several children, whose ages are similar to the ones in the magazine, have been observed playing at the ____ residence. The suspect is a teacher in the community and is in charge of children in the same age group as those depicted in the magazines.

SUSPECT:

J ____, L ____

WMA, 37 years, (date of birth)

6'0", 175 lbs., brn/blu

CDL# M____

SEE ATTACHED PHOTO

Addresses of:  991 L____, Palo Alto, and

Dock__, Berth__, R____ Municipal

Marina, ____ Blvd., R____

## Exhibit 8.5   (continued)

OPERATION OUTLINE:

A controlled delivery of pornography will be done at the suspect's post office box at the Hamilton post office. A postal inspector and Palo Alto Police Department detective will watch the box until the parcel is picked up. Once it is retrieved, the suspect will be followed. If he goes to the 991 _____ address and carries the parcel into the house an agent at the San Jose Federal Building will be advised by radio and the search warrant signed for that location.

If the suspect fails to bring the parcel into the house, we will keep the house under surveillance until the suspect leaves. He will then be followed. Based on recent surveillance, the suspect may return to his boat at the R_____ Municipal Marina. The suspect lives at that location alone.

The warrant will then be signed for the boat and vehicle. Once the warrant is signed, the agent will transport it to the location where it will be served by U.S. Customs and the Palo Alto Police Department.

PERSONNEL:

To assist in the service of the search warrant and surveillance, a total of eight law enforcement officials will be used.

*Palo Alto Police Department:*

Detective Bob S____

Detective Chris L____

Detective Sergeant Judy D____

Two uniformed officers   (1 from the Palo Alto Police Department and I from the R____ Police Department, if needed)

*U.S. Customs:*

Agent W. S____

Agent C. D____

Agent F. G____

*Santa Clara County District Attorney's Office:*

Inspector Seth Goldstein

*U.S. Postal Inspector:*

To be named.

HOURS OF OPERATION

0700–1900 hours from 23 July, until 25 July.

EQUIPMENT:

1. Unmarked van—provided by U.S. Secret Service (one)
2. Palo Alto Police Department portable radios (eight) or eight Federal radios
3. Palo Alto Police Department bulletproof vests (eight)
4. Authorized duty weapons
5. Camera equipment
6. Evidence collection kits
7. Palo Alto Police Department jackets or caps

---

## EXHIBIT 8.5   (CONTINUED)

---

RESIDENCE:

99 L____ is occupied by D____ and H____ S____ and their 4-year-old daughter. They have no criminal history. They have no weapons registered to them.

CAUTION: The suspect J____ has no criminal history. He has no weapons registered to him.

ADDITIONAL:

Agent S____ will coordinate the search warrant with the U.S. Attorney. If the suspect does not take the contraband to 991 L____ , a search warrant will be obtained for his "drop off" point.

### OPERATION AFT DECK

SITE LOCATION AND NAME:

| | |
|---|---|
| 991 L____ : | Site #1 |
| Municipal Marina__ T____ : | Site #2 |
| Hamilton Post Office: | P/O |
| Federal Building __ San Jose: | San Jose |

SUSPECT:

| | |
|---|---|
| J____ , L____ : | Player #1 |
| S____ , D____ : | Player #2 |
| S____ , H____ : | Player #3 |

ASSIGNMENTS:

| Assignment | Detective | Call # | Vehicle |
|---|---|---|---|
| Post Office | H____ | 500 | Ford van, cream |
| | D____ | 545 | Plymouth, 4-door, blk/blu |
| Boat | G____ | 558 | Chrysler, blk/sil |
| L____ | Goldstein | 499 | Chevy, tan, 2-door |
| Tail units | S____ | L-11 | Blue Zephyr |
| | L____ | L-29 | White Monte Carlo |
| | D____ | X-11 | Blue Cougar |
| Federal Building,<br>San Jose | S____ | 543 | |

GATE COMBINATION:

Gate "C"

2-1-5-4-3

(Courtesy of Palo Alto Police Department.)

# Need to Share Information Discovered with Other Agencies

In investigations that disclose information about other potential or known offenders and victims from other police jurisdictions, the investigator should share that information. The police agency responsible for the jurisdiction in which the children or offenders live should be given the information so that it can initiate action. Once a name is obtained, much can result if the proper efforts are made. For example, in Canada, as a result of a tip from a local police agency in the United States, a teacher suspected of molesting his class members was subsequently arrested after a search turned up over 250 child pornography magazines and films. Canadian officials, acting on the seizure lists of materials from foreign countries, searched the homes of the persons whose names appeared on the list as receiving child pornography and found "substantial" amounts of child pornography.

In this country, acting on a mailing list found in possession of one molester, police in several other states made arrests of individuals who names were provided them by the original investigating police agency. Through the use of the proactive, nonintrusive, investigative techniques described in this chapter, such as surveillance and covert operations, simply providing the name of a possible offender should be enough to initiate an investigation that may result in the identification of new, unreported crimes and the protection of innocent children.

Law enforcement has both a moral and ethical obligation to follow through with this type of information. If it is not done, it subjects the children of that other community to unnecessary peril and may be perpetuating the abuse of children. In a case that involved several federal agencies and numerous different local police and protective service agencies within the state of California, a man was allowed to continue molesting children even though his inclinations were known for several years by several of the agencies, because they never communicated with one another.

The man's name came up in an investigation in New Mexico, found in letters to a known child molester in which he talked of his sexual escapades with children. His address at the time was in Southern California. The federal agency investigating the case never communicated that information to the law-enforcement agency responsible for the area where the man lived.

Several years later, the man was discovered to be having pornographic photographs of children developed. He was investigated by the local police department, who dismissed the case as nonpriority because the pictures only depicted children in lewd poses, with no sexual activity to speak of. However, it was found that he was running a daycare center licensed by the state through the county in which he lived. Because of the nature of the photographs, the country demanded that he turn in his daycare license and told him to leave the county. He did, and moved to Northern California, where he and his wife opened another daycare facility in her name, again licensed by the state.

When U.S. Customs seized some child pornography destined for the man's postal box, within a year after his move to Northern California, they notified the local sheriff's office responsible for the area where the man lived. A subsequent controlled delivery and search warrant disclosed that the man had been molesting his own children and those of the people who brought their children to his daycare facility. He was also found to have over 50,000 color slides of his molesting children in Vietnam while he was there, as well as a host of commercial and homemade child pornography.

Some of the incidents of molest were found to have occurred after the dates of the investigation conducted in New Mexico, and most after the move to Northern California. However, numerous incidents were described by the children in his family that were before the move to the north and around the time of the New Mexico investigation. There is a good chance that had the federal agency reported its discoveries, the molestation of the family members would have been discovered and others prevented. There is no doubt that had they communicated their discoveries at the time they found them, the Southern California police agency would have had more to work with when it discovered the photographs that were being developed.

In this case, a multimillion dollar suit was filed against the State of California and the Southern California county in which the man lived when the photographs were found, for negligent investigative and licensing practices. They settled out-of-court for a hefty sum.

## The Investigation Must Not Officially Endanger Children

Stringent ethical guidelines must be created and adhered to when considering the use of children to "develop cause to arrest" offenders. The use of children as operatives may raise questions of civil and criminal liability. This also applies to the use of children in getting evidence of abuse for the police. However, the use of children in face-to-face confrontations to elicit incriminating statements should be used with great discretion and carefully planned. It should never be allowed to involve situations where the child is out of the immediate presence of someone who can step in to protect him should something go wrong or he become endangered. Officially placing a child in a position of peril may constitute a crime as defined in criminal statutes that define child endangerment. Certainly the examples that follow fit this criterion.

In one case, a law-enforcement agency wanted to find a child who was involved in sexual exploitation of children and was missing. It employed the services of an informant operative who claimed to know what was going on in the local underground. Over a long period of time the investigator working the case repeatedly hounded the operative to "get him a kid." Finally, after being rebuked for not "coming across" as promised, the operative went to a neighboring city and kidnapped a child and brought him to the investigator.

In another case, a retarded child was suspected of being molested by a therapist she was seeing. She was unable to articulate what had happened to her or identify the offender. The local police agency that investigated the crime tried to figure out a way in which an officer or some other individual could witness the event without anyone involved knowing about it. They were able to conceal an officer inside a closet in the therapist's office where the officer would be able to observe a session between the child and the therapist. Fearing discovery of the concealed officer, the door of the closet was nailed shut with the officer inside before the session began, unbeknownst to the therapist. During the session, the officer observed the child and therapist in several acts of molestation. After the child left, the police released the officer from his hiding place and the offender was arrested. He was subsequently convicted of the acts, which wouldn't have been established without the testimony of the officer.

Another police agency working with their local prosecutor's office discovered that an officer in their own agency was molesting a teenaged boy. So adamant were they to obtain evidence of the acts that they sent the boy into the offender's home with a concealed tape recorder in hopes of getting an incriminating statement. The boy was out of their view and control for a period of time long enough for the officer to molest him again.

In each of the cases cited above, the need to obtain evidence was great, and the ideas that were tried were creative efforts to obtain incriminating evidence or to establish a crime. The problem is the ethics used in doing so. In the first case, the law-enforcement agency clearly went beyond the limit in trying to get a handle on the problem by encouraging the operative to "find" a child. The operative should have been prevented from committing a crime in order to provide what the agency asked of him. In the case with the retarded child, some signal could have been arranged to alert those outside the session that a crime was about to occur or was occurring, and the session could have been interrupted in a manner that wouldn't have traumatized the child. In the case of the police officer offender, a phone call might have been a better first try. Then, if necessary, a "wire" (radio transmitter) could have been used in the face-to-face meeting, which would have allowed the surveilling officers to know that the child was in jeopardy and allow them to take action. The confrontation itself may have been troublesome for the child, so the technique must be carefully thought out and the consequences considered.

## Handling the Media During High-Profile Cases

The press will want as much of the details of a major investigation as it can get its hands on. It will print or run almost anything, regardless of its accuracy, just to make headlines or the evening news. It will get in the way of an ongoing investigation if it catches wind of it and it will question every step an investigator makes. The problem that all this creates is that, if unprepared, a police agency can unwittingly fall victim to the desires of the press to "inform the public."

It should be decided as soon as possible exactly what information will be given to the press. Consideration must be given to what the effect will be on the families involved, given the fact that they may be identified on the screen or in the paper. The families may not want their relatives and close friends to have the "details," and disclosure to the press may violate their privacy. It should also be kept in mind that if the press isn't informed, it is likely to go out and find its own facts, which may not jibe with the truth and may be "bad press" for the victim. This may create more pressure on the victim and his family and result in a loss of cooperation on their part. This is mentioned in this chapter because to manage this element of the case may require a public information officer should the case draw a great deal of media attention.

## Steps for Investigating and Uncovering the Underground

Steps taken during investigations should be with an eye to finding other offenses, offenders, victims, and breaking into the underground. Here are some steps that have proven helpful in the past.

1. Monitor phone calls made by children and offenders who have been arrested and record phone numbers.
   - Child will call offender to pick him up or get him out of trouble.
   - Offender will call another child molester to bail him out, get an attorney, or warn that the police are coming.

**Comment.**  On several occasions, children arrested for either criminal or noncriminal offenses (runaway, truancy, etc.) have called their "benefactors," representing them as their "uncle" or a "family friend" instead of their parents. Unknowingly, the police have released the children to them, only to later discover their mistake.

2.  Copy and maintain lists of names and phone numbers from those persons arrested.
    • Provide the police agency that has jurisdiction with the information found. The information you have may close a case they are carrying or, more importantly, supply the information needed to prevent the abuse of other children.

**Comment.**   In one case, a man was arrested for a non-sex offense and was discovered to have an interest in boys. First names, phone numbers, and pictures of boys were found in his wallet and address book. He admitted his involvement with boys and divulged the identity of some of the boys in his book who lived in another county. He also provided the names of other adults who were abusing children in the other county. Copies of the names, the information given by the man, and his identity and predisposition were sent to the county in question. Within several weeks, that county had charged the man with multiple counts of child molest.

3.  Review all correspondence at the offender's home for leads to others.
    • cassette tapes
    • letters
    • pictures
    • offender's diary
    • Ads in papers found in the offender's home.
4.  Subscribe to and read books and publications published by the underground with classified ads in them, such as swinger magazines, video magazines, sex journals, and legitimate local papers with classified sections.
    • publish ads of your own.

**Comment.**   The pitfall in this type of investigation is that an investigator, morally and ethically, *must act on information as soon as the violation or reasonable suspicion of abuse is developed.* As stated earlier, it will mean that a "sting" may have to fold if a child is found to be endangered.

5.  Using a pseudonym, write to selected names from evidence found.
    • check with the local postal inspector and police agency before starting to write to determine that the subject is not a police officer.

**Comment.** Rather than wasting valuable time writing to someone who is undercover, it is important that the investigator make a brief background check.

6. Monitor graffiti on walls of bathrooms, juvenile "hang-outs," and pick-up locations.
7. Use interviews with victims and offenders to provide new leads to more offenses and other people involved, sources of child pornography, and locations where activities are taking place.
8. Informants.
    - runaways
    - children on the street
    - offenders

**Comment.** Runaways have to spend their time somewhere. They need to eat, sleep, and have clothing. When on the run, they find a way to satisfy these needs. Often their needs are catered to by the pedophile/child molester/pornographer. In a case involving a home for disturbed children, "the word was out" that when children ran away from the home, a particular individual would give them refuge and supply their needs. This individual was discovered after several children ran from the home and were found in Southern California, over 600 miles away from their home. Interviews with the children revealed that the man whose home they had run to had supplied them with the connections to Southern California, as well as narcotics. He had them engage in homosexual sex acts with adults before sending them to Southern California.

In a case in Wareham, Mass., two adults and two runaways were arrested when the police raided the home of an underground group member who was found to have over 200 pounds of child pornography. Connected to that same case, within the month authorities in Vermont arrested two more adults linked to the kidnapping of a 13-year-old boy. Some of the information that generated the two cases had come from runaways who were interviewed after they were recovered.

9. During routine investigations and during daily patrol activity, be attuned to:
    a. unusual groupings or frequency of the same adults in places where children generally congregate or play.
    b. watching for both adult and child porn where children can see it or where it is available to them.
    c. watching for nude statues, paintings, pictures, or drawings of naked people or children in places where children would or could see them.
    d. sexual aids available to children.

    e.   cutout pictures of children.

    f.   crimes involving children.

**Comment.** In property crimes (burglaries and thefts) where juveniles are responsible, certain questions must be answered.

    a.   Why was this person selected as a target?

    b.   Did the children know just where to go to get what they were after (dope, money)?

    c.   In cases where the reporting person is not the victim himself, did the child pick the target because he felt the offender wouldn't report the crime?

    d.   In cases where the offender reports an auto theft and has all of the identifying information on the juvenile thief, how did the child get the car and why is the "victim" reporting it? Is he suddenly worried about civil liability because the car hasn't returned?

In a case in Berkeley, a boy was arrested for shoplifting eye shadow. Investigation revealed that he was a runaway from Philadelphia and that he was working in a porn house in San Francisco where he and other boys were involved in sex acts.

10.   Identify locations for activity and surveil.

    a.   amusement centers

    b.   beaches

    c.   bowling alleys, pool halls

    d.   swap meets, flea markets

    e.   parks

**Comment.** The individual who seeks children in these types of settings will be seen repeatedly over periods of time making contact with different children. After watching these locations for a while, he will become apparent. Surveillance is one of the best investigative methods to use because there is less chance the investigation will be revealed. Its pitfall is that it eats up manpower and time. In a case in Baldwin Park, N.Y., a man was arrested and found to have over 50 reels of 8-mm film and 300 videocassettes of hardcore child porn. Neighbors reported that he had an "endless stream" of 10- to 14-year-old boys coming and going from his apartment. Investigation revealed that many boys came from out of state to be involved in sex acts and filming.

11.  Contact photo outlets that send out and use machine photo processing let them know what to look for and what to do with it when they find it.

**Comment.**  In Mississippi, a roll of pornographic film was accidentally dropped off at a reproducing lab, resulting in the uncovering of a sex ring and the recovery of over 200 pornographic photographs. Boys were brought to a farm in the area from both coasts and throughout the country. Many cases are generated as a result of the diligence of photo reproduction company employees who report suspected child pornography.

12.  Prepare and execute search warrants in every case.
     a.  Contact vice, property, narcotics, and juvenile units in order to be aware of when they do their search warrants.
13.  Monitor cyberspace on computer internet.

## Dispositions and Investigations

Multiple dispositions are possible, several of which may be appropriate at the same time. For example, the case may be referred for prosecution *and* juvenile court for dependency proceedings. The case may not have sufficient evidence for criminal prosecution, yet, have enough to meet the standards of evidence for a dependency hearing. The case may be unfounded — that is, the allegations are disproved or found to have no merit. In any case, it is important for the investigator to realize that not every case will be able to be referred to a prosecutor and not every case referred for prosecution will have charges filed.

## References and Notes

1.  *Life Magazine*, May, 1988.
2.  *APSAC Advisor*, Chicago, IL.
3.  Child Victim Witness Judicial Advisory Committee's *Final Report* to the California Attorney General's Office, Oct. 1988.
4.  *Research and Evaluation Final Report*, California Attorney General's Office, July 1994.
5.  U.S. Department of Justice, Office of Juvenile Justice and Delinquency Prevention, Washington, D.C., Oct. 1994.
6.  Dana Gassaway in *Law Enforcement Quarterly*, Nov. 1994 to Jan. 1995.
7.  Conversation with Terry Hall of the Indianapolis P.D. May, 1995.
8.  Adapted from the case files of Terry Hall.
9.  Hubert H. Humphrey, III. *Report on the Scott County Investigations*. St. Paul., Minn., Attorney General's Office, State of Minnesota, Feb. 1985.

11. See the discussion in *Evidence in Child Abuse and Neglect Cases* by John Myers, Wiley, New York, 1992 p.225.

12. "Summary of Findings From the Sexual Abuse Allegations Project," Nancy Theonnes, The Association of Family and Conciliation Courts Research Unit, Denver, Co., in *Sexual Abuse Allegations in Custody and Visitation Cases*, E. Nicholson, et al., American Bar Association, Washington, D.C., 1988, p. 4.

13. J. Bulkley, citing AFCC study in *Think Tank Report: Allegations of Sexual Abuse in Child Custody and Visitation Situations*, The National Resource Center on Child Sexual Abuse, Huntsville, Alabama, 1989, p. 17.

14. "The Extent, Nature, and Validity of Sexual Abuse Allegations in Custody/ Visitation Disputes," N. Thoennes, et al., in *Child Abuse and Neglect*, Vol. 14, p. 153, 1990.

15. *Achieving Equal Justice For Women and Men in the Courts, the Draft Report of the Judicial Council Advisory Committed on Gender Bias in the Courts*, California Judicial Council, Administrative Office of the Courts, San Francisco, March, 1990.

16. Ibid, p. 43.

17. For two excellent discussions on this subject see *Handling Child Custody, Abuse and Adoption Cases*, Ann Haralambie, McGraw Hill 1983 and *Evidence In Child Abuse and Neglect Cases*, John E. B. Myers, Wiley, N.Y., 1992.

18. Charles Wilson and Donna Pence, *Team Investigation of Child Sexual Abuse: the Uneasy Alliance*, Sage, 1994.

19. *Joint Investigations of Child Abuse: Report of a Symposium*, National Institute of Justice, Office for Victims of Crime, Office of Juvenile Justice and Delinquency Prevention, (Pub. #NCJ142056) July 1993..

20. Da.vid Lloyd, "The Corroboration of Sexual Victimization of Children." in *Child Sexual Abuse and the Law*, Bulkley, Josephine, ed. Washington D.C., Amer ican Bar Association, 1981, p. 103.

21. Because this book will eventually find its way into the hands of members of the underground, the specific details of this technique will not be discussed. For more information on this technique, contact may be made with any of the law-enforcement agencies which use it, including the U.S. Postal Service.

## Additional Reading

American Bar Association, National Legal Resource Center for Child Advocacy and Protection, *Sexual Abuse Allegations in Custody and Visitation Cases*, Nicholson, E. Bruce, ed., Washington, D.C., Feb., 1988.

Attorney General's Task Force on Family Violence. *Final Report*. Washington, D.C., United States Department of Justice, Sept. 1984.

Bronx County Grand Jury, Bronx County, New York. *Report of the November 1984 Bronx County Grand Jury: An Inquiry into Child Maltreatment in the City of New York. The New York City Experience with Child Abuse: A Lesson for the Nation.* New York, Nov. 1984.

Bulkley, Josephine (ed). *Child Sexual Abuse and the Law.* Washington, D.C.: American Bar Association, 1981.

Commission on Peace Officer Standards and Training, State of California. *Guidelines for the Investigation of Sexual Exploitation and Sexual Abuse of Children.* Sacramento, CA., June 1983.

Commission on Peace Officer Standards and Training, State of California. *Investigation of Child Abuse and Neglect: Guidelines for California Law Enforcement Agencies.* Sacramento, CA, Jan. 1980.

Depanfilis, Diane, & Salus, Marsha, *A Coordinated Response to Child Abuse and Neglect: A Basic Manual,* U.S. Department of Health and Human Services, National Center for Child Abuse and Neglect, Washington, D. C., 1992.

Faller, Kathleen Coulborn, *Child Sexual Abuse: Intervention and Treatment Issues,* U.S. Department of Health and Human Services, National Center for Child Abuse and Neglect, Washington, D. C., 1993.

Los Angeles Police Department. *Preliminary Investigation of the Sexual Exploitation/Abuse of Children.* Parts I and II, Vol. X, Issues 18 and 19. Aug. 1978.

National Judicial Education Program to Promote Equality for Women and Men in the Courts, *Adjudicating Allegations of Child Sexual Abuse When Custody is In Dispute,* New York, 1996.

National Resource Center on Child Sexual Abuse, *Think Tank Report: Allegations of Sexual, Abuse in child Custody and Visitation Situations,* Huntsville, AL., March, 1989.

Peterson, Marilyn Strachan, & Urquiza, Anthony J., *The Role of Mental Health Professionals in the Prevention and Treatment of Child Abuse and Neglect,* U.S. Department of Health and Human Services, National Center for Child Abuse and Neglect, Washington, D.C., 1993.

President's Task Force on Victims of Crime. *Final Report.* Washington, D.C., Dec. 1982.

United States Department of Health and Human Services, Office of Human Development Services, Administration for Children, Youth, and Families, Children's Bureau, National Center on Child Abuse and Neglect. *The Role of Law Enforcement in the Prevention and Treatment of Child Abuse and Neglect.* Washington, D.C., Sept. 1984.

*Webster's Deluxe Unabridged Dictionary,* 2nd ed. New York: Simon and Schuster, 1983.

# Appendix I

Your affiant, detective T—— J——, is a police officer with the City of Los Altos assigned to the detective division. Your affiant has been a police officer for six years and is presently the investigating officer with respect to a child molest that occurred at the ——Day Care Center in Los Altos. the victim of this molest is J—— M——, age nine. Your affiant has prepared a nine-page police report pertaining to your affiant's investigation. Said police report is incorporated herein as People's Exhibit No. 1. Your affiant believes that the contents of the police report are true and accurate. Your affiant believes that the statement of J—— M—— is true.

Your affiant has discussed this case with J—— A——, who is the Program Director for the Child Assault Prevention Program at the YWCA, and who has (as stated in the police report) interviewed J—— M——. Your affiant learned from Miss A—— that she has been Program Director of the Child Assault Prevention Program at the YWCA for two years, and as Program Director, she has lectured at numerous schools and civic programs about how to prevent child sexual abuse. Your affiant learned from J—— A—— that she has an Associate of Arts Degree from Duchess Community College in Poughkeepsie, New York and a Bachelor of Arts Degree in history and elementary education and special education from Marist College in Poughkeepsie, New York. Your affiant also learned from Miss A—— that she is presently in the second year of a graduate program at the University of Santa Clara in child therapy. Your affiant learned from Miss A—— that she worked as a special education teacher in the Marlboro District in New York for four years. Your affiant learned from Miss A—— that she has counseled in excess of 75 children who were sexually abused, as well as hundreds of adults who were sexually abused.

Miss A—— told your affiant that she believes J—— M—— and bthe statement contained in the police report is a truthful statement by J—— M——. Miss A—— told your affiant that she believes J—— M–the following:

1. The adult nature of the language which J—— M—— used to describe the sexual attack on him by "L——," which is not common for a child of this age.

463

2.  The way J—— M—— could describe the episodes of sexual abuse, including the reaction of his friends and their facial expressions.
3.  The amount of detail that J—— M—— used to describe the sexual assault, plus J—— M——'s affect and anxiety at the time he was telling Miss A—what happened to him.

Your affiant also discussed this case with Detective Jeffrey Miller of the Los Gatos Police Department. Your affiant learned from Detective Miller that he has been a police officer for approximately six years and has been assigned to the investigative division of the Los Gatos Police Department as the juvenile investigator for the past 18 months. Your affiant learned from Detective Miller that his duties include the investigation of sexual assaults on children. Your affiant learned from Detective Miller that he has investigated in excess of 40 cases involving child sexual abuse. Your affiant learned from Detective Miller that he has attended a 40-hour course given by the California Youth Authority on the subject of juvenile investigation, a 15-hour course given by the Sexual Assault Investigation Association on the subject of sexual abuse of juveniles, and a 35-hour course given by the Sexual Assault Investigators School of the San Jose State University on the subject of sexual assault investigation, as well as an 8-hour course given by the United States Customs Service on the production and importation of child pornography and methods used to combat child pornography. Your affiant learned that Detective Miller has testified as an expert witness on sexual abuse before the Superior Court in Santa Clara County. Your affiant has given Detective Miller the opportunity to review the police report (People's No. 1) pertaining to this incident, and your affiant also was present with Detective Miller when your affiant discussed this case with J —— A ——. Your affiant has also discussed the details of this case with Detective Miller.

Your affiant believes, based upon his conversation with Detective Miller, that he will find in L —— D ——'s home at —— V ——photographs described by the victim, J —— M ——, because in Detective Miller's experience, persons who take photographs tend to keep them, usually in their residence. Your affiant also believes, based upon your affiant's conversation with Detective Miller, that L —— D —— is a pedophile, who is an adult who procures children for his own sexual satisfaction and takes photographs of children for his own satisfaction. Your affiant learned from Detective Miller that it is likely that L —— D —— has photographs, movies, video tapes, negatives, and slides depicting sexual activities involving adults and juveniles. Your affiant learned from Detective Miller that pedophiles often subscribe to magazines and newspapers that specialize in child pornography and maintain correspondence with other pedophiles who have a similar interest in child pornography.

# Appendix II

## Identification of Affiant

Affiant R.P. "Toby" Tyler is a duly sworn Deputy Sheriff in and for the County of San Bernardino. Affiant was appointed as a Reserve Deputy Sheriff in 1967. Affiant has been employed on a full-time basis as a Deputy Sheriff since June 14, 1969.

Affiant has completed in excess of 70 college semester units in the field of Police Science. Affiant has attended and completed the San Bernardino County Sheriff's Basic Academy and has attended regular in-service training since attendance at the basic academy in 1969 and 1970. Affiant has attended four advanced officer academies, receiving training in various law enforcement subjects, since graduation from the Basic Academy.

Affiant was a patrol deputy assigned the West End Sheriff's Station and the Rancho Cucamonga Sheriff's Station until February 1979. The last two years as a patrol officer were completed as the San Bernardino County Sheriff's first School Resource Officer, assigned to the schools within the City of Rancho Cucamonga.

Affiant has received the P.O.S.T. Basic Certificate and also the P.O.S.T. Intermediate Certificate. Affiant is eligible and qualified for the P.O.S.T. Advanced Officer Certification.

## Expertise of Affiant: Maltreatment of Children

Affiant has received extensive training in the field of child maltreatment. This has included courses provided during the Sheriff's Basic Academy and Advanced Officer Academies. In-service training has also been provided in this specific field. In addition, affiant has attended and completed the following specialized programs in the field of Child Maltreatment:

    University of Southern California
        Delinquency Control Institute (update) program
    University of Southern California
        Child Abuse program
    College of The Redwoods

Sexual Exploitation of Children
Orange Coast College
  Parents United: Sexual Abuse Intervention
Orange County District Attorney/California Youth Authority
  Sexual Abuse and the Sexual Exploitation of Children
University of California , San Diego
  Rape and the Sexual Abuse/Assaults of Children
Riverside City College
  Child Abuse/Sexual Abuse


Numerous other one- to three-day seminars/symposiums in the field of child abuse, sexual abuse, and sexual exploitation of children (a minimum of one program per month) are attended and completed by affiant as well.

Affiant was promoted to the rank of Detective in February 1979 and was at that time assigned to the Sheriff's Juvenile Division. Affiant was instrumental in the formation and development of the Crimes Against Children Unit and is the senior investigator within said unit, assigned specifically to the Sexual Abuse/Sexual Exploitation Team.

Affiant is the instructor for the Sheriff's Basic Academy in the field of child abuse, sexual abuse and sexual exploitation of children. In addition, affiant has provided lectures/training and/or served as consultant to numerous law enforcement, medical, social service, and educational departments and agencies, including:

Office of Criminal Justice Planning
California Youth Authority
California Sexual Assault Investigators' Association
Kaiser Foundation Medical Center
San Antonio Hospital
Needles School District
Riverside City College
Barstow Unified School District
Victor Valley School District
Palm Springs Womens' Press Club
Redlands Unified School District
Department of Mental Health, San Bernardino
Bear Valley School District
Mental Health Association, San Bernardino
San Bernardino County Schools
San Bernardino City Schools
College of the Desert
Valley College

University of California , Riverside
University of California , Los Angeles
City of San Francisco, Sexual Abuse Council of the Mayor's Office
Walnut Creek Community Action Council
United States Postal Inspection Service
Loma Linda University

In addition, affiant is scheduled as an invited plenary speaker at the Fourth International Congress on Child Abuse and Neglect in Paris, France in September 1982.

Affiant is a member of the faculty at Loma Linda University (the School of Medicine). Affiant was appointed to the position of Clinical Instructor, Department of Pediatrics, effective January 1982.

Affiant has served as a consultant to numerous law enforcement and prosecution agencies in the field of maltreatment of children.

Affiant has testified before a joint committee of the California Legislature in the field of Child Maltreatment.

Affiant has served as a consultant/validator to the family court services in San Bernardino and Los Angeles Counties.

Affiant has served as an affiant or co-affiant on more than ten previous search warrant affidavits in pedophile/child molest investigations.

Affiant has qualified in both Municipal and Superior Court as an expert in Child Maltreatment. This has been in both criminal and civil proceedings and as a defense and prosecution witness. Affiant has also qualified as an expert before a State of California Labor Commission hearing.

Affiant has read and studied over 80 books/publications in the field of child maltreatment.

Affiant is a member/consultant to five multidisciplinary Child Protective Teams.

Affiant is a founding member of the national Foundation for America's Sexually Exploited Children, Inc., a nonprofit public benefit corporation, and is presently the Vice-President of the Foundation.

## Definition: Pedophile

A pedophile is a child molester. The word *pedophile* is Greek in origin, and means literally child (*pedo*) love or lover (*phile*). The word may also be spelled "paedophile" or "pedofile" and not be inaccurate.

## Expertise of Affiant: Photography

Affiant has been involved in the field of photography for more than 28 years. This includes continuous experience as a photographer, and has included the use of various brands and models of cameras, both still, movie, and instant photo cameras. Affiant has worked, as a youth, in photo finishing laboratories and has recently toured several commercial photo finishing laboratories. In addition, affiant has owned and worked in his own private darkroom facility, developing, printing and enlarging photographs.

## Expertise of Affiant: Video Tape

Affiant has studied consumer video tape products since 1973. Affiant has owned and utilized video tape products, both recorders and cameras, for more than four years. Affiant is familiar with all current consumer video tape formats.

## Expertise of Affiant: Child Pornography

Affiant has viewed in excess of ten thousand photographs of children in nude and lewd sexual poses. These have included private collections that have been seized as the result of investigations that affiant has participated in and commercial publications that depict children engaging in every possible sex act. Affiant utilizes child pornography in training and lectures and is familiar with the history of and the use of such material. Affiant's paper to be presented before the Fourth International Conference On Child Abuse and Neglect is titled: "Child Pornography, The International Exploitation Of Children." Affiant has consulted with numerous law enforcement agencies in the gathering and sharing of intelligence and information relating to victims, offenders, and methods of operation of child pornographers.

## Expertise of Affiant: Age Identification and Developmental Characteristics of Children

While assigned as the School Resource Officer in the City of Rancho Cucamonga, affiant had daily contact with several thousand children from four years of age through their late teens. In addition, affiant has reviewed medical publications which explain and depict children photographically in various developmental stages and ages. This includes the "Growth Patterns at Adolescence" paper by J.M. Tanner. Affiant has had occasion to interview hundreds of child victims during the course of assignment within and without the Crimes Against Children Unit of the San Bernardino County Sheriff's Department.

## Some Characteristics of the Pedophile

As a result of the training, experience, and education that affiant has received, it has been learned that pedophiles almost always photograph their victims.

victims. In addition, many pedophiles collect nude, sexually suggestive and sexually explicit material featuring children. This material includes but is not limited to:

1. Photographs.
2. Movies.
3. Photographic slides.
4. Video tapes.
5. Books and magazines, depicting children in various nude, lewd, and sexually suggestive poses as well as children engaging in explicit sexual activity.

Pedophiles are also frequently found to have and use "sex toys," such as rubber penises, strap-on dildoes, and vibrators that are the same or similar shape as a male penis. They are found to have these items in various sizes, from a three or four inch item to more than twelve inches in length, with a like variation in the diameter of said items. These items may be used by the pedophile on himself for self-gratification, on the child victim as a different form of perverse sexual activity, or the pedophile may have the child victim utilize these items in performing sexual acts upon or with the body of the pedophile.

These materials are gathered both for the sexual gratification of the pedophile and also to arouse and incite the sexual urges of the target victim(s). These items will also be used to arouse the curiosity and to lower the inhibitions of the target child victims, so that they will participate in subjecting themselves to similar activity and also allow themselves to be photographed in activity such as is depicted in the child pornography displayed to them.

Pedophiles rarely, if ever, dispose of their sexually explicit material or nude photographs of children, especially when it is used in the seduction of their target victims. These sexually explicit materials are treated as prized possessions by pedophiles. While affiant has participated in a large number of investigations involving child pornography, affiant has never discovered a pedophile who has destroyed any of his child pornography material. In one such case for example, a pedophile began collecting such material in the 1940's and when a search was conducted, he was found to have acquired so much material that he had even rented a garage for the specific purpose of retaining his entire collection of material.

Pedophiles will frequently use "instant" picture cameras such as those made by Polaroid and Kodak to produce sexually explicit photographs of children. Pedophiles will often take nude but not sexually explicit photographs of victims with regular negative and slide type films, producing the explicit photos with instant cameras. Some pedophiles are ignorant of the photographic laboratories' methods and will use print film for producing explicit photographs, not knowing that all photographs are seen by a quality control employee of the laboratory and they may therefore be reported as suspected child sex abusers.

Pedophiles who are familiar with photographic film-developing processes will also feel safer using slide film and movies to record explicit sex acts involving children as these types of films are viewed at a relatively fast speed and are not nominally handled by hand in the modem laboratory. Movie film is in fact nominally checked for quality control at such a rapid speed that a viewable image is not seen, but rather a blurred image is seen which will facilitate the determination of the quality of the chemicals used in such processing.

Pedophiles will often take one or more rolls of pictures of their victims in nude but not explicit poses, send them off for processing to determine whether they will be resumed or reported, and if such nude photographs are resumed, will then send explicit photographic film taken at the same time as the nonexplicit nudes.

In recent years, many pedophiles have acquired video tape recorders and cameras. These are instruments which record both video (picture) and audio (sound) onto reusable and erasable magnetic tape. Cameras are available with black and white or with color capability. In modem video tape products, the camera is the determining factor as to whether color or black and white images are recorded.

Many pedophile photographers will also maintain a collection of nude and sexually explicit photographs and/or commercial publications that depict such activity in their vehicles. These can then be used for chance encounters with potential new victims.

Pedophiles also are found to carry an example of such material on their person, frequently in their wallet, for encounters they may have while pedestrian.

Knowledgeable pedophile photographers will maintain their movies, video tapes, slides and negatives inside a building, rather than in an automobile, as the heat buildup that takes place in parked cars is capable of causing permanent destruction of such items. Most dwellings offer relatively consistent and safe temperatures for the safe storage of such items.

Many pedophiles photograph their victims and these photographs serve the purposes listed above plus many pedophiles will exchange, trade, or sell such photographs to other pedophiles. In fact many pedophiles maintain an extensive correspondence with other pedophiles who have the same interest (children of various age or developmental stages), and these pedophiles do nominally trade and exchange material that feature children in explicit acts.

The trading of such material enables pedophiles to increase their own private collections of such material and provides not only material for seducing additional victims, but material which can be traded to still other pedophiles.

Many pedophiles maintain a diary, detailing the activity and the date of the activity, the age of the victim, and the date of occurrence. These diaries may or may not contain photographic reminders of the activity, or in some cases, a photographic rather than written diary will be maintained by the pedophile. Some pedophiles are now maintaining a computerized diary of their victims and activity.

Most pedophiles prefer a particular age and/or developmental range in their target victims, peculiar to each individual pedophile.

Most pedophiles will engage in activity that is of interest to their victims or potential victims that they are trying to seduce. This may include trips to recreation areas, arcades, etc. The pedophile seduces the child in a way that is similar to adults seducing adults, but at a clearly different (juvenile) level.

Married pedophiles will normally go to great lengths to conceal their collections of explicit or suggestive materials and correspondence. The reason for the great effort to conceal is to prevent discovery by their spouse or other routine visitors to their homes.

Single pedophiles will often leave some of their material in plain sight so that visiting children (potential victims) will see and view the material in the hope that it will lead to their curiosity and willingness to participate in the depicted activity on the part of the child.

Many pedophiles maintain post office boxes where they receive correspondence from other pedophiles and also where they can receive their explicit material that has been processed or traded. They will often utilize a fictitious name or slightly change their own name when obtaining the P.O. box assignment. Most commercial child pornography that is imported from the European producers (the primary source of such commercial material) is sent to P.O. boxes as well.

Commercial child pornography is primarily published and distributed on an international scale from Europe. The providers of the original material (master print for movies, slides, negatives or photographs for pictures) are pedophile pornographers, not just pornographers. In fact, such original material is used to increase private collections of such material by trading such material for past or future publications/movies, tapes, etc. This commercial material is distributed all over the world by the producers, who solicit new original material through advertisements in their respective publications.

# Appendix III

Municipal Court of California Santa Clara County Judicial District
San Jose Facility

State of California   } ss.   *Affidavit in Support*
County of Santa Clara }        *of Search Warrant*

Personally appeared before me this —— day of May, 1985, SETH
GOLDSTEIN who, on oath, makes complaint, and deposes and says that
there is just, probable and reasonable cause to believe, and that he does
believe, that there is now in the possession of JOHN JONES, on the premises
located at 123 Anywhere Street, San Jose, County of Santa Clara, California,
which premises consist of: a single story, single family dwelling, beige or light
salmon in color, with brown trim on the front porch; the numerals "123"
with the numeral "1" missing are affixed to the front of the house on the
right side of the garage; the numerals "123" are painted in black and white
on the curb in front of the house; the house is located on the north side of
Anywhere Street between Coffee and Tea Avenues; including basements,
attics, storage spaces, appurtenant buildings, surrounding grounds and all
containers therein and thereon which could contain any of the items sought;
    AND THE PERSON of JOHN JONES, Latino male adult, D.O.B. 9-24-40,
5'9", 150 pounds, black hair, brown eyes;
    AND THE FOLLOWING VEHICLES:

A blue 1981 Ford pickup truck with a camper, California license 1234567;
A 1978 Buick sedan, California license ABCDEF;
A 1983 Chevrolet station wagon, California license XYZ1234; personal
property described as follows:

1.  Camera equipment and video equipment intended for the taking,
    producing, and reproducing of photographic images, including but
    not limited to: cameras, instant and otherwise, video production
    equipment, lenses, enlargers, photographic papers, film, chemicals;

473

2. Phone books, phone registers, correspondence or papers with names, addresses or phone numbers which would tend to identify a Latino male juvenile, approximately 16 years old, 5′ to 5′6″ in height, 120 to 125 in weight, dark short hair approximately collar length, "skinny"; an unknown-race male juvenile, 16 to 18 years old; an unknown-race male juvenile, approximately 15 years old; an unknown-race male, approximately 11 years old; or any other juvenile;

3. Photographs, movies, video tape, negatives, slides and/or undeveloped film depicting nudity and/or sexual activities involving juveniles with juveniles, juveniles with adults, which would tend to identify a Latino male juvenile, approximately 16 years old, 5′ to 5′6″ in height, 120 to 125 in weight, dark short hair approximately collar length, "skinny"; an unknown-race male juvenile, 16 to 18 years old; an unknown-race male juvenile, approximately 15 years old; an unknown-race male, approximately 11 years old; or any other juvenile or adult;

4. Photographs, movies, slides, video tape, negatives, drawings, and/ or undeveloped film which would tend to identify a Latino male juvenile, approximately 16 years old, 5′ to 5′6″ in height, 120 to 125 in weight, dark short hair approximately collar length, "skinny"; an unknown-race male juvenile, 16 to 18 years old; an unknown-race male juvenile, approximately 15 years old; an unknown-race male, approximately 11 years old; or any other juvenile or adult;

5. Correspondence, diaries, and any other writings, tape recordings or letters relating to any juvenile and/or adults which tend to show the identity of juveniles and adults and sexual conduct between juveniles with juveniles or adults;

6. Magazines, books, movies, video tapes, and photographs depicting nudity and/or sexual activities of juveniles or adults, as well as collections of newspaper, magazine, and other publication clippings of juveniles which tend to demonstrate a particular sex and age preference of JOHN JONES;

7. Magazines, newspapers, classified ads, and other publications or writings which contain names, addresses, and phone numbers of individuals who have similar sexual interests and which would tend to identify persons, adult and juvenile, who are involved with JOHN JONES;

8. Sexual aides consisting of "sex toys" such as rubber penises, dildos of various sizes, shapes and construction, vibrators of similar design and construction;

9. Articles of personal property, toys, drawings played with, belonging to or made by a Latino male juvenile, approximately 16 years old, 5′ to 5′6″ in height, 120 to 125 in weight, dark short hair approximately collar length, "skinny"; an unknown-race male juvenile, 16 to 18 years

old; an unknown-race male juvenile, approximately 15 years old; an unknown-race male, approximately 11 years old; or any other juvenile or adult;

10. Safe deposit keys, bank statements, billings and checks, tending to show the location and identity of safe deposit boxes and storage facilities or any person involved in the sexual exploitation of children through child molestation, child pornography, and child prostitution, consisting of, but not limited to: file cabinets, mail envelopes, items of mail;

11. Indicia of occupancy consisting of articles of personal property tending to establish the identity of the person or persons in control of the premises located at 123 Anywhere St., San Jose, including, but not limited to: rent receipts, canceled mail, keys, utility bills and telephone bills.

Your Affiant says that the facts in support of the issuance of the search warrant are as follows:

( *Followed by expertise section.*)

As a result of the above-mentioned training and experience, I have learned that the following characteristics are, generally, found to exist in varying combinations and be true in cases involving people who buy, produce, trade, or sell child pornography, who molest children, and/or who are involved with child prostitutes:

1. There are persons whose sexual objects are children. They receive sexual gratification and satisfaction from actual, physical contact with children and from fantasy involving use of pictures, other photographic or art mediums, and writings on or about sexual activity with children;

2. These people collect sexually explicit materials consisting of photographs, magazines, motion pictures, video tapes, books, and slides which they use for their own sexual gratification and fantasy;

3. These people use sexually explicit materials including those listed above for lowering the inhibitions of children, sexually stimulating children and themselves, and for demonstrating the desired sexual acts, before, during and after sexual activity with children;

4. These people rarely, if ever, dispose of their sexually explicit materials, especially when it is used in the seduction of their victims, and those materials are treated as prize possessions;

5. These people often correspond or meet with one another to share information and identities of their victims as a means of gaining status, trust, acceptance, and psychological support;

6. These people rarely destroy correspondence received from other people with similar interests unless they are specifically requested to do so;

7. The majority of these people prefer contact with children of one sex,
as well as in a particular age or developmental range peculiar to each
individual;

8. These people engage in activity or gravitate to programs which will
be of interest to the type of victims they desire to attract and will
provide them with easy access to these children;

9. These people obtain, collect, and maintain photographs of the children they are or have been involved with. These photos may depict
children fully clothed, in various states of undress, or totally nude, in
various activities, not necessarily sexually explicit. These photos are
rarely, if ever, disposed of and are revered with such devotion that they
are often kept upon the person's person in wallets and such. If a picture
of a child is taken by such a person depicting the child in the nude,
there is a high probability the child was molested before, during, or
after the photo-taking session, because the act of posing is such a great
stimulus for the individual.

10. These people use such photos as described above as a means of reliving
fantasies or actual encounters with the depicted children. They also
utilize the photos as keepsakes and as a means of gaining acceptance,
status, trust, and psychological support by exchanging, trading, or
selling them to other people with similar interests. These photos are
carried and kept by these people as a constant threat to the child of
blackmail and exposure;

11. These people cut pictures of children out of magazines, newspapers,
books, and other publications which they use as a means of fantasy
relationships. These "cut-outs" help to identify the age and sexual
preference of the person under investigation;

12. These people collect books, magazines, newspapers, and other writings on the subject of sexual activities with children. They maintain
these as a way of understanding their own feelings towards children;

13. The people who are afraid of discovery often maintain and run their
own photographic production and reproduction equipment. This may
be as simple as the use of "instant" photo equipment such as Polaroid
makes, video equipment, or as complex as a completely outfitted
photo lab;

14. These people go to great lengths to conceal and protect from discovery,
theft, and damage their collections of illicit materials. This often
includes the rental or use of safe deposit boxes or other storage facilities
outside their immediate residence;

15. These people often collect, read, copy or maintain names, addresses, phone numbers or lists of persons who have similar sexual interests. These may have been collected by personal contact or through advertisements in various publications. These contacts are maintained as a means of personal referral, exchange, and commercial profit. These names may be maintained in the original publication, in phone or note books, or merely on scraps of paper;

16. These people often keep the names of the children they are involved with or with whom they have had sexual contact. They maintain these names in much the same manner as that described in the preceding paragraph and for much the same reasons;

17. These people use sexual aides such as dildos fashioned after a man's penis of various sizes and shapes in addition to other sexual aides in the seduction of their victims. They often utilize these as a means of exciting their victims and of arousing the curiosity of the children;

18. These people maintain diaries of their sexual encounters with children. These accounts of their sexual experiences are used as a means of reliving the encounter when the offender has no children to molest. Such diaries might consist of a notebook, scraps of paper, or a formal diary; depending upon the resources available to the. offender, they may be contained on audio tape or computer entries in a "home computer;"

19. These people collect and maintain books, magazines, articles, and other writings on the subject of sexual activity. These books and materials may be on the topics of human sexuality and sexual education, or consist of sex manuals discussing or showing various sexual acts, positions, or sexual activities. These books and materials are used as a means of seduction of the victim by arousing curiosity, demonstration of propriety of the acts desired, explaining or demonstrating what the offender desires to be done, and as a means of sexual arousal on the part of the offender—particularly when naked children are shown or depicted in the materials;

20. These people often use drugs as a means of inducement to get a child to a particular location such as the offender's home. Alcohol is also used in this fashion. Both drugs and alcohol are also used as a means of seduction reducing the child's inhibitions and for sexual excitement;

21. These people often collect and maintain artifacts, statues, paintings, or other art media which depict children or young perverts in nude poses or sexual acts. These are kept or "left" in places where the victims can find or "discover" them;

22. These people obtain and keep things of interest to their victims. These may consist of magazines, books, and toys for the age level of the

victims they desire to attract and may be as complicated as video games, toy train sets, and computers;

23. These people often keep mementos of their relationship with specific children as a means of remembrance. These may consist of underwear or other garments or things which are unique to the relationship they had with the child;

24. All of the materials requested for seizure will identify children who are being sexually exploited through child molestation, child pornography, and/or child prostitution. The materials will also identify other adults who are engaging in the sexual exploitation of children by these means. In addition, these materials will demonstrate the sexual proclivity, inclination, preference, and activities of the person(s) under investigation, providing evidence that will tend to show that the person(s) under investigation has committed felonies, to wit: Penal Code Sections 288(a) and 311.3.

In Your Affiant's capacity as the investigator assigned to the Sexual Assault Unit, Your Affiant had occasion to review San Jose Police report #85-123-0456, originally investigated by Officer J. M——, badge #——, and followed up by Officer R. F——, badge #——. This incident occurred on March 2, 1985; a copy of the aforementioned police report is attached hereto and incorporated herein for reference as Exhibit A.

According to Officer M——'s preliminary interview as reported in the supplemental report dated 3-2-85, GEORGE O. RODRIGUEZ, Mexican male juvenile, 13 years old (d.o.b. 8-03-71), 123 Castle Court, San Jose, reported that JONES was at his apartment repairing a glass pane in the front door of the apartment in which he lives with his family. He said that JONES asked him to assist him in doing the maintenance work. They went to an upstairs bathroom at which point JONES closed the door. While working on the sink, JONES engaged GEORGE O. RODRIGUEZ in conversation which led to questions about the size and length of GEORGE O. RODRIGUEZ' penis as well as activities with girls of his age.

RODRIGUEZ told Officer M—— that at one point JONES told him to "pull your pants down and let me see it just once. I won't tell anyone." RODRIGUEZ also told Officer M—— that JONES told him not to be embarrassed on several occasions during the incident. While working on the sink, RODRIGUEZ said that JONES grabbed his "genitals" and said, "Didn't that feel good."

On 3-5-85, Officer F—— reported in his supplemental of the same date that he interviewed RODRIGUEZ once again. According to Officer——'s report, RODRIGUEZ said that JONES specifically asked him to repair the door and then, specifically, asked him to assist in repairing the bathroom sink.

RODRIGUEZ told Officer F——— that upon reaching the bathroom, JONES immediately closed the door behind him. As they began repairing the sink, JONES asked RODRIGUEZ about whether or not he had any girl friends. He then asked what kind of sexual experiences he had with them.

RODRIGUEZ told Officer F——— that JONES asked him if he had a "best friend" and that JONES asked him his name. He then asked if RODRIGUEZ did "stuff" with him when no one else was around. RODRIGUEZ told Officer——— that JONES also asked him, "Do you blow on it," referring to his penis. He also said, "Don't be shy, just tell me: I used to do it with my cousin." RODRIGUEZ said that JONES then began asking him about the size of his penis, asking, "How long is it," and "How big is the head." RODRIGUEZ told Officer——— that JONES then asked him about whether or not he had hair "all over."

RODRIGUEZ told Officer F——— that JONES asked to "let me see it, don't be shy," at which point, after being rebuked, JONES reached with his hand and grabbed ahold of RODRIGUEZ' penis through the clothing and squeezed it. After touching RODRIGUEZ, RODRIGUEZ said that JONES asked him if it "felt good."

On 5-24-85, Your Affiant interviewed RODRIGUEZ at the District Attorney's Office. He said that in addition to the information he had given Officer F——— and Officer M——— as related above, JONES talked of masturbating with RODRIGUEZ' best friend. He told Your Affiant that JONES asked him who his best friend was and, when RODRIGUEZ identified him by name, JONES asked RODRIGUEZ if he engaged in masturbation with him. RODRIGUEZ told Your Affiant that JONES told him that JONES had done that with his own cousin when he was a child.

RODRIGUEZ also told Your Affiant that his brothers Ricardo (16 years) and Eugene (15 years) told him, after this incident came to light, that JONES had talked to them about the same things.

RODRIGUEZ also told Your Affiant that two months before this incident he saw JONES at the apartment complex in the company of a 16-year-old, who is described as a Latino male juvenile, approximately 16 years old, 5' to 5'6" in height, 120 to 125 in weight, dark short hair approximately collar length, "skinny."

He said that he also saw him with other boys on at least two or three occasions, describing them as being approximately 15 to 16 years of age, when JONES was working at the apartment house.

On the same date, Your Affiant talked to RODRIGUEZ' father, Richardo RODRIGUEZ, Sr. Mr. RODRIGUEZ said that he also remembers the occasion which his son referred to regarding the 16-year-old described as above. On this occasion, Mr. RODRIGUEZ said that he spoke with JONES and that JONES specifically told him that the 16-year-old was not his son.

Mr. RODRIGUEZ also told Your Affiant that after this incident surfaced, both his sons, Ricardo and Eugene, told him that JONES had made similar advances to them as described by GEORGE.

On the same date, Your Affiant spoke with RODRIGUEZ' mother, Margarita RODRIGUEZ. Mrs. RODRIGUEZ said that on at least three occasions she had seen JONES at the apartment house with three different boys. She remembers one incident as being between the months of August and September, 1984, when she saw JONES in the company of a male juvenile, she could not remember what race, aged approximately 16 to 18 years. She said that she spoke to JONES regarding this individual, and JONES told her that this person was an "exchange student." She described another incident being in the summer of 1984 when she saw JONES in the company of an 11-year-old boy, no further description. The last incident she remembers occurred during a school day, in May or June of 1984, wherein she saw JONES in the company of a 15-year-old boy, no further description.

Officer F———'s police report, dated 3-7-85, indicates that on 3-685 Officer F——— interviewed JONES at the San Jose Police Department. According to Officer F———'s report, Officer F——— told JONES that he was investigating an incident, without describing the particulars. Without prompting, JONES admitted that he believed the incident in question was that which has been previously described by GEORGE O. RODRIGUEZ.

JONES told Officer F——— that he owns the apartment house in which the RODRIGUEZ' parents rent an apartment. He admitted repairing the door on the apartment, assisted by GEORGE RODRIGUEZ. He also told Officer F——— that he asked GEORGE to come upstairs to the bathroom with him to repair the sink. He told Officer F——— that GEORGE walked into the bathroom and sat on the edge of the bath tub, watching him fix the sink. He admitted talking with GEORGE about possible girl friends and said that when GEORGE told him that he had a boy friend, he was "surprised to hear this and was considering informing GEORGE's father of this information."

JONES told Officer F——— that while he was working on the sink he needed a tool which was out of his reach, and he asked GEORGE to get it. He said that at the same time he reached out across to the tool box and his hand "inadvertently" struck GEORGE's groin area. He told Officer F——— that he apologized to GEORGE for touching him. He also told Officer F——— that he did not deliberately touch the boy in a sexual manner and that it was a "complete accident."

Your Affiant contacted Detective Dave S——— of the San Bruno Police Department. Detective S——— told Your Affiant that, according to San Jose police reports, JONES was involved in an accident on 5-5-76 wherein he listed the Anywhere Street address as his home. Detective S——— told Your Affiant that on 7-13-76 JONES reported a burglary, listing the Anywhere

Street address as his home. Detective S——— said at the address listed as 123 Anywhere Street, he found a JOSEPHINE JONES, D.O.B. 3-8-43, was involved in an accident on 5-20-82.

Detective S——— told Your Affiant that he checked with the San Jose Water Department and that the San Jose Water Department billing shows JONES as the current billee. Detective S——— told Your Affiant that he also checked with the San Jose Cable Television Company and that they show JONES as recently disconnecting their service at the Anywhere Street address.

Detective S——— told Your Affiant that he checked with the Tax Assessor of Santa Clara County and found that JONES is listed as the owner and mailing is listed as 123 Anywhere Street. According to Detective S———, the Tax Assessor also lists 132 San Jose Avenue, San Jose, 378 North Chicago, San Jose, and 437 Elmwood Street, Milbrea, as being owned by JONES.

Detective S——— told Your Affiant that JONES is a teacher at Eastside School, a junior high school in San Jose. Detective S——— told Your Affiant that the ages of the children in the school are consistent with the age of GEORGE O. RODRIGUEZ and some of the other children described by GEORGE and his father.

Detective S——— told Your Affiant that on May 28, 1985, he went to 123 Anywhere Street, San Jose, and obtained a description of the house. At the same time, he observed a blue pickup truck with a camper, California license 1234567, parked in front.

Your Affiant checked with the California State Department of Justice, Command Center, and was told that JONES is listed as an applicant in 1965 for a San Jose recreation leader, San Jose Police Department application #12345.

Your Affiant checked with the Department of Motor Vehicles through the use of the District Attorney's teletype terminal and found driver's license #N1234567 as being listed in the name of JOHN JONES, d.o.b. 9-24-40, 123 Anywhere Street. The license was issued on 6-22-81 and expires on 6-22-85. Through the same means, Your Affiant learned that JONES is the registered owner, along with JOSEPHINE JONES, of a 1981 Ford pickup, California license 1234567, at the 123 Anywhere Street address; registration expiration date is 5-31-86, having been issued 5-14-85. Your Affiant also learned that JONES is the registered owner, with JOSEPHINE JONES, of a 1978 Dodge sedan, California license ABCDEF, at the 123 Anywhere Street address; expiration date of this license is 12-4-85, having been issued on 1-18-82.

Your Affiant also learned in the same manner that JONES is the registered owner, with JOSEPHINE JONES, of a 1983 Chevrolet station wagon, California license 1234567, at the 123 Anywhere Street address; registration of this car expires April 24, 1986, and was issued on May 14, 1985.

Your Affiant has learned through training and experience that to prevent discovery, to protect, to transport, and to conceal and store the items listed for seizure in this affidavit, people who molest children often use their vehicles.

Through training and experience Your Affiant also knows that people who molest children often carry the types of things listed for seizure in this affidavit on their person.

Based upon the above facts, Your Affiant prays that a Search Warrant be issued with respect to the above locations for the seizure of said property, and that the same be held under California Penal Code section 1536 and disposed of according to law.

SETH GOLDSTEIN
Affiant

Subscribed and sworn to before me this ——— day of May, 1985.

_____

JUDGE OF THE SUPERIOR COURT

# Appendix IV

[Preceded by listing of expertise]

On January 23, at 1000 hrs., while assigned to the Juvenile Bureau, I interviewed E—— B——, 2—— California, ——, WMJregarding his knowledge of A—— K——, whom he knew as D—— K–told me that he first met K—— the previous winter when he was going to Odyssey School. He said that, at that time, K—— lived at 10th & University. He said that he saw K—— on approximately 3–4 occasions each week and that he bought marijuana from him. He told me that on numerous occasions K—— would make sexual advances to him, talking about oral and anal intercourse.

He told me, prior to K——'s move to Dwight Way (—— #B Dwight) that he saw several photographs (approximately ten) of three or four different boys, age 15–16 years, depicted in nude poses in a house.

He told me that K—— had given him a book which K—— had inscribed "love D"over the summer and that he had given him a necklace. In addition, he wrote him a letter, telling him how much K—— loved him.

I interviewed Michael P. B—— and his wife, Nancy B——, of ——hey lived directly above the apartment rented by K—— at the Dwight Way address.

Among other things, B—— told me that virtually every night, white male juveniles, age 13 to 18, would be constantly going in and out of the rear door of K——'s apartment. He told me that he observed that the traffic began in the late afternoons, around 3 p.m., and would increase as the evening progressed. he said that in one week, there were approximately twenty boys going in and out of K——'s apartment in a single night.

I interviewed Peter C——, —— C——, WMJ, dob —— that he and his friend, David D——, —— WMJ, dob ——62, had run away in November. He said that they stayed at the Donough Arms Hotel on Shattuck Avenue, Sleeping in the hallway.

He said that at approximately 6:15 in the morning, he awoke to find that K—— was giving him a "blow job" (performing oral sex on him). He told me that, at that time, he didn't know who he was, however, later came to know him as K——.

He said that after this, K——— took him to his home on Dwight Way, where K——— gave him cocaine in return for engaging in mutual oral copulation. A copy of the written statement he offered at that time is attached hereto and incorporated herein for reference.

I reinterviewed C——— regarding his experience at K———'s house for further details. C——— told me more of the specifics regarding the sexual acts which occurred between he and K——— and also told me of the observations he had made inside the apartment.

C——— told me that he had seen some photographs of boys, estimated to be about 15 or 20 in number, ranging in age from 17 to 22 years old. He described the pictures as depicting the boys fully clothed.

He also told me of some other pictures which he had seen in K———'s bedroom, which were black and white photographs of boys aged 17 to 19, some with clothing on and two with their clothes off.

He described to me one of the pictures, telling me that it depicted a white boy, age 17–19 years with a half shirt on and nothing else. He described the others as being pictures of boys of similar ages, in various stages of nudity.

He also told me that he had seen some pictures which depicted men and boys engaged in homosexual acts. A copy of the written statement which I took at that time is also attached hereto and incorporated herein for reference.

I had interviewed D——— D———, at which time he had told me about the incident involving K——— and C———. A copy of that statement is attached hereto and incorporated herein for reference.

On January of 1981, E——— S———, owner of E——— Van & Storage, ——— ——— St., 524———, called me and gave me some slides which he said were taken from the property of K———. He said that the Alameda County Sheriff's Office had deposited, with E——— Van & Storage, the possessions of K——— after he was evicted from Dwight Way. He told me that in July, he began disposing of all of the items, having placed an ad in the Independent Gazette, on (day and date) and receiving no response. He told me that while disposing of the items of property, he came upon numerous items of homosexual pornography involving the depicting of boys and men in sexual acts. He told me that among the items he found were the slides which he gave me and a lot of correspondence and other writings belonging to and identifying the owner of the property as being K———.

I examined the content of these slides, approximately fifteen in number, and saw that they depicted boys aged 13–15 in the nude, in various poses. All of the slides depicted the same two boys.

Attention was called to the investigation of Berkeley Police Department case #———83 (the report of investigation attached hereto and incorporated herein for reference) by Sgt. John Houpt. He asked that I review that case because it involved K———. I reviewed that report and found that

Off. Sanchez #57 responded to a call at 1425 hrs., made by K———, who lived at 3——— R———. The narrative of that report is not available, however, I spoke with Off. Sanchez. He told me that K——— told him that the three individuals, listed in the supplemental report written by Off. Avila, had kicked in the door of K———'s apartment, after being involved in an argument over K———'s involvement with a young boy.

I reviewed Off. Avila's report and saw that he had arrested Lawrence Eugene J———, WMA, dob 3-24-63, ——— ——— Drive, San Leandro, 351 ———; Jason –, WMA, dob 1-16-61, 3———, no phone;and David Arlin H———, WMA, dob 12-29-62, ——— ———, San Leandro, 483——— for assault and other charges. Off. Avila's report only briefly alludes to the supposed homosexual acts with young boys. Sgt. Houpt told me that he had spoken to the suspects in this case and that they had told him about K———'s involvement with young boys. Sgt. Houpt directed me to interview the subjects who were still in custody, at which time I contacted C——— and J———.

Subsequent to the brief interviews which I conducted on Monday, I conducted in detail interviews with C———, H———, J———, and one of their associates "Billy" E. S———, ——— ——— Drive, San Leandro, ———their statements was reduced to writing and are attached hereto and incorporated herein for reference.

In brief, C——— told me that he has known K——— since approximately July of last year, having lived in the same house with him, He described their housing arrangements as a cooperative affair, a conversion of a formerly single family dwelling into fourteen rented rooms. It has community kitchen and bath facilities and a common living room.

He said that he first met K——— when K——— complained about C———hygiene and noise. He said that he knows him as D——— and that D——— also goes by the name of F———.

He said that soon after he moved in, K——— told him that he was gay and that he liked to have sex with boys under 18 years old.

He said that over the seven months, he has seen eight different boys in D———'s company, ranging in age from 12 years old to 17 years old. He said that most of the boys were 15–17 years old in age range, possibly as young as 14. He said that the Sunday he was arrested was the first time he had ever seen a boy who was 12 or 13 years old.

He said that over the seven months that he had lived there, D——— had told him on 3–4 occasions that he likes to have sexual relations with boys and that on other occasions he has told him that he likes boys under the age of 18 years old. He said that as recently as two months ago K——— had said "I suck little boys' cocks."

C——— told me that on several occasions he has seen K——— wearing a T-shirt which says "Big Boss" on the front and "Bad Little Boys" on the back.

He said that approximately two weeks ago, he had seen D——— with a boy who was 16 or 17 years old. He said that the boy went into D———'s room after knocking on the door. He said that the boy had red hair, was approximately 5'11", approximately 160–170 lbs. and was slim in build. He said that he had also seen him with D——— approximately 4–5 months ago.

He said that most of the time, the boys come to visit K——— approximately 9 p.m. in the evening to 12 p.m. in the evening and stay until approximately 10–11 the next morning.

He said that for the past several months he has lived in the apartment directly adjacent to K———'s.

He said that approximately four or five months ago, he had occasion to be inside K———'s room. He saw, opposite the door, on a wall, five or six 12" × 12", black and white pictures, depicting boys showing their genitalia. He said that the pictures depicted boys who were 6–12 years old, without pubic hair, showing them from the navel to the knees. He said that they were mounted on thick, white construction paper and that in the picture the background was dark.

He also saw a plaque, which he said was similar to a nameplate which one would have on an office desk, which said "I Love Little Boys." This plaque was white with red letters.

He said that approximately two months ago, a boy whom he only knew as Nathan and who was a friend of D———, told him that D——— had given him $50.00 and some cocaine when he visited K——— on an occasion approximately two months ago. C——— said that Nathan told him that he fell asleep on the floor, after taking the cocaine and that when he awoke, he found K——— unzipping his pants and trying to take them off.

C——— told me that K——— talks about cocaine use "all the time" and on two ocasions, the most recent being the night before he was arrested, people had come to the house at R——— Street asking him if they knew where K——— was in order that they might buy cocaine from K———.

He said that on an occasion approximately two months ago, he saw a white male, 25 years, with K——— in the living room of the apartment house. He said that he saw the white male give D——— some money and that D——— gave him a package of what he thought was cocaine, in a "snow seal."

C——— told me that he always smells ether coming from D———'s room and that the most recent time that he had smelled ether (used in the ingestion of cocaine in a "free base" method) was Friday night, before he was arrested.

C——— told me that he has used cocaine for approximately 2–3 years, using it approximately 5–7 times in that time span. He said that during his military and civilian life, he has been present approximately fifty times when cocaine has been used by others. He said that he has seen it "snorted" (inhaled), injected through needles, and smoking it. He has seen it packaged and mixed and is familiar with the manner in which it is prepared using mirrors and "kits."

He said that on the Sunday he was arrested, at approximately 11:30 in the morning, he saw K——— with a boy who was approximately 12 years old. He said the boy was white, had freckles, straight, sandy blond colored hair, length to below the ears. He said the boy was wearing a brown or tan T-shirt and blue jeans. he said that the boy was approximately 5'2" and weighed approximately 100–120 lbs.

He said that when the boy emerged from K———'s room with K———, his head was covered with a blue down jacket, however when he took it off, he saw the boy's eyes were glassy, red, and that the pupils were wide.

He said that when this happened, he was in the living room with his friends listed above.

He described the boy's hair as being "messed up" and said that so was K———'s. He said that K——— was wearing a T-shirt, blue jeans; however, he was not wearing any shoes.

He said that when someone in his group of friends asked how old the boy was, that K——— replied he was 12 years old. C——— told me that K——— alhing similar to "I popped his sugar."

H——— told me that he has known Jason for approximately 6–7 months, having visited him at the R——— Street address about two to three times each month since that time. He said that he had never seen K——— prior to the Sunday that the incident in question occurred.

He said that the Sunday in question, he had gone to visit C——— and took with him his friends Larry J———, Billy ———, and Dave H———.

When they arrived, they stayed in a room outside D———'s room and began drinking beer. He said that while they were drinking, Colley had told him about K———'s preference for boys.

He said approximately 10–15 minutes after they arrived, a young boy came out of D———'s room with D———. He told me that he saw the boy had a coat over his head, but was able to see that the boy was approximately 10–12 years old, had sandy blond hair, was approximately 4'5" to 4'6" and wore Levis and tennis shoes.

He said that K——— went outside with the boy and a short while later returned without the boy. He said that someone asked him how old the boy was and that K——— told him he was 12 years old and something similar to "I just got his sugar." K——— then said, "do you want some." At this, everybody got mad and an argument started. At some point K——— said something similar to "I love little boys." Both J——— and S——— basically said the same things as C——— andreviously mentioned, their statements were reduced to writing and have been attached hereto and incorporated herein for reference.

I then called Off. Sanchez and spoke to him regarding his investigation. He said that while investigating the complaint of malicious damage and the allegations that K—— admitted to Off. Sanchez that he was a homosezual. He also said something similar to "it doesn't matter what age they are."

Off. Sanchez told me that while he was inside K——'s room, investigating the malicious damage report, he saw on a wall, opposite the door, the same photographs described by C——. In addition, Off. Sanchez told me that he saw a book entitled, *The Boy, A Photographic Essay* and a book on anatomy described as being blue or red with a leather binding.

According to C——, K—— has been using a red AMC Javelin, with lots of dents and a green interior. He said that he had last seen him using this car on the Saturday night prior to his arrest.

I called K—— at the number listed in Off. Sanchez's report and confirmed that his apartment number is 13. Off. Sanchez and David H—— told me that K——'s apartment is immediately on the right as one enters the front door from R—— Street. It is in the northeast quadrant of the house at —— R——.

Wherefore, your affiant prays that such search warrant be issued, based upon the above facts, for the seizure of said property.

# Appendix V

[Preceded by listing of expertise]
In your Affiant's capacity as the Investigator assigned to the District Attorney's Sexual Assault Unit, your Affiant had occasion to review L——— Police Report #84 authored by Detective Jeff Miller. A copy is attached hereto as Reference "A".

According to Detective Miller's report, he met with and discussed this case with the mother of Sara R———, ——— A——— Place, L———nile, DOB ——— 79 (5 years), Beth R———, ——— A———ite female adult, DOB ———51. She told Detective Miller that her daughter attended the home of a babysitter located at ——— C———, L———, run b—, beginning in November of 1983. She said that her daughter had been taken to the babysitters on a daily basis during the month of November and approximately 6 times between November 1983 and the time of their discussion in May of 1984.

Your Affiant spoke with Detective Miller regarding this contact with Mrs. R——— and the information he obtained during that interview. Detective Miller told your Affiant that the reason Mrs. R——— took her daughter out of the program was because she had found other arrangements. According to the report, Mrs. R——— also told Detective Miller that when her daughter, Sara, was at the babysitters she played a game which she called the "hands game" with "a man." Her daughter described the game of consisting of her daughter touching parts of her body while the man touched parts of his body. She told Detective Miller that her daughter had said that one of the parts of the body which she touched was her own genitalia. She also told Detective Miller that her daughter said that both she and the man were fully clothed during the "game".

Mrs. R——— told Detective Miller that her daughter described the man as being "about the age of her daddy." Detective Miller learned from Mrs. R——— that her husband is 42 years old.

In addition, Mrs. R——— told Detective Miller that Julia said the man who played the game with Julia had a beard.

On May 30 and June 1, Detective Miller and your Affiant interviewed Sara R——— regarding the facts previously related in his police report. She repeated the account of the "game," demonstrating with the use of dolls and on her own body how she touched herself and where the "man" touched himself. She started first touching her head and parts of her body above her waist, slowly working down to her feet and then back again. The game would entail saying which part she would toch as she did so simultaneously while the man would do the same thing.

On June 1, 4, 7, and 12, Detective Miller and I interviewed Beth R———'s son, R. J. R———, DOB ———80 (4 years old).

At first, R.J. told us that he couldn't talk about what happened at the babysitters'. Through the use of toys, your Affiant and Detective Miller were finally able to get R.J. to explain what happened. He said that the babysitter gave him a bath. He also told us that he had been spanked, but was unable to identify the person who did these things in either circumstance.

He also told of playing the "naked game," telling us that it occurred in the house which he lived in prior to his living at the A——— Place home, his new house (A——— Place), and his friend Cameron's (Cameron C———) home.

He described the naked game as taking his clothes off whereupon he was kissed all over his body including his genitalia.

When your Affiant presented the anatomically correct dolls which bore clothing of like size, at his instigation and demonstration, R.J. began taking the clothes off the small boy dall, asking "Whose pee pee is this?" pointing to the doll's "penis."

After repeated questioning, R.J. told your Affiant that the person who played the "naked game" with him was Cameron.

Your Affiant watched Detective Miller use some of R.J.'s toys, one of which was a Mickey Mouse doll, as the means of getting R.J. to discuss the case. It was through the character of Mickey Mouse that R.J. was able to articulate what had occurred to him.

After our interview, conducted on June 7 with R.J., using the Mickey Mouse doll, R.J.'s mother told both your Affiant and Detective Miller that he told her that "Mickey Mouse was bad for telling what happened."

At one point during the use of the anatomically correct dolls, Detective Miller asked R.J. who the "bad person was" and R.J., in response, said "Raggedy Andy" and went to his room, bringing out a Raggedy Ann and Andy doll set.

On May 9, 1984, according to Detective Miller's report, he met with Sue C———, mother of Cameron C———, white male juvenile, DOB ———80 (3 years), —— told Detective Miller that her son was taken to the babysitter at ——— C——— on every Wednesday (all day) in September and October of 1983. Beginning in November of 1983, she began taking him to another babysitter and has not brought him back since.

She told Detective Miller that Cameron was removed from the C——— address babysitter because he seemed afraid of the place and did not want to go there. She told Detective Miller that Cameron would cry "I don't want to go. I'm not going there." She told Detective Miller that since he had been removed from the babysitter, he occasionally would seek reassurance that he is not going to be taken back.

Sue C——— told Detective Miller that she has noticed Cameron no longer appears to be affectionate to her. She told Detective Miller that on or about January or February of 1984, she discovered her son with his pants down, trying to insert his penis between the legs of a doll, simulating sexual intercourse.

On June 29, July 3, 11, 12, 13 and 16, your Affiant interviewed Cameron C——— with Detective Miller. Whenever Detective Miller and I would begin to discuss the babysitter, Cameron became evasive, changing the subject repeatedly and beginning to play with toys away from us. He would stop talking or quietly play by himself, turning away from us. Sometimes, he left the room.

One one occasion, we asked Cameron who "was a bad person." He responded by saying "Raggedy Andy", after going to a shelf and pulling down a Raggedy Andy doll.

While playing with Cameron, when we chose characters to play using his toys, Cameron would only assume the character of "evil" or "bad" character toys during the play interview.

Then, during the play interview, Cameron would not allow the "good" characters to prevail, severely restricting their ability to "combat" or "win" the game.

He steadfastly refused to play a "good" character or accept an award for being a "good guy."

Mrs. C——— told your Affiant that after our interviews, Cameron told her that "Mr. A——— took my clothes off." He also told her that he had received a spanking and was given a bath, but did not identify the person who did these things with him. He also told his mother about playing the "naked game," saying it was necessary to have "a bed" and that in order to play the naked game he would have to take his clothes off.

Your Affiant and Detective Miller were never able to get Cameron to tell us the things that he told his mother, listed in the above paragraph.

According to Detective Miller's report, on May 9, 1984, he spoke with Martha K———, mother of Julia K———, white female juvenile, DOB ———81 (3 years), , L———, ———. She told Detective Miller that her daughter, Julia, had been attending the babysitter at ——— C———, L——— since September of 1her daughter had recently indicated that she did not want to go to the babysitter's. She told Detective Miller that her daughter was having nightmares, talking about "the man." She said that she has seen her daughter "pulling out her hair and screaming."

Mrs. K——— told Detective Miller that she has noticed that when Julia kisses her or her husband that Julia has done so in a "passionate, very sexual" way, wrapping her arms around the parent and kissing with an open mouth.

Mrs. K——— told Detective Miller that approximately one month prior to his interview (April) she had picked up Julia from the babysitter's at which point Julia said "only girls eat penis."

She told Detective Miller that Julia had not been to the babysitter's since the first week in May of 1984.

Detective Miller and your Affiant interviewed Julia K——— on July 17, 26, 27, and 30, August 2, and August 8.

Through the use of anatomically correct dolls, Julia demonstrated the activity she engaged in with a person she described as "a man," which occurred up a flight of stairs. She demonstrated that she was made to take off her clothes at the "man's direction." She also demonstrated that the man took his clothes off and reenacted an act of oral copulation whereupon the adult male would orally copulate with her placing his head in her genital area.

She demonstrated how she was told to masturbate the man, placing her hand over the man's penis and rubbing it.

She demonstrated penetration of her vagina, showing the placing of the adult male's hand into the area of her vagina, saying that it "hurt."

She also demonstrated an act of sexual intercourse, showing the adult male's penis coming in contact with the vagina of the young girl doll, which she identified as being herself and said was an act done to her.

According to Detective Miller's report, he interviewed Evelyn M——— on ———, 1984, mother of Anne M———, ——— M———, L——— DOB 81 (2 years).

Mrs. M——— told Detective Miller that she had place her daughter in the babysitting program in September of 1983 and kept the child there until the first week of May 1984. She told Detective Miller that since December of 1983 she had noticed some strange behavior in her daughter.

She told Detective Miller that since December her daughter's had frequent nightmares, waking up screaming "I'm afraid, I'm afraid." She said that her daughter was afraid of "the ducks" and of "the man."

Mrs. M——— told Detective Miller that prior to December of 1983, her daughter had no trouble sleeping and usually slept soundly throughout the night.

Mrs. M——— also told Detective Miller that her daughter usually cooperated and enjoyed taking a bath; however, since the December time period, she no longer likes to bathe.

Mrs. M——— told Detective Miller that she has found her daughter trying to scratch her forearms with "such intensity" as to draw blood.

She described to Detective Miller an incident that occurred in the first week of May involving the gardener, who is known to Anne. She said that she saw her daughter, when she encountered the gardener, throw herself on the ground, place her hands over genital area and scream "Don't hurt me, don't hurt me."

Mrs. M——— told Detective Miller that her daughter is normally very friendly with people, including the gardener, and that she has noticed her daughter to become withdrawn and avoid contact with others.

Mrs. M——— told Detective Miller that her daughter complained of pain when urinating.

Detective Miller interviewed Anne M——— through her mother acting as an interpreter (she speaks only French) and she told Detective Miller that "the man" hurt her and that the man was "at A——— 's." Detective Miller also states in his report that Anne M——— repeatedly said "A———' was done" which is, accordo her mother's interpretation, her way of saying that she is no longer going back to the babysitter's.

Detective Miller told your Affiant that since his interview in May, he spoke to Mrs. M———, and that she told him that while on vacation in France, from May 11 through June 10, her daughter took a ruler and stuck it between her aunt's (Chislaine M———) legs in the area of the vagina and said, "The man put his finger there."

Detective Miller also told your Affiant that Mrs. M——— told him that when they went away on vacation her daughter returned to her normal behavior pattern and did not have any nightmares until ———, 1984 when they went to the beach in Santa Cruz.

Detective Miller told your Affiant that Mr. and Mrs. M——— told him that on the aforementioned date, Mr. M——— was walking with his daughter down the beach when they encountered R——— A———, a man whom Mr. M——— knows to b—'s son and whom he knows to live at ——— C———. Mr. M———ller that as soon as his daughter saw Mr. A——— she became "terrified," grabbing and hiding behind his legs, saying "I'm scared, I'm scared."

He told Detective Miller that they went back to where they had their towels on the beach and he and his wife spoke with their daughter about Mr. A ——— and she said, "I'm afraid, I'm afraid of the man." They then left without pursuing it any further.

Detective Miller said that the M ———'s told him that their daughter's nightmares resumed in the extreme that night and have remained since.

Detective Miller told your Affiant that Mrs. M ——— told him that in July she was giving her daughter a bath and that her daughter told her not to put her finger in her vagina.

She also told Detective Miller that on the night of the ———th, in a nightmare, she heard her daughter say, "It hurts, it hurts, finger, it hurts."

Mrs. M ——— also told Detective Miller that on ———, 1984, they took their daughter to the ——— Plaza, ——— ——— Avenue, L ———which contains an office Mr. A ——— uses.

Without telling their daughter where they were going, they began walking around the complex and when they got to Mr. A ———'s office, their daughter started screaming and crying saying, "I'm afraid, I'm afraid." At some time during this incident, she said her daughter looked into the office and said, "The man's not there."

Detective Miller told your Affiant that on ———, 1984, he spoke with Mr. M ——— at lunchtime. He said his daughter told him that "the man did head in the bottom." He also told Detective Miller that his daughter has began coming up to people in their home and exposing herself, pulling her pants down before them.

Detective Miller also told your Affiant that he spoke with Mrs. K ——— and that she said she and her husband were in their bedroom one recent evening when their daughter came into the room. She said that her husband was wearing a robe and nothing else, at which point her daughter came to her husband and started trying to lift the robe. She said that when they questioned her about why she had done what she did with her father's robe, Julia replied that she had done it "with the man at A ———'s. They were never able to get her to describe the robe or the incident any further.

Detective Miller told your Affiant on the ——— he spoke to Julia's parents who described another incident which occurred on ———. He said that they told him that they and Julia were talking about the robe incident and that Julia described something she saw at "A ———'s" (the babysitter's). She said that a man and lady were fighting and that the man hit the lady.

Detective Miller told your Affiant that the parents described how Julian demonstrated what she saw, telling him that she described the woman as laying on her back with her legs in the air, legs spread apart.

They told him that she said, "The lady ate the man's penis." They also said that Julia said the man was wearing "a black bathing suit," also describing it as black pants and a suit like "daddy wears."

Detective Miller said that the parents told him that Julia said that there were boys and girls present at this incident and that they didn't like it and were "crying." Julia also said Anne M——— was there.

Detective Miller also told your Affiant that on ———, 1984, Anne M ———'s father, Jean ——— M ———, told him that on the weekend of ——— and –d his family were at the beach and had met several French women. The women wanted to take Anne's picture; however, Anne said "No" and refused to stand still or pose for a photograph.

Detective Miller told your Affiant that on ———, 1984 he brought both the M ——— family and the K——— family to Valley Medical Center where Dr. H——— examied Julia and Anne.

Detective Miller told me that Dr. H——— told him that he found a slight scar near the opening of Anna's vagina, which had healed. He told me that Dr. H——— told him that this was "unusual for a child her age."

Detective Miller also told me that Dr. H——— told him that he found a reaction in Julia's anus consistent with "stimulation." He also told Detective Miller that he found a mark at the opening of her vagina, which was inconclusive.

Your Affiant has learned from experience and training that children who have been abused sexually often have a feeling of being "unclean." This manifests itself in behavior wherein they constantly wash themselves or scratch or rub the area where they were touched or other parts of their body, often to the point of causing bleeding or disfiguring themselves.

Your affiant has also learned through experience and training that children who have been sexually abused feel that if they make themselves unattractive, perhaps the abuser will not be interested in them any longer. This manifests itself in behavior such as cutting themselves or, often, pulling out their hair, as described earlier in this Affidavit.

Your Affiant has also learned through experience and training that children who have been sexually abused have a poor self-image. Quite often this manifests itself by their association with "bad characters," similar to that experienced in the interviews with Cameron C———.

Your Affiant has also learned through experience and training that children who have been sexually abused often disgress in developmental behavior. This often consists of things similar to potty training reversal, wherein the child is no longer able to control its bowels, or infantile behavior similar to that experienced with Anne M——— in this case.

Your Affiant has also learned through experience and training that children who have been sexually abused also show signs of being abused in refusal to engage in similar activities which surrounded their abuse. This would consist of refusal to take baths, such as that in this case wher Anne M——— refused to be bathed and was fearful of being injured during the taking of a bath, as well as her refusal to pose for photographs.

Your Affiant has also learned through experience and training that children who have been sexually abused experience recurring sleep disorders such as the nightmares mentioned in this case by the various victims.

Your Affiant has also learned through experience and training that these children also experience a fear of adults similar to that of their gardener described by Anne M———'s mother.

Your Affiant has also learned through experience and training that sexually abused children have drastic behavior and mood changes wherein they become nervous, not happy and, in general, fearful of more common experiences, consistent with the behavior described by the parents of the children in this case.

Your Affiant has also learned through experience and training that children experience physical pain following molestation, consistent with the behavior described by Anne M——— during urination.

Your Affiant has also learned through experience and training that children will often reenact the offense with others in their own peer group or of lesser age similar to that described as occurring with R.J. R——— and Cameron C———.

Your Affiant has also learned through experience and training that children who have been molested often exhibit inappropriate behavior for their age group, in particular regarding sexual activity. This may manifest itself in kissing in a very passionate way similar to that described in the instances of Anne and Julia and simulation of intercourse with a doll as described by Cameron C———'s parents. This may also manifest itself in inappropriate language that is sexual in nature, similar to the statement made by Julia about girls engaged in oral copulation. It also could appear in the form of an action similar to that described by Anne's mother regarding the sticking of the ruler between her aunt's legs. Another form of this behavior could be the replaying of a game such as "the naked game" described by Cameron.

Your Affiant has also learned through experience and training that children who have been molested often display other behaviors consistent with being abused. This is often called "avoidance behavior," wherein when the subjects are addressed by parents or others they change the subject, refuse to discuss it, or go about playing as though no discussion was occurring. They also display a fear of returning to the place where the incidents occurred, similar to that wherein all of the children refused to go back to the babysitter's, as well as Anne M———'s reaction approaching the office of R——— A——— at ——— Plaze.

Your Affiant has also learned through experience and training that children who have been abused feel extremely guilty after making disclosure. This may manifest itself in a sudden mood swing or be consistent with behavior described by R.J.'s parents after he told your Affiant and Detective Miller about what happened to him.

Your Affiant has also learned through experience and training that the medical findings as described by Dr. H——— in this case are extremely common in abuse cases such as this and are a significant finding in determining whether or not a child has been sexually assaulted.

Your Affiant has also learned through experience and training that the offender in a case such as this usually engages in "normal" activity, which then digresses through the legitimate play or activity to sexual contact. Such behaviors as those described in this case are extremely consistent with that type of activity. The use of dolls or games to seduce children such as that previously described is a consistent trademark in this type of an offense.

Detective Miller told your Affiant that all of the parents told him that they had taken their children to the home of A——— A——— at ——— C–babysitting. Detective Miller told your Affiant that he checked the phone book and found that A. P. A——— is listed with the same phone number as given him by the parents.

Detective Miller told your Affiant that Mr. M——— identified the person at the beach whom his daughter identified as being the man at the babysitter's as being R——— A———, the son of A——— A———.

Detective Miller showed your Affiant a copy of a certified copy of a driver's license, California ———, in the name of R——— A———, ——te male adult, DOB ———43, physical description consisting of brown hair, hazel eyes, 6', 205 pounds, wearing a full beard.

On August 8, you Affiant, Detective Miller, and J——— K——— went to Mr. A——'s business at the Mall in L———. Detective Miller and your Affiant saw Mr. A——— in his office and saw that he had no beard.

Detective Miller told your Affiant that all of the parents who knew R——— A——— said that they had seen him at the C——— Avenue address.

Your Affiant checked the phone book and found that R——— A——— is listed as the ——— agent at ———, L———. Your Affiant went to ——o be ——— Plaze, and A——— in the ——— office on the second floo

\*\*\*

That based upon the above facts, your Affiant prays that a Search Warrant be issued with respect to the above location for the seizure of said property, and that the same be held under California Penal Code section 1536 and disposed of according to law.

SETH L. GOLDSTEIN
Affiant
Subscribed and sworn to before me
this ——— day of ——— 1984.
JUDGE OF THE MUNICIPAL COURT

[Preceded by listing of expertise]

In early December, Postal Inspector William H—— of the San Francisco Postal Office, called me and told me that both he and the U.S. Customs had made seizures of child pornography destined for a J—— B——, P.O. Box 2——A, 94702. H—— told me that he had checked the postal box application completed by B—— and found that B—— had listed himself and another name, D——, as the names which mail would be received for at the postal box. H—— also told me that B—— had listed his California driver's license number as ——.

I checked with DMV and found that under that number the following person was listed as possessing a driver's license: J—— —— B——, —erkeley, 94702, white male, brn hair, blue eyes, 5′8″, 140, birth date ——.

I sent for and received a copy of his driver's license picture.

I checked the BPD alpha files and found that, BPD case ——79, B—— had reported, to the police, a noise complaint using the address of —— A——.

I found that, BPD case #——81, he reported to the police that a 16-year-old boy had punctured the tires of his car at the school he teaches at. He told the officer investigating the complaint (according to the report) that he lived at —— A——.

I checked the Juvenile Bureau files and found that the FBI had told me that B——'s name was found on the mailing list of a child pornography operation they closed down, called All American Studios. I have seen the publications distributed by this operation and can testify that they are primarily homosexual in nature, depicting adults with adults engaging in sexual acts, boys with adults, and boys with boys engaging in sexual acts.

I ran B——'s name in the computer and found that he has a VW sedan, 5—— ——C, registered to him. I went by his home and saw that it was a beige "bug," seeing it parked in the rear of the duplex at —— A——.

Officer Bob N——, of the Juvenile Bureau, called the —— School, ——, and spoke to B——. N—— told me that he spoke to B—— old him that he still teaches at the school. N—— told me that B—— told him that the school hosts grades 5–12 (ages 11–18).

Ofc. N——— and myself went to the U.S. Customs office and met with Insp. H——— and Special Agent James J. H——— of the Customs Service. H——— showed me the five seizures made by the Customs Service. They were as follows:

1.  Dated 12-22-82, one 8mm film on a plastic reel wrapped in cellophane between two post cards. I viewed the film and it depicts a young boy, estimated to be approximately 15–18, masturbating. The package which contained it was addressed to B——— at his PO Box ———.
2.  Dated 12-22-82, two pornographic magazines entitled *Chicken 9* and *Chicken 11*, wrapped in brown paper. I examined these magazines and saw that they depict boys, estimated to be 10–14 (no older), engaged in oral copulation, anal intercourse, and masturbation. The package was addressed to ——— A———.
3.  Dated 12-22-82, two film boxes for 8mm film, entitled *Golden Boy 75* and *Golden Boy 79*. They contained no film and the covers depicted boys, estimated to be 15–18, engaged in masturbation and in the nude. It was addressed to ——— A———.
4.  Dated 12-27-82, two pornographic magazines entitled *Super Boy 12* and *Wonder Boy 26* wrapped in brown paper. These depicted individual boys, shown in the nude, of various ages. It was addressed to PO Box ———.
5.  Dated 12-30-82, two pornographic magazines entitled *Mini Boys Nr5* and *Picolo 38*, wrapped in brn paper. These magazines depicted boys, estimated to be aged 10–14 (no older), engaged in anal intercourse, oral copulation, and masturbation. It was addressed to ——— A———.

I spoke with the postal carrier who delivers mail to ——— A———, R———, Route ———. He told me that he has often delivered packages to ——— A———hich are consistent with the packaging of magazines and large photographs. He said that he had a package at that time which was exactly like the ones he had delivered in the past. He showed me that package and I saw that it was exactly like the one listed as #1 above. It appeared to contain a reel of film and was addressed in the same fashion and handwriting as item #1 listed above.

Since receiving the photograph of B——— from DMV, I have seen him on several occasions. Once was on Jan. 4th, at approx 1500 hrs. He was leaving the Post Office at Addison and San Pablo. I saw him enter and drive away in the previously described VW. I have seen him on two other occasions, also driving the car, once driving into the driveway to ——— A———.

Ofc. Bob N———, myself, Insp. H———, Special Agent H———, and Sgt. H——— of the Berkeley Police Dept., served a federal search warrant after making a controlled delivery to B——— at his home. During the course of the service of that warrant we found the following:

1. A dresser full of pornographic magazines depicting boys in nude, pornographic poses, engaged in sexual acts with adults and other boys. Some of the titles were: *Ball Boys; Big Boys; Boy Meat; C.O.D. Boys; Boy Land; Teenage Sex; Young Boys and Sex,* among others. There appeared to be hundreds of magazines of similar titles. This dresser also contained hundreds of 8mm films. Titles were similar to these, which I found: *Randy and Lunch Break; Golden Boys; Little Brothers Comming Out; I'll do it if you do.* The boxes these films were contained in depicted boys involved in sexual acts and in lewd poses.

2. A cardboard box full of home variety photographs depicting boys of the ages 13–18 engaged in oral copulation, anal insertion, anal intercourse, and in lewd poses. They were in envelopes and banded together with rubber bands. There were over a thousand such pictures.

3. Under the couch we found the items listed above which were seized by Customs and delivered in a controlled delivery to his home (Items #2, 3, and 5 listed on page six). We also found under a couch cushion several other child pornography magazines of similar titles.

4. Two (2) video recorders hooked up in tandem to enable copying of video tapes.

5. Hundreds of video tapes with titles similar to these I found: *Boy Edition 1 through 4.*

6. Thousands of 35mm slides. One box I viewed contained pictures of young boys in lewd, nude poses.

7. Camera, 35mm, Pentax and two slide projectors.

8. Correspondence with pornography outlets and individuals who said they were interested in sex with children. One of the entries listed in a file of such correspondence was this one: "16 Nov., '76 Requested Chicken Catalog/8-4-82 Wrote for new catalog"

9. Books on the benefits and good aspects of sex with children. Some of the titles were: *Men and Their Boys, Sexual Aspect of Paedophile Relations, Paedophilia, The Radical Case.* (*Paedophilia* is the European spelling.)

10. Dildos of various sizes, shaped in the form of the male sex organ. One of these was the size of a young boy's erect penis, estimated to be approx. 3″ long.

Through training and experience I have found that pedophiles use sexual aides such as those described in item #10 above in the seduction of their victims. Often they utilize these as a means of exciting their victims and of arousing the curiosity of the children.

Wherefore, Affiant prays that a search warrant be issued, based upon the above facts, for the seizure of said property.

# Appendix VII

On August 24, Inspector Bill H———, Postal Inspector, P.O. Box 822000, San Francisco, 550———, sent me a note informing me that he had gone through the correspondence of a person by the name of Raymond T———, arrested by the San Carlos Police Department for selling child pornography. H——— told me that he had read some letters written to T——— by a person identified as Pat D———, 1———, Berkeley, CA 94704, ———. H——— told me that he had read one of the rs that D——— had written and that in it D——— said that he had collected child pornography for fourteen years. H——— told me that among the correspondence he found samples which had been sent T——— by D——— which were dated February 2, and February 6.

I conducted a records check through the Berkeley Police Department files and found that John Patrick D———, aka Patrick D———, aka R——— D———, FBI #———, CII #———, WMA, DOB: 12/–/19, 6-2, 190, gray hair, 1——— P———, ———, had been arrested for drunk driving in Berkeley University of California Police, in February 1982. He also had reported traffic problems in the area of the P——— address, using that address under case numbers ———81, ———81, ———80 and was involved in the accident for which he was arrested under case number ——— 82. At that time he was driving a 1980 Honda, 7——— P———.

On December 4, using a Post Office Box in the State of Washington, and the alias of ——— C———, I sent D——— a letter which asked him where a friend of mine was in the City of Berkeley.

Receiving no response, on April 23, 1983, using the same ruse, I sent D——— another letter making the same inquiry. This time I mentioned that the other individual and I were "exchanging things from our collections." Shortly thereafter, D——— sent me a letter dated May 2, postmarked May 24, through the Oakland Post Office, telling me, in part, that he would "be very interested in exchanging items (or) simply prepaying for material you can describe. Photos, cassettes, descriptive writing." He also asked that I give him an indication of "what you have and how you would prefer to set up a mutual regarding association."

In an undated letter postmarked August 1, enclosing five photocopies of pictures depicting boys and girls appearing to range in age from 6 to 12 or

14 engaged in oral copulation and masturbation of one another, D——
wrote to me, saying in part:

> I've enclosed just a sample of the kind of material I have.... . I'm getting a
> lot of material copied right now from original prints... You work in an
> elementary school? Doesn't that give you a chance occasionally to see or
> caress a sweet girlish bun or dear suttle [sic] hairless cunt or maybe fondle
> a handful of boyish balls and prick for a moment? ...I've sent...you...orig-
> inal story...true, in the main, and shows you some of the aspects of this
> fascinating interest which turn me on... If you feel you can send me one
> of your mags (magazines)...do you know a source of cassettes or even of
> special books...[signed in closing] to a long and satisfying exchange!

In a postscript he writes "glad, of course, to reimburse you for the use of
your mag, but I would, in any case send you back some extra prints."

The original story he refers to is a graphic description of how he orally
copulated and had a twelve year old girl orally copulate him whom he identified as "C——," a daughter of a friend of his. He alludes to a photograph
which was included in the letter; however, none was accompanying the material. In response to his request for magazines, on August 12, I sent him three
nudist magazines (*Young and Naked* number 1, *Young and Naked* number 2
and *Nudist Encore* number 5).

D—— responded with an undated letter postmarked August 23,
marked "Monday." In his letter he said he had "found a reliable person who
will photograph and reprint collections like mine." In this letter he included
a photocopy of a photograph depicting a young girl appearing to be between
ages twelve and fifteen, standing with her breasts exposed. The numbers "170"
appear written on the back of the photocopy.

He had also included two copies of hand drawn pictures, one marked
number six. This depicted an adult male engaged in sexual intercourse with
a young girl who shows no pubic hair or breasts. The second drawing,
numbered seven, depicts an adult man with a young girl orally copulating
him.

His letter identifies the aforementioned photocopy of the photograph:
"photo of little girl with outstanding girlish breasts is B——, my niece, let
me tell you about her first sexual encounter with an older person—her aunt
S——." His letter goes on to describe how he had inserted his finger in her
vagina and how he orally copulated her.

He identifies her as twelve years old and himself as fifty-eight years old.

In his closing paragraph he asks, "Do you know the contact in Mariposa,
California?"

I returned his letter with one of our own dated September 12, 1983 enclosing a copy of *Lolita* magazine marking the magazine number 120 on the back. I also included a copy of *Joyboy* number 6, marked number 214.

I drove by the address on P——— and saw parked in a lower level garage, a gold Honda, 7——— P———. I ran the registration for that license plate and learned that it is registered to K——— D———, 1——— P——

On October 7, I spoke with Diane R——— of the Juvenile Bureau, Berkeley Police Dept. She updated the files on D———, learning that he had only one contact since the file check I had performed in August of. In February of (———83) Pat D——— was involved in a dispute at the Oaks Theatre in Berkeley.

[Preceded by listing of expertise]
The probable cause in this case is as follows: Mr. —— contacted Captain Schuyler of the Sheriff's Department. Mr. —— and Captain Schuyler are neighbors living in the city of San Bernardino. Mr. —— is employed by Fox Photo, a photo-finishing firm in the city of Pico Rivera, County of Los Angeles. Mr. —— indicated to Captain Schuyler that they had received photographs depicting a very young child in various nude poses and that they were alarmed by these pictures and wished to obtain an expert opinion as to whether or not they were indicators of sexual abuse. Mr. —— subsequently took these pictures to his residence, which is located in the city of San Bernardino. I met with him at his residence at approximately 5:05 pm, 8/3/81. I viewed these photographs, which he provided to me for my opinion. these photographs feature two girls. One of the girls appears to be approximately 12 years old. She is Caucasian, has brown hair, and in the pictures where she is wearing normal clothes, she is wearing a shiny green top and green shorts. She is also pictured wearing what appears to be a pair of white panties and a button-up shirt. In some of the photographs, this shirt is unbuttoned and lying as if to suggest the breast development the child has experienced. There is a second child pictured also, and she appears to be approximately nine years old and also appears to be wearing a pair of panties and a top which is possibly a pajama top. Both of these children are depicted in some of the photographs together. There were numerous photographs of the 12-year-old girl which show her in various nude poses inside of a dwelling. These poses include the victim standing in front of a piano, sitting on a stool in front of the piano, sitting on a dresser which has a mirror mounted on it, and lying on a sofa in nude poses, and also she is seen lying on the floor in various poses. These photographs were mailed into Fox Photo for processing. It was a print film, 35 millimeter in size. The return address on the envelope was ——. As a result of my experience and my knowledge of the field of pedophilia, these pictures represent a strong suspicion that at least one child and possibly two are being sexually abused by the person who took these photographs, apparently ——.

(Courtesy of Sgt. Toby Tyler, San Bernardino Police Dept.)

# Appendix IX

[Preceded by listing of expertise]

On January 6, Detective Lee L—— of the Los —— Police Department called your Affiant and asked for advice for a case he was investigating.

Detective L—— told your Affiant that he was contacted by Officer M—— of the South San Francisco Police Department and told that George M——, the manager of the Berkey Photo Processing Firm, brought him a roll of film that had been developed and printed that contained possible child pornography under the definitions of California Penal Code Section 311.4(c). Officer M—— told Detective L—— that the roll of film had been submitted by the C—— Camera Shop of L——. Officer M—— told Detective L—— that the envelope submitted contained the name "S. T——" and the telephone number 941——.

Detective L —— told your Affiant that he went to the South Francisco Police Department and picked up the aforementioned envelope and photographs, determining the envelope to be Receipt No. 213582 dated "12-31". Detective L—— told your Affiant that he observed the name and phone number as described by Officer M——.

Detective L—— told your Affiant that he picked up the film from South Francisco on January 3. Detective L—— told your Affiant that he then went to the Camera Shop on the same date and spoke to Maureen W——, who said that she had received the roll of film which was contained in the envelope previously mentioned from a customer whom she knows to have frequented her business on several occasions as "Jill T——." She told Detective L—— that she had placed the roll offilm in the Camera Shop envelope and submitted it for processing.

Detective L—— told your Affiant that W—— also told him that she had taken a second roll of film on the same date and that that film had been returned from the processing firm already printed. She provided Detective L—— with a second envelope. Receipt No. 213583, containing 35 printed photographs and negatives, which was filled out exactly the same as the one previously mentioned.

For purposes of identification, your Affiant will refer to the first roll of film given to the authorities by the Berkey Color Processing Firm as Roll "A."

Your Affiant will refer to the second roll of film picked up at the L——— Photo Firm as Roll "B."

Detective L——— told your Affiant that they opened the envelope containing Roll B and found that the photograph that your Affiant has marked as B-3 depicted a woman whom Detective L——— told your Affiant that W——— identified as being "Jill T———".

On January 6, Detective L——— met with your Affiant to show your Affiant the pictures as well as to discuss the case with your Affiant.

On the same date, Detective L——— prepared a search warrant for phone records of the Telephone Company in San Francisco signed by the Honorable Judge R ——— A ———. A copy of that search warrant is attached hereto and incorporated by reference as Exhibit A.

Detective L——— told your Affiant that Mark F ——— of Pacific Bell told him that the phone number was listed to Robert T ———, ———, ———.

Detective L——— and your Affiant numbered the photographs that were printed Series A-0 through B-2 through B-36.

Your Affiant noted that there are nine different individuals depicted in all of the series of photographs. Your Affiant noted that a girl, heretofore referred to as Subject No. 1, appears in photographs B-5, B-13 through B-15, B-19, B-22, B-24, B-29, and B-30. She also appears in photographs A-5 through A-9, A-11 and A-12, A-16, A-19, A-21, A-22, and A-31. In photograph number B-5, Subject No. 1 appears with Subject No. 2 (to be further described) wearing a dark sweater and light blouse. She is standing in a room that contains a lighted Christmas tree, wood paneling along one wall, and light-colored curtains. Also appearing in the photograph with her is a young boy (to be further identified as Subject No. 4). The photograph is out of focus. The exposure is also too dark.

In photographs B-13 through B-29 she appears in a pink bathrobe and yellow T-shirt. All of the pictures appear to be in a living room with similar wall paneling as previously described and curtains.

All of the aforementioned pictures except B-5 depict Subject No. 1, along with other individuals who will be later described, opening packages wrapped in Christmas wrap.

Photograph number B-30 depicts Subject No. 1 holding onto a stroller containing two Cabbage Patch dolls. She is dressed in a light-colored blouse and light-colored pants. She is seated on the floor of an interior room that is covered in the same colored carpet as in the photographs she appears in previous to that exposure.

She next appears in photograph A-5 wearing nothing but a bra, panties, two white bracelets, and a gold necklace. In the series of photographs A-5 through A-31, she is depicted in less and less clothing and in sexually suggestive poses.

The wall behind Subject No. 1 in Photograph A-5 appears to have a multicolored wall paper with a purple, green, blue, and magenta flower pattern. She is depicted resting her right elbow and right foot on the banister on a wrought iron railing which is painted white and bronze. To her right is a multi-colored pink and white wall paneling. In the second photograph, in this series, photograph number A-6, she is seen leaning over the banister of the railing, and to the lower left of the photograph can be seen the corner of a bathtub with soap and bottles consistent with the packaging of shampoos, etc.

In photographs A-21 and A-22 she is seen standing in front of a wall vent, with no clothes on, on top of a purple "belour"-like bath mat. On top of the bath mat is a blue-with-black polkadot pattern piece of material that is the same pattern as a pullover shirt worn by Subject No. 2 in photographs taken previous to this series, which will be described further below.

Your Affiant noticed in looking at the photographs of Subject No. 1 that she has little, or no, pubic hair and no breast development. She also appears, in several of the pictures, to be wearing braces.

Subject No. 2 first appears, as previously mentioned, in photograph number B-5. She is similarly dressed in this photograph to Subject No. 1. Subject No. 2 next appears in photograph A-4, wearing the previously mentioned blue-with-black polka dot pullover shirt seen in photograph number A-22 and a pair of slacks with a gray paisley print. She is holding a group of Cabbage Patch dolls, two of which are the same as the Cabbage patch dolls held by Subject No. 1 in photograph number B-30. The dolls are dressed in green with white blouses, and one has the words "Cabbage Patch" across the left breast and the other not. She is seated on a couch that has a similar design to that depicted in photograph number B-15, with a red poinsettia plant in the background, which is also seen on a similarly described table with a lamp adjacent to it in photograph B-15. In the background in the photograph is a set of beige curtains, which is also consistent with the curtains depicted in B-15. Subject No. 2 next appears in photograph A-10 wearing only the blue-with-black polkadot pullover. She is seatee on the same banister as previously described in photographs A-5 through A-9 and before the same background. In photograph A-10 the shower head of a shower can be seen along the back wall, behind her.

Subject No. 2 next appears in photographs A-13 through A-15 in various poses at that same location. She next appears in photograph A-17, standing in the bathtub. She is wearing only a pair of panties and has a bra dangling from her right hand. Her left arm is held over her hand grasping the aforementioned shower head. She next appears in photograph A-18, seated at the bottom of the bathtub, with a towel wrapped around her waist. She next appears in photograph A-23 with no clothes on at all, holding a brush in her right hand, leaning against the rail previously described.

Your Affiant observed the photographs of Subject No. 2, and she has a sparse growth of very light, fine pubic hair, is wearing a gold necklace, and has braces.

Subject No. 1 is a white female, approximately nine to twelve years old, light brown or drak blonde hair cut with bangs.

Subject No. 2 is a white female, approximately ten to thirteen years old, light brown or dirty blonde hair, below-the-shoulder length. In all of the prints, Subject No. 2 appears to have redder lips, consistent with lipstick.

Subject No. 3 appears in photographs A-34 through A-36. She is wearing a blue sweater and a blue-and-beige plaid long-sleeve shirt. She has braces and what appears to be light brown hair.

Subject No. 4 appears in photographs number B-4 through B-7, B-16, B-18, B-21, B-23, B-24 through B-26, B-31, and B-32. He appears in A-0 and A-33. He is approximately eight or nine years old and is depicted in pictures B-4 and B-5 wearing a dark-colored, partly red shirt, long sleeved, and in B-16 through B-32 wearing a red-with-blue striped jumpsuit with a hood and with an alligator on the left breast. He is also wearing a blue, short-sleeved T-shirt with the letters *USA* across the front. In photograph A-0 he appears wearing a red, white, and dark-colored long-sleeved shirt with a pair of blue pants. The blue pants have a patch on the left thigh that has a white background and a blue-and-red emblem, similar to a United Airlines emblem. He is looking at a "Weekly Reader." This photograph is taken in a room that has a kitchen sink with white tiling and dark grout. This photograph is consistent with the tile on both the counter, as previously described, and back walls, which is red and gold with dark grout, and the two photographs B-34 and B-35. He next appears in A-33, in the same room which contained the couch and curtains, poinsettia plant, lamp, and Christmas tree. He is wearing a grey long-sleeved shirt, green slacks, and grey tennis shoes. He has blond or light brown hair, cut in a "shag."

Subject No. 5 who appears in photographs B-3 and A-1 was identified, as described above, as "Jill T———."

Subject No. 6 appears in photographs B-17, B-27, B-28, and A-1. He is wearing the same clothes in all of the photographs. In photograph A-1 he appears with Jill T———, who is wearing a bathrobe, light in color. He is wearing a white-and-blue shirt with light blue trousers.

Subject No. 6 appears in photos B-17, B-28, and A-1. He is wearing the same white-and-blue plaid shirt and light blue slacks in all photographs. He is approximately 50 to 60 years old, clean shaven, and balding and wears dark-rimmed prescription glasses.

He is depicted seated in the same room with the green rug, couch, poinsettia plant, and wood paneling. In one set of photographs, he appears in front of wood paneling that appears to conform to a circle or curved wall.

Subject No. 7 is an elderly woman, in her mid- to late 50s, and is depicted in photos B-20, B-21, and B-34 through B-36. She is wearing a blue blouse with blue trim in the latter prints and the same blouse with a light-colored sweater in photographs B-20 and B-21.

Subject No. 8 is a white male in his early to his mid-40s, depicted in photographs B-23 through B-25 wearing a brown, knee-length bathrobe. He is depicted standing in the aforementioned room with a green rug, wood paneling, etc.

Subject No. 9 appears in photos B-19, B-26, B-36, And A-2, a white female adult, early to mid-50s, light brown or dirty blonde hair, wearing a green long-sleeved top and red pants. She also appears in photograph B-26 wearing the same attire and in B-36 and A-2 is seen wearing a blue and black patterned blouse and glasses. She is depicted in the kitchen in both photographs B-36 and A-2.

Your Affiant examined the photographs depicted in the series A-5 through A-31. Your Affiant noted that in the photograph A-9, Subject No. 1}s panties were pulled down exposing the break in the cheeks of the buttocks. In photograph A-8, Subject No. 1 poses in a position that accentuates the breasts and is consistent with a model's pose. In photograph A-7, she is depicted bending over with her buttock facing the camera looking over her right shoulder. In photograph number A-10 she is depicted with ler leg up on the bathroom vent with no panties on, looking at the camera over her right shoulder. In photograph A-12 she appears again, posed in a manner deemed, consistent with your Affiant's experience and training, to be sexually suggestive, wearing only a bra and what appears to be a piece of white material the size of toilet paper. In photograph A-16 she wears a pair of "backless" panties judged, consistent with your Affiant's experience and training, to be the type of suggestive lingerie sold by Frederick's of Hollywood. In photograph A-19 she appears tootally naked, facing the camera, and in A-21 and A-22 poses, again looking at the camera, looking over her right shoulder, exposing her buttock and covering her breasts. Your Affiant last sees her in photograph A-31, where she is standing in the bathtub with her foot on the sink, facing the mirror, covering her eyes.

Your Affiant examined photos A-24 through A-30 and saw that photographs A-25, A-26, and A-29 depict a young girl with no pubic hair and what appears to be red irritation in a pattern deemed, consistent with your Affiant's training and experience, to indicate abuse. A red ring appears around the vagina in photograph A-29, which appears to be the size of a man's penis. Only the goin and/or anus is displayed in the series of shots.

Photographs number A-24, A-27, and A-30 depict a young girl who has very light, fine public hair like that previously described on Subject No. 2. Again, based on your Affiant's training and experience, the vagina in photograph A-30 appears to be irritated, consistent with possible abuse. Only the groin and/or anus is displayed in these shots.

Photographs A-29 and A-30 depict two girls seated on a purple, "velour-like" rug similar to that depicted on the floor in photographs A-11, A-12, and A-22, in the same bathroom in which Subjects No. 1 and No. 2 are seen. Also, behind the girl seated in the picture in photograph A-29 is a floor pattern consistent with the floor pattern of the aforementioned bathroom.

Your Affiant also noted the following other common characteristics of the two sets of photographs. In photographs A-1 and B-22, a portrait of a man, which is black and white in color, rests on a television in the background of the pictures. In photographs B-27, B-28 and A-32, the rounded walls appear in the background.

The long-sleeved knit blouse worn by Subject No. 1 in photo B-30 is consistent with a piece of clothing draped over the edge of the bathtub in photo A-18.

Detective L——— told your Affiant that the scalloped ceiling depicted in photograph A-32 is consistent with a roof line that he saw at the house when he drove by the house on January 7, 1986. He also told your Affiant that the rounded walls depicted in the previously described photographs are also consistent with the construction of the house, which is described on the face of this affidavit.

Detective L——— told your Affiant that the scenery depicted in photographs B-14, B-15, B-26, and B-33 is also consistent with the type of foilage and terrain outside the house that he observed on January 7.

Detective L——— told your Affiant that he ran the name Robert T——— in his computer, which is tied to the State of California Department of Motor Vehicles, and learned that a Robert T———, date of birth March 3, 19———, has a California Driver's license ———, listing an address of ——— Lane, L———, L———, with a physical description of male, brown hair, brown eyes, 6 foot, 175 pounds. On that same DMV printout, which he gave to your Affiant, is listed a violation date of July 18, 1984 with a vehicle license number of ———. This vehicle is registered as a 1983 Mercury sedan, to Robert T———, ———.

In addition, Detective L——— told your Affiant that he found, using the Department of Motor Vehicle's computer, that a 1971 Toyota, California license ———, and a 1978 Jeep, California license ———, were registered in the names Jill or Robert T——— at the ——— Lane address. He also found a 1979 Jeep, California license ———, registered in the name of Robert T———, at the ———

Detective L——— told your Affiant that he saw a black Jeep, unknown year, a brown Jeep, unknown year, a light blue BMW, and a light blue Mercury parked on the property in the driveway and the carport of the ——— Lane address. He was unable to see the license plate numbers from his points of observation.

Your Affiant checked with Pacific Gas and Electric Company, speaking with Carolyn D———, and learned that the electricity bill is being sent to the ——— Lane address billed to Robert T———.

Detective L——— told your Affiant that he checked with the County Assessor and was told that the tex biil is mailed to the ——— Lane address in care of Jill and Robert T———. Your Affiant ran Jill T———'s name through the DMV computer located in the District Attorney's Office and learned that a Jill T——— holds a driver's license number ———, listing a date of birth of October ———, 19— and an address of ——— Lane; physical description: brown hair and brown eyes, 5 feet 3 inches, 113 pounds.

Through your Affiant's training and experience, your Affiant has learned that those who sexually exploit or molest children do so in a progressive pattern. Each step becomes more and more explicit or oriented towards sexual activity. This is often seen in the progression of the photographs taken by those who molest children. For example, your Affiant observed the sequence of photographs involving Subject No. 1 and Subject No. 2 to progress in a very clear pattern and progression from wearing clothing to disrobing, posing in sexually provocative and suggestive ways to explicitly displaying the genitalia, consistent with the last series of photographs of the girls' genital areas in photographs A-24 through A-30.

Your Affiant has also learned through experience and training that children who are being molested or exploited through pornography often pose willingly for child pornography, even to the point of being involved in explicit sexual acts.

Your Affiant has also learned through experience and training that it is not uncommon for the children to initiate the sexual activity or posing on their own in order to please the offender or produce the material for someone else.

It is also your Affiant's experience and training that children of the ages depicted in the photographs in question in this case are often shown pornography, both child and adult pornography, in order to give them an idea of how to pose for the camera. It is your Affiant's belief, based on his experience and training, that similar materials would be found that would depict children or adults posing in similar ways to those depicted in the photographs of the children in this case.

Further, it is your Affiant's experience and training which leads him to believe that evidence will be found at the home and in the vehicles described above which will identify the children who are being abused through the taking of sexually explicit photographs and by sexual molestation, as well as evidence which would tend to identify those who are perpetrating those acts.

Furthermore, through your Affiant's experience and training, he believes that in seeking to identify the home in which these photographs were taken,

we will learn the proper jurisdiction and reveal the identities of those perpetrating these acts.

Your Affiant, through his training and experience, knows that individuals
who molest and photograph children use their vehicles as a means of transportation of both the children and the material they garner from the abuse.
He also is aware of the fact that hose who molest children and exploit them
through child pornography often use vehicles as a means of storing their
explicit material and to protect it from being discovered by members of their
family and professional associates.

Your Affiant also knows through experience and training that those who
molest children and exploit them through child pornography often carry
address books, ledgers, and other writings on their person that contain the
identities of the persons they are involved with sexually and that would tend
to identify others in similar activities with the children involved.

Your Affiant also knows through experience and training that those who
molest children in their own family often carry photographs of their children
on their person.

Your Affiant has also learned through experience and training that those
who photograph children in sexually explicit conduct often use the services
of photo processing firms similar to that which was utilized in this case. In
order to prevent discovery, the offending party will try to conceal the content
of the roll of film by first photographin normal, conventional scenes as was
done in the photograph series in Roll A.

Affiant also believes that the above-mentioned property, evidence of the
commission of felonies, to wit: violation of California Penal Code Section
311.4(c) (Child Pornography) and California Penal Code Section 288(a)
(Lewd and Lascivious Conduct Upon Child), and property used in the commission of these felonies will be located on the premises, persons, and vehicles
above described.

Based on the above facts, your Affiant prays that a search warrant be
issued with respect to the above location, persons, and vehicles for seizure
of said property, and that the same be held under California Penal Code
Section 1536 and disposed of according to law.

INSPECTOR SETH GOLDSTEIN

Subscribed and sworn to befor me
this ——— day of January.

_____

JUDGE OF THE SUPERIOR COURT

# Appendix X

[Preceding by listing of experience]

On March 30, K—— H——, white male adult, 32 years, DOB 10——s arrested by Officer H—— of the Berkeley Police Department for possession of stolen property and possession of a stolen credit card. Your affiant reviewed the case written by Officer H—— and found that Officer H—— was informed by the Alameda Police Department that H —— was in Berkeley and was arrestable for several sex offenses which they were, at the time, investigating.

Your affiant discovered that H—— was booked by Officer H—— for the aforementioned property charges and a hold placed him for the sex charges from Alameda Police Department.

Your affiant spoke with H—— in his jail cell at the Berkeley Police Department jail regarding his activities and contacts with individuals who are sexually active with boys under the age of 18 years of age. Since that time, your affiant has spoken with H—— on no less than three (3) occasions and on 4-10- your affiant took a written statement regarding the business known as —— Works, —— Street and possible violations of the law there as they constitute crimes defined in the California Penal Code Section 311.2, Subsection (b) (person who knowingly possesses with intent to exhibit child pornography to others for commercial consideration) and Section 313 (allowing a minor to view "harmful matter"). That statement is attached hereto and incorporated herein for reference.

H—— told your affiant that he has been living in Berkeley for the past 11 years, off and on. H—— told your affiant that he has been going to —— Works three or four times a week ever since it opened, approximately four years ago. H—— told your affiant that he stayed there for three weeks during the time in which his apartment was being refurbished. H—— told your affiant that —— Works is located at —— Street, without having to refer to any notes or a phone directory.

H—— told your affiant that he had gained entry to —— Works on many occasions, paying a $5 rate each time for a room for a period of 12 hours. H—— told your affiant that the most recent time he was at —— Works and had paid the $5 entry fee was on the date he was arrested by

Officer H———. H——— told your affiant that he had paid the $5 admission, which enabled him to have access to all of the facilities at ——— Works. H——— told your affiant that ———s many rooms with beds in them; a large room with a TV in it; a sauna bath; a Jacuzzi; showers; a "bunk house" room; an "orgy room"; a "maze"; locker room; and a movie room.

H——— described the movie room to your affiant as being set up with different levels, much like a movie theater, with the lowest level near where the screen is and the highest near the wall where the projection booth is. H——— told your affiant that the different levels within the room are used for sitting or lying on while viewing the movies.

H——— told your affiant that on the many occasions he has gone to ——— Works the establishment was showing movies on a constant basis, except between the hours of 0130–0730 in the morning. H——— told your affiant that all of the movies he has seen depict men engaged in homosexual acts. H——— told your affiant that those homosexual acts range from anal intercourse, oral copulation, "fist fucking," anal insertion, and any number of sadomasochistic acts.

H——— told your affiant that he had personally seen boys who appeared to be under the age of 18 years old in the movie room watching the films. H——— told your affiant that he has seen this occur at least 20–25 occasions a week. H——— also told your affiant that he personally knows seven boys whom he knows to be under 18 who have seen the aforementioned movies.

H——— described, to your affiant, a movie which he believes is entitled "Mechanics" or something similar. He described it as being about two adult auto mechanics who are in their early 30s or late 20s and their experiences with a "high school" student who comes to their shop in the evening hours. H——— told your affiant that the boy in the movie looks to be about 16 years old—at most 17 years old. H——— told your affiant that he felt that this was the case because the actor in the movie had very little pubic hair or body hair and when he heard his voice it was very much like someone who was young.

H——— told your affiant that the movie begins with the two mechanics working on separate cars and the young boy comes in and talks to the mechanics. They then take off the boy's clothes and have him orally copulate each of them. They then take off their clothes and each perform sodomy on him while he is orally copulating the other adult. H——— said that the film is approximately 10–15 minutes long and it ends when everybody appears to be tired. H——— told your affiant that he is not certain of the title of the movie. H——— also told your affiant that the last time he saw this movie was the night he was arrested by Officer H———. H——— told your affiant that that night he had paid the customary $5 to gain entry to the establishment and the movie room.

H——— also told your affiant that ——— Works keeps some of its movies in the building, in the projection room behind the "movie room." H——— stated to your affiant that he has personally seen them stored on shelves on the walls of the projection room. H——— also told your affiant that he has personally seen the movie he previously described in that room.

H——— told your affiant that he has seen the film on one of the shelves in the projection room, in a gray can with a tape label around the edge. H——— told your affiant that he has seen other films in this room which are also so labeled. H——— told your affiant that some of the headings he has seen on the shelves were "Leather," "S and M," "Water Sports," and "Young Studs."

H——— reiterated to your affiant that the only way someone can get into the movie room is to pay the entrance fee and that there is no one there who checks who goes into the room to watch the movies.

On 4-10- your affiant learned that H——— appeared in Berkeley–Albany Municipal Court before Judge G——— where he pled guilty to the possession of stolen property and stolen credit card charges.

Your affiant also read the report written by Officer T. A——— of the Alameda Police Department regarding the sex charges against H———. Your affiant learned that a 17 year old boy, R——— G———, ———, Alameda, ——— that H——— on Monday, 3-26- at approximately 1930 hours, had taken him to ——— Works at ——— and had had sexual relations with him consisting of anal sex and oral copulation. A copy of the Alameda report is attached hereto and incorporated herein for reference.

On 4-3- your affiant took a statement from G———, a copy of which is attached hereto and incorporated for reference. G——— told your affiant that he had gone to ——— Works with H——— and when he got there H——— paid $5 for to enter. G——— told your affiant that he filled out a registration card in his own name, but that H——— told him to use H———'s address of ——— G——— described the card as being about 3" × 5" in size with the words "——— Works" printed on it as well as a section that was for logging the time into the establishment and out.

Your affiant has asked H——— if he knew of any juveniles who have been in ——— Works and he listed four names: C——— E———, NMJ, 15 or 16 years old, ——R——— G——— (listed above); Frank, NMJ, 15–16; and C——— (ph16. H——— told your affiant that all, except G———, have been in the movie room and seen the movies.

Your affiant has been specially trained in matters pertaining to juveniles and has investigated and supervised the investigation of numerous sex-related cases involving juveniles, among them child pornography. Your affiant has been specially trained in the investigation and identification of incidents of child abuse, sexual exploitation involving children, child pornography, and child prostitution. Additionally, your affiant has had specialized training in the areas of laws pertaining to said offenses. This training includes attending an eight-hour training seminar covering topics such as "sexual abuse of children... investigation procedure involving molest... ways children are sexually exploited, and managing investigations involving sexually exploited children," as well as a 40-hour juvenile officers' training course which included areas of child abuse and related problems. Furthermore, your affiant has attended a 40-hour (one-week) training course on child abuse and its investigation, dealing specifically with the aforementioned types of offenses.

It is from this training and experience that your affiant has found that business establishments, such as that described and currently in business as ———— Works, keep or store movies such as those described above on the premises for exhibition to their clientele.

It is through experience and training that your affiant knows that businesses, such as that doing business as ———— Works, keep records of the time their clients spend in their establishments for the purposes of charging their clients for the use of their facilities. Such records may consist of the type of cards described by G———— and these records are retained by the establishment for bookkeeping or other purposes. For these reasons, your affiant feels that such records may be found at ———— Works with the names of C———— E————, R—and C————.

# Appendix  XI

STATEMENT OF PROBABLE CAUSE

Your Affiant says that the facts in support of the issuance of the search warrant are as follows:

Your Affiant is a peace officer, employed as an Investigator for the Napa County District Attorney since September 1986. Prior to that, I was an Investigator for the Santa Clara County District Attorney's Office, for three years, assigned to Sexual Assault Investigations. Prior to working for the District Attorney's Office, I was a police officer, employed by the Berkeley Police Department, for ten years, having been assigned to the Patrol Division and Detective Divisions of the police department. While working the Detective Division, I was assigned to the Juvenile Bureau for two years. Prior to my promotion to patrolman in 1973, I was a cadet for three years.

What follows is a partial list of the training courses I have taken on the subject of child abuse, sexual assault, sexual abuse, child sexual assault, and sexual exploitation of children:

> Men in Sexual Abuse of Children, San Francisco, 1984;
>
> Sexual Assault Seminar, California Sexual Assault Investigators Association, San Jose, 1984;
>
> Assessment and Treatment of the Sex Offender, Fred Berlin, A.N. Groth, San Francisco, March, 1985;
>
> California District Attorneys Association, Child Sexual Abuse Conference, San Francisco, 4/17/85;
>
> Southeast Symposium on Sexual Abuse of Children, Huntsville, Alabama, 2/20-22/85;
>
> U.S. Department of Justice, Third Annual Conference on Sexual Victimization of Children, Washington, D.C., 4/27/84;
>
> Santa Clara County Child Abuse Seminar, San Jose, California 4/13/84;
>
> The Male Victim of Sexual Assault and the Juvenile Sex Offender, N. Groth, Ph.D., San Francisco, 1982;
>
> Sexual Assault: Rape, Incest and Child Molestation—The Psychology of the Offender, N. Groth, Ph.D., 1982;

Sexual Abuse Conference, Alameda County Child Abuse Council, 1980;
  Child Pornography Seminar, Alameda County Sex Crimes Investiga-
  tors, 1980;
Child Sexual Abuse Seminar, California Association of Diversion and
  Youth Service Counselors, San Jose, 1979;
Child Abuse Seminar, California State Juvenile Officers Association, 8
  hours, Sacramento, 1977;
P.O.S.T. Child Abuse Training Seminar, 8 hours, Richmond, 1980;
P.O.S.T. Sexual Exploitation of Children Seminar, 24 hours, Eureka, 1980;
P.O.S.T. Delinquency Control Institute, Child Abuse Seminar, 40-hour
  school, Morro Bay, 1979;
P.O.S.T. Juvenile Officers Training, 40-hours school, Oakland, 1977;
P.O.S.T., Sexual Assault Investigators, 40-hour course on Sexual Assault,
  San Jose, 1984;
Children's Hospital National Medical Center, Washington, D.C., Seminar
  on Child Sexual Assault;
FBI Academy, Seminars on Sexual Exploitation of Children, 1983/1984.

Your Affiant is an instructor at several police academies, presenting on
the subject of child sexual assault, sexual exploitation of children, and sexual
assault. I have lectured to police groups throughout the country, including
the FBI Academy and appeared at seminars throughout the State of California. I have developed a 40-hour seminar on the subject of sexual assault,
child pornography investigation, and child prostitution investigation. I have
taught for the FBI, the United States Department of Justice, the California
Youth Authority, the International Association of Chiefs of Police, the California District Attorneys Association, the California State Juvenile Officers
Association, the California State Sexual Assault Investigators Association, the
Colorado State Juvenile Officers Association; prosecutors' offices in California, Alabama and Florida, as well as numerous other law enforcement organizations.

In 1985 I was called to the White House to confer with President Ronald
Reagan on the subject of child sexual abuse.

I am consultant to the International Association of Chiefs of Police. I
have consulted on numerous investigations conducted by police agencies
across the country, in addition to those conducted in the State of California.
I have been consulted by District Attorneys' Offices throughout California,
as well as in Alaska, Florida, Wyoming, Colorado and Alabama.

I co-authored investigative guidelines and police academy curicula on
the topics of sexual abuse, sexual exploitation of children, and sexual assault
for California Law enforcement, through the California Department of Justice's Commission on Peace Officer Standards and Training.

I have authored several articles, one of which received an American Bar Association Gavel Award. Three of these articles have been published on the national level. I have written a book on the subject of the sexual exploitation of children entitled *The Sexual Exploitation of Children*, published by CRC Press, Boca Raton, FL.

I have testified before the Alameda County Grand Jury and qualified as an expert witness before the Contra Costa Superior Court, Sonoma County Superior Court, Monterey County Superior Court, Santa Clara County Superior and Municipal Courts, Napa County Superior Court, and in a teacher termination hearing, Professional Competency Commission, Eastside Union High School District, San Jose, California. I have testified before numerous state legislative subcommittees and at governmental commission and committee meetings.

I have been the author and affiant of numerous other search warrants on investigations of child sexual assault and sexual exploitation.

I have read and studied over 200 books and articles on the subject of child sexual assault, sexual exploitation of children, child prostitution, and child pornography.

I was the Chairman of the Northern California Juvenile Officers Association Committee on Sexual Abuse and Sexual Exploitation of Children. IN that capacity, I authored numerous legislative proposals, many of which were adopted by the California State Legislature.

I was a founding member of the Berkeley based group, Citizens Against Sexual Abuse of Children.

I am on the Board of Directors and a trainer for the National Center for Missing and Exploited Children, Washington, D.C.

I was a member of the Board of Directors of the nonprofit group Future Educational Films, Incorporated, producers of "Breaking Silence," an award winning film on sexual abuse of children.

I was named "Man of the Month" by Odyssey Institute's Morality in Media in New York, New York, for my work researching the problem of child sexual exploitation and its attendant crime problems; pedophilia, child prostitution, and child pornography.

I reviewed, investigated, consulted on or supervised the investigation of over 500 cases of child sexual assault, pedophilia, child prostitution, and child pornography. I created an investigative procedure for the tracking of child molestation cases in the City of Berkeley, which is followed to this day.

I have viewed thousands of sexually explicit pictures of children, depicting them in the nude, in sexually provocative poses, lewd poses, and engaged in virtually every sex act conceivable. I have seen children as young as two months old depicted as being engaged in oral copulation and sexual intercourse.

As a Juvenile Officer and on my own, I have had contact with a wide variety of children of various ages. I have taken a course on child development and read several articles on the developmental states of children which has assisted me in recognizing and identifying the age of children.

I have viewed thousands of magazines depicting children in the nude, in sexually provocative poses, in lewd poses, and engaged in virtually every conceivable sex act. I have seen the manner in which these magazines are packaged for mailing and have learned how they are mailed for distribution in this country. I have seen magazines published in Europe and those published in the United States and seen that, although some of the publications were printed and distributed in Europe, the photography and pictures depicted therein had actually come from this country. Many of the children shown in the pornographic magazines are those from local communities, such as Napa County; their photographs sent to the magazines by people who have taken them.

I have seen numerous movies and video tapes depicting children in the same activities and poses as previously described above. These films and video tapes are both commercially produced in Europe and in the United States as well as in the same manner as previously described above for pornographic magazines.

I have read and examined various publications written and distributed by people who molest children and their organizations which described the acts they desire to commit upon children. I have read various publications produced by the same individuals which seek to encourage sexual relations with children. These same publications spell out the manner in which people seduce their victims and outline the ways to seek out, find and successfully molest children.

I have talked with over 50 people who have confessed to me their attraction to children and told me the manner in which they seek out, find, and molest their victims.

I have talked to over 100 persons, both adult and children, who have told me of the manner in which they have been victimized as children.

I have corresponded with at least 20 persons who have identified themselves as people who molest children and told me of their sexual interests and experiences. I have read over 200 letters of persons who have written about their sexual experiences with children and been involved in the exchange of child pornography. I have discussed or reviewed the investigations of at least 100 cases where correspondence was involved. In these cases the persons involved wrote about their sexual experience with children and/or were involved in exchange or sale of child pornography.

As a result of the above-mentioned training and experience, I have learned that the following characteristics are, generally, found to exist in varying combinations and be true in cases involving people who buy, produce, trade, or sell child pornography; who molest children and/or who are involved with child prostitutes:

1. There are persons whose sexual objects are children. They receive sexual gratification and satisfaction from actual, physical contact with children and from fantasy involving use of pictures, other photographic or art mediums, and writings on or about sexual activity with children;

2. These people collect sexually explicit materials consisting of photographs, magazines, motion pictures, video tapes, books, and slides which they use for their own sexual gratification and fantasy;

3. These people use sexually explicit materials, including those listed above for lowering the inhibitions of children, sexually stimulating children and themselves, and for demonstrating the desired sexual acts, before, during and after sexual activity with children;

4. These people rarely, if ever, dispose of their sexually explicit materials, especially when it is used in the seduction of their victims, and those materials are treated as prize possessions;

5. These people often correspond or meet with one another to share information and identities of their victims as a means of gaining status, trust, acceptance, and psychological support;

6. These people rarely destroy correspondence received from other people with similar interests unless they are specifically requested to do so;

7. The majority of these people prefer contact with children of one sex, as well as in a particular age or developmental range peculiar to each individual;

8. These people engage in activity or gravitate to programs which will be of interest to the type of victims they desire to attract and will provide them with easy access to these children;

9. These people obtain, collect, and maintain photographs of the children they are or have been involved with. These photos may depict children fully clothed, in various states of undress or totally nude, in various activities, not necessarily sexually explicit. these photos are rarely, if ever, disposed of and are revered with such devotion that they are often kept upon the person's person in wallets and such. If a picture of a child is taken by such a person depicting the child in the nude, there is a high probability the child was molested before, during, or after the photo taking session, because the act of posing is such a great stimuli for the individual.

10. These people use such photos as described above as a means of reliving fantasies or actual encounters with the depicted children. They also

utilize the photos as keepsakes and as a means of gaining acceptance, status, trust, and psychological support by exchanging, trading, or selling them to other people with similar interests. These photos are carried and kept by these people as a constant threat to the child of blackmail and exposure;

11.  These people cut pictures of children out of magazines, newspapers, books, and other publications which they use as a means of fantasy relationship. These "cutouts" help to identify the age and sexual preference of the person under investigation;

12.  These people collect books, magazines, newspapers, and other writings on the subject of sexual activities with children. They maintain these as a way of understanding their own feelings towards children;

13.  The people who are afraid of discovery often maintain and run their own photographic production and reproduction equipment. This may be as simple as the use of "instant" photo equipment such as Polaroid makes, video equipment, or as complex as a completely outfitted photo lab;

14.  These people go to great lengths to conceal and protect from discovery, theft, and damage, their collections of illicit materials. This often includes the rental or use of safe deposit boxes or other storage facilities outside their immediate residence;

15.  These people often collect, read, copy or maintain names, addresses, phone numbers or lists of persons who have similar sexual interests. These may have been collected by personal contact or through advertisements in various publications. These contacts are maintained as a means of personal referral, exchange, and commercial profit. These names may be maintained in the original publication, in phone or note books, or merely on scraps of paper;

16.  These people often keep the names of the children they are involved with or with whom they have had sexual contact. They maintain these names in much the same manner as that described in the preceding paragraph and for much the same reasons;

17.  These people use sexual aides such as dildos fashioned after a man's penis or various sizes and shapes in addition to other sexual aides in the seduction of their victims. They often utilize these as a means of exciting their victims and of arousing the curiosity of the children;

18.  These people maintain diaries of their sexual encounters with children. These accounts of their sexual experiences are used as a means of reliving the encounter when the offender has no children to molest. Such diaries might consist of a notebook, scraps of paper, or a formal diary; depending upon the resources available to the offender, they may be contained on audio tape or computer entries in a "home computer;"

19. These people collect and maintain books, magazines, articles, and other writings on the subject of sexual activity. These books and materials may be on the topics of human sexuality, sexual education, or consist of sex manuals discussing or showing various sexual acts, positions, or sexual activities. These books and materials are used as a means of seduction of the victim by arousing curiosity, demonstration of propriety of the acts desired, explaining or demonstrating what the offender desires to be done, and as a means of sexual arousal on the part of the offender - particularly when naked children are shown or depicted in the materials;

20. These people often use drugs as a means of inducement to get a child to a particular location such as the offender's home. Alcohol is also used in this fashion. Both drugs and alcohol are used as a means of seduction reducing the child's inhibitions and for sexual excitement;

21. These people often collect and maintain artifacts, statues, paintings, or other art media which depict children or young persons in nude poses or sexual acts. These are kept or "left" in places where the victims can find or "discover" them;

22. These people obtain and keep things of interest to their victims. These may consist of magazines, books, and toys for the age level of the victims they desire to attract and may be as complicated as video games, toy train sets, and computers;

23. These people often keep momentos of their relationships with specific children as a means of remembrance. These may consist of underwear or other garments or things which are unique to the relationship they and with the child;

24. All of the materials requested for seizure will identify children who are being sexually exploited through child molestation, child pornography, and/or child prostitution. The materials will also identify other adults who are engaging in the sexual exploitation of children by these means. In addition, these materials will demonstrate the sexual proclivity, inclination, preferences, and activities of the person(s) under investigation, providing evidence that will tend to show that the person(s) under investigation has committed felonies, to wit, section 283(a) Penal Code, 289 PC, and Misdemeanors 311.3 PC, 647a PC, and 314 PC.

As a result of the above mentioned training and experience, I have also learned that there are characteristics which may be examined to help to predict what kind of evidence may be present in a given case or to assess the type of offender under investigation. These are defined by the Federal Bureau of Investigation as consisting of four major groups of characteristics. The first involves long term and consistent patterns of behavior. The second, an identifiable preference for children as sexual objects or the objects of sexual advances and acts. The third are well developed techniques for obtaining victims. Finally, there are sexual fantasies focusing on children.

Indicators of the characteristics of long term and persistent patterns of behavior include the circumstances wherein more than one child is reporting sexual improprieties committed by the subject under investigation. A second manifestation of this characteristic is the presence of planned, repeated, and often high risk attempts or actual molestations of children. The bolder the attempt, often committed in the presence of other children or witnesses, if repeated more than once and carried out in a cunning and skillful manner, the stronger the indications are that the subject under investigation will possess traits similar to those listed in numbers 1 through 23 above on pages 14 through 18.

The second characteristic, children as preferred sexual objects, manifests itself in many ways, among them an excessive interest in children. This manifestation may include an individual who has no children of his own, yet, whose home is a magnet for neighborhood children. Another manifestation is the socializing with children wherein the subject under investigation is usually seen associating with or having a circle of friends who are young, much younger than he. This may be where they frequent places where children may be found or where they provide the location and invitation. Lastly, is the manifestation of an age and gender preference or victim target group. This involves an identifiable gender and age target, wherein the offender is sexually involved only with children of a particular group. The age span may range anywhere from 2 to 4 years and the offender may only target particular children within that age group.

The third characteristic, having well developed techniques for obtaining victims includes manifestations of an individual's ability to better identify with children than with people in his or her own peer group. In this situation, an offender surrounds himself with children who are nonthreatening and easily impressed. Another manifestation of this characteristic is the access to children. It is not uncommon for an individual to either move into a particular neighborhood which already has children within his target group or to utilize the neighborhood as a pool to draw victims from. The further manifestation of this characteristic is the involvement in activities with children which often exclude other adults. Here the individual tries to get children into situations where there are no other adults present. In addition, this individual seduces children with attention, affection, and providing them with gifts. Here they literally seduce the children by befriending them, talking to them, listening to them, paying attention to them, spending time with them, and buying gifts for them which includes, but is not limited to candy.

A further characteristic of this offender is a developed skill at manipulating children. Her, in order to be sexually involved with numerous children, simultaneously, this individual uses seduction techniques, competition, peer pressure, child and group psychology, motivation techniques, threats, and blackmail. It often involves the molestation of children in front of other children, the threat of what the offender will do if the children tell, and the warning of the child of disclosure or negative consequences on the part of their telling. Furthermore, another manifestation of this characteristic is the hobbies and interests the individual possesses which appeal to children. This most frequently occurs in situations where the offender has material things which the children do not have normal access to such as computers, video games, athletic equipment, or toys.

Another manifestation of this characteristic is the use of what ostensibly is legitimate physical contact used as a means of securing both sexual stimulation and reducing the reluctance to having been physically touched or molested. This type of activity is most frequently manifested by the offender engaging the children in tickling or horse play.

Lastly, is the manifestation of the display of sexually explicit material to children. Here, as described in paragraphs numbered 2 through 4 on page y above, the material is used to seduce the child.

Lastly, the characteristic of sexual fantasies focusing on children involve, among other things, youth oriented decorations or furnishings contained where the children will be frequenting. Through experience and training, I have seen such places which could only be described as miniature amusement parks.

Your Affiant has also learned through experience and training that there are certain characteristics surrounding the interview of young children which will influence the manner in which disclosure is made and what information is obtained regarding what has happened to them. One of the most common characteristics in the victimization of young children is that when disclosing, children don't always tell everything in initial interviews. What happens is that after the child finally comes to grips with what has happened to him or her the account slowly unravels. Subsequent interviews reveal more detail and new information about what had originally transpired.

In addition, your Affiant has discovered through experience and training, that when dealing with young victims in the age group involved in this case, unless specific questions are asked regarding certain events or circumstances, the children will not comprehend the nature of the inquiry and therefore not reveal what has happened to them or understand the connections which the inquirer is trying to make or establish. This explains the ability to obtain further information in subsequent interviews from those that were initially made by initial investigators.

In addition, through experience and training, I have found that when dealing with young children the time that the interview is initiated is extremely important in the ability of the child to recall and relate the events which have transpired. Interviews conducted in late afternoon or evening hours are often non-productive and produce confusing, if not, misleading information.

On October 16, 1987, in my capacity as the investigator assigned to the Napa County District Attorney's Office, Child Abuse Vertical Prosecution Program, I reviewed Napa Sheriff's Department report number 87- written by Detective William Lacey of the Napa County Sheriff's Department. This report was made to the Sheriff's Office on October 2, 1987, and involves a child molestation investigation involving R—— D—— a white female juvenile, eight years old, S——, a white female juvenile, M—— M——, a white female juvenile, nine years old, 7 years, and J—— S——, a white male adult, 38 years. A copy of that investigation report is attached hereto and incorporated herein for reference as Exhibit "A."

At the request of Deputy District Attorney Lynn Young, I reviewed this case for the purpose of reinterviewing the children involved to establish specifics for charging and the preparation of this affidavit.

According to Detective Lacey's report, he interviewed S—— D——, mother of R—— D—— on October 2, 1987. Mrs. D—— told Detective Lacey that at approximately 7:00 p.m. on the previous evening, her nine year old daughter, L——, brought her a school journal belonging to R——. Mrs. D—— said that she discovered two pages wherein her daughter, R——, had written passages stating that J—— S——, a neighbor of theirs, had shown R—— and another neighbor S—— E—— pornographic movies, showed them his penis, and let them play with what R—— called S——'s "bottom." The specific pages described by Detective Lacey were retained by him as evidence and are attached hereto as part of Exhibit A.

According to Detective Lacey, Mrs. D—— said that she and the family moved to their present residence approximately eight years ago and became friends with S—— and his wife, J——, approximately 3 or 4 years ago. She said that occasionally their families would get together for barbeques at the S——'s home and that her children and other neighborhood children would frequently go over to S——'s house to play in his hot tub, play his video games, and jump on his small trampoline.

Mrs. D—— said that toward the end of summer of 1987, her daughter, R——, was frequently asking if she could go to S——'s home "all the time." She said that R—— returned from S——'s home on a few occasions with candy.

Mrs. D—— told Detective Lacey that approximately two weeks prior to his interview with her, R—— has returned from S——'s house with the crotch of her shorts that she was wearing torn. She said that when asked by R——'s father, R—— said that she had torn her shorts while jumping on S——'s trampoline and having been "tickled by J—— S——." She said that R—— said that S—— had "touched her" in what Mrs. D—— remembers as being described as S—— putting his hands or hand on R——'s pants. Mrs. D—— said that after this, R—— was not allowed to return to the S——'s. Nothing else was done or said about it until the journal was discovered.

According to Detective Lacey's report, on the same date, he interviewed J—— D——, R——'s father regarding the incidents described by R——'s mother. Essentially he repeated the same information.

On the same date, at approximately 5:07 P.M., Detective Lacey interviewed R—— D——. On 1/7/88, 1/8/88, and 1/13/88, in the morning hours, I reinterviewed R—— D—— to clarify, elaborate on certain points, and determine the prospects of preparation of this affidavit.

According to Detective Lacey's report, on 10/2/87 R—— told him that "J——" had touched her in "a way she though was wrong." Detective Lacey said that R—— identified J—— as an adult man, approximately 36 years old "that lives across the street." Detective Lacey said that R—— pointed out S——'s residence as being the place where "J——" lived. When I reinterviewed her, she said that she guessed at S——'s age due to his looks.

According to Detective Lacey's report, R—— said that during the mid portion of September, 1987, on an afternoon, she was with her friend S—— B——. She said that they had gone to S——'s house and were playing with a slot machine which she later described to me as operating with nickels, a lever action arm, and the rotating "fruit bars" which indicate whether one wins or not. She said that the slot machine was located in a "room with beer and wine" which she later told me was a room with a bar. She described the game that she played on the slot machine to Detective Lacey as being called "Jackpot."

She said that while sitting on the living room couch, later, S—— asked both she and E—— if they would like to see his "weenie." She told Detective Lacey that S—— then unfastened the front of his pants and exposed his "weenie" which she both identified to Detective Lacey and myself as being S——'s penis.

R—— also told Detective Lacey that after exposing himself, he asked them if they wanted to see a "gross movie" which S—— then showed them. She told Detective Lacey that S—— then played two VCR movies on his VCR which depicted men and women in various sexual acts including intercourse and oral copulation. She later further described these movies to me as being shown on the living room, big screen, t.v. which had a VCR on top of it. On top of the VCR were 3 to 4 tapes, two of which S—— played for them depicting the aforementioned activities. R—— told me that he told them that he had bought the tapes and described them as containing the following: The first had a man on a white floor who she described as a white male, younger than her father whom she believed was 40 years old. She said the man had no clothes on and that he appeared with a woman, who had long, dark, hair. She described the activity which was depicted as the woman sitting on the man's groin and rocking her hips. She described these both to Detective Lacey and myself by using dolls and toy bears. She described the second movie as containing a white male adult and a white female adult and the action as having "sucked each others butt." She indicated oral copulation had occurred by demonstrating both touching the faces of the dolls which she was demonstrating with to the genitals and anal areas of the dolls.

At the time of Detective Lacey's original interview, R—— told him that during the movies S—— was talking about "butts" and that he "explained that the movie showed that what happens after men and women marry and connect bottoms to have babies." Detective Lacey said that R—— told him that S—— had rubbed his "weenie" and at some point tried to have S—— touch his genitals. She said that he then tried to have her do the same thing.

According to Detective Lacey, R—— then said that S—— replaced his genitals into his pants until S—— asked him to pull it out again at which point he then exposed himself once again. He said that R—— said that both she and S—— again returned to playing the slot machine and were allowed to keep the money that they operated it with. After doing this, they then went to S——'s back yard where S—— was cleaning his hot tub. Later in the day, R—— said that they returned to the living room where S—— again exposed himself and that he "showed the girls the black hair around his "weenie."

According to Detective Lacey, R—— also told him that she recalled that before she and S—— left S——'s home, S—— briefly rubbed their clothed vaginal areas and that S—— bought them candy and root beer bubble gum. He then told them, after giving them the candy, "don't tell anybody because I'll get in trouble and have to go to court and you'll have to sit in a chair and be assistants (sic)." When I reinterviewed R——, she remembered only S—— touching her and not S——. She did not remember how he had touched them either, indicating that she was not sure whether it was over or under her clothes.

According to Detective Lacey, R—— described another incident which occurred on an afternoon approximately one or two days after the previously mentioned incident. She described to Detective Lacey going to S——'s residence wherein they watched a war movie for approximately 5 minutes. She described this war movie to me as containing a story about "dirty" soldiers who had guns. She said the part that they watched had approximately 4 soldiers and was bout one of them being shot in the chest. She said that they were smoking and that one of the soldiers shared his cigarette with another. This was in the living room on the previously described VCR and large screen television. Again, he had retrieved the tapes from on top of the television.

R—— told Detective Lacey that during the time they watched this movie, S—— pulled out his "weenie" for a short time and then put it back in his pants. During this time period, S—— began talking to the children and exposed himself once again and began talking to R—— about sexual matters which she described as "gross things about getting together." She described both to Detective Lacey and myself that to her "getting together" meant engaging in sexual intercourse, which she described to both of us using dolls and teddy bears.

R—— described to Detective Lacey another incident which occurred on a different afternoon approximately one week after the above described incidents. On this occasion, she told Detective Lacey that she had gone to S——'s residence by herself. She said that while sitting on a living room couch with S——, he had her stand up and that he pulled her pants and panties down. On this occasion, S—— talked to her about having sexual intercourse and that he briefly rubbed the outer area of her vagina for awhile and then inserted his fingers inside her vagina for "one or two seconds." She also told Detective Lacey that she thought that he had also rubbed her breasts on the outside of her shirt at the same time and may have told her that "you're getting big up here."

She also told Detective Lacey that on another incident, within the time period described above, she, S——, and her sister L—— were playing on S——'s trampoline. She said that during this occasion S—— tickled her sister and looked up her shorts while playing with her.

When I interviewed R——, she described the very first incident which occurred with S—— as having occurred after school had started for her third grade which I later determined from her mother to have occurred on August 31, 1987. She said this incident occurred in the room which contained the bar and that they had been playing with the "Jackpot" game. She said that at this time she was alone with S—— and that he was by the game with her.

She said that after playing for awhile, S—— invited her into his living room to have a snack. While she was sitting on the couch, S—— sat next to her and pulled down his pants to below his knees. She said that he had underwear on then and that he had pulled them down while he was sitting down. She described the pants as being red with stripes.

She said that S—— told her to "look" and pointed at his "weenie." She told me that she was repulsed at what she saw and that he immediately pulled his pants back up and told her not to tell anyone. She did not remember if he said what would happen if she did. She told me that on this occasion, before he told her not to tell anyone, he gave her some applies and some tomatoes to take home to her parents. She said that that never happened after that and that that was the only time that he had ever done such a thing.

I later spoke with R——'s mother and she said that she did remember a time when R—— had brought apples to her which she had used to make applesauce but did not remember her bringing any tomatoes. She said there was only one occasion that this occurred, however, was unable to place it in time.

R—— also further described the incident where the war movie was shown as occurring during the evening hours and in S——'s living room on a couch. She said that S—— was sitting on that same couch, next to the victim at the time of the sexual activity. She did not remember for certain, but believed that S—— was present and that they did talk about school. She said that the defendant had rubbed her "boobies" which she demonstrated on a doll as being her breasts. She described the action performed by S—— by rubbing, over her clothes, the area of her own breasts. At that time she did not remember the details about how she arrived or how she left.

She also said that on many occasions S—— would give she and her friends candy of varying types. She said that he would not give it to her or her friends on every occasion.

I discussed with R—— the portion of Detective Lacey's report wherein he discusses the occasion that she was wearing pants that were torn. She said that at that time she did not remember all of the details however, she still had the shorts which she showed me.

R—— also told me that she had seen a scar on S——'s penis which she drew a picture of. She said that she wasn't certain on just which occasions that she had seen it, however said that S—— has shown it to her repeatedly. A copy of that drawing is attached hereto and incorporated herein as reference as Exhibit B.

According to Detective Lacey's report on October 2, 1987, he interviewed S—— E—— at approximately 8:00 p.m. She described an incident to him which occurred in S——'s truck. According to Detective Lacey, S—— told him that she and R—— were playing in S——'s truck. After playing for a while, S—— entered the truck. According to Detective Lacey's report, S—— said that R—— pulled down the back of S——'s shorts to his "crack" and told him "let us seen your private." She said at this point, S—— pulled up one leg of his shorts and exposed his "private." When I reviewed the report with her she told me that she did not tell Detective Lacey that R—— had said what is recorded in Lacey's report. She did identify the private as where "you go to the bathroom" and that men have different "privates" than women.

According to Detective Lacey's report, S—— told him that S—— "rubbed his private" and that "R—— touched the hairy part." When I reviewed this portion with her she remembered this incident and this activity.

She said that S—— had also asked her if she wanted to touch it. She remembers that S—— told both she and R—— not to tell bout what had happened or that they wouldn't be able to see his "private" again.

According to Detective Lacey's report, S—— also said that on another afternoon, around the same time as the previously mentioned incident in the truck, she and R—— were at S——'s house when his wife was gone. On this occasion they played with his slot machine, watched him clean the hot tub that he had and that he had shown them two pornographic movies which she described as men and women "putting their privates together." When I tried to clarify with her exactly what she had seen, she at that time, was unable to describe it in any more detail than had been done in Detective Lacey's report. She said that while showing the movies, she had seen R——'s mother walking up the steps to the house at which point S—— turned off the movies.

According to Detective Lacey's report, on October 5, 1987, at 1039 hours, he reinterviewed R—— regarding the incident in the truck. She said that she did recall an afternoon, possibly the same day that he showed the pornographic movies where she, S——, and S—— were sitting in his pickup truck. She said that during this incident, S—— played a "musical horn" which she described as an electronic horn in his truck." During that time, he also "pulled out his weenie." She was not able to describe much else in the way of activity but believed that he was wearing dark red pants at the time without underwear.

According to Detective Lacey's report, on October 5, 1987, at 10:52 A.M., Detective Lacey interviewed R——'s sister, L——. She told him that during the summer, possibly on a weekend several weeks prior to the interview she was having with him, they were at S——'s house playing. She indicated that she was with R—— and that on this occasion she was jumping on S——'s trampoline in his living room. At that time, R—— and S—— were sitting on a couch.

She said that when she was tired from jumping, she laid face up on the trampoline, at which point S—— began to tickle her. She said that he picked her up by the ankles, with her head down, and looked down her pants. She said that she tried to prevent him from doing so by grabbing the sides of her pants and pulling them tight against her body.

On this same occasion, she remembers that R——'s shorts had a hole in them over the vaginal area. She said that she saw S—— poking at it with his index finger, talking about the existence of the hole. She does not remember if he actually touched her, however.

According to Detective Lacey's report, on October 5, 1987, at approximately 11:15 in the morning, he spoke with M—— M——, a neighbor and friend of R—— and S——'s. She said that she would often go the the S——'s house and that on at least one occasion, during the summer of 1986, S——— exposed his penis to her.

According to Detective Lacey's report, on October 5, 1987, he interviewed S——— who identified himself as described in the Search Warrant and Affidavit. He denied that he had exposed himself to any children and, on the contrary, claimed that on two occasions, once when he was unloading groceries from his vehicle and once when he was in his hot tub, "the D——— girl" pulled down his shorts. He said that he did not have underwear because he doesn't wear it. In addition, he said that recently he was watching pornographic movies that he had rented when two neighborhood girls walked into his house and that he immediately turned them off. At this point Detective Lacey admonished S——— of his Constitutional rights per the Miranda decision at which point he elected to invoke those rights.

When I initially interviewed R——— D———, she said that she remembered at least two times when S——— had touched her "boobies" and "bottom." She estimated that at least ten times she had seen his "weenie." She believed there was only one time that he had actually tried to get her to touch his "weenie." In addition, she believed there was at least one occasion where he had asked that she and he "get together."

When I interviewed, she estimated that she had gone to S———'s house on at least three occasions and that on each time she went there something sexual would happen. She further described an incident not mentioned in Detective Lacey's report where she was sitting on his porch and that he had exposed himself to her.

# Appendix

On June 2, 19–, I received a letter from a persona named N——. It was in response to an ad I placed in an underground newspaper. He used the address of —— W—— Street, ——, Hayward, California. In the letter he stated that he lived in Oakland, the Dimond District, but that he received certain letters in Hayward. He said a friend kept the letters for him. He indicated that he was interested in both boys and girls but that he preferred girls. He let me know what age range he was interested in with the following analogy, "I know what I like! Like to play craps? My favorite numbers are 5 thru 10—I like to bet and sometimes win." In the letter he included four cutouts from magazines of girls ranging from five to ten years old. In the letter N—— indicated that he corresponds with several people, seeking people who are interested in pedophilia. N—— also stated that he has a friend who has a large collection of films, magazines and pictures. He said that the collection was the "real McCoy." He stated that he wanted to meet me face to face rather than dealing through the mails.

I contacted Inspector Brad Reeves of the United States Postal Inspection Office because I recalled that he was working a pedophile case with the suspect being a N—— L—— using a Hayward address. R—— informed me that it was in fact L—— that was his suspect and that he was using the ——W—— Street, ——, Hayward, California, as his address. He also told me that another person by the name of D—— D—— was writing him from the same address that L—— writes from. R—— stated that both L—— and D—— joined the Postal Service's sting operation. Both filled out Questionnaires in which they indicate their sexual preferences. L—— indicated that he was interested in having sex with seven to ten year old girls. D—— indicated that he liked girls from eleven to early teens as sex partners. R—— stated that L—— answered several ads in the Postal Inspections's sting operation. He also stated that D—— placed an ad in the paper which reads as follows: WHITE GENTLEMAN 42, SINGLE 6'6" STRAIGHT, CLEAN, HEALTHY AND EMPLOYED WISHES TO SWING WITH AFFECTIONATE WHITE LADIES AND COUPLES. ALSO WITH FAMILY WITH DAUGHTER 10 AND UP. REGULAR HOT SEX. NO RUFF STUFF. ALSO LOVE TO GIVE ORAL AND ANAL SEX IF DESIRED. WEEKENDS, CAN TRAVEL BY

CAR IN S.F. BAY AREA AND NO. CAL. OR HAVE OVERNITE GUESTS. MOST SINCERE, PLEASE SEND PHOTO, NUDE NOT NECESSARY.

On June 10, 19-, I wrote back to L' leading him to believe that I shared the same interest in pedophilia as he did. I also told him that I was interested in seeing the collection that his friend has. I told him that I would be happy to meet him but that I was not willing to give out my phone number. I asked for a number to contact him or to have him set up a date and location where I could meet him.

On June 23, 19- I received a second letter from L——. In it he enclosed three more cutouts from a magazine. There was no letter in the envelope.

On June 11, 19-, I write back to L—— asking him why there was not letter with the cutouts. I told him that I was still very interested in meeting him. I also asked him if he was still interested in corresponding with me.

On August 25, 19-, I received another letter from L——. He had set up a meet with me on Sunday, August 24, 1986, at the 1/4 LBER Burger at 37th Ave and E. 14th Street. I had just returned from vacation so I missed the meet.

On August 28, 19-, I wrote to L—— and apologized for missing the meeting. I asked him to set up another meeting and I assured him that I would not miss the meeting.

On September 9, 19-, I received another letter from L—— setting up another meet at the Giant 1/4lber at 27th Ave and E. 14th on September 12, 1986. He said that he said that he would be there at three different times (1:30PM, 5:30PM and 7:00PM) on that date. He said that he would wait a half hour at each of those times. He described himself as 50 years old and having very scarce hair. He said that he would be wearing a white jacket with "Mountain Meadow Ranch, Staff" printed on it. This was the last letter received from L——. Copies of all correspondence through the mail attached to this affidavit as Exhibits 1-7.

On September 12, 19-, as arranged by L—— I met with him at the Giant 1/4lber at 37th Ave and E. 14th Street. We met at approximately 1:30PM. We sat in an undercover van used by the Vice Division. He told me that he was into Child Pornography but he referred to it as "KP" (kiddie Porn). He told me that he lived in the Dimond District and was a widower. He stated that while he was married he had a 14 year old step-daughter. He said the following about his step-daughter, "I didn't get into her pants but it wasn't because I didn't try. Boy did I try." L—— stated that he had a lot of child pornography but he threw it away because he was afraid that his wife might find it. L—— stated that all the child pornography that he had available to him was at his friend's house in Hayward. L—— stated that his friend's name was D——. L—— stated that he used to room with D—— but moved out when D—— got a live-in girlfriend. L—— stated that lately D—— has been having problems with his girlfriend. D—— stated that the only reason that

D—— was keeping the girlfriend around was because she has two daughters six and eight years old who are suppose to move in with him. He is supposedly putting up with the girlfriend so that he can get his hands on the daughters. L—— stated that D—— keeps his child pornography locked in a safe in the closet. L—— stated that he and D—— have a mutual friend by the name of Ken who lives in San Francisco. L—— stated that Ken took pictures of himself having sexual intercourse with his daughter. L—— stated that D—— has several of these photographs in his safe. L—— also stated that D—— has homemade movies of adults having sex with children.

L—— stated that his favorite age range was 7-8 years old. He told me that he frequents a bar at 40th and San Pablo, The Bank Club. He said that the owner has a 7-8 year old daughter who is always around the bar. He said the girl's name is Tia and that she is blind. L—— stated that he is sure that the father is having sex with the girl. He said, "Watching her eat a hot dog I know she is good at sucking dick." L—— gave me his home phone number —— and asked me to call him the following week.

On September 15, 1986, I contacted L—— via the telephone at the number that he gave me ——. He again talked about his interests in pedophilia. He told me that he had access to all the material that D—— has in his possession. He stated that D—— had a movie of a girl having sex with an adult. He said that it was the real thing, that it was not an adult female made up to look like a juvenile. He told me that he was going to contact D —— and set up a meeting for Friday or Saturday, September 19 and 20 respectively. He told me to call him on Thursday (September 18, 19-).

On September 19, 19-, I again contacted L—— via telephone at the same number. He stated that he contacted D—— and that D—— was interested in meeting me. He gave me D——'s phone number, ——, and told me to call him. He also gave me D——'s address as —— W—— St., Hayward, California. He also gave me directions on how to get to D——'s home. He offered to go with me if I wanted him to but that he would rather not because he did not get along with D——'s girlfriend.

On September 19, 19-, I telephoned D—— at —— in the 415 area cod. He said that he was interested in meeting me. He said that we could exchange notes, pictures and magazines. He said to call him at approximately 10:00 AM on September 20, 19-, to set up a date and location. At not time did we discuss the type of magazines and photographs that we were interested in. He was totally relying on the information that L—— gave him about me.

On September 20, 19-, at approximately 10:00am, I phoned D—— at ——. He asked me if I had spoken to N—— (L—— lately. I told him no. He said that he was going to try to get ahold of L—— so that the three of us could meet. He was having an argument with his girlfriend, which I could hear over the phone, so he asked me to call him back in about an hours. I phoned him back about an hour later and we set up a meet at Denny's Restaurant. Again we did not discuss our interest in magazines and photographs.

All phone conversations between myself, L—— and D—— were recorded with the tape being kept in the case file.

On September 20, 19-, I met with D—— in the parking lot of Denny's Restaurant at 15015 Freedom Ave, San Leandro, California. He was waiting in a 78 Dodge silver with California License ——. I pulled along side him and we spoke through the windows. He then got out of his vehicle removing a brown paper bag and he then got into the blue undercover van that I was driving. He introduced himself as Dennis and told me that he was not really into meeting single men. He told me that he likes couples with children or mother-daughter teams, D—— said, "I like 11-13 year old girls but that's not to say that I would pass up a 5 or 6 year old girl. I like them a little older so that their pussies aren't so tight and I can actually fuck them.' D—— told me that he once met a woman through the Berkeley Barb who had a 13 year old daughter. He said that he told the lady that he was interested in the daughter. D—— stated that he confessed his desire for the daughter because he was afraid the mother would see the way he was looking at the daughter. He stated that the mother did not seem to be disturbed by his desire for the daughter but that he somehow let the opportunity slip through his fingers.

D—— then pulled two magazines out of the brown paper bag and asked to see what I had. I showed him several magazines that were confiscated from other cases. He had Lolita 1 and Lolita 17 both child pornography. He went through the magazines that I brought and picked out a magazine named Loving Children. He traded Lolita 17 for the Loving Children magazine. The Lolita 17 contained 31 photographs of female juveniles 7-13 years old in sexually explicit situations. D—— stated that he has other magazines and films at home. Copies of the covers of Lolita 17 and Loving Children attached to this affidavit as Exhibits 8 and 9.

D—— then stated that he advertised in the Swingers Digest to meet couples with children. He current girlfriend answered the ad and came up from Southern California and the next thing he knew she was living with him. He stated that she was angry this morning when I called because he was leaving her out of the meeting. He stated that she wanted to get involved. D—— said that his girlfriend's name was N——. He said that when she was a child that she had sexual intercourse with a couple of her uncles. He told me that she would be interested in swapping partners if I had someone who was interested. D—— stated that his girlfriend's children were living in G—— with the grandparents. He stated that they might send for the children.

D—— stated that L—— had quite a collection of child pornography. He stated that L—— called him one night and told him that he dumped his collection. L—— had told me that same story, that he was afraid that this wife might find them. D—— said that L—— had the collection long after his wife died.

On September 22, 19-, I searched through copies of Swinger Digest which I had available to me and found D——'s ad in the —— issue. It was on page 16 in the first column. The ad read as follows: HAYWARD-FRIENDLY W/M, SINCERE, 43, 6'2", 230, SINGLE, SINSIBLE, WELL-MANNERED & DISCREET, WISH TO HAVE HOT HORNY SEX WITH A FEW W/F OR W/C TO AGE 50. LOVE FRENCHING, MAYBE GREEK, OPEN MINDED TO FAMILY SEX ARRANGEMENT OR MOTHER/DAUGH-TER(TEEN*OLDER), T.L.C., LIKE PICNICS, BEACH, MOVIES, MUSIC ON DOING NOTHING AT ALL. WARM LONG FRIENDSHIP DESIRED. AM CLEAN, DISEASE FREE, STRAIGHT, VIRILE, 7 1/2", YOUR PLACE OR MINE. WILL TRAVEL 100+ MI. CALL FOR LOCAL WEEKNIGHT & DISTANT WEEKEND MEETING AND FUN. HAYWARD ——. D——'s photograph, standing in the nude was included, in the ad. The phone number in the ad is the same that L—— game me as D——'s number and the same number I called to reach D——. A copy of the ad from Swingers Digest —— issue attached to this affidavit as Exhibit 10.

On September 23, 19-, I again contacted L—— via telephone ——. He asked me about my meeting with D——. He wanted to know if I thought he was exaggerating about D——'s collection. I told him that D—— only brought two magazines. He said that D——is probably being careful. L—— stated that he wanted to meet with me again. He said that he was going to have the house to himself for the next two weeks. L—— requested that I bring my collection to his house so that he could view it. He gave me his address as # —— V——, Oakland, California. He also gave me direction on how to get to his home. L—— when talking about child pornography almost always refers to it as "KP" (Kiddie Porn). He has been saying that he destroyed his collection but during our last phone conversation he slipped and said when talking about collections, "But the kind of material that I have, you have..." leading me to believe that he still has his collection. Also the two different stories that L—— told D—— and myself about when he got rid of his collection.

All my contact with D—— was arranged by L——. I never told D—— what my interests were and yet he showed up to the meeting with child pornography. L—— is responsible for the meeting and informing each of us that the other was interested in child pornography.

I believe that both L—— and D—— are a danger to children in the areas that they live. Through my contacts with both L—— and D—— I believe that each of them in the past have molested children and given the opportunity will continue to molest them in the future.

I contacted Pacific Bell Security to ascertain If L———'s and D———'s phone numbers were listed. Both were in fact listed. L———, was listed at ———, the address that L—— gave as his home. D———'s ——9 listed at —— W——.

Based on my training and experience and the above information, I am of the opinion that both L—— and D—— are involved in the sexual exploitation of children. They are in violation of Child Molesting (288PC), Child Molesting (647A PC), and/or the producing, distributing, selling, trading, or the exchanging of child pornography (311 and its attendant subsections of the Penal Code), and Contributing to the Delinquency of a Minor (272 PC). 288 PC and some sections of 311 PC are felonies. Therefore, I request a search for all indicia and evidence of pedophilia which are located in the following locations: #15 V—— W—, Oakland, California, (L———'s residence) and —— W—— St., ———, Hayward, California (D———'s residence).

I also know that persons involved in pedophilia activity will often times keep and/or transport any materials and photographs in their vehicle, as D—— did when meeting me on the September 20, 1986. Therefore, I request a search of the following vehicle which is registered to D———, D———: 78 Dodge Silver California L——. The registration was verified through a record check of California Department of Motor Vehicles.

# Appendix XIII

Search Warrant Affidavit Supporting Search of Offender's Home

(Summary of expertise and experience of the affiant)
(Summary of the crimes in the series including the MO traits listed below, see example paragraph)
(listing of characteristics of offenders in Appendix III)
(sample description of an offense in series)
Case # 1234-91 (Knoxville P.D.) On 4-22-1991, at approximately 0400 hours, Gena Baxter, White, Female, 8 yrs, awoke to see a man standing under the light in the hallway just outside of her bedroom. Her bedroom is located on the ground level, in the northwest corner of the house with a door opening onto the patio in the back of the house. The house is a single story, single family residence, located in a residential neighborhood of the small town of Knoxville, There is an alley immediately behind the residence which connects with the streets on either end of the block in which the house sits.

The man was holding a flashlight in his right hand and one of the toy dolls in his left hand. She recognized the doll as one she had kept on a bookcase just inside the door of her bedroom.

She called out "Who's there?" and the man dropped the doll and fled through the bedroom and out of the door onto the back patio.

She described the man as white, approx 5'6", slim build, wearing a blue watch cap and a white scarf with a pattern of straight black threads through it. He was wearing dark, fingerless gloves and a navy blue blazer with a double row of brass buttons down the front, gray pants and black shoes.

The man's face was wrapped and concealed by the scarf.

Officer Jones spoke to Gena's mother, whose bedroom is located in the northeast ground level bedroom of the house. She had been asleep with the bedroom door closed.

She awoke to see that her bedroom door was slowly being re-closed. She looked at her clock and saw that it was 3:16AM.

Case 2577-91 (Knoxville P.D.) On June 5, 19-, Officer Jones was again called to the Baxter home at 3:15 AM. This time Gena reported that she had awoke to find a man standing over her with his fingers inside her vagina... (crime described further with similar description as above).

Case #91-4578 (Prichard P.D.)...

(Herein were listed other offenses where the same or similar offenses were reported in four cities over a five year period, all with no suspects identified.

After a review of the 25 reported offenses occurring in the four cities in this county, your affiant has identified 18 unusual modus operandi factors that are present throughout the reports. These distinctive factors are:

1.  the responsible commits a nighttime residential burglary/prowl/child molestation;
2.  the residences involved are all single level homes located in areas with a street or alley immediately behind them;
3.   the residences are located in small residential communities;
4.  the time element for the offenses is between 3:00 AM and 4:00 AM on Tuesday or Wednesday mornings;
5.  the responsible is described as a white male, 5'8", medium build;
6.  the responsible often wears a knit watch cap;
7.  the responsible often wears a "mask" covering his face below the eyes;
8.  the responsible wears dark clothing;
9.  the responsible wears gloves with the fingers exposed;
10. the responsible targets residences where a pre-adolescent female child lives;
11. the responsible enters the residence through an unlocked window;
12. the responsible prowls the residence examining children's toys and effects before any sexual contact;
13. the responsible takes children's toys and personal effects;
14. once inside the responsible locates that child's bedroom and fondles or digitally penetrates the child;
15. the responsible says nothing during the assault;
16. the responsible often repeatedly returns to the same victim on different occasions;
17. the responsible uses a small flashlight and frequently shines it in the victim/witness's eyes when discovered to avoid being identified;
18. the responsible flees when the child awakens or when confronted by a resident of the house;

In case #1234-91, MO factors, #1, #2, #5, #7, #8, #9, #11, #12, #13, #14, #15, #16, #17 appear.
In case #91-4578, MO factors, #1, #2, #5, #7, #8, #13, #14, #15, #16, #17, #18 appear.
In case #...
(Each case is analyzed and identified for the traits it matches in the series)

On JUly 6, 1991, at 3:40 AM, Officer Donnell was dispatched to the report of an in-progress prowler call at 231 Farwest Dr., Petton Jnct, a small residential community. While responding to the call, the dispatcher of his agency reported that a resident was in pursuit of the prowler running towards Main Street. The reporting party was See E Mall.

When Officer Donnell arrived on Farwest, she was flagged down by a resident, Dave Witt, who told her that his neighbor was holding the prowler in the backyard of 241 Farwest.

Officer Donnell went to 241 Farwest and found Robert Catcher holding a man, later identified at Prowl N. Tuch, on the ground.

Officer Donnell saw a flashlight next to Tuch's right hand, lying on the ground. It was dry to the touch, as opposed to the dew drenched grass upon which it lay. Mr. Catcher said it was not his and that it had dropped from Tuch when Catcher grabbed him.

Mr. Mall was brought to the scene of the detention and he identified Tuch as the man he chased from inside his house.

Tuch was wearing a black and blue plaid long-sleeved shirt, tan pants and black tennis shoes.

Tuch told Officer Donnell that he had been walking home from checking his mail box in West View (a neighboring town). Tuch said that he often takes the back roads to his residence to avoid contact with the police. Tuch claimed that he was walking home on Farwest when Mall ran after him and was threatening him. Tuch had no wallet, keys, or any identification on him at the time of his arrest.

Mall said that he had fallen asleep at approximately 12:30 AM and that he had awakened at approx 1/ 1/2 hours later due to some noises. Mall said that as he lay awake he heard some footsteps coming up the stairs that lead from the ground to the porch. Mall stated that he got up to investigate the noises. As he looked down the stairs that lead to the porch, he saw the subject later identified as Tuch crouched on the top steps just below the porch. He gave chase and caught him in the yard where Officer Donnell found them.

Mall's house is a single-story, single-family dwelling, with a narrow street located immediately behind the property. Mall has a 9-year-old daughter whose bedroom is adjacent to his overlooking the porch described above.

Your affiant has stopped and observed Tuch driving the following vehicle in the early morning hours in and around the neighborhoods described in the above paragraphs over the past four years: 1965, Ford, Van, Blue, 123XYZ.

At the end of the street running behind Mall's house, Officer Donnell found the aforementioned van, parked with the keys in the ignition.

Visible in the rear of the van were children's toys consisting of dolls, stuffed animals, and other personal effects.

A search of the vehicle found photographs of pre-adolescent, white girls, in various candid poses.

A diary/journal was found, written in the hand of its author, describing a trip taken and some dreams. One is as follows;

Aug 9 dream (morn. 10th)... I was in the far North. The scene was the farthest north any trees grow, which was in a narrow valley. There were large carved statues of ice some of them humanoid that no one discovered yet... I saw a young girl (about 11) sitting naked in a small tub of warm water. She was enjoying playing with her right nipple which was more developed than her left. I played with it and then stuck my finger in her pussy...

Your affiant checked the arrest record of Tuch and found that he has been previously arrested for prowling and burglary of residences wherein young, pre-adolescent, white, children live. On one occasion he was tried and acquitted of the same offense as that in the Baxter case described above in the same neighborhood in which the Baxter's live.

He was identified as a suspect, having been stopped in the vicinity of the following hot-prowl burglary...

He was stopped at 4:00 AM in the area of 1234 Lakewood, the week before Jenny Farber, WFJ, 10-years, reported having been digitally penetrated by a prowler described as...

He was arrested for...

(*listed in the same fashion as the sample cases above, are the cases Tuch was suspected of being involved in describing the scene of the crimes, the MO traits and characteristics, and the investigative leads that point towards Tuch*)

(*List of items to search for and seize*)

# Appendix XIV

Your affiant, Detective Franklin Clark has been a Police Officer for the Fresno Police Department for the past 23 years 10 months and has been assigned as a Detective in the Economic/Computer Crimes unit for the past 5 years 8 months.

Your affiant has investigated dozens of computer related crimes over the past 5 years including those involving telecommunications and computer bulletin boards.

Your affiant has received the below listed training specifically in the area of computers and computer crime investigation.

*(list training here)*

Your affiant is familiar with computer usage, software, modems, bulletin boards and the methods used to store and transmit date from computer to computer via modem.

Your affiant has investigated, written and/or served numerous search warrants on computer bulletin boards and computers with modems involved in various crimes including those involved in selling stolen property, those involved in hacking (illegally obtaining long distance telephone calling codes and illegally obtaining and or using stolen credit card numbers and bulletin boards involved in the photographing, distributing and selling of pornographic pictures of minors via modem to other computer users.

Your affiant is a member of and active in the following national computer crime investigative organizations: The Federal Computer Investigators Committee, the High Tech Crime Investigators Association and the Communications Fraud Control Association.

February 2nd. 1992 I was advised by a citizen (who is known to your affiant as being involved in the use of computers and modems) that said citizen had picked up a phone number for a computer bulletin board run by M—— (F——) he was not sure of the spelling of the spelling of the last name.

This citizen told your affiant that he has met M—— F—— and M—— advertises in the paper for young male models, and that he believes F—— sells preteen pictures to magazines in the L.A. area and he believes F—— is a pedophile. This citizen stated he believes F—— is taking lewd pictures of

juveniles and selling them to magazines and putting them on the bulletin
board as graphics files.

This citizen gave the bulletin board phone number as 442 ——.

Your affiant is familiar with computer bulletin boards which are computers, connected to one or more phone lines via a modem. Other persons
with a computer and modem can then call the bulletin board computer and
leave electronic mail, copy files and pictures and send the bulletin board
computer files and pictures. Bulletin Boards are often called "BBS" or bulletin
board systems.

A modem is a device that converts computer signals into signals the
telephone can understand, sends the data by phone line to another modem
which reconverts the information into a computer signal again.

A computer bulletin board uses special software (computer program) to
control access into the computer by outside persons. The software can require
names, passwords and limit access to the various areas on the computer.

The computer bulletin board operator is called "SYSOP" or system operator and he has control of the computer and all its files. He can see all the
files and break in at any time on any caller.

Graphics files are actual images which are scanned into the computer
much like a paper is copied in a photocopier machine or input into the
computer by a digital camera or video camera. These images can be still or
moving video and black and white or color. They appear on a quality computer screen very much as they would appear on a tv screen when displaying
a video movie.

February 11, 1992 0710 hrs. Your affiant called 442 —— by computer
and modem. The line was answered by computer and modem with "Designer
BBS which described itself as a Alternative Lifestyle Bulletin Board Gay-Bi-
Sexual-Lesbian date matching-Echo Mail-International. I was asked several
questions about my sex and sexual preferences and hung up on without
gaining access to the bulletin board.

Your affiant talked with Warwick Township PA. Chief of Police, Al Olsen
about Designer BBS.

Chief Olsen is known by your affiant to have extensive experience in both
in the of sex crimes and computer crimes investigations.

Chief Olsen called Designer BBS at (209) 442—— and was accepted as
a member of the bulletin board. Chief Olsen logged onto Designer BBS as
"B——" account code B——, password wbird from L——, —. He stated in
the introduction that he was a Gay male looking for long distance friends.

Chief Olsen saved each computer session on disk as a readable file and
copied each graphic he obtained from Designer BBS and sent them to your
affiant.

Chief Olsen told your affiant that there were no security procedures in place on Designer BBS to insure that minors do not get on the board or have access to pornographic photos. In fact there are numerous sexually explicit questionnaires to fill out which ask if you prefer under 18, without hair etc.

Chief Olsen found that Designer BBS had a lot of pictures in "GIF" format. (Gif is a method of storing photos in graphics form on a computer so they can be viewed with special software on a computer screen as a photo.) The photos which Chief Olsen copied from Designer BBS depict men from an estimated 15 years old to 50 years old engaged in various sex acts from sodomy to fellatio, sometimes with more than 2 participants in the acts. See attachments 1 through 10 for a black and white print out of these color pictures off a laser printer by your affiant.

The graphic photos have names as listed on the bulletin board such as:

1. Ramit-13.gif which is described as "teen boy is getting some hot hunk's butt in the backroom...ohhhh fuckit!!!".
2. AF&S.gif "A very hot pic of gorgeous blond boy getting fucked and sucked!!!!new addition!!!
3. Ram-12.gif "Teen boy fucking the hell out of Blond Chad, he's in ecstacy, the boys really hung!!!
4. Chad-5.gif "Blond Chad lying on blanket getting fucked by pretty teen boy...he's moaning-groaning, the boy is pretty big...

Chief Olsen also stated that Designer BBS advertises as being connected to other Gay BBS and the SYSOP M—— claims he is a video photographer and sells his pictures to magazines in LA.

Designer BBS is divided into different areas of interest such as:

1. Personal Mail
3. Fast Fuck
5. Hot Desires
7. General Info
8. Graphics
9. Publishers Info
10. Astro Match
12. Windows related file
13. Male Modeling
14. Shareware Programs
16. Grafik Utils
17. Fantasy Notes
21. Gay-Bi-Hetero Match

24. Graphics Programs
25. X-Stories
26. Members Pictures
40. Private Uploads
48. Grakiks II
61. Gay X Pics

Designer BBS has three incoming phone lines 442——, 442—— and 442——. These numbers were given to him by the SYSOP M——. M—— also told him that this bulletin board charges for its services in increments and checks must be sent to: M—— F—— Suite ——, ——, Fresno, Ca.

The SYSOP M—— also has a section on the bulletin board called "Fast Fuk" which as a questionnaire for under 18 years old and a "Date with the SYSOP" with a similar questionnaire. M—— has sections in the bulletin board which sets up appointments for photo sessions with the SYSOP.

M—— F—— sent Chief Olsen a GIF of himself titled "Sysop-1.gif" and requested Chief Olsen post this picture and information on Designer BBS on other adult Bulletin boards on the east coast. Sysop-1.gif shows a white male adult approx. 40 years with blonde hair lying on his stomach with nothing on below the waist. This picture has the words "Sargent Video Capture Magic by M——" on the picture and at the bottom right side "M—— (sysop). See attachment A11 for a printed copy of that color graphic.

M—— F—— talked several times to Chief Olsen on the computer and told him he was in Sacramento but had to come to Fresno to take care of his ailing mother and his brother who was injured in an car accident and confined to a wheel chair. M—— F—— complained that he was stuck at home all the time with these chores.

Chief Olsen told your affiant that in his training and experience he believed that some of the males in the sex act gif's on Designer BBS were under 18 years of age and that the bulletin board was set up with to enable the SYSOP to locate males for the SYSOP to photograph and have sex with. Those under 18 were not excluded by what he observed on the BBS.

Chief Olsen also told your affiant that he could look around the different areas of the BBS and that the Sysop M—— writes lewd stories about forcing sex on 5 ft. 6 in. 135 lbs. blonde high school boys.

During the entire investigation and in 7 different times your affiant logged onto Designer BBS as S—— a 15 year old 5 ft. 6 in. blonde high school kid I was never allowed to look around or access the stories or even my own mail. The SYSOP controlled my entire session on the BBS.

Your affiant is aware that there are many "adult" bulletin boards and most adult bulletin boards have specific warnings stating you must be over

21 to access XXX photos and even require a photo ID be sent to the SYSOP before you have access to sexually explicit graphics.

March 4, 1992 at 14:30 hrs. your affiant called Designer BBS at 442—— via a computer and modem.

Your affiant logged onto the bulletin board as S—— G——, DOB Oct. 12, 1976 (a 15 yr. old juvenile) —— Fresno, Ca. —— phone —— using the account code "look" password "friend" and handle of "S——".

Your affiant was immediately contacted on the computer by the SYSOP M—— who wanted to know how I found his BBS. I told him I saw a photo of a good looking blonde guy and phone number on English Palace BBS back east. he asked how old the guy was and I replied 30 to 35 years. M—— stated the picture was him. The sysop M—— then told me to hand up and he would call me by phone to verify my identity.

M—— called back almost immediately. Your affiant had a confidential informant talk to M—— on the phone. This conversation was recorded with Det. Danisi monitoring the tape recording. See a transcript of the conversation attachments B 1 through B 5. In this conversation M—— verified how "S——" had gotten his BBS number and gave instructions for using the BBS.

M—— asked·Steve to fill out the questionnaire on 38 and asked his physical description as well as if he had ever had any liaisons with a guy or anything? Had he ever done anything, yet?

S—— replied Yeah and was comforted by M—— who told him he was there for him and they were family.

Your affiant then completed the sexually explicit questionnaire on the bulletin board. The questionnaire asked questions as to how I wanted to be "fucked and sucked" as well my age including under 18 and other physical information. I filled this information out as requested by M—— including listing myself as under 18.

I called back to Designer BBS at approx. 1545 hrs. The sysop came back on line immediately. He talked about how safe the BBS was as he had a good friend Deputy Sheriff who was gay and if he had any trouble he would get in uniform and contact the trouble makers.

Everyone knew him and if someone messed up he would get a baseball bat and go to their home and straighten things out.

He asked about my having sex before and I told him sometimes with a friend at school. I commented on being scared and new to gay life. He stated what I needed was some friends that felt the same way I did. He felt that way before he came out and he would be that friend so welcome home.

I commented on the fact that I liked his picture and his voice made me feel comfortable. he stated good he was nice on the phone and nicer in person and when it cam to sex he was a gentle romantic. He was clean and safe he worked out and rode a bicycle to keep in shape. He couldn't speak for others but I did not need to worry around him. He asked me if I had sex with others like me. I told him sometimes with B——. He asked if B—— was gay. I told him I thought so but B—— would not admit it.

He stated he wanted to meet me and introduce me to some friends. Was I free Friday night he would pick me up and take to to his house to meet some gay friends, some older, some younger.

I said my folks wanted me in early. He said he would pick me up and bring me back early. He would show me all his wookies, he has lots of GIF's to look at and he had his video camera and capture board there connected to his computer.

We talked about needing guidance as I discovered who I was and a possible meeting. He said he would be on the board for me anytime and to call back after my folks went to sleep. He gave me a new phone number of 442—— to call back on.

3-4-92 Chief Olsen called. He talked to M—— F—— last night and F—— was talking excitedly about his kid "L——" who signed on after seeing the photo in English Palace. He thanked Olsen for placing the ad.

3-5-92 Olsen downloaded S—— —— —— "match" showing his age (15) and sexual preferences I had filled out the day before. This list showing my age as 15 and name and sexual preferences was posted on the BBS for all members to see.

3-5-92 11:00 I called the BBS and looked around as the SYSOP had left his residence, the activity was "dumped" to a log and printed. I was not allowed access to photos, I left SYSOP a message I would call him Fri. (See attachment C1 through C20.)

3-6-92 14:18 I called the BBS and talked with M——. He asked me about my having sex with B——. He then told me he wanted to have sex with me. He asked me to talk to B—— about a foursome with C—— and himself. M—— said he would like to fuck me for a long time as he can hold back. He said his friend C—— was interested in having sex with B——. M—— sent me a photo of C—— by computer. See attachment D1 through D20. The photo of C—— was not a nude sex photo.

3-9-92 13:53 I called the BBS and C—— had sent me some mail, before I could read it the SYSOP M—— cut me off and talked about having sex again. He agreed to send me a picture of guys my age (15) doing it when I told him pictures turn B—— on. M—— gave me a pic of 3 boys having sex. One was being screwed in the rear while getting a blow job by another male. I was to call him tomorrow about our meeting later this week for sex. See attachment E1 through E-14.

3-10-92 Your affiant called Designer BBS again. M—— had left me a message to download Suckem-1.gif described as a hot blond boy sucking a nice fat dick. He wanted me to fill out another questionnaire on "Date with the SYSOP" to get him really excited for our date.

He also wanted me to tell B—— that C—— was getting wild to get B—— to come along. M—— came on the computer and wanted to make arrangements for a motel etc. for our date. We set the time as 3 PM. Friday March 13, 1992.

I filled out the sexually explicit questionnaire and M—— came back on the computer talking about having sex with me even if B—— wouldn't and asking the size of B—— I told him 7 inches and M—— told me I was gonna get a little increase in size. I copied Suckem-1.Gif. A log of this conversation, the sex questionnaire and a print of Suckem-1.gif are attached as attachments F1 through F17.

3-11-92 I received information from Chief Olsen that M—— was now advertising an escort service on Designer BBS. In this service M—— states C—— has the boys and he'll bring them over and he'll video digitize them then they will collect a small fee for a chance to chose a boy of their choice for a date.

He also sent me a copy of his continuing use of Designer BBS and his conversations with M——.

3-10-92 While your affiant was on Designer BBS copying the picture suckem-1.gif I was also on the telephone with Chief Olsen. Chief Olsen called Designer BBS on another line and immediately was talked to on the computer by M—— who was bragging he couldn't believe his luck he had a date with "L——" (Your affiant's account name on the BBS). M—— went on to say that he and C—— were going to pick the boys up then bring them by the house and get some good pics of them both. Then take them to the motel for a four way. See attachment G1. for a partial printout of the conversation.

3-10-92 Chief Olsen 17:00 hrs. Chief Olsen called Designer BBS. He talked with the Sysop who talked about his date Friday. He told Olsen he hoped to get pics… he was sure S—— wouldn't mind but was not sure about B——. M—— went on to talk about the boys finding out about a hot fuck on the BBS and he was the big hot fucker. See attachment H1 a faxed copy of that computer conversation Chief Olsen sent your affiant.

3-11-92 13:28 hrs. Your affiant as "S——" called Designer BBS. I was contacted immediately by the SYSOP M—— as I was starting to read my mail. He told me there was no need to read the mail from other members and began talking about our date on Friday. He told me he had to be careful about who looked at my pictures we would take on Friday because I was under 18.

He also told me he would pick me up in an —— Nissan Sentra Wagon Creme tan with woody side and a chrome rack on top. This is the same description vehicle your affiant has seen at —— N. B—— and Detectives

Danisi and Conrad have seen M—— F—— driving. He directed me to a picture 3Friends.gif. This graphic shows a young man being entered from the rear by one young man while placing his mouth on the penis of another young man. See attachment #I1 through I18 for a printout of the computer activity and a copy of 3Friends.gif.

Based on your affiant's training, experience and the information contained in this affidavit your affiant believes that Mark F—— with knowledge that "S—— C——" is a minor and that "B——" is a minor did send harmful matter as defined in California Penal Code 313 to a minor with the intent of arousing, appealing to, or gratifying the lust or passions or sexual desires of that person or of the minor, with the intent, or for the purpose of seducing the minor.

Your affiant also believes and has probable cause to believe that M—— F—— after giving said harmful matter to "S—— C——" has made an date with S—— C—— a minor with the intent of having sexual intercourse with him.

Your affiant also believes that further evidence of this and other crimes dealing with pornographic pictures of minors, seduction of minors and the evidence of the identity of said minors, as well as the distribution and sale of said pornographic photos and graphics images is to be found at —— N. ——, County of Fresno, City of Fresno, State of California.

# Index

## A

ABA, *see* American Bar Association

Abduction, 94, 98, 107, 114–115

Abel, Dr. Gene, 39

*A Brief Manifesto on Behalf of Child Sexual Relating*, 33

Accused, 54 *see also* Offenders; Defenses

Act, *see* Conduct

Admissions, 130

Adolescent, 8, 15, 235–236, 256, 258 *see also* Child victim

    offender(s), 25, 95, 109

        criteria for distinguishing criminal vs. innocent act, 109

Adult bookstores, 45

Affection as means of seduction/victimization, 7

Africa, 45, 173

Age preferences, 100

Age-of-consent laws,

    abolition lobbied for, 23, 31

    pornography investigation, *see* Child pornography

Alcohol abuse, 65, *see also* Case management; MO

    supplying to children, 103

Alibi, *see* Case management; Defense

Alternative causes for allegations, 53

American Bar Association (ABA), 387, 432

American Prosecutor's Research Association, 245

American Psychiatric Association, 62

American sex tours, 46

Asia, 45–46, 173, 187, 189

Anal intercourse, 27, *see also* Sodomy

Angel(s), 28

*APSAC Advisor*, 318, 376

Attention as means of seduction/victimization, 7

Australia, 39, 45,126

Authenticity of allegation, 53

Authority as method of victimization, 7

## B

Backlash, 16–18

    bureaucratic resistance, 17

    counter-movement, 17

    inertial opposition, 17

Barry, Robert, 167

Behavior, *see* Individual (offender/child)

Berkeley, California, 32, 40, 48, 339

Bias, 2, 11–12, 17, *see also* Investigation/investigator

Bisexual, 24

Blackmail, 44, 57, *see also* MO; Victimization

*Blue Lagoon, The*, 158

Bondage, 94–95

Boy-Love, 31–32

Boy-lovers, 27–28, *see also* Offenders

Boys as victims, 8, 37, 86, *see also* Male

*Boys Will Be Boys*, 189

Bradbury, Michael D., 270

Brazil, 46

Brainwashing into doing acts and maintaining secret, 62, *see also* MO; Victimization

*Brooke Book, The*, 156

Broken homes, 7

Bross, Don, 18

Bulletin boards, *see* Computers

Burgess, Ann, 3, 61–62, 108

## C

Cambodia, 46

CAMEL, 29

California Judicial Council, 390

Canada, 38, 189

Case failures, 18

Case management, 2, 19, 136

    alcohol, questions to determine manner used, 437

    alliances, getting information before formed, 372

    alpha-name file, 442, 444, Appendices IV, VI, XIII

    approaches, 19

    arrest of offender, 411–412

    background checks, 369, 392, 445

    biological evidence, 385, 398

    case summary, 415, 417, 428